NINTH EDITION

JUSTICE ADMINISTRATION

POLICE, COURTS, AND CORRECTIONS MANAGEMENT

Kenneth J. Peak
University of Nevada, Reno

Andrew L. Giacomazzi
Boise State University

Pearson 330 Hudson Street, NY NY 10013

Vice President, Portfolio Management: Andrew Gilfillan
Portfolio Manager: Gary Bauer
Editorial Assistant: Lynda Cramer
Field Marketing Manager: Bob Nisbet
Product Marketing Manager: Heather Taylor
Director, Digital Studio and Content Production: Brian Hyland
Managing Producer: Jennifer Sargunar
Content Producer: Rinki Kaur
Manager, Rights Management: Johanna Burke
Operations Specialist: Deidra Smith
Creative Digital Lead: Mary Siener
Managing Producer, Digital Studio: Autumn Benson
Content Producer, Digital Studio: Maura Barclay
Full-Service Management and Composition: Integra Software Services Pvt. Ltd.
Full-Service Project Manager: Gowthaman Sadhanandham
Cover Designer: StudioMontage
Cover Art (or Cover Photo): Atomazul/Shutterstock
Printer/Binder: LSC Communications, Inc.
Cover Printer: Phoenix Color/Hagerstown
Text Font: Times LT Pro

Library of Congress Cataloging-in-Publication Data

Justice Administration
Library of Congress Cataloging in Publication Control Number: 2017030716

1 17

Pearson

ISBN 10: 0-13-487140-5
ISBN 13: 978-0-13-487140-0

Dedication

To the late Sam Chapman—longtime professor, police practitioner, and true expert in the field. Sam was notably an enduring friend and associate of the great August Vollmer; indeed, it was Sam who, while on duty, would be summoned to Gus' backyard and hold him as Vollmer neared death. A more true, loyal, interesting, and dedicated friend I have never known. Thanks for everything, Sam.

—K. P.

To my mother, Monika Giacomazzi. While not planned, I wrote the last of my words to this edition on the 8th anniversary of her passing. From my mother, I gained a great appreciation for hard work and a thirst for knowledge, not to mention a sometimes wicked sense of humor. To you, mom; I know you're already reading! "Always Loving, Always Loved."

—A. G.

THE CRIMINAL

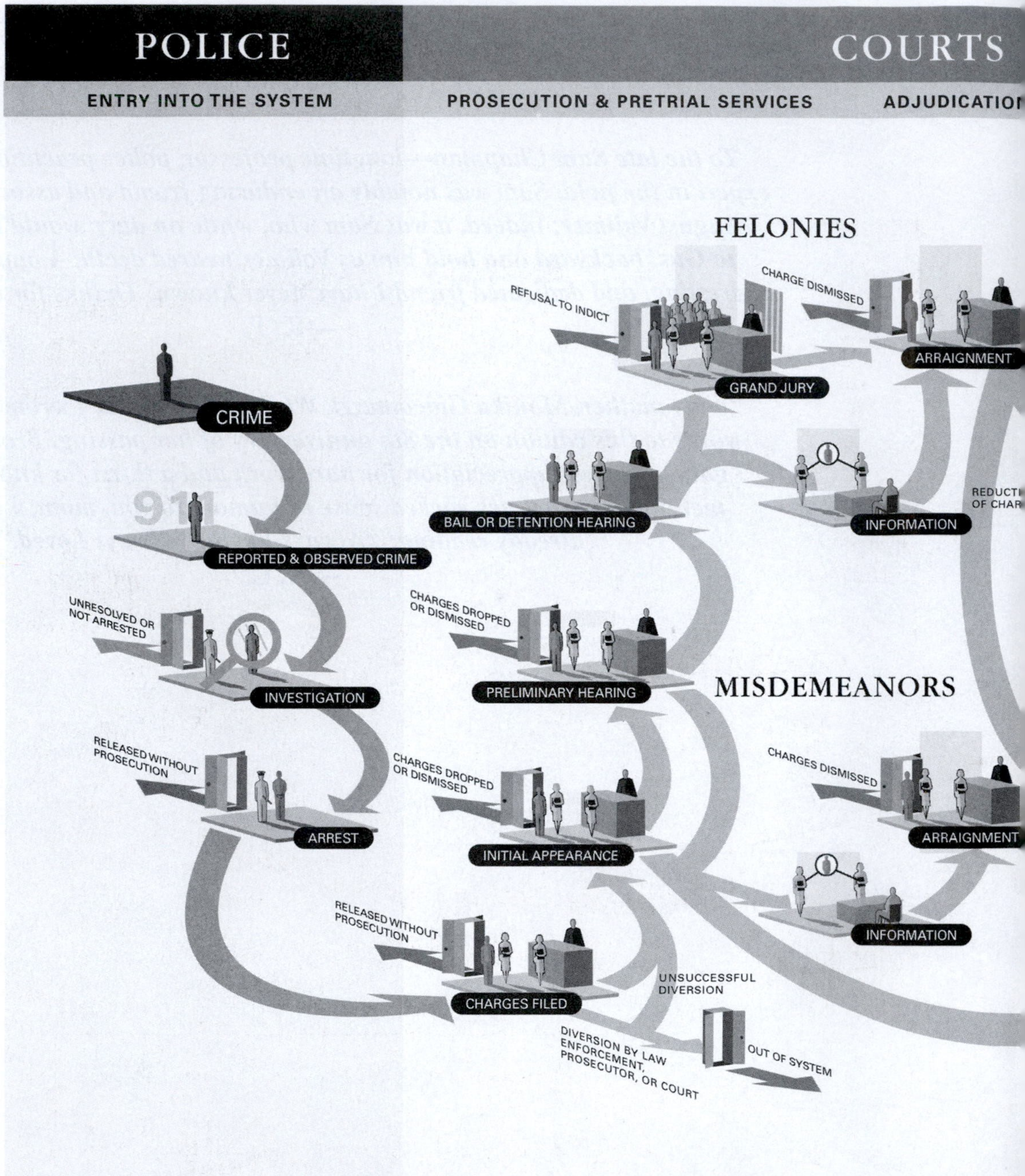
POLICE
COURTS
ENTRY INTO THE SYSTEM
PROSECUTION & PRETRIAL SERVICES
ADJUDICATIO
FELONIES
MISDEMEANORS
CRIME
911
REPORTED & OBSERVED CRIME
UNRESOLVED OR NOT ARRESTED
INVESTIGATION
RELEASED WITHOUT PROSECUTION
ARREST
REFUSAL TO INDICT
GRAND JURY
CHARGE DISMISSED
ARRAIGNMENT
BAIL OR DETENTION HEARING
INFORMATION
REDUCTI OF CHAR
CHARGES DROPPED OR DISMISSED
PRELIMINARY HEARING
CHARGES DROPPED OR DISMISSED
INITIAL APPEARANCE
CHARGES DISMISSED
ARRAIGNMENT
INFORMATION
RELEASED WITHOUT PROSECUTION
CHARGES FILED
UNSUCCESSFUL DIVERSION
DIVERSION BY LAW ENFORCEMENT, PROSECUTOR, OR COURT
OUT OF SYSTEM

JUSTICE SYSTEM

CORRECTIONS

SENTENCING & SANCTIONS | PROBATION | PRISON | PAROLE

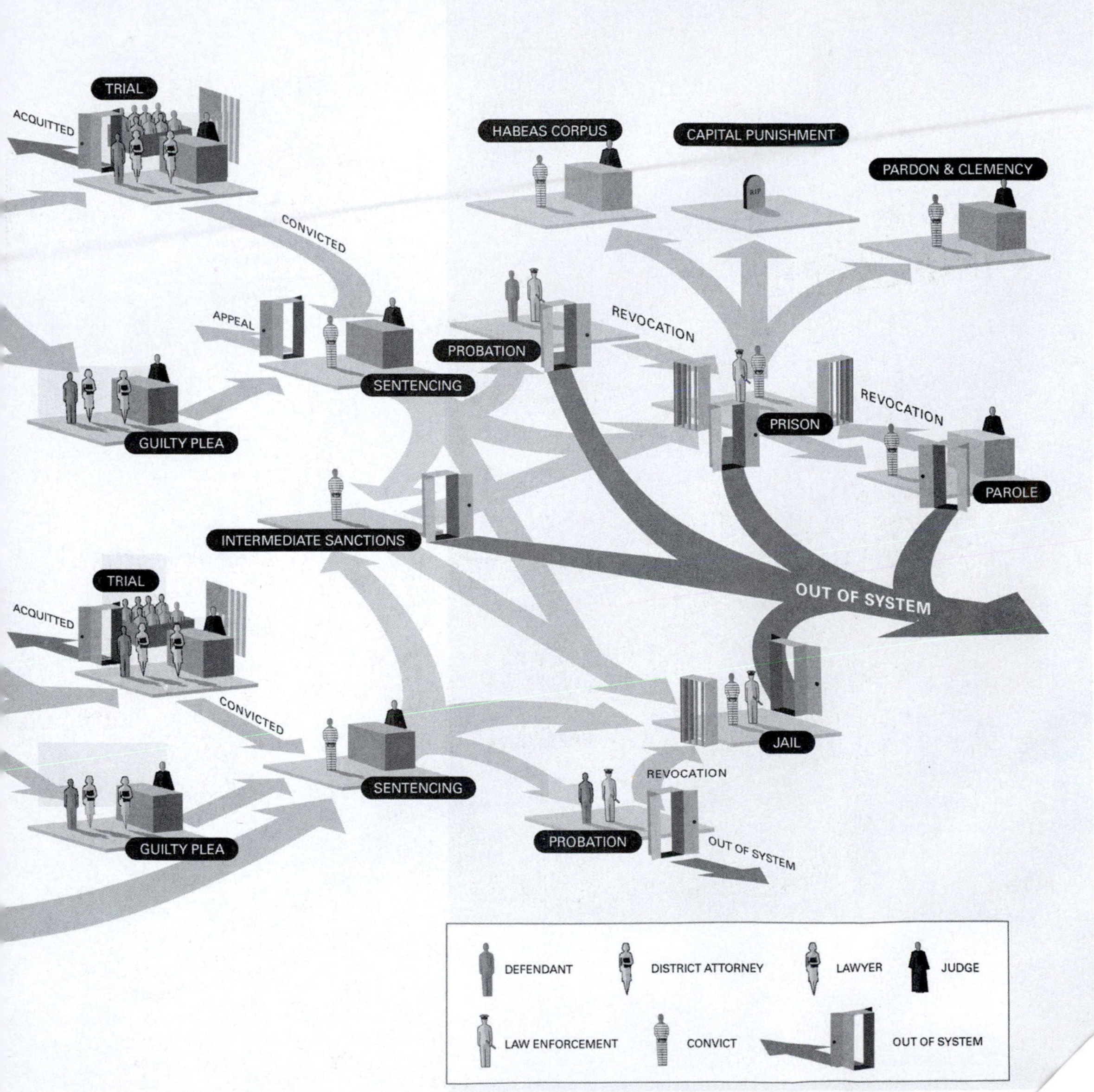

Brief Contents

Contents

Preface

New to This Edition

In addition to the general updated information provided throughout the book, the following are other substantively new additions to this revised ninth edition:

Chapter 1: Redefining performance measures in the criminal justice system; expanded material on strategic planning; consequences for not planning for change

Chapter 2: Closed versus open systems; external communications: use of social media; situational leadership theory; Ouchi's Theory Z; motivation through job enrichment; expanded discussion of Generation Y in the workforce

Chapter 3: Updates on federal laws, generally; Lilly Ledbetter Fair Pay Act; impact of Affordable Care Act; dress codes, tattoos, and Millennials (material concerning uniforms moved here from Chapter 6)

Chapter 4: New materials on procedural justice; a new professionalism; constitutional policing and legitimacy; responding to mass demonstrations; achieving harmony; CompStat

Chapter 5: Preparing for a chief executive career; profile of today's police chief; navigating the political arena; chiefs under fire and being fired; a chief's apology to minorities; debating the "Ferguson effect" (also, material concerning diversity and sexual harassment has been moved here from Chapter 6)

Chapter 6: Police shootings—need for a national database, posting related information, demand for and pros/cons of body cameras, and de-escalating crises; dealing with officers' PTSD; civilian review boards; use of consent decrees; hazards confronting officers and developing a formal, agency-wide wellness program (previous edition's terrorism material is now moved to new Chapter 17)

Chapter 7: Comparing federal and state court systems; expanded material on court unification

Chapter 8: Expanded section on methods of judicial selection; what makes for good judging; expanded material on court clerks and evaluating court administrators

Chapter 9: Updated research on the CSI effect and courthouse violence; new material on mental health courts; expanded information on alternative dispute resolution; use of reverse waiver

Chapter 10: Updated new trends in California's decarceration effort; the controversy of the supermax; updated cases in "Constitutional Rights of Inmates"; community jails

Chapter 11:	New research on prison wardens; Boston Marathon bomber update; traits of successful corrections officers/supervisors; added material on stressors in jails
Chapter 12:	Hostage rescue protocol; latest information on the state of solitary confinement; expanded section on the aging of inmates; video visitation; private prisons in Trump Era; effectiveness of house arrest/electronic monitoring
Chapter 13:	Seven case studies and ethical dilemmas (including one based on the federal investigation of Ferguson, Missouri)
Chapter 14:	New material concerning the "blue flu," civil lawsuit settlements, police unions, and early intervention systems; possible issues concerning legalized recreational use of marijuana; example of agency policy governing officer conduct
Chapter 15:	Enhancing budgets, stretching resources; performing job analyses and surveying similar agencies; utilizing growth, grants, civilianization, sensational incidents; mobilizing stakeholders; strategic planning; uniqueness of court budgets; methods of reforming corrections (reducing prison populations and expenditures)
Chapter 16:	Entirely new chapter on homeland security
Chapter 17:	Selecting proper police technologies based on functions performed; pros and cons of body-worn cameras; crime mapping and real-time crime centers; using social media and civic apps; legal, moral, and practical considerations involving IT in policing; status of electronic control devices, drones, facial recognition, fingerprinting, robots, and apps for crime-fighting; technologies and ECDs, drones, robots, cold cases; the courts' goal of becoming paperless; new technologies found in a model courtroom; technology replacing court reporters; how unified management systems are making courts more efficient; corrections' uses of biometrics, inmate scanning; how *not* to adopt IT; the continuing problem of contraband cellphones in prison

▶ Introduction

Famed educator John Dewey advocated the "learn by doing" approach to education, or problem-based learning. Another contemporary, popular learning method, espoused by Benjamin Bloom and known as "Bloom's taxonomy," called for "higher-order thinking skills"—critical and creative thinking that involves analysis, synthesis, and evaluation.

This ninth edition of *Justice Administration: Police, Courts, and Corrections Management* attempts, to the extent possible, to adhere to such philosophy and practice from start to finish while continuing to examine all facets of the criminal justice system as well as several related matters of interest to prospective and current administrators. The authors have held numerous administrative and academic positions in their criminal justice careers; thus, this book's 17 chapters contain a palpable real-world flavor not found in most textbooks. Furthermore, this edition's continuing use of the exercises in Learn by Doing and the Case Study sections in nearly all chapters greatly enhance the text's applied nature as well as the reader's problem-solving capabilities and the practical application of information provided in the chapters; furthermore, these scenarios and activities place the reader in hypothetical—yet typically real-world—situations, creating opportunities to practice skills in communication and examining and addressing current community issues. Again, readers are encouraged to become engaged in some or all of these scenarios and activities.

In addition to the chapters concerning police, courts, and corrections administration, the book includes chapters on personnel and financial administration, rights of criminal justice employees, discipline and liability, ethics, homeland security, technologies. A practice continued in this edition is the listing of chapter learning objectives, which appear at the beginning of each chapter, and key terms and concepts at each chapter's end.

There is an appendix at the book's end that provides some writings of three noted early philosophers: Confucius, Machiavelli, and Lao-Tzu.

Criminal justice is a people business. This book reflects that fact as it looks at human foibles and some of the problems of personnel and policy in justice administration. Thanks to many innovators in the field, a number of exciting and positive changes are occurring. The general goal of the book is to inform the reader of the primary people, practices, and terms that are utilized in justice administration.

Finally, there may well be activities, policies, actions, and our own views with which the reader will disagree. This is not at all bad, because in the management of people and agencies, there are few absolutes. From the beginning to the end of the book, the reader is provided with a comprehensive and penetrating view of what is certainly one of the most difficult and challenging positions that one can occupy in the United States: the administration of a criminal justice agency. We solicit your input concerning any facet of this textbook; feel free to contact us with recommendations for improving it.

Instructor Supplements

Instructor's Manual with Test Bank. Includes content outlines for classroom discussion, teaching suggestions, and answers to selected end-of-chapter questions from the text. This also contains a Word document version of the test bank.

TestGen. This computerized test generation system gives you maximum flexibility in creating and administering tests on paper, electronically, or online. It provides state-of-the-art features for viewing and editing test bank questions, dragging a selected question into a test you are creating, and printing sleek, formatted tests in a variety of layouts. Select test items from test banks included with TestGen for quick test creation, or write your own questions from scratch. TestGen's random generator provides the option to display different text or calculated number values each time questions are used.

PowerPoint Presentations. Our presentations are clear and straightforward. Photos, illustrations, charts, and tables from the book are included in the presentations when applicable.

To access supplementary materials online, instructors need to request an instructor access code. Go to **www.pearsonhighered.com/irc**, where you can register for an instructor access code. Within 48 hours after registering, you will receive a confirming e-mail, including an instructor access code. Once you have received your code, go to the site and log on for full instructions on downloading the materials you wish to use.

Alternate Versions

eBooks. This text is also available in multiple eBook formats. These are an exciting new choice for students looking to save money. As an alternative to purchasing the printed textbook, students can purchase an electronic version of the same content. With an eTextbook, students can search the text, make notes online, print out reading assignments that incorporate lecture notes, and bookmark important passages for later review. For more information, visit your favorite online eBook reseller or visit www.mypearsonstore.com.

Acknowledgments

This edition, like its eight predecessors, is the result of the professional assistance of several people. First, it continues to benefit by the guidance of the staff at Pearson Education. This effort involved: Gary Bauer, Product Manager; Gowthaman Sadhanandham, Project Manager; and Rinki Kaur, Program Manager. Copyediting was masterfully accomplished by Pradheepa Balasubramanian. We also wish to acknowledge the invaluable assistance of the following reviewers: Karen Murray, Southern Regional Technical College; Donald Ricker, Southwestern Michigan College; and Billy Wilson, Campbellsville University. Their careful reading and input made to a much more informed and overall improved ninth edition.

About the Authors

Kenneth J. Peak is Professor Emeritus and former chairman of the Department of Criminal Justice, University of Nevada, Reno, where he was named "Teacher of the Year" by the university's Honor Society (and served a stint as Director of Police Services). After serving for several years as a municipal police officer in Kansas, Ken subsequently held positions as a nine-county criminal justice planner for southeast Kansas, Director of a four-state Technical Assistance Institute for the Law Enforcement Assistance Administration, Director of University Police at Pittsburg State University, and Assistant Professor of Criminal Justice at Wichita State University. He has authored or coauthored 38 textbooks and 2 historical books (on Kansas bootlegging and temperance). His other books include *Policing America: Methods, Issues, Challenges*, 9th ed.; *Community Policing and Problem Solving: Strategies and Practices*, 7th ed. (with R. W. Glensor); *Managing and Leading Today's Police: Challenges, Best Practices, & Case Studies,* 4th ed. (with L. K. Gaines and R. W. Glensor); and *Women in Law Enforcement Careers* (with V. B. Lord). He also has published more than 60 monographs, journal articles, and invited chapters on a variety of policing topics. Ken has held several national and regional criminal justice offices and continues to be very active in academia. He holds a doctorate from the University of Kansas and received two gubernatorial appointments to statewide criminal justice committees while residing in Kansas.

Andrew L. Giacomazzi is Associate Dean in the School of Public Service and Professor of Criminal Justice at Boise State University. Prior to assuming that role, Andy was the chair of the Department of Criminal Justice. He worked extensively with the Western Regional Institute of Community Oriented Public Safety to conduct assessments of police departments and sheriff's offices in the western United States, and also worked at the Spokane Police Department in leadership development. Andy received his bachelor's degrees in Social Ecology and German from UC Irvine, and his master's and Ph.D. (Criminal Justice and Political Science, respectively) from Washington State University. He is coauthor of *Community Policing in a Community Era: An Introduction and Exploration* and is coeditor of a book entitled *Controversial Issues in Policing*. He has more than 65 other publications including refereed journal articles, book chapters, and technical reports. His research interests include community policing, organizational change, family violence, and juvenile intervention programs. In May 2015, Andy was named Faculty Member of the Year by the Residential Housing Association at Boise State, and in 2016 won Boise State's Golden Apple Award for excellence in teaching. Andy lives on the Boise State University campus, serving in the capacity of Faculty Member in Residence in the Leadership & Engagement Living-Learning Community.

PART 1

Justice Administration

An Introduction

This part consists of three chapters and sets the stage for the later analysis of criminal justice agencies and their issues, problems, functions, and challenges in Parts 2 through 5. Chapter 1 examines the scope of justice administration and why we study it. Chapter 2 discusses organization and administration in general, looking at both how organizations are managed and how people are motivated. The rights of criminal justice employees are reviewed in Chapter 3. The introductory section of each chapter previews the specific chapter content.

ER_09/Shutterstock

1 The Study and Scope of Justice Administration

LEARNING OBJECTIVES

After reading this chapter, the student will be able to:

1. *explain and distinguish between the concepts of* administration, manager, *and* supervisor
2. *understand and distinguish among criminal justice process, network, and nonsystem*
3. *understand system fragmentation and how it affects the amount and type of crime*
4. *understand consensus and conflict theorists and their theories*
5. *understand the two goals of the U.S. criminal justice system (CJS)*
6. *distinguish between extrinsic and intrinsic rewards and how they relate to the CJS*
7. *explain the differences between planned change and unplanned change in an organization*

▶ Introduction

The overarching theme of this book is that administration is far too important than to be left to on-the-job training or to one's personal idiosyncrasies and ideals. Concisely put, today's leaders must know their people, the current trends and issues of the day, how to deal with related challenges (e.g., financial administration), and the legal underpinnings of their work. Unfortunately, many readers of this book have had to suffer an administrator, manager, or supervisor who was not educated, trained, or well prepared in these daunting tasks.

This first chapter explains in more detail this book's purposes and general approach, and why it is important and essential to study criminal justice administration. Included are discussions of the criminal justice system itself—whether or not there is a true "system" of justice, how and why the U.S. justice system was founded, and some differences between public and private administration. After a review of planned change and policymaking in justice administration, the chapter concludes with review questions and exercises in the Deliberate and Decide, Learn by Doing, and Case Study sections.

▶ Why Study Justice Administration?

Recent events highlighted by national media attention suggest that the American system of criminal justice is broken.[1] And while the brunt of this attention has focused on the front gate of the system—the police—the grand jury system, prosecutors, and corrections' administrators have not been immune to criticism. According to Conrad Black, reform legislation in the federal government has been scant, but should include recommitting to Bill of Rights guarantees, including fair and speedy trials, reasonable bail, and plea bargaining reform.[2]

Many of us may find it difficult when we are young to imagine ourselves assuming a leadership role in later life. As one person quipped, we may even have difficulty envisioning ourselves serving as captain of our neighborhood block watch program. The fact is, however, that organizations increasingly seek people with a high level of education and experience as prospective administrators. The college experience, in addition to transmitting knowledge, is believed to make people more tolerant and secure and less susceptible to debilitating stress and anxiety than those who do not have this experience. We also assume that administration is a science that can be taught; it is not a talent that one must be born with. Unfortunately, however, administrative skills are often learned through on-the-job training; many of us who have worked for a boss with inadequate administrative skills can attest to the inadequacy of this training.

Purpose of the Book and Key Terms

As indicated in the Preface, this textbook attempts to follow, to the extent possible, an applied, practical approach as espoused by famed educator John Dewey, who advocated the "learn by doing" approach to education, or problem-based learning. Another contemporary, popular learning method is also followed, which was espoused by Benjamin Bloom and known as "Bloom's taxonomy," which called for "higher-order thinking skills"—critical and creative thinking that involves analysis, synthesis, and evaluation.

This book alone, as is true for any other single work on the subject of administration, cannot instantly transform the reader into a bona fide expert in organizational behavior and administrative techniques. It alone cannot prepare someone to accept the reins of administration, supervision, or leadership; formal education, training, and experience are also necessary for such undertakings.

Many good basic books about administration exist; they discuss general aspects of leadership, the use of power and authority, and a number of specialized subjects that are beyond the reach of this book. Instead, here we simply consider some of the major theories, aspects, and issues of administration, laying the foundation for the reader's future study and experience.

Many textbooks have been written about *police* administration; a few have addressed administering courts and corrections agencies. Even fewer have analyzed justice administration from a *systems* perspective, considering all of the components of the justice system and their administration, issues, and practices. This book takes that perspective. Furthermore, most books on administration are immersed in pure administrative theory and concepts; in this way, the *practical* criminal justice perspective is often lost on many college and university students. Conversely, many books dwell on minute concepts, thereby obscuring the administrative principles involved. This book, which necessarily delves into some theory and specialized subject matter, focuses on the practical aspects of justice administration.

Justice Administration is not written as a guidebook for a major sweeping reform of the U.S. justice system. Rather, its primary intent is to familiarize the reader with the methods and challenges of criminal justice administrators. It also challenges the reader, however, to consider what reform is desirable or even necessary and to be open-minded and visualize where changes might be implemented.

administrator the person whose focus is on the overall organization, its mission, acquisition and use of resources, and agency relationship with external organizations and groups.

manager a person in the intermediate level of management, responsible for carrying out the policies and directives of upper-level administrators and supervising subordinate managers and employees.

supervisor typically the lowest position of leadership in an organization, one who plans, organizes, and directs staff members in their daily activities.

Although the terms *administration, manager*, and *supervisor* are often used synonymously, each is a unique concept that is related to the others. Administration encompasses both management and supervision; it is the process by which a group of people is organized and directed toward achieving the group's objective. The exact nature of the organization will vary among the different types and sizes of agencies, but the general principles and the form of administration are similar. **Administrators** focus on the overall organization, its mission, and its relationship with other organizations and groups external to it. In a hierarchical organization, they typically hold such ranks as police chief/sheriff, and assistant chief or undersheriff, warden and associate warden, and so on, and include those persons who are in a policymaking position.

Managers, often termed middle management or mid-level managers, are typically the intermediate level of leadership in a hierarchical organization, reporting to the higher echelon of administrators and responsible for carrying out their policies and the agency's mission while also supervising subordinate managers and employees to ensure a smooth functioning organization; they are typically the ranks of captains and lieutenants. **Supervisors** (also sometimes termed *first-line supervisors*) occupy the lowest position of leadership in an organizational hierarchy, and typically plan, organize, and direct staff members in their daily activities. They are typically sergeants in a hierarchical organization.

In policing (or in prisons, or wherever there is a paramilitary rank structure), for example, although we tend to think of the chief executive as the administrator, the bureau chiefs or commanders as managers, and the sergeants as supervisors, it is important to note that on occasion all three of these roles are required of one administrator; such may be the case when a critical situation occurs, such as a hostage or barricaded-subject incident, and a single person is responsible for all of these levels of decision making.

The terms *police* and *law enforcement* are generally used interchangeably. Many people in the police field believe, however, that the police do more than merely enforce laws; they prefer to use the term *police*.

Organization of the Book

To understand the challenges that administrators of justice organizations face, we first need to place justice administration within the big picture; thus, in Part 1, Justice Administration: An Introduction, we discuss the organization, administration, and general nature of the U.S.

justice system; the state of our country with respect to crime and government control; the evolution of justice organization and administration in all of its three components: police, courts, and corrections; and the rights of criminal justice employees.

Parts 2, 3, and 4 discuss contemporary police, courts, and corrections administration, respectively, and follow the same organizational theme: The first chapter of each part deals with the *organization and operation* of the component, followed in the next chapter by an examination of the component's *personnel roles and functions*, and in the third chapter a discussion of *issues and practices* (including future considerations).

Part 5 examines administrative problems and factors that influence the entire justice system, including ethical considerations, financial administration, technology for today and the future, and the threat of terrorism.

This initial chapter sets the stage for later discussions of the criminal justice system and its administration. We first consider whether the justice system comprises a process, a network, a nonsystem, or a true system. A discussion of the legal and historical bases for justice and administration follows (an examination of what some great thinkers have said about governance in general is provided at the end of the book, in appendix). The differences between public and private sector administration are reviewed next, and the chapter concludes with a discussion of policymaking in justice administration. After completing this chapter, the reader will have a better grasp of the structure, purpose, and foundation of our CJS.

▶ A True *System* of Justice?

What do justice administrators—police, courts, and corrections officials—actually *administer*? Do they provide leadership over a system that has succeeded in accomplishing its mission? Do individuals within the system work amiably and communicate well with one another? Do they all share the same goals? Do their efforts result in crime reduction? In short, do they compose a *system*? We now turn to these questions, taking a fundamental yet expansive view of justice administration.

The U.S. CJS attempts to decrease criminal behavior through a wide variety of uncoordinated and sometimes uncomplementary efforts. Each system component—police, courts, and corrections—has varying degrees of responsibility and discretion for dealing with crime. Often a federal, state, or local system component fails, however, to engage in any coordinated planning effort; hence, relations among and between these components are often characterized by friction, conflict, and deficient communication. Role conflicts also serve to ensure that planning and communication are stifled.

For example, one role of the police is to arrest suspected offenders. Police typically are not judged by the public on the quality (e.g., having probable cause) of arrests but on their number. Prosecutors often complain that police provide case reports of poor quality. Prosecutors, for their part, are partially judged by their success in obtaining convictions; a public defender or defense attorney is judged by success in getting suspected offenders' charges dropped. The courts are very independent in their operation, largely sentencing offenders as they see fit. Corrections agencies are torn between the philosophies of punishment and rehabilitation and, in the view of many, wind up performing neither function with a large degree of success. These agencies are further burdened with overcrowded conditions, high caseloads, and antiquated facilities.[3] Unfortunately, this situation has existed for several decades and continues today.

This criticism of the justice system or process—that it is fragmented and rife with role conflicts and other problems—is a common refrain. Following are several views of the CJS as it currently operates: the process, network, and nonsystem points of view. Following the discussion of those three points of view, we consider whether criminal justice truly represents a system.

A Criminal Justice Process?

criminal justice process the decisions and actions by an institution, offender, victim, or society that influence the offender's movement into, through, or out of the justice system.

What is readily seen in the foregoing discussion is that our CJS may not be a system at all. Given its current operation and fragmentation, it might be better described as a **criminal justice process**. As a process, it involves the decisions and actions taken by an institution, offender, victim, or society that influence the offender's movement into, through, or out of the justice system.[4] In its purest form, the criminal justice process functions as shown in Figure 1-1 ■. Note that the horizontal effects result from factors, such as the amount of crime, the number of prosecutions, and the type of court disposition affecting the population in correctional facilities and rehabilitative programs. Vertical effects represent the primary system steps or procedures.[5]

At one end of this process are the police who understandably may view their primary role as getting lawbreakers off the street. At the other end of the process are the corrections officials who may see their role as being primarily custodial in nature. Somewhere in between are the courts that try to ensure a fair application of the law to each case coming to the bar.

As a process, the justice system cannot reduce crime by itself, nor can any of the component parts afford to be insensitive to the needs and problems of the other parts. In criminal justice planning jargon, "You can't rock one end of the boat." In other words, every action has a reaction, especially in the justice process. If, say, a bond issue for funds to provide 10 percent more police officers on the streets is passed in a community, the additional arrests made by those added police personnel will have a decided impact on the courts and corrections components. Obviously, although each component operates largely on its own, the actions and reactions of each with respect to crime will send ripples throughout the process.

Much of the failure to deal effectively with crime may be attributed to organizational and administrative fragmentation of the justice process. Fragmentation exists among the components of the process, within the individual components, among political jurisdictions, and among persons.

A Criminal Justice Network?

criminal justice network a view that the justice system's components cooperate and share similar goals but operate independently and compete for funding.

Other observers contend that U.S. justice systems constitute a **criminal justice network**.[6] According to Steven Cox and John Wade, the justice system functions much like a television or radio network whose stations share many programs but in which each station also presents programs that the network does not air on other stations. The network appears as a three-dimensional model in which the public, legislators, police, prosecutors, judges, and correctional officials interact with one another and with others who are outside the traditionally conceived CJS.[7]

Furthermore, the criminal justice network is said to be based on several key yet erroneous assumptions, including the following:

1. The components of the network cooperate and share similar goals.
2. The network operates according to a set of formal procedural rules to ensure uniform treatment of all persons, the outcome of which constitutes justice.
3. Each person accused of a crime receives due process and is presumed innocent until proven guilty.
4. Each person receives a speedy public trial before an impartial jury of his or her peers and is represented by competent legal counsel.[8]

Cox and Wade asserted that these key assumptions are erroneous for the following reasons:

1. The three components have incompatible goals and are continually competing with one another for budgetary dollars.
2. Evidence indicates that blacks and whites, males and females, and middle- and lower-class citizens receive differential treatment in the criminal justice network.

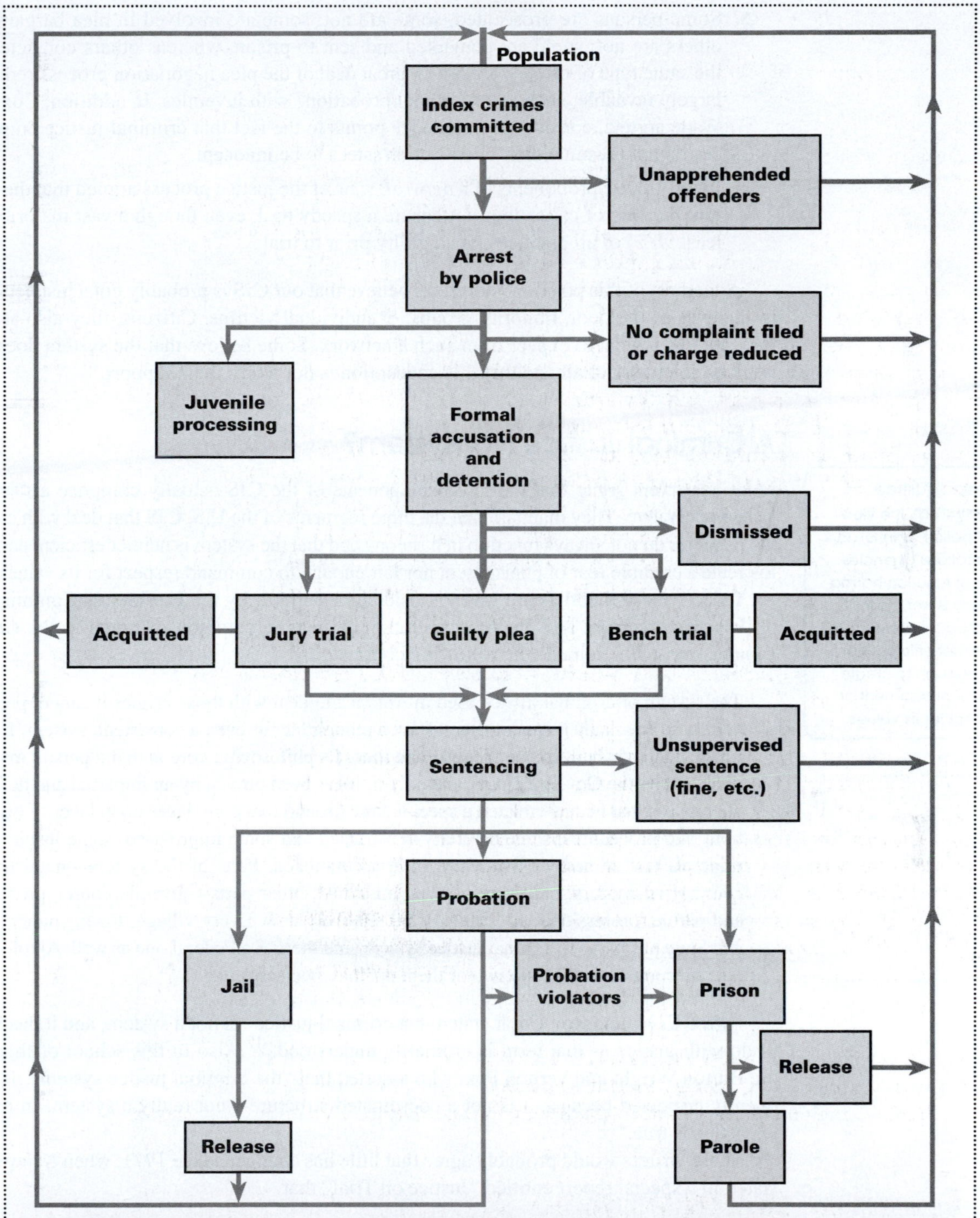

FIGURE 1-1 Criminal Justice Model

Source: Adapted in part from the President's Commission on Law Enforcement and Administration of Justice, *The Challenge of Crime in a Free Society* (Washington, DC: U.S. Government Printing Office, 1967), pp. 262–263.

3. Some persons are prosecuted, some are not; some are involved in plea bargaining, others are not; some are convicted and sent to prison, whereas others convicted of the same type of offense are not. A great deal of the plea negotiation process remains largely invisible, such as "unofficial probation" with juveniles. In addition, Cox and Wade argued, considerable evidence points to the fact that criminal justice employees do not presume their clients or arrestees to be innocent.
4. Finally, these proponents of a *network view* of the justice process argued that the current backlog of cases does not ensure a speedy trial, even though a vast majority (at least 90%) of all arrestees plead guilty prior to trial.[9]

Adherents of this position, therefore, believe that our CJS is probably not a just network in the eyes of the poor, minority groups, or individual victims. Citizens, they also assert, may not know what to expect from such a network. Some believe that the system does not work as a network at all and that this conception is not worth their support.[10]

A Criminal Justice Nonsystem?

criminal justice nonsystem the view that police, courts, and corrections agencies do not function harmoniously is not a coordinated structure, and is neither efficient nor fair enough to create fear of punishment or respect for its values.

Many observers argue that the three components of the CJS actually comprise a **criminal justice nonsystem**. They maintain that the three segments of the U.S. CJS that deal with criminal behavior do not always function in harmony and that the system is neither efficient enough to create a credible fear of punishment nor fair enough to command respect for its values.

Indeed, these theorists are given considerable support by the President's Commission on Law Enforcement and the Administration of Justice (commonly known as the *Crime Commission*), which made the following comment:

> The system of criminal justice used in America to deal with those crimes it cannot prevent and those criminals it cannot deter is not a monolithic, or even a consistent, system. It was not designed or built in one piece at one time. Its philosophic core is that a person may be punished by the Government, if, and only if, it has been proven by an impartial and deliberate process that he has violated a specific law. Around that core, layer upon layer of institutions and procedures, some carefully constructed and some improvised, some inspired by principle and some by expediency, have accumulated. Parts of the system—magistrates, courts, trial by jury, bail—are of great antiquity. Other parts—juvenile courts, probation and parole, professional policemen—are relatively new. Every village, town, county, city, and State has its own criminal justice system, and there is a Federal one as well. All of them operate somewhat alike, no two of them operate precisely alike.[11]

Alfred Cohn and Roy Udolf stated that criminal justice "is not a system, and it has little to do with justice as that term is ordinarily understood."[12] Also in this school of thought are Burton Wright and Vernon Fox, who asserted that "the criminal justice system…is frequently criticized because it is not a coordinated structure—not really a system. In many ways this is true."[13]

These writers would probably agree that little has changed since 1971, when *Newsweek* stated in a special report entitled "Justice on Trial" that

> America's system of criminal justice is too swamped to deliver more than the roughest justice—and too ragged really to be called a system. "What we have," says one former government hand, "is a non-system in which the police don't catch criminals, the courts don't try them, and the prisons don't reform them. The system, in a word, is in trouble. The trouble has been neglect. The paralysis of the civil courts, where it takes five years to get a judgment in a damage suit—the courts—badly managed, woefully undermanned and so inundated with cases that they have to run fast just to stand still."[14]

Unfortunately, in many jurisdictions, those words still ring true. Too often, today's justice administrators cannot be innovators or reformers but rather simply "make do." As one law professor stated, "Oliver Wendell Holmes could not survive in our criminal court. How can you be an eminent jurist when you have to deal with this mess?"[15]

Those who hold that the justice system is in reality no system at all can also point to the fact that many practitioners in the field (police, judges, prosecutors, correctional workers, and private attorneys) and academicians concede that the entire justice system is in crisis, even rapidly approaching a major breakdown. They can cite problems everywhere—large numbers of police calls for service, overcrowded court dockets, and high prison populations. In short, they contend that the system is in a state of dysfunction, largely as a result of its fragmentation and lack of cohesion.[16]

system fragmentation the view that members of police, courts, and corrections agencies have tremendous discretion and their own perception of the offender, resulting in goal conflict.

System fragmentation is largely believed to directly affect the amount and type of crime that exists. Contributing to this fragmentation are the wide discretionary powers possessed by actors in the justice system. For example, police officers (primarily those having the least experience, education, and training) have great discretion over whom they arrest and are effectively able to dictate policy as they go about performing their duties. Here again, the Crime Commission was moved to comment as follows, realizing that how the police officer moves around his or her territory depends largely on this discretion:

> Crime does not look the same on the street as it does in a legislative chamber. How much noise or profanity makes conduct "disorderly" within the meaning of the law? When must a quarrel be treated as a criminal assault: at the first threat, or at the first shove, or at the first blow, or after blood is drawn, or when a serious injury is inflicted? How suspicious must conduct be before there is "probable cause," the constitutional basis for an arrest? Every [officer], however sketchy or incomplete his education, is an interpreter of the law.[17]

Judicial officers also possess great discretionary latitude. State statutes require judges to provide deterrence, retribution, rehabilitation, and incapacitation—all in the same sentence. Well-publicized studies of the sentencing tendencies of judges—in which participants were given identical facts in cases and were to impose sentences based on the offender's violation of the law—have demonstrated considerable discretion and unevenness in the judges' sentences. The nonsystem advocates believe this to be further evidence that a basic inequality exists—an inequality in justice that is communicated to the offender.[18]

Finally, fragmentation also occurs in corrections—the part of the criminal justice process that the U.S. public sees the least of and knows the least about. Indeed, as the Crime Commission noted, the federal government, all 50 states, the District of Columbia, and most of the country's 3,047 counties now engage in correctional activities of some form. Each level of government acts independently of the others, and the responsibility for the administration of corrections is divided within the given jurisdictions as well.[19]

With this fragmentation comes polarity in identifying and establishing the primary goals of the system. The police, enforcing the laws, emphasize community protection; the courts weigh both sides of the issue—individual rights and community needs; and corrections facilities work with the individual. Each of these groups has its own perception of the offender, creating goal conflict; that is, the goal of the police and the prosecutor is to get the transgressor off the street, which is antithetical to the caretaker role of the corrections worker who often wants to rehabilitate and return the offender to the community. The criminal justice process does not allow many alternative means of dealing with offenders. The nonsystem adherent believes that eventually the offender will become a mere statistic, more important on paper than as a human being.[20]

Because the justice process lacks sufficient program and procedural flexibility, these adherents argue that its workers either can circumvent policies, rules, and regulations or adhere to organizational practices they know are, at times, dysfunctional. (As evidence of the former, they point to instances of *informal* treatment of criminal cases; e.g., a police officer "bends" someone's constitutional rights in order to return stolen property to its rightful owner, or a juvenile probation officer, without a solid case but with strong suspicion, warns a youth that any further infractions will result in formal court-involved proceedings.)

Or, Is It a True Criminal Justice System?

That all of the foregoing perspectives on the justice system are grounded in truth is probably evident by now. In many ways, the police, courts, and corrections components work and interact to function like a process, a network, or even a nonsystem. However, the justice system may still constitute a true system. As Willa Dawson stated, "Administration of justice can be regarded as a system by most standards. It may be a poorly functioning system but it does meet the criteria nonetheless. The systems approach is still in its infancy."[21] J. W. La Patra added, "I do believe that a criminal justice system [CJS] does exist, but that it functions very poorly. The CJS is a loosely connected, nonharmonious, group of social entities."[22]

To be fair, however, perhaps this method of dealing with offenders is best after all; it may be that having a well-oiled machine—in which all activities are coordinated, goals and objectives are unified, and communication between participants is maximized, all serving to grind out justice in a highly efficacious manner—may not be what we truly want or need in a democracy.

From Nonsystem to System: Redefining Performance Measures

Despite being a decentralized system with considerable system fragmentation, one can argue that a set of common goals for the CJS gets us closer to what a true system represents. John J. DiIulio argues for criminal justice performance measures beyond those we traditionally associate with the system, such as crime rates and recidivism.[23] As such, DiIulio advocates for a democratic vision of the CJS that includes doing justice, promoting secure communities, restoring crime victims, and promoting noncriminal options.[24] The challenge, as DiIulio puts it, is to see whether justice officials can rally around performance measures that go beyond the traditional CJS "bottom line."

We hope that we have not belabored the subject; however, it is important to establish early in this book the type of system and the components that you, as a potential criminal justice administrator, may encounter. You can reconcile for yourself the differences of opinion described earlier. In this book, we adhere to the notion that even with all of its disunity and lack of fluidity, what criminal justice officials administer in the United States is a system. Nonetheless, it is good to examine its operation and shortcomings and, as stated earlier, confront the CJS's problems and possible areas for improvement.

Now that we have a systemic view of what it is that criminal justice managers actually administer, it would be good to examine briefly how they go about doing it. We first consider the legal and historical bases that created the United States as a democracy regulated by a government and by a system of justice; we include the consensus–conflict continuum, with the social contract on one end and the maintenance of the status quo/repression on the other. Next, we distinguish between administration and work in the public and private sectors because the styles, incentives, and rewards of each are, by their very nature, quite different. This provides the foundation for the final point of discussion, a brief examination of the policymaking process in criminal justice agencies.

The Foundations of Justice and Administration: Legal and Historical Bases

Given that our system of justice is founded on a large, powerful system of government, the following questions must be addressed: From where is that power derived? How can governments presume to maintain a system of laws that effectively governs its people and, furthermore, a legal system that exists to punish persons who willfully suborn those laws? We now consider the answers to those questions.

The Consensus versus Conflict Debate

U.S. society has innumerable lawbreakers. Most of them are easily handled by the police and do not challenge the legitimacy of the law while being arrested and incarcerated for violating it. Nor do they challenge the system of government that enacts the laws or the justice agencies that carry them out. The stability of our government for more than 200 years is a testimony to the existence of a fair degree of consensus as to its legitimacy.[25] Thomas Jefferson's statements in the *Declaration of Independence* are as true today as the day when he wrote them and are accepted as common sense:

> We hold these truths to be self-evident, that all men are created equal, that they are endowed by their Creator with certain inalienable Rights, that among these are Life, Liberty, and the pursuit of Happiness—That to secure these rights, Governments are instituted among Men, deriving their just powers from the consent of the governed. That whenever any Form of Government becomes destructive of these ends, it is the Right of the People to alter or abolish it.

The principles of the *Declaration* are almost a paraphrase of John Locke's *Second Treatise on Civil Government*, which justifies the acts of government on the basis of Locke's theory of social contract. In the state of nature, people, according to Locke, were created by God to be free, equal, independent, and with inherent inalienable rights to life, liberty, and property. Each person had the right of self-protection against those who would infringe on these liberties. In Locke's view, although most people were good, some would be likely to prey on their fellows, who in turn would constantly have to be on guard against such evildoers. To avoid this brutish existence, people joined together, forming governments to which they surrendered their right of self-protection. In return, they received governmental protection of their lives, property, and liberty. As with any contract, each side has benefits and considerations; people give up their right to protect themselves and receive protection in return. Governments give protection and receive loyalty and obedience in return.[26]

Locke believed that the chief purpose of government was the protection of property. Properties would be joined together to form the commonwealth. Once the people unite into a commonwealth, they cannot withdraw from it, nor can their lands be removed from it. Property holders become members of that commonwealth only with their express consent to submit to the government of the commonwealth. This is Locke's famous theory of *tacit consent*: "Every Man ... doth hereby give his *tacit Consent*, and is as far forth obliged to Obedience to the Laws of the Government."[27] Locke's theory essentially describes an association of landowners.[28]

Another theorist connected with the **social contract** theory is Thomas Hobbes, who argued that all people were essentially irrational and selfish. He maintained that people had just enough rationality to recognize their situation and to come together to form governments for self-protection, agreeing "amongst themselves to submit to some Man, or Assembly of men, voluntarily, on confidence to be protected by him against all others."[29] Therefore, they existed in a state of consensus with their governments.

social contract
a belief that people are essentially irrational and selfish, but have enough rationality to come together to form governments for self-protection.

Jean-Jacques Rousseau, a conflict theorist, differed substantively from both Hobbes and Locke, arguing that "Man is born free, but everywhere he is in chains."[30] Like Plato, Rousseau associated the loss of freedom and the creation of conflict in modern societies with the development of private property and the unequal distribution of resources. Rousseau described conflict between the ruling group and the other groups in society, whereas Locke described consensus within the ruling group and the need to use force and other means to ensure the compliance of the other groups.[31]

Thus, the primary difference between the consensus and conflict theorists with respect to their view of government vis-à-vis the governed concerns their evaluation of the legitimacy of the actions of ruling groups in contemporary societies. Locke saw those actions as consistent with natural law, describing societies as consensual and arguing that any conflict was illegitimate and could be repressed by force and other means. Rousseau evaluated the actions of ruling groups as irrational and selfish, creating conflicts among the various groups in society.[32]

This debate is important because it plays out the competing views of humankind toward its ruling group; it also has relevance with respect to the kind of justice system (or process) we have. The system's model has been criticized for implying a greater level of organization and cooperation among the various agencies of justice than actually exists. The word *system* conjures an idea of machinelike precision in which wasted effort, redundancy, and conflicting actions are nearly nonexistent; our current justice system does not possess such a level of perfection. As mentioned earlier, conflicts among and within agencies are rife, goals are not shared by the system's three components, and the system may move in different directions. Therefore, the systems approach is part of the **consensus model** point of view, which assumes that all parts of the system work toward a common goal.[33] The **conflict model**, holding that agency interests tend to make actors within the system self-serving, provides the other approach. This view notes the pressures for success, promotion, and general accountability, which together result in fragmented efforts of the system as a whole, leading to a criminal justice nonsystem.[34]

consensus model the view of the criminal justice system in which it is assumed that all parts of the system work toward a common goal.

conflict model holds that actors within the criminal justice system are self-serving, with pressures for success, promotion, and general accountability and resulting in fragmented efforts.

This debate also has relevance for criminal justice administrators. Assume a consensus–conflict continuum, with social contract (the people totally allow government to use its means to protect them) on one end and class repression on the other. That our administrators *do not* allow their agencies to drift too far to one end of the continuum or the other is of paramount importance. Americans cannot allow the compliance or conflict that would result at either end; the safer point is toward the middle of the continuum, where people are not totally dependent on their government for protection and maintain enough control to prevent totalitarianism.

Crime Control through Due Process

In 1968, Herbert Packer described two now-classic models of the criminal justice process (see Figure 1-2 ■) in terms of two competing value systems: crime control and due process.[35] The **due process model**—likened to an "obstacle course" by some authors—essentially holds that criminal defendants should be presumed innocent, that the courts' first priority is protecting the constitutional rights of the accused, and that granting too much freedom to law enforcement officials will result in the loss of freedom and civil liberties for all Americans; therefore, each court case must involve formal fact-finding to uncover mistakes by the police and prosecutors. This view also stresses that crime is not a result of individual moral failure, but is the result of social influences (such as unemployment, racial discrimination, and other factors that disadvantage the poor); thus, courts that do not follow this philosophy are fundamentally unfair to these defendants. Furthermore, rehabilitation will prevent further crime.

due process model the ideal that the accused should be presumed innocent and have his/her rights protected, while police must act only in accordance with the Constitution.

Crime Control Model

1. The repression of crime is of utmost importance, to provide order.
2. CJ focus should be on helping victims rather than on defendants' rights.
3. Police powers should be expanded, legal technicalities eliminated, for ease of arrest, search and seizure, conviction.
4. The CJ process should operate like an assembly line, moving cases through swiftly.
5. There should generally be a presumption of guilt of the accused (and police/prosecutors' views trusted).

Due Process Model

1. CJ must provide due process, fairness, and a focus on defendants' rights, as provided in the Bill of Rights.
2. Police powers should be limited to prevent oppression.
3. Constitutional rights aren't "technicalities," so police/prosecutors should be held accountable to ensure fairness.
4. The CJ process should resemble an obstacle course, with impediments/safeguards to protect the innocent and convict the guilty.

FIGURE 1-2 Herbert Packer's Crime Control/Due Process Models of Criminal Justice: A Synopsis

Note: No city will be wholly in one or the other; also, the political climate determines which model shapes criminal justice policy at a specific point in time.

In contrast is the **crime control model**, which is a much more traditional philosophy and which Packer likened to an "assembly line." This model views crime as a breakdown of individual responsibility. It places the highest importance on repressing criminal conduct and thus protecting society. Persons who are charged are presumed guilty, and the courts should not hinder effective enforcement of the laws; rather, legal loopholes should be eliminated and offenders swiftly punished. Under this philosophy, the police and prosecutors should have a high degree of discretion. Punishment will deter crime, so there must be speed and finality in the courts to ensure crime suppression.

crime control model a philosophy that states crime must be repressed, the accused presumed guilty, legal loopholes eliminated, offenders swiftly punished, and police and prosecutors given a high degree of discretion.

Although Packer indicated that neither of these models would be found to completely dominate a particular community or control U.S. crime policy,[36] even to say that one of these models is superior to the other requires an individual to make a value judgment. How much leeway should be given to the police? Should they be allowed to "bend" the laws just a little bit in order to get criminals off the streets? Does the end justify the means? These are important questions. Note that these questions will be revisited in discussions of ethics in Chapter 4 and police discretion in Chapter 6.

▶ Public versus Private Sector Administration

The fact that people derive positive personal experiences from their work has long been recognized.[37] Because work is a vital part of our lives and carries tremendous meaning in terms of our personal identity and happiness, the right match of person to job has long been recognized as a determinant of job satisfaction.[38] Factors such as job importance, accomplishment, challenge, teamwork, management fairness, and rewards become very important.

People in both the public (i.e., government) and private (e.g., retail business) sectors derive personal satisfaction from their work. The means by which they arrive at those positive feelings and are rewarded for their efforts, however, are often quite different. Basically, whereas private businesses and corporations can use a panoply of *extrinsic* (external) rewards to motivate and reward their employees, people working in the public sector must achieve job satisfaction primarily through *intrinsic* (internal) rewards.

Extrinsic rewards include perquisites such as financial compensation (salary and a benefits package), a private office, a key to the executive washroom, bonuses, trips, a company car, awards (including designations such as the employee of the month or the insurance industry's "million-dollar roundtable"), an expense account, membership in country clubs and organizations, and a prestigious job title. The title assigned to a job can affect one's general perceptions of the job regardless of the actual job content. For example, the role once known disparagingly as "grease monkey" in a gasoline service station has commonly become known as "lubrication technician," garbage collectors have become "sanitation engineers," and so on. Enhancement of job titles is done to add job satisfaction and extrinsic rewards to what may often be lackluster positions.

Corporations often devote tremendous amounts of time and money to bestowing extrinsic rewards, incentives, and job titles on employees to enhance their job satisfaction. These rewards, of course, cannot and do not exist in the public sector anywhere near the extent that they do in the private sector.

As indicated earlier, public sector workers must seek and obtain job satisfaction primarily from within—through intrinsic means. These workers, unable to become wealthy through their salaries and to be in a position that is filled with perks, need jobs that are gratifying and that intrinsically make them feel good about themselves and what they accomplish. Practitioners often characterize criminal justice work as intrinsically rewarding, providing a sense of worth in making the world a little better place in which to live. These employees also seek appreciation from their supervisors and coworkers and generally enjoy challenges.

To be successful, administrators should attempt to understand the personalities, needs, and motivations of their employees and attempt to meet those needs and provide motivation to the extent possible. Sometimes this can occur in unconventional locations. As a case in point, Boise, Idaho, police chief William Bones frequently rides a police bicycle along the city's vast greenbelt along the Boise River near Boise State University. Chief Bones uses these opportunities not only to know better his community constituents but also to speak and interact with park rangers and other officers assigned to the downtown area. Nontraditional administrator–subordinate interactions can certainly break down traditional barriers between employees and top-level managers.

▶ Planned Change and Policymaking in Justice Administration

Planning Interventions

In past decades and simpler times, change in criminal justice agencies typically occurred slowly and incrementally. Continuous change is now a constant rather than an exception, however, and the pace and frequency of change have increased. While change is not bad in itself, if unplanned, programs will often fail and even result in negative consequences in the workplace—absences, tardiness, medical or stress leaves, high turnover rates, and even sabotage. Remember, too, that a major change occurring in one component of the justice system can have severe repercussions on the others if not anticipated and planned for. Oftentimes, major changes are enacted without due consideration given to planning, design, implementation, and evaluation; a good example is the initial "three-strikes" laws, initiated in California in 1994, which had a very different structure and outcome than originally intended. The short-lived "team policing" initiative in the 1970s also has provided numerous opportunities to reflect on the importance of planned change in the criminal justice arena.

Obviously, then, change in criminal justice should not and typically does not occur accidentally or haphazardly. Justice administrators must know how to plan, implement, and evaluate interventions that address problems in their organizations and systems while taking into account components such as time frame, target population, outcomes, and normative values—guiding assumptions about how the CJS *ought* to function. **Planned change**, therefore, involves problem analysis, setting goals and objectives, program and policy design, developing an action plan, and monitoring and evaluation.

planned change rational approach to criminal justice planning that involves problem analysis, setting goals and objectives, program and policy design, developing an action plan, and monitoring and evaluation.

As examples, specific programs and policies have been developed to address domestic violence; prostitution; drug abuse; gang activities; repeat offenders; the availability of handguns; prison overcrowding; and the efficacy of statutory enactments, such as the "three-strikes" law.

The most complex and comprehensive approach to effecting planned change in criminal justice is to create a *policy*. Policies vary in the complexity of the rule or guidelines being implemented and the amount of discretion given to those who apply them. For example, police officers are required to read *Miranda* warnings to suspects before they begin questioning them if the information might later be used in court against the defendant. This is an example where discretion is relatively constrained, although the Supreme Court has formulated specific exceptions to the rule. Sometimes policies are more complex, such as "the social policy" of President Lyndon Johnson's War on Poverty in the 1960s. Organizations, too, create policies specifying how they are going to accomplish their mission, expend their resources, and so on.[39]

Imagine the following scenario. Someone in criminal justice operations (e.g., a city or county manager, or a municipal or criminal justice planner) is charged with formulating an omnibus policy with respect to crime reduction. He or she might begin by trying to list all the related variables that contribute to the crime problem: poverty; employment; demographics of people residing within the jurisdiction; environmental conditions (such as housing density and conditions and slum areas); mortality, morbidity, and suicide rates; educational levels of the populace; and so on.

The administrator would request more specific information from each justice administrator within the jurisdiction to determine where problems might exist in the practitioners' view of the police, courts, and corrections subsystems. For example, a police executive would contribute information concerning calls for service, arrests, and crime data (including offender information and crime information—time of day, day of week, methods, locations, targets, and so on). The status of existing programs, such as community policing and crime prevention, would also be provided. From the courts, information would be sought concerning the sizes of civil and criminal court dockets and backlogs ("justice delayed is justice denied"). Included in this report would be input from the prosecutor's office concerning the quality and quantity of police reports and arrests, as well as data on case dismissals and conviction rates at trial. From corrections administrators would come the average officer caseload and the recidivism and revocation rates. Budgetary information would certainly be solicited from all subsystems, as well as miscellaneous data regarding personnel levels, training levels, and so on. Finally, the administrator would attempt to formulate a crime policy, setting forth goals and objectives for addressing the jurisdiction's needs.

As an alternative, the policymaker could approach this task in a far less complex manner, simply setting, either explicitly or without conscious thought, the relatively simple goal of "keeping crime down." This goal might be compromised or complicated by other factors, such as an economic recession. This administrator could in fact disregard most of the other variables discussed earlier as being beyond his or her current needs and interest and would not even attempt to consider them as immediately relevant. The criminal justice practitioners would not be pressed to attempt to provide information and critical analyses. If pressed for time (as is often the case in these real-life scenarios), the planner would readily admit that these variables were being ignored.[40]

Because executives and planners of the alternative approach expect to achieve their goals only partially, they anticipate repeating endlessly the sequence just described as conditions and aspirations change and as accuracy of prediction improves. Realistically, however, the first of these two approaches assumes intellectual capacities and sources of information that people often do not possess; furthermore, the time and money that can be allocated to a policy problem are limited. Public agencies are in effect usually too hamstrung to practice the first method; it is the second method that is followed. Curiously, however, the literature on decision making, planning, policy formulation, and public administration formalizes and preaches the first approach.[41] The second method is much neglected in this literature.

At the organizational level, the first method is akin to formalized "strategic planning," a process for planned change that involves convening key stakeholders (both inside and outside the organization) to develop organizational mission and vision statements, and from there realistic goals, objectives, and strategies to achieve the mission and vision. For example, say a police chief is interested in revisiting a mission statement from decades ago that stressed law enforcement as the mission of his or her agency. Here, a strategic planning group might be convened (comprised of both commissioned and civilian employees as well as community stakeholders) to revise the mission, rethink the vision, and develop goals, objectives, and activities to meet the organization's new priorities.

This group might first start with a SWOT analysis, which focuses on the organization's Strengths, Weaknesses, Opportunities, and Threats. SWOT analysis requires the collection of considerable information important to the organization, which, as described above, may be incomplete for a variety of reasons, including time and access. SWOT analysis is typically a first step in the creation of a strategic plan.

Back to our macro view, probably no part of government has attempted a comprehensive analysis and overview of policy on crime (the first method described). Thus, making crime policy is at best a rough process. Without a more comprehensive process, we cannot possibly understand, for example, how a variety of problems—education, housing, recreation, employment, race, and policing methods—might encourage or discourage juvenile delinquency. What we normally engage in is a comparative analysis of the results of similar past policy decisions. This explains why justice administrators often believe that outside experts or academics are not helpful to them—why it is safer to "fly by the seat of one's pants." Theorists often urge the administrator to go the long way to the solution of his or her problems, following the scientific method, when the administrator knows that the best available theory will not work. Theorists, for their part, do not realize that the administrator is often, in fact, practicing a systematic method.[42] So, what may appear to be mere muddling through is both highly praised as a sophisticated form of **policymaking**—the formal development of ideas or plans that are then used by an organization or government to guide decision making—and soundly denounced as no method at all. What society needs to bear in mind is that justice administrators possess an intimate knowledge of past consequences of actions that outsiders do not. Although seemingly less effective and rational, this method, according to policymaking experts, has merit. Indeed, this method is commonly used for problem-solving in which the means and ends are often impossible to separate, aspirations or objectives undergo constant development, and drastic simplification of the complexity of the real world is urgent if problems are to be solved in reasonable periods of time.[43]

policymaking
(1) developing plans that are then used by an organization or government as a basis for making decisions; (2) establishing rules, principles, or guidelines to govern actions by ordinary citizens and persons in positions of authority.

Force-Field Analysis

There will always be barriers and resistance to change in criminal justice organizations. Such barriers may be physical, social, financial, legal, political, and/or technological in nature. One useful technique for identifying sources of resistance (and support) is called **force-field analysis**. This technique, developed by Kurt Lewin, is based on an analogy to

force-field analysis
a process of identifying forces in support of change and those resisting change.

physics: A body will remain at rest when the sum of forces operating on it is zero. When the forces pushing or pulling it in one direction exceed the forces pushing or pulling it in the opposite one, the body will move in the direction of the greater forces. (Note, however, that in criminal justice administration, change involves *social* forces rather than *physical* ones.) Generally, we focus on reducing rather than overcoming resistance.

Three steps are involved in a force-field analysis:

1. Identifying driving forces (those supporting change) and restraining forces (those resisting change)
2. Analyzing the forces identified in Step 1
3. Identifying alternative strategies for changing each force identified in Step 1; focus on reducing forces of resistance[44]

Take, for example, the forces at work concerning whether or not one will attend a university that is some distance away. Forces favoring the decision might be parents' and friends' encouragement to attend, the opportunity to meet new people and to experience new places and cultures, the prospect of attaining a desirable career with higher income, and the acquisition of far greater knowledge. Forces in opposition might be the costs of tuition, books, and living expenses; the financial loss while attending school and not working; unexceptional high school grades; the number of years required to graduate; and perhaps going to a strange locale and leaving friends, family, and other support groups behind. To reduce the opposing pressures, the student might obtain financial aid or scholarships, plan to call family and friends often, visit the school and community first to try to become more comfortable with them, and so on.

Consequences of Not Planning for Change

You might imagine, then, that there could be rather negative consequences to not planning for change. For one, as alluded to earlier, new programs or initiatives may not be successful. Our example of team policing earlier in this chapter is a case in point. While the idea of bringing police officers both physically and symbolically closer to the citizens they serve seems beneficial, team policing suffered from a lack of planning, which resulted in poor implementation and unclear goals. Critics of this 1970s initiative suggest that it disappeared as quickly as it appeared.[45]

Proactive planning for change can be advantageous over forced change based on events that already have occurred (reactionary change). In our team policing example, change efforts in policing to become closer to its constituents resulted from a deterioration of police–minority relationships in the 1960s and claims of institutional racism. As such, the short-lived change to team policing was reactionary change that was not well planned nor implemented.

Summary

This chapter presented the foundation for the study of justice administration. It also established the legal existence of governments, laws, and the justice agencies that administer them. It demonstrated that the three components of the justice system are independent and fragmented and often work at odds with one another toward the accomplishment of the system's overall mission. Our discussion concluded with a review of the importance of planning for justice administrators and policymakers.

Key Terms and Concepts

Administrator, p. 4
Conflict model, p. 12
Consensus model, p. 12
Crime control model, p. 13
Criminal justice network, p. 6
Criminal justice nonsystem, p. 8
Criminal justice process, p. 6
Due process model, p. 12
Force-field analysis, p. 16
Manager, p. 4
Planned change, p. 15
Policymaking, p. 16
Social contract, p. 11
Supervisor, p. 4
System fragmentation, p. 9

Questions for Review

1. Do the three justice components (police, courts, and corrections) constitute a true system, or are they more appropriately described as a process or a true nonsystem? Defend your response.
2. What are the legal and historical bases for a justice system and its administration in the United States? Why is the conflict versus consensus debate important?
3. What are some of the substantive ways in which public and private sector administration are similar? How are they dissimilar?
4. What is a SWOT analysis and how can this be helpful in the strategic planning process?
5. What elements of planned change must the justice administrator be familiar with in order to ensure that change is affected rationally and successfully?
6. Why is planned change preferred over reactionary change?
7. Which method, a rational process or just muddling through, appears to be used in criminal justice policymaking today? Which method is probably best, given real-world realities? Explain your response.

Deliberate and Decide 1

Is Our Justice System Always "Just"?[46]

Nancy Black, a California marine biologist, also captains a whale watching ship. She was with some watchers in 2005 when a member of her crew whistled at a nearby humpback whale, hoping the whale would linger. Meanwhile, on land one of Black's employees contacted a national oceanographic organization to see if the whistling was in fact harassment of a marine mammal—an environmental crime. Black provided a videotape of the incident, slightly edited to show the whistling; for the editing, she was charged with a felony under the 1863 False Claims Act. She was also charged with a federal crime involving the feeding of killer whales (orcas)—having rigged an apparatus that would stabilize a slab of blubber to better photograph the orca while feeding on a dead gray whale. Since the charges were filed, Black has spent more than $100,000 in legal fees and could be sentenced to 20 years in prison.

Questions for Discussion

1. Does this case represent the conflict or consensus model of justice?
2. Assume Black were to be convicted: Would the end justify the means? Conversely, would the means justify the end result (i.e., having such federal laws, compelling such exorbitant legal fees)?
3. Do you believe politics played a part in this case?
4. Should the prosecutor have the discretion to drop all charges in this case?

Deliberate and Decide 2

The Sovereign Citizen Movement[47]

Recently, a 50-year-old Arizona man who rejects government authority as a member of the "sovereign movement" was sentenced to more than 8 years in a federal prison and ordered to forfeit more than $1.29 million in assets. He was convicted on 1 count of conspiracy to commit money laundering, 13 counts of money laundering, and 4 counts of failure to appear, and ordered to pay $98,782 in restitution once he leaves prison.

This man is heavily involved in the sovereign movement, whose members believe that the U.S. government is illegitimate and that they should not have to pay taxes or be subject to federal laws. Most of them have their own constitution, bill of rights, and government officials. Sovereign citizens can be dangerous and violent, and have been tied with a number of shoot-outs with and killings of police officers. Furthermore, members often commit financial fraud crimes as well.

It is estimated that hundreds of thousands of sovereign citizens currently live throughout the United States. They are such a threat that the FBI maintains a website on these citizens.

Questions for Discussion

1. Based on this chapter's discussions of the foundations of governments and their criminal justice systems, what determination would you make concerning such a movement's legitimacy and legality?
2. Looking at their beliefs, are such people truly American "citizens"?
3. Do you believe any of their beliefs have any redeemable merit?
4. What types and amounts of punishment, if any, do you believe are justified for members of such movements?

Learn by Doing

1. Your criminal justice professor asks you to consider the CJS flowchart displayed on the inside cover of the text. Then, after reading this chapter, you are asked to prepare a paper concerning how this chart implies that criminal justice agencies constitute both a *system* and a *non*system. What will be your response? Alternatively, do you believe that the CJS most closely resembles a *network* or *process*? Explain.
2. It is announced that because of financial shortfalls, your local police department must eliminate 10 percent of its officer positions through layoffs and retirements.
   a. Given the criminal justice planning adage that "you cannot rock one end of the boat," what might be the effects of such position reductions on your local criminal justice system?
   b. Assume instead that local revenues have *increased* in your jurisdiction, and your local police department is told it can add 10 percent more officers' positions. What possible impacts on your local CJS might result?
3. Your criminal justice professor says her department is undergoing a strategic planning process. She asks you for some ideas on how to organize a session related to the departments' strengths, weaknesses, opportunities, and challenges. How would you help her organize this session? Who are the most important people of whom to ask these questions?
4. The head of your state department of corrections wants to close the state's oldest prison, now located in the state capitol; constructed in the 1920s, it is now extremely dangerous as well as very expensive to operate. Although the new location would be in a community that is 50 miles away, it would be nearer the state capitol and offer a considerably larger labor pool of prospective prison employees as well as a much better public transportation system. Being politically astute, the director asks you and several of your fellow staff members to conduct a force-field analysis, looking at *both* communities to determine opposition and support for the move. Identify at least three forces or factors that are likely to *support* the decision to relocate the prison and three that are likely to *oppose* it.

Case Study

We Should Have Planned for This!

You are a resident in a town of 50,000 in the Midwestern United States. Over the years, you have seen great growth in your town, while at the same time, you have seen considerable negative change in your neighborhood. Once a close-knit community, your neighborhood has been experiencing considerable turnover. Families don't know one another very well anymore; neighborhood kids aren't playing outside; you feel fearful walking alone in your own neighborhood at night; and residential and vehicle burglaries are on the increase. The crime rate in your town, while very low when you were growing up there, has now skyrocketed. Violent crimes are up 10 percent over a 10-year period, and larceny/theft is up over 50 percent. Now understanding that something different needs to be done, your local police chief plans to hold a town hall meeting, a first step in a strategic planning process to try some innovative, yet undefined, ways to reduce crime and improve neighborhood life in your town. As a longtime resident, you have been invited to the meeting.

Questions for Discussion

1. Do you plan to attend the initial strategic planning meeting? Why or why not?
2. What kinds of contributions do you feel you could make that could affect change at your local police department?
3. What barriers do you think exist that might lead to little or no change at your police department?

Notes

1. James Downie, "Yes, the American Justice System Is Broken," *The Washington Post* (December 5, 2014).
2. Conrad Black, "Baltimore's Problem, and America's," *National Review* (May 6, 2015).
3. Michael E. O'Neill, Ronald F. Bykowski, and Robert S. Blair, *Criminal Justice Planning: A Practical Approach* (San Jose, CA: Justice Systems Development, 1976), p. 5.
4. Ibid., p. 12.
5. Ibid.
6. Steven M. Cox and John E. Wade, *The Criminal Justice Network: An Introduction*, 2nd ed. (Dubuque, IA: William C. Brown, 1989), p. 1.
7. Ibid., p. 4.
8. Ibid., p. 12.
9. Ibid., pp. 13–14.
10. Philip H. Ennis, "Crime, Victims, and the Police," *Transaction* 4 (1967): 36–44.
11. The President's Commission on Law Enforcement and the Administration of Justice, *The Challenge of Crime in a Free Society* (Washington, DC: U.S. Government Printing Office, 1967), p. 7.
12. Alfred Cohn and Roy Udolf, *The Criminal Justice System and Its Psychology* (New York: Van Nostrand Reinhold, 1979), p. 152.
13. Burton Wright and Vernon Fox, *Criminal Justice and the Social Sciences* (Philadelphia, PA: W. B. Saunders, 1978).
14. "Justice on Trial: A Special Report," *Newsweek* (March 8, 1971): 16.
15. Ibid., p. 18.
16. Alan R. Coffey and Edward Eldefonso, *Process and Impact of Justice* (Beverly Hills, CA: Glencoe Press, 1975), p. 32.
17. The President's Commission, *Challenge of Crime in a Free Society*, p. 5.
18. Coffey and Eldefonso, *Process and Impact of Justice*, p. 35.
19. Ibid., p. 39.
20. Ibid., p. 41.
21. Willa Dawson, "The Need for a System Approach to Criminal Justice," in Donald T. Shanahan (ed.), *The Administration of Justice System—An Introduction* (Boston, MA: Holbrook, 1977), p. 141.
22. J. W. La Patra, *Analyzing the Criminal Justice System* (Lexington, MA: Lexington Books, 1978), p. 75.
23. John J. DiIulio, "Rethinking the Criminal Justice System: Toward a New Paradigm," in Discussion Papers from the BJS-Princeton Project, *Performance Measures for the Criminal Justice System* (Washington, DC: U.S. Department of Justice, 1993).
24. Ibid.
25. Alexander B. Smith and Harriet Pollack, *Criminal Justice: An Overview* (New York: Holt, Rinehart and Winston, 1980), p. 9.
26. Ibid., p. 10.
27. Ibid., p. 366.
28. Thomas J. Bernard, *The Consensus–Conflict Debate: Form and Content in Social Theories* (New York: Columbia University Press, 1983), p. 78.
29. Thomas Hobbes, *Leviathan* (New York: E. P. Dutton, 1950), pp. 290–291.
30. Jean-Jacques Rousseau, "A Discourse on the Origin of Inequality," in G. D. H. Cole (ed.), *The Social Contract and Discourses* (New York: E. P. Dutton, 1946), p. 240.
31. Bernard, *Consensus–Conflict Debate*, pp. 83, 85.
32. Ibid., p. 86.
33. Frank Schmalleger, *Criminal Justice Today*, 10th ed. (Upper Saddle River, NJ: Prentice Hall, 2009), pp. 16–17.
34. One of the first publications to express the nonsystem approach was the American Bar Association, *New Perspective on Urban Crime* (Washington, DC: ABA Special Committee on Crime Prevention and Control, 1972).
35. Herbert L. Packer, *The Limits of the Criminal Sanction* (Stanford, CA: Stanford University Press, 1968).
36. Herbert L. Packer, *Two Models of the Criminal Process*, 113 U. PA. L. REV. 1, 2 (1964).
37. Fernando Bartolome and Paul A. Lee Evans, "Professional Lives versus Private Lives: Shifting Patterns of Managerial Commitment," *Organizational Dynamics* 7 (1982): 2–29; Ronald C. Kessler and James A. McRae, Jr., "The Effect of Wives' Employment on the Mental Health of Married Men and Women," *American Sociological Review* 47 (1979): 216–227.
38. Robert V. Presthus, *The Organizational Society* (New York: Alfred A. Knopf, 1962).
39. Wayne N. Welsh and Philip W. Harris, *Criminal Justice Policy and Planning*, 2nd ed. (Cincinnati, OH: LexisNexis Anderson, 2004), p. 5.
40. This scenario is modeled on one set out by Harvard economist Charles E. Lindblom, "The Science of 'Muddling Through,' " *Public Administration Review* 19 (Spring 1959): 79–89.
41. Ibid., p. 80.
42. Ibid., p. 87.
43. Ibid., p. 88.
44. Kurt Lewin, *Field Theory in Social Science* (New York: Harper and Row, 1951).
45. Lawrence Sherman, Catherine Milton, Thomas V. Kelly, and Thomas F. MacBride, *Team Policing: Seven Case Studies* (Washington, DC: Police Foundation, 1973).
46. For more information, see "Nancy Black, Indicted Marine Biologist, Denies Feeding Orcas," *Huffington Post*, February 1, 2012, http://www.huffingtonpost.com/2012/02/01/indicted-marine-biologist-nancy-black_n_1247284.html.
47. See William D'Urso, "Sovereign Citizen Gets 8 Years in Money Laundering Case," *Las Vegas Sun*, March 20, 2013, http://www.lasvegassun.com/news/2013/mar/20/sovereign-citizen-gets-8-years-money-laundering-ca/; also see Nadine Maeser, "Special Report: A Closer Look at Sovereign Citizens," *WECT*, http://www.wect.com/story/21237082/special-report-sovereign-citizens.

Reshavskyi/Shutterstock

2 Organization and Administration

Principles and Practices

LEARNING OBJECTIVES

After reading this chapter, the student will be able to:

1. *define organizations and the types of organizations*
2. *understand the evolution of organizational theory, including scientific management, human relations, systems, and bureaucratic management*
3. *understand the major components of organizational structure, such as span of control and unity of command*
4. *explain the uniqueness of communication within police organizations*
5. *describe the primary components of communication, such as its process, barriers, cultural cues, and upward/downward/horizontal forms*
6. *comprehend the primary leadership theories and skills, including the characteristics and skills of America's best leaders*
7. *describe the challenges and implications of new generations of workers who are entering the workplace*
8. *describe the rights and interests—and legal aspects—concerning both employees and employers regarding employees' personal appearance at the workplace*

Introduction

Michael Scott, the title character of NBC's long-running comedy *The Office*, was a regional manager at the fictitious Dunder-Mifflin paper company in Scranton, PA. Scott, along with an ensemble cast of his subordinates, depicted the antithesis of a pleasant and inviting workplace. Scott's top-down management approach and often highly inappropriate behavior served as the basis of most episodes. Employees of Dunder-Mifflin were stuck at their desks, tied to their corded phones, while Scott on numerous occasions belittled them, including the HR manager, Toby Flenderson, who was frequently depicted as the recipient of Scott's unpredictable wrath. Leading and managing a diverse workforce, as depicted in *The Office*, can lead to workplace hostility, low motivation, and low job satisfaction. But, as we will see, it does not have to be so.

This chapter—one of the lengthiest in this book and certainly one of the most essential chapters in terms of providing the foundation of administration—examines organizations and the employees within them and how they should be managed and motivated. The underlying theme is that *administrators must know their people*, and the chapter offers a general discussion of organizations, focusing on their definition, theory and function, and structure. Included are several approaches to managing and communicating within organizations.

Also, as indicated in Chapter 1, the initial chapters of Parts 2, 3, and 4 of this book discuss the organization and operation of police, courts, and corrections agencies, respectively. Similarly, countless books and articles have been written about organization and administration in general (many of them in the business and human resources disciplines); therefore, in this chapter, we will attempt to discuss the major elements of organization and administration that apply to the field of criminal justice administration. Then, we review the evolution of organizational theory, including scientific, human relations, systems, and bureaucratic management.

Next, we consider the structure of organizations (including concepts such as span of control and unity of command). We then focus on one of the most important aspects of organizations: communication. After defining what constitutes communication, we consider its process, barriers, role, some cultural cues, and the uniqueness of communication within police organizations. Next is a discussion of leadership and primary theories of how to lead the organization; included is an overview of the characteristics and skills of America's best leaders. Following is a discussion of several classical motivational techniques that are used with employees, which includes major theorists in the field such as McGregor, Maslow, Katz, and Herzberg.

Then, we examine some of the unique challenges posed by the coming generation of criminal justice employees—the so-called Generation Y (or Millennial) employees—including the world into which they were born, the influences of technologies on their worldview, their penchant for bodily adornment, and the implications for the criminal justice workplace. The chapter concludes with review questions and exercises in the Deliberate and Decide, Learn by Doing, and Case Study sections.

Defining Organizations

Like *supervision* and *management,* the word *organization* has a number of meanings and interpretations that have evolved over the years. We think of organizations as entities of two or more people who cooperate to achieve an objective(s); it can therefore be a company, business, club, and so forth, which engages in planning and arranging the different parts of the group toward accomplishing a fundamental mission. In that sense, certainly, the concept of organization is not new. Undoubtedly, the first organizations were primitive hunting parties. Organization and a high degree of coordination were required to bring down huge animals, as revealed in fossils from as early as 40,000 years ago.[1]

An **organization** may be formally defined as "a consciously coordinated social entity, with a relatively identifiable boundary, that functions on a relatively continuous basis to achieve a common goal or set of goals."[2] The phrase *consciously coordinated* implies management. **Social entity** refers to the fact that organizations are composed of people who interact with one another and with people in other organizations. **Relatively identifiable boundary** alludes to the organization's goals and the public served.[3] Using this definition, we can consider many types of formal groups as full-blown organizations. Four different types of formal organizations have been identified by asking the question "Who benefits?" Answers include (1) mutual benefit associations, such as police labor unions; (2) business concerns, such as General Motors; (3) service organizations, such as community mental health centers, where the client group is the prime beneficiary; and (4) commonweal (e.g., those that exist for the public good or welfare) organizations, such as the Department of Defense and criminal justice agencies, where the beneficiaries are the public at large.[4] The following analogy is designed to help the reader understand organizations.

organization entities of two or more people who cooperate to achieve an objective(s).

social entity an organization composed of people who interact with one another and with other people.

relatively identifiable boundary an organization's goals and the public it is intended to serve.

An organization corresponds to the bones that structure or give form to the body. Imagine that the hand is a single mass of bone rather than four separate fingers and a thumb made up of bones joined by cartilage to be flexible. The single mass of bones could not, due to its structure, play musical instruments, hold a pencil, or grip a baseball bat. A criminal justice organization is analogous. It must be structured properly if it is to be effective in fulfilling its many diverse goals.[5]

It is important to note that no two organizations are structured or function exactly alike, nor is there one best way to run an organization.

▶ The Evolution of Organizational Theory

Next, we discuss the evolution of **organizational theory**, which is the study of organizational designs and structures, the relationship of organizations with their external environment, and the behavior of administrators and managers within organizations.

organizational theory the study of organizational designs and structures that includes the behavior of administrators and managers within organizations.

According to Ronald Lynch,[6] the history of management can be divided into three approaches and time periods: (1) scientific management (1900–1940), (2) human relations management (1930–1970), and (3) systems management (1965–present). To this, we would add another important element to the concept of organizations: bureaucratic management, which is also discussed in this section.

Scientific Management

Frederick W. Taylor, who first emphasized time and motion studies, is known today as the father of **scientific management**—a school of management thought that is concerned primarily with the efficiency and output of the individual worker. Spending his early years in the steel mills of Pennsylvania, Taylor became chief engineer and later discovered a new method of making steel; this allowed him to retire at the age of 45 years to write and lecture. He became interested in methods for getting greater productivity from workers and was hired in 1898 by Bethlehem Steel, where he measured the time it took workers to shovel and carry pig iron. Taylor recommended giving workers hourly breaks and going to a piecework system, among other adjustments. Worker productivity soared; the total number of shovelers needed dropped from about 600 to 140, and worker earnings increased from $1.15 to $1.88 per day. The average cost of handling a long ton (2,240 pounds) dropped from $0.072 to $0.033.[7]

scientific management a school of management thought that is concerned primarily with the efficiency and output of an individual worker.

PLANNING: working out in broad outline what needs to be done and the methods for doing it to accomplish the purpose set for the enterprise

ORGANIZING: the establishment of a formal structure of authority through which work subdivisions are arranged, defined, and coordinated for the defined objective

STAFFING: the whole personnel function of bringing in and training the staff and maintaining favorable conditions of work

DIRECTING: the continuous task of making decisions, embodying them in specific and general orders and instructions, and serving as the leader of the enterprise

COORDINATING: the all-important duty of interrelating the various parts of the organization

REPORTING: informing the executive and his or her assistants as to what is going on, through records, research, and inspection

BUDGETING: all that is related to budgeting in the form of fiscal planning, accounting, and control

FIGURE 2-1 Gulick's POSDCORB

Source: Luther Gulick and Lyndall Urwick, *Papers on the Science of Administration* (New York: Institute of Public Administration, 1937).

Taylor, who was highly criticized by unions for his management-oriented views, proved that administrators must know their employees. He published the book *The Principles of Scientific Management* in 1911. His views caught on, and soon emphasis was placed entirely on the formal administrative structure; terms such as *authority, chain of command, span of control*, and *division of labor* were coined.

POSDCORB an acronym for planning, organizing, staffing, directing, coordinating, reporting, and budgeting; this philosophy was emphasized in police management for many years.

In 1935, Luther Gulick formulated the theory of **POSDCORB**, an acronym for planning, organizing, staffing, directing, coordinating, reporting, and budgeting (Figure 2-1 ■). This philosophy was emphasized in police management for many years. Gulick stressed the technical and engineering side of management, virtually ignoring the human side.

The application of scientific management to criminal justice agencies was heavily criticized. It viewed employees as passive instruments whose feelings were completely disregarded. In addition, employees were considered to be motivated by money alone.

Human Relations Management

Beginning in the 1930s, people began to realize the negative effects of scientific management on the worker. A view arose in policing that management should instill pride and dignity in officers. The movement toward human relations management began with the famous studies conducted during the late 1920s through the mid-1930s by the Harvard Business School at the Hawthorne plant of the Western Electric Company.[8] These studies, which are discussed in more detail later in this chapter, found that worker productivity is more closely related to *social* capacity than to physical capacity, noneconomic rewards play a prominent part in motivating and satisfying employees, and employees do not react to management and its rewards as individuals but as members of groups.[9]

In the 1940s and 1950s, police departments began to recognize the strong effect of the informal structure on the organization; agencies began using techniques such as job enlargement and job enrichment to generate interest in policing as a career. Studies indicated that the supervisor who was "employee centered" was more effective than one who was "production centered." Democratic or participatory management began to appear in police agencies. The human relations approach had its limitations, however. With the emphasis placed on the employee, the role of the organizational structure became secondary; the primary goal seemed to many to be social rewards, with little attention given to task accomplishment. Many police managers saw this trend as unrealistic. Employees began to give less and expect more in return.[10]

Systems Management

In the mid-1960s, features of the human relations and scientific management approaches were combined in the *systems management* approach. Designed to bring the individual and the organization together, it attempted to help managers use employees to reach desired production goals. The systems management approach recognized that it was still necessary to have some hierarchical arrangement to bring about coordination, that authority and responsibility were essential, and that overall organization was required.

The systems management approach combined the work of Abraham Maslow,[11] who developed a hierarchy of needs; Douglas McGregor,[12] who stressed the general theory of human motivation; and Robert Blake and Jane Mouton,[13] who developed the "managerial grid," which emphasized two concerns—for task and for people—that managers must have. In effect, the systems management approach holds that to be effective, the manager must be interdependent with other individuals and groups and have the ability to recognize and deal with conflict and change. More than mere technical skills are required; managers require knowledge of several major resources: people, money, time, and equipment.[14] Team cooperation is required to achieve organizational goals.

Several theories of leadership and means of motivating employees have also evolved over the past several decades; we discuss several of them in the following sections.

Bureaucratic Management

Criminal justice agencies certainly fit the description of an organization. First, they are managed by being organized into a number of specialized units. Administrators, managers, and supervisors exist to ensure that these units work together toward a common goal (each unit working independently would lead to fragmentation, conflict, and competition). Second, these agencies consist of people who interact within the organization and with external organizations, and they exist to serve the public. Through a mission statement, policies and procedures, a proper management style, and direction, criminal justice administrators attempt to ensure that the organization maintains its overall goals of crime treatment and suppression, and that it works amicably with other organizations and people. As the organization becomes larger, the need becomes greater for people to cooperate to achieve organizational goals.

Criminal justice organizations are *bureaucracies,* as are virtually all large organizations in modern society. The idea of a pure **bureaucracy** was developed by Max Weber, a German sociologist and the "father of sociology," who argued that if a bureaucratic structure is to function efficiently, it must have the following elements:

bureaucracy structuring of an organization so as to function efficiently; it includes rules, division of labor, hierarchy of authority, and expertise among its members.

1. ***Rulification and routinization.*** Organizations stress continuity. Rules save effort by eliminating the need for deriving a new solution for every problem. They also facilitate standard and equal treatment of similar situations.

2. ***Division of labor.*** This involves the performance of functions by various parts of an organization along with providing the necessary authority to carry out these functions.
3. ***Hierarchy of authority.*** Each lower office is under the control and supervision of a higher one.
4. ***Expertise.*** Specialized training is necessary. Only a person who has demonstrated adequate technical training is qualified to be a member of the administrative staff.
5. ***Written rules.*** Administrative acts, decisions, and rules are formulated and recorded in writing.[15]

First, many people today view bureaucracies in negative terms, believing that all too often, officials tell clients "That's not my job," or appear to be "going by the book"—relying heavily on rules and regulations, and policies and procedures ("red tape"). Second, they are said to stifle the individual freedom, spontaneity, and self-realization of their employees.[16] James Q. Wilson referred to this widespread discontent with modern organizations as the "bureaucracy problem," where the key issue is "getting the frontline worker … to do 'the right thing.' "[17]

Weber's ideal bureaucracy, however, as described earlier, was designed to eliminate inefficiency and waste in organizations. As shown for each of the earlier principles, many of the characteristics that he proposed years ago are found in today's criminal justice agencies as well as in other bureaucracies (e.g., political parties, churches, educational institutions, and private businesses).

The administration of most police and prison organizations is based on the traditional, pyramidal, quasi-military organizational structure containing the elements of a bureaucracy: specialized functions, adherence to fixed rules, and a hierarchy of authority. (This pyramidal organizational environment is undergoing increasing challenges, especially as a result of departments implementing community policing, as will be seen in Chapter 4.)

Organizational Inputs/Outputs

inputs an organization's committing such resources as funds, personnel/labor, and equipment toward accomplishing a goal or mission.

outputs an organization's desired outcome, goods, or services.

Another way to view organizations is as systems that take **inputs** (e.g., committing resources as funds, personnel/labor, and equipment needed for accomplishing a goal or mission), process them, and thus produce **outputs** (the desired outcome, goods, or services). A police agency, for example, processes reports of criminal activity and, like other systems, attempts to satisfy the customer (crime victim). Figure 2-2 ■ demonstrates the input/output model for the police and private business. There are other types of inputs by police agencies; for example, a robbery problem might result in an input of newly created robbery surveillance teams, the processing would be their stakeouts, and the output would be the number of subsequent arrests by the team. Feedback would occur in the form of conviction rates at trial.

▶ Organizational Structure

Primary Principles

All organizations have an organizational structure or table of organization, be it written or unwritten, very basic or highly complex. An experienced manager uses this organizational chart or table as a blueprint for action. The size of the organization depends on the demands placed on it and the resources available to it. Growth precipitates the need for more personnel, greater division of labor, specialization, written rules, and other such elements.

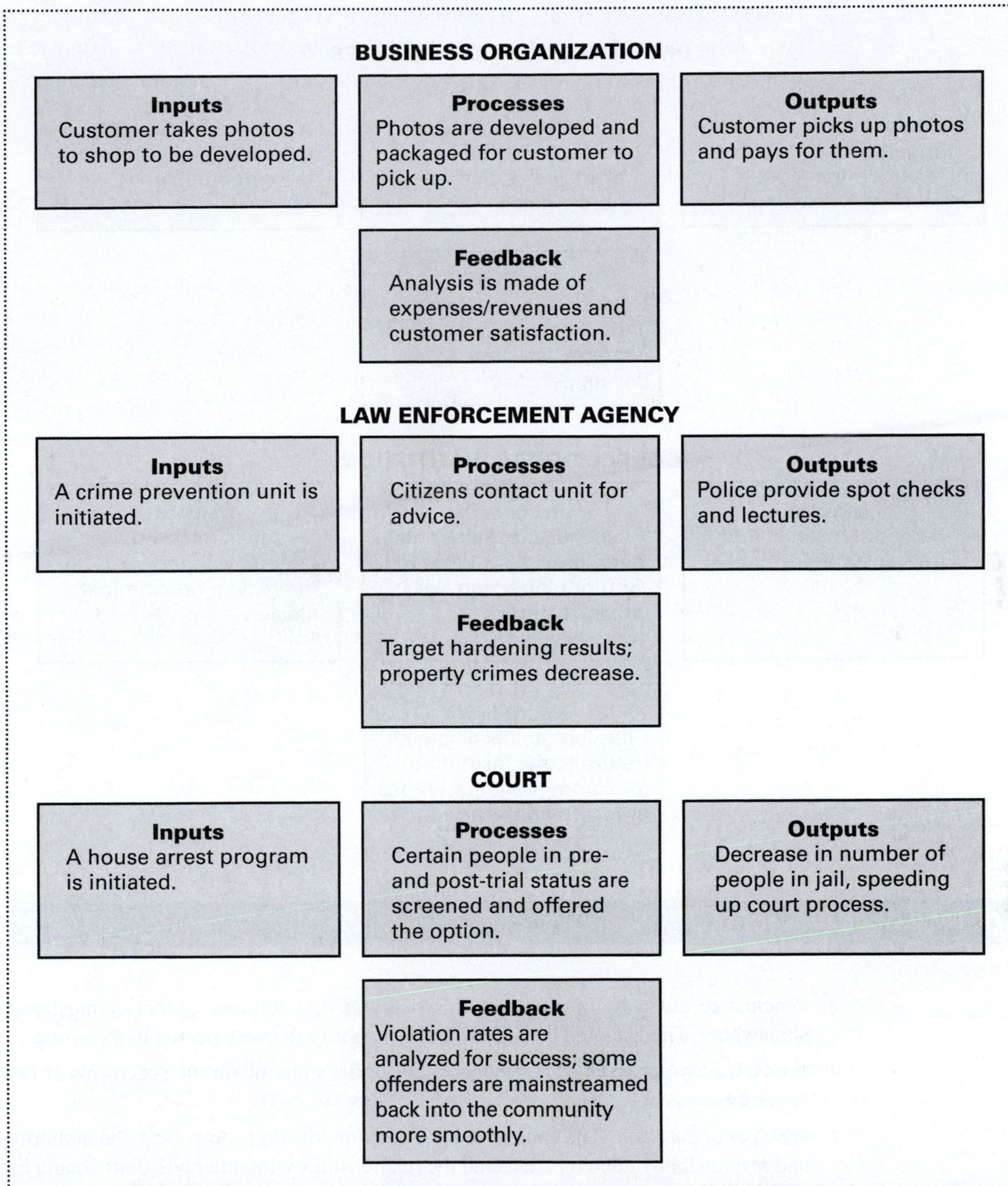

BUSINESS ORGANIZATION
Inputs
Customer takes photos to shop to be developed.
Processes
Photos are developed and packaged for customer to pick up.
Outputs
Customer picks up photos and pays for them.
Feedback
Analysis is made of expenses/revenues and customer satisfaction.
LAW ENFORCEMENT AGENCY
Inputs
A crime prevention unit is initiated.
Processes
Citizens contact unit for advice.
Outputs
Police provide spot checks and lectures.
Feedback
Target hardening results; property crimes decrease.
COURT
Inputs
A house arrest program is initiated.
Processes
Certain people in pre- and post-trial status are screened and offered the option.
Outputs
Decrease in number of people in jail, speeding up court process.
Feedback
Violation rates are analyzed for success; some offenders are mainstreamed back into the community more smoothly.

FIGURE 2-2 The Organization as an Input–Output Model

In building the organizational structure, the following principles should be kept in mind:

1. ***Principle of the objective.*** Every part of every organization must be an expression of the purpose of the undertaking. You cannot organize in a vacuum; you must organize for something.
2. ***Principle of specialization.*** The activities of every member of any organized group should be confined, as far as possible, to the performance of a single function.

PROBATION/PAROLE AGENCIES

Inputs	Processes	Outputs
Parole guidelines are changed to shorten length of incarceration and reduce overcrowding.	Qualified inmates are contacted by parole agency and given new parole dates.	A higher number of inmates are paroled into the community.

Feedback
Parole officer's caseload and revocation rates might increase; less time to devote per case.

CORRECTIONAL INSTITUTION

Inputs	Processes	Outputs
Person is incarcerated for felony offense(s).	Prison incapacitates and often provides counseling, GED or higher; job skills; other treatment or programming.	Person is released—generally supervised—to maintain a noncriminal lifestyle.

Feedback
Does inmate recidivate (return to the institution for committing new crimes or for violating parole conditions)?

FIGURE 2-2 *(continued)*

3. ***Principle of authority.*** In every organized group, the supreme authority must rest somewhere. There should be a clear line of authority to every person in the group.
4. ***Principle of responsibility.*** The responsibility of the superior for the acts of his or her subordinates is absolute.
5. ***Principle of definition.*** The content of each position, the duties involved, the authority and responsibility contemplated, and the relationships with other positions should be clearly defined in writing and published for all concerned.
6. ***Principle of correspondence.*** In every position, the responsibility and the authority to carry out the responsibility should correspond.
7. ***Span of control.*** No person should supervise more than six direct subordinates whose work interlocks.[18]

span of control the number of subordinates a chief executive, manager, or supervisor in a criminal justice organization can effectively supervise.

Span of Control and Unity of Command

The last concept in the preceding list, **span of control**, has recently been revisited in the literature and deserves additional commentary. How many subordinates can a chief executive, manager, or supervisor in a criminal justice organization effectively supervise?

The answer will depend on factors such as the capacity of the leader and the persons supervised, the type of work performed, the complexity of the work, the area covered, distances between elements, the time needed to perform the tasks, and the types of persons served. Normally, a police patrol sergeant will supervise 6–10 officers, while a patrol lieutenant may have 4 or 5 sergeants reporting to him or her.[19]

Several authors now argue for even higher spans of control, however, to afford reductions in the distortion of information as it flows through the organization; more rapid, effective decision making and action; fewer functional roadblocks and "turf protection"; greater emphasis on controlling the bureaucracy rather than on customer service; and reduced costs because of the lower number of managers and management support staff. Some also argue that rank-and-file employees favor higher spans of control because they receive less detailed and micromanaged supervision, greater responsibility, and a higher level of trust by their supervisors.[20]

A related, major principle of hierarchy of authority is **unity of command**, which refers to placing one and only one superior officer in command or in control of every situation and employee. When a critical situation occurs, it is imperative that only one person should be responsible and in charge. The unity of command principle ensures, for example, that multiple and/or conflicting orders are not issued to the same police officers by several superior officers. For example, a patrol sergeant might arrive at a hostage situation, deploy personnel, and give all appropriate orders, only to have a shift lieutenant or captain come to the scene and countermand the sergeant's orders with his or her own orders. This type of situation would obviously be counterproductive for all concerned. All officers must know and follow the chain of command at such incidents. Every person in the organization should report to one and only one superior officer. When the unity of command principle is followed, everyone involved is aware of the actions initiated by superiors and subordinates. A simple structure indicating the direct line of authority in a chain of command is shown in Figure 2-3 ■.

> **unity of command** the principle holding that only one person should be in command or control of a situation or an employee.

An organization should be developed through careful evaluation of its responsibilities; otherwise, the agency may become unable to respond efficiently to clients' needs. For example, the implementation of too many specialized units in a police department (e.g., community relations, crime analysis, media relations) may obligate too many

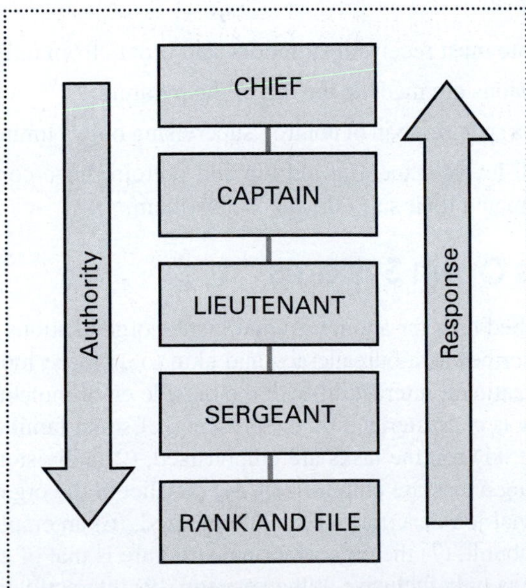

FIGURE 2-3 Chain of Command

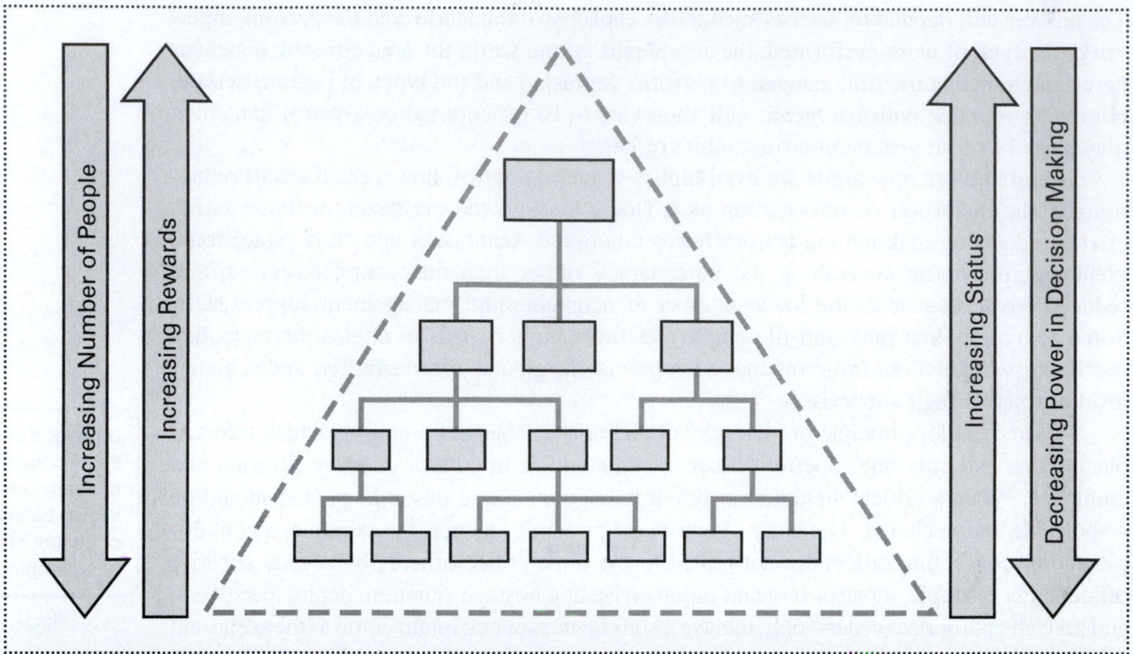

FIGURE 2-4 Organizational Pyramid

Source: Sayles & Strauss, *Human Behavior in Organizations*, 1st Ed., © 1966. Reprinted and Electronically reproduced by permission of Pearson Education, Inc., Upper Saddle River, New Jersey., p. 349.

personnel to these functions and result in too few patrol officers. Today, 56 to 90 percent of all sworn personnel are assigned to patrol.[21]

The classic pyramidal design is shown in Figure 2-4 ■. The pyramidal structure has the following characteristics:

1. Nearly all contacts take the form of orders going *down* and reports of results going *up* the pyramid.
2. Each subordinate must receive instructions and orders from only one boss.
3. Important decisions are made at the top of the pyramid.
4. Superiors have a specific span of control, supervising only a limited number of people.
5. Personnel at all levels, except at the top and bottom, have contact only with their boss above them and their subordinates below them.[22]

Closed versus Open Systems

What we have described thus far about criminal justice organizations is largely consistent with what Weber describes as a bureaucracy and akin to a closed model system. In these organizations, organizational interaction with the outside environment is minimal and this model of bureaucracy is characterized by the presence of some familiar Weberian themes, such as the following: (1) routine tasks are emphasized, (2) a division of labor is central, (3) the means for doing a task are emphasized, (4) conflict in the organization is managed from the top, (5) formal job descriptions are emphasized, (6) an employee's sense of loyalty is to his or her subunit, (7) the organizational structure is that of a hierarchy, (8) organizational knowledge is only inclusive at the very top, (9) interaction among employees is generally vertical, (10) clear superordinate/subordinate relationships are emphasized, and (11) status is determined by rank.[23]

While a closed system is closely aligned with bureaucratic management, open systems are more closely aligned to human relations management, which we discussed earlier as an employee-centered management approach, focused on participatory management. In contrast to closed systems, open systems focus on the following: (1) nonroutine tasks, (2) specialized knowledge can contribute to common tasks, (3) getting the job done (the ends) are emphasized over the means, (4) organizational conflict is resolved among peers, (5) the sense that all organizational members can contribute to organizational needs, (6) one's sense of responsibility is to the organization as a whole rather to an employee's subunit, (7) the organization is seen as a fluidic structure rather than a pyramid, (8) knowledge can be located anywhere in the organization, (9) interaction tends to be horizontal rather than exclusively vertical, (10) interactions between managers and employees tend to be friendly and advice oriented, and (11) one's status in the organization is dependent upon abilities and reputation, rather than rank.[24]

▶ Communication within the Organization

Import and Consequence

communication the use of words, sounds, signs, bodily cues, or other actions to convey or exchange information, or to express ideas, to another person or group.

Communication is obviously important in every segment of our society. As Mark Twain put it, "The difference between the right word and the almost right word is the difference between lightning and lightning bug."[25]

And to that we might add one more quote, by the noted Italian-American linguist Mario Pei,[26] who wrote about the essential nature of proper communication in general:

> Rightly or wrongly, most people consider language as an index of culture, breeding, upbringing, personality, sometimes even of intelligence, decency, and integrity. Under the circumstances, it is unwise, not to say harmful, to pay no heed to your language. Ignorance or improper use of language can easily interfere with your success and advancement. It can take money out of your pocket.

Certainly there is no discipline where communication is more important than that of criminal justice, where people communicate in and through offense reports; in affidavits; via general orders, policies, procedures, rules, and regulations; on the courtroom witness stand; and in competency, parole, or probation hearings. Indeed, it might be fairly said that communication is the foundation of criminal justice organization and administration.

Communication also becomes exceedingly important and sensitive in criminal justice organizations because of the nature of information that is processed by practitioners—particularly police officers, who often see people at their worst and when they are in the most embarrassing and compromising situations. To communicate what is known about these kinds of behaviors could be devastating to the parties concerned. A former Detroit police chief lamented several decades ago that "many police officers, without realizing they carry such authority, do pass on rumors. The average police officer doesn't stop to weigh what he says."[27] Certainly the same holds true today and extends to courts and corrections personnel, especially in view of the high-tech communications equipment now in use.

Process and Characteristics

Today, we communicate via e-mail, videoconferencing, smart phones and text messages, satellite dishes, and many other forms. We converse orally, in written letters and memos, through our body language, via television and radio programs, and through newspapers and meetings. Even private thoughts—which occur four times faster than the spoken word—are communication. Every waking hour, our minds are full of ideas. Psychologists say that nearly 100,000 thoughts pass through our minds every day, conveyed by a multitude of media.[28]

Studies have long shown that communication is the primary problem in administration and lack of communication is employees' primary complaint about their immediate supervisors.[29] Indeed, managers are in the communications business. It has been said that

> [o]f all skills needed to be an effective manager/leader/supervisor, skill in communicating is *the* most vital. In fact, research has shown that 93 percent of police work is one-on-one communication. Estimates vary, but all studies emphasize the importance of communications in everyday law enforcement operations.[30]

Several elements comprise the communication process: encoding, transmission, medium, reception, decoding, and feedback.[31]

Encoding. To convey an experience or idea, we translate, or encode, that experience into symbols. We use words or other verbal behaviors or nonverbal behaviors such as gestures to convey the experience or idea.

Transmission. This element involves the translation of the encoded symbols into some behavior that another person can observe. The actual articulation (moving our lips, tongue, and so on) of the symbol into verbal or nonverbal observable behavior is transmission.

Medium. Communication must be conveyed through some channel or medium. Media for communication include sight, hearing, taste, touch, and smell. Some other media are television, telephone, paper and pencil, and radio. The choice of the medium is important; for example, a message that is transmitted via a formal letter from the CEO will carry more weight than the same message conveyed via an administrative assistant's memo.

Reception. The stimuli, the verbal and nonverbal symbols, reach the senses of the receiver and are conveyed to the brain for interpretation.

Decoding. The individual who receives the stimuli develops some meaning for the verbal and nonverbal symbols and decodes the stimuli. These symbols are translated into some concept or experience for the receiver. Whether or not the receiver is familiar with the symbols, or whether or not interference such as noise or a physiological problem occurs, determines how closely the message that the receiver has decoded approximates the message that the sender has encoded.

Feedback. After decoding the transmitted symbols, the receiver usually provides some response or feedback to the sender. If someone appears puzzled, we repeat the message or we encode the concept differently and transmit some different symbols to express that concept. Feedback that we receive acts as a guide or steering device and lets us know whether the receiver has interpreted our symbols as we intended. Feedback is obviously a crucial element in guaranteeing that the sender's intended meaning was in fact conveyed to the receiver.

An organization's systems of communication are usually created by establishing formal areas of responsibility and explicit delegations of duties, including statements of the nature, content, and direction of the communications that are necessary for the group's performance. Most criminal justice administrators prefer a formal system, regardless of how cumbersome it may be, because they can control it and because it tends to create a record for future reference. Several human factors, however, affect the flow of communication. Employees typically communicate with those persons who can help them to achieve their aims; they avoid communicating with those who do not assist, or may retard, their accomplishing those goals; and they tend to avoid communicating with people who threaten them and make them feel anxious.[32] Other barriers to effective communication are discussed later.

Communication within a criminal justice organization may be downward, upward, or horizontal. There are five types of *downward* communication within a criminal justice organization:

1. ***Job instruction.*** Communication relating to the performance of a certain task
2. ***Job rationale.*** Communication relating a certain task to organizational tasks
3. ***Procedures and practice.*** Communication about organizational policies, procedures, rules, and regulations (discussed as they relate to police, in Chapter 4)
4. ***Feedback.*** Communication appraising how an individual performs the assigned task
5. ***Indoctrination.*** Communication designed to motivate the employee[33]

Other reasons for communicating downward—implicit in this list—are opportunities for administrators to spell out objectives, to change attitudes and mold opinions, to prevent misunderstandings from lack of information, and to prepare employees for change.[34]

Upward communication in a criminal justice organization may be likened to a trout trying to swim upstream: With its many currents of resistance, it is a much harder task than to float downstream. Several deterrents restrict upward communication. The physical distance between superior and subordinate impedes upward communication. Communication is often difficult and infrequent when superiors are isolated and seldom seen or spoken to. In large criminal justice organizations, administrators may be located in headquarters that are removed from the operations personnel. The complexity of the organization may also cause prolonged delays of communication. For example, if a corrections officer or a patrol officer observes a problem that needs to be taken to the highest level, normally this information must first be taken to the sergeant, then to the lieutenant, captain, deputy warden or chief, and so on. At each level, these higher-level individuals will reflect on the problem, put their own interpretation on it (possibly including how the problem might affect them professionally or even personally), and possibly even dilute or distort the problem. Thus, delays in communication are inherent in a bureaucracy. Delays could mean that problems are not brought to the attention of the CEO for a long time. The more levels the communication passes through, the more it is filtered and diluted in its accuracy.

There is also the danger that administrators have a "no news is good news" or "slay the messenger" attitude, thereby discouraging the reception of information. Unless the superior does in fact maintain an open-door atmosphere, subordinates are often reluctant to bring, or will temper, bad news, unfavorable opinions, and mistakes or failures to the superior.[35] Administrators may also believe that they know and understand what their subordinates want and think, and that complaints from subordinates are an indication of disloyalty.

For all of these reasons, administrators may fail to take action on undesirable conditions brought to their attention; this will cause subordinates to lose faith in their leaders. Many time-consuming problems could be minimized or eliminated if superiors took the time to listen to their employees.

Horizontal communication thrives in an organization when formal communication channels are not open.[36] The disadvantage of horizontal communication is that it is much easier and more natural to achieve than vertical communication and therefore it often replaces vertical channels. The horizontal channels are usually informal in nature and include the grapevine, discussed next. The advantage is that horizontal communication is essential if the subsystems within a criminal justice organization are to function in an effective and coordinated manner. Horizontal communication among peers may also provide emotional and social bonds that build morale and feelings of teamwork among employees.

Communicating in Police Organizations: Consequence, Jargon, and the Grapevine

Because of their 24/7 work schedules, decentralized nature, unique jargon, and the gravity of what they encounter on the streets, let's briefly consider communications in policing. Police officers must possess the ability to communicate internally and externally regarding policies and procedures that affect daily operations. The ability of the police to communicate effectively using both oral and written means is also paramount because of the damage that can be done by, say, not completing an offense report properly or failing to convey accurately to one's supervisors, to the district attorney, or in court what actually happened in a criminal matter. Officers must also be prepared to converse with highly educated people in their day-to-day work.

Like people in other occupations and professions, the police have their own jargon, dialect, and/or slang that they use on a daily basis. To the police, an offender might be a "perp" (perpetrator); a "subject" is simply someone of interest whom they are talking with, while a "suspect" is someone suspected of having committed a crime. In an "interview," the officer attempts to obtain basic information about a person (name, address, date of birth, and so forth), while an "interrogation" involves questioning an individual about his or her knowledge of, or possible involvement in, a crime. Such jargon and slang help officers to communicate among themselves.

Such slang (or argot) tends to occur among groups, can differ depending on the location of the groups, changes over time, and is widely used in policing for informal, internal communications. In 1993, the *Chicago Tribune* noted some common and other criminal justice organizations argot used among Chicago police officers, including "hype," an intravenous drug user, "501," a drunk driver (from the Illinois Revised Statues), "smoker," a stolen vehicle, and "spot," a location where drugs are sold.[37] And while Chicago police officers use the word "head" to describe an arrest, New York City police officers use the word "collar."[38]

The police also communicate with one another by listening and talking on the police car radio/police officer worn radio, or communicating digitally using a mobile data terminal (MDT). Agencies generally have detailed instructions and dos and don'ts in their policies and procedures regarding the use of a radio. Supervisors must ensure that officers' radio transmissions are as concise, complete, and accurate as possible; officers are to refrain from making unprofessional, rude, sarcastic, or unnecessary remarks while on their radio; and those who fail to abide by these rules will quickly be admonished or even disciplined.

Police communicate on their radios using codes and have done so since the 1920s. The police also communicate with the use of a phonetic alphabet, which was designed to avoid confusion between letters that sound alike, such as when radioing in the name of a person or a license plate number to the dispatcher. For example, a *d* might easily be confused with a *b* or an *m* with an *n*. So, if radioing in a license plate number that is "DOM-123," the officer would say "David Ocean Mary 1-2-3." This eliminates any possible confusion on the receiver's part.

grapevine an informal means of circulating and communicating information or gossip.

In addition to the several barriers to effective communication just discussed, the so-called **grapevine**—an informal means of circulating and communicating information or gossip, and so called because it zigzags back and forth across organizations—can also hinder communication. Communication includes rumors, and probably *no* type of organization in our society has more grapevine "scuttlebutt" than police agencies. Departments even establish *rumor control* centers during major crisis situations. Increasing the usual barriers to communication is the fact that policing, prisons, and jails are 24-hour, 7-day operations, so that rumors are easily carried from one shift to the next.

The grapevine's most effective characteristics are that it is fast, it operates mostly at the place of work, and it supplements regular, formal communication. On the positive side, it can be a tool for management to gauge employees' attitudes, to spread useful information, and to help employees vent their frustrations. However, the grapevine can also carry untruths and be malicious. Without a doubt, the grapevine is a force for administrators to reckon with on a daily basis.

Oral and Written Communication

Our society tends to place considerable confidence in the written word within complex organizations. Writing establishes a permanent record, but transmitting information this way does not necessarily ensure that the message will be clear to the receiver. Often, in spite of the writer's best efforts, information is not conveyed clearly. This may be due in large measure to shortcomings with the writer's skills. Nonetheless, criminal justice organizations seem to rely increasingly on written communication, as evidenced by the proliferation of written directives found in most agencies.

This tendency for organizations to promulgate written rules, policies, and procedures has been caused by three contemporary developments. First is the *requirement for administrative due process* in employee disciplinary matters, encouraged by federal court rulings, police officer bill of rights legislation, and labor contracts. Another development is *civil liability*. Lawsuits against local governments and their criminal justice agencies and administrators have become commonplace; written agency guidelines prohibiting certain acts provide a hedge against successful civil litigation.[39] Written communication is preferred as a medium for dealing with citizens or groups outside the criminal justice agency. This means of communication provides the greatest protection against the growing number of legal actions taken against agencies by activists, citizens, and interest groups.

Finally, a third stimulus is the *accreditation movement*. Agencies that are either pursuing accreditation or have become accredited must possess a wealth of written policies and procedures.[40]

In recent years, electronic mail (e-mail) and text messaging have proliferated as a communication medium in criminal justice organizations. Such messages are easy to use and are almost instantaneous communication—in upward, downward, or horizontal directions. For all their advantages, however, such messages can lack security and can be ambiguous—not only with respect to content meaning but also with regard to what they represent. Are such messages to be given the full weight of an office letter or memo, or should they be treated more as offhand comments?[41]

Other Barriers to Effective Communication

In addition to the barriers just discussed, several other potential barriers to effective communication exist. Some people, for example, are not good listeners. Unfortunately, listening is one of the most neglected and the least understood of the communication arts.[42] We allow other things to obstruct our communication, including time constraints, inadequate or excessive information, the tendency to say what we think others want to hear, failure to select the best word, prejudices, and strained sender–receiver relationships.[43] In addition, subordinates do not always have the same "big picture" viewpoint that superiors possess and do not always communicate well with someone in a higher position who is perhaps more fluent and persuasive than they are.

Cultural Cues

It is important to note that at least 90 percent of communication is *nonverbal* in nature, involving posture, facial expressions, gestures, tone of voice ("it's not what you say but how you say it"), and so on.[44] People learn to interpret these nonverbal messages by growing up in a particular culture, but not every culture interprets nonverbal cues in the same way.

For example, in some cultures, avoiding eye contact by looking at the ground is meant to convey respect and humility. Making what to some people are exaggerated hand gestures may be a normal means of communication in some cultures, and social distance for conversation in some societies may be much closer than it is in the United States. Someone from Nigeria, for example, may stand less than 15 inches from someone while conversing, whereas about two feet is a comfortable conversation zone for Americans. These few examples demonstrate why criminal justice practitioners must possess cultural empathy and understand the cultural cues of citizens from other nations.

External Communications: Use of Social Media

You might recall from our earlier discussion in this section that the choice of medium for communications is important. With the proliferation of social media, criminal justice agencies are turning to such platforms as Facebook and Twitter to communicate externally with their constituents.[45] Historically, external communications to the public went first to the media, then were pushed out via newspapers, television, and radio. But this type of communication typically is one-sided, with little ability of the public to directly interact with criminal justice agencies.

Social media includes a number of varied platforms, including Microblogs (e.g., Twitter), social networking sites (e.g., Facebook), professional networks (e.g., LinkedIn), video sharing (e.g., YouTube), and content-driven communities (e.g., Wikipedia).[46] In a 2015 study, the International Association of Chiefs of Police reported that 96 percent of the law enforcement agencies it surveyed used social media, the great majority of which (94 percent) used Facebook.[47] Almost 89 percent of those police agencies used Facebook to communicate to the public about criminal investigations, oftentimes seeking the public's help in the investigation.[48] In a statewide study completed in Idaho in 2015, Jacob Kabrud found that law enforcement agencies use Facebook to communicate with the public for a variety of reasons, including public interest posts, crime-related posts, and alert-related posts.[49]

As criminal justice agencies move away from being closed, bureaucratic, insular organizations to those that are more open and responsive to community needs, external communications and interactions with the community become more and more paramount. Social media appears to be the driving force of this communication in the twenty-first century.

▶ Primary Leadership Theories

What Is Leadership?

Over 20 years ago, Peter Drucker, often referred to as the *business guru,*[50] conducted a study of the Los Angeles Police Department; among Drucker's findings was: "You police are so concerned with doing things right that you fail to do the right things." Drucker added, "Managers do things right; leaders do the right thing." Another leadership guru, Warren Bennis, has said essentially the same thing. In other words, administrators cannot be so concerned with managing that they fail to lead.[51] We now examine theories underlying leadership and what leaders can do to motivate their subordinates. Probably since the dawn of time, when cave dwellers clustered into hunting groups and some particularly dominant person assumed a leadership role over the party, administrators have received advice on how to do their jobs from those around them. Even today, manuals for leaders and upwardly mobile executives abound, offering quick studies in how to govern others. Although many have doubtlessly been profitable for their authors, most of these how-to primers on leading others enjoy only a brief, ephemeral existence.

To understand **leadership**, we must first define the term. This is an important and fairly complex undertaking, however. Perhaps the simplest definition is to say that leading is "getting things done through people." In general, it may be said that a manager operates in the status quo, but a leader takes risks. Managers are conformers; leaders are reformers. Managers control; leaders empower. Managers supervise; leaders coach. Managers are efficient; leaders are effective. Managers are position oriented; leaders are people oriented. In sum, administrators must be both skilled managers and effective leaders.[52]

leadership influencing and working with and through individuals or a group to generate activities that will accomplish organizational goals.

Other definitions of leadership include the following:

- "The process of influencing the activities of an individual or a group in efforts toward goal achievement in a given situation"[53]
- "Working with and through individuals and groups to accomplish organizational goals"[54]
- "The activity of influencing people to strive willingly for group objectives"[55]
- "The exercise of influence"[56]

Conversely, it has been said that the manager may be viewed as a team captain, parent, steward, battle commander, fountain of wisdom, poker player, group spokesperson, gatekeeper, minister, drill instructor, facilitator, initiator, mediator, navigator, candy-store keeper, linchpin, umbrella-holder, and everything else between nurse and Attila-the-Hun.[57]

In criminal justice organizations, leaders take the macro view; their role might best be defined as "the process of influencing organizational members to use their energies willingly and appropriately to facilitate the achievement of the [agency's] goals."[58] We discuss leaders and managers in greater length later in this chapter and in Chapter 5 (the Mintzberg Model of CEOs).

Next, we discuss what kinds of activities and philosophies constitute leadership.

Trait Theory

Trait theory was popular until the 1950s, but it raises important questions for us today. This theory was based on the contention that good leaders possessed certain character traits that poor leaders did not. Those who developed this theory, Stogdill and Goode, believed that a leader could be identified through a two-step process. The first step involved studying leaders and comparing them to nonleaders to determine which traits only the leaders possessed. The second step sought people who possessed these traits to be promoted to managerial positions.[59]

trait theory a theory based on the notion that good leaders possess certain character traits that poor leaders do not.

A study of 468 administrators in 13 companies found certain traits in successful administrators. They were more intelligent and better educated; had a stronger need for power; preferred independent activity, intense thought, and some risk; enjoyed relationships with people; and disliked detail work more than their subordinates.[60] Figure 2-5 ■ shows traits and skills commonly associated with leader effectiveness, according to Gary Yuki. Following this study, a review of the literature on trait theory revealed the traits most identified with leadership ability: intelligence, initiative, extroversion, a sense of humor, enthusiasm, fairness, sympathy, and self-confidence.[61]

Trait theory has lost much of its support since the 1950s, partly because of the basic assumption of the theory that leadership cannot be taught. A more important reason, however, is simply the growth of new, more sophisticated approaches to the study of leadership. Quantifiable means to test trait theory were limited. What does it mean to say that a leader must be intelligent? By whose standards? Compared with persons within the organization or within society? How can traits such as a sense of humor, enthusiasm, fairness, and the others listed earlier be measured or tested? The inability to measure these factors was the real flaw and the reason for the decline of trait theory.

Traits	Skills
Adaptable to situations	Clever (intelligent)
Alert to social environment	Conceptually skilled
Ambitious and achievement oriented	Creative
Assertive	Diplomatic and tactful
Cooperative	Fluent in speaking
Decisive	Knowledgeable about group task
Dependable	Organized (administrative ability)
Dominant (desire to influence others)	Persuasive
Energetic (high activity level)	Socially skilled
Persistent	
Self-confident	
Tolerant of stress	
Willing to assume responsibility	

FIGURE 2-5 Traits and Skills Commonly Associated with Leader Effectiveness

Source: Yukl, Gary A., *Leadership in Organizations,* 1st Ed., © 1981, pp. 70, 121-125. Adapted and Electronically reproduced by permission of Pearson Education, Inc., Upper Saddle River, New Jersey.

Style Theory

A study at Michigan State University investigated how leaders motivated individuals or groups to achieve organizational goals. The study determined that leaders must have a sense of the task to be accomplished as well as the environment in which their subordinates work. Three principles of leadership behavior emerged from the Michigan study:

1. Leaders must give task direction to their followers.
2. Closeness of supervision directly affects employee production. High-producing units had less direct supervision; highly supervised units had lower production. Conclusion: Employees need some area of freedom to make choices. Given this, they produce at a higher rate.
3. Leaders must be employee oriented. It is the leader's responsibility to facilitate employees' accomplishment of goals.[62]

style theory a theory that focuses on what leaders do, and argue that leaders engage in two distinct types of behaviors: those relating to task and relationships.

In the 1950s, Edwin Fleishman began studies of leadership at Ohio State University. After focusing on leader behavior rather than personality traits, he identified two dimensions or basic principles of leadership that could be taught: *initiating structure* and *consideration* (Figure 2-6 ■).[63] Initiating structure referred to supervisory behavior that focused on the achievement of organizational goals, and consideration was directed toward a supervisor's openness to subordinates' ideas and respect for their feelings as persons. High consideration and moderate initiating structure were assumed to yield higher job satisfaction and productivity than high initiating structure and low consideration.[64]

The major focus of style theory is the adoption of a single managerial style by a manager based on his or her position in regard to initiating structure and consideration. Three pure leadership styles were thought to be the basis for all managers: autocratic, democratic, and laissez-faire.

autocratic leader leaders who are primarily authoritarian in nature and prefer to give orders rather than invite group participation.

The autocratic style is leader centered and has a high initiating structure. An autocratic leader is primarily authoritarian in nature and prefers to give orders rather than invite group participation. Such a leader has a tendency to be personal with criticism. This style

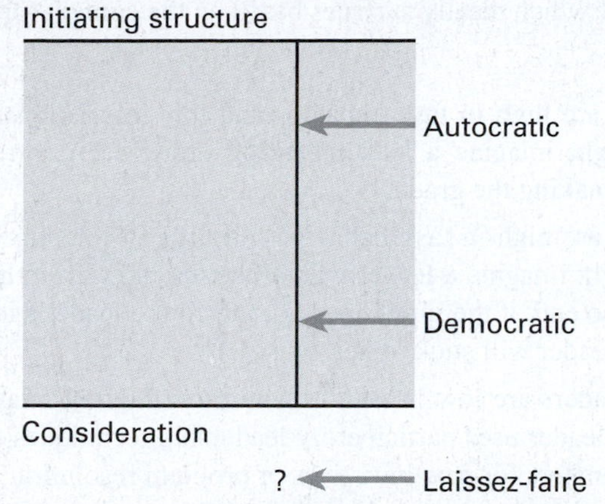

FIGURE 2-6 Style Theory

Source: Holden, Richard, *Modern Police Management*, 1st Ed., © 1986, p. 50. Reprinted and Electronically reproduced by permission of Pearson Education, Inc., Upper Saddle River, New Jersey.

works best in emergency situations in which strict control and rapid decision making are needed. The problem with autocratic leadership is the organization's inability to function when the leader is absent. It also stifles individual development and initiative because subordinates are rarely allowed to make an independent decision.[65]

In the democratic style, the **democratic leader** tends to focus on working within the group and strives to attain cooperation from group members by eliciting their ideas and support. Democratic managers tend to be viewed as consideration oriented and strive to attain mutual respect with subordinates. These leaders operate within an atmosphere of trust and delegate much authority. The democratic style is useful in organizations in which the course of action is uncertain and problems are relatively unstructured. It often taps the decision-making ability of subordinates. In emergency situations requiring a highly structured response, however, democratic leadership may prove too time-consuming and awkward to be effective. Thus, although the worker may appreciate the strengths of this style, its weaknesses must be recognized as well.[66]

democratic leader leaders who stress working within the group and strive to attain cooperation from group members by eliciting their ideas and support.

In the laissez-faire style, the **laissez-faire leader** has a hands-off approach in which the leader is actually a nonleader. The organization in effect runs itself, with no input or control from the manager. This style has no positive aspects, as the entire organization is soon placed in jeopardy. In truth, this may not be a leadership style at all; instead, it may be an abdication of administrative duties.

laissez-faire leader a hands-off approach to leadership, in which the organization essentially runs itself.

Situational Leadership Theory

Similar to style theory, situational leadership theory (SLT), popularized by Hersey and Blanchard, assumes that leaders are most effective when they are adaptable. Rather than trait theory's focus on ideal leadership characteristics, SLT suggests that the best leadership style is situationally dependent based on the interaction of task behavior and relationship behavior. Task behavior refers to the extent to which leaders define the roles of members of their group—leaders who essentially tell their group members what to do and when to do it. Relationship behavior, on the other hand, refers to the extent to which leaders form relationships with members of their group—leaders who essentially provide emotional support and psychological strokes.[67]

From the interaction between task behavior and relationship behavior, four leadership styles emerge, each of which ideally surfaces based on the context (or situation) before the leader.

- "Telling" leaders are high in task behavior and low in relationship behavior. In this scenario, you might imagine a leader barking orders at a correctional officer who repeatedly is not making the grade.
- "Selling" leaders are high in task behavior and high in relationship behavior. In this scenario, you might imagine a leader who seeks the input from her captain to solve a problem, but in the end, if the input does not match the leader's ideas on how to solve the problem, the leader will stick to her guns.
- "Participating" leaders are low in task behavior and high in relationship behavior. In this scenario, the leader uses participatory leadership techniques that create buy-in by organizational members for new initiatives or problem resolution.
- "Delegating" leaders are low in task behavior and low in relationship behavior. Here, a leader might outline broad goals to a working group and ask group members to devise ways to attain the goals with little interference.

The key features of SLT include the interaction between task behavior and relationship behavior, which is dictated by both employee readiness (the extent to which the employee is ready to do the job) and psychological readiness (the extent to which the employee can assume responsibility for getting the job done).[68]

▶ Characteristics and Skills of America's Best Leaders

"Good in Their Skin"

Given today's deep-seated skepticism and distrust of leaders—often justified by public- and private-sector leaders' ethical violations, fraud, and cover-ups—it may seem that there is a complete dearth of leadership. But who are the leaders making a difference? A national panel sifted through nominations and agreed on a small group of men and women who embody the more important traits of leadership. The survey determined that there is not a lack of leadership, but rather a "wrong-headed notion of what a leader is," causing leaders to be hired for their style rather than substance and their image instead of integrity. It was also learned that there is no shortage of people with the capacity to lead who are just waiting for the opportunity.[69]

The survey found that twenty-first-century authentic leaders know who they are; they are "good in their skin," so they do not feel a need to impress or please others. They inspire those around them and bring people together around a shared purpose and a common set of values. They know the "true north" of their moral compass and are prepared to stay the course despite challenges and disappointments. They are more concerned about serving others than about their own success or recognition. By acknowledging their weaknesses, failings, and errors, they connect with people and empower them to take risks. Usually authentic leaders demonstrate the following five traits: pursuing their purpose with passion, practicing solid values, leading with their hearts as well as their heads, establishing connected relationships, and demonstrating self-discipline.[70]

For a less contemporary, classical view of what skills leaders need to possess, we consider the views of Robert Katz.

Katz's Three Skills

Robert Katz, in 1975, identified three essential skills that leaders should possess: technical, human, and conceptual. Katz defined a *skill* as the capacity to translate knowledge into action in such a way that a task is accomplished successfully.[71] Each of these skills (when performed effectively) results in the achievement of objectives and goals, which is the primary task of management.

Technical skills are those a manager needs to ensure that specific tasks are performed correctly. They are based on proven knowledge, procedures, or techniques. A police detective, a court administrator, and a probation officer have all developed technical skills directly related to the work they perform. Katz wrote that a technical skill "involves specialized knowledge, analytical ability within that specialty, and facility in the use of the tools and techniques of the specific discipline."[72] This is the skill most easily trained for. A court administrator, for example, has to be knowledgeable in areas such as computer applications, budgeting, caseload management, space utilization, public relations, and personnel administration; a police detective must possess technical skills in interviewing, fingerprinting, and surveillance techniques.[73]

Human skills involve working with people, including being thoroughly familiar with what motivates employees and how to utilize group processes. Katz visualized human skills as including "the executive's ability to work effectively as a group member and to build cooperative effort within the team he leads."[74] Katz added that the human relations skill involves tolerance of ambiguity and empathy. *Tolerance of ambiguity* means that the manager is able to handle problems when insufficient information precludes making a totally informed decision. *Empathy* is the ability to put oneself in another's place. An awareness of human skills allows a manager to provide the necessary leadership and direction, ensuring that tasks are accomplished in a timely fashion and with the least expenditure of resources.[75]

Conceptual skills, Katz said, involve "coordinating and integrating all the activities and interests of the organization toward a common objective."[76] Katz considered such skills to include "an ability to translate knowledge into action." For example, in a criminal justice setting, a court decision concerning the admissibility of evidence would need to be examined in terms of how it affects detectives, other court cases, the forensic laboratory, the property room, and the work of the street officer.

Katz emphasized that these skills can be taught to actual and prospective administrators; thus, good administrators are not simply born but can be trained in the classroom. Furthermore, all three of these skills are present in varying degrees at each management level. As one moves up the hierarchy, conceptual skills become more important and technical skills less important. The common denominator for all levels of management is *human* skills. In today's litigious environment, it is inconceivable that a manager could neglect the human skills.

▶ Motivating Employees

One of the most fascinating subjects throughout history has been how to motivate people. Some have sought to do so through justice (Plato), others through psychoanalysis (Freud), through conditioning (Pavlov), through incentives (Taylor), and still others through fear (any number of dictators and despots). From the Industrial Revolution to the present, managers have been trying to get a full day's work from their subordinates. The controversy in the early 1990s caused by Japanese businessmen who stated that American workers were lazy certainly raised our collective ire; many U.S. businesspeople and managers would probably agree that better worker motivation is needed. As Donald Favreau and Joseph Gillespie stated, "Getting people to work, the way you want them to work, when you want them to work, is indeed a challenge."[77]

Many theories have attempted to explain motivation. Some of the best known are those resulting from the Hawthorne studies and those developed by Abraham Maslow, Douglas McGregor, and Frederick Herzberg, all of which are discussed here along with the expectancy and contingency theories.

The Hawthorne Studies

Hawthorne effect
a theory meaning that employees' behavior may be altered if they believe they are being studied—and that management *cares.*

Another important theory that criminal justice leaders must comprehend is that of the **Hawthorne effect**, which essentially means that employees' behavior may be altered if they believe they are being studied—and that management *cares*; this was demonstrated in the following research project.

As mentioned earlier, one of the most important studies of worker motivation and behavior, launching intense interest and research in those areas, was the Western Electric Company's study in the 1920s. In 1927, engineers at the Hawthorne plant of Western Electric near Chicago conducted an experiment with several groups of workers to determine the effect of illumination on production. The engineers found that when illumination was increased in stages, production increased. To verify their finding, they reduced illumination to its previous level; again, production increased. Confused by their findings, they contacted Elton Mayo and his colleague Fritz Roethlisberger from Harvard to investigate.[78] First, the researchers selected several experienced female assemblers for an experiment. Management removed the women from their formal group and isolated them in a room. The women were compensated on the basis of the output of their group. Next, researchers began a series of environmental changes, each discussed with the women in advance of its implementation. For example, breaks were introduced and light refreshments were served. The normal six-day workweek was reduced to five days, and the workday was cut by one hour. *Each* of these changes resulted in increased output.[79] To verify these findings, researchers returned the women to their original working conditions; breaks were eliminated, the six-day workweek was reinstituted, and all other work conditions were reinstated. The results were that production again increased!

Mayo and his team then performed a second study at the Hawthorne plant. A new group of 14 workers—all men who performed simple, repetitive telephone coil-winding tasks—were given variations in rest periods and workweeks.[80] The men were also put on a reasonable piece rate—that is, the more they produced, the more money they would earn. The assumption was that the workers would strive to produce more because it was in their own economic interest to do so.

The workers soon split into two informal groups on their own, each group setting its own standards of output and conduct. The workers' output did not increase. Neither too little nor too much production was permitted, and peers exerted pressure to keep members in line. The values of the informal group appeared to be more powerful than the allure of bigger incomes:

1. Don't be a "rate buster" and produce too much work.
2. If you turn out too little work, you are a "chiseler."
3. Don't be a "squealer" to supervisors.
4. Don't be officious; if you aren't a supervisor, don't act like one.[81]

Taken together, the Hawthorne studies revealed that people work for a variety of reasons, not just for money and subsistence. They seek satisfaction for more than their physical needs at work and from their coworkers. For the first time, clear evidence was gathered to support workers' social and esteem needs. As a result, this collision between the human relations school, begun in the Hawthorne studies, and traditional organizational theory sent researchers and theorists off in new and different directions. At least three major new areas of inquiry evolved: (1) what motivates workers (leading to the work of Maslow and Herzberg), (2) leadership (discussed earlier), and (3) organizations as behavioral systems.

Maslow's Hierarchy of Needs

Abraham H. Maslow (1908–1970), who argued for the application of the **humanistic school** of psychology—which basically stressed the importance of growth and self-actualization and argued that people are innately good—conducted research on human behavior at the Air University, Maxwell Air Force Base, Alabama, during the 1940s. His approach to motivation was unique in that the behavior patterns analyzed were those of motivated, happy, and production-oriented people—achievers, not underachievers. He studied biographies of historical and public figures, including Abraham Lincoln, Albert Einstein, and Eleanor Roosevelt; he also observed and interviewed some of his contemporaries—all of whom showed no psychological problems or signs of neurotic behavior.

humanistic school
a school of psychological thought that stressed the importance of growth and self-actualization and argued that people are innately good.

Maslow hypothesized that if he could understand what made these people function, it would be possible to apply the same techniques to others, thus achieving a high state of motivation. His observations were coalesced into a **hierarchy of needs**.[82]

hierarchy of needs
Maslow's belief that people's basic and primary needs or drives are physiological (survival), safety or security, social, ego (self-esteem), and self-realization or actualization.

Maslow concluded that because human beings are part of the animal kingdom, their basic and primary needs or drives are physiological: air, food, water, sex, and shelter. These needs are related to survival. Next in order of importance are needs related to safety or security, protection against danger: murder, criminal assault, threat, deprivation, and tyranny. At the middle of the hierarchy is belonging, or social needs: being accepted by one's peers and associating with members of groups. At the next level of the hierarchy are the needs or drives related to ego: self-esteem, self-respect, power, prestige, recognition, and status. At the top of the hierarchy is self-realization or actualization: self-fulfillment, creativity, becoming all that one is capable of becoming.[83] Figure 2-7 ■ depicts this hierarchy.

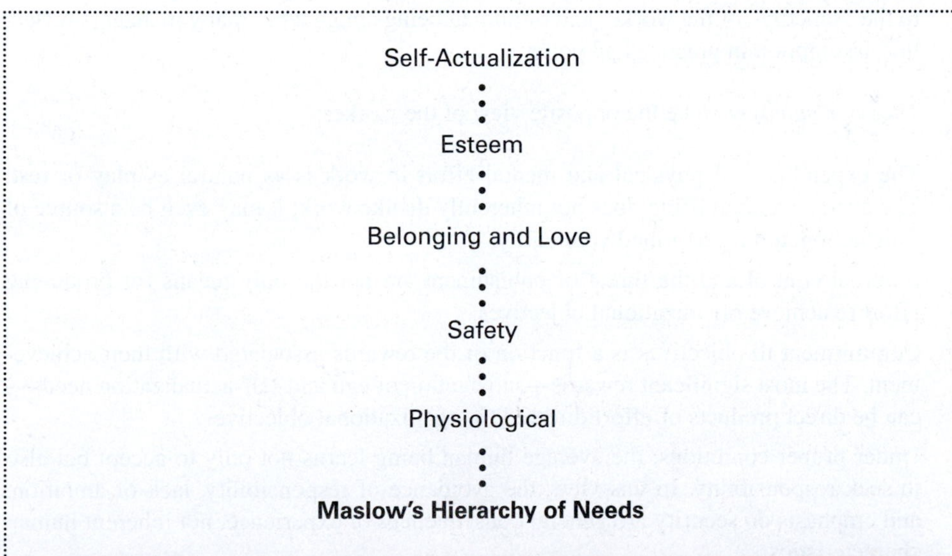

FIGURE 2-7 Maslow's Hierarchy of Human Needs
Source: Maslow's Hierarchy of Human Needs based on *Motivation and Personality*, edited by Kenneth J. Peak..

Unlike the lower needs, the higher needs are rarely satisfied. Maslow suggested that to prevent frustration, needs should be filled in sequential order. A satisfied need is no longer a motivator. Maslow's research also indicated that once a person reaches a high state of motivation (i.e., esteem or self-realization levels), he or she will remain highly motivated, will have a positive attitude toward the organization, and will adopt a "pitch in and help" philosophy.

McGregor's Theory X/Theory Y

Douglas McGregor (1906–1967), who served as president of Antioch College and then on the faculty of the Massachusetts Institute of Technology, was one of the great advocates of humane and democratic management. At Antioch, McGregor tested his theories of democratic management. He noted that behind every managerial decision or action are assumptions about human behavior. He chose the simplest terms possible with which to express them, designating one set of assumptions as **Theory X** and the other as **Theory Y**.[84]

Theory X the management view holding that people inherently dislike work and will avoid it, and thus negative reinforcements (punishments) and other "drivers" must be used as motivators.

Theory Y the management view holding that people inherently like to work, seek greater responsibility, and are inherently motivated rather than by punishment.

Theory X managers hold traditional views of direction and control, such as the following:

- The average human being has an inherent dislike of work and will avoid it if possible. This assumption has deep roots, beginning with the punishment of Adam and Eve and their banishment into a world where they had to work for a living. Management's use of negative reinforcement and the emphasis on "a fair day's work" reflect an underlying belief that management must counter an inherent dislike for work.[85]
- Because of their dislike of work, most people must be coerced, controlled, directed, or threatened with punishment to get them to put forth adequate effort to achieve organizational objectives. Their dislike of work is so strong that even the promise of rewards is not generally enough to overcome it. People will accept the rewards and demand greater ones. Only the threat of punishment will work.[86]
- The average human being prefers to be directed, wishes to avoid responsibility, has relatively little ambition, and wants security above all. This assumption of the "mediocrity of the masses" is rarely expressed so bluntly. Although much lip service is paid to the "sanctity" of the worker and of human beings in general, many managers reflect this assumption in practice and policy.

Theory Y managers take the opposite view of the worker:

- The expenditure of physical and mental effort in work is as natural as play or rest. The average human being does not inherently dislike work; it may even be a source of satisfaction, to be performed voluntarily.
- External control and the threat of punishment are not the only means for producing effort to achieve organizational objectives.
- Commitment to objectives is a function of the rewards associated with their achievement. The most significant rewards—satisfaction of ego and self-actualization needs—can be direct products of effort directed to organizational objectives.
- Under proper conditions, the average human being learns not only to accept but also to seek responsibility. In this view, the avoidance of responsibility, lack of ambition, and emphasis on security are general consequences of experience, not inherent human characteristics.
- The capacity to exercise a high degree of imagination, ingenuity, and creativity in the solution of organizational problems is widely, not narrowly, distributed in the population.

- Under the conditions of modern industrial life, the intellectual potential of the average human being is only partially utilized.

What's interesting to note here are the parallels that you may be realizing between a closed-model organization and McGregor's Theory X, and an open-model organization and McGregor's Theory Y.

Ouchi's Theory Z

William Ouchi popularized Theory Z, which essentially takes McGregor's Theory Y further by emphasizing the importance of participatory decision making in organizations.[87] Core elements of Theory Z include collective decision making, job security, generalized (vs. specialized) understanding of organizational goals, an emphasis on training and performance improvement, concern for the employee, and individual responsibility for shared accomplishments.[88] As you already may have noted, open-model organizations are congruent not only with McGregor's Theory Y conceptions of human behavior but also with Ouchi's Theory Z approach to management.

Herzberg's Motivation-Hygiene Theory

During the 1950s, Frederick Herzberg conducted a series of studies in which he asked workers, primarily engineers, to describe the times when they felt particularly good and particularly bad about their jobs. The respondents identified several sources of satisfaction and dissatisfaction in their work. Then, from these findings, Herzberg isolated two vital factors found in all jobs: maintenance or hygiene factors and motivational factors.

Maintenance or hygiene factors are those elements in the work environment that meet an employee's hedonistic need to avoid pain. These factors include the necessities of any job (e.g., adequate pay, benefits, job security, decent working conditions, supervision, interpersonal relations). Hygiene factors do not satisfy or motivate; they set the stage for motivation. They are, however, a major source of dissatisfaction when they are inadequate.[89]

maintenance or hygiene factors elements of one's career that provide one with their need to avoid pain (e.g., adequate pay, benefits, job security, decent working conditions, supervision, interpersonal relations).

Motivational factors are those psychosocial factors that provide intrinsic satisfaction and serve as an incentive for people to invest more of their time, talent, energy, and expertise in productive behavior. Examples include achievement, recognition, responsibility, the work itself, advancement, and potential for growth. The absence of motivators does not necessarily produce job dissatisfaction.[90]

motivational factors those psychosocial factors providing intrinsic satisfaction on the job, serving as an incentive to devote more of their time, energy, and expertise in productive behavior.

Although these needs are obviously related, they represent totally different dimensions of satisfaction.

Expectancy and Contingency Theories

In the 1960s, **expectancy theory** was developed, focusing on certain beliefs that can influence effort and performance. As examples, if an employee believes that his or her efforts will result in a certain level of performance leading to a desired reward, then that employee will likely take action accordingly. Of course, the opposite is true as well: If an employee perceives a low correlation between effort or performance and reward, then the result may well be inaction. Essentially, expectancy theory holds that employees will do what their managers or organizations want them to do if the following are true:

expectancy theory a theory that certain beliefs can influence effort and performance.

1. The task appears to be possible (employees believe that they possess the necessary competence).
2. The reward (outcome) offered is seen as desirable by the employees (intrinsic rewards come from the job itself; extrinsic rewards are supplied by others).

3. Employees believe that performing the required behavior or task will bring the desired outcome.

4. There is a good chance that better performance will bring greater rewards.[91]

Expectancy theory will work for an organization that specifies what behaviors it expects from people and what the rewards or outcomes will be for those who exhibit such behaviors. Rewards may be pay increases, time off, chances for advancement, a sense of achievement, or other benefits. Managers and organizations can find out what their employees want and see to it that they are provided with the rewards they seek. Walter Newsom[92] said that the reality of the expectancy theory can be summarized by the "nine Cs": (1) capability (does a person have the capability to perform well?), (2) confidence (does a person believe that he or she can perform the job well?), (3) challenge (does a person have to work hard to perform the job well?), (4) criteria (does a person know the difference between good and poor performance?), (5) credibility (does a person believe the manager will deliver on promises?), (6) consistency (do subordinates believe that all employees receive similar preferred outcomes for good performance, and vice versa?), (7) compensation (do the outcomes associated with good performance reward the employee with money and other types of rewards?), (8) cost (what does it cost a person, in effort and outcomes foregone, to perform well?), and (9) communication (does the manager communicate with the subordinate?).

contingency theory
an effort to determine the fit between the organization's characteristics and its tasks and the motivations of individuals.

Later, in the 1970s, Morse and Lorsch built on McGregor's and Herzberg's theories with their theory of motivation called **contingency theory**. This theory sought to determine the fit between the organization's characteristics and its tasks and the motivations of individuals. The basic components of the contingency theory are that (1) among people's needs is a central need to achieve a sense of competence, (2) the ways in which people fulfill this need will vary from person to person, (3) competence motivation is most likely to be achieved when there is a fit between task and organization, and (4) a sense of competence continues to motivate people even after competence is achieved. In essence, we all want to be competent in our work. Contingency theory contends that people performing highly structured and organized tasks perform better in Theory X organizations and that those who perform unstructured and uncertain tasks perform better under a Theory Y approach. This theory tells managers to tailor jobs to fit people or to give people the skills, knowledge, and attitudes they will need to become competent.[93]

Motivation through Job Enrichment

Motivation, among other desirable employee behaviors in an organization, can also be achieved by creating enriched jobs.[94] Enriched jobs include the following five characteristics: (1) skill variety (the extent to which a job requires a number of different skills and talents), (2) task identity (the extent to which a job requires completion of an entire piece of work), (3) task significance (the impact of one's work), (4) autonomy (the level of independence of one's work), and (5) feedback (the extent of information the employee receives about effective performance).[95]

Redesigning jobs to emphasize the above five characteristics influences three psychological states, which can lead to higher levels of motivation, satisfaction, and productivity, as well as lower levels of employee absenteeism and turnover. These three critical work-related states include the following: (1) experienced meaningfulness of work, (2) experienced responsibility, and (3) knowledge of results.[96] In the criminal justice system, a good example of a redesigned job is that of a community policing officer engaged in problem-solving, who when compared to an incident-driven traditional police officer may possess more of the desired elements of a redesigned job.

Preparing for Employees Now and in the Future: Generation Y

Changing Demographics and Mind-Set

American workers, although working longer, are aging and approaching retirement. In fact, over the next 20 years, 10,000 people will turn age 65 each day; 75 million baby boomers (people born between 1946 and 1964) are poised to retire and will leave large gaps in the workforce.[97] Certain administrators of the criminal justice system—particularly those in police and corrections (i.e., jails, prisons, probation and parole) agencies—must be prepared for a literal "changing of the guard" that is being realized right now.[98] They are already being replaced by persons born in what is termed Generation X, or Gen Xers (those born between 1965 and 1979), as well as the so-called **Generation Y** (sometimes termed the Millennials, or those born between 1980 and 2000).[99]

Generation Y sometimes termed the Millennials, persons born between 1980 and 2000.

Gen Yers were raised in an environment where they received awards just for showing up. Their parents have emphasized self-esteem building and feelings of success rather than keeping score of winners and losers. Generation Y is more team oriented and the most technically literate workers ever to hit the job market; they also prefer to work to live, rather than live to work. Gen Yers think nothing of leaving their job for a year to work as a volunteer in Africa. They already give signs of viewing the workplace as a means to an end and do not allow their career and job title to define them. Gen Y employees want to find immediate fulfillment and respect at the workplace, and are not willing to wait 20 years to pay their dues. They expect educational opportunities both in and outside the job, a balanced work and play life, and recognition on the job.

Coming Challenges

How must justice administrators adapt their views and organizational cultures in order to meet these new employees of the future? Should they attempt to mold the Gen Y police officer or prison corrections officer to fit the traditional, "correct" attitude and ways of behaving at the work site? Or should the administrator change his or her approach to leadership in order to attract and keep these coming employees? Matt Kenyon suggests that Gen Yers can make significant contributions in the field of criminal justice, particularly in policing, but administrators must play to the characteristics and strengths of Millennials if they are to be successfully recruited and retained.[100] For example, Kenyon suggests police departments develop mentorship programs for Millennials, based on survey research suggesting the Gen Yers tend to be more loyal to agencies when they offer training for leadership positions.[101] In addition, Kenyon suggests that departments attempt to encourage conversation, which would allow Millennials to voice their opinions, which could improve departmental policies.[102] Essentially, Kenyon is suggesting that police administrators think seriously about adjusting some traditional police structures to accommodate the ever-growing Millennial workforce.

Kelly Sharp offered five challenges for administrators in finding, training, and keeping these employees, as well as some recommendations for their body art and technological skills.[103]

> ***Challenge 1:*** Finding Them—Think electronically. The agency must attract Gen Yers via social media, or some type of police blog if substantial recruitment is to be realized. The agency must have an up-to-date, attractive website and social media presence.
>
> ***Challenge 2:*** Training Them—The agency's training program must also be designed to keep Gen Yers, who were raised on video games and television and thus expect rapid

access to information and will quickly become bored. Training should be interactive and entertaining, as well as educational, and include the ability to brainstorm with each other and to engage in problem-solving.

Challenge 3: Keeping Them—The workplace should be a fun, flexible environment. The days of "do it my way or hit the highway" management style will not suffice. While pay is important to the Gen Y employee, he or she is seeking an environment in which to learn and grow—and one that includes volunteerism and educational opportunities. Gen Yers also prefer feedback that is informal and immediate, so agencies should adjust their evaluation process accordingly.

Challenge 4: Body Art—Gen Y employees will likely display a very casual attitude toward unusual body art and piercings among their coworkers—a normal form of expression among Gen Yers. Therefore, the traditional militaristic, standardized look (and dress code) may be jeopardized when every applicant comes decorated with body art. Dress codes may thus have to be rewritten at some point, or at least allow the option of softening the more stringent requirements.

Challenge 5: Technology—Gen Y employees, being surrounded by technology since birth, cannot imagine life without it. Indeed, their approaching any task without technologies to use may well baffle them. They were also raised online and inundated with reality TV, so it is natural for them to wish to record and broadcast their lives. The Internet, their smart phones, and their iPods and tablets are viewed in the same manner as earlier generations viewed pen and pencil or typewriters. As a result, administrators may need to rethink policies that prohibit "surfing the Web at work."

As baby boomers retire at rapid rates across criminal justice agencies, Gen Yers are being criticized for some of their "nontraditional" attitudes, such as impatience with existing hierarchies and social contracts that mandate respect between generations.[104] But Althea Olson and Mike Wasilewski argue that the criticisms that some administrators have toward Gen Yers may be overly generalized and simply unfair.[105] In fact, some of the attributes associated with Millennials might benefit and improve law enforcement, especially their proficiency with technology, creativity, and their questioning of tradition.

California POST's Career Pipeline Program is one way to address an emerging "human resource crisis."[106] This program targets students in grades 5–8 and uses educators and criminal justice employees to teach the values of sportsmanship and citizenship along with vocation-based learning.[107] While not a panacea, the Career Pipeline Program is an innovative attempt to create a "hook" into the law enforcement profession. But if one of these pipeline students ultimately finds his or her way into a POST academy, no one should be surprised if the student asks whether his or her police report must be fewer than 140 characters!

Becoming a Learning Organization

In sum, the criminal justice workplace is changing in dramatic ways. Understanding the Millennials is important not only for developing future leaders but also for basic workplace effectiveness and employee retention.

learning organization an organizational culture that looks to the future to continually experiment, improve, and adapt so as to meet the challenges of a more complex role.

Agency administrators must promote what is termed a "**learning organization**" culture, where communication and collaboration are promoted so that everyone is engaged in identifying and solving problems. This culture will enable organizations of the future to continually experiment, improve, adapt to generational differences, and meet the challenges of a more complex role. The learning organization will prize equity, open information, reduced hierarchy, and a culture that encourages personnel being adaptive and seizing opportunities for growth and handling crises.[108]

Summary

Most young people entering the labor force would probably like to retain their individuality, feel free to express themselves, have a sense of being an important part of the team, and realize both extrinsic and intrinsic rewards from their work. The reality is, however, that a majority of people entering the job market will work within the structure of an organization that will not meet all of their personal needs.

We have seen that many organizations have a highly refined bureaucracy. Whether an organization will meet an employee's needs depends largely on its administrative philosophy. Therefore, the discussions in this chapter covered the structure and function of organizations and, just as important, how administrators and subordinates function within them. Also shown to be of major importance are the need for effective communication and the ability to work effectively with future generations who are now entering the workforce.

The point to be made above all else is that administrators *must know their people*. In addition to covering several prominent theories that have withstood the test of time, we pointed out some approaches that have not succeeded. One can learn much from a failed approach or even from a poor boss who failed to appreciate and understand subordinates and used improper or no motivational techniques.

Key Terms and Concepts

Autocratic leader, p. 38
Bureaucracy, p. 25
Closed versus open systems, p. 30
Communication, p. 31
Contingency theory, p. 46
Democratic leader, p. 39
Expectancy theory, p. 45
External Communications: Use of Social Media, p. 36
Generation Y, p. 47
Grapevine, p. 34
Hawthorne effect, p. 42
Hierarchy of needs, p. 43
Humanistic school, p. 43
Inputs, p. 26
Job enrichment, p. 46
Laissez-faire leader, p. 39
Leadership, p. 37
Learning organization, p. 48
Maintenance or hygiene factors, p. 45
Motivational factors, p. 45
Organization, p. 23
Organizational theory, p. 23
Outputs, p. 26
POSDCORB, p. 24
Relatively identifiable boundary, p. 23
Scientific management, p. 23
Situational leadership theory, p. 39
Social entity, p. 23
Span of control, p. 28
Style theory, p. 38
Theory X, p. 44
Theory Y, p. 44
Theory Z, p. 45
Trait theory, p. 37
Unity of command, p. 29

Questions for Review

1. Define *organization*. What is its function and structure?
2. Explain the evolution of organizational theory, including scientific, human relations, systems, and bureaucratic management theories.
3. Define *span of control* and *unity of command*.
4. What is situational leadership theory? What are the four types of leaders?
5. How does Ouchi's Theory Z differ from Theory Y?
6. What does *communication* mean? What is its importance in organizations? Explain cultural cues, the nature and uniqueness of police communications, and some of the major barriers to effective communication.
7. Objectively assess what kind of leader you would likely be. Is it an effective style? What are some of the possible advantages and disadvantages of that style?
8. What can criminal justice administrators do to attract and retain Generation Y employees into the workforce?

Deliberate and Decide

A Communication Conundrum

Communication and budgetary problems have beset your state's Secretary of Corrections and the area's prison warden. First, costs for your county's new prison far exceeded the budget, and the warden never sought or obtained the corrections or budget director's authorization for cost overruns. The warden added a second prison drug dog program and sent the dog and a correctional officer for training without the director's authorization. And, despite his assertions to the contrary, it appears that a new program for geriatric inmates would not be covered entirely by grants and instead cost the state $75,000; the warden also hired a personal acquaintance to run this program—an employee from another prison. The warden also bought a van with personal funds and registered it to the state without authorization.

Questions for Discussion

1. What are the issues involved in this situation?
2. What should the secretary do about them?
3. What must the secretary do to prevent such situations from occurring in the future?

Learn by Doing

1. As part of a criminal justice class project concerning government careers, you are assigned to examine bureaucracies. What would you say are some of the specific characteristics and criticisms of bureaucracies? What could happen in criminal justice if these characteristics were applied in the extreme?
2. You are contacted by a friend who belongs to a local civic club that is planning a Labor Day luncheon to recognize all workers in the community. Knowing of your background and prior study of organizational theory, she asks you to speak at this luncheon concerning the scientific management approach to organizational theory—particularly the career of Frederick W. Taylor and his contributions and primary motivations regarding management. What will you report?
3. Your prison duty shift's middle manager (a lieutenant) comes to you saying he has personally observed a number of problems concerning the manner in which communication is occurring from one duty shift to another. These problems appear to primarily involve inaccurate information being disseminated, a grapevine that seems bent on carrying incorrect, malicious information, and a diverse group of employees with language and cultural barriers. You are assigned to look at the problem as well as recommend means by which communications could be improved. How would you proceed, and what kinds of ideas might you put forth?

Case Study

My Door is Always Open

As a veteran sheriff's deputy, you've seen sheriffs in your agency come and go. But the most recently elected sheriff is someone different—someone whose way of doing business has really impressed you. During her first week on the job, Sheriff Harkness made sure to make the rounds, not only in the office but also at all patrol and jail briefings. She introduced herself with confidence and stressed a team orientation that was quite refreshing. As the weeks and months passed, Sheriff Harkness made it clear that her philosophy is to hire and retain good people, and "get out of their way" so they can do their jobs. She implemented an internal advisory board, which allows both civilian and sworn employees to have input into organizational processes and policies. Despite how busy she is, Sheriff Harkness has an open-door policy for all of her team members. Patrol and jail deputies (as well as civilian staff) have access to the sheriff, as she has dispensed with the formal, vertical communication processes that had existed in the agencies for many years. Sheriff Harkness also pays special attention to employees in need and assists in organizing shared leave, when needed.

Questions for Discussion

1. What leadership traits do you see in Sheriff Harkness?
2. Would you describe Sheriff Harkness as a situational leader? Why or why not?
3. What obstacles do you believe Sheriff Harkness will have in continuing to implement her leadership philosophy?

Notes

1. David A. Tansik and James F. Elliott, *Managing Police Organizations* (Monterey, CA: Duxbury Press, 1981), p. 1.
2. Stephen P. Robbins, *Organizational Theory: Structure, Design and Applications* (Upper Saddle River, NJ: Prentice Hall, 1987).
3. Larry K. Gaines, John L. Worrall, Mittie D. Southerland, and John E. Angell, *Police Administration*, 2nd ed. (New York: McGraw-Hill, 2002), p. 8.
4. Peter W. Blau and W. Richard Scott, *Formal Organizations* (Scranton, PA: Chandler, 1962), p. 43.
5. Gaines et al., *Police Administration,* p. 12.
6. Ronald G. Lynch, *The Police Manager: Professional Leadership Skills*, 3rd ed. (New York: Random House, 1986), p. 4.
7. Samuel C. Certo, *Principles of Modern Management: Functions and Systems,* 4th ed. (Boston: Allyn and Bacon, 1989), p. 35.
8. See Elton Mayo, *The Human Problems of an Industrial Civilization* (New York: Macmillan, 1933).
9. Paul M. Whisenand and Fred Ferguson, *The Managing of Police Organizations,* 3rd ed. (Upper Saddle River, NJ: Prentice Hall, 1989), pp. 218–219.
10. Lynch, *Police Manager,* pp. 5–6.
11. Abraham H. Maslow, *Motivation and Personality* (New York: Harper & Row, 1954).
12. Douglas McGregor, *The Human Side of Enterprise* (New York: McGraw-Hill, 1960).
13. Robert R. Blake and Jane S. Mouton, *The Managerial Grid* (Houston, TX: Gulf, 1964).
14. Lynch, *Police Manager,* pp. 7–8.
15. Max Weber, *The Theory of Social and Economic Organization,* trans. A. M. Henderson and Talcott Parsons (New York: Oxford University Press, 1947), pp. 329–330.
16. James Q. Wilson, *Varieties of Police Behavior* (Cambridge, MA: Harvard University Press, 1968), pp. 2–3.
17. Ibid., p. 3.
18. Lyndall F. Urwick, *Notes on the Theory of Organization* (New York: American Management Association, 1952).
19. Troy Lane, "Span of Control for Law Enforcement Agencies," *The Associate* (March–April 2006): 19–31.
20. Ibid.
21. Gaines et al., *Police Administration,* p. 12.
22. Leonard R. Sayles and George Strauss, *Human Behavior in Organizations* (Upper Saddle River, NJ: Prentice Hall, 1966), p. 349.
23. Nicholas Henry, *Public Administration & Public Affairs* (Upper Saddle Creek, NJ: Prentice Hall, 2001).
24. Ibid.
25. Charles R. Swanson, Leonard Territo, and Robert W. Taylor, *Police Administration,* 2nd ed. (New York: Macmillan, 1988), p. 308.
26. Mario Pei, *Language for Everybody: What It Is and How to Master It* (Greenwich, CT: Devin-Adair Co., 1961), pp. 4–5.
27. Louis A. Radelet, *The Police and the Community: Studies* (Beverly Hills, CA: Glencoe, 1973), p. 92.
28. Swanson et al., *Police Administration,* p. 86.
29. Institute of Government, University of Georgia, *Interpersonal Communication: A Guide for Staff Development* (Athens: Author, 1974), p. 15.
30. Wayne W. Bennett and Karen Hess, *Management and Supervision in Law Enforcement* (St. Paul, MN: West, 1992), p. 72.
31. See R. C. Huseman, quoted in ibid., pp. 21–27. Material for this section was also drawn from Swanson et al., *Police Administration,* pp. 309–311.
32. Swanson et al., *Police Administration,* pp. 312–313.
33. D. Katz and R. L. Kahn, *The Social Psychology of Organizations* (New York: Wiley, 1966), p. 239. As cited in P. V. Lewis, *Organizational Communication: The Essence of Effective Management* (Columbus, OH: Grid, 1975), p. 36.
34. Lewis, *Organizational Communication,* p. 38.
35. Swanson et al., *Police Administration,* p. 315.
36. See R. K. Allen, *Organizational Management Through Communication* (New York: Harper & Row, 1977), pp. 77–79.
37. Anne Keegan, "There is a Definite Lingo the Chicago Police Use, an Argot…," *Chicago Tribune* (December 22, 1993), http://articles.chicagotribune.com/1993-12-22/features/9312220213_1_police-officer-police-radio-drugs.
38. Ibid.
39. Swanson et al., *Police Administration*, p. 343.
40. Stephen W. Mastrofski, "Police Agency Accreditation: The Prospects of Reform," *American Journal of Police* 5(3) (1986): 45–81.
41. Alex Markels, "Managers Aren't Always Able to Get the Right Message across with E-mail," *The Wall Street Journal* (August 6, 1996), p. 2.
42. Robert L. Montgomery, "Are You a Good Listener?" *Nation's Business* (October 1981): 65–68.
43. Bennett and Hess, *Management and Supervision in Law Enforcement,* p. 82.
44. G. Weaver, "Law Enforcement in a Culturally Diverse Society," *FBI Law Enforcement Bulletin* (September 1992): 1–10.
45. Kourtnie Rodgers, *A Content Analysis of Social Media Policies of Police Departments and Sheriffs' Offices in the State of Idaho: Congruency to the Model Policy* (Boise, ID: Boise State University, 2016).
46. P. Walaski, "Social Media: Powerful Tools for SH&E Professionals," *Professional Safety* 48(4) (2013): 40–49.

47. International Association of Chiefs of Police *About the Initiative* http://www.iacpsocialmedia.org/AboutTheInitiative.aspx.
48. Ibid.
49. Jacob S. Kabrud, *Facebook and Law Enforcement in the State of Idaho: A Descriptive Content Analysis* (Master's Thesis. Boise, ID: Boise State University, 2015).
50. Certo, *Principles of Modern Management*, p. 103.
51. Wayne W. Bennett and Karen M. Hess, *Management and Supervision in Law Enforcement*, 4th ed. (Belmont, CA: Wadsworth, 2004), p. 52; Warren Bennis and Burt Nanus, *Leaders* (New York: Harper & Row, 1985).
52. Bennett and Hess, *Management and Supervision in Law Enforcement*, 4th ed., pp. 53–54.
53. Paul Hersey and Kenneth H. Blanchard, *Management of Organizational Behavior,* 3rd ed. (Upper Saddle River, NJ: Prentice Hall, 1977), p. 12.
54. Ibid.
55. Bennett and Hess, *Management and Supervision in Law Enforcement,* 4th ed., p. 52.
56. Ibid.
57. Roger D. Evered and James C. Selman, "Coaching and the Art of Management," *Organizational Dynamics* 18 (Autumn 1989): 16.
58. Charles R. Swanson, Leonard Territo, and Robert W. Taylor, *Police Administration: Structures, Processes, and Behavior,* 6th ed. (Upper Saddle River, NJ: Prentice Hall, 2005), p. 272.
59. Richard Holden, *Modern Police Management,* 2nd ed. (Upper Saddle River, NJ: Prentice Hall, 1994), p. 47.
60. Thomas A. Mahoney, Thomas H. Jerdee, and Alan N. Nash, "Predicting Managerial Effectiveness," *Personnel Psychology* 13(2) (Summer 1960): 147–163.
61. Joe Kelly, *Organizational Behavior: An Existential Systems Approach,* rev. ed. (Homewood, IL: Richard D. Irwin, 1974), p. 363.
62. Bennett and Hess, *Management and Supervision in Law Enforcement*, 4th ed., p. 57.
63. Edwin Fleishman, "Leadership Climate, Human Relations Training and Supervisory Behavior," *Personnel Psychology* 6(1953): 208–222.
64. Stephen M. Sales, "Supervisory Style and Productivity: Review and Theory," in Larry Cummings and William E. Scott (eds.), *Readings in Organizational Behavior and Human Performance* (Homewood, IL: Richard D. Irwin, 1969), p. 122.
65. Holden, *Modern Police Management,* pp. 39–40.
66. Ibid., pp. 41–42.
67. Paul Hersey, Kenneth H. Blanchard, and Dewey E. Johnson, *Management of Organizational Behavior: Utilizing Human Resources*, 7th ed. (Upper Saddle River, NJ: Prentice Hall, 1996).
68. Ibid.
69. Bill George, "Truly Authentic Leadership," *U.S. News & World Report* (October 30, 2006): 52.
70. Ibid.
71. Robert L. Katz, "Skills of an Effective Administrator," *Harvard Business Review* 52(1975): 23.
72. Ibid., p. 23.
73. Dan L. Costley and Ralph Todd, *Human Relations in Organizations* (St. Paul, MN: West, 1978).
74. Ibid., p. 24.
75. James M. Higgins, *Human Relations: Concepts and Skills* (New York: Random House, 1982).
76. Ibid., p. 27.
77. Favreau D. F. and Gillespie J. E., *Modern Police Administration* (Englewood Cliffs, NJ: Prentice Hall, 1978), p. 85.
78. Warren R. Plunkett, *Supervision: The Direction of People at Work* (Dubuque, IA: Wm. C. Brown, 1983), p. 121.
79. Elton Mayo, *The Social Problems of an Industrial Civilization* (Boston: Division of Research, Graduate School of Business Administration, Harvard University, 1945), pp. 68–86.
80. Favreau and Gillespie, *Modern Police Administration,* pp. 100–101.
81. Frederick J. Roethlisberger and William J. Dickson, *Management and the Worker* (Cambridge, MA: Harvard University Press, 1939), p. 522.
82. Favreau and Gillespie, *Modern Police Administration*, p. 87.
83. Ibid.
84. Ibid., p. 88.
85. Ibid., p. 89.
86. Ibid.
87. Jeanne Dininni, "Management Theory of William Ouchi," *Business.com*, http://buisness.com/management/management-theory-of-william-ouchi/.
88. Ibid.
89. Harry W. More and W. Fred Wegener, *Behavioral Police Management* (New York: Macmillan, 1992), pp. 163–164.
90. Frederick Herzberg, "One More Time: How Do You Motivate Employees?" *Harvard Business Review Classic* (September–October 1987), http://hbr.org/2003/01/one-more-time-how-do-you-motivate-employees/.
91. Randall S. Schuler, *Personnel and Human Resources Management* (St. Paul, MN: West, 1981), pp. 41–43.
92. Walter B. Newsom, "Motivate, Now!" *Personnel Journal* 14 (February 1990): 51–55.
93. Plunkett, *Supervision,* pp. 131–132.
94. J. R. Hackman and G. R. Oldham, *Work Redesign* (Reading, MA: Addison-Wesley, 1980).
95. Ibid.
96. Ibid.
97. Dave Bernard, "The Baby Boomer Number Game," *U.S. News and World Report*, http://money.usnews.com/money/blogs/On-Retirement/2012/03/23/the-baby-boomer-number-game.
98. Kelly Sharp, "Recruiting Generation Y," *Law and Order* 60(8) (August 2012): 58–60.
99. Matt Rosenberg, "Names of Generations," *About.com: Geography*, http://geography.about.com/od/populationgeography/qt/generations.htm.

100. Matt Kenyon, "The Next Generation: Recruiting and Retaining *Millennials*," June 20, 2016 http://www.powerdms.com/blog/the-next-generation-recruiting-and-retaining-millenials/
101. Ibid.
102. Ibid.
103. Sharp, "Recruiting Generation Y," pp. 59–60.
104. Althea Olson and Mike Wasilewski "More than a Cop: 7 Things Police Leaders Need to Know about Millennials," *PoliceOne.com*, http://www.policeone.com.
105. Ibid.
106. Sid Smith, "A Crisis Facing Law Enforcement: Recruiting in the 21st Century," *The Police Chief* 83 (June 2016), p. 6, http://www.policechiefmagazine/org/a-crisis-facing-law-enforcement-recruiting-in-the-21st-century/.
107. Ibid., p. 5.
108. Tommy York, Andy Whitford, and Brian Williams, "Command and Control Meets the Millennials," *American Jails* 26(2) (May/June 2012): 23–24, 26–31.

Igorstevanovic/Shutterstock

3 Rights of Criminal Justice Employees

LEARNING OBJECTIVES

After reading this chapter, the student will be able to:

1. *describe laws and rights affecting criminal justice employees*
2. *delineate and describe several aspects and rights of the employment relationship, such as proper recruitment and hiring, disparate treatment, affirmative action, property rights, pay and benefits, and providing a safe workplace*
3. *explain the elements of a due process claim under U.S. Section 1983*
4. *define the impact of the Fair Labor Standards Act on criminal justice employees*
5. *delineate the nature and impact of workplace harassment in criminal justice*
6. *review the eligibility requirements for Family and Medical Leave Act benefits*
7. *describe the Americans with Disabilities Act*
8. *explain the authority of criminal justice administrators to govern employees' appearance and maintain dress codes*

▶ Introduction

In the last few decades, the rights and obligations of criminal justice employees, like those of workers in the private sector, have changed dramatically. Changes in values, demographics, law, and technology have blurred the line dividing the manager and the managed in enforcement, judicial, and correctional agencies. Today's criminal justice employee is far more sophisticated about employee rights.[1] For that reason, and because of attendant liability considerations (discussed in Chapter 14), contemporary criminal justice administrators must be more aware of employees' legal rights.

After an overview of the relevant employment laws, we discuss recruitment and hiring issues, age discrimination, affirmative action, discipline and discharge, pay and benefits, and safe workplace issues. Then, we examine constitutional rights of criminal justice employees as determined by the courts regarding free speech, searches and seizures, self-incrimination, religious practices, sexual misconduct, residency requirements, moonlighting, misuse of firearms, alcohol and drugs in the workplace, workplace harassment, and the Americans with Disabilities Act. Finally, we review the authority of criminal justice administrators to govern employees' appearance and maintain dress codes, focusing on challenges posed by Millennials coming to the workplace and their penchant for body modifications (particularly tattooing). The chapter concludes with review questions and exercises in the Deliberate and Decide, Learn by Doing, and Case Study sections.

▶ Overview

Law and litigation affecting criminal justice employees can arise out of federal and state constitutions, statutes, administrative regulations, and judicial interpretations and rulings. Even poorly written employee handbooks or long-standing agency customs or practices may create vested rights. The ripple effect begun by improper or illegal hiring, training, discipline, or discharge can lead not only to poor agency performance and morale but also to substantial legal and economic liability. It should become apparent in the following overview and the court decisions that follow that utilizing good common sense as well as a sense of fairness will go a long way toward preventing legal problems in the employment relationship.[2]

It should also be noted that the Civil Rights Act of 1991, like its predecessors, may result in further amended versions and changes in public and private sector employment; however, it will take several years for significant decisions to wind their way through the courts for a final determination by the Supreme Court of the intent and reach of the Act. Therefore, this section focuses on presenting the issues rather than on attempting to settle the law in these areas.

- ***Fair Labor Standards Act (FLSA; at 29 U.S.C. 203 et seq.).*** This Act provides minimum salary and overtime provisions covering both public and private sector employees. Part 3(a) contains special provisions for firefighters and police officers. I discuss the FLSA more fully later.
- ***Title VII of the Civil Rights Act of 1964 and its amendments (42 U.S.C. 2000e).*** This broadly based Act establishes a federal policy requiring fair employment practices in both the public and private sectors. It prohibits unlawful employment discrimination in the hiring process, discharge, discipline, and working conditions and the unlawful provision of benefits based on race, color, religion, sex, and national origin. Its provisions extend to "hostile work environment" claims based on sexual, racial, or religious harassment.

EXHIBIT 3.1

ATTACKING PAY DISCRIMINATION: THE LILLY LEDBETTER FAIR PAY ACT

Women today who work full time in the United States are paid 80 cents for every dollar paid to men; the gap is even wider for women of color.[3] However, in 2009 a major piece of legislation was enacted that provides women the right to seek legal redress when they believe their job duties and wages, being comparable to men's in their workplace, are lacking in parity.

Lilly Ledbetter, a female supervisor at a Goodyear plant in Alabama, learned that her salary was substantially lower than 15 male managers who did similar work and had equal or less seniority. She filed a complaint with the Equal Employment Opportunity Commission (EEOC), her case went to trial, and the jury awarded her back pay and approximately $3.3 million in compensatory and punitive damages. However, a federal appeals court overturned the jury verdict on the ground that her case was filed too late.[4]

Because the appeals court's decision ran against a long-standing congressional goal of eliminating discrimination in the workplace, within two years both the U.S. House and Senate passed, and in January 2009 President Obama signed, the Lilly Ledbetter Fair Pay Act, helping to ensure that individuals subjected to unlawful pay discrimination are able to assert their claims.[5]

While having a major influence in the private sector, the law's effect has been felt in the public sector as well. For example, the law has granted wage parity at a police department in Pennsylvania;[6] a university in Pennsylvania, involving salaries of male and female professors;[7] and a university in Louisiana, involving tenure-track professors in different departments who performed similar duties.[8]

- ***Equal Pay Act (29 U.S.C. 206(d)).*** This legislation provides an alternative remedy to Title VII for sex-based discrimination in wages and benefits when men and women do similar work. It applies the simpler Fair Labor Standards Act procedures to claims. Note that the Equal Pay Act does not mean "comparable worth"—an attempt to determine wages by requiring equal pay for employees whose work is of comparable worth even if the job content is totally different. Exhibit 3.1 discusses a major related piece of legislation enacted in 2009.
- ***The Pregnancy Discrimination Act of 1978 (42 U.S.C. Section 2000e(k)).*** This Act is an amendment to the scope of sexual discrimination under Title VII. It prohibits unequal treatment of women because of pregnancy or related medical conditions (e.g., nausea). The Act requires that employers treat pregnant women like other temporarily disabled employees. The U.S. Supreme Court decided a major case in 1991 that limited employers' ability in excluding women who are pregnant or of childbearing years from certain jobs under a fetal protection policy.[9]
- ***Age Discrimination in Employment Act (29 U.S.C. 623).*** This Act generally prohibits the unequal treatment of applicants or employees based on their age, if they are age 40 years or older, in regard to hiring, firing, receiving benefits, and other conditions of employment.
- ***Americans with Disabilities Act of 1990 (ADA) (42 U.S.C. 12112).*** The goal of this legislation is to remove barriers that might prevent otherwise qualified individuals with disabilities from enjoying the same employment opportunities as persons without disabilities. Before the ADA, the Rehabilitation Act of 1973 (see 29 U.S.C. 701) and its amendments prevented similar disability discrimination among public agencies receiving federal funds. The ADA is discussed more fully later.
- ***Section 1983 (codified as Title 42, U.S. Code Section 1983).*** This major piece of legislation is the instrument by which an employee may sue an employer for civil rights violations

based on the deprivation of constitutional rights. It is the most versatile civil rights action and is also the most often used against criminal justice agencies. Section 1983 is discussed in more detail in Chapter 14.

In addition to the legislative enactments and state statutes that prohibit various acts of discrimination in employment, there are remedies that have tremendous impact on public sector employees. Tort actions (a tort is the infliction of a civil injury) may be brought by public sector employees against their employer for a wide variety of claims, ranging from assault and battery to defamation. Contractual claims may grow out of collective bargaining agreements, which may include procedures for assignments, seniority, due process protections (such as in the Peace Officers' Bill of Rights, discussed later), and grievance procedures. Often the source of the right defines the remedy and the procedure for obtaining that remedy; for example, statutes or legal precedents often provide for an aggrieved employee to receive back pay, compensatory damages, injunctive relief, or punitive damages.

▶ The Employment Relationship

Recruitment and Hiring

Numerous selection methods for hiring police and corrections officers have been tried over the years. Issues in recruitment, selection, and hiring also often involve internal promotions and assignments to special units, such as a special weapons team in a police agency. Requirements concerning age (e.g., the FBI will hire no one older than 37 years), height, weight, vision, education, and possession of a valid driver's license have all been utilized over the years in criminal justice. In addition, tests are commonly used to determine intelligence, emotional suitability and stability (using psychological examinations and oral interviews), physical agility, and character (using polygraph examinations and extensive background checks).[10] More recently, drug tests became a frequently used part of the employee screening process as well (drug tests are discussed more fully later).

The critical question for such tests is whether they validly test the types of skills needed for the job. A companion concern is whether the tests are used for discriminatory purposes or have an unequal impact on protected groups (e.g., minorities, the physically challenged). As a result of these considerations, a number of private companies provide valid, reliable examinations for use by the public sector.

Disparate Treatment

It should be emphasized that there is nothing in the law that states that an employer must hire or retain incompetent personnel. In effect, the law does not prohibit discrimination; thus, for positions that require driving, it is not unlawful to refuse to hire people who have a record of driving while intoxicated. What is illegal is to treat people differently because of their age, gender, sex, or other protected status, that is, **disparate treatment**. It is also illegal to deny equal employment opportunities to such persons, that is, disparate impact.[11] Federal equal opportunity law prohibits the use of selection procedures for hiring or promotion that have a discriminatory impact on the employment opportunities of women, Hispanics, African Americans, or other protected classes. An example of overt discriminatory hiring is reflected in a court decision in 1987 arising out of a situation in a sparsely populated county in Virginia. Four women sued because they were denied positions as courtroom security officer, deputy, and civil process server because of their gender. Sheriffs had refused to hire the women, justifying their decision by contending that

disparate treatment treating people differently because of their age, gender, sex, or other protected status.

bona fide occupational qualifier (BFOQ) in certain situations, a rationale for discriminating on the basis of a business necessity.

being male was a **bona fide occupational qualifier (BFOQ)** (i.e., in certain situations it is lawful and reasonable to discriminate because of a business necessity, such as a female corrections facility maintaining at least one female staff member on duty at all times to assist inmates in toileting, showering, and disrobing) for the positions and that because the positions were within the "personal staff" of the sheriff, they were exempt from the coverage of Title VII. The Fourth Circuit overturned a lower court decision, finding that the sheriff did not establish that gender was a BFOQ for the positions and that the positions were not part of the sheriff's personal staff (the positions were not high level, policymaking, or advisory in nature). Thus, the refusal to hire the women violated Title VII.[12] There may, however, be a "business justification" for a hiring policy even though it has a disparate impact. For example, in one case an employer required airline attendants to cease flying immediately on discovering they were pregnant. The court upheld the policy on the ground that pregnancy could affect one's ability to perform routine duties in an aircraft, thereby jeopardizing the safety of passengers.[13]

A classic example of an apparent neutral employment requirement that actually had a disparate impact on gender, race, and ethnicity was the once-prevalent height requirement used by most public safety agencies. Minimum height requirements of 5 feet, 10 inches or above were often advertised and effectively operated to exclude most women and many Asians and Hispanics from employment.[14] Such a requirement has gradually been superseded by a "height in proportion to weight" requirement.

Nonetheless, other existing physical agility tests serve to discriminate against women and small men with less upper-body strength. One wonders how many push-ups a police officer must do on the job or be able to do to perform his or her duties adequately, or how many 6-foot walls, ditches, and attics officers must negotiate. (Occasionally, preemployment physical abilities testing becomes ludicrous. For example, one of the authors once allowed a recruiter from a major western city to recruit students in an upper-level criminal justice course. The recruiter said the city's physical test included scaling a 6-foot wall; however, he quickly pointed out that testing staff would boost all female applicants over it.)

Litigation is blossoming in this area. In a western city, a woman challenged the police department's physical abilities test as discriminatory and not job related, prompting the agency to hire a Canadian consultant who developed a job-related preemployment agility test (currently used by the Royal Canadian Mounted Police and other agencies across Canada) based on data provided by officers and later computer analyzed for incorporation into the test. In other words, recruits were soon tested in terms of the physical demands placed on police officers in that specific community. (No push-ups or 6-foot walls are included.)[15]

Discrimination may also exist in promotions and job assignments. As an example of the former, a Nebraska female correctional center worker brought suit alleging that her employer violated her Title VII and equal protection rights by denying her a promotion. The woman was qualified for the higher-level position (assistant center manager for programming), and she also alleged that the center treated women inequitably and unprofessionally, that assertiveness in women was viewed negatively, and that women were assigned clerical duties not assigned to men. The court found that she was indeed denied a promotion because of her sex, in violation of Title VII and the equal protection clause of the Fourteenth Amendment; she was awarded back pay and front pay biweekly until a comparable position became available, general damages, and court costs.[16]

With respect to litigation in the area of job assignments, four female jail matrons who were refused assignments to correctional officer positions in Florida even though they had been trained and certified as jail officers were awarded damages. It was ruled that a state regulation prohibiting females in male areas of the jail was discriminatory without proof that gender was a BFOQ.[17] However, a particular assignment may validly exclude one gender. An assignment to work as a decoy female prostitute demonstrates a business necessity for women.[18]

How Old Is "Too Old" in Criminal Justice?

State and public agencies are not immune from age discrimination suits, in which arbitrary age restrictions have been found to violate the law. In Florida, a police lieutenant with the state highway patrol with 29 years of service was forced by statute to retire at age 62. The Equal Employment Opportunity Commission brought suit, alleging that Florida's statute violated the Age Discrimination in Employment Act (ADEA). The court held that age should not be a BFOQ because youthfulness is not a guarantee of public safety. Rather, a physical fitness standard would better serve the purpose of ensuring the ability to perform the tasks of the position.[19]

Indeed, the U.S. Supreme Court rejected mandatory retirement plans for municipal firefighters and police officers.[20] Until 1985, the city of Baltimore had relied on a federal police officer and firefighter statute (5 U.S.C. 8335b), an exemption to the ADEA, to establish age limits for appointing and retiring its fire and police officers; the city also contended that age was a BFOQ for doing so. The U.S. Supreme Court said that although Congress had exempted federal employees from application of the ADEA, another agency cannot just adopt the same standards without showing an agency-specific need. Age is not a BFOQ for nonfederal firefighters (or, by extension, police officers). The Court also established a "reasonable federal standard" in its 1984 decision in *EEOC v. Wyoming,*[21] in which it overturned a state statute providing for the mandatory retirement of state game wardens at age 55; it held that the ADEA did not require employers to retain unfit employees, only to make individualized determinations about fitness.

Criminal Justice and Affirmative Action

Probably no single employment practice has caused as much controversy as **affirmative action**—actions or policies favoring persons or groups who have suffered from discrimination, particularly in employment or education. The very words bring to mind visions of quotas and of unqualified people being given preferential hiring treatment.[22] Indeed, quotas have been at the center of legal, social, scientific, and political controversy for more than four decades.[23] However, the reality of affirmative action is substantially different from the myth; as a general rule, affirmative action plans give preferred treatment only to affected groups when all other criteria (e.g., education, skills) are equal.[24]

affirmative action actions or policies that favor persons or groups who have suffered from discrimination, particularly in employment or education.

The legal question (and to many persons, a moral one) that arises from affirmative action is, When does preferential hiring become **reverse discrimination** (where, it is argued, the aforementioned affirmative action policies have resulted in unfair treatment for members of majority groups)? The leading case here is *Bakke v. Regents of the University of California*[25] in 1978, in which Allan Bakke was passed over for medical school admission at the University of California, Davis, partly because the school annually set aside a number of its 100 medical school admissions slots for "disadvantaged" applicants. The Supreme Court held, among other things, that race could be used as a criterion in selection decisions, but it could not be the only criterion.

reverse discrimination the argument that affirmative action policies have resulted in unfair treatment for members of majority groups.

In a series of cases beginning in 1986,[26] the Supreme Court considered the development and application of affirmative action plans, establishing a two-step inquiry that must be satisfied before an affirmative action plan can be put in place. A plan must have (1) a remedial purpose to correct past inequities, and (2) there must be a manifest imbalance or significant disparity to justify the plan. The Court, however, emphasized that such plans cannot completely foreclose employment opportunities to nonminority or male candidates.

The validity of such plans is generally determined on a case-by-case basis. For example, the District of Columbia Circuit Court held in 1987 that an affirmative action plan covering the promotion of African Americans to management positions in the police department was justified because only 174 of the 807 positions (22 percent) above the rank of sergeant were filled by African American in a city where 60 percent of the labor market was African American.[27] Twenty-one past and present nonminority male detectives of the Metropolitan Police Department who were passed over for promotion challenged the department's voluntary affirmative action plan designed to place "special emphasis" on the hiring and advancement of females and minorities in those employment areas where an "obvious imbalance" in their numbers existed.[28]

The plaintiffs believed that their failure to be promoted was attributable to illegal preferential treatment of African Americans and women (reverse discrimination) that violated their rights under Title VII and the due process clause of the Fifth Amendment. The court held that the nonminority and male employees of the department failed to prove that the plan was invalid; a considerable body of evidence showed racial and sexual imbalance at the time the plan was adopted. Also, the plan did not unnecessarily trammel any legitimate interests of the nonminority or male employees because it did not call for displacement or layoff and did not totally exclude them from promotion opportunities.[29]

In summary, then, whenever a criminal justice employer wishes to implement and maintain job requirements, they must be job related. Furthermore, whenever a job requirement discriminates against a protected class, it should have a strong legitimate purpose and be the least restrictive alternative. Finally, attempts to remedy past hiring inequities by such means as affirmative action programs need substantial justification to avoid reverse discrimination.[30]

Property Rights in Employment

The Fourteenth Amendment to the U.S. Constitution provides in part that

> No state shall make or enforce any law which shall abridge the privileges or immunities of citizens of the United States; nor shall any State deprive any person of life, liberty, or property without due process of law; nor deny to any person within its jurisdiction the equal protection of the law.

Furthermore, the Supreme Court has set forth four elements of a due process claim under Section 1983: (1) A person acting under color of state law (2) deprived an individual (3) of constitutionally protected property (4) without due process of law.[31]

A long line of court cases has established the legal view that public employees have a property interest in their employment. This flies in the face of the old view that employees served "at will" or until their employer, for whatever reason, no longer needed their services. The Supreme Court has provided some general guidance on how the question of a constitutionally protected property interest is to be resolved:

> To have a property interest in a benefit, a person clearly must have more than an abstract need or desire for it. He must have more than a unilateral expectation of it. He must, instead, have a *legitimate claim of entitlement to it.* It is a purpose of the ancient institution of property to protect those claims *upon which people rely in their daily lives, reliance that must not be arbitrarily undermined* [emphasis added].[32]

The Court has also held that employees are entitled to both a pretermination hearing (setting forth the reasons and supporting evidence prompting the proposal to terminate the employee) and a posttermination notice,[33] as well as an opportunity to respond, and that state legislators are free to choose not to confer a property interest in public employment.

The development of a property interest in employment has an important ramification: It means that due process must be exercised by a public entity before terminating or interfering with an employee's property right. What has been established, however, is that a probationary employee has little or no property interest in employment; for example, the

Ninth Circuit held that a probationary civil service employee ordinarily has no property interest and could be discharged without a hearing or even "good cause." In that same decision, however, the court held that a woman who had passed her 6-month probationary period and who had then been promoted to a new position for which there was a probationary period had the legitimate expectation of continued employment.[34]

Normally, however, policymaking employees (often called exempt appointments) possess an automatic exception to the contemporary property interest view. These personnel, often elected agency heads, are generally free to hire and fire those employees who are involved in the making of important decisions and policy. Examples of this area include new sheriffs who appoint undersheriffs and wardens who appoint deputy wardens. These subordinate employees have no property interest in their positions and may be asked at any time to leave the agency or revert back to an earlier rank.

The property right in one's employment does not have to involve discipline or discharge to afford an employee protections. The claim of a parole officer that he was harassed, humiliated, and interfered with in a deliberate attempt to remove him from his position established a civil rights action for deprivation of property.[35] This decision, against the Illinois Department of Corrections, resulted from allegations that the department engaged in "a deliberate and calculated effort to remove the plaintiff from his position by forcing him to resign, thereby making the protections of the personnel code unavailable to him." As a result, the plaintiff suffered anxiety and stress and eventually went on disability status at substantially reduced pay.[36]

The key questions, then, once a property right is established, are: (1) What constitutes adequate grounds for interference with that right and (2) what is adequate process to sustain that interference?[37]

Pay and Benefits

The **Fair Labor Standards Act (FLSA)** has had a major impact on criminal justice agencies. One observer referred to the FLSA as the criminal justice administrator's "worst nightmare come true."[38] Enacted in 1938 to establish minimum wages and to require overtime compensation in the private sector, amendments were added in 1974 extending its coverage to state and local governmental employees and including special work period provisions for police and fire employees. In 1976, however, the U.S. Supreme Court ruled that the extension of the Act into traditional local and state governmental functions was unconstitutional.[39] In 1985, the Court reversed itself, bringing local police employees under the coverage of the FLSA. In this major (and costly) decision, *Garcia v. San Antonio Transit Authority,*[40] the Court held, 5 to 4, that Congress could impose the requirements of the FLSA on state and local governments.

Fair Labor Standards Act (FLSA) a federal law establishing minimum wages and requiring overtime compensation in the private sector as well as state and local governmental employees.

Criminal justice operations take place 24 hours per day, 7 days per week, and often require overtime and participation in off-duty activities such as court appearances and training sessions. The FLSA comes into play when overtime salaries must be paid. It provides that an employer must pay employees time and a half for all hours worked over 40 per week. Overtime must also be paid to personnel for all work in excess of 43 hours in a 7-day cycle or 171 hours in a 28-day period. Public safety employees may accrue a maximum of 240 hours of compensatory or "comp" time, which, if not utilized as leave, must be paid on separation from employment at the employee's final rate of pay or at the average pay over the last 3 years, whichever is greater.[41] Furthermore, employers usually cannot require employees to take compensatory time in lieu of cash.

A recent decision by the U.S. Supreme Court favored administrators in this regard, however. A county in Texas became concerned that after employees reached their cap on comp time accrued, it would be unable to afford to pay them for overtime worked. So, the county sought to reduce accrued comp time and implemented a policy under which the employees' supervisor set a maximum number of compensatory hours that could be accumulated. When an employee's accrued amount of comp time approached that maximum, the employee would be asked to take some compensatory time off so as to reduce his or her number of comp hours. If the employee did not do so voluntarily, the supervisor would order the employee to use his or her comp time at specified times. This policy was challenged in the Court by 127 deputy sheriffs. The Court held that nothing in the FLSA prohibited employers from instituting such a policy.[42]

An officer who works in the night shift must now receive pay for attending training or testifying in court during the day. Furthermore, officers who are ordered to remain at home in anticipation of emergency actions must be compensated. Notably, however, the FLSA's overtime provisions do not apply to persons employed in a bona fide executive, administrative, or professional capacity. In criminal justice, the Act has generally been held to apply to detectives and sergeants but not to those of the rank of lieutenant and above.

A companion issue with respect to criminal justice pay and benefits is that of equal pay for equal work. Disparate treatment in pay and benefits can be litigated under Title VII or statutes such as the Equal Pay Act or the equal protection clause. An Ohio case involved matron/dispatchers who performed essentially the same job as jailers but were paid less. This was found to be in violation of the Equal Pay Act and, because discriminatory intent was found, Title VII.[43]

Other criminal justice employee benefits are addressed in Title VII, the ADEA, and the Pregnancy Discrimination Act (PDA). For example, it is illegal to provide less insurance coverage for a female employee who is more likely to use maternity leave or for an older employee who is more liable to use more coverage. In addition, an older person or a woman could not be forced to pay higher pension contributions because he or she might be paying in for a shorter period of time or would be expected to live longer. Regarding pregnancy, the PDA does not require an employer to discriminate in favor of a pregnancy-related condition. It demands only that the employer not treat pregnancy differently from any other temporary medical condition. For example, if an agency has a 6-month leave policy for officers who are injured or ill from off-duty circumstances (on-duty circumstances would probably be covered by workers' compensation), that agency would have to provide 6 months' leave (if needed) for a pregnancy-related condition.[44]

Criminal Justice and a Safe Workplace

It is unclear what duties are owed by public employers to their employees in providing a safe workplace. Federal, state, and local governments are exempted from the coverage of the Occupational Safety and Health Act (OSHA), in 29 U.S.C. 652. Nonetheless, criminal justice work is often dangerous, involving the use of force and often occurring in locations outside governmental control. Therefore, workplace safety issues in criminal justice are more likely to revolve around adequacy of training and supervision than physical plants.[45]

The Supreme Court has noted the unique nature and danger of public service employment. In one case, the Court specifically stated that an employee could not bring a Section 1983 civil rights action alleging a workplace so unsafe that it violated the Fourteenth Amendment's due process clause. In this matter, a sewer worker was asphyxiated while clearing a sewer line. His widow alleged that the city knew the sewer was dangerous and that the city had failed to train or supervise the decedent properly.[46]

Other federal courts, especially the federal circuits, however, have ruled inconsistently on the safe workplace issue. One federal circuit held that a constitutional violation could be brought if it was proven that the city actively engaged in conduct that was "deliberately indifferent" to the employee's constitutional rights.[47]

However, the Fifth Circuit held differently in a Louisiana case, based on a failure to comply with a court order to have three officers on duty at all times in a prison disciplinary unit.[48] Here, a prison correctional officer in Baton Rouge was the only guard on a dangerous cellblock. While attempting to transfer a handcuffed inmate, the guard got into a scuffle with the inmate and was injured, although not severely. However, he claimed that he received insufficient medical attention and that as a result he became permanently disabled and that the institution "consciously" and with wanton disregard for his personal safety conspired to have him work alone on the cellblock. He invoked 42 U.S.C. 1983 in his charges, claiming that the institution acted in an indifferent, malicious, and reckless manner toward him, and that he suffered "class-based discrimination." The court held that the guard had no cause of action (no federal or constitutional grounds for litigation).

Liability for an employee's injury, disability, or death is a critical concern for criminal justice agencies. In particular, police and correctional officers often work in circumstances involving violent actions. Although state workers' compensation coverage, disability pensions, life insurance, and survivor pensions are designed to cover such tragedies, such coverage is typically limited and only intended to be remedial. On the other hand, civil tort actions in such cases can have a devastating impact on governmental budgets. Clearly, this is a difficult and costly problem to resolve. It is an area with moral dilemmas as well. For example, what should be done with a prison intelligence unit that has knowledge of an impending disturbance but fails to alert its officers (who are subsequently injured)? And, might a police department with knowledge that its new police vehicles have defective brakes fail to take immediate action for fear that its officers will refuse to drive the vehicles, thus reducing available personnel?[49]

Constitutional Rights of Criminal Justice Employees

Freedom of Speech and Association

Many criminal justice executives have attempted to regulate what their employees say to the public; executives develop and rely on policies and procedures designed to govern employee speech. On occasion those restrictions will be challenged; a number of court decisions have attempted to define the limits of criminal justice employees' exercise of free speech.

Although the right of freedom of speech is one of the most fundamental of all rights of Americans, the Supreme Court has indicated that "the State has interests as an employer in regulating the speech of its employees that differ significantly from those it possesses in connection with regulation of the speech of the citizenry in general."[50] Thus, the state may impose restrictions on its employees that it would not be able to impose on the citizenry at large; however, these restrictions must be reasonable.[51]

There are two basic situations in which a police regulation may be found to be an unreasonable infringement on the free speech interests of officers.[52] The first occurs when the action is overly broad. A Chicago Police Department rule prohibiting "any activity, conversation, deliberation, or discussion which is derogatory to the Department" is a good example, because such a rule obviously prohibits all criticism of the agency by its officers, even in private conversation.[53] A similar situation arose in New Orleans, where the police department had a regulation that prohibited a police officer from making statements that "unjustly criticize or ridicule, or express hatred or contempt toward, or which may be detrimental to, or cast suspicion on the reputation of, or otherwise defame, any person."[54] The regulation was revised and later ruled constitutional.[55]

The second situation in which free speech limitations may be found to be unreasonable is in the way in which the governmental action is applied. Specifically, a police department

EXHIBIT 3.2

NOT "POLITICS AS USUAL": THE HATCH ACTS[59]

All federal executive branch and civil service employees (except the president and vice president) are subject to the **Hatch Act**, which limits partisan political activities of governmental employees. Federal employees who are "further restricted"—working in several key federal law enforcement agencies—cannot run for office in a partisan election, solicit, or encourage political activity of those doing business with their agency, or use their official authority to affect the outcome of an election. In addition, political contributions may not be received from subordinates, and covered employees may not participate in political fund-raising, canvass for votes, or endorse or oppose a candidate in political literature. They may, however, vote in all partisan elections and express opinions on political topics, work in nonpartisan campaigns, attend political meetings, donate money to political parties and candidates, and sign nominating petitions.

State and local agency employees are also covered by the law, often known as "Little Hatch Acts," if they perform duties connected to programs financed totally or in part by federal funds—that is, in programs funding homeland security, training, employment, overtime, community development, emergency preparedness. Such employees may, however, run for public office in nonpartisan elections, hold office in political organizations, and actively campaign for candidates for public office (as well as engage in drafting speeches, write letters, contribute money to political organizations, and attend political fund-raisers).

The Office of Special Counsel investigates alleged Hatch Act violations by federal employees, and the state or local levels of government will investigate those of their employees.

may be unable to demonstrate that the statements by an officer being disciplined actually adversely affected the operation of the department. A Baltimore regulation prohibiting public criticism of police department action was held to have been unconstitutionally applied to a police officer who was president of the police union and had stated in a television interview that the police commissioner was not leading the department effectively[56] and that "the bottom is going to fall out of this city."[57]

Hatch Acts legislation that limits partisan political activities by governmental employees.

A related area is that of political activity. The most protected type of speech is political speech. However, governmental agencies may restrict the political behavior of their employees—and the U.S. Supreme Court has upheld the constitutionality of laws that do so.[58] Exhibit 3.2 discusses how the Hatch Act operates at the federal, state, and local levels.

Although it may appear that Supreme Court decisions have lain to rest all controversy in this area, such has not been the case. Two recent cases show lower courts opting to limit the authority of the state to restrict political activities of their employees. In Pawtucket, Rhode Island, two firefighters ran for public office (mayor and city council member), despite a city charter provision prohibiting all political activity by employees (except voting and privately expressing their opinions). The Rhode Island Supreme Court issued an injunction against enforcing the charter provision, on the ground that the provision applied only to partisan political activities.[60] In a similar Boston case, however, the court upheld the police department rule on the basis that whether the partisan–nonpartisan distinction was crucial was a matter for legislative or administrative determination.[61]

In a Michigan case, a court declared unconstitutional, for being overly broad, two city charter provisions that prohibited contributions to or solicitations for any political purpose by city employees.[62] Clearly, although the Supreme Court seems to be supportive of governmental attempts to limit the political activities of its employees, lower courts seem just as intent to limit the Supreme Court decisions to the facts of those cases.

Could a police officer be disciplined, even discharged, because of his or her political affiliations? The Supreme Court ruled on that question in a case arising out of the Sheriff's

Department in Cook County, Illinois.[63] The newly elected sheriff, a Democrat, fired the chief deputy of the process division and a bailiff of the juvenile court because they were Republicans. The Court ruled that it was a violation of the employees' First Amendment rights to discharge them from nonpolicymaking positions solely on the basis of their political party affiliation.[64]

Nonpolitical associations are also protected by the First Amendment; however, it is common for police departments to prohibit officers from associating with known felons or others of questionable reputation, on the ground that "such associations may expose an officer to irresistible temptations to yield in his obligation to impartially enforce the law, and . . . may give the appearance that the police are not themselves honest and impartial enforcers of the law."[65]

However, rules against association, as with other First Amendment rights, must not be overly broad. A Detroit Police Department regulation prohibiting associating with known criminals or persons charged with crimes, except in connection with regular duties, was declared unconstitutional. The court held that it prohibited some associations that had no bearing on the officers' integrity or public confidence in the officer (e.g., an association with a fellow church member who had been arrested on one occasion years ago, or the befriending of a recently convicted person who wanted to become a productive citizen).[66]

Occasionally, a criminal justice employee will be disciplined for improper association even though it was not demonstrated that the association had a detrimental effect on the employee or the agency. For example, a Maryland court held that a fully qualified police officer who was a nudist could not be fired simply on that basis.[67] On the other hand, a court upheld the discharge of an officer who had had sexual intercourse at a party with a woman he knew to be a nude model at a local "adult theater of known disrepute."[68]

An individual has a fundamental interest in being free to enter into certain intimate or private relationships; nevertheless, freedom of association is not an absolute right. For example, a federal district court held that the dismissal of a married police officer for living with another man's wife was a violation of the officer's privacy and associational rights.[69] Other courts, however, have found that off-duty sexual activity can affect job performance. When a married city police officer allegedly had consensual, private, nonduty, heterosexual relations with single adult women other than his wife in violation of state law criminalizing adultery, the adultery was not a fundamental right. Thus, the officer's extramarital affairs were not protected and the intimate relationship affected the public's perception of the agency.[70]

In another case, a police officer became involved with a city dispatcher who was the wife of a sergeant in the same department. The adulterous officer became eligible for promotion and scored high on the exam. The chief, confirming via an investigation that the officer had in fact been involved in an adulterous relationship with the dispatcher, refused on that basis to promote the officer, as he "would not command respect and trust" from rank-and-file officers and would adversely affect the efficiency and morale of the department. The Texas Supreme Court held that the officer's private, adulterous sexual conduct was not protected by state or federal law; the U.S. Supreme Court denied the appeal.[71]

Finally, the U.S. Court of Appeals for the Sixth Circuit held that a police department could conduct an investigation into the marital sexual relations of a police officer accused of sexual harassment.[72] In this case, there were allegations that the married officer had sexually harassed coworkers and had dated a gang member's mother. The department investigated the accusations, and the officer and his wife brought a Section 1983 action, alleging that the investigation violated their constitutional rights to privacy and freedom of association. The court held that the agency's investigation was reasonable, and, furthermore, that the police department would have been derelict in not investigating the matter.

In summary, police administrators have the constitutional authority to regulate employees' off-duty associational activities, including off-duty sexual conduct that involves a supervisory–subordinate relationship and associations that impact adversely employees' ability to do their jobs or impair the effectiveness and efficiency of the organization.[73]

The First Amendment's reach also includes means of expression other than verbal utterances. The Supreme Court upheld the constitutionality of a regulation of the Suffolk County, New York, Police Department that established several grooming standards (regarding hair, sideburn, and moustache length) for its male officers. In this case, *Kelley v. Johnson,*[74] is discussed below.

Searches and Seizures

The Fourth Amendment to the U.S. Constitution protects "the right of the people to be secure in their persons, houses, papers, and effects, against unreasonable searches and seizures." In an important case in 1967, the Supreme Court held that the amendment also protected individuals' reasonable expectations of privacy, not just property interests.[75]

The Fourth Amendment usually applies to police officers when they are at home or off duty in the same manner as it applies to all citizens. Because of the nature of their work, however, police officers can be compelled to cooperate with investigations of their behavior when ordinary citizens would not. Examples include searches of equipment and lockers provided by the department to the officers. There, the officers have no expectation of privacy that affords or merits protection.[76] Lower courts have established limitations on searches of employees themselves. The rights of prison authorities to search their employees arose in a 1985 Iowa case, in which employees were forced to sign a consent form for searches as a condition of hire; the court disagreed with such a broad policy, ruling that the consent form did not constitute a blanket waiver of all Fourth Amendment rights.[77]

Police officers may also be forced to appear in a lineup, a clear "seizure" of his or her person. Appearance in a lineup normally requires probable cause, but a federal appeals court upheld a police commissioner's ordering of 62 officers to appear in a lineup during an investigation of police brutality, holding that "the governmental interest in the particular intrusion [should be weighed] against the offense to personal dignity and integrity." Again, the court cited the nature of the work, noting that police officers do "not have the full privacy and liberty from police officials that [they] would otherwise enjoy."[78]

Self-Incrimination

The Supreme Court has also addressed questions concerning the Fifth Amendment as it applies to police officers who are under investigation. In *Garrity v. New Jersey,*[79] a police officer was ordered by the attorney general to answer questions or be discharged. The officer testified that information obtained as a result of his answers was later used to convict him of criminal charges. The Supreme Court held that the information obtained from the officer could not be used against him at his criminal trial because the Fifth Amendment forbids the use of coerced confessions.

In *Gardner v. Broderick,*[80] a police officer refused to answer questions asked by a grand jury investigating police misconduct because he believed his answers might tend to incriminate him. The officer was terminated from his position as a result. The Supreme Court ruled that the officer could not be fired for his refusal to waive his constitutional right to remain silent. The Court added, however, that the grand jury could have forced the officer to answer or be terminated for his refusal provided that the officer was informed that his answers would not be used against him later in a criminal case.

As a result of these decisions, it is proper to fire a police officer who refuses to answer questions that are related directly to the performance of his or her duties provided that the officer has been informed that any answers may not be used later in a criminal proceeding. Although there is some diversity of opinion among lower courts on the question of whether an officer may be compelled to submit to a polygraph examination, the majority of courts that have considered the question have held that an officer can be required to take the examination.[81]

Religious Practices

Criminal justice work requires that employees of police, corrections, and even some court organizations be available and on duty 24 hours per day, 7 days a week. Although it is not always convenient or pleasant, such shift configurations require that many criminal justice employees work weekends, nights, and holidays. It is generally assumed that one who takes such a position agrees to work such hours and to abide by other such conditions (e.g., carrying a weapon, as in a policing position); it is usually the personnel with the least seniority on the job who must work the most undesirable shifts.

There are occasions when one's religious beliefs are in direct conflict with the requirements of the job. Conflicts can occur between work assignments and attendance at religious services or periods of religious observance. In these situations, the employee may be forced to choose between his or her job and religion. One of the authors is acquainted with a Midwestern state trooper whose religion posed another related cause of job–religion conflict: His religion (with which he became affiliated after being hired as a trooper) banned the carrying or use of firearms. The officer chose to give up his weapon, and thus his job. A number of people have chosen to litigate the work–religion conflict rather than accept agency demands.

Title VII of the Civil Rights Act of 1964 prohibits religious discrimination in employment. The Act defines religion as including "all aspects of religious . . . practice, as well as belief, unless an employer . . . is unable to reasonably accommodate to an employee's . . . religious . . . practice without undue hardship on the conduct of the employer's business."[82] Thus, Title VII requires reasonable accommodation of religious beliefs, but not to the extent that the employee has complete freedom of religious expression.[83] For example, an Albuquerque firefighter was a Seventh Day Adventist and refused to work Friday or Saturday nights because such shifts interrupted his honoring the Sabbath. He refused to trade shifts or take leave with (as vacation) or without pay, even though existing policy permitted his doing so. Instead, he said that the *department* should make such arrangements for coverage or simply excuse him from his shifts. The department refused to do either, discharging him. The court ruled that the department's accommodations were reasonable and that no further accommodation could be made without causing an undue hardship to the department. His firing was upheld. The court emphasized, however, that future decisions would depend on the facts of the individual case.[84]

Religious practices can also conflict with state law. For example, a circuit court held that the termination of a Mormon police officer for practicing plural marriage (polygamy) in violation of state law was not a violation of his right to freely exercise his religious beliefs.[85]

Another issue relating to religious expression concerns the display of religious items on one's uniform. In a Texas case, a police veteran wished to wear a small gold cross pin on his uniform as well as on plainclothes attire "as a symbol of his evangelical Christianity." The agency forbade officers from doing so unless approved by the police chief; the chief offered the plaintiff several other accommodations, such as wearing a cross ring or bracelet instead of the pin, or wearing the pin under his uniform shirt or collar. Refusing such accommodations, the plaintiff was fired for insubordination. The Fifth Circuit Court of Appeals upheld his firing, agreeing that a police uniform "is not a forum for . . . expressing one's personal beliefs," that the constitution is not violated when a department bars religious symbols, and that the plaintiff had "myriad alternative ways to manifest this tenet of his religion."[86]

Finally, policies prohibiting the wearing of beards have also been challenged on First Amendment grounds. Two devout Sunni Muslim police officers challenged the Newark, New Jersey, Police Department's banning of beards, arguing that in their religion the lack of a beard is a "major sin"; they also noted that the department had made several medical exemptions to the policy (some officers were allowed to grow beards because of a skin condition called *folliculitis barbae*, which affects up to 60 percent of African American men; this condition is exacerbated by shaving). The Third Circuit Court of Appeals accepted the plaintiff's arguments and struck down the no-beards provision as it applied to the Muslim officers. The court determined that because the department granted exemptions for nonreligious reasons, closer scrutiny was warranted; the court concluded that the policy simply could not stand up under that scrutiny.[87]

Sexual Misconduct

To be blunt, criminal justice employees have ample opportunity to become engaged in sexual affairs, incidents, trysts, dalliances, or other behavior that is clearly sexual in nature. History and news accounts have shown that wearing a uniform, occupying a high or extremely sensitive position, or being sworn to maintain an unblemished and unsullied lifestyle does not mean that all people will do so for all time. Some people are not bashful about their intentions: Several officers have told us they aspired to police work because they assumed that wearing a uniform made them sexually irresistible. On the civilian side, there are police "groupies" who chase police officers and others in uniform.

Instances of sexual impropriety in criminal justice work can range from casual flirting while on the job to becoming romantically involved with a foreign agent whose principal aim is to learn delicate matters of national security. There have been all manner of incidents between those extremes, including the discipline of female police officers who posed nude in magazines. Some major police departments have even been compelled by their mayors to recruit officers for their sexual preference (i.e., homosexuality).

This is a delicate area, one in which discipline can be and has been meted out as police managers attempt to maintain high standards of officer conduct. It has also resulted in litigation because some officers believe that their right to privacy has been intruded on.

Officers may be disciplined for impropriety involving adultery and homosexuality. Most court decisions of the 1960s and 1970s agreed that adultery, even when involving an off-duty police officer and occurring in private, could result in disciplinary action[88] because such behavior brought debilitating criticism on the agency and undermined public confidence in the police. The views of the courts in this area, however, seem to be moderating with the times. A case involving an Internal Revenue Service agent suggested that to uphold disciplinary action for adultery, the government would have to prove that the employing agency was actually discredited.[89] The U.S. Supreme Court more recently appeared to be divided on the issue of extramarital sexual activity in public employment. In 1984, the Sixth Circuit held that a Michigan police officer could not be fired simply because he was living with a woman to whom he was not married (a felony under Michigan law).[90]

The issue of homosexual activity as a ground for termination of public employees arose in an Oklahoma case, in which a state law permitted the discharge of schoolteachers for engaging in "public homosexual activity."[91] A lower court held the law to be unconstitutionally restrictive, and the Supreme Court agreed.[92] Another federal court held that the firing of a bisexual guidance counselor did not deprive the counselor of her First or Fourteenth Amendment rights. The counselor's discussion of her sexual preferences with teachers was not protected by the First Amendment.[93]

Residency Requirements

In the 1970s and 1980s, interest in residency requirements for governmental employees heightened, especially in communities experiencing economic difficulties.[94] Many governmental agencies now specify that all or certain members in their employ must live within the geographical limits of their employing jurisdiction. In other words, employees must reside within the county or city of employment. Such residency requirements have often been justified by employing agencies, particularly in criminal justice, on the grounds that employees should become familiar with and be visible in the jurisdiction of employment and that they should reside where they are paid by the taxpayers to work. Perhaps the strongest rationale given by employing agencies is that criminal justice employees must live within a certain proximity of their work in order to respond quickly in the event of an emergency.

Prior to 1976, numerous challenges to residency requirements were raised, even after the Michigan Supreme Court ruled that Detroit's residency requirement for police officers was not irrational.[95] In 1976, when the U.S. Supreme Court held that Philadelphia's law requiring firefighters to live in the city did not violate the Constitution, the challenges subsided. The cases now seem to revolve around the question of what constitutes residency. Generally, the police officer must demonstrate that he or she spends a substantial amount of time at the in-city residence.[96] Strong arguments have been made, however, that in areas where housing is unavailable or is exceptionally expensive, a residency requirement is unreasonable.[97]

Moonlighting

The courts have traditionally supported criminal justice agencies placing limitations on the amount and kind of outside work their employees can perform.[98] For example, police department restrictions on moonlighting range from a complete ban on outside employment to permission to engage in certain forms of work, such as investment counseling, private security, and teaching police science courses. The rationale for agency limitations is that "outside employment seriously interferes with keeping the [police and fire] departments fit and ready for action at all times."[99]

In a Louisiana case, however, firefighters successfully provided evidence that moonlighting had been a common practice for 16 years before the city banned it. No firefighters had ever needed sick leave as a result of injuries acquired while moonlighting, there had never been a problem locating off-duty firefighters to respond to an emergency, and moonlighting had never caused a level of fatigue that was serious enough to impair a firefighter's work. With this evidence, the court invalidated the city ordinance that had sought to prohibit moonlighting.[100]

Misuse of Firearms

Because of the need to defend themselves or others and be prepared for any exigency, police officers are empowered to use lethal force when justified. Although restricted by the Supreme Court's 1985 decision in *Tennessee v. Garner*[101] (deeming the killing of unarmed, nondangerous suspects as unconstitutional), the possession of, and familiarity with, firearms remains a central aspect of the contemporary officer's role and function. Some officers take this responsibility to the extreme, however, becoming overly reliant on and consumed with their firepower.

Thus, police agencies typically attempt to restrain the use of firearms through written policies and frequent training in "Shoot/Don't Shoot" scenarios. Still, a broad range of potential and actual problems remains with respect to the use and possible misuse of firearms, as the following shows.

In the face of extremely serious potential and real problems and the omnipresent specter of liability suits, police agencies generally have policies regulating the use of handguns and other firearms by their officers, both on and off duty. The courts have held that such regulations need only be reasonable and that the burden rests with the disciplined police officer to show that the regulation was arbitrary and unreasonable.[102] The courts also grant considerable latitude to administrators in determining when their firearms regulations have been violated.[103] Police firearms regulations tend to address three basic issues: (1) requirements for the safeguarding of the weapon, (2) guidelines for carrying the weapon while off duty, and (3) limitations on when the weapon may be fired.[104]

Courts and juries are becoming increasingly harsher in dealing with police officers who misuse their firearms. The current tendency is to "look behind" police shootings to determine whether the officer acted negligently or the employing agency inadequately trained and supervised the officer/employee. In one case, a federal appeals court approved a $500,000 judgment against the District of Columbia when a police officer who was not in adequate physical shape shot a man in the course of an arrest. The court noted that the District officer had received no fitness training in 4 years and was physically incapable of subduing the victim. The court also noted that had the officer been physically fit and adequately trained in disarmament techniques, a gun would not have been necessary. In his condition, however, the officer posed a "foreseeable risk of harm to others."[105]

Courts have awarded damages against police officers and/or their employers for other acts involving misuse of firearms: An officer shot a person while intoxicated and off duty in a bar,[106] an officer accidentally killed an arrestee with a shotgun while handcuffing him,[107] an unstable officer shot his wife five times and then committed suicide with an off-duty weapon the department required him to carry,[108] and an officer accidentally shot and killed an innocent bystander while pursuing another man at night (the officer had had no instruction on shooting at a moving target, night shooting, or shooting in residential areas).[109]

Alcohol and Drugs in the Workplace

Alcoholism and drug abuse problems have taken on a life of their own in contemporary criminal justice; employees must be increasingly wary of the tendency to succumb to these problems, and administrative personnel must be able to recognize and attempt to counsel and treat these problems.

Indeed, in the aftermath of the early 1990s beating death of Malice Green by a group of Detroit police officers, it was reported that the Detroit Police Department had "high alcoholism rates and pervasive psychological problems connected with the stress of policing a city mired in poverty, drugs, and crime."[110] It was further revealed that although the Detroit Police Department had paid $850,000 to two drug-testing facilities, the department did not have the counseling programs many other cities offer their officers. A psychologist asserted, "There are many, many potential time bombs in that department."[111]

It is obvious, given the extant law of most jurisdictions and the nature of their work, that criminal justice employees must be able to perform their work with a clear head, unaffected by alcohol or drugs.[112] Police departments and prisons will often specify in their manual of policy and procedures that no alcoholic beverages be consumed within a specified period prior to reporting for duty.

Such regulations have been upheld uniformly because of the hazards of the work. A Louisiana court went further, upholding a regulation that prohibited police officers from consuming alcoholic beverages on or off duty to the extent that it caused the officer's behavior to become obnoxious, disruptive, or disorderly.[113] Enforcing such regulations will occasionally result in criminal justice employees being ordered to submit to drug or alcohol tests, discussed next.

Drug Testing

The courts have had several occasions to review criminal justice agency policies requiring employees to submit to urinalysis to determine the presence of drugs or alcohol. It was held as early as 1969 that a firefighter could be ordered to submit to a blood test when the agency had reasonable grounds to believe he was intoxicated, and that it was appropriate for the firefighter to be terminated from employment if he refused to submit to the test.[114]

In March 1989, the U.S. Supreme Court issued two major decisions on drug testing of public employees in the workplace. *Skinner v. Railway Labor Executives Association*[115] and *National Treasury Employees Union v. Von Raab*[116] dealt with drug-testing plans for railroad and U.S. Customs workers, respectively. Under the Fourth Amendment, governmental workers are protected from unreasonable search and seizure, including how drug testing can be conducted. The Fifth Amendment protects federal, state, and local workers from illegal governmental conduct.

In 1983, the Federal Railway Administration promulgated regulations that required railroads to conduct urine and blood tests on their workers following major train accidents. The regulations were challenged, one side arguing that because railroads were privately owned, governmental action, including applying the Fourth Amendment, could not legally be imposed. The Supreme Court disagreed in *Skinner,* ruling that railroads must be viewed as an instrument or agent of the government.

Three of the most controversial drug-testing issues have been whether testing should be permitted when there is no indication of a drug problem in the workplace, whether the testing methods are reliable, and whether a positive test proves on-the-job impairment.[117] The *Von Raab* case addressed all three issues. The U.S. Customs Service implemented a drug-screening program that required urinalysis for employees desiring transfer or promotion to positions that were directly involved in drug interdiction, where carrying a firearm was necessary, or where classified material was handled. Only 5 of 3,600 employees tested positive. The Treasury Employees Union argued that such an insignificant number of positives created a "suspicionless search" argument; in other words, drug testing was unnecessary and unwarranted. The Supreme Court disagreed, ruling that although only a few employees tested positive, drug use is such a serious problem that the program could continue.

Furthermore, the Court found nothing wrong with the testing protocol. An independent contractor was used. The worker, after discarding outer garments, produced a urine specimen while being observed by a member of the same sex; the sample was signed by the employee, labeled, placed in a plastic bag, sealed and delivered to a lab for testing. The Court found no "grave potential for arbitrary and oppressive interference with the privacy and personal security of the individuals" in this method.

Proving the connection between drug testing and on-the-job impairment has been an ongoing issue. Urinalysis cannot prove when a person testing positive actually used the drug. Therefore, tests may punish and stigmatize a person for extracurricular drug use that may have no effect on the worker's on-the-job performance.[118] In *Von Raab,* the Court indicated that this dilemma is still no impediment to testing. It stated that the Customs Service had a compelling interest in having a "physically fit" employee with "unimpeachable integrity and judgment."

Together, these two cases may set a new standard for determining the reasonableness of drug testing in the criminal justice workplace. They may legalize many testing programs that formerly would have been risky. *Von Raab* presented three compelling governmental interests that could be weighed against the employee's privacy expectations: the integrity of the workforce, public safety, and protection of sensitive information. *Skinner* stated that railroad workers also have diminished expectations of privacy because they are in an industry that is widely regulated to ensure safety.[119]

Rights of Police Officers

Delineated earlier were several areas (e.g., place of residence, religious practice, freedom of speech, search, and seizure) in which criminal justice employees, particularly the police, may encounter treatment by their administrators and the federal courts that is quite different from that received by other citizens. One does give up certain constitutional rights and privileges by virtue of wearing a justice system uniform. This section looks at how, for the police at least, the pendulum has swung more in the direction of the rank and file.

Peace Officers' Bill of Rights (POBR) legislation mandating due process rights for peace officers who are the subject of internal investigations that could lead to disciplinary action.

In the last decade, police officers have insisted on greater procedural safeguards to protect themselves against what they perceive as arbitrary infringement on their rights. These demands have been reflected in statutes enacted in many states, generally known as the **Peace Officers' Bill of Rights (POBR)**. This legislation mandates due process rights for peace officers who are the subject of internal investigations that could lead to disciplinary action. These statutes identify the type of information that must be provided to the accused officer, the officer's responsibility to cooperate during the investigation, the officer's right to representation during the process, and the rules and procedures concerning the collection of certain types of evidence. Following are some common provisions of state POBR legislation:

Written notice: The department must provide the officer with written notice of the nature of the investigation, summary of alleged misconduct, and name of the investigating officer.

Right to representation: The officer may have an attorney or a representative of his or her choosing present during any phase of questioning or hearing.

Polygraph examination: The officer may refuse to take a polygraph examination unless the complainant submits to an examination and is determined to be telling the truth. In this case, the officer may be ordered to take a polygraph examination or be subject to disciplinary action.

Officers expect to be treated fairly, honestly, and respectfully during the course of an internal investigation. In turn, the public expects that the agency will develop sound disciplinary policies and conduct thorough inquiries into allegations of misconduct.

It is imperative that administrators become thoroughly familiar with statutes, contract provisions, and existing rules between employer and employee so that procedural due process requirements can be met, particularly in disciplinary cases in which an employee's property interest might be affected.

Police officers today are also more likely to file a grievance when they believe their rights have been violated. Grievances may cover a broad range of issues, including salaries, overtime, leave, hours of work, allowances, retirement, opportunity for advancement, performance evaluations, workplace conditions, tenure, disciplinary actions, supervisory methods, and administrative practices. The preferred method for settling officers' grievances is through informal discussion: The employee explains his or her grievance to the immediate supervisor. Most complaints can be handled in this way. Those complaints that cannot be dealt with informally are usually handled through a more formal grievance process, which may involve several different levels of action.

Workplace Harassment

Although sexual harassment has been a major concern in the nation for several decades—and is even outlawed in the Code of Federal Regulations (see 29 C.F.R. 1604.11[a])—the more contemporary approach is for agencies to have a broader policy that applies to all forms of **workplace harassment**. All such harassment is a form of discrimination that violates Title VII of the Civil Rights Act of 1964 and other federal laws.

workplace harassment unwelcome verbal or physical conduct (whether or not of a sexual nature) that creates a hostile work environment, or a change in an employment status or benefits.

Unwelcome verbal or physical conduct based on race, color, religion, sex (whether or not of a sexual nature), national origin, age (40 years and older), disability (mental or physical), sexual orientation, or retaliation constitutes harassment when:

1. The conduct is sufficiently severe to create a hostile work environment, or
2. A supervisor's harassing conduct results in a change in an employment status or benefits (such as demotion, termination, or failure to promote).[120]

Hostile work environment occurs when unwelcome comments or conduct based on sex, race, or other legally protected characteristics unreasonably interferes with an employee's work performance or creates an offensive work environment. Examples of such actions can include:

- Leering in a sexually suggestive manner
- Making offensive remarks about looks, clothing, body parts
- Touching in a way that makes an employee uncomfortable, such as patting, pinching, brushing against another's body
- Sending or telling suggestive letters or notes, or telling sexual or lewd jokes
- Using racially derogatory words, phrases, epithets

A claim of harassment generally requires that the complaining party be a member of a statutorily protected class and was subjected to unwelcome verbal or physical conduct, that the unwelcome conduct complaint is based on his or her membership in that protected class, and that the unwelcome conduct affected a term or condition of employment and unreasonably interfered with his or her work performance. Any employee wishing to initiate an Equal Employment Complaint (EEO) arising out of the prohibited conduct described earlier must contact an EEO official within 45 days of the incident.

Still, however, sexually related improprieties can and do occur; police supervisors and managers must be vigilant of such inappropriate behaviors, seven types of which have been identified:[121]

1. ***Nonsexual contacts that are sexually motivated.*** An officer will stop another citizen without legal justification to obtain information or get a closer look at the citizen.
2. ***Voyeuristic contacts.*** Police officers attempt to observe partially clad or nude citizens. They observe apartment buildings or college dormitories. In other cases, they roust citizens parked on lovers' lanes.
3. ***Contacts with crime victims.*** Crime victims generally are emotionally distraught or upset and particularly vulnerable to sexual overtures from officers. In these instances, officers may make several return visits and calls with the intention of seducing the victim.
4. ***Contacts with offenders.*** In these cases, officers may conduct body searches, frisks, and pat-down searches. In some cases, officers may demand sexual favors. Offenders' complaints of sexual harassment will not be investigated by a department without corroborating evidence, which seldom exists.
5. ***Contacts with juvenile offenders.*** In some cases, officers have exhibited some of the same behaviors with juveniles that they have with adults, such as patdowns, frisks, and sexual favors. There have also been cases in which officers assigned as juvenile or school liaison officers have taken advantage of their assignment to seduce juveniles.

6. ***Sexual shakedowns.*** Police officers demand sexual services from prostitutes, homosexuals, and others engaged in criminal activity as a form of protection.
7. ***Citizen-initiated sexual contacts.*** Some citizens are attracted to police officers and attempt to seduce them. They may be attracted to the uniform, authority, or the prospect of a "safe" sexual encounter. In other cases, the citizen may be lonely or may want a "break" when caught violating the law.

Family and Medical Leave Act

Eligibility Requirements

Family and Medical Leave Act (FMLA) legislation that entitles eligible employees to take unpaid, job-protected leave for specified family and medical reasons.

The **Family and Medical Leave Act (FMLA),** enacted by Public Law 103-3, became effective in August 1993 and is administered and enforced by the U.S. Department of Labor's Wage and Hour Division. FMLA applies to all public agencies, including state, local, and federal employers; local schools; and private sector employers with 50 or more employees in 20 or more workweeks and who are engaged in commerce. FMLA entitles eligible employees to take up to 12 weeks of unpaid, job-protected leave in a 12-month period for specified family and medical reasons.

To be eligible for FMLA benefits, an employee must:

- work for a covered employer
- have worked for a covered employer for at least 12 months (and have worked at least 1,250 hours during that time)

A covered employer must grant an eligible employee unpaid leave for one or more of the following reasons:

- For the birth and care of a newborn child of the employee
- For placement with the employee of a child for adoption or child care
- To care for an immediate family member with a serious health condition
- To take medical leave when the employee is unable to work because of a serious health condition

A serious health condition means an illness, injury, impairment, or physical or mental condition that involves either any period of incapacitation or treatment, or continuing treatment by a health care provider; this can include any period of inability to work, attend school, or perform regular daily activities.

Amendments to the Act

In 2013, the U.S. Supreme Court in *United States v. Windsor*[122] struck down section 3 of the Defense of Marriage Act (DOMA), saying that interpreting "marriage" and "spouse" to apply only to opposite-sex unions was unconstitutional. A so-called Final Rule became effective on March 27, 2015, revising the regulatory definition of spouse under the FMLA, so that eligible employees in legal same-sex marriages will be able to take FMLA leave to care for their spouse or family member, *regardless of where they live*. This change ensures that the FMLA affords spouses in same-sex marriages the same ability as all spouses to fully exercise their FMLA rights.

Earlier, the 2009 and 2010 amendments to the FMLA[123] addressed hardships being placed on military families. Two new categories of leave were created in the amendments—qualifying exigency leave and military caregiver leave—which are designed to ease the strains.

Qualifying exigency leave is designed to allow family members of deployed regular Armed Forces personnel to take time away from work to provide for the exigencies that arise out of a military deployment. Such leave is triggered only when the deployed military member is the employee's spouse, son, daughter, or parent. Military caregiver leave is triggered when a family member must help a wounded soldier on his return home; it also imposes new obligations on employers. An eligible employee—including a spouse, son, daughter, parent, or next-of-kin of a covered service member—is entitled to this type of leave in order to care for a member of the Armed Forces as well as National Guard or Reserves who has a serious injury or illness that was incurred in the line of duty on active duty and requires ongoing medical treatment, recuperation, or therapy.[124]

▶ The Americans with Disabilities Act (ADA)

Americans with Disabilities Act legislation making it illegal to discriminate against persons with disabilities in their recruitment, hiring, and promotion practices.

The **Americans with Disabilities Act (ADA)** was signed into law in 1990. Although certain agencies in the federal government, such as the Federal Bureau of Investigation, are exempt from the ADA, state and local governments and their agencies are covered by the law. It is critical for administrators to develop written policies and procedures consistent with the ADA and have them in place before a problem arises.[125]

Under the law, criminal justice agencies may not discriminate against qualified individuals with disabilities. A person has a disability under the law if he or she has a mental or physical impairment that substantially limits a major life activity, such as walking, talking, breathing, sitting, standing, or learning.[126] Title I of the ADA makes it illegal to discriminate against persons with disabilities. This mandate applies to the agency's recruitment, hiring, and promotion practices. ADA is not an affirmative action law, so persons with disabilities are not entitled to preference in hiring.

Employers are to provide reasonable accommodation to disabled persons. A reasonable accommodation can include modifying existing facilities to make them accessible, job restructuring, part-time or modified work schedules, acquiring or modifying equipment, and changing policies.[127] Hiring decisions must be based on whether an applicant meets the established prerequisites of the position (e.g., experience or education) and is able to perform the essential functions of the job. Under the law, blanket exclusions of individuals with a particular disability (such as diabetes) are, in most cases, impermissible.

Corrections agencies—jails, prisons, and detention facilities—are also covered by the ADA; programs offered to inmates must be accessible. For example, if a hearing-impaired inmate wished to attend Alcoholics Anonymous meetings, the corrections facility would need to make reasonable accommodation to allow him or her to do so, through such means as providing a sign language interpreter or writing notes as needed.[128]

▶ Related Laws—And Possible Changes in the Offing

In 2010, as part of the Patient Protection and Affordable Care Act (also known as Obamacare, which became law in March 2010),[129] providing break time for nursing mothers to express milk in "a place, other than a bathroom, that is shielded from view and free from intrusion from coworkers and the public" should be available for employees. The fate of the Act in general as well as such individual provisions remain unclear under the Trump administration.

In May 2016, the Obama administration attempted to expand the receipt of overtime pay eligibility to millions of Americans. If enacted, employees earning a salary of less than

$913 per week would be paid overtime; however, in November 2016, a federal judge imposed an injunction, barring the rule's enforcement nationwide. Similarly, several attempts were made by the Obama administration to increase the federal minimum wage for all employees, but (like the Affordable Care Act and overtime laws) those attempts are presently politically unsettled.[130]

▶ Addressing Grooming and Appearance: Uniform Codes, Beards, and Tattoos

Employers' Rights

As noted in Chapter 2, the needs of newer generations of people now entering the labor market are changing employers' views and perks for these employees in the workplace. Similarly, they are bringing new views with respect to workers' appearance, particularly where policing and prison employment are concerned. Concurrently, changes in agency **dress codes**—a set of rules, usually set forth in the agency's policy and procedure manual, specifying the required manner of dress and appearance for employees in an organization—may be coming in terms of what should be permitted concerning one's appearance and body modifications.

dress code
a set of rules, usually written as policy, specifying the required manner of dress and appearance for employees in an organization.

Succinctly stated, criminal justice administrators have long been able to regulate the appearance of their officers. In *Kelley v. Johnson*,[131] 1976, the U.S. Supreme Court held that police agencies have a legitimate, "rational" interest in establishing such rules and regulations. (The case involved a police department's grooming standards for male officers as to style and length of hair, sideburns, and mustaches; also, beards and goatees were prohibited.) The court upheld such regulations on the grounds they "make police officers readily recognizable to the members of the public, or [maintain] a desire for the esprit de corps. Either one is a sufficiently rational justification for regulations . . ."[132]

Certainly, the police or correctional officer uniform is important, as it conveys power and authority while also identifying persons who have the power to arrest and use force. Therefore, many, if not most, such agencies have general orders or policies constituting a dress code so as to

> promote a professional image to the community served; have uniformed officers be consistently attired to reflect their authority, respective assignment, and rank within the agency; require the wearing of agency approved uniforms; have officers be properly groomed and his/her uniform clean, pressed, and in proper condition.[133]

In addition to hair and beard/goatees standards (and whether or not they are permitted), such codes can address types of sunglasses to be worn (mirrored, for example, are often banned) and tattoos (discussed below). Regulations might also spell out prohibitions against the wearing of items of clothing with an identifying logo, so the jurisdiction is not viewed as endorsing a particular name (brand).

Employees' Rights: Tattoos and Millennials

An increasing sticking point in criminal justice and for dress codes concerns tattooing (a related matter is body piercings). Certainly the entry of the Millennials—persons born in the 1980s—into the workplace creates some challenges and new ways of viewing appearance in criminal justice. Millennials' penchant for tattoos is well known, as 40 percent of them sport at least one tattoo. With tattoos also becoming more socially acceptable, it has therefore become more difficult for criminal justice administrators to take a totally anti-tattoo position. Furthermore, we may be approaching a point where treating employees differently because of their tattoos will be illegal. For example, in California tattoos are generally considered protected speech under the First Amendment.[134] Lawsuits are challenging such policies as the one in Des Moines, Iowa, which states that any tattoos, branding, and intentional scarring on the face, head, neck, hands, and exposed arms and legs are prohibited.[135] Even prospective police employees are filing suit, such as the northeastern Pennsylvania man who claimed his rights were violated when he was not hired with the state police because he would not have his arm tattoo removed (he lost his federal lawsuit in which he claimed his First Amendment and equal-protection rights had been violated).[136]

The matter of tattoos and body modifications may well pose increasing challenges for criminal justice administrators in years to come. It should be emphasized, however, that employers still have a right to regulate employee appearance at work. The aforementioned *Kelley v. Johnson* case remains intact, and administrators are free to determine that body modifications create an unprofessional appearance.[137]

Summary

After providing an overview of related legislation, this chapter examined several areas of criminal justice employee rights, including the issues of drug testing, privacy, hiring and firing, sexual harassment, disabilities, and peace officers' rights. Criminal justice employers' responsibilities were also discussed.

Being an administrator in the field of criminal justice has never been easy. Unfortunately, the issues facing today's justice administrators have probably never been more difficult or complex.

This chapter clearly demonstrated that these are challenging and, occasionally, litigious times for the justice system; one act of negligence can mean financial disaster for an individual or a supervisor.

Key Terms and Concepts

Americans with Disabilities Act (ADA), p. 75
Affirmative action, p. 59
Bona fide occupational qualifier (BFOQ), p. 58
Disparate treatment, p. 57
Dress code, p. 76
Fair Labor Standards Act (FLSA), p. 61
Family and Medical Leave Act (FMLA), p. 74
Hatch Acts, p. 64
Peace Officers' Bill of Rights (POBR), p. 72
Reverse discrimination, p. 59
Workplace harassment, p. 73

Questions for Review

1. What are criminal justice employees' rights in the workplace according to federal statutes?
2. What is the general employee–employer relationship in criminal justice regarding recruitment and hiring and affirmative action?
3. It has been stated that criminal justice employees have a "property interest" in their jobs as well as a right to a safe workplace. What does this mean?
4. What constitutional rights are implicated for criminal justice employees on the job? (In your response, address whether rights are held regarding freedom of speech, searches and seizures, self-incrimination, and religion.)
5. In what regard is a greater standard of conduct expected of criminal justice employees? (In your response, include discussions of sexual behavior, residency, moonlighting, use of firearms, and alcohol/drug abuse.)

6. What kinds of behaviors can lead to charges of workplace harassment in a criminal justice agency?
7. What are the protections afforded criminal justice employees under the Family and Medical Leave Act (including its amendments) and the Americans with Disabilities Act?
8. What purposes do agency dress codes serve, and what is the current and future stance concerning body modification (i.e., tattooing)?

Deliberate and Decide 1

When to Dole Out Discipline

Officer Seymour is a 9-year veteran of your police agency, experienced in both the patrol and detective divisions. He takes pride in being "old school," but his hard-nosed style alienates a lot of officers. At times he responds to calls for service without requesting cover units or backup, has had several complaints of brutality lodged during the last 3 years, and is borderline insubordinate when dealing with supervisors, leading to some of past and present supervisors even commenting that he is a "walking time bomb" who is unpredictable.

One day while on patrol, Seymour responds to a shooting in a home just outside of his city's jurisdiction, where county sheriff, fire, and medical personnel are working on a man with a head wound who is lying on the floor. He informs the dispatcher that he is out "assisting." Nearby on a wall divider is a large, unique, foreign-made handgun; awed by it, he picks it up and examines it. A fire department captain yells at him, "Hey! Put that down, this might become a homicide case!" so he places the revolver back on the shelf. Later, the fire captain informs you, Seymour's supervisor, of his actions, and so you require that he write a report of his actions. He denies both verbally and in writing that he touched or picked up the handgun. Looking at his personnel file, you find his performance evaluations for the past 9 years have been "standard" or above—average to above average; he has never been suspended from duty. Although verbally expressing concerns and general unhappiness with his work and attitude, his former supervisors never expressed such in writing.

Questions for Discussion

1. What are the primary issues in this situation?
2. Do sufficient grounds exist for bringing disciplinary action against Seymour? If so, what would be the specific charges and the type/level of punishment?
3. Do grounds exist for termination even though his past supervisors have rated him as standard for 9 years?

Deliberate and Decide 2

You are a new university police chief in a medium-sized city, and today is a huge football game at your university. You have just received information from a patrol sergeant that one of your male officers, Spicer, is at the football stadium working overtime and wearing an earring and sporting a new, visible (and rather risqué) tattoo on his arm. The sergeant says both are highly visible, and that a rudimentary dress code exists in your agency but does not cover earrings. You are aware that the other officers are anxiously watching the situation to see what you do. Spicer, the recipient of many letters of reprimand and filer of many grievances, is fully aware of what he can and cannot do, and no doubt aware that there is no specific prohibition against either earrings or tattoos under the agency's dress code, and that he is merely "expressing" himself under the First Amendment.

Questions for Discussion

1. What, if any, action will you take regarding the earring?
2. Can you legally regulate the appearance of the employees in the workplace and require a "professional" appearance?
3. Can you use to advantage any U.S. Supreme Court decisions in response to this matter?

Learn by Doing

1. As an administrator in your probation and parole office, you have long been supportive of your subordinates and appreciate their hard work. Lately, however, the effects of budget cutbacks have taken a serious toll on your organization, with no new hiring occurring and positions being frozen when someone retires or resigns. Your officers have sent you a letter stating that they are very upset with the work environment now that there are too fewer employees, resulting in their having to be on-call for prolonged

amounts of time, caseloads being extremely high, their paperwork being excessive, and their home visits with clients now seemingly much more dangerous—particularly when someone's probation or parole is revoked and he or she must be arrested and taken to jail. Clearly, they perceive that the workplace is unsafe and their morale is low. How will you attempt to address their concerns?

2. You are a mid-manager in a campus police organization. During the fall semester, you and your personnel are quite challenged with special events—students returning to campus, football games, concerts, and other activities—that require officers to work a lot of overtime. A sergeant comes to you with a problem: Two of his day-shift officers are refusing to work overtime for evening and weekend events. Their reason is that they are very busy (and making a lot of extra money) moonlighting, one for a private security firm and the other installing fencing for a home developer. This is causing a major problem in terms of filling required overtime needs at special events on campus. How will you address this problem?

Case Study

You are a lieutenant working night shift in your office when a female officer, Jenkins, comes in and is visibly upset. She says that she just left a meeting with her supervisor, Sgt. Montgomery, in which they discussed in detail her annual performance evaluation. She is irate and complains that Montgomery evaluated her unfairly. She also asserts that she and Montgomery have been "intimate" for several months, but she recently broke off their relationship upon learning that he was seeing other women. She believes that now, as a result, he is vengeful and biased in his evaluation, thereby putting a blot on her personnel record and harming future chances for promotion. Jenkins leaves, and you summon Sgt. Montgomery to your office. He comes in with a very different account of the situation. First, he maintains that the two have never dated (because, he says that would be in violation of agency policy). Second, he believes he was fair in Jenkins' evaluation, and that she actually slapped his face before she left his office. He demands to know what you, as their commander, are going to do about her and this "assault."

Questions for Discussion

1. Does this situation justify your conducting an immediate investigation into either a sexual harassment complaint or an assault?
2. If so, what would be your *first* course of action (remember that there can be multiple parts to an initial action)?
3. Assuming there will be an Internal Affairs investigation at some point (because one of the parties is obviously lying), what kinds of information would you consider important to obtain concerning both the officer and sergeant, and how would you go about obtaining it?

Notes

1. Robert H. Chaires and Susan A. Lentz, "Criminal Justice Employee Rights: An Overview," *American Journal of Criminal Justice* 13 (April 1995): 259.
2. Ibid.
3. American Association of University Women, *The Simple Truth about the Gender Pay Gap*, Fall 2016, pp. 1, 3, http://www.aauw.org/aauw_check/pdf_download/show_pdf.php?file=The-Simple-Truth.
4. National Women's Law Center, "Lilly Ledbetter Fair Pay Act," January 29, 2013, http://nwlc.org/resources/lilly-ledbetter-fair-pay-act/; also see National Women's Law Center, "The Lilly Ledbetter Act Five Years Later – A Law That Works," January 29, 2014, http://nwlc.org/resources/lilly-ledbetter-act-five-years-later-law-works/.
5. Ibid.
6. See *Mikula v. Allegheny County of Pennsylvania,* 583 F.3d 181 (3d Cir. 2009), *where* a grants coordinator was paid $7,000 less per year than a male counterpart.
7. See *Schengrund v. Pennsylvania State University*, 705 F.Supp.2d 425 (M.D. Penn. 2009).
8. *Herster v. Board of Supervisors of Louisiana State University*, No. 13–139–JJB, 2013 WL 2422893 (M.D. La. June 3, 2013).
9. *United Autoworkers v. Johnson Controls,* 111 S.Ct. 1196 (1991).
10. Kenneth J. Peak, *Policing America: Challenges and Best Practices,* 7th ed. (Upper Saddle River, NJ: Prentice Hall, 2012), Chapter 4, generally.
11. Chaires and Lentz, "Criminal Justice Employee Rights," p. 260.
12. *U.S. v. Gregory,* 818 F.2d 114 (4th Cir. 1987).
13. *Harris v. Pan American,* 649 F.2d 670 (9th Cir. 1988).
14. Chaires and Lentz, "Criminal Justice Employee Rights," p. 267.
15. Ken Peak, Douglas W. Farenholtz, and George Coxey, "Physical Abilities Testing for Police Officers: A Flexible,

Job-Related Approach," *The Police Chief* 59 (January 1992): 52–56.
16. *Shaw v. Nebraska Department of Corrections,* 666 F.Supp. 1330 (ND February 1987).
17. *Garrett v. Oskaloosa County,* 734 F.2d 621 (11th Cir. 1984).
18. Chaires and Lentz, "Criminal Justice Employee Rights," p. 268.
19. *EEOC v. State Department of Highway Safety,* 660 F.Supp. 1104 (ND Fla.: 1986).
20. *Johnson v. Mayor and City Council of Baltimore* (105 S.Ct. 2717, 1985).
21. 460 U.S. 226, 103 S.Ct. 1054, 75 L.Ed.2d 18 (1983).
22. Chaires and Lentz, "Criminal Justice Employee Rights," p. 269.
23. Paul J. Spiegelman, "Court-Ordered Hiring Quotas after *Stotts:* A Narrative on the Role of the Moralities of the Web and the Ladder in Employment Discrimination Doctrine," *Harvard Civil Rights–Civil Liberties Law Review* 20 (1985): 72.
24. Chaires and Lentz, "Criminal Justice Employee Rights," p. 269.
25. *Regents of the University of California v. Bakke,* 98 S.Ct. 2733, 438 U.S. 265, 57 L.Ed.2d (1978).
26. *Wygant v. Jackson Board of Education,* 106 S.Ct. 1842 (1986).
27. Chaires and Lentz, "Criminal Justice Employee Rights," p. 269.
28. *Ledoux v. District of Columbia,* 820 F.2d 1293 (D.C. Cir. 1987), at 1294.
29. Ibid.
30. Chaires and Lentz, "Criminal Justice Employee Rights," p. 270.
31. *Parratt v. Taylor,* 451 U.S. 527, 536–537, 101 S.Ct. 1908, 1913–1914, 68 L.Ed.2d 420 (1981).
32. *Board of Regents v. Roth,* 408 U.S. at 577, 92 S.Ct. at 2709.
33. *Cleveland Board of Education v. Loudermill,* 470 U.S. 532, 541 (1985).
34. *McGraw v. City of Huntington Beach,* 882 F.2d 384 (9th Cir. 1989).
35. *McAdoo v. Lane,* 564 F.Supp. 1215 (ND Ill., 1983).
36. Ibid., at 1217.
37. Chaires and Lentz, "Criminal Justice Employee Rights," p. 273.
38. Lynn Lund, "The 'Ten Commandments' of Risk Management for Jail Administrators," *Detention Reporter* 4 (June 1991): 4.
39. *National League of Cities v. Usery,* 426 U.S. 833 (1976).
40. 105 S.Ct. 1005 (1985).
41. Charles R. Swanson, Leonard Territo, and Robert W. Taylor, *Police Administration: Structures, Processes, and Behavior,* 6th ed. (Upper Saddle River, NJ: Prentice Hall, 2005), p. 599
42. *Christiansen v. Harris County,* 529 U.S. 576, 120 S. Ct. 1655, 146 L.Ed.2d 621 (2000).
43. *Jurich v. Mahoning County,* 31 Fair Emp. Prac. 1275 (BNA) (ND Ohio, 1983).
44. Chaires and Lentz, "Criminal Justice Employee Rights," p. 280.
45. Ibid.
46. *Collins v. City of Harker Heights,* 112 S.Ct. 1061 (1992).
47. *Ruge v. City of Bellevue,* 892 F.2d 738 (1989).
48. *Galloway v. State of Louisiana,* 817 F.2d 1154 (5th Cir. 1987).
49. Chaires and Lentz, "Criminal Justice Employee Rights," pp. 280–283.
50. *Pickering v. Board of Education,* 391 U.S. 563 (1968), p. 568.
51. *Keyishian v. Board of Regents,* 385 U.S. 589 (1967).
52. Swanson, Territo, and Taylor, *Police Administration,* p. 394.
53. *Muller v. Conlisk,* 429 F.2d 901 (7th Cir. 1970).
54. *Flynn v. Giarusso,* 321 F.Supp. 1295 (ED La.: 1971), at p. 1299.
55. *Magri v. Giarusso,* 379 F.Supp. 353 (ED La.: 1974).
56. Swanson, Territo, and Taylor, *Police Administration,* p. 395.
57. *Brukiewa v. Police Commissioner of Baltimore,* 263 A.2d 210 (MD: 1970).
58. See Hatch Reform Act Amendments of 1993, Pub. L. No. 103-94, 107 Stat. 1001 (1993) (codified at 5 U.S.C. Secs. 1501-1503); also see *United Public Workers v. Mitchell,* 330 U.S. 75 (1947).
59. Adapted from Michael Bulzomi, "Casting More Than Your Vote: The Hatch Act and Political Involvement for Law Enforcement Personnel," *FBI Law Enforcement Bulletin* 77(12) (2008): 16–25.
60. *Magill v. Lynch,* 400 F.Supp. 84 (R.I. 1975).
61. *Boston Police Patrolmen's Association, Inc. v. City of Boston,* 326 N.E.2d 314 (MA: 1975).
62. *Phillips v. City of Flint,* 225 N.W.2d 780 (MI: 1975).
63. *Elrod v. Burns,* 427 U.S. 347 (1976); see also *Ramey v. Harber,* 431 F.Supp 657 (WD Va., 1977) and *Branti v. Finkel,* 445 U.S. 507 (1980).
64. *Connick v. Myers,* 461 U.S. 138 (1983); *Jones v. Dodson,* 727 F.2d 1329 (4th Cir. 1984).
65. Swanson, Territo, and Taylor, *Police Administration,* p. 397.
66. *Sponick v. City of Detroit Police Department,* 211 N.W.2d 674 (MI: 1973), p. 681; but see *Wilson v. Taylor,* 733 F.2d 1539 (11th Cir. 1984).
67. *Bruns v. Pomerleau,* 319 F.Supp. 58 (D. Md. 1970); see also *McMullen v. Carson,* 754 F.2d 936 (11th Cir. 1985), where it was held that a Ku Klux Klansman could not be fired from his position as a records clerk in the sheriff's department simply because he was a Klansman. The court did uphold the dismissal because his active KKK participation threatened to negatively affect the agency's ability to perform its public duties.
68. *Civil Service Commission of Tucson v. Livingston,* 525 P.2d 949 (Ariz. 1974).
69. *Briggs v. North Muskegon Police Department,* 563 F.Supp. 585 (WD Mich., 1983), affd. 746 F.2d 1475 (6th Cir. 1984).

70. *Oliverson v. West Valley City,* 875 F.Supp. 1465 (D. Utah, 1995).
71. *Henery v. City of Sherman,* 116 S.Ct. 1098 (1997).
72. *Hughes v. City of North Olmsted,* 93 F.3d 238 (6th Cir., 1996).
73. Michael J. Bulzomi, "Constitutional Authority to Regulate Off-Duty Relationships: Recent Court Decisions," *FBI Law Enforcement Bulletin* (April 1999): 26–32.
74. 425 U.S. 238 (1976).
75. *Katz v. United States,* 389 U.S. 347 (1967).
76. *People v. Tidwell,* 266 N.E.2d 787 (IL: 1971).
77. *McDonell v. Hunter,* 611 F.Supp. 1122 (SD Iowa, 1985), affd. as mod., 809 F.2d 1302 (8th Cir., 1987).
78. *Biehunik v. Felicetta,* 441 F.2d 228 (1971), p. 230.
79. 385 U.S. 483 (1967).
80. 392 U.S. 273 (1968).
81. *Gabrilowitz v. Newman,* 582 F.2d 100 (1st Cir. 1978). Cases upholding the department's authority to order a polygraph examination for police officers include *Eshelman v. Blubaum,* 560 P.2d 1283 (Ariz.: 1977); *Dolan v. Kelly,* 348 N.Y.S.2d 478 (1973); *Richardson v. City of Pasadena,* 500 S.W.2d 175 (Tex.: 1973); *Seattle Police Officer's Guild v. City of Seattle,* 494 P.2d 485 (Wash.: 1972); *Roux v. New Orleans Police Department,* 223 So.2d 905 (La.: 1969); and *Farmer v. City of Fort Lauderdale,* 427 So.2d 187 (Fla.: 1983), cert. den., 104 S.Ct. 74 (1984).
82. 42 U.S.C. 200e(j).
83. *United States v. City of Albuquerque,* 12 EPD 11, 244 (10th Cir. 1976); see also *Trans World Airlines v. Hardison,* 97 S.Ct. 2264 (1977).
84. *United States v. Albuquerque,* 545 F.2d 110 (10th Cir. 1977).
85. *Potter v. Murray City,* 760 F.2d 1065 (10th Cir. 1985).
86. *Daniels v. City of Arlington, Texas*, 246 F.3d 500 (5th Cir. 2001), *cert. denied*, 122 S. Ct. 347 (2001).
87. *Fraternal Order of Police Newark Lodge No. 12 v. City of Newark*, 170 F.3d 359 (3rd Cir. 1999), *cert. denied*, 120 S. Ct. 56 (1999).
88. *Faust v. Police Civil Service Commission,* 347 A.2d 765 (Pa. 1975); *Stewart v. Leary,* 293 N.Y.S.2d 573 (1968); *Brewer v. City of Ashland,* 86 S.W.2d 669 (Ky. 1935); *Fabio v. Civil Service Commission of Philadelphia,* 373 A.2d 751 (Penn.: 1977).
89. *Major v. Hampton,* 413 F.Supp. 66 (1976).
90. *Briggs v. City of North Muskegon Police Department,* 563 F.Supp. 585 (6th Cir. 1984).
91. *National Gay Task Force v. Bd. of Ed. of Oklahoma City,* 729 F.2d 1270 (10th Cir. 1984).
92. *Board of Education v. National Gay Task Force,* 53 U.S.L.W. 4408, No. 83-2030 (1985).
93. *Rowland v. Mad. River Sch. Dist.,* 730 F.2d 444 (6th Cir. 1984).
94. David J. Schall, *An Investigation into the Relationship between Municipal Police Residency Requirements, Professionalism, Economic Conditions, and Equal Employment Goals,* Unpublished dissertation, University of Wisconsin–Milwaukee, 1996.
95. *Detroit Police Officers Association v. City of Detroit,* 190 N.W.2d 97 (1971), appeal denied, 405 U.S. 950 (1972).
96. *Miller v. Police Board of City of Chicago,* 349 N.E.2d 544 (Ill.: 1976); *Williamson v. Village of Baskin,* 339 So.2d 474 (La.: 1976); *Nigro v. Board of Trustees of Alden,* 395 N.Y.S.2d 544 (1977).
97. *State, County, and Municipal Employees Local 339 v. City of Highland Park,* 108 N.W.2d 898 (1961).
98. See, for example, *Cox v. McNamara,* 493 P.2d 54 (Ore.: 1972); *Brenckle v. Township of Shaler,* 281 A.2d 920 (Penn.: 1972); *Hopwood v. City of Paducah,* 424 S.W.2d 134 (Ken.: 1968); *Flood v. Kennedy,* 239 N.Y.S.2d 665 (1963).
99. Richard N. Williams, *Legal Aspects of Discipline by Police Administrators* (Traffic Institute Publication 2705) (Evanston, IL: Northwestern University, 1975), p. 4.
100. *City of Crowley Firemen v. City of Crowley,* 264 So.2d 368 (La.: 1972).
101. 471 U.S. 1, 105 S.Ct. 1694, 85 L.Ed.2d 1 (1985).
102. *Lally v. Department of Police,* 306 So.2d 65 (La. 1974).
103. See, for example, *Peters v. Civil Service Commission of Tucson,* 539 P.2d 698 (Ariz. 1977); *Abeyta v. Town of Taos,* 499 F.2d 323 (10th Cir. 1974); *Baumgartner v. Leary,* 311 N.Y.S.2d 468 (1970); *City of Vancouver v. Jarvis,* 455 P.2d 591 (Wash.: 1969).
104. Swanson, Territo, and Taylor, *Police Administration,* p. 433.
105. *Parker v. District of Columbia,* 850 F.2d 708 (1988), at 713, 714.
106. *Marusa v. District of Columbia,* 484 F.2d 828 (1973).
107. *Sager v. City of Woodlawn Park,* 543 F.Supp. 282 (D. Colo.: 1982).
108. *Bonsignore v. City of New York,* 521 F.Supp. 394 (1981).
109. *Popow v. City of Margate,* 476 F.Supp. 1237 (1979).
110. Eloise Salholz and Frank Washington, "Detroit's Brutal Lessons," *Newsweek* (November 30, 1992): 45.
111. Ibid.
112. *Krolick v. Lowery,* 302 N.Y.S.2d 109 (1969), p. 115; *Hester v. Milledgeville,* 598 F.Supp. 1456, 1457 (MD Ga.: 1984).
113. *McCracken v. Department of Police,* 337 So.2d 595 (La.: 1976).
114. *Krolick v. Lowery.*
115. 489 U.S. 602 (1989).
116. 489 U.S. 656 (1989).
117. Robert J. Alberts and Harvey W. Rubin, "Court's Rulings on Testing Crack Down on Drug Abuse," *Risk Management* 38 (March 1991): 36–41
118. Ibid., p. 38.
119. Ibid., p. 40.
120. Federal Communications Commission, "Understanding Workplace Harassment," August 21, 2014, http://www.fcc.gov/encyclopedia/understanding-workplace-harassment-fcc-staff.
121. Allen D. Sapp, "Sexual Misconduct by Police Officers," in T. Barker and D. Carter (eds.), *Police Deviance* (Cincinnati: Anderson, 1994), pp. 187–200.

122. *U.S. v. Windsor*, 570 U.S. ____ (2013) (Docket No. 12-307).
123. The amendments were contained in the National Defense Authorization Act for Fiscal Year 2008 (2008 NDAA), which became effective on January 16, 2009; the 2009 amendments were expanded again by amendments contained in the National Defense Authorization Act for Fiscal Year 2010 (2010 NDAA); see Public Law 110-181 and Public Law 111-84, respectively.
124. See Richard G. Schott, "Family and Medical Leave Act Amendments: New Military Leave Entitlements," *FBI Law Enforcement Bulletin* 79(6) (June 2010), August 21, 2014, http://www.fbi.gov/stats-services/-publications/law-enforcement-bulletin/june-2010/family-and-medical-leave-act-amendments.
125. Paula N. Rubin and Susan W. McCampbell, "The Americans with Disabilities Act and Criminal Justice: Providing Inmate Services," *U.S. Department of Justice, National Institute of Justice Research in Action* (July 1994): 2.
126. Paula N. Rubin, "The Americans with Disabilities Act and Criminal Justice: An Overview," *U.S. Department of Justice, National Institute of Justice Research in Action* (September 1993): 1.
127. "Health and Criminal Justice: Strengthening the Relationship," *U.S. Department of Justice, National Institute of Justice Journal, Research in Action* (November 1994): 40.
128. Ibid., p. 41
129. For an overview of the Affordable Care Act and its ten titles, see the U.S. Department of Health & Human Services, "About the Law," https://www.hhs.gov/healthcare/about-the-law/index.html
130. See The White House, "Raise the Wage," https://www.whitehouse.gov/raise-the-wage.
131. 425 U.S. 238 (1976).
132. Ibid., pp. 247–248.
133. Based on the Watertown, South Dakota, Police Department General Order A-170, http://www.watertownpd.com/images/pdf_files/a-170%20personnel%20dress%20code%20and%20uniform%20regulations.pdf.
134. Stefanie K. Vaudreuil, "Tattoos. Piercings. The Workplace. Like It or Not, the Millennials are the Future Workforce," *Labor & Employment Blog*, April 7, 2015, http://www.calpublicagencylaboremploymentblog.com/employment/tattoos-piercings-the-workplace-like-it-or-not-the-millennials-are-the-future-workforce/; see also *Los Angeles Times*, "Tattoos are free speech protected by Constitution, U.S. appeals court rules," September 9, 2010, http://latimesblogs.latimes.com/lanow/2010/09/tattoos-free-speech.html
135. "Des Moines Police Ban New Tattoos," http://www.foxnews.com/story/0,2933,379203,00.html.
136. "Tattooed State Police Job Applicant Sues over Policy," http://www.wpxi.com/news/20567045/detail.html; also see David L. Hudson, Jr., "Pa. tattoo-removal policy challenge rejected," *First Amendment Center*, http://www.firstamendmentcenter.org/pa-tattoo-removal-policy-challenge-rejected/.
137. See, for example, Riggs v. City of Fort Worth, No. CIV.A.4-00-CV-816-Y. (N.D. Texas, 2002), where the federal district court upheld the police chief's decision that an officer's tattoos created an unprofessional appearance and thus he could be removed from a bicycle patrol assignment.

PART **2**

The Police

This part consists of three chapters Chapter 4 examines the organization and operation of police departments, Chapter 5 covers police personnel roles and functions, and Chapter 6 discusses police issues and practices. The introductory section of each chapter previews the specific chapter content.

TFoxFoto/Shutterstock

4 Police Organization and Operation

LEARNING OBJECTIVES

After reading this chapter, the student will be able to:

1. *understand why and how police leaders must examine—and possibly change—agency culture*
2. *explain what is meant by constitutional policing, legitimacy, and procedural justice*
3. *review some new approaches for addressing mass demonstrations*
4. *describe how police might work toward achieving harmony with their communities*
5. *understand why police agencies are arranged into organizations, to include grouping of activities and division of labor*
6. *explain the primary components of a basic police organizational structure*
7. *identify the seven elements of police organizational structure*
8. *define the purposes of policies, procedures, rules, and regulations in police organizations*
9. *explain community policing and problem-solving, and why it is a predominate police management philosophy and practice*

⑩ *define the four emerging management paradigms that complement community policing and are used in addressing crime and neighborhood disorder*

⑪ *describe what is needed to transform a good police organization into a great one*

⑫ *relate how and why a police organization would seek to become accredited*

Introduction

To be succinct, this chapter is a blunt, critical look at the need for police leaders to transform their organizations and operations in order to better meld with the communities they serve. Given the current chasm that exists between many citizens and their police in our nation, exacerbated by police shootings, reform in many, if not most, agencies must come sooner rather than later; toward that end, several approaches and methods are discussed, including the organization's culture, change, becoming more constitutional and legitimate in affording procedural justice, and some ideas for addressing mass demonstrations and achieving harmony. That is the first general topic of discussion in this chapter.

Next, because things "don't just happen" in police organizations and they must be structured so as to accomplish their mission and values, we consider the basic elements of police organizational structure, look at examples of a basic as well as a more specialized organizational structure, and review how policies, procedures, and rules and regulations provide guidelines for organizations. Then, we briefly examine what is now the dominant concept in police philosophy and operations: community policing and problem-solving; this strategy has caused many changes in the organization and administration of police agencies. In this connection, we will also examine four emerging paradigms that complement this strategy: CompStat, smart policing, intelligence-led policing (ILP), and predictive policing. Following is a look at what experts say is needed in order to transform a good police organization into a great one, and next is a discussion of how a police organization may become accredited and the benefits of doing so. The chapter concludes with review questions and Deliberate and Decide, Learn by doing, and Case Study exercises. Note that several related topics are discussed in Chapter 6, most notably the outcry for body-worn cameras and several aspects regarding police use of force.

No More "Business as Usual": Changing Police Culture

It is obvious that these are unusually difficult and challenging times for police–community relations and trust. As the 2015 President's Task Force on 21st Century Policing[1] put it, this is due to "recent events that have exposed rifts in the relationships between local police and the communities they protect and serve."[2] These "recent events" are in fact a number of highly publicized and controversial police shootings of unarmed suspects that began with the shooting death of Michael Brown in Ferguson, Missouri, in mid-2014. The Task Force added that "Trust between law enforcement agencies and the people they protect and serve is essential in a democracy. It is key to the stability of our communities, the integrity of our criminal justice system, and the safe and effective delivery of policing services."[3]

A Change in Mind-Set

What is needed in many of today's police and sheriff's departments is a change in mind-set. As Kansas City, Missouri, police officer Octavio Villalobos put it, "You don't have to look like the people you police, you just have to care."[4]

As one police executive put it, a good beginning point for that change is in diversity training, to:

- Focus on seeing all others as people with value and worth and deserving of unconditional respect
- Contribute to personal development and expand the intellect while touching the hearts of officers
- Remember that adults learn best by doing and participating in an experience
- Provide tools and skills that can be practiced and applied to daily work
- Make educational sessions one part of a continuing process of learning that reinforces a philosophy ultimately leading to a culture shift.[5]

Change and innovation in some police agencies has been felt to be nearly impossible—even being described by Dorothy Guyot in 1975 as akin to "bending granite."[6] Although that is generally an unfair statement in light of the kinds of changes now occurring in policing (several of them are discussed below and in later chapters), the fact remains that many of today's police chief executives remain stagnant—merely hoping, as one former police chief stated, "just to survive until Friday night." Such an attitude does not bode well when agency leaders should have a three- to five-year vision of where the agency needs to be and how to get there. This is called strategic planning.

What are the hindrances to cultural and organizational change in policing? Actually, there are several, a few of them being: chief executives not wishing to explore and commit to a new direction or vision or engage in the extensive planning required to develop strategies for meeting intended goals; not being knowledgeable of how to best implement planned strategies or monitor the steps as it unfolds; the failure of past attempts to change; organizational inertia; and existing policies and procedures that are outdated and reinforce tradition. As one person described it, in its simplest form, a police culture means "This is how we do things around here." At a more complex level, a police organization's culture is derived from its mission, values, customs, and rituals, all of which are drawn from the organization's history and how its members interact with one another and with those outside of the organization. Organizational culture is also influenced by how leaders reward, recognize, or discipline behaviors.

This is why a few organizations are highly professional and respected, while some are constantly receiving citizens' complaints, being sued for excessive force, and so on. And, while some police chief executives can project and maintain departmental integrity and ethics, this message must be conveyed (and rewarded), lest the officers do something altogether different on the street.

The culture of policing is also important to the proper exercise of officer discretion and the use of force and authority. The agency's values and ethics will guide officers in their decision-making process on the street; indeed, they cannot just rely on agency rules and policies to act in encounters with the public. Good police executives know that good policing is more than just complying with the law. Sometimes actions are perfectly permitted by policy and law, but that does not always mean an officer should take those actions (such as shooting a juvenile who stole a car).

EXHIBIT 4.1

MISSION AND VALUES STATEMENTS, ST. LOUIS COUNTY, MISSOURI, POLICE DEPARTMENT

Mission Statement

The mission of the St. Louis County Police Department is to work cooperatively with the public, and within the framework of the Constitution to enforce the laws, preserve the peace, reduce fear and provide a safe environment in our neighborhoods.

Statement of Values

The St. Louis County Police Department exists to serve the community by protecting life and property; by preventing crime; by enforcing the laws; and by maintaining order for all people.

Central to our mission are the values which guide our work and decisions. These help us contribute to the high quality of life in St. Louis County.

The public trust and confidence given to those in the police service requires the adoption and compliance of stated values, which are the foundation upon which our policies, goals and operations are built.

In fulfilling our mission, we need the support of citizens and elected officials in order to provide the quality of service our values commit us to providing.

We, the men and women of the St. Louis County Police Department, value:

Human Life—We value human life and dignity, as guaranteed by the Constitution.

Integrity—We believe that integrity is the basis for community trust.

Laws and Constitution—We respect the principles that are embodied in the Constitution of the United States. We recognize the authority of federal, state and local laws.

Excellence—We strive for personal and professional excellence.

Accountability—We are accountable to the people in the community, and each other.

Cooperation—We believe that cooperation with the community and the members of our organization will enable us to combine our diverse backgrounds, skills and styles to achieve common goals beneficial to the community and the St. Louis County Police Department.

Problem-Solving—We are most effective when we can identify and solve community problems.

Ourselves—We are dedicated, caring and capable people who are performing important and satisfying work for the people of St. Louis County.[8]

Source: St. Louis County, Missouri, Police Department, "Values: Our Mission Statement and Codes of Ethics," retrieved from http://www.stlouisco.com/LawandPublicSafety/PoliceDepartment/AboutUs/Values. Used with permission from St. Louis County.

Adopting Procedural Justice

Adopting **procedural justice** as the guiding principle for policies and practices can be the underpinning of a change in culture and should also contribute to building trust and confidence in the community. Succinctly put, procedural justice revolves around four central principles: (1) treating people with dignity and respect; (2) giving individuals "voice" during encounters; (3) being neutral and transparent in decision making; and (4) conveying trustworthy motives.[7]

It is therefore imperative that each organization develop, publicize, convey, and practice its values and mission statements, such as those shown in Exhibit 4.1 for the St. Louis County, Missouri, Police Department.

A New Professionalism

Given the contemporary problems that exist between the police and the communities they serve, particularly with minorities, there is a movement growing within the police service to be seen as true protectors of the community, without bias or favor—what is termed a New Professionalism.

New Professionalism includes stricter accountability in terms of police effectiveness and conduct while also increasing legitimacy in the eyes of those they serve. Following are four principles that compose this effort.

1. *A commitment to accountability* means having an obligation to account for police actions—not only internally but also to civilian review boards (discussed in Chapter 6), city councils and county commissioners, state legislatures, and courts. Police agencies might also conduct public surveys in order to learn about crime and disorder and fear of crime. It is also hoped that the New Professionalism will bring reductions in the use of force as police departments become more proficient in analyzing events leading up to use-of-force incidents to determine if the officers were justified in using such tactics.
2. *A commitment to legitimacy* includes a determination to engage in policing activities with the consent, cooperation, and support of the community. The New Professionalism emphasizes professional integrity and public trust. Traditionally, police often measured their legitimacy in terms of the numbers of civilian complaints that were lodged against them. This measure is highly problematic, because relatively few people actually make a formal complaint. Legitimacy is discussed in detail below.
3. *A commitment to innovation* means actively experimenting with new ideas and changing policies and procedures accordingly. Such agencies look for practices that work as they attempt to both prevent crimes and solve problems. Knowledge—its creation, dissemination, and practical application—is essential to genuine professionalism. Police must measure their outcomes, encourage independent evaluations of their policies and tactics, and design experiments that rigorously test new ideas.
4. *National coherence* means that leaders exemplifying the New Professionalism participate in national conversations about professional policing. They train their officers, supervisors, and managers in successful practices and theories. Such organizations as the Police Foundation, the Police Executive Research Forum, the federal COPS Office, the Major Cities Chiefs Association, and others generate national conversations among practitioners and researchers.

Are We "Guardians" or "Soldiers"?

The contemporary chasm between police and minorities, and many people in society at large, often revolves around how the police are now too often being seen as "soldiers" or "warriors." Certainly the recent killings by police of young African American men and others have caused many people to ask whether or not there exists within the police culture a "warrior mind-set." Given that, it is time for police executives to consider the sort of image they project to the public and to minority communities in particular. The 21st Century Task Force stated:

> Law enforcement culture should embrace a guardian mindset to build public trust and legitimacy. Toward that end, police and sheriffs' departments should adopt procedural justice as the guiding principle for internal and external policies and practices to guide their interactions with the citizens they serve.[9]

There is a significant distinction between the two roles; former Shoreline, Washington, police chief Susan Rahr questioned this distinction:

> Why are we training police officers like soldiers? Although police officers wear uniforms and carry weapons, the similarity ends there. The missions and rules of engagement are

completely different. The soldier's mission is that of a warrior: to conquer. The rules of engagement are decided before the battle. The police officer's mission is that of a guardian: to protect. The rules of engagement evolve as the incident unfolds. Soldiers must follow orders. Police officers must make independent decisions. Soldiers come into communities as an outside, occupying force. Guardians are members of the community, protecting from within.[10]

"In Boston, we don't train our recruits to be a military force. I want my officers to come out as problem-solvers, not an occupying force," thus stated Boston police commissioner William Evans. And, as Kansas City, Missouri, chief Terry Zeigler put it, "For a long time, the police academy has been based on a military boot camp type of philosophy. That is missing the point. Policing is mostly about manners and courtesy."[11]

Taking on a warrior's mentality is only good with incidents like active shooter situations where officer survival is paramount. According to Camden County (New Jersey) police chief Scott Thomson, "It's a question of the 'crime-fighter' versus the 'community-builder' mentality. We need to have a cultural shift in policing to the latter to regain the trust and legitimacy that has been recently lost." Use of force is discussed more thoroughly in Chapter 6.

Related Concepts: Constitutional Policing and Legitimacy

As noted above, several race-related events from 2014 to present have led to a careful review of police practices and calls for reform. At the heart of this issue are questions of race relations, compelling many police leaders to look at their agency's culture in a new light. Protests and riots have centered on the experiences of minority communities with police and questions of disparate treatment, particularly with respect to the use of deadly force.

Police chief executives are now becoming much more heavily involved in what is termed **constitutional policing**—a cornerstone of community policing and problem-solving efforts. When a police agency develops policies and practices that advance the constitutional goals of protecting citizens' rights and providing equal protection under the law, then, as New Haven (Connecticut) police chief Dean Esserman put it, "The Constitution is our boss. We are not warriors, we are guardians. The [police] oath is to the Constitution."[12]

constitutional policing policing operates within the parameters of the U.S. Constitution, state constitutions, and the body of court decisions.

Constitutional policing, then, forms the foundation of community policing. Police agencies cannot form positive and productive relationships with the citizens they serve if those communities do not trust the police or if the communities do not believe that the police see their mission as protecting civil rights as well as public safety. Too often, concerns with constitutional aspects of policing occur only after the fact—when police officials, community members, and the courts look at an officer's actions to determine whether or not laws, ordinances, or agency policies were violated. Now, there is a growing recognition among police leaders that constitutional policing should be on the minds of all agency members on an everyday basis.

A related yet different concept is that of police legitimacy: the extent to which the community believes that police actions are appropriate, proper, and just. If the police have a high level of perceived legitimacy in a community, members of the community tend to be more willing to cooperate with the police and to accept the outcome of their interactions with the police.

Legitimacy, like procedural justice discussed above, is reflected in several ways. First, people want to have an opportunity to explain their situation or tell their side of the story to a police officer. Second, people want the police authorities to be neutral—make decisions based on consistently applied legal principles and the facts of an incident, not based on an officer's personal opinions and biases. Third, people want to be treated with dignity and

legitimacy the extent to which the community believes that police actions are appropriate, proper, and just.

politeness, and have their rights respected. Finally, people focus on cues that indicate trustworthiness—the belief that their police are benevolent, caring, and sincerely trying to do what is best for the people with whom they are dealing.

In sum, police leaders need to think about their role in a new way, focusing on the influence that their values, mission, policies, and practices have on public views about their legitimacy—how citizens view police practices and deem as appropriate, reasonable, and just.

Changing "Optics" and Responding to Mass Demonstrations

Also to be placed under consideration is the "optics" of a police response to mass gatherings. Certainly much controversy was generated concerning the use of the state's national guard and military equipment and tactics in Ferguson, Missouri, and later in other communities. Many people are upset about the millions of pieces of surplus military equipment that have been given to local police departments across the country airplanes. This means police should avoid bringing heavy equipment to the scene of a demonstration or wearing protective riot gear if there is no indication that a demonstration will be violent. Also, police have learned through trial and error that interacting with people—such as asking them kindly to move along if necessary—is much more effective.[13]

The rage and violence involved in several of the 2014 and later riots and protests in many cities also changed how many police agencies react to such matters; as Pittsburgh, Pennsylvania, police chief Cameron McLay stated, "How you approach a crowd of demonstrators will determine what you will get back from the crowd."

In furthering constitutional policing and legitimacy, a "soft" approach is now recommended in dealing with demonstrations, beginning with police communicating with protest leaders before and during the event to deter any violence by agitators and ensure that protests can be conducted peacefully. Police leaders are finding that responses are to be measured and proportional to what is happening during a demonstration. As Boston police commissioner William Evans said, "If we go looking for a fight with demonstrators, that's what we'll get."

The Nashville Police Department emphasized the "we're not looking for a fight" approach when engaging protesters during a protest when demonstrators marched for a couple of miles to police headquarters. Police met them not with numerous officers in riot gear, but with three officers and coolers full of ice water. On another occasion, when there were protests following the grand jury decision in Ferguson, it was cold outside, so police met them with hot chocolate and coffee.

Achieving Harmony

What is the solution for those many cities that have witnessed rioting and unrest in the wake of police shootings? How can police executives hope to bridge the gap between their agencies and their communities, particularly their minority neighborhoods—especially when many underlying social problems in our communities have taken many years if not decades to build to a boiling point? If someone had the perfect answer to that question, he or she would probably be very wealthy. But perhaps a good starting point is to make every effort to recruit, train, and diversify the agency to reflect their community makeup, and thus provide a means for giving people a voice.

Other reform ideas that ensued after the recent riots and protests have included that police stop blurring the lines with the military, begin wearing body cameras (discussed in Chapter 6), investigate police shootings to determine whether any civil rights violations occurred, implement training on racial profiling, and create programs to address vestiges of segregation, dehumanization, and stereotyping in our society.[14]

In addition, greater emphasis has been placed on police transparency, particularly given the near total lack of national information concerning police shootings. As a result, in the wake of the police shooting death of Michael Brown in Ferguson, Missouri, legislation was introduced to initiate a national database tracking such shootings in the United States. A White House panel was appointed to require states to report the deaths of all people in police custody or during arrest to the federal government. The Death in Custody Reporting Act (Pub. L. No. 113–242) was signed into law in December 2014, mandating that all states report quarterly to the attorney general information regarding the death of any person in the process of arrest or who is otherwise in law enforcement custody, including jails, prisons, and juvenile facilities.[15]

▶ Police Agencies as Organizations

Having discussed how to examine and make necessary and desired changes in agency culture, next we turn to the importance of having a properly organized agency for accomplishing its mission, achieving its vision, and conveying its values.

As noted above, things don't "just happen" in police organizations; personnel and their functions must be organized for the greatest efficiency and equity.

The Grouping of Activities

As stated in Chapter 2, an organization is an artificial structure created to coordinate either people or groups and resources to achieve a mission or goal.[16] Certainly, police agencies fit this definition. First, the organization of these agencies includes a number of specialized units (e.g., patrol, traffic, investigation, records). The role of chief executives, middle managers, and first-line supervisors is to ensure that these units work together to reach a common goal; allowing each unit to work independently would lead to fragmentation, conflict, and competition and would subvert the entire organization's goals and purposes. Second, police agencies consist of people who interact within the organization and with external organizations.

Through mission statements and policies and procedures (discussed later), as well as management style, among other factors, police administrators attempt to ensure that the organization meets its overall goals of investigating and suppressing crime and that the organization works amicably with similar organizations. As the organization becomes larger, the need for people to cooperate to achieve the organizational goals increases. Formal organization charts assist in this endeavor by spelling out areas of responsibility and lines of communication and by defining the chain of command.

Police administrators often modify or redesign the structure of their organization to fulfill their mission. An organizational structure reflects the formal organization of task and authority relationships determined to be best suited to accomplishing the police mission (organizational structures are discussed and shown later in this chapter).

The Division of Labor

The larger an agency, the greater the need for specialization and the more vertical (taller) its organizational chart becomes. Some 2,300 years ago, Plato observed that "each thing becomes . . . easier when one man, exempt from other tasks, does one thing."[17]

Specialization, or the **division of labor**, is one of the basic features of traditional organizational theory.[18] Specialization produces different groups of functional responsibilities, and the jobs allocated to meet these different responsibilities are held by people who are considered to be especially well qualified to perform those jobs. Thus, specialization is crucial to effectiveness and efficiency in large organizations.[19]

division of labor a basic feature of traditional organizational theory, where specialization produces different groups of functional responsibilities.

Specialization can also make the organization more complex, however, by complicating communication, increasing the number of units from which cooperation must be obtained, and creating conflict among different units. Specialization creates an increased need for coordination because it adds to the hierarchy, which can lead to narrowly defined jobs that stifle the creativity and energy of those who hold them. Overall, however, personnel tend to enjoy the opportunity to rotate into various assignments and be given additional responsibilities that challenge them. For example, in even a medium-sized department—say, one serving a community of 100,000 or more—a police officer or deputy sheriff with 10 years of experience may have had the opportunities to serve as a dog handler, motorcycle officer, detective, and/or traffic officer while being a member of special weapons or hostage negotiation teams.

Other advantages to specialization in police and sheriff's departments include the following:

- ***Placement of responsibility.*** The responsibility for performing given tasks can be placed on specific units or individuals. For example, the traffic division investigates all accidents, and the patrol division handles all calls for service.
- ***Development of expertise.*** Those who have specialized responsibilities receive specialized training. Homicide investigators can be sent to forensic pathology classes; special weapons and tactics teams train regularly to deal with terrorists or hostage situations.
- ***Group esprit de corps.*** Groups of specially trained persons share camaraderie and depend on one another for success; this leads to cohesion and high morale.
- ***Increased efficiency and effectiveness.*** Specialized units have a high degree of proficiency in performing job tasks. For example, a specially trained financial crimes unit normally is more successful in handling complex fraud cases than a general detective division.[20]

Elements of Police Organizational Structure

organizational structure how an organization divides up its work and establishes lines of authority and communication.

According to Henry Mintzberg, an **organizational structure** can be defined simply as the sum total of the ways in which the organization divides its labor into distinct tasks and then achieves coordination among them.[21] This definition translates into measures that are relatively easy to compute.

Maguire et al. accomplished an excellent analysis of organizations and structural change in large police agencies. Essentially, they determined that there are seven specific elements of law enforcement organizational structure; the first four are types of structural differentiation, or methods of dividing labor. These elements are (1) functional, (2) occupational, (3) spatial and (4) vertical differentiation, (5) centralization, (6) formalization, and (7) administrative intensity:[22]

1. ***Functional differentiation*** is the degree to which tasks are broken down into functionally distinct units. A police agency with a homicide unit, an accident reconstruction unit, and a juvenile division is more functionally differentiated than one that only employs patrol officers. Today's larger agencies have several bureaus, divisions, and specialized units to perform separate functions as needs dictate.[23]
2. ***Occupational differentiation*** measures distinctions within the staff (job titles) and the extent to which an organization relies on specially trained workers from distinct occupational groups. Civilianization has increased in policing, and today, civilian police employees represent a separate occupational group.[24]
3. ***Spatial differentiation*** is the extent to which an organization is spread geographically. A police agency with a headquarters and several precinct stations is more spatially

differentiated than a department that operates out of a single police facility; agencies that carve the jurisdiction into a large number of small beats, with mini stations scattered throughout the jurisdiction and district stations in different areas of the community, are the most spatially differentiated.[25]

4. ***Vertical differentiation*** focuses on the hierarchical nature of an organization's command structure, including its (a) segmentation, (b) concentration, and (c) height. Organizations with elaborate chains of command are more vertically differentiated than those with flatter command structures. *Segmentation* is the number of command levels in an organization, from the lowest ranking to the highest. *Concentration* is the percentage of personnel located at various levels, and *height* is the social distance between the lowest- and the highest-ranking employees in the organization.[26]
5. ***Centralization*** is the extent to which the decision-making capacity within an organization is concentrated in a single individual or a small, select group. Organizations in which lower-ranking employees are given the autonomy to make decisions are less centralized than those in which senior administrators make most decisions.
6. ***Formalization*** is the extent to which employees are governed by specific rules and policies. Some factors in law enforcement, including liability issues and accreditation, are likely to encourage increase in formalization.
7. ***Administrative intensity*** refers to the proportion of organizational resources committed to administration. Organizations with high levels of administrative intensity are often thought of as being more bureaucratic.[27]

▶ Examples of Police Organization

The Basic Organizational Structure

As noted previously, an organizational structure helps police and sheriff's departments carry out the many complex responsibilities. It should be noted, however, that organizational structures vary from one jurisdiction to another and are fluid in nature. The highly decentralized nature and the different sizes of police and sheriff's departments in the United States, as well as the turnover in the chief executive officer (chief of police or sheriff) position, cause these structures to change. It is possible, however, to make certain general statements about all agencies to characterize a typical police organization.

The police traditionally organize along military lines, with a rank structure that normally includes the patrol officer, sergeant, lieutenant, captain, and chief. Many departments, particularly larger ones, employ additional ranks, such as corporal, major, and deputy chief, but there is a legitimate concern that these departments will become top-heavy. The military rank hierarchy allows the organization to designate authority and responsibility at each level and to maintain a chain of command. The military model also allows the organization to emphasize supervisor–subordinate relationships and to maintain discipline and control.

Every police agency, regardless of size, has a basic plan of organization. In addition, every such agency, no matter how large or small, has an organizational structure. A visitor to the police station or sheriff's office may even see this organizational structure displayed prominently on a wall. Even if it is not on paper, such a structure exists. A basic organizational structure for a small agency is shown in Figure 4-1 ■.

Operational or line elements involve policing functions in the field and may be subdivided into primary and secondary line elements. The patrol function—often called the "backbone" of policing—is the primary line element because it is the major law enforcement responsibility within the policing organization. Most small police agencies, in fact,

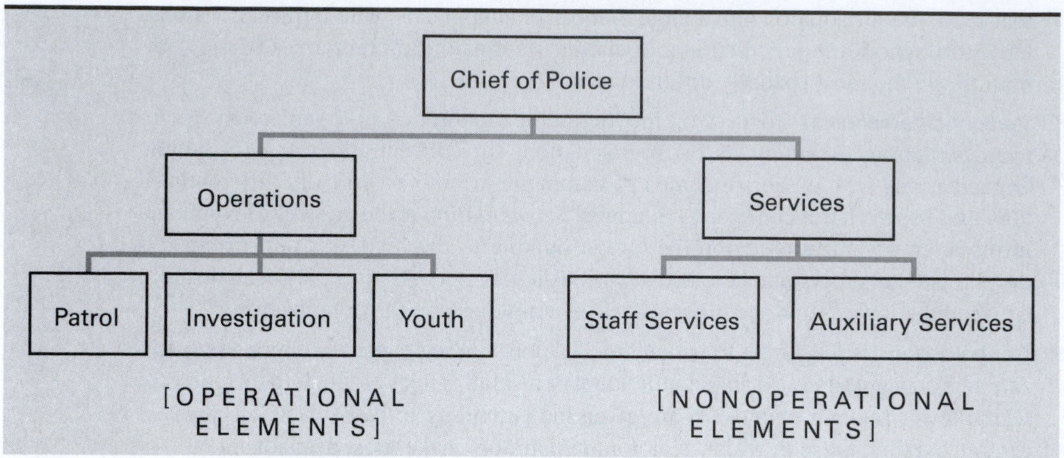

FIGURE 4-1 Basic Police Organizational Structure

can be described as patrol agencies, with the patrol forces responsible for all line activities. Such agencies provide routine patrols, conduct criminal and traffic investigations, and make arrests. These agencies are basically generalists. In a community that has only one policing employee—a city marshal, for example—he or she obviously must perform all the functions just listed. This agency's organizational chart is a simple horizontal one with little or no specialization.

Investigative and youth activities are the secondary line elements. These functions would not be needed if the police were totally successful in their patrol and crime prevention efforts—an obviously impossible goal. Time and area restrictions on the patrol officers, as well as the need for specialized training and experience, require some augmenting of the patrol activity.

The nonoperational functions and activities can become quite numerous, especially in a large community. These functions fall within two broad categories: *staff services* (also known as *administrative*) and *auxiliary* (or *technical*) *services*. Staff services are usually people oriented and include recruitment, training, promotion, planning and research, community relations, and public information services. Auxiliary services involve the types of functions that a nonpolice person rarely sees, including jail management, property and evidence handling, crime laboratory services, communications (dispatch), and records and identification. Many career opportunities exist for persons interested in police-related work who cannot or do not want to be a field officer.

Consider the organizational structure for a larger police organization, such as that of the Portland (Oregon) Police Bureau (PPB) (see Figure 4-2 ■). Portland has a population of about 610,000, but the metropolitan area (consisting of five counties) has about 2.35 million people.[28] The PPB has about 1150 sworn personnel.[29] As with all organizations, especially those that are medium or large in size, some of the PPB functions are unique to that organization.[30]

Portland's and other cities' police department organizational structures are designed to fulfill five functions: (1) apportioning the workload among members and units according to a logical plan; (2) ensuring that lines of authority and responsibility are as definite and direct as possible; (3) specifying unity of command throughout so that there is no question as to which orders should be followed; (4) placing responsibility and authority, and if responsibility is delegated, holding the delegator responsible; and (5) coordinating the

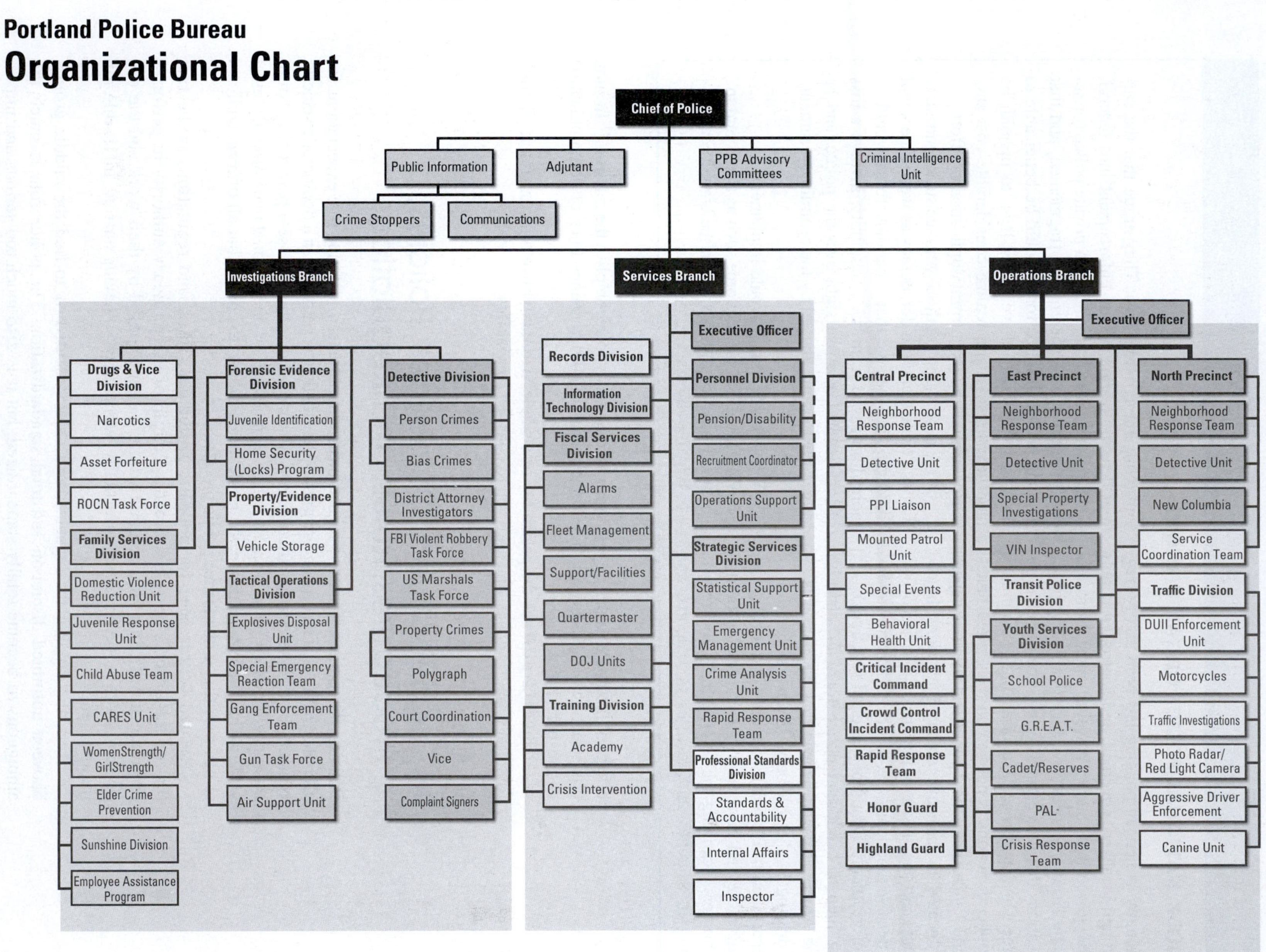

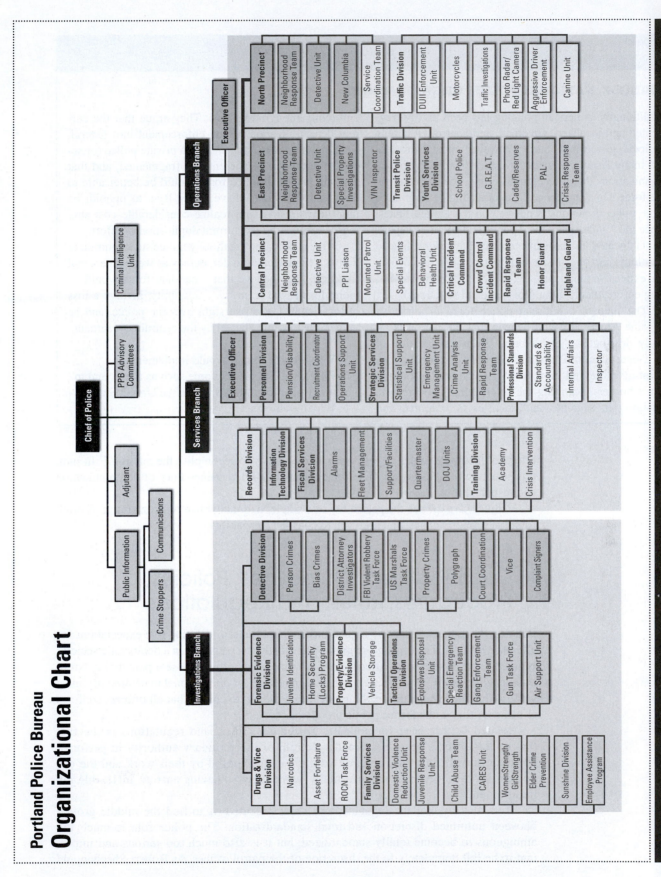

FIGURE 4-2 Portland Police Bureau Organizational Chart

Source: Take from p.16 of Portland Police Bureau Annual Report, 2014, retrieved from : https://www.portlandoregon.gov/police/article/548323. Used with permission from Portland Police Bureau.

EXHIBIT 4.2

A SINGLE, NATIONAL POLICE ORGANIZATION?

Traditionally, American policing has been highly fragmented and localized, governed, and controlled largely by local governing boards; however, most European and many Asian countries have historically had police organizations that are centralized into one national police force. On a smaller scale, centralizing or combining some police functions is not new in the United States. Since the 1960s, many local police and sheriff's departments located in the same county have consolidated their units into one, thus avoiding the duplication of several expensive functions (e.g., records, communications, drug enforcement, extraditions, and jail functions).

The idea of a national police force is attractive to some Americans who believe that the nation is already drifting in that direction given the creation of the Department of Homeland Security and local police devoting more and more energy to protecting the nation's borders, scanning the Internet for cybercrimes, engaging in searches and seizures at seaports, and enforcing immigration laws. They argue that the current decentralization of law enforcement into federal, state, municipal, county, and even private police (or security) entities is inefficient and fragmented, and that a single, national police force would be better able to train their personnel, have fewer laws to uphold, be more accountable, and realize considerable cost savings if eliminating the current duplication of effort.

In the other camp are those who see such centralization as a huge danger to democracy as well as personal freedom. They believe that a national force would be more disengaged from the community, involve a loss of local control and oversight over the police, and be vulnerable to being abused by the central government.

1. What do you think? Would implementing a single, national police force such as that found in many other countries work in the United States? Why or why not?

efforts of members so that all will work harmoniously to accomplish the mission.[31] In sum, this structure establishes the chain of command and determines lines of communication and responsibility.

Exhibit 4.2 explores the possibility of a single, national police organization as is often found in foreign venues, and asks you to consider its viability.

▶ Organizational Guidelines: Policies, Procedures, Rules, and Regulations

Policies, procedures, rules, and regulations are important for defining role expectations for all police officers. The officers are granted unusually strong power in a democratic society; because they possess such extraordinary powers, police officers pose a potential threat to individual freedom. Thus, because police agencies are service oriented in nature, they must work within well-defined, specific guidelines designed to ensure that all officers conform to behavior that will enhance public protection.[32]

Related to this need for policies, procedures, rules, and regulations is the fact that police officers possess a broad spectrum of discretionary authority in performing their duties. This fact, coupled with the danger posed by their work and the opportunities to settle problems informally, works against having narrow, inflexible job requirements.

Thus, the task for the organization's chief executive is to find the middle ground between unlimited discretion ɪnd total standardization. The police role is much too ambiguous to become totally standardized, but it is also much too serious and important to be left completely to the discretion of the patrol officer. As Robert Sheehan and

Gary Cordner put it, the idea is for chief executives to "harness, but not choke, their employees."[33]

Organizational **policies** are more general than procedures, rules, or regulations; they serve as basic guides to the organization's philosophy and mission and help in interpreting their elements to the officers.[34] Policies should be committed to writing, then modified according to the changing times and circumstances of the department and community. An example would be a police or prison policy stating that employees are prohibited from "posting or transmitting any photographs or video or audio recordings that specifically identifies (name of agency) on any personal or social networking website or web page, without the express written permission of the (police chief/sheriff/warden)." Some policies are dictated by federal or state law or court decisions, such as the prohibition against police officers placing juveniles in any form of institutional confinement without a specific order from a juvenile judge in the jurisdiction. Another example is the Supreme Court's 1985 decision in *Tennessee v. Garner*, which allows officers to use deadly force only when a "suspect threatens the officer with a weapon or there is probable cause to believe that [the suspect] has committed a crime involving the infliction or threatened infliction of serious physical harm."[35] Thus, the "policy" governing the use of deadly force provides that it only be used when the officer's or citizen's life is threatened.

policies written guidelines that are general in nature and serve to further the organization's philosophy and mission and help in interpreting their elements to the officers.

Procedures are more specific than policies; they serve as guides to action. A procedure is "more specific than a policy but less restrictive than a rule or regulation. It describes a method of operation while still allowing some flexibility within limits."[36] Many organizations are awash in procedures; examples are written directives that inform employees how to conduct investigations, patrol, arrests, and suspect bookings; engage in radio communications; prepare reports; arrive at roll call or start-of-shift briefings; counsel employees about the proper use of sick leave; and many other related activities. Such procedures are not totally inflexible, but they do describe in rather detailed terms the preferred methods for carrying out policy.

procedures specific guidelines that serve to direct employee actions, such as how to prepare investigations and conduct patrol, bookings, radio communications, and prepare reports.

Some police executives have attempted to run their departments via flurries of memos containing new procedures. This method is often fraught with difficulty. An abundance of standardized procedures can stifle initiative and imagination, as well as complicate jobs.[37] On the positive side, procedures can decrease the time wasted in figuring out how to accomplish tasks and thereby increase productivity. As they do with policies, chief executives must seek the middle ground in drafting procedures and remember that it is next to impossible to have procedures that cover all possible exigencies.

Rules and regulations are specific managerial guidelines that leave little or no latitude for individual discretion; they require action (or, in some cases, inaction). Some require officers to wear their hats when outside their patrol vehicle, check the patrol vehicle's oil and emergency lights before going on patrol, not consume alcoholic beverages within 4 hours of going on duty, and arrive in court 30 minutes before sessions open or at roll call 15 minutes before scheduled duty time. Rules and regulations are not always popular, especially if perceived as unfair or unrelated to the job. Nonetheless, they contribute to the total police mission of community service.

rules and regulations specific managerial guidelines for officers, such as not smoking in public or types of weapons to be carried on duty.

Rules and regulations should obviously be kept to a minimum because of their coercive nature. If they become too numerous, they can hinder action and send the message that management believes that it cannot trust the rank and file to act responsibly on their own. Once again, the middle ground is the best. As Thomas Reddin, former Los Angeles police chief, stated:

> Certainly we must have rules, regulations and procedures, and they should be followed. But they are no substitutes for initiative and intelligence. The more a [person] is given an opportunity to make decisions and, in the process, to learn, the more rules and regulations will be followed.[38]

► Existing and Emerging Paradigms in Policing

Next, we discuss a major management philosophy and strategy in policing today—community policing and problem-solving—and then review several relatively new and intertwined administrative tools—crime-fighting paradigms that can complement that philosophy: CompStat, smart policing, intelligence-led policing, and predictive policing. These paradigms complement the analysis phase of the SARA problem-solving model, discussed below.

Community Policing and Problem Solving

Rationale and Definition

Community policing and problem-solving has emerged as the dominant philosophy and strategy of policing. It is an approach to crime detection and prevention that provides police officers and supervisors with new tools for addressing recurrent problems that plague communities and consume a majority of police agency time and resources. The California Department of Justice provided the following definition of this strategy:

> Community-oriented policing and problem solving is a philosophy, management style, and organizational strategy that promotes proactive problem solving and police–community partnerships to address the causes of crime and fear as well as other community issues.[39]

Using a four-step SARA problem-solving process, the police have the tools necessary to accomplish these tasks.

The SARA Process

SARA for *S*canning, *A*nalysis, *R*esponse, *A*ssessment—the logical framework for officers to respond to crime and neighborhood disorder.

SARA (*S*canning, *A*nalysis, *R*esponse, *A*ssessment) (see Figure 4-3 ■) provides officers with a logical, step-by-step, long-term crime-fighting framework in which to identify, analyze, respond to, and evaluate crime, fear of crime, and neighborhood disorder.

Scanning: Problem Identification

Scanning involves problem identification, where the police conduct a preliminary inquiry to determine whether a problem really exists and whether further analysis is needed. A problem may be defined as a cluster of two or more similar or related incidents that are of substantive concern to the community and to the police.

Analysis: Determining the Extent of the Problem

Analysis is the heart of the problem-solving process, as officers gather as much information as possible from a variety of sources. Tools used for analysis include crime analysis

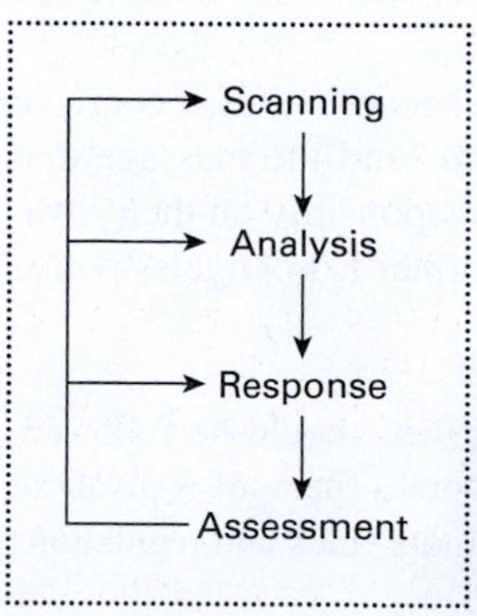

FIGURE 4-3 A Problem-Solving Process

Source: John E. Eck and William Spelman, *Problem-Solving: Problem-Oriented Policing in Newport News* (Washington, DC: U.S. Department of Justice, National Institute of Justice, 1987), p. 43.

(collecting, collating, analyzing, and disseminating data relating to crime), criminal offenders, victims, and locations. Mapping and geographic information systems (GIS) can identify patterns of crime and "hot spots." Police offense reports can also be analyzed for suspect characteristics, victim characteristics, and information about high-crime areas and addresses. Computer-aided dispatch (CAD) is also a reliable source of information, as it collects data on all incidents and specific locations from which an unusual number of incidents require a police response. (A career profile concerning crime analysis is provided below.)

Response: Formulating Tailor-Made Strategies

Once a problem has been clearly defined, officers may seek the most effective responses. Responses to substantive problems rarely involve a single agency or tactic; arrest is often viewed as the only response to a problem, even though it is rarely sufficient to provide permanent solutions. More appropriate responses often involve the police and public and other appropriate actors, including businesses, private and social service organizations, and other government agencies.

Assessment: Evaluating Overall Effectiveness

The final stage of the SARA process is assessment. Here, officers evaluate the effectiveness of their actions (looking at calls for service, arrest data, reductions in crime, and so on) and may use the results to revise their responses, collect more data, or even redefine the problem. Evaluations provide knowledge; key decision makers in the jurisdiction need a gauge of the strategy's impact and cost-effectiveness.

Contributory Strategies: CompStat, Smart Policing, Intelligence-Led Policing, Predictive Policing

A crime management tool developed by the New York City Police Department in 1994 is known as CompStat (for "comparative or computer statistics"), which is said to be "revolutionizing law enforcement management and practice,"[40] and others have called it "perhaps the single most important organizational/administrative innovation in policing during the latter half of the 20th century."[41]

CompStat requires police commanders to generate frequent crime activity reports, so officers begin proactively thinking about ways to deal with crime in terms of suppression, intervention, and prevention. Commanders must explain at CompStat meetings what tactics they have employed to address crime patterns, what resources they have and need, and with whom they have collaborated.[42]

smart policing a policing approach that emphasizes the use of data and analytics as well as improved crime analysis, performance measurement, and evaluation research.

Smart policing emphasizes the use of data and analytics as well as improved crime analysis, performance measurement, and evaluation research. In June 2009, the federal Bureau of Justice Assistance (BJA) began soliciting grant proposals for "smart policing" initiatives (SPI), seeking proposals that would identify or confirm crime-reduction techniques that were effective and efficient (i.e., reasonably affordable) for most agencies to replicate.[43]

Perhaps the most important element of SPI was to be research partnerships, which BJA emphasized in the call for proposals, with police and academics working together to test solutions that were informed by crime science theories and assessed with sound evaluation. Since BJA made its first 10 SPI awards to police agencies in 2009, to date, grants have been awarded to 33 local law enforcement agencies conducting 36 SPI projects.

Because the initial SPI did not prescribe any particular policing model or approach, an impressive array of strategies and tactics were developed and implemented by the local SPI sites. For example, while some sites focused primarily on hot spot and place-based policing strategies, others focus primarily on offender-based approaches (e.g., focused deterrence through identification of prolific offenders and strategic application of suppression and social support strategies). Some first identified hot spots and then pinpointed the prolific offenders within them. Some sites begin with a distinct problem-oriented policing approach (e.g., application of the SARA process), and others adopted a distinctly community-oriented policing approach (e.g., strong emphasis on community and victim engagement); again, some sites combine these two approaches. Several sites have implemented initiatives with a strong predictive-analytic approach, others have incorporated elements of intelligence-led policing or have implemented strategies to move their entire agency toward an intelligence-led policing model, and others have adopted technological approaches to improving police operations (e.g., strategic use of surveillance cameras, enhanced crime analysis capabilities, enhancements to "real-time crime centers," or enhanced predictive analytic capabilities).

IN THEIR OWN WORDS

ADMINISTRATIVE ADVICE FROM THE FIELD

Police Officer/Crime Analyst

Name: Eric W. Drifmeyer

Current position: Police Officer/Crime Analyst

City, State: Barnstable, Massachusetts

College attended/academic major: Western New England University, Springfield MA. Bachelor of Science in Criminal Justice.

How long have you been a practitioner in this criminal justice position? Seven years as a crime analyst and 27 years in law enforcement.

My primary duties and responsibilities as a practitioner in this position: A crime analyst can be many different things to many different law enforcement agencies. Generally, the most common duties involve four fundamental types of analysis: tactical, strategic, administrative, and intelligence. Tactical analysis is the process of weighing the characteristics of criminal events (i.e., time of day, day of week, and geographic proximity) to determine and identify the presence of a crime series or pattern. This type of analysis transforms raw crime data into actionable information to then develop strategies for deployment in the field—which will in turn provide measurable outcomes for reanalysis. Strategic analysis involves comparable techniques but looks at data spanning months or years in an effort to identify crime trends on a long-term basis. It is typically used to identify target areas for long-term projects specifically designed to address a particular crime or quality-of-life issue. Administrative analysis is the maintenance of crime statistics of a specific organization; it is used to assist the agency in accurate reporting practices, determining staffing levels, organizational planning, deployment of resources, and to justify the agency's qualification for state and federal grant funding. Finally, intelligence analysis identifies those offenders who work within criminal enterprises, such as street gangs, by analyzing relationships between people, places, and objects. The analyst uses the resulting data to create visual charts depicting the organizational structure, which in turn provides officers with vital information to deploy on the street.

The qualities/characteristics that are most helpful in this career: By policing's very nature, its essential characteristics include high integrity and a good moral compass. A crime analyst must apply these qualities in everything he or she does. An analyst may very well hold the reputation of an agency in his or her hands, as law enforcement and policing are continually measured by a "scorecard," and scrutinized for any perceived inconsistencies. The analyst must possess strong analytical skills. He or she must be a critical thinker and a problem-solver, have excellent communication skills, and be able to accurately relay valuable information to the decision makers of the agency. Crime analysis has also evolved into a technology-based career. Advances in data storage, data querying, and geo-based applications have placed the crime analyst in a position of technological expertise. These skills are forever advancing and require lifelong learning.

In general, this is what a typical day looks like for a practitioner in this career: First, a good analyst will want to work with the immediate needs of the agency, knowing the fundamental necessities every officer needs to perform his or her duties and providing analytical products to support that effort. Many crime analysts create up-to-date intelligence and crime bulletins, activity summaries, or daily reports, which are usually derived from crime reports and require extensive data mining and refinement. Second, an analyst may focus on long-term trends, which could include the use of open-source databases, media outlets, government websites, or nonprofit organizations. Long-term analysis is not as time-sensitive and allows the analyst to put on his or her thinking cap and to delve deeply into the data. Lastly, a smart analyst will reserve a small amount of time for personal development, reading and understanding current trends in policing, data analysis, and organizational management. Having a broad-based knowledge of policing will translate into more detailed and useful analytical products.

My advice to someone either wishing to study, or now studying, criminal justice or wanting to become a practitioner in this career: Crime analysis is a relatively new field within an old and noble occupation. Many agencies have adopted crime analysis as part of their policing philosophies, while others are just beginning to recognize its value and potential. Over the past decade, crime analysis has become more and more prevalent in every part of the country, and so too have the educational opportunities. Many universities now offer crime analysis programs, built within criminal justice majors, or separate crime analysis certificate programs that supplement the criminal justice major. Both options provide students with the analytical skills necessary for the crime analysis profession. These programs can be instrumental in preparing an individual for a career as a crime analyst and will provide sought-after qualifications for students when they enter the workforce. Beyond a formal education, analysts and students also have access to nonprofit professional organizations such as the International Association of Crime Analysts. These organizations provide training, certification programs, and international networking opportunities with crime analysts from around the world. The key to a fulfilling and rewarding career as a crime analyst is a commitment to lifelong learning and personal development.

Source: Used with permission from Eric W. Drifmeyer.

Findings thus far suggest that smart policing programs can significantly reduce violent crime (Philadelphia); creative use of crime analytics and crime analysis resources, coupled with targeted problem-solving approaches, can also reduce violent crime in historically violent police districts (Los Angeles); and problem-solving teams can prevent violence in stubborn chronic hot spots (Boston) and reduce service calls and property crime at troubled high-traffic convenience stores (Glendale, Arizona).

intelligence-led policing a style of policing that combines crime analysis (where the "who, what, when, and where" of crime is analyzed) with intelligence analysis (which looks at the "who" of crime—the crime networks and individuals).

Intelligence-led policing originated in Great Britain, where police believed that a relatively small number of people were responsible for a comparatively large percentage of crimes; they believed that officers would have the best effect on crime by focusing on the most prevalent offenses occurring in their jurisdiction.[44]

The word *intelligence* is often misused; the most common mistake is to consider intelligence as secretly collected data that were analyzed. Intelligence is information; furthermore, "information plus analysis equals intelligence," and without analysis, there is no intelligence. Intelligence is what is produced after the collected data were evaluated and analyzed by a trained intelligence professional.[45]

To better comprehend intelligence-led policing, let's break it down into its core components. For example, many police agencies have both crime analysts and intelligence analysts. Crime analysts keep their fingers on the pulse of crime in the jurisdiction: which crime trends are up, which ones are down, where the hot spots are, what type of property is being stolen, and so on. Intelligence analysts, on the other hand, are likely to be more aware of the specific *people* responsible for crime in the jurisdiction—who they are, where they live, what they do, who they associate with, and so on. Integrating these two functions—crime analysis and intelligence analysis—is essential for obtaining a comprehensive grasp of the crime picture. *Crime analysis* allows police to understand the "who, what, when, and where," while *intelligence analysis* provides an understanding of the "who"—the crime networks and individuals.

predictive policing a policing strategy that integrates crime analysis, technology, intelligence-led policing, and other tactics to inform forward thinking crime prevention strategies.

The term **predictive policing**, according to the U.S. Department of Justice (DOJ), is a relatively new law enforcement concept that "integrates approaches such as cutting-edge crime analysis, crime-fighting technology, intelligence-led policing, and more to inform forward thinking crime prevention strategies and tactics." The DOJ states that, ultimately, predictive policing is intended as a framework to advance strategies like community policing, problem-oriented policing, intelligence-led policing, and hot spots policing.[46]

The police have always known that robberies surge near check-cashing businesses, that crime spikes on hot days and plummets during the rain, that residential burglaries often occur on Sunday mornings (while people are attending church services), and that Super Bowl Sunday is usually the slowest crime day of the year.[47] But officers' minds can store and remember only so much data. So when the police monitor crime data and query a computer system for historical and real-time patterns, they can predict, more systematically, over a bigger area, and across shifts and time spans, where crimes are likely to occur. More important, the crime-analysis software does not forget details, get sick, take vacation, or transfer to a different precinct.

So if commercial robberies were high in, say, March 2011, their software will predict another spike in March 2012, and the police can then look at the types of businesses that were hit, their locations, and time of day. The system can even analyze a robber's modus operandi—what was said, type of weapon used, and so on.[48]

▶ Moving a Police Organization from "Good" to "Great"

In 2001, Jim Collins wrote a book entitled *Good to Great: Why Some Companies Make the Leap and Others Don't*.[49] Collins and his associates spent more than 10 years studying 11 companies and how their organization tended to make them great. Four years later, he published a monograph entitled *Good to Great and the Social Sectors*,[50] shifting his attention to government agencies.

Collins coined the term *Level 5 leader* to describe the highest level of executive capabilities (Levels 1 through 4 are, respectively, highly capable individual, contributing team member, competent manager, and effective leader). Level 5 leaders are ambitious, but their ambition is directed first and foremost to the organization and its success, not to personal renown. **Level 5 leaders**, Collins stressed, are "fanatically driven, infected with an incurable need to produce results."[51]

level 5 leader the highest level in a hierarchy, where the leader's skills transforms the organization from mediocrity to excellence.

Such leaders, Collins found, do not exhibit enormous egos; instead, they are self-effacing, quiet, reserved, even shy. Unlike business executives, police leaders have to answer to the public; unions and civil service systems further inhibit their power, therefore, Level 5 leadership in a police organization may involve a greater degree of legislative-type skills—relying heavily on persuasion, political currency, and shared interests to create the conditions for the right decisions to happen.[52]

Collins also likes to use a bus metaphor when talking about igniting the transformation from good to great:

> The executives who ignited the transformations . . . did not first figure out where to drive the bus and then get people to take it there. No, they *first* got the right people on the bus (and the wrong people off the bus) and *then* figured out where to drive it. (emphasis in the original).[53]

In fact, Collins wrote, "The main point is not about assembling the right team—that's nothing new." Rather, the main point is that great leaders assemble their teams *before* they decide where to go. The executive who hires the right people does not need to waste time looking for ways to manage and motivate them; the right people will be self-motivated. Good-to-great organizations, Collins found, also have a "culture of discipline," in which employees show extreme diligence and intensity in their thoughts and actions, always focusing on implementing the organization's mission, purpose, and goals.[54]

People are not an organization's most important asset; rather, the *right* people are. When police executives are appointed or promoted, they inherit nearly all of their personnel, including poor performers who are unenthusiastic about the organization's vision and philosophy. Some of these people may be near retirement (about ready to "get off the bus"). Collins states that picking the right people and getting the wrong people off the bus are critical: "By whatever means possible, personnel problems have to be confronted in an organization that aspires to greatness."[55]

This is why performance evaluations are so critical. Unfortunately, however, many police departments still have not created evaluation tools that adequately reflect the work police do. The tendency is to measure what is easy to measure: orderliness (neatness, attendance, punctuality) and conformity to organizational rules and regulations. A consultant to a Texas police agency asked how employees could be expected to act like supervisors, managers, and leaders when everyone in the organization was evaluated by an instrument that was "designed to control a 20-year-old, high-testosterone male who was armed with a gun and given a fast car to drive."[56] Until police agencies invest in valid and reliable instruments for measuring the real work of policing, it will remain very difficult to move the nonperformers out of the organization.

Agency Accreditation

In 1979, the accreditation of police agencies began slowly with the creation of the Commission on Accreditation for Law Enforcement Agencies (CALEA), located in Fairfax, Virginia. CALEA is a nonprofit organization that has developed and administers standards that cover the role and responsibilities of the agency; its organization and administration; law enforcement, traffic, and operational support; prisoner- and court-related services; and auxiliary and technical services. Accreditation, a voluntary process, is quite expensive, both in dollars and in human resources; it often takes 12–18 months for an agency to prepare for the assessment.[57] Today, there are nearly 750 agencies accredited or recognized in one of the commission's various programs, with several hundred others working toward their first award.[58]

accreditation a voluntary effort by a criminal justice agency where it seeks to meet national standards in its field and thus be officially designated as accredited.

In 2011, CALEA adopted a tiered accreditation model that allows police agencies to choose between levels of accreditation based on budget situations and staff reductions. One level is comprised of 177 standards specifically linked to life, health, and safety issues as well as those standards that are essential to the effective delivery of services for contemporary law enforcement agencies. The second level represents the full complement of CALEA's *Standards for Law Enforcement Agencies*, and there are currently 464 standards.[59]

Two unanticipated consequences of the accreditation process have emerged. First, some departments report decreased insurance costs as a result of accreditation. Also, the accreditation self-assessment process provides many opportunities to institutionalize community policing. Not only do the accreditation standards help to weave community policing into an agency's internal fabric, but they also provide a way to integrate such objectives into external service delivery.[60]

In comparing accredited and nonaccredited police agencies, Kimberly A. McCabe and Robin G. Fajardo found that accredited police agencies (1) provided more training for their officers and required higher minimum educational requirements for new officers, (2) were nearly twice as likely to require drug testing for sworn applicants, and (3) were more likely to operate special units for the enforcement of drug laws and laws against child abuse.[61]

Summary

This chapter explored the importance and elements of police organizational culture and structure, including the bureaucratic nature of such organizations; division of labor; and the policies, procedures, rules, and regulations that are a part of such organizations. Included was an examination of the current era and the organizational paradigm of policing, community-oriented policing, and problem-solving. In considering this topic, we examined several related aspects, including Smart Policing Initiatives, intelligence-led policing, and predictive policing. We also considered how a police organization may become great rather than merely being good, and in a related vein, we looked at how police agencies become accredited and the benefits of doing so.

Perhaps what was most clearly demonstrated in this chapter is the extent to which modern policing is changing, and how its organizational elements must also be viewed as fluid in nature and must be modified in order to adapt to and provide the foundation for today's demands on the police.

Clearly, the traditional reactive, unilateral approach to addressing crime and disorder is not suited for today's police organization and administration. The manner in which the organization remains fluid as needs arise and its structures and functions are of paramount concern to police administrators.

Key Terms and Concepts

Accreditation, p. 103
Community policing and problem-solving, p. 98
Constitutional policing, p. 89
Division of labor, p. 91
Intelligence-led policing, p. 101
Legitimacy, p. 89
Level 5 leader, p. 102
Mass demonstrations, p. 90
Organizational structure, p. 92
Policies, p. 97
Predictive policing, p. 102
Procedures, p. 97
Procedural justice, p. 87
Rules and regulations, p. 97
SARA problem-solving process, p. 98
Smart policing, p. 99

Questions for Review

1. What is meant by police culture, how does it affect policing, and how might it be changed when necessary?
2. How can a police leader influence the agency to adopt a new policing mind-set and become more constitutional, practicing legitimacy and affording procedural justice?
3. What practices might police leaders adopt for addressing mass demonstrations?
4. How might police work toward achieving harmony with their communities?
5. Why are police agencies arranged into organizations, and what are the primary components of a basic police organizational structure?
6. How would you describe the seven elements of police organizational structure?
7. What purposes are served by policies, procedures, and rules and regulations in police organizations?
8. How does community policing and problem-solving and its related problem-solving process work as a strategy for addressing crime and disorder?
9. How are four management tools—CompStat, smart policing, intelligence-led policing, and predictive policing—being put to use in solving crime problems?
10. What do experts say is needed to transform a good police organization into a great one?
11. How and why would a police organization seek to become accredited?

Deliberate and Decide

Changing Agency Organization and Culture

Your local police department is in a rapidly growing city of close to 250,000 residents, lying 30 miles to the east of a large Midwestern city. With 350 officers and another 120 civilians, the department is among the largest in the region and was once viewed as the premier law enforcement agency in the state. At the beginning of the 2000s, the city began undergoing major changes in its local government, including the appointment of a new, reform-minded city manager, and greater openness and emphasis on accountability on the part of its city council. These changes, however, also brought to light many problems that existed in the local police department.

The former police chief—who was promoted from within—sought to meet these challenges in the early 2000s but left behind a complicated legacy. On the one hand, she was able to revamp the agency's technologies, modernizing the communications and budgeting systems; however, she refused to lay the foundation for community policing and problem-solving. Officers thus have little dialogue with citizens outside of reactive, individual calls for service, and there is not much in the way of an informative departmental website; a recent university survey found that while 65 percent of white citizens rated the agency's performance in a positive manner, "fair" or "poor" ratings were given by 54 percent of African Americans and 31 percent of Latinos.

Retiring officers often tell the Human Resources office that the department has become too top-heavy and loosely administered, while lacking direction. Regarding agency operations, some in the city also worry that the department has become overly specialized, with far too many persons out of patrol and working in various types of offices, in investigations and special assignments. Furthermore, patrol beats are not divided in a meaningful fashion according to workload or demands for service, so while some officers are backlogged on calls during their shifts, others have little to do. The patrol lieutenants and sergeants have little inclination to change the aforementioned; nor do they appear to support officers engaged in problem-solving projects.

The basic problems, then, are that the department is loosely organized and has weak leaders, operating in an informal manner. About half of the agency's middle managers and first-line supervisors are nearing retirement and appear to be "retired on the job." The policies and procedures manual has not been revised for 20 years; no one even knows what the department's disciplinary process consists of. Finally, while the department's mandatory recruit training meets state standards, its in-service training programs are poor and more than one-third of the force is close to being out of compliance with state training requirements.

The police union membership voted "no confidence" in the former police chief, indicating its frustration with the agency's lack of direction. The city manager is trying to decide whether to open up the search for the chief's position to outside applicants or to promote again from within. In the latter case, there appears to be a dearth of qualified people to promote up to the first-line supervisor and middle manager ranks, much less the chief's position.

Questions for Discussion

1. What seems to be the trappings of this agency's culture, and what are the major issues that exist?
2. What needs to be done to move the agency from where it is to where it can become a "great" organization?
3. What changes in the agency's organization seem warranted?[62]

Learn by Doing

1. Your county law enforcement executive has become increasingly concerned with the number of allegations of improper use of force on all shifts. Accordingly, she tasks you (as chief deputy) to prepare a draft mission and vision statement to convey your agency's goals and purposes. You are told to avoid mere "buzz words," while being powerful in conveying how your organization will view and treat members of the public. It should be clear and able to guide officers' decision-making efforts. Your draft will be shown to a number of stakeholders, including agency staff, area boards, business people, and members of the community. How will you proceed, and how will your mission statement look.
2. Your chief executive has assigned you as head of the agency's research, planning, and analysis unit, the task of developing a comprehensive report containing recommendations for establishing intelligence-led policing. Explain what your report would contain.

Case study

Scanning—On an early August morning—the peak of harvest season—15 farm workers climbed into a 1983 van to drive to work; soon thereafter the van slammed into a commercial vehicle making a U-turn on the road, killing 13 of the van's passengers. The van's driver, who had a lengthy record of driving violations, was arrested for operating the vehicle while under the influence. After learning of this fatal accident you decide to employ the SARA methodology to see if this is a problem area. Scanning also reveals that collisions among farm labor vehicles are not uncommon in this area, especially during the peak harvesting season (May through September), when about 300,000 farm labor jobs are available. With this increase in temporary employment come increased traffic congestion, road infractions, the operating of unsafe vehicles, and incidents of DUI.

Analysis—Although farm labor vehicle collisions prove challenging to document due to shortcomings in how data are recorded, at a minimum you determine that an estimated 187 farm labor collisions, with 20 fatalities and 121 injuries, occurred during the past 3 years. On average, traffic fatalities are 42 percent higher in the area during the peak harvest months and that many accidents involve DUI charges. Examination of relevant statutes and regulatory laws shows room for improvement: farm labor vehicles are exempt from the state's mandatory seat belt law, language barriers create problems, understanding the farm-working culture, and the fact many workers are not permanent citizens have affected outreach efforts and hindered efforts to improve farm worker safety.

Questions for Discussion

1. What possible responses might you develop for dealing with the problem (consider legislative responses as well as those related to law enforcement and public information)?
2. What assessment strategies would you devise for measuring whether or not your responses have been effective?

Notes

1. The President's Task Force on 21st Century Policing was charged by President Barack Obama in December 2014 with identifying best practices and offering recommendations on how policing practices can promote effective crime reduction while building public trust.
2. President's Task Force on 21st Century Policing, *Interim Report of the President's Task Force on 21st Century Policing*, Office of Community Oriented Policing Services, March 4, 2015, p. 1, http://www.cops.usdoj.gov/pdf/taskforce/Interim_TF_Report.pdf.
3. Ibid.
4. Quoted in Tracie Keesee, "Fairness and Neutrality: Addressing the Issue of Race in Policing," *The Police Chief,* March 2011, http://www.policechiefmagazine.org/magazine/index.cfm?fuseaction=display_arch&article_id=2334&issue_id=32011.
5. Quoted in Ibid.
6. Dorothy Guyot, "Bending Granite: Attempts to Change the Rank Structure of American Police Departments," *Journal of Police Science and Administration* 7 (1979): 253–284.
7. Quoted in President's Task Force on 21st Century Policing, *Interim Report of the President's Task Force on 21st Century Policing*, p. 9.
8. St. Louis County, Missouri, Police Department, "Values: Our Mission Statement and Codes of Ethics," http://www.stlouisco.com/LawandPublicSafety/PoliceDepartment/AboutUs/Values.
9. President's Task Force on 21st Century Policing, *Final Report*, Office of Community Oriented Policing Services, March 2015, p. 1,
10. Quoted in ibid., p. 11.
11. Quoted in Police Executive Research Forum, *Constitutional Policing as a Cornerstone of Community Policing* (Washington, DC: Author, April 2015), p. 18.
12. Quoted in Ibid., p. 2.
13. Ibid.
14. The Leadership Conference, *Lessons from Ferguson, Missouri—The Need for Sensible Law Enforcement Reform* (n.d.), http://www.civilrights.org/publications/reports/civil-rights-act-report-december-2014/lessons-from-ferguson.html.
15. See Congress.gov, "H.R.1447—Death in Custody Reporting Act of 2013," https://www.congress.gov/bill/113th-congress/house-bill/1447/actions.
16. Wayne W. Bennett and Karen M. Hess, *Management and Supervision in Law Enforcement*, 4th ed. (Belmont, CA: Wadsworth, 2004), p. 2.
17. *The Republic of Plato*, trans. Allen Bloom (New York: Basic Books, 1968), p. 7.
18. Luther Gulick and L. Urwick (eds.), *Papers on the Science of Administration* (New York: Augustus M. Kelley, 1969).
19. Charles R. Swanson, Leonard Territo, and Robert W. Taylor, *Police Administration: Structures, Processes, and Behavior*, 6th ed. (Upper Saddle River, NJ: Prentice Hall, 2005), pp. 232–233.
20. Ibid., p. 233.
21. Henry Mintzberg, *The Structure of Organizations* (Upper Saddle River, NJ: Prentice Hall, 1979), p. 253.
22. Edward R. Maguire, Heunhee Shin, Zihong Zhao, and Kimberly D. Hassell, "Structural Change in Large Police

Agencies during the 1990s," *Policing: An International Journal of Police Strategies & Management* 26(2) (2003): 251–275.
23. Ibid., p. 255.
24. Ibid., p. 259.
25. Ibid., p. 261.
26. Ibid., pp. 266–267.
27. Ibid., pp. 268–270.
28. Portland, Oregon, population statistics from Metro Regional Government, http://library.oregonmetro.gov/files//msa_popdata1990_2010.pdf.
29. "Portland Police Bureau Statistical Report 2014," https://www.portlandoregon.gov/police/article/548323, p. 17.
30. In the Portland Police Bureau (PPB) organizational structure shown in Figure 4-2 ■, the Sunshine Division includes personnel who work to provide food, clothing, and toys to needy families, and WomenStrength/GirlsStrength is a program that teaches women and girls self-defense tactics.
31. President's Commission on Law Enforcement and Administration of Justice, *Task Force Report: The Police* (Washington, DC: U.S. Government Printing Office, 1967), p. 46.
32. Robert Sheehan and Gary W. Cordner, *Introduction to Police Administration*, 2nd ed. (Cincinnati, OH: Anderson, 1989), pp. 446–447.
33. Ibid., p. 449.
34. Ibid.
35. 471 U.S. 1 (1985).
36. O. W. Wilson and Roy C. McLaren, *Police Administration*, 3rd ed. (New York: McGraw-Hill, 1972), p. 79.
37. Raymond O. Loen, *Manage More by Doing Less* (New York: McGraw-Hill, 1971), pp. 86–89.
38. Thomas Reddin, "Are You Oriented to Hold Them? A Searching Look at Police Management," *The Police Chief* (March 1966): 17.
39. California Department of Justice, *COPPS: Community-Oriented Policing and Problem Solving. Office of the Attorney General, Crime Violence Prevention Center* (Sacramento, CA: Author, 1995).
40. Daniel DeLorenzi, Jon M. Shane, and Karen L. Amendola, "The CompStat Process: Managing Performance on the Pathway to Leadership," *The Police Chief* 73 (September 2006), http://www.policechiefmagazine.org/magazine/index.cfm?fuseaction=display&article_id=998&issue_id=92006.
41. Ibid.
42. Heath B. Grant and Karen J. Terry, *Law Enforcement in the 21st Century* (Boston, MA: Allyn & Bacon, 2005), pp. 329–330.
43. Information concerning the origins and initial grant funded test sites for SPI was obtained from the following sources: James R. Coldren Jr., Alissa Huntoon, and Michael Medaris, "Introducing Smart Policing: Foundations, Principles, and Practice," *Police Quarterly* 16(3) (September 2014): 275–286; and Nola M. Joyce, Charles H. Ramsey, and James K. Stewart, "Commentary on Smart Policing," *Police Quarterly* 16(3) (September 2014): 358–368. This special issue of *Police Quarterly* contains a number of other, site-specific articles that discuss SPI.
44. U.S. Department of Justice, Office of Justice Programs, Bureau of Justice Statistics, *Intelligence-Led Policing: The New Intelligence Architecture* (Washington, DC: Author, 2005), p. 9.
45. Ibid., p. 3.
46. U.S. Department of Justice, National Institute of Justice, "Predictive Policing Symposium: The Future of Prediction in Criminal Justice," http://www.nij.gov/topics/law-enforcement/strategies/predictive-policing/symposium/future.htm.
47. Ellen Perlman, "Policing by the Odds," *Governing*, December 1, 2008, www.governing.com/article/policing-odds.
48. Ibid.
49. Jim Collins, *Good to Great and the Social Sectors: A Monograph to Accompany Good to Great* (New York: HarperCollins, 2005).
50. Ibid.
51. Chuck Wexler, Mary Ann Wycoff, and Craig Fischer, *Good to Great: Application of Business Management Principles in the Public Sector* (Washington, DC: Office of Community Oriented Policing Services and the Police Executive Research Forum, 2007), p. 5.
52. Ibid., p. 7.
53. Ibid., p. 6.
54. Ibid.
55. Ibid., p. 22.
56. Ibid., p. 24.
57. Steven M. Cox, *Police: Practices, Perspectives, Problems* (Boston, MA: Allyn & Bacon, 1996), p. 90.
58. See the CALEA website, http://www.calea.org.
59. Commission on Accreditation for Law Enforcement Agencies, "CALEA Announces Tiered Law Enforcement Accreditation Program," http://www.calea.org/calea-update-magazine/issue-105/calea-announces-tiered-law-enforcement-accreditation-program
60. Fulton County, Georgia, Sheriff's Office, "CALEA Law Enforcement Accreditation," p. 2.
61. Kimberly A. McCabe and Robin G. Fajardo, "Law Enforcement Accreditation: A National Comparison of Accredited versus Nonaccredited Agencies," *Journal of Criminal Justice* 29 (2001): 127–131.
62. This case study is loosely adapted from David Thatcher, National COPS Evaluation Organizational Change Case Study: Riverside, California, Program in Criminal Justice Policy and Management, John F. Kennedy School of Government, Harvard University, https://www.ncjrs.gov/nij/cops_casestudy/riversid.html. Case Study Prepared for the Urban Institute.

NicoElNino/Shutterstock

5 Police Personnel Roles and Functions

LEARNING OBJECTIVES

After reading this chapter, the student will be able to:

1. *describe each of Mintzberg's three main roles of the chief executive officer (CEO)*
2. *explain how one might go about preparing for a career as a police chief executive officer to include the kinds of activities that compose an assessment center process*
3. *define the duties placed upon chiefs of police, how they must navigate the political arena, and today's tendency to criticize—and fire—chiefs*
4. *define the duties performed by the sheriff's office*
5. *review the tasks performed by middle managers (captains and lieutenants)*
6. *describe the roles and tasks of a first-line supervisor (patrol sergeant)*
7. *identify the tasks of patrol officers, the traits that make a good officer, and the means of recruiting quality personnel*
8. *describe the ongoing problem of sexual harassment in police agencies*

▶ Introduction

Some of the most significant and grueling challenges facing executives in any position today are those confronting police leadership (several of those issues will be discussed in Chapter 6). It is probably fair to say that given the current police–community climate in the aftermath of events occurring in Ferguson, Missouri, in mid-2015 (discussed in Chapter 4) and since in other venues, and the ongoing volatility of that climate, this may well be the most difficult time in the history of policing in which to be a police leader. Indeed, as Chuck Wexler, executive director of the Police Executive Research Forum, has pointed out, today's "policing profession faces one of the biggest challenges in memory: creating a new, 'post-Ferguson' model of policing, one that prevents unnecessary uses of force and is built on community trust."[1]

This chapter examines some of the challenges confronting law enforcement chief executives (chiefs of police and county sheriffs), middle managers (typically including captains and lieutenants), first-line supervisors (sergeants), and patrol officers. First, we examine, in general terms, the roles of law enforcement chief executive officers, using Henry Mintzberg's model for chief executive officers (CEOs) as a guide. Next, we review how one might prepare for a career as a police chief executive as he or she faces the interview and assessment center processes.

Next, we explore more specifically the expectations and functions of chiefs of police and sheriffs, and then consider the roles and functions of middle managers (captains and lieutenants) supervisors (sergeants). Next is a discussion of a "theory" that has been debated in government and media for some time: whether or not—given the public's angst over police shootings and the possibility that officers are becoming less proactive as a result (leading to more violence)—there exists a "Ferguson effect" in policing that chief executives must acknowledge and deal with. This concept is discussed in this chapter because, if it exists, it potentially affects police personnel at all levels. And then we review the role of patrol officers, focusing on the traits that executives should look for and methods used when trying to recruit quality personnel. After a review of problems that still exist with sexual harassment in some agencies, the chapter concludes with review questions and exercises in the Deliberate and Decide, Learn by Doing, and Case Study sections.

▶ Roles of the Police Executive: The Mintzberg Model for CEOs

Any attempt to discern what roles are occupied and functions are performed by a police **chief executive officer (CEO)** would do well to begin by looking at a model developed in 1975 by Henry Mintzberg.[2] And, while the **Mintzberg model for CEOs** could therefore be applied to courts and corrections administrators as well as to the police, it is most easily applied and understood when used with the latter; therefore, following is an examination of the three primary roles of the police chief executive—the chief of police or sheriff—according to Mintzberg: the interpersonal, the informational, and the decision-maker roles.

> **chief executive officer (CEO)** the highest-ranking executive or administrator in an organization, who is in charge of its overall operation.

> **Mintzberg model for CEOs** a model that delineates and defines the primary roles of a chief executive officer.

The Interpersonal Role

The *interpersonal* role has three components: (1) the figurehead, (2) leadership, and (3) liaison duties.

In the figurehead role, the CEO performs various ceremonial functions. He or she rides in parades and attends civic events; speaks to school and university classes and civic organizations; meets visiting officials and dignitaries; attends academy graduations, swearing-in ceremonies, and certain weddings and funerals; and visits injured officers. Like a city's mayor, whose public responsibilities include cutting ribbons and kissing babies, the police CEO performs these duties simply because of his or her title and position within the organization. Although the chiefs or sheriffs are not expected to attend the grand opening of every retail or commercial business and other such events to which they are invited, they are certainly obligated from a professional standpoint to attend many civic functions and ceremonies.

The leadership role requires the CEO to motivate and coordinate workers while achieving the mission, goals, and needs within the department and the community. A chief or sheriff may have to urge the governing board to enact a code or ordinance that, whether or not popular, is in the best interest of the jurisdiction. For example, a chief in a Western state recently led a drive to pass an ordinance that prohibited parking by university students in residential neighborhoods surrounding the campus. This was a highly unpopular undertaking, but the chief was prompted by the complaints of hardships suffered by the area residents. The CEO also may provide leadership by taking stands on bond issues (seeking funds to hire more officers or build new buildings, for example) and by advising the governing body on the effects of proposed ordinances.

The liaison role is undertaken when the CEO of a police organization interacts with other organizations and coordinates work assignments. It is not uncommon for executives from a geographical area—the police chief, sheriff, ranking officer of the local highway patrol office, district attorney, campus police chief, and so on—to meet informally each month to discuss common problems and strategies. The chief executive also serves as liaison to regional law enforcement councils, narcotics units, crime labs, dispatching centers, and so on. He or she also meets with the representatives of the courts, the juvenile system, and other criminal justice agencies.

The Informational Role

Another role identified by Mintzberg's model is the *informational* one. In this capacity, the CEO engages in tasks relating to (1) monitoring/inspecting, (2) dissemination, and (3) spokesperson duties.

In the monitoring/inspecting function, the CEO constantly reviews the department's operations to ensure that it is operating smoothly (or as smoothly as police operations can be expected to be). This function is often referred to as "roaming the ship"; many CEOs who isolated themselves from their personnel and the daily operations of the agency can speak from sad experience of the need to be involved and present. Many police executives use daily staff meetings to acquire information about their jurisdictions, especially criminal and other activities during the previous 24 hours.

Dissemination tasks involve distributing information to members of the department via memoranda, special orders, general orders, and policies and procedures as described in Chapter 3. The spokesperson function is related to the dissemination task but is focused more on providing information to the news media. This is a difficult task for the chief executive; news organizations, especially television and the print media, are competitive businesses that seek to obtain the most complete news in the shortest amount of time, which often translates into wider viewership and therefore greater advertising revenues for them. From one perspective, the media must appreciate that a criminal investigation can be seriously compromised by premature or excessive coverage. From the other perspective, the public has a right to know what is occurring in the community, especially matters relating to crime; therefore, the prudent police executive attempts to have an open and professional relationship with the media in which each side knows and understands its responsibilities. The prudent chief executive also remembers the power of the media and does not alienate them; as an old saying goes, "Never argue with someone who buys his ink by the barrel."

The Decision-Maker Role

In the decision-maker role, the CEO of a police organization serves as (1) an entrepreneur, (2) a disturbance handler, (3) a resource allocator, and (4) a negotiator.

In the capacity of entrepreneur, the CEO must sell ideas to the members of the governing board or the department—perhaps helping them to understand a new computer or communications system, the implementation of a policing strategy, or different work methods, all of which are intended to improve the organization. Sometimes roles blend, as when several police executives band together (in their entrepreneurial and liaison functions) to lobby the state attorney general and the legislature for new crime-fighting laws.

As a disturbance handler, the executive's tasks range from resolving minor disputes between staff members to dealing with major events, such as riots, continued muggings in a local park, or the cleanup of the downtown area. Sometimes, the executive must solve intradepartmental disputes, which can reach major proportions. For example, the executive must intervene when friction develops between different units, as when the patrol commanders' instruction to street officers to increase arrests for public drunkenness causes a strain on the resources of the jail division's commander.

As a resource allocator, the CEO must clearly understand the agency's budget and its priorities. The resource allocator must consider requests for funds from various groups. Personnel, for example, will ask for higher salaries, additional officers, and better equipment. Citizens may complain about speeding motorists in a specific area, which would require the allocation of additional resources to that neighborhood. In the resource allocator role, the CEO must be able to prioritize requests and to defend his or her choices.

As a negotiator, the CEO resolves employee grievances and, through an appointed representative at the bargaining table, tries to represent the best interests of both the city and labor during collective bargaining. In this role, the CEO must consider the rank and file's request for raises and increased benefits as part of budget administration. If funds available to the jurisdiction are limited, the CEO must negotiate with the collective bargaining unit to reach an agreement. At times, contract negotiations reach an impasse or a deadlock. We will elaborate on some of these chief executive functions later in the chapter; labor relations—including unionism and collective bargaining—are discussed more fully in Chapter 14.

Preparing for a Career as Law Enforcement Executive

Next, we consider how an individual should prepare for the position of law enforcement chief executive and the prevailing means that are used for selecting people for these positions.

Vying for a Law Enforcement Executive's Position: What Works

Although their roles are quite different and the means by which they obtain their positions are quite different—it has been said that "a sheriff is elected for four years, but a chief of police runs for office every day"—there are many similarities between the two positions. Following are some tips for preparing for and succeeding in a law enforcement chief executive's position—most if not all of which would apply at the federal or state levels as well. A recent national survey of more than 300 police chiefs by the Police Executive Research Forum provided these recommendations.

However, before viewing these recommendations, one should recognize that if employed in a police agency and wanting to become a chief elsewhere at some point, career development support from higher-ups is virtually nonexistent; too often, when colleagues learn that an employee is contemplating higher career options, he or she might be viewed as disloyal to their agency and thus jeopardize their career standing. Still, to the extent possible, the following measures can and should be taken to prepare for a chief executive's position:

- Education is key, so work in all divisions and take on special assignments to get well rounded; obtain an undergraduate (and preferably a graduate) degree, read police literature to stay abreast of trends and "what works" in the field, and stay current with laws, procedures, and best practices.
- Know what CALEA (discussed in Chapter 4) requires for an agency to become accredited.
- Get to know the technological aspects of the job.
- Don't be afraid to ask for assistance, and work closely with people who will challenge you.
- Have a secure retirement in place before striking out for a chief's position.
- Develop critical thinking skills as well as communication skills.
- Look for mentors and ask others for advice.[3]

It is also recommended that police chief candidates negotiate for such professional development provisions as tuition reimbursement (and higher pay for a graduate degree), attendance at conferences, outside employment opportunities (not having a conflict of interest or job interference), and provision for time off for consulting, teaching, speaking for a set amount of time each year.[4]

Tips and Preparation for the Assessment Center

assessment center a process used for promoting and hiring personnel that may include oral interviews, psychological tests, group and in-basket exercises, and writing and role-playing exercises.

To obtain the most capable people for chief executive positions (and also for middle-management and even supervisory positions) in policing, the **assessment center** method has proved to be an efficacious means of hiring and promoting personnel. (*Note:* Sheriffs, being normally elected, are thus not subjected to the assessment center process.) The assessment center method is now increasingly utilized to select people for all management or supervisory ranks. The process may include interviews; psychological tests; in-basket exercises; management tasks; group discussions; role-playing exercises, such as simulations of interviews with subordinates, the public, and news media; fact-finding exercises; oral presentation exercises; and written communications exercises.[5]

The first step is to identify behaviors important to successful performance in the position. Job descriptions listing responsibilities and skills should exist for all executive, middle management, and supervisory positions (such as chief, captain, lieutenant, and sergeant). Then, each candidate's abilities and skill levels should be evaluated using several of the techniques mentioned.

Individual and group role-playing are valuable hands-on exercises during the selection process. Candidates may be required to help solve simulated police–community problems (they conduct a "meeting" to hear the concerns of local minority groups), to react to a major incident (explaining what they would do and in what order in a simulated shooting or riot situation), to hold a news briefing, or to participate in other such exercises. They may be given an in-basket situation in which they receive an abundance of paperwork, policies, and problems to be prioritized and dealt with in a prescribed amount of time. Writing abilities may also be evaluated Candidates may be given a specified amount of time to develop a use-of-force policy for a police agency, to examine their written communications skills and to determine how they think cognitively and can build a proposal.

EXHIBIT 5.1

HIRING THE BEST: THE POLICE CHIEF'S INTERVIEW

When an agency conducts interviews toward hiring a permanent police chief, the interview should be conducted in a structured and thorough manner. It is an optimal time to determine if the applicant is the right fit and possesses the right values and abilities for the agency, and to impart the agency's mission, values, and expectations. John Gray, who possesses 12 years as a police chief, recommends that the following sequence of questions be used for these purposes.[6]

The interview might begin by saying, "I have your application and resume. So, tell me in about two minutes, what is the most important thing I should know about you." This allows applicants to talk about themselves and affords an opportunity to judge their communication style under the stress of time. As follow-up questions, applicants might be asked to describe their work experience, their three most important accomplishments in policing, hobbies, interests, and so on. During this time, the interviewer(s) is also observing the applicants' verbal and nonverbal communication skill and style.

Next, Gray recommends discussing the agency's mission, values, and culture, to include a summary of the challenges and accomplishments of the agency. Included here might be any nonnegotiable job behaviors, such as performance levels, service and integrity, and what specific behaviors will lead to termination.

Then, applicants might be asked questions that can reveal any character flaws: what is in their background would they not want others to know about them, what other agencies or supervisors might say about them, and what kinds of things do they publicly display (profiles, statements, and photos on a social networking site, a blog, and so on).

Last are questions that are geared toward learning the applicant's real motivation for and degree of commitment to the position, as well as true passions. "Why do you want this job?" "Assume that policing had never happened for you. What would have been your Plan B?" It is also appropriate to ask candidates if they are applying or testing for other agencies (applicants who are applying at a number of other agencies are probably not highly committed to this particular one; also, the best applicants will often get hired rapidly elsewhere).

During each exercise, several assessors or raters analyze each candidate's performance and record some type of evaluation; when the assessment center process ends, each rater submits his or her rating information to the person making the hiring or promotion decision. Assessment center procedures are logistically more difficult to conduct, as well as more labor-intensive and costly, than traditional interviews, but they are well worth the extra investment. This process can help to avoid selecting the wrong person and can prevent untold problems for years to come.

Exhibit 5.1 provides tips for interviewing a police chief.

▶ Chiefs of Police

Expectations and Advocacy

The **chief of police** (also given the title of *commissioner* or *superintendent*) is generally considered to be one of the most influential and prestigious persons in local government. Indeed, people in this position often amass considerable power and influence in their jurisdiction. Mayors, city managers and administrators, members of the agency, labor organizations, citizens, special-interest groups, and the media all have differing role expectations of the chief of police that often conflict.

chief of police the title given to the top official in the chain of command of a municipal police department.

The mayor also expects the chief to communicate with city management about police-related issues and to be part of the city management team; to communicate city management's policies to police personnel; to establish agency policies, goals, and objectives and put them in writing; to develop an administrative system for managing people, equipment, and the budget in a professional and businesslike manner; to set a good example, both personally and professionally; to administer disciplinary action consistently and fairly when required; and to select personnel whose performance will ably and professionally promote the organization's objectives.

Members of the agency expect their chief executive to be their advocate, supporting them when necessary and representing the agency's interests when dealing with judges and prosecutors who may be indifferent or hostile. Citizens tend to expect the chief of police to provide efficient and cost-effective police services while keeping crime and tax rates down (often an area of built-in conflict), while preventing corruption and illegal use of force.

Special-interest groups expect the chief to advocate policy positions that they favor. For example, Mothers Against Drunk Driving (MADD) would desire strong anti-DUI measures by the police. Finally, the media expect the chief to cooperate fully with their efforts to obtain fast and complete information on crime.

Who Is Today's Police Chief: A Profile

The aforementioned survey by the Police Executive Research Forum revealed much in terms of a profile of today's police chief executive, based on input from more than 330 respondents.

First, a large majority (82%) held a graduate degree; those chiefs having a graduate degree or who had completed one of the programs below tended to have higher salaries (and those from the Western states earn about 17% more than others, on average, while those in the Southern states earn about 10% less).[7] Such training was typically obtained from widely recognized programs as PERF's Senior Management Institute for Police, the FBI's National Academy and the Law Enforcement Executive Development Association (LEEDA), Harvard University's Senior Executives program, Southern Police Institute's Administrative Officers Course, and Northwestern University's School of Police Staff and Command. Attendance at these programs allows one to stand out from the competition.

Today's chiefs tend to be older than previous surveys found; for example, most chiefs today are in the 56–60 age category, while a decade ago they tended to be 46–50. The typical chief has been in office for 4.3 years—about a year less time in office than another PERF study found in the mid-1980s, which was 5.5 years. This short tenure of police chiefs has several negative consequences. It prevents long-range planning, results in frequent new policies and administrative styles, and prohibits the development of the chief's political power base and local influence.

Only about a third of the chiefs had a contract or employment agreement (the most common length of time of the contract being 3 years); those that did tended to be in smaller agencies. About 86 percent of the respondents reported that they were vested in a retirement plan before becoming a chief, and more than half (60%) were hired from outside the department rather than being promoted from within.[8]

Promote from Within, or Hire from Outside?

Many cities finding themselves in need of a police chief have to consider whether it would be better to promote someone from within the ranks or hire from outside (perhaps using the assessment center process described earlier). Although it is perhaps more economical and certainly less trouble to select a police chief from within the organization than to use an assessment center, both methods have advantages and disadvantages. One study of police chiefs promoted from within or hired from outside indicated only one significant difference in qualification: educational attainment. The outsiders were more highly

IN THEIR OWN WORDS

ADMINISTRATIVE ADVICE FROM THE FIELD

Name: Debora Black

Current position/City/State: Police Chief, Prescott, Arizona Police Department

College attended/academic major/degree(s): Bachelor of Science and Master in Public Administration, Arizona State University; Certificate in Legal Studies, Phoenix College; Senior Executives in State and Local Government Program, Kennedy School of Government at Harvard.

My primary duties and responsibilities in this position include: responsibility for leading all 540 sworn and civilian members of the department to achieve our mission of protecting the lives and property of the people we serve. Internal and external communications are incredibly important in my position. Administrative responsibilities also include planning, establishing policy, budget management, procurement, and managing complex radio communication and technology systems. Staffing and hiring are critical responsibilities, as well as maintaining high levels of accountability and integrity throughout the organization. Community outreach is essential to accomplishing our mission, so cultivating relationships and feedback mechanisms require continuous attention.

Personal attributes/characteristics that have proven to be most helpful to me in this position are: perseverance, creativity, and humility.

My three greatest challenges in this administrative role include: severe budget reductions spanning several years. Although public safety is considered an essential service provided by municipal government, the impact of the Great Recession has required organizational restructuring and realignment of existing staff to absorb additional duties as the employee base is reduced. The resulting instability and decline in employee morale has required contentious communication and the identification of non-monetary rewards to maintain employee engagement. Due to the ongoing nature of our reductions, retention of highly skilled workers has been an ongoing challenge.

Personal accomplishments during my administrative career about which I am most proud are: formalizing leadership development and mentoring programs within my organization, which has encouraged incredibly talented individuals to assume new roles and take on additional responsibility in the organization. Identifying creative solutions, such as alternative funding sources, establishing new partnerships, and advancing technology efficiencies, has been the cornerstone of my tenure as police chief. My goal of inspiring individual employees is to focus on service to others while connecting to our mission and values defines the organizational culture I am creating today and the leadership legacy I hope will remain long after I leave.

Advice for someone who is interested in occupying an administrative position such as mine would be: Know your individual strengths and those of your team; fill gaps as soon as you identify them. Develop people and invest in systems that support their work, not the other way around. Establish high expectations for individual and organizational excellence. Treat people with dignity and respect, and never stop growing.

Source: Used with permission from Debora Black.

educated. No differences were found with respect to other aspects of their background, attitudes, salary, tenure in their current position or in policing, the size of the agency or community, and their current budget.[9]

Navigating the Political Arena

As noted above, as a rule, police chiefs and sheriffs obtain their positions in very different fashion (appointed and elected, respectively); nevertheless, both learn early on in their careers that politics is involved in everything they do—and not only the partisan kind. They must, each day, confront a number of constituencies and stakeholders, both informal (community groups, ethnic minorities, and special interests) and formal (elected public officials and representatives of political groups) individuals and entities, while also addressing the needs, requests, and demands of agency personnel.

The history of policing is so replete with politics that it even experienced a political "era" in the United States, roughly from the 1840s to the 1930s. Still, this is an aspect of policing that is often overlooked and has had both good and bad elements. Politics colors nearly everything, and political influence can range from major policy, personnel, and budgetary decisions to the overzealous governing board member who wishes to micromanage the police agency and even appears unexpectedly at night at a crime scene (overheard on the police scanner) to "assist" the officers.

Norm Stamper, former chief of police in Seattle, Washington, gave perhaps the best, succinct description of the power and influence of politics over policing. Stamper wrote that "*everything* about policing is ultimately political. Who gets which office: political. Which services are cut when there's a budget freeze: political. Who gets hired, fired, promoted: political, political, political."[10] Stamper also observed that there is both good and bad politics: "I hire my brother-in-law's cousin, a certifiable doofus, because he's got a bass boat I wouldn't mind borrowing—bad politics. I promote a drinking buddy—bad politics. I pick an individual because he or she will add value to the organization and will serve the community honorably—good politics."[11]

Several aspects of police administration that involve the political arena—for example, changing the culture, philosophy, and practice of the agency to accommodate community policing and problem-solving; developing policies and training to address the use of force; dealing with the public in the aftermath of a critical incident; navigating the waters of labor relations and collective bargaining—are discussed in other chapters.

Today's Chief: Under Fire and Being Fired

Largely as a result of some of the issues discussed in Chapter 6 (i.e., the public's angst with police shootings and use of force in general calls for body-worn cameras), a number of police chiefs have been ousted in the wake of racially charged episodes, civil unrest, or internal strife. Included in that list of replaced chiefs are those in Ferguson; San Francisco; Baltimore; Chicago; Cincinnati; Baton Rouge, Louisiana; and Salt Lake City, Utah. According to Darrel Stephens, former chief in Charlotte-Mecklenburg, North Carolina Police Department, and now the executive director of the Major Cities Chiefs Association, "Never has the job been more difficult."[12]

Certainly the chief executive's job is made more difficult by today's close and sustained scrutiny of all facets of police operations, the result being that many governing boards are willing to cut ties with their established police leaders. There seems to be little patience with changes in police agency culture and operations. In some cities, a U.S. Department of Justice investigation of the agency (see Chapter 6) has resulted in the chief's ouster. Of course, chiefs may be forced out for other reasons as well; for example, in 2016 chiefs were terminated for reasons relating to allegations of sexual harassment and sex scandals, low morale and a hostile work environment, and accusations of improper budget management or record keeping. In sum, police chiefs have been under the magnifying glass for 2 years, and there appears to be no end in sight.

In a significant address, in October 2016, the president of the International Association of Chiefs of Police (Chief Terrence Cunningham of Wellesley, Massachusetts) issued an apology for the role police officers played in "society's historical mistreatment of communities of color." Cunningham also noted that police officers should not be blamed for the racial injustices of the past, but that laws enacted in decades past at all levels of government put officers in a position of having to perform "unpalatable tasks" such as maintaining legalized discrimination.[13]

▶ The Sheriff

The position of **sheriff** has a long tradition, rooted in the time of the Norman conquest of England (in 1066), and it played an important part in the early law enforcement activities of colonial America. Unfortunately, because of television and movie depictions, many people today view the county sheriff as a bumbling, cruel, overweight, or corrupt individual wearing a cowboy hat and sunglasses while talking with a Southern drawl (see, e.g., reruns of movies such as *Smokey and the Bandit*, *Mississippi Burning*, *The Dukes of Hazzard*, and *Walking Tall*). This image is both unfair and highly inaccurate. Next, we examine the role of today's county sheriffs.

sheriff the title given to the top official in the chain of command of a county law enforcement agency.

According to a June 2016 federal report, there are an estimated 3,012 sheriffs' offices employing about 189,000 full-time sworn officers (those with general arrest powers) and 163,000 full-time nonsworn or civilian employees. Most agencies also operate local jails and provide court bailiff/security services.[14]

Because of the diversity of sheriffs' offices throughout the country, it is difficult to describe a typical sheriff's department; these offices run the gamut from the traditional, highly political, limited-service office to the modern, fairly nonpolitical, full-service police organization. It is possible, however, to list functions commonly associated with the sheriff's office (in addition to jail and court security functions):

1. Serving and/or implementing civil processes (divorce papers, liens, evictions, garnishments and attachments, and other civil duties, such as extradition and transportation of prisoners)
2. Collecting certain taxes and conducting real estate sales (usually for nonpayment of taxes) for the county
3. Performing routine order-maintenance duties by enforcing state statutes and county ordinances, arresting offenders, and performing traffic and criminal investigations[15]

Sheriffs, therefore, have a unique role in that they typically serve all three components of the justice system: (1) law enforcement (with patrol, traffic, and investigative functions), (2) the courts (as civil process servers and bailiffs), and (3) corrections (in the local jails). In many urban areas, civil process duties consume more time and resources than those involving law enforcement.[16]

There are no sheriffs in Alaska, and the office was essentially abolished in 2000 in Connecticut; Hawaii does not have a traditional sheriff's position, as there are two statewide sheriff's departments (sheriffs being appointed by the Department of Public Safety). In Rhode Island, the governor appoints the sheriff,[17] and in some consolidated jurisdictions also, such as Miami–Dade County, Florida, sheriffs are appointed; thus, they tend to be aligned with a political party. As elected officials, sheriffs are important political figures and, in many rural areas, represent the most powerful political force in the county. As a result, sheriffs are far more independent than appointed municipal police chiefs, who can be removed from office by the mayors or city managers who appoint them; however, because they are elected, sheriffs receive considerable media scrutiny and are subject to state accountability processes.

The sheriff enjoys no tenure guarantee, although one study found that sheriffs (averaging 6.7 years in office) had longer tenure in office than chiefs of police (5.4 years). The politicization of the office of sheriff can result in high turnover rates of personnel who do not have civil service protection. The uncertainty concerning their tenure, as with police chiefs, is not conducive to long-range (strategic) planning. Largely as a result of the political nature of the office, sheriffs tend to be older, less likely to have been promoted through the ranks of the agency, and less likely to be college graduates and to have specialized training than police chiefs. Research has also found that sheriffs in small agencies have more difficulty with organizational problems (field activities, budget management) and that sheriffs in large agencies find dealing with local officials and planning and evaluation to be more troublesome.[18]

IN THEIR OWN WORDS

ADMINISTRATIVE ADVICE FROM THE FIELD

Name: Scott R. Jones

Current position/City/State: Sheriff, Sacramento County, California

College attended/academic major/degree(s): Bachelor of Science, Criminal Justice, California State University, Sacramento; Juris Doctor (JD), Lincoln Law School, Sacramento.

My primary duties and responsibilities in this position include: overseeing a very large Sheriff's Department with nearly 1,300 sworn officers, 2,000 total employees, and an annual budget over $400 million; providing not only first-responder public safety to over 580,000 persons but also overseeing corrections and other county-wide services for the entire county of 1.4 million people.

Personal attributes/characteristics that have proven to be most helpful to me in this position are: the ability to seek input on decisions when possible, but make decisions quickly and decisively when necessary; having a diminished ego; recognizing as a personal mantra that "there is no best, only better"; having a vision and drive for innovation and NOT the status quo.

My three greatest challenges in this administrative role include: (1) trying to effectuate change in a large, decentralized, diverse workforce; (2) creating "growth" without additional resources; looking inward for growth solutions through better technologies, strategies, deployment of resources, and partnerships; and (3) trying to be available to all the myriad of stakeholders in the community, with limited time to do so.

Personal accomplishments during my administrative career about which I am most proud are: creating the first dedicated youth services unit in our history, to better foster early relationships with our youth; creating an annual strategic planning process that establishes our priorities year by year, becoming an engine that drives our department forward despite external challenges; creating a multijurisdictional team to combat youth and gang violence that is truly intelligence-led and one-of-a-kind in the nation; protecting our employees from layoffs and re-hiring all those personnel that were laid off during our downsizing; and creating and maintaining an air of transparency and trust for our department with the public and the media.

Advice for someone who is interested in occupying an administrative position such as mine would be: don't be too concerned with where you want to be; instead focus on where you are and make your decisions and guide your actions on how best to accomplish your current role, not some future role. Never be satisfied that anything you do or see is the best it can be; once you open yourself to the paradigm that ANYTHING can be improved, you'll be surprised at the vision that comes from yourself AND others. Never have an ego about who or what you are; you are the same person you were before you became "important." And always be human; you are dealing not with gears in a machine, but rather human beings with their own limitations, challenges, motivations, priorities, and so on.

Source: Used with permission from Scott R. Jones.

middle manager typically a captain or lieutenant, one who coordinates agency units' activities and sees that the administrative strategies and overall mission are carried out.

Middle Managers: Captains and Lieutenants

Few police administration books contain information about the **middle managers** of a police department: the captains and lieutenants. This is unfortunate because they are too numerous and powerful within police and other paramilitary organizations to ignore. Opinions concerning these middle-management personnel vary, however, as will be seen in the following discussion.

Leonhard Fuld, one of the early progressive police administration researchers, said in 1909 that the captain is one of the most important officers in the organization. Fuld believed that the position had two broad duties—policing and administration. The captain was held responsible for preserving the public peace and protecting life and property within the precinct. Fuld defined the captain's administrative duties as being of three kinds: clerical, janitorial, and supervisory.[19]

Middle managers are generally (as mentioned in Chapter 1) the intermediate level of leadership in a hierarchical organization, reporting to the higher echelon of administrators and responsible for carrying out their policies and the agency's mission while also supervising subordinate managers and employees to ensure a smooth functioning organization. In a mid-sized or large police agency, a patrol shift or watch may be commanded by a captain who will have several lieutenants reporting to him or her. The lieutenants may assist the captain in running the shift, but when there is a shortage of sergeants as a result of vacations or retirements, the lieutenant may assume the duties of a first-line supervisor. In some respects, the lieutenant's position in some departments is a training ground for future unit commanders (the rank of captain or higher).

Perhaps the best way to understand what these shift commanders do is to examine the tasks they perform in a medium-sized police department. First, we examine the tasks generally performed by the captain, using the Lexington, Kentucky, Police Department as an example. The 15 most important tasks performed by captains are as follows:[20]

1. Issuing assignments to individuals and units within the section
2. Receiving assignments for the section/unit
3. Reviewing incoming written complaints and reports
4. Preparing routine reports
5. Reviewing the final disposition of assignments
6. Ensuring that subordinates comply with general and special orders
7. Monitoring crime and other activity statistics
8. Evaluating the work of individuals and units within the section
9. Maintaining sector facilities
10. Discussing concerns and problems with people
11. Attending various staff meetings
12. Maintaining working contacts and responding to inquiries from other sections of the division
13. Reviewing and approving overtime in the section/unit
14. Monitoring section/unit operations to evaluate performance
15. Fielding and responding to complaints against subordinates

Captains spend a substantial amount of time coordinating their units' activities with those of other units and overseeing the operation of their units. As an officer progresses up the chain of command, his or her responsibilities become more administrative. At the same time, captains also have supervisory responsibilities (tasks 1, 3, 5, 6, 8, and 15). Whereas a sergeant or lieutenant may be supervising individual officers, a captain is more concerned with individual tasks, unit activities, and the overall performance of the officers under his or her command.

Next, we examine the tasks generally performed by the lieutenant, again using the Lexington Police Department as an example. The 15 most important responsibilities for lieutenants include the following, based on the frequency with which they are performed and their urgency:[21]

1. Assisting in supervising or directing the activities of the unit
2. Performing the duties of a police officer
3. Ensuring that departmental and governmental policies are followed
4. Preparing the duty roster
5. Reviewing the work of individuals or groups in the section
6. Responding to field calls requiring an on-scene commander
7. Holding the roll call
8. Preparing various reports
9. Reviewing various reports
10. Coordinating the activities of subordinates on major investigations
11. Meeting with superiors concerning unit operations
12. Maintaining time sheets
13. Notifying the captain/bureau commander of significant calls
14. Answering inquiries from other sections/units, divisions, and outside agencies
15. Serving as the captain/bureau commander in the latter's absence

Note that lieutenants perform the duties of a police officer (task 2). With their supervisory and managerial responsibilities, they engage in a limited amount of police work, however. One potential problem that police leaders must avoid is that of the organization becoming "top-heavy," with too many administrative, management, and supervisory personnel in general or too many who are working in offices and not on the streets. Too often, middle managers become glorified paper pushers, especially in the present climate that requires myriad reports, budgets, grants, and so on.

The agency should determine what administrative, management, and supervisory functions are essential and how many captains, lieutenants, and sergeants are needed to perform them. Some communities, such as Kansas City, Missouri, have eliminated the rank of lieutenant; they found that this move had no negative consequences.[22]

▶ First-Line Supervisors: The Patrol Sergeant

Seeking the Gold Badge

first-line supervisor the lowest yet a very important level of leadership, the supervisor directs, controls, and evaluates the work of field personnel, ensures that agency policies and procedures are followed, counsels and places employees where resources are most needed, resolves employee conflicts, and performs related duties.

Sometime during the career of a patrol officer (provided that he or she acquires the minimal number of years of experience), the opportunity for career advancement is presented—the chance to wear the sergeant's "gold badge." This is a difficult position to occupy because at this lowest leadership level, **first-line supervisors** are caught between upper management and the rank-and-file officers.

This initial opportunity to attain the rank of sergeant is normally quite attractive. It is not uncommon for 60–65 percent or more of those who are eligible to take the test for promotion; thus, competition for the sergeant openings in most departments is quite keen.

Becoming a sergeant often involves an assessment center process, discussed earlier, and departmental and civil service procedures that are intended to guarantee legitimacy and impartiality in the process. Officers are often told that it is best to rotate into different assignments before testing for sergeant to gain exposure to a variety of police functions and supervisory responsibilities. The promotional system, then, favors well-rounded officers; furthermore, being skilled at test taking is often of tremendous assistance, so even if one fails the first or several tests, going through the testing process can be invaluable. As with the chief executives' hiring process, an assessment center, which includes critical-incident, problem-solving, in-basket, disciplinary problems, role-playing exercises, and/or other components, will provide candidates with valuable training and testing experience. Other factors that might come into play as part of the promotional process include education and training, years of experience, supervisory ratings, psychological evaluations, and departmental commendations.

Assuming the Position: General Roles and Functions

Administrative personnel know that a good patrol officer is not automatically a good supervisor. Because supervisors are promoted from within the ranks, they are often placed in charge of their friends and peers. Long-standing relationships are put under stress when a new sergeant suddenly has official authority over former equals. Leniency or preferential treatment is often expected of new sergeants by their former peers.

When new supervisors attempt to correct deficient behavior, their previous performance may be recalled as a means of challenging the reasonableness or legitimacy of their supervisory action. Supervisors with any skeletons in their closets can expect to hear those skeletons rattling as they begin to use their new-found authority. This places a great deal of pressure on the supervisor. A new supervisor, therefore, must go through a transitional phase to learn how to exercise command and get cooperation from subordinates.

The new supervisor is no longer responsible solely for her or his behavior but also for the behavior of several other employees. The step from officer to supervisor is a big one and calls for a new set of skills and knowledge largely separate from those learned at lower levels in the organization.

Supervision is challenging not only in policing but also in corrections, where supervisors must follow federal and state laws and court decisions that concern the custody, care, and treatment of inmates. Their subordinates, however, expect them to be understanding, to protect them from prison management's potentially unreasonable expectations and arbitrary decisions, and to represent their interests.

The supervisor's role, put simply, is to get his or her subordinates to do their very best. This task involves a host of actions, including communicating, motivating, leading, team building, training, appraising, counseling, and disciplining. Getting them to do their very best includes figuring out each subordinate's strengths and weaknesses; defining good and bad performance; measuring performance; providing feedback; and making sure that subordinates' efforts coincide with the organization's mission, values, goals, and objectives.

Supervising a group of subordinates is made more difficult because of the so-called human element. People are complex and sometimes unpredictable. Rules and principles for communicating, leading, and other supervisory tasks are rarely hard and fast because different people react differently. What works for a supervisor in one situation may not work for that supervisor in another situation, much less for some other supervisor. Thus, supervisors have to learn to "read" subordinates and diagnose situations before choosing how to respond. Supervisors have to become students of human behavior and of behavioral science disciplines, such as psychology and sociology.

Effective supervision is also difficult because the job is dynamic, not static. One's subordinates change over time as they age, grow, mature, and experience satisfaction and dissatisfaction in their personal and work lives. In addition, attrition is common, as personnel retire, promote, and transfer into other units within the department. When new

TABLE 5-1 **Management's and Officers' Expectations of Supervisors**

MANAGEMENT'S EXPECTATIONS
• Interpret departmental policies, procedures, and rules and ensure that officers follow them
• Initiate disciplinary action when officers fail to follow policies
• Ensure that officers' paperwork and reports are accurate and filed on a timely basis
• Train officers when they are deficient or unskilled
• Complete performance evaluations
• Ensure that officers treat citizens respectfully, professionally, and impartially
• Ensure that officers' equipment and appearance are in order
• Back up officers and review their performance when officers answer calls for service
• Take charge of high-risk or potential critical-incident situations
• Make assignments to ensure that the objectives of the unit are met
OFFICERS' EXPECTATIONS
• Interpret departmental policies, procedures, and rules to meet the needs of the officers
• Handle disciplinary actions informally rather than taking direct action, especially regarding minor infractions
• Advocate for officers when they request a vacation or time off
• Support them when there is a conflict with citizens
• Provide them with support and backup at high-risk calls
• Assist them in getting better assignments and shifts
• Emphasize law enforcement activities over other activities such as providing services, community policing activities, or mundane assignments such as traffic control
• Understand that officers need to take breaks and sometimes attend to personal needs while on duty

subordinates come under the supervisor's wing, the supervisor must learn the best way to handle them and also be attuned to the new officers' effects on other subordinates and on the work group as a whole.

Table 5-1 ■ shows the expectations that both managers and rank-and-file officers have of first-line supervisors.

Basic Tasks

The following nine tasks are most important for police supervisors, in order of importance:[23]

1. Supervise subordinate officers in the performance of their duties
2. Disseminate information to subordinates
3. Ensure that general and special orders are followed
4. Review and approve various reports
5. Listen to problems voiced by officers
6. Answer calls
7. Keep superiors apprised of ongoing situations
8. Provide direct supervision for potential high-risk calls or situations
9. Interpret policies and inform subordinates

Types of Supervisors

Robin S. Engel[24] studied police supervisors and found four distinct types: traditional, innovative, supportive, and active. Each of these types can be found in any police department. A particular supervisor's style is largely dependent on his or her experiences on the job, his or her training, and the department's organizational climate.

The first type, *traditional,* is law enforcement oriented. Traditional supervisors expect their subordinates to produce high levels of measurable activities, such as traffic citations and arrests. They expect officers to respond to calls for service efficiently, place a great deal of emphasis on reports and other paperwork, and provide officers with a substantial amount of instruction and oversight. They tend to be task oriented and place greater emphasis on punishment than rewards and often believe that they do not have a great deal of power in the department. These supervisors see their primary role as controlling subordinates, and thus can have morale and motivation problems with their subordinates.

The second type is the *innovative* supervisor, who is most closely associated with community policing. Innovative supervisors generally do not place a great deal of emphasis on citations or arrests. They also depend more on developing relationships with subordinates than on using power to control or motivate. Innovative supervisors usually are good mentors, and they tend to coach rather than order. They are open to new ideas and innovations, and try to develop officers who can solve problems and have good relations with citizens.

The third type of supervisor is the *supportive* supervisor, who, like the innovative supervisor, is concerned with developing good relations with subordinates. The primary difference is that supportive supervisors are concerned with protecting officers from what are viewed as unfair management practices. They see themselves as a buffer between management and officers. They attempt to develop strong work teams and motivate officers by inspiring them. A potential shortcoming is seeing themselves as "one of the troops," and they sometimes neglect emphasizing departmental goals and responsibilities.

The final category of supervisors, according to Engel, is the *active* supervisor, who tends to work in the field. Active supervisors sometimes are police officers with stripes or rank. They often take charge of field situations rather than supervise them, although they are active supervisors in most situations. They are able to develop good relations with subordinates because they are perceived as being hardworking and competent. Their shortcoming is that, by being overly involved in some field situations, they do not give their subordinates the opportunity to develop.

▶ Should Police Leaders Give Credence to a "Ferguson Effect"?

In Chapter 4 we discussed the chasm that now exists in many communities between the police and citizens they serve in the "post-Ferguson environment" and at a time when many see their police as "soldiers" or "warriors" rather than as guardians and protectors; in Chapter 5, the problem of police shootings and their general use of force is specifically addressed.

All of this has led to a debate concerning whether or not there now exists what is termed a "Ferguson effect"—a term coined by St. Louis police chief Sam Dotson in 2014. We discuss it in this chapter as it concerns police personnel of all ranks.

Former FBI director James Comey, known to be outspoken, ignited the debate by asserting in a speech that there is a link between the spike in violent crimes in some cities and the heightened scrutiny of police in recent years. (The 56 largest U.S. cities saw 17% ore homicides in 2015 than in 2014—and in 10 of those cities, homicides were up by more than 60%.)[25] Comey argued that with the ubiquitous cellphones now recording many police actions that wind up on social media and result in public outcry, many police officers now feel they are "under siege." Comey believes this, in turn, leads to a "de-policing" or slowdown in proactive beat work, which brings about greater violence in many cities.[26]

Comey stated at a news conference that "police are less likely to do the marginal additional policing that suppresses crime—the getting out of your car at 2 in the morning and saying to a group of guys, 'What are you doing here?'"[27]

Agreeing with Comey and the existence of such an "effect" are many conservatives, such as political commentator Heather MacDonald, author of a 2016 book, *The War on Cops: How the New Attack on Law and Order Makes Everyone Less Safe*,[28] "Policing is political. If a powerful segment of society sends the message that proactive policing is bigoted, the cops will eventually do less of it. This is not unprofessional; police take their cues, as they should, from the messages society sends about expected behavior."[29]

Conversely, lacking scientific testing or basis, the claim of such an "effect" has been criticized by many in the ranks of policing—including the head of the 330,000-member National Fraternal Order of Police—who disagree with the notion that officers are afraid to do their jobs.[30] Similarly, many progressives disagree with this theory, insisting that there is no evidence that large-scale protests that occurred in several cities are to blame for their increases in violence.[31] Others, like Daniel Denvir, believe there is simply no way that protesters are cowling police because it has no "causal mechanism": if in fact police are afraid of being proactive because of the fear of public backlash, "there is no explanation as to how that information would be conveyed to criminals so as to cause them to quickly make decisions to fire their guns with more frequency."[32] Even former President Barack Obama disputed the notion of such an effect while speaking at a police conference, saying people should not "cherry-pick data or use anecdotal evidence."[33]

Indeed, much of the "evidence" of a Ferguson effect is anecdotal. An example is the *Washington Post* report of a Chicago police officer who was savagely beaten at a car accident scene and did not draw her gun on her attacker—allegedly because she was afraid of the media attention that would come if she shot him and she "didn't want her family or the department to go through the scrutiny the next day on the national news."[34]

Perhaps all that police leaders can do at this point is be aware of the theory in order to observe any changes in their agency's style of police. As many studies have shown—those concerning the broken windows theory, the benefits of community policing and problem-solving, and foot patrol, to name a few—changes in policing do affect crime rates. Indeed, they must remember that "proactive" policing methods such as these, particularly those where police build relationships with their residents, are one of the most effective approaches an agency can take to prevent crime.

▶ The Patrol Officer

Countless books and articles have been written about, and other chapters in this book deal, in part, with the beat officer. Here, we briefly discuss the nature of this position. Included is a review of their basic tasks, some traits of good officers, hiring the best personnel possible, and some basic training methods.

Basic Tasks

Many people believe that the police officer has the most difficult job in the United States. In fundamental terms, the police perform four basic functions: (1) enforcing the laws, (2) performing services (such as maintaining or assisting animal control units, reporting burned-out street lights or stolen traffic lights and signs, delivering death messages, checking the welfare of people in their homes, delivering blood), (3) preventing crime (patrolling, providing the public with information on locks and lighting to reduce the opportunity for crime), and (4) protecting the innocent (by investigating crimes, police systematically remove innocent people from consideration as crime suspects).[35]

Because police officers are solitary workers, spending much of their time on the job unsupervised, and because those officers who are hired today will become the supervisors of the future, police administrators must attempt to attract the best individuals possible and select people who are self-motivated.

What Traits Make a Good Officer?

Although it may be difficult for the average police administrator to describe the qualities he or she looks for when recruiting, training, and generally creating a good officer, some psychological characteristics can be identified. According to psychologist Lawrence Wrightsman,[36] it is important that good officers be *incorruptible*, of high moral character. They should be *well adjusted* and able to carry out the hazardous and stressful tasks of policing without cracking up, and thick-skinned enough to operate without defensiveness. They should also be *people oriented* and able to respond to situations without becoming overly emotional, impulsive, or aggressive; they need to exercise restraint. They also need *cognitive skills* to assist in their investigative work. And, of course, they must possess good oral and written communications skills, have good judgment, and not cower in the face of danger.

Addressing a Front-End Problem: Recruiting Quality Officers

Certainly, the recruitment of quality police officers is the key to the success, values, and culture of any police organization. However, recruitment is exacerbated in many cities by a competitive job market and struggles to retain diversity.[37] Furthermore, this crunch comes at a time when today's police need a stronger focus on problem-solving skills, ability to collaborate with the community, and a greater capacity to use technology.[38] Adding to the problems are today's higher incidence of obesity, major debt, drug use, and criminal records that are found among potential recruits.[39]

However, there are several recruiting measures that can be adopted toward generating a satisfactory applicant pool:

- Consider the academy dropout rate: Are recruiters signing up the most promising candidates for the academy?[40]
- Publicize hiring campaigns on business cards, use department vehicles as billboards, and make the agency websites more effective by emphasizing the positive reasons for joining (rather than focusing on the challenges faced by police officers).
- Limit recruiting trips to those locations where candidates are likely to be found, such as areas with economic difficulties; out-of-town recruiting trips are generally not effective.[41]
- Look at the academy program to see if something is hindering diversity and in effect "washing out" candidates, particularly those whose native language is not English.[42]
- Make recruiting efforts focus on the positives of police work, such as job security, the satisfaction of public service, and superior pay and benefits.[43]
- Include an online sample test on the agency website to give recruits an idea of the types of questions they will be facing.

The Kansas City, Missouri, Police Department attempts to recruit and hire the best personnel using the process described in Exhibit 5.2; then, Exhibit 5.3 demonstrates how police agencies are using social networking sites to perform background checks on recruits.

EXHIBIT 5.2

THE POLICE HIRING PROCESS IN KANSAS CITY, MISSOURI[44]

Following are the types of examinations and activities involved in the hiring process for the Kansas City, Missouri, Police Department (KCPD) (as well as many other police agencies). The entire process, which includes a substance abuse questionnaire (not shown), may require several months to complete.

- ***Written examination.*** All applicants begin with and must take the Police Officer Selection Test (POST). A review for this examination is generally given within 1 month prior to the written examination, and a sample test is available upon request.
- ***Physical abilities test.*** This is an obstacle course designed to simulate challenges that could be encountered during an officer's tour of duty. Applicants must demonstrate their ability to maneuver through the course with minimal errors.
- ***Pre-employment polygraph examination.*** The polygraph examination is administered by a qualified polygraph examiner and covers criminal activity, drug usage, integrity, truthfulness, and employment history.
- ***Background investigation.*** The background investigation will cover pertinent facts regarding the applicant's character, work history, and any criminal or traffic records.
- ***Ride-along.*** To expose applicants to the actual duties performed by KCPD officers, during the background investigation, the applicant will be required to ride with an officer on a weekend for a full tour of duty during the evening or night shift.
- ***Oral board.*** This interview consists of questions designed to allow the KCPD to assess an applicant's overall abilities, which are related to the field of law enforcement.
- ***Psychological examination.*** This interview is conducted by a certified psychologist, after a job offer has been made.
- ***Physical examination.*** Applicants undergo a complete medical and eye examination performed by a licensed physician, after a job offer has been made.

EXHIBIT 5.3

USING SOCIAL NETWORKING SITES FOR BACKGROUND CHECKS[45]

Police agencies are using social networking sites to perform background checks, requesting that candidates sign waivers allowing investigators access to their Facebook, MySpace, YouTube, Twitter, and other personal Internet accounts. Some agencies also demand that applicants provide private passwords, Internet pseudonyms, text messages, and e-mail logs to allow the agency even greater access to information for the hiring process.

Among the findings on use of social networking sites are the following:

- In Massachusetts, an agency requested electronic message logs and found a recruit's text messages revealed past threats of suicide, resulting in disqualification.
- A New Jersey agency disqualified a candidate for posting racy photographs of himself with scantily clad women.
- Inappropriate officers' postings have been found that range from sexually explicit photographs to racially charged commentary.

Sexual Harassment: Enigma Wrapped in Anachronism

In Chapter 3, we briefly defined and discussed workplace harassment in general; here, it is discussed more in terms of its occurrence in police agencies—and because it still looms large as police agencies attempt to hire more women.

It is almost impossible to fathom that, in this century, sexual harassment still exists in our society, particularly in an occupation as tightly controlled with policies and procedures as policing. Yet it does occur, and is in fact "alive and well." A 2013 study by Lonsway et al.[46] estimated that between one-half and three-fourths of all women working in law enforcement have experienced some form of sexually harassing behavior in their workplace, and about 84 percent of their respondents indicated they had experienced such behavior in the past year. Lonsway et al.[47] found that most of these behaviors involved "dirty stories or jokes," statements that "put women down," were typically performed by a coworker, and were most likely unreported (only about 5% filing a formal complaint). More disturbingly, unwanted sexual attention that was physical in nature and *quid pro quo* harassment (where one offers another person a condition of employment or job-related benefits, such as promotion, salary increases, shift or work assignments, in exchange for sexual favors), although less frequently experienced by the respondents, was more likely to be committed by a supervisor. Furthermore, about half of the respondents who had filed a formal complaint experienced retaliation as a result.[48]

Clearly, supervisors and administrators in policing (and, where it occurs, in courts and in prisons) should be aware that this study demonstrates a "high incidence" of such behaviors can and does still occur. Such administrators must, as Lonsway et al. conclude, "ensure that sexually harassing behaviors are not committed or tolerated within their organizations and, when they do occur, that retaliation does not result."[49]

Summary

This chapter has generally described the challenges, traits, and duties of today's law enforcement executives, middle managers, first-line supervisors, and patrol officers. Clearly, these individuals occupy positions of tremendous responsibility. Police executives, managers, and supervisors must decide what the best leadership method is, both inside and outside their organizations. They must be concerned with their agency's performance and standing with the community, governing board, and rank and file. Their abilities will be challenged in additional ways.

Key Terms and Concepts

Assessment center, p. 112
Chief executive officer (CEO), p. 109
Chief of police, p. 113
First-line supervisor, p. 120
Middle manager, p. 118
Mintzberg model for CEOs, p. 109
Sheriff, p. 117

Questions for Review

1. What are some of the primary roles of a police executive? (Use the three major categories of the Mintzberg model of CEOs in developing your response.) What expectations are placed on them?
2. How does one prepare to enter a law enforcement executive position, and how does one approach the interview and assessment center processes?
3. How do chiefs and sheriffs differ in roles and background?

4. How do the roles and functions of middle managers and sergeants differ?
5. What are examples of "good politics" and "bad politics"?
6. What are the basic tasks and desired traits of patrol officers, and how might leaders go about recruiting and hiring quality personnel?
7. How would you describe the various parts of the "hurdle" (recruitment and hiring) process used by the Kansas City, Missouri, Police Department?
8. How would you define and describe sexual harassment, the extent of the problem in policing, and some possible solutions?

Deliberate and Decide

In recent months, it has become increasingly apparent to your deputy chief of operations that the watch commanders (lieutenants)—and, by extension, sergeants—are not communicating, coordinating, or cooperating well. Specifically, three issues are at the core of the matter:

1. Officers' report writing: two patrol lieutenants have been attempting to improve the quality of officers' reports by rejecting those written efforts that are deemed unacceptable. Other lieutenants, however, believe that, with all of the other pressures on officers to perform, this concern about reports is far too "nitpicky."
2. "Supervisor shopping": due to the above issues with reports, several sergeants and patrol officers, observing the differences in how lieutenants view the report matter, have been "shopping" for lieutenants who are more "sensitive" to their side and will approve their reports.
3. Use of mobile data computers: one year ago all patrol vehicles in the department were equipped with mobile data computers (MDCs) to improve officer efficiency in the field and to relieve the burden on the communications section. Now, however, sharp differences of opinion exist about when it is practical and appropriate to use the MDCs; the deputy chief has learned that officers in fact use them infrequently in the field, and practically never during traffic stops—resulting once again on a heavy workload for dispatchers. Some lieutenants have differences of opinion about when/how MDCs should be used.

Questions for Discussion

1. What is your evaluation of the overall problem and causal factors?
2. If left unchecked, what affect can these problems have on the agency?
3. What recommended changes would you propose to correct the problems, especially as they relate to interaction between management, supervision, and the rank and file.

Learn by Doing

1. Your criminal justice professor has been hired as a consultant with an area police agency to develop and help conduct an assessment center for a sergeant's promotional examination. You are asked to assist him in doing so. What kinds of testing activities would you believe should be included at minimum, and how will you arrange to have the candidates' performance evaluated?
2. You are guest lecturing before a group of university students in a criminal justice organization and administration class. One of the students indicates confusion about the use of organizational structures in general as well as the roles of middle managers (captains and lieutenants) in specific. Provide an explanation.

Case Study

Applying the Mintzberg Model for CEOs

You have been the Park City police chief for 6 months, overseeing an agency of 60 sworn officers in a community of 80,000 people; your city abuts another larger city, with a population of 160,000. These populations are deceptive, however, soaring during the summertime, because your area is a tourist-based gaming destination. Today is July 3, and at 8:00 A.M. you briefly attend a staff meeting of detectives, led by a deputy chief of operations, to learn the latest information concerning a highly publicized kidnapping. In the afternoon, you plan to deliver a news release concerning the case status. Then you will give the graduation speech at the area police academy, which is followed by your attending a meeting of the Tri-County Regional Major Case Squad, where you will discuss the latest intelligence information concerning a ring of circulating slot machine cheaters in your jurisdiction. You then learn from Dispatch that one of your motorcycle officers has gone down, and you speed to the hospital emergency room to wish him well. You then meet with your events staff and other city officials to finalize security and traffic plans for tomorrow's huge fireworks display because last year's event resulted in huge numbers of alcohol-related traffic and fighting arrests. You are also scheduled to ride in a car in the holiday parade. At day's end, you make final preparations for your July 5 presentation to the city council concerning the need for a modern, 800-megahertz communications system, which you hope to convince the council to purchase. You also will be attending a special ceremony at a city park that honors area law enforcement officers who have been killed in the line of duty.

Questions for Discussion

1. Using Mintzberg's model for CEOs, how would you classify each of the functions described into the interpersonal, informational, decision-maker—as well as any subcategory—roles.
2. Which of these roles, if any, do you believe to be more "weighty" and important for the chief executive officer?

Notes

1. Police Executive Research Forum, *Advice from Police Chiefs and Community Leaders on Building Trust: "Ask for Help, Work Together, and Show Respect,"* March 2016, p. 1, http://www.policeforum.org/assets/policecommunitytrust.pdf.
2. Henry Mintzberg, "The Manager's Job: Folklore and Fact," *Harvard Business Review* 53 (July–August 1975): 49–61.
3. Adapted from William E. Kirchoff, Charlotte Lansinger, and James Burack, *Command Performance: Career Guide for Police Executives,* 2nd ed. (Washington, DC: Police Executive Research Forum, 2015), pp. 149–151.
4. Ibid., p. 148.
5. For a comprehensive look at the assessment center process and tips for how to participate as a candidate, see John L . Coleman, *Police Assessment Testing: An Assessment Center Handbook for Law Enforcement Personnel* (Springfield, IL: Charles C Thomas, 2002).
6. John Gray, "The Chief's Interview," *Law and Order* 59 (10) (October 2011): 82–85; much of this discussion and several interview items are also based on the author's experiences with assessment centers and oral boards.
7. Kerchoff et al., *Command Performance*, p. 151.
8. Ibid., pp. 156–157.
9. Janice K. Penegor and Ken Peak, "Police Chief Acquisitions: A Comparison of Internal and External Selections," *American Journal of Police* 11 (1992): 17–32.
10. Norm Stamper, *Breaking Rank: A Top Cop's Exposé of the Dark Side of American Policing* (New York: Nation Books, 2005), p. 185.
11. Ibid.
12. Kevin Johnson, "Amid Heightened Scrutiny, It's 'A Precarious Time' for U.S. Police Chiefs," *USA Today*, May 24, 2016, http://www.usatoday.com/story/news/nation/2016/05/23/police-chiefs-ferguson-san-francisco/84785128/
13. John Bacon, "Top Cop Sorry for 'Historical Mistreatment' of Minorities," *USA Today*, October 18, 2016, http://www.usatoday.com/story/news/nation/2016/10/18/top-cop-sorry-historical-mistreatment-minorities/92348646/.
14. Bureau of Justice Statistics, *Sheriff's Office Personnel*, 1993–2013 (June 2016), http://www.bjs.gov/content/pub/pdf/sop9313_sum.pdf.
15. Clemens Bartollas, Stuart J. Miller, and Paul B. Wice, *Participants in American Criminal Justice: The Promise and the Performance* (Englewood Cliffs, NJ: Prentice Hall, 1983), p. 35.
16. Charles R. Swanson, Leonard Territo, and Robert W . Taylor, *Police Administration: Structures, Processes, and Behavior,* 6th ed. (Upper Saddle River, NJ: Prentice Hall, 2005), pp. 129–130.
17. National Sheriffs Association, "Elected Office of the Sheriff: Executive Summary" (n.d.), https://www.sheriffs.org/sites/default/files/tb/The_Elected_Office_of_Sheriff_-_An_Executive_Summary.pdf;
18. Colin Hayes, "The Office of Sheriff in the United States," *The Prison Journal* 74 (2001): 50–54. For data concerning demographic makeup and employment trends of persons employed by the nation's sheriffs' offices, see U.S. Department of Justice, Bureau of Justice Statistics, *Sheriffs' Office Personnel, 1993–2013,* June 2016, http://www.bjs.gov/content/pub/pdf/sop9313.pdf
19. Leonhard F. Fuld, *Police Administration* (New York: G. P. Putnam's Sons, 1909), pp. 59–60.
20. See Kenneth J. Peak, Larry K. Gaines, and Ronald W. Glensor, *Police Supervision and Management: In an Era of Community Policing,* 2nd ed. (Upper Saddle River, NJ: Prentice Hall, 2004), pp. 33–34.
21. Ibid., p. 33.
22. Richard N. Holden, *Modern Police Management,* 2nd ed. (Upper Saddle River, NJ: Prentice Hall, 1994), pp. 294–295.
23. Peak et al., *Police Supervision and Management,* Chapter 2 generally.
24. Robin S. Engel, "Patrol Officer Supervision in the Community Policing Era," *Journal of Criminal Justice* 30 (2002): 51–64.
25. Dara Lind, "The 'Ferguson Effect,' A Theory That's Warping the American Crime Debate, Explained," *Vox*, http://www.vox.com/2016/5/18/11683594/ferguson-effect-crime-police.

26. Alex Altman, "Is the Ferguson Effect for Real? Obama and the FBI Director Square Off," *Time*, November 9, 2015, pp. 7–8.
27. Quoted in Heather MacDonald, "The Nationwide Crime Wave Is Building," *The Wall Street Journal*, May 16, 2016, http://www.wsj.com/articles/the-nationwide-crime-wave-is-building-1464045462.
28. New York: Encounter Books, 2016.
29. Quoted in Heather MacDonald, "The Nationwide Crime Wave Is Building."
30. Eric Lichtblau, "F.B.I. Director Says 'Viral Video Effect' Blunts Police Work," *The New York Times*, May 11, 2016, http://www.nytimes.com/2016/05/12/us/comey-ferguson-effect-police-videos-fbi.html.
31. Neil Gross, "Is There a 'Ferguson Effect'"? *The New York Times*, September 30, 2016, http://www.nytimes.com/2016/10/02/opinion/sunday/is-there-a-ferguson-effect.html?_r=0.
32. Daniel Denvir, "The Ferguson Effect Debunked: The Theory Not Only Lacks Evidence, It Makes No Sense," *Salon*, June 30, 2016, http://www.salon.com/2016/06/03/the_ferguson_effect_debunked_the_theory_not_only_lacks_evidence_it_makes_no_sense/.
33. Altman, "Is the Ferguson Effect for Real?" p. 8.
34. Derek Hawkins, "'Ferguson Effect'? Savagely Beaten Cop Didn't Draw Gun for Fear of Media Uproar, Says Chicago Police Chief," *The Washington Post*, October 7, 2016, https://www.washingtonpost.com/news/morning-mix/wp/2016/10/07/ferguson-effect-savagely-beaten-cop-didnt-draw-gun-for-fear-of-media-uproar-says-chicago-police-chief/.
35. Kenneth J. Peak, *Policing America: Challenges and Best Practices,* 8th ed. (Columbus, OH: Pearson Education, Inc., 2015), p. 71.
36. Lawrence S. Wrightsman, *Psychology and the Legal System* (Monterey, CA: Brooks/Cole, 1987), pp. 85–86.
37. Jeremy M. Wilson and Clifford A. Grammich, *Police Recruitment and Retention in the Contemporary Urban Environment: A National Discussion of Personnel Experiences and Promising Practices from the Front Lines* (Santa Monica, CA: RAND Corporation, 2009), p. 5; also available at: http://www.rand.org/pubs/conf_proceedings/2009/RAND_CF261.pdf.
38. Ibid., p. 2.
39. Stephanie Slahor, "RAND Study Suggests Strategies to Address Recruiting Shortage," *Law and Order* (December 8, 2008): 32.
40. Ibid., p. 18.
41. Ibid., pp. 18–19.
42. Ibid.
43. Slahor, "RAND Study Suggests Strategies to Address Recruiting Shortage," pp. 32–38.
44. Excerpt from Careers: Law Enforcement Hiring Process. Copyright by Kansas City, Missouri, Police Department. Used by permission of Kansas City, Missouri, Police Department.
45. Based on Kevin Johnson, "Cops Get Screened for Digital Dirt," *USA TODAY*, November 12, 2010, http://www.usatoday.com/tech/news/2010-11-12-1-Afacebookcops12_ST_N.htm; also see Martha Stonebrook and Rick Stubbs, "Social Networking in Law Enforcement," International Association of Chiefs of Police 2010 Annual Conference, Orlando, Florida, http://www.aele.org/los2010s&s.pdf.
46. Kimberly A. Lonsway, Rebecca Paynich, and Jennifer N. Hall, "Sexual Harassment in Law Enforcement: Incidence, Impact, and Perception," *Police Quarterly* 16(2) (June 2014): 177–210.
47. Ibid.
48. Ibid.
49. Ibid.

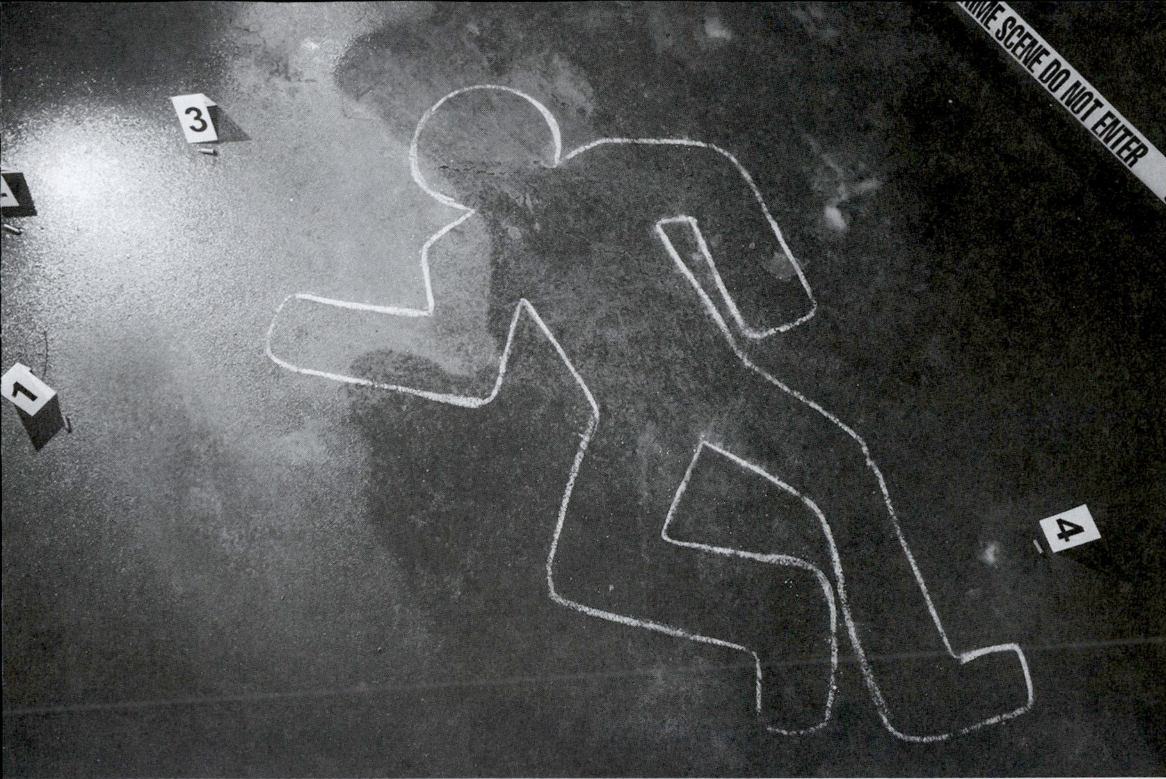

Fer Gregory/Shutterstock

6 Police Issues and Practices

LEARNING OBJECTIVES

After reading this chapter, the student will be able to:

1. *explain reasons for the national uproar with police shootings*
2. *provide rationales for a national database of police uses of force and examples of the kinds of policies needed for governing it*
3. *review reasons in favor of, and militating against, police use of body-worn cameras*
4. *explain how and why police leaders must implement de-escalation training*
5. *describe how to better manage officers' use of force, including identifying the types of officers and situations that tend to foster it, use-of-force continuums, using force with persons having mental disorders, and vehicle pursuits*
6. *review reasons for and against units of government having citizen review boards*
7. *describe how use of consent decrees for police agencies can foster constitutional policing*
8. *explain the new police approaches to active shooters*

9. *describe some of the hazards of and the personal toll taken on police officers as a result of their occupation*
10. *explain the meaning of officer wellness, the steps for developing an agency wellness campaign, and how training, policies, and technologies relate to officer wellness*

Introduction

Other chapters of this book focused, or will focus, on some of the pressing issues and contemporary practices of law enforcement executives, specifically issues relating to police organization, operations, and personnel; later chapters, for example, will focus on ethics, liability, financial administration, and the application of new technologies.

This chapter looks at some issues that are equally—if not more—challenging. Many years ago someone said, with tongue in cheek, that to be a police officer one needed "a size 3 hat and a size 43 jacket." Given the kinds of topics that are discussed in this chapter, this description could not be further from the truth today. In several ways, the police have increasingly been placed under the microscope with regard to how they deal with (and are viewed by) the public, exercise their force prerogative, and generally deal with crisis situations. At the same time, they are confronted with many dangers and physical/mental illnesses that take a toll as a result of doing their job. These are the foci of this chapter.

The chapter begins with an examination of what is certainly at the forefront of public concern regarding police practices: shooting deaths by police and use of force against the public. Included are the need for a related database, the demand for body-worn cameras, and how to de-escalate crisis situations. Then we consider several facets of how law enforcement executives must manage the use of force, including how they deal with active shooter situations and mentally ill individuals. Finally, we review the types of dangers that confront police officers and the means of prioritizing and developing a formal agency-wide wellness and safety program for them. We conclude the chapter with review questions and exercises in the Deliberate and Decide, Learn by Doing, and Case Study sections.

Police Shootings: Conundrum and Controversy

As indicated above, nothing can inflame a community and raise tensions like deaths by police shootings, such as those in Ferguson, Missouri, and other U.S. cities (discussed in Chapters 4 and 5). Certainly the police, for their part, can employ a use-of-force continuum (as described below) and engage in a variety of "shoot/don't shoot" training sessions to better understand when to unholster and use their firearms. However, on the public's side, these highly publicized police shootings represent much broader issues of accountability, prejudicial behavior against minority group members, a serious lack of shooting data, and declining police–community relations in general.

America's Angst

By the end of 2015, the number of people killed by law enforcement in the United States had reached 1,000 after officers in Oakland, California, shot dead a man who allegedly pointed a replica gun at them; the media would inform Americans that African Americans were more than twice as likely to be unarmed as white Americans when killed by police.[1]

It would certainly be difficult for anyone to argue that all such shootings were unlawful or unjustified, such as the case of a 77-year-old man in a high-rise apartment in

Birmingham, Alabama, who police shot when he answered his door with a gun. But then there are cases such as the 17-year-old girl gunned down by police while joyriding in a stolen car in Denver.[2]

These incidents that also involve minority group members will often heighten the tension and lead to charges of racism against the entire police agency. One *Washington Post* columnist offered that "it is the police culture, more than race, that is at the crux of the problem . . . a mentality of brutality."[3] In this same regard, Human Rights Watch stated the following:

> The excessive use of force by police officers, including unjustified shootings, severe beatings, fatal chokings, and rough treatment, persists because overwhelming barriers to accountability make it possible for officers who commit human rights violations to escape due punishment and often to repeat their offenses.[4]

Wanted: A National Use-of-Force Database

As indicated in Chapter 4, there is great concern with transparency regarding police shootings. Inexplicably, no one knows the actual number of police shooting deaths, incidents causing serious bodily injury, or discharge of firearm—or how many of them were deemed unjustified.

Until now no one has been required to submit this information; therefore, many police departments choose not to.[5] Certainly from policymakers', police trainers', and researchers' perspectives, having to rely on guesswork concerning the nature and extent of police use of force is less than ideal. For this reason, the President's Task Force on 21st Century Policing recommended in 2015 that "agencies should have comprehensive policies on the use of force that include training, investigations, prosecutions, data collection, and information sharing. These policies must be clear, concise, and openly available for public inspection."[6]

The FBI announced in late 2016 that in early 2017 it would be launching a pilot program to collect data on police shootings and other incidents of nonlethal force. As a direct result of the persistent, racially charged incidents from 2014 to present, data will be collected in these areas first in federal law enforcement agencies and eventually from state and local agencies. This effort will go beyond the Death in Custody Reporting Act of 2014, which only requires reporting of civilian *deaths* during police encounters or custody.[7]

The Importance of Use-of-Force Policymaking

At first blush, the development of policies concerning use of force might seem insignificant, at least in terms of how such policies are applied in the field, when officers must often make split decisions. However, a breakdown of use-of-force incidents can lead to informed and improved policymaking and even dramatically reduce deadly encounters.[8]

For example, several years ago a New York City Police Department prohibited officers from shooting at or from a moving vehicle, unless a person in the vehicle is using or threatening deadly force. That policy resulted in an immediate, sharp reduction in uses of lethal force in New York City.[9] Following are other examples of use-of-force policies that have been enacted:

- The use of deadly force is prohibited against individuals who pose a danger only to themselves and not to other members of the public or to officers.
- All critical police incidents resulting in death or serious bodily injury will be reviewed by specially trained personnel. Other uses of force should be investigated by the officer's supervisor and reviewed through the chain of command.
- Supervisors should respond to the scene of any use-of-force incident to initiate the investigation.
- All non-training-related firearms discharges will be investigated, regardless of whether the subject was struck.
- The agency will publish regular reports on their officers' use of force, including officer-involved shootings, deployment of less-lethal options, and use of canines.

- The agency will periodically check to make sure that the academy training is consistent with such policies.
- The use of force should embrace the sanctity of human life, with de-escalation as agency policy and a duty to intervene with officers who may be using excessive force.
- Officers have a duty to intervene when observing colleagues using excessive force.[10]

Posting Information about Police Shootings

Some police agencies now demonstrate complete openness regarding officer-involved shootings. An example is provided in Exhibit 6.1; it shows facts and outcomes of such a shooting as provided by the Dallas, Texas, Police Department's website.

EXHIBIT 6.1

DALLAS POLICE DEPARTMENT'S POSTINGS OF INFORMATION CONCERNING OFFICER-INVOLVED SHOOTINGS[11]

On Monday, December 9, 2013, at approximately 3:11 P.M., plainclothes deployment officers were conducting surveillance on a vehicle at 9524 Military Parkway that had been taken in a robbery offense. The vehicle became occupied by two individuals and a felony traffic stop supported by uniformed officers in marked vehicles was attempted outside the apartment complex. The vehicle did not stop and turned back into the complex. The driver fled on foot and the passenger remained in the vehicle. One officer approached the vehicle, pulled her weapon, and fired one time at the B/M/19 suspect striking him. The suspect was injured and transported to Baylor Hospital.

Suspect was unarmed. The officer was terminated for violation of departmental policy and later indicted by a Dallas County Grand Jury for aggravated assault. No officer was injured.

One officer fired 1 round. Involved Officer: W/F 12 years, 3 months service.

The Cry Heard Round the Country: "Wear Body Cameras!"

Two national ramifications of the recent rash of controversial police shootings across the United States have been an examination of police methods and an emphasis on greater police transparency—both of which include a cry for police **body-worn cameras** (BWC). With peoples' cellphones often recording what appear to many people to be questionable cases of police use of force, many politicians and activists argue that all officers should be compelled to use BWC.

EXHIBIT 6.2

BORDER AGENTS OPT NOT TO WEAR BODY CAMERAS

Even in the face of national cry for police body-worn cameras, in late 2015 the federal U.S. Customs and Border Protection agency decided against requiring its agents to wear them. After a yearlong internal study, administrators said a full-scale deployment on every person is not necessary. They argue that the cameras will not work for agents in the brush, only lasting a few months before they became gummed up with dirt; also noted was the cost: wide-scale deployment of the cameras would cost tens of millions of dollars.[12]

As is often the case with the implementation of new criminal justice policies and procedures, however, "the devil is in the details." Putting such a practice into effect carries a number of hidden issues and problems (see, for example, Exhibit 6.2). Indeed, according to Cindy Shain, director of the Southern Police Institute at the University of Louisville, the following issues accompany police use of body-worn cameras and must be addressed:[13]

1. ***Legal issues (privacy):*** certainly many kinds of potentially sensitive images can be captured, of both citizens and police. Should videos be made that are publicly embarrassing, such as people who are being arrested or are intoxicated? Would videos be made of strip searches and interviews of suspects? Of innocent child victims, witnesses, confidential informants, and bystanders? People who are suspects but not yet charged with a crime? What about officers' reasonable right to privacy, such as during bathroom or lunch breaks or in private conversations? Finally, who should be allowed to view the videos?[14]
2. ***Storage and related costs:*** as one expert put it, the "800-pound gorilla in the room" with BWC is that unless state laws are changed, the ability of, and cost for, police to dedicate personnel and equipment to store, redact, and provide videos for all open-records requests (to include those by defense attorneys) would be extremely challenging if not impossible. Therefore, body cameras can carry tremendous costs—not only from the equipment itself but also from the time required to store and edit the videos. A related issue is that Freedom of Information Act (FOIA) requests are often from individuals or companies wishing to post police activity on YouTube and sell advertising space.[15]
3. ***Personnel considerations:*** relating to the above cost considerations is the added—possibly exorbitant—cost of increased staffing to handle all the requests related to evidence, redaction, preparing evidence for court, and open records requests. See Exhibit 6.3.
4. ***Policies and procedures concerning the equipment:*** directives must be established and include protocols concerning how the equipment will be deployed, generally. At minimum, they should include where the cameras will be worn (e.g., hat, sunglasses, chest); who will maintain, charge, and issue new cameras; training to be provided in when to activate and deactivate cameras; where data will be stored and safeguarded; how to protect and document the chain of custody; and the process for releasing recorded data to the public (including redaction processes).[16]

EXHIBIT 6.3

CELLPHONES MAY SOON REPLACE BODY CAMERAS

Perhaps not surprisingly, a new smartphone app has been announced as a solution for police agencies seeking more accessible and inexpensive means for officers to record audio and video. In mid-2017 the Jersey City, New Jersey, Police Department announced its testing of the app with 250 officers.[17]

The officers simply had to download the app on a smartphone, strap the phone onto their chest, and simply push a button to begin recording; the video is streamed live to supervisors who can monitor the recording from their offices. The entire encounter is then saved onto a server, saving officers having to download all of their shift video at end of shift. The app is free to any police department, thus offsetting a major barrier to body camera use: the cost. Test runs of the app already done in Rio de Janeiro, South Africa, and Bulgaria show that officers are quick to adapt to the app.[18]

De-escalating Crises: No "Line in the Sand"

Sometimes the best course of action for police officers is to take *no action*. That is the general idea behind the current emphasis (following the aforementioned spate of police shootings and riots) on de-escalation training for officers—an area of training identified by a national think tank that has been sorely underserved.

Police officers are probably, for the most part, action-oriented, take charge, no-retreat individuals and thus constitute a culture that encourages engagement when someone is endangering themselves or others. Indeed, police culture can overshadow agency policy. The mentality of "We need to draw a line in the sand—we can't wait around forever"[19] can take hold; certainly that mentality can kick in prior to officer-involved shootings.

Certainly a rush to action is justified in some circumstances, such as those involving active shooters, discussed above, or at felony crimes in progress where the public's safety is in jeopardy. But in many other instances—particularly those involving a mentally ill person who is having difficulty understanding what officers want them to do or why—undue haste can lead to tragic and unnecessary consequences. In addition, rushing to action can endanger the officers themselves. In short, the idea is that officers should not unnecessarily escalate situations themselves.

When officers can maintain a safe distance from a person who is holding a knife or throwing rocks while trying to defuse the situation through communication and other de-escalation strategies, they are in a better position to avoid lethal force or impose serious physical injury to anyone, including themselves.[20]

The Police Executive Research Forum, in its publication *Guiding Principles on Use of Force*, maintains that this type of approach involves a concept termed *proportionality*, which takes into account whether a particular police use of force is proportional to the threat posed by the subject and is appropriate given the totality of the circumstances. Here, the officer is to consider various available levels of force for mitigating the threat, and whether there is a less injurious option available. Under proportionality, the officer should also consider how his or her actions will be viewed by their own agencies per its policy, as well as by the general public, given the circumstances.[21]

This does *not* mean that officers are to attempt to "stop the action" and hesitate or dwell at length on options or how the agency and public might react.[22] And certainly officers should never jeopardize their own safety. The agency and public understand that, in some circumstances, deadly force is a proportional response. In other situations, however, such as a person with mental illness holding a knife at his side, a proportional response might be tactically repositioning (i.e., moving away from the threat and using cover, such as a squad car), bringing in additional resources, and communicating with the person.[23]

EXHIBIT 6.4

DE-ESCALATION TRAINING

In mid-2015 the NYPD launched a four-day program that was incorporated into standard training and issued a requirement that officers take annual refresher courses. The department already had a small, highly trained unit of officers for dealing with mentally ill individuals, but the new four-day training program is meant to give more officers a better chance at de-escalating crisis situations.[24]

Managing the Use of Force: Issues, Practices, Controversies

The International Association of Chiefs of Police (IACP) has defined force as "that amount of effort required by police to compel compliance from an unwilling subject."[25] Next we discuss police **use of force** in several contexts: its lawful application; types; the characteristics of officers and situations in which force is more heavily involved; use with persons who have mental disorders, new responses to active shooters, vehicle pursuits, use-of-force continuums, and reporting and investigating occurrences.

use of force the amount of effort required by police or other criminal justice functionary to compel compliance by an unwilling subject.

Power to Be Used Judiciously

Certainly the events (riots, looting, protests, and shootings) that ensued following the August 2014 police killing of Michael Brown—a young, unarmed African American—in Ferguson, Missouri, underscored the ongoing volatility and controversial nature of police shootings and use of force. There, police reactions to the community's unrest, which included activating the state's national guard, also revived the debate about whether the police are becoming too militarized (discussed in Chapter 4).[26] The Ferguson shooting's aftermath—reminiscent of the rage and disorder occurring in the United States during the 1960s and 1970s—also laid bare the fact that much work remains to be done with respect to police–minority relations in many cities of this nation.

Americans bestow a tremendous amount of authority on their police officers. Indeed, the police are the only element of our society (except for the military, under certain circumstances) that is allowed to use force against its citizens, up to and including lethal force. The *quid pro quo*, however, is that the police are given this power and authority with the expectation that they will use it judiciously, only when necessary, and as a last resort. A serious problem arises when officers deploy this force improperly.

Regardless of the type of force used, police officers must use it in a legally acceptable manner. The U.S. Supreme Court ruled that the use of force at arrest must be

> [o]bjectively reasonable in view of all the facts and circumstances of each particular case, including the severity of the crime at issue, whether the suspect poses an immediate threat to the safety of the officers or others, and whether he is actively resisting arrest or attempting to evade arrest by flight.[27]

However, determining what constitutes "objectively reasonable" is not an easy task; we discuss this concept more below.

A Typology of Abuse of Authority

The use-of-force continuum (discussed below) shows the range of force that officers can employ. David Carter[28] looked at officers' conduct and provided a typology of abuse of authority, which includes (1) physical abuse/excessive force, (2) verbal/psychological abuse, and (3) legal abuse/violations of civil rights.

- ***Physical Abuse and Excessive Force***: Police use of physical force often results in substantial public scrutiny. Local incidents may not receive national media coverage, but they often have the same dramatic, chilling effect in a community. The application of deadly force can be a form of excessive force. When a police officer deliberately kills someone, a determination is made as to whether the homicide was justified to prevent imminent death or serious bodily injury to the officer or another person. As discussed earlier, in 1985, the U.S. Supreme Court ruled that the shooting of any unarmed, nonviolent fleeing felony suspect violates the Fourth Amendment to the Constitution.[29] As a result, almost all major urban police departments enacted restrictive policies regarding deadly force.

- ***Verbal and Psychological Abuse***: Police officers sometimes inflict verbal and psychological abuse on citizens by berating or belittling them. One of the most common methods used by police officers to verbally abuse citizens is through the use of profanity. Unfortunately, profanity has become a part of the police culture and of many officers' everyday speech. When profanity is used liberally in the work setting, it increases the likelihood that it will be used inappropriately.
- ***Legal Abuse and Violations of Civil Rights***: Certain police actions violate citizens' constitutional or statutory rights, such as false arrest, false imprisonment, and harassment. Supervisors and managers play a key role in preventing legal abuse and violations of citizens' civil rights. Supervisors should ensure that officers' decisions to arrest are based on probable cause, not some lesser standard. They should also review arrest reports and question officers when arrests are not observed to ensure that they meet the probable cause standard.

Use-of-Force Continuums

use-of-force continuum a graphic depiction of levels of force used by police to determine the type of force that is appropriate for certain types of citizen resistance.

Use-of-force continuums have been evolving for over three decades; they serve as a guideline that officers can use to determine the type of force that is appropriate for certain types of citizen resistance they encounter.

Graphically, continuums can be depicted as a simple staircase or ladder to a more elaborate wheel or matrix. A simple linear use-of-force continuum might contain the following five escalating steps: officer presence/verbal direction, touch control, empty-hand tactics and chemical agents, handheld impact weapons, and lethal force.[30]

Today, many police executives and researchers are uncomfortable with the above simplistic, sequential depiction of the force continuum, believing that use of force cannot always be determined and employed in such a sequential fashion. So the question remains: How much force is reasonable for a police officer to use against a suspect? Force continuums also fail to represent properly the dynamic encounter between the officer and a resistant suspect vis-à-vis the wide array of tools (e.g., a baton, pepper spray, electronic control device, or other, less lethal weapons) that are available to officers.

Instead, many agencies now require their officers to be "objectively reasonable" in their use of force, defined by the International Association of Chiefs of Police as "based upon the totality of the circumstances known or perceived by him or her at the time force was used."[31]

A new approach to determine proper use of force has recently been developed by two special agents of the Federal Bureau of Investigation (FBI), which is felt to "more accurately reflect the intent of the law and the changing expectations of society" and provide officers with "simple, clear, unambiguous, and consistent guidelines in the use of force."[32]

Known as the dynamic resistance response model, or DRRM, this approach combines a use-of-force continuum with the behaviors of suspects. *Dynamic* indicates that the model is fluid, and *resistance* demonstrates that the suspect controls the interaction. In sum, the suspect's level of resistance determines the officer's response. The model in Figure 6-1 ■ shows how suspects' actions are divided into one of four categories.

As shown in Figure 6-1, if a passively resistant suspect fails to follow commands and perhaps attempts to move away from the officer or escape, appropriate responses include using a firm grip, control holds, and pressure points to gain compliance. Conversely, an aggressively resistant suspect—one who is attempting to push, throw, strike, tackle, or physically harm the officer—would call for such responses as the use of personal weapons

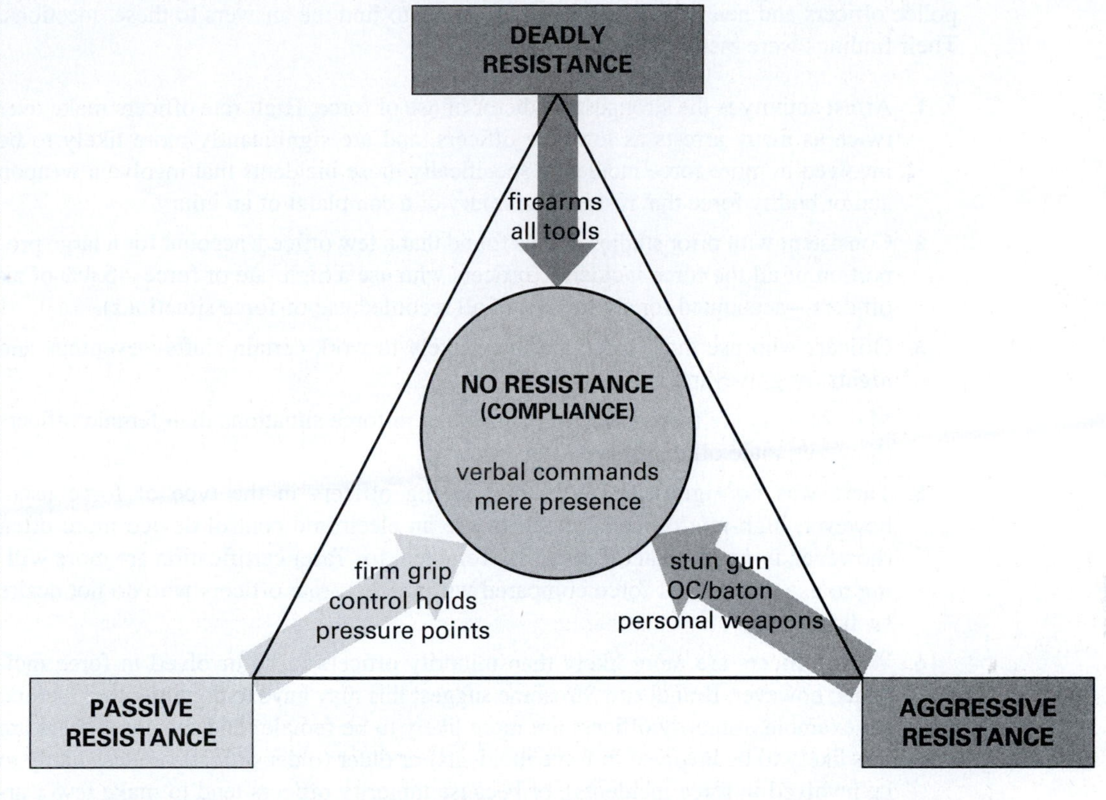

Typical configuration of the dynamic resistance response model with traditional use-of-force options

FIGURE 6-1 Dynamic Resistance Response Model

Source: From Charles Joyner and Chad Basile, "The Dynamic Resistance Response Model," *FBI Law Enforcement Bulletin*, September 2007, p. 19.

(hands, fists, and feet), batons, pepper spray, and a stun gun. Finally, because a deadly resistant (i.e., lethal force is being or is about to be utilized) suspect can seriously injure or kill the officer or another person, the officer is justified in using force, including deadly force, as is *objectively reasonable* to overcome the offender. In the model, a suspect's lack of resistance (compliance) is in the center of the triangle, which is emphasized as the goal of every encounter. However, if a suspect's resistance level places him or her on one of the three corners of the triangle, the officer's response is intended to move the suspect's behavior to the center of the triangle and compliance.

Does a Particular "Type" of Officer Use More Force?

Do certain characteristics—"types"—of officers predispose them to be more (or less) likely to engage in the use of force? Are there differences in terms of officer gender, race, type and place of assignment, length of service, and so on? These are important policy questions that can, if answered, certainly affect how agencies recruit, hire, train, and assign their officers.

A recent study by Steven Brandl and Meghan Stroshine[33] analyzed more than 1,000 police officers and nearly 500 use-of-force reports to find the answers to these questions. Their findings were instructive:

1. Arrest activity is the strongest predictor of use of force. High-rate officers make over twice as many arrests as low-rate officers, and are significantly more likely to be involved in more force incidents, specifically those incidents that involve a weapon and/or bodily force that result in an injury or a complaint of an injury.
2. Consistent with prior studies, it was found that a few officers account for a large proportion of all the force incidents (officers who use a high rate of force—5.4% of all officers—accounted for about 32% of all recorded use-of-force situations).
3. Officers who use more force are more likely to work certain shifts—evenings and nights (or graveyard).
4. Male officers are more likely to be involved in force situations than female officers (however, male officers make more arrests).
5. There was no significant difference among officers in the type of force used; however, high-rate officers tended to use an electronic control device more often (however, it may be that officers who volunteer for Taser certification are more willing to use any type of force compared with the low-rate officers who do not desire such training).
6. White officers are more likely than minority officers to be involved in force incidents; however, Brandl and Stroshine suggest this may have to do with other factors; for example, minority officers are more likely to be female (and female officers are less likely to be involved in force incidents) or older (older officers are less likely to be involved in force incidents), or because minority officers tend to make fewer arrests, they might have less likelihood of being involved in force situations.

Previous research also indicates that the location/type of patrol assignment may be related to use of force, as high-crime areas may foster conditions where use of force is more frequently necessary. There are also indications that time of day may be correlated with use-of-force incidents: serious crime and arrests are more likely to occur during the late evening/early morning hours. Finally, it is indicated that officers who are more active (in terms of the number of arrests made) may be more often involved in use-of-force situations.[34]

Use of Force on Persons with Mental Disorders

A topic that has recently gained considerable attention concerns police treatment of persons suffering from mental disorders. Several studies have attempted to determine the extent to which officers encounter such persons, and if force is used by, and against, the police in such encounters. First, findings suggest that many police believe that dealing with persons having mental disorders is dangerous, because such individuals are more likely to use violence (although this belief is not borne out by the existing research; rather, studies show that it is primarily when people are under the influence of drugs—rather than mental illness or alcohol—that police must use force). Police have also reported that they use more severe levels of force on suspects who appear to be mentally unstable—force which is justified because of the suspects' more aggressive behavior. It has also been suggested that police disproportionately use pepper spray against such individuals.[35]

It is clear that although the proportion of incidents of use of force with persons having actual mental disorders is relatively small, it remains that dealing with such persons is a significant portion of the police workload; therefore, because such persons may seem irrational and unstable, and threaten to use (and may actually use) weapons on the police, officers need to be trained in communicating and verbally de-escalating incidents with people who are mentally disordered to minimize the likelihood of either party being injured. It is suggested that such training be standardized, focusing on risk assessment and management, while emphasizing the importance of cordoning and managing such situations and thus avoid situations where force must be deployed.[36] This training and overall policy development can be developed through partnering with mental health agencies.

Vehicle Pursuits

Another policing matter that is at the heart of police use of force concerns high-speed **vehicle pursuits** where police attempt to apprehend someone in a fleeing vehicle who has indicated he or she does not intend to stop or yield. Civil litigation arising out of collisions involving police pursuits reveals it to be a high-stakes undertaking with serious and sometimes tragic results. Several hundred people are killed each year during police pursuits[37]; many of the resulting deaths and injuries involve innocent third parties or stem from minor traffic violations. The U.S. Supreme Court, as discussed in the next section, has strengthened most progressive chase policies, but the Court has also conferred responsibility on the police. The responsibility for ensuring that proper policies and procedures exist rests squarely with the chief executive officer (CEO) of the agency.

vehicle pursuit police attempts to apprehend someone in a fleeing vehicle who has indicated he or she does not intend to stop or yield.

Vehicle pursuits involve a delicate balancing act. On the one hand is the need to show that flight from the law is no way to freedom. If a police agency completely bans high-speed pursuits, its credibility with both law-abiding citizens and law violators may suffer; public knowledge that the agency has a no-pursuit policy may encourage people to flee, decreasing the probability of apprehension.[38]

On the other hand, the high-speed chase threatens everyone within range of the pursuit, including suspects, their passengers, and other drivers or bystanders. One police trainer tells officers to ask themselves a simple question to determine whether to continue a pursuit: "Is this person a threat to the public safety other than the fact that the police are chasing him?" If the officer cannot objectively answer "yes," the pursuit should be terminated.[39]

The following incidents demonstrate the dangerous nature of police pursuits:

- In Omaha, Nebraska, a 70-mile-per-hour pursuit through a residential neighborhood of a motorcyclist for expired license plates ended when the motorcyclist ran a stop sign, crashing into another vehicle and killing the female passenger on the motorcycle.
- A sheriff's deputy in Florida intentionally rammed a vehicle during a pursuit for an outstanding misdemeanor warrant, causing a collision and killing a backseat passenger.
- A police officer pursuing a shoplifter in Mobile, Alabama, crashed into a mall security vehicle, seriously injuring the guard.

In May 1990, two Sacramento County, California, deputies observed a motorcycle with two riders approaching their vehicle at high speed; turning on their red lights, they ordered the driver to stop. The motorcycle operator began to elude the officers, who initiated a pursuit reaching speeds of more than 100 miles per hour over about 1.3 miles. The pursuit ended when the motorcycle crashed; the deputies' vehicle could not stop in time and struck the bike's passenger, killing him. His family sued, and in May 1998, the U.S. Supreme Court, in *County of Sacramento v. Lewis*,[40] held that the proper standard to be employed in these cases is whether the officer's conduct during the pursuit was conscience shocking; it further determined that high-speed chases with no intent to harm suspects do not give rise to liability under the Fourteenth Amendment.[41]

In such pursuits, the field supervisor is responsible for ensuring that proper methods are employed by patrol officers during pursuits, whether the pursuit involves simply a primary pursuing officer and a backup or a more elaborate scenario. Furthermore, it is the responsibility of command personnel and supervisors to ensure that officers thoroughly understand and comply with pursuit policies. Factors to be considered by the courts in evaluating pursuit liability include the following:

- ***The reason for the pursuit.*** Does it justify the actions taken by the officer?
- ***Driving conditions.*** Any factor that could hinder an officer's ability to safely conduct a pursuit should be considered sufficient reason to terminate it.
- ***The use of police warning devices.*** Typically, lights and siren are required by state statutes.
- ***Excessive speed.*** This often depends on the conditions of the environment. For example, a 30-mile-per-hour pursuit in a school zone may be considered excessive and dangerous.
- ***Demonstrations of due regard in officers' actions.*** Officers must create the least danger to all parties affected and maintain the highest degree of protection from liability.
- ***The use of deadly force.*** There are few instances in which officers can justify driving tactics that result in the death of a fleeing driver; such situations include roadblocks, boxing in (which involves police pursuit vehicles surrounding a violator's moving vehicle, and then slowing the violator's vehicle to a stop), and ramming.
- ***Departmental policies and state law.*** These must be obeyed; to do otherwise greatly increases the potential liability of both the officer and the department.[42]

The Early Intervention System: Identifying Problem Employees

An Early Intervention System (EIS) is a computer database police management tool designed to identify officers whose behavior is problematic, as indicated by preselected performance indicator fields determined by the agency. The focus is on helping employees by providing intervention in a voluntary and non-disciplinary format. The program is "early" in the sense that an agency acts on the basis of performance indicators that suggest an officer may be having problems on the job but do not necessarily warrant formal disciplinary action as the initial organizational response. The identification, coupled with a menu of remedial actions, increases agency accountability and offers employees a better opportunity to succeed in their organizations. Evaluations enable supervisors to meet with an employee, discuss his or her performance, and formally record strengths, weaknesses, and expectations. Evaluations also provide supervisors with an opportunity to coach, mentor, and praise desired behavior and to notify employees when unacceptable behavior has been reported.

Most EIS use computer systems or databases to track employee records are housed as a separate entity from the disciplinary system (usually within Internal Affairs units), and are intended to track employee behaviors and any interventions by supervisors. These programs rely on a broad array of performance indicators, including use-of-force incidents, citizen complaints, department and community commendations and awards, court appearances, and arrest reports. Supervisors must be adequately prepared to review the data and, as with traditional performance evaluations, conduct appropriate interventions and follow-up with the employee.[43]

Dealing with Officers' Pain: PTSD

Police officers are necessarily involved with many of the kinds of horrific experiences described above and even, for some, mass shootings (discussed below). Behavioral health experts warn that there is often a "second wave" of suffering that flows from such violent events when, as first responders or survivors, officers struggle with what they have witnessed. One can hardly imagine the level of officers' trauma after being involved with, say, a mass killing like that in Orlando, Florida, in 2016 (49 dead) or the 2012 Sandy Hook Elementary School murders in Newton, Connecticut (26 children and teachers killed).

No amount of training can prepare officers for such critical incidents, so police leaders must understand and be prepared to provide assistance to those officers suffering from post-traumatic stress syndrome (PTSD)—the levels of which can compare with those found in troops who have been to war.[44]

▶ Civilian Review Boards: Blessing—Or Curse?

Extent and Rationale

Given the wisdom of community policing's bringing together citizens and police to address crime and disorder and solve problems, it would seem logical that civilian (or citizen) review boards (CRBs) should be used in order to involve citizens in investigating and overseeing police activities. This is a commonly discussed approach to police accountability, often arising in the wake of fatal police shootings or corruption scandals. It is commonly argued that the public expects—and that CRBs will provide—the kind of independent and transparent oversight of policing that is needed today. There is even a national organization devoted to such boards, the National Association of Civilian Oversight of Law Enforcement, that provides a website, programs, training, conferences, and a number of other resources in this regard.[45]

Today there are more than 200 such entities around the country, though their powers to investigate and punish officers vary.[46] Some such boards are used to investigate disciplinary actions regarding the use of force and in-custody deaths, but also review their police agency's budget and policies, and how police are using body-worn cameras.

Police Distrust

However, there remains a robust debate about whether or not CRBs are beneficial, and if so, which model of citizen oversight should be adopted. Tensions run high when this subject is discussed,[47] and the fact that so few jurisdictions use such boards would indicate that police are winning this debate, arguing that the boards are often politicized and unfair to them.

In the words of Jim Pasco, the executive director of the Fraternal Order of Police, civilians simply are not qualified to judge whether a police officer followed a department's rules governing use of force:

> The fact of the matter is, an officer has to make a split-second decision involving life or death. And the civilian review boards tend to, by definition, be made up of civilians who have no particular experience or insight into what went through that officer's mind… what the circumstances were.[48]

Even the establishment and power of such boards can be tricky, especially where they are independently elected officials who are not accountable to a governing body. In addition, some states' laws protect personnel records of police officers from most public disclosure and block access to investigative records.[49]

In sum, it seems the verdict is apparently still out on whether or not local units of government are helped or hindered by having such citizen input. The President's Task Force on 21st Century Policing has viewed the concept of CRBs favorably: "Some form of civilian oversight of law enforcement is important in order to strengthen trust with the community. Every community should define the appropriate form and structure of civilian oversight to meet the needs of that community."[50]

EXHIBIT 6.5

LESSONS LEARNED: CIVILIAN OVERSIGHT IN BOSTON

The Boston Police Department (BPD) sought to better understand and improve civilian oversight in the complaint review process while also understanding the best practices of complaint and use-of-force review nationally.

Some of the key principles drawn from the inquiry were:

1. The community has a role in complaint review and oversight, and strong civilian oversight models increase communication with the public.
2. Oversight works best when it is triggered automatically.
3. Oversight should be transparent.
4. There is no one best model—models must fit the local needs, structure, and history.

The BPD inquiry found that the use of force by officers is low compared with other departments of similar sizes.[51]

Fostering Constitutional Policing: Use of the Consent Decree

How does a police agency having serious problems involving improper use of force and other inappropriate behaviors alter its entire culture and foster an environment of constitutional policing and legitimacy? One of the ways to foster such meaningful change was made possible by the 1994 Violent Crime Control and Law Enforcement Act, which gives the U.S. Department of Justice's (DOJ) Civil Rights Division authority to investigate state and local law enforcement agencies that it believes have unconstitutional policies or engage in unconstitutional patterns or practices of conduct.[52]

The law allows the DOJ to sue any police agency if it has exhibited a "pattern and practice" of using excessive force and/or violating people's civil rights. Furthermore, such agencies can be compelled to change those practices through what is known as a consent decree (also known as a memorandum of agreement).[53]

Over the past two decades, consent decrees have become critical in forcing police departments to transform what were often brutal, racist, and unaccountable cultures. As noted in Chapter 4, fomenting change in police cultures is often a very daunting task, often requiring many years for officers to understand that they have been operating in an improper and illegal fashion. Exacerbating this change is the fact that police culture often involves bad habits that are handed down from one police generation to the next, and many officers simply eschew change.[54]

So dozens of cities have found themselves placed under consent decree by a court and compelled to change in such areas as policies and training, collecting and analyzing data to allow for the assessment of officer activity, obtaining the necessary technology to effectively track officer activities, and even developing community policing strategies to help rebuild the relationship between the agency and the various stakeholders it serves. If unwilling to comply, the agency can be sued by the DOJ, and possibly even be placed under a receiver who has total control over its operations.[55]

In short, consent decrees can provide an essential blueprint for policing constitutionally, providing detailed goals to be met. This is typically accomplished under the watchful eye of an outside federal monitor (usually a team) and a federal judge, for measuring whether the purposes of the agreement are being achieved.[56] The costs associated for a court-appointed monitor can be very high, with most cities spending at least $1 million per year.[57] However, some cities' cost can exceed several million dollars per year. But on a positive note, a consent decree can often be leveraged so that the DOJ helps with funding such resources as an early intervention system and underlying technology infrastructure to support it.[58]

How should police leaders view consent decrees? Their appropriate mind-set should not be "How do we keep the DOJ from investigating our department?" but rather, "How do we deliver police services in an effective manner that complies with the Constitution and builds public confidence?"[59]

It is also notable that because the DOJ has a lengthy track record of such investigating local police, and each case has produced publicly available information in the form of consent decrees and investigative findings detailing the reforms that were undertaken, no police department should in theory find itself in a position where it can be sued by the federal government.[60]

▶ New Approaches to Active Shooters: A Sea Change

Certainly a topic that is related to police use of force is the concern with mass shootings, particularly those that have occurred in the nation's schools. Still emblazoned in the public conscience are such acts of terrorism as the aforementioned June 2016 shooting deaths of 49 people (53 others being wounded) inside a nightclub in Orlando, Florida, as well as the murders of 14 people (22 seriously wounded) in December 2015 at a government facility in San Bernardino, California.

Such attacks are not of recent origin, going back several decades. What is relatively new, however, is the change in how police address such mass-killer situations, which—because they are defined as incidents in which four or more people are killed by the attacker—actually occur in the United States on average about once every day.[61]

Indeed, much has changed in the decade since the April 1999 mass murders by two shooters at Columbine High School in Golden, Colorado, where 13 people were killed while on-scene officers waited 45 minutes for an elite SWAT team to arrive. As seen in the aforementioned Sandy Hook Elementary School shootings, police have greatly modified their protocols for dealing with such critical incidents. The most immediate change in protocol calls for police across the country to react swiftly to an **active shooter** situation, where an individual is actively engaged in killing or attempting to kill people in a confined and populated area, is that responding officers are being trained to rush toward gunfire and, if necessary, even step over victims in order to stop the active shooter before more lives are lost. Such training is grounded on the assumption that a gunman, in a mass shooting, kills a person every 15 seconds. The old approach, prior to Columbine, was for police to take a contain-and-wait strategy, intended to prevent officers and bystanders from getting killed; first responders would establish a perimeter to contain the situation and then wait for the special-weapons team to go in and neutralize the shooter(s). Now, however, police typically employ so-called contact teams, where officers from any jurisdiction quickly band

active shooter an individual who is actively engaged in killing or attempting to kill people in a confined and populated area.

together to enter a building in formation and confront the shooters. Thus, officers shift the shooter's focus *from* persons in the building *to* the officers. Then the SWAT teams enter to search for any remaining shooters or to attempt to rescue any hostages.

Another change wrought by Columbine is that special-weapons teams now typically have armed medics and rescue teams trained to remove wounded persons under fire.[62]

▶ Officer Wellness and Safety: A Top Priority

An "Uneasy" Time

There is a side of policing, and its administration, that we would prefer to not have to discuss: the harms that are done to officers by virtue of the hazards of their work. Indeed, for more than a century, people have written about the hazards of policing. In 1879, Sir William Gilbert observed that "When constabulary duty's to be done, the policeman's lot is not a happy one."[63] Furthermore, William A. Westley, who performed one of the first sociological studies of police subculture, observed that "[t]he policeman's world is spawned of degradation, corruption and insecurity. He walks alone, a pedestrian in Hell."[64] Finally, we might also borrow a line from Shakespeare's play "King Henry IV" (1597), in which he wrote, "Uneasy lies the head that wears the crown." With a little variation, the same might also be said for today's police officer: "Uneasy lies the head that wears the badge."

The job of policing has never been easy, but the danger and frustration that have always accompanied the work of policing seem to be at higher levels today than ever before, as they daily confront heavily armed, arrogant, and often mentally disturbed offenders. Furthermore, as will be seen later, exacerbating this situation is the fact that even their own organizations and policies and practices generate tremendous levels of stress for officers.

In addition, the recent Great Recession translated into safety and wellness issues for the police, as budget cuts often resulted in layoffs, furloughs, hiring freezes, retirement incentives, as well as reduction or elimination of police training and health prevention programs. Such cutbacks also resulted in larger patrol areas to cover, declines in the number of available backup officers, and increased stress levels.

Therefore, police administrators must be concerned with the health and well-being of their employees, ensuring that employees are mentally and physically prepared for the challenges of the workplace. Protecting our police officers—the agency's greatest investment—is a moral and practical imperative. For many agencies, a complete change in agency culture is required (a number of administrators choosing to ignore the signs, or believing that officers should just "tough it out"); however, there is too much at stake, and a holistic approach is needed. That is a recurring theme of this chapter.

Occupational Hazards: The Issues

Although it is now a *statistically* safer time in which to serve in policing than the decade of the 1970s, when 1,114 officers were feloniously killed[65]—as compared with 541 officers murdered during the 2000s[66]—for the reasons noted above, policing has never been more dangerous than it is today. On average, one law enforcement officer is killed in the line of duty somewhere in the United States every 61 hours.[67] Indeed, the occupational fatality rate for law enforcement is three to five times greater than the national average for the working population.[68]

Furthermore, in recent years our nation has observed a shocking increase in felonious assaults on officers. Over the past decade, there has been an average of 58,930 assaults a year on officers, resulting in 15,404 injuries. Each loss of a police officer also results in long-term negative ramifications for the family and agency survivors.[69]

In addition, the mere fact of performing their duties places officers at particularly high risk for early deaths, heart attacks, and other health-related problems. Aside from the most obvious and well-known risks that arise, that is, assaults by suspects and other assailants, police officers also face elevated risks from vehicle crashes, accidental injuries resulting from foot pursuits and other common police activities, exposure to hazardous substances and communicable diseases, stress and fatigue, poor nutrition, and a variety of other physical and mental health risks.[70]

The mental well-being of officers is also an important consideration, especially when one suffers from post-traumatic stress disorder or severe depression, which can lead to suicide. PTSD can be triggered by experiencing traumatic events, such as crime scenes or exceptionally heinous acts, and can affect returning military veterans who experienced combat trauma.[71]

Given these occupational risks, there is a need for programs that promote health, wellness, and safety among police officers, focusing on all of these issues and addressing cardiovascular fitness, chronic disease prevention, alcohol and drug use and abuse, nutrition, weight management, exercise and conditioning, injury prevention, safe driving, stress management, and resilience to trauma.[72]

A Wellness and Safety Plan—and Change of Agency Culture

Police leaders must recognize that accountability to their officers is the number one factor in providing the best safety and wellness practices. Leaders are responsible, for example, to see that constant equipment compliance checks, proper weapons deployment, and policy and procedure enforcement are performed in order to minimize officer injuries and fatalities. Such ongoing monitoring and the enforcing of compliance will set the tone for meeting high standards, expectations, and practices for ensuring officer safety. Following is a description of how to develop a well-rounded program of officer wellness.

First, however, it should be noted that developing a wellness and safety program can be approached either proactively or reactively. When an organization acts **proactively**, it anticipates issues and attempts to ward off problems; a proactive campaign can also encourage employees to use existing services, such as the Philadelphia Police Department does with its health and wellness programs (both proactive approaches are described in Exhibit 6.6). When an agency is **reactive**, it develops campaigns, policies, and training programs to address a problem or issue that has emerged, such as when there has been a surge in officer injuries resulting from preventable traffic crashes.[73]

EXHIBIT 6.6

PROACTIVE APPROACHES TO WELLNESS CAMPAIGNS: PHOENIX AND PHILADELPHIA[74]

Bouts of oppressive heat can create a host of issues: dehydration, heatstroke, fatigue, cramps, and rash. Given their location in a desert climate, Phoenix, Arizona, police officers are especially vulnerable to these threats. The police department launched its "Beat the Heat" campaign to educate officers on the risks of heat-related injury and ways to mitigate those risks. The department produced a "Beat the Heat" training video for officers (see www.youtube.com/watch?v=ywgd8Gs9KI4). Furthermore, during major incidents, the agency's Safety Unit ensured adequate hydration was available for responding officers. Overall, the campaign ran for 1 year, during which the department saw no reports of heat-related injuries.

The Philadelphia Police Department launched several initiatives designed to proactively address ailments adversely affecting police personnel and their families. This holistic approach to health and wellness seeks to reduce the number of members who are impacted by serious ailments or are unavailable to work while managing health problems within their family. Each health and wellness program is disseminated through the police department's intranet, bulletins, and a general message is read at roll calls for three consecutive days. A suicide prevention course is conducted to help officers and supervisors recognize the signs of suicidal peers and educate them on available resources and appropriate actions. Psychologists provide confidential mental health services in areas such as marriage counseling, parenting, bullying, and other job-related or personal stresses. A drug and alcohol awareness program, seminars to support families with children with autism and special needs, and a health fair provide employees and family members with eye care, cardiovascular, pulmonary, blood pressure, cholesterol, and cancer tests. Employees can receive fitness and nutrition counseling, and a nutritionist meets with officers to adjust dietary habits in coordination with a fitness plan.

Developing a wellness campaign—fostering a safe working environment, protecting the safety of officers, and supporting health and wellness priorities—involves the following steps:[75]

1. ***Identify and analyze issues:*** first, assess the agency's health and wellness problems and what must be done to reduce them. Also, consider the existing culture: does there appear to be any incentives or concern with employee health and fitness? In addition, certain types of data can be examined: agency trends with regard to employee sickness, car crashes, alcohol-related offenses, suicide, lost days due to illness, or declines in officer fitness. Finally, employees themselves can be asked to indicate any wellness-related concerns and suggested improvements; surveys and focus groups can also be employed. Doing so will inform the leaders while also involve officers in the problem-solving process.
2. ***Establish goals and objectives:*** a goal is general (e.g., decreasing the numbers of employees getting injured on on-duty car crashes), while objectives are the means of reaching the goal (e.g., using training, posters, shift briefings on such things as use of safety belts, not exceeding speed limits, and being more attentive to safe driving). Note, however, that some wellness goals may involve increases in agency budgets (e.g., increasing the numbers of officers who obtain a yearly physical exam); funding is discussed in detail below.
3. ***Develop strategies:*** with goals and objectives in mind, a strategy can be crafted for putting the plan into action. This moves the program to the blueprint phase and must include how the program will be communicated, funded, implemented, and so on.
4. ***Consider key messages, branding, and design:*** assigning a name to the campaign will define why it exists. It should involve a visual identity, to include a logo and a name so the initiative will stand out and gain employee interest, buy-in, and participation. See Exhibit 6.7.

EXHIBIT 6.7

DEVELOPING A MESSAGE: "ARRIVE ALIVE"[76]

In Prince George's County, Maryland, fatal automobile accidents involving officers became one of the top three causes of officer fatalities. Therefore, police leaders were compelled to consider what efforts might be taken to help reduce such fatalities. The agency determined that many factors played a role in collisions: distractions in the patrol vehicle, excessive speed, and officers not wearing their seatbelts. Although policy required officers to wear their seatbelts while their vehicle was in motion, many officers believed seatbelts would make it more difficult for them to respond effectively to ambushes or other situations, as well as making access to their sidearm more difficult.

Simply ordering officers to wear their seatbelts was not seen as an effective solution, so police executives sought a way to change officers' viewpoints. The result was a safety initiative called "Arrive Alive," which involved showing a video to each officer in the department (featuring graphic footage of department crashes, along with heartfelt testimonials from eight survivors of officers killed in crashes); parking a demolished cruiser near the gas pumps where officers fill up their gas tanks that displayed safety messages (to buckle up, slow down, pay attention, and arrive alive); and issuing a weekly driver-safety message over the radio.

5. ***Identify a budget and resources:*** as noted above, additional funding may be required for certain fitness campaigns; however, police agencies can be very resourceful (e.g., many have obtained private funds for purchasing body armor, police dogs). Agencies might develop partnerships with various community and professional organizations as well as seek grants; public health organizations, physicians' organizations, and insurance providers may be approached as well.
6. ***Establish evaluations and measurements:*** finally, the agency must try to avoid the "We did these things, and believe they worked, but we're not sure" kind of program evaluation—especially where the tax dollars are concerned. The department should attempt to show—with empirical data—that its fitness program achieved its goals. Such an assessment may not be within the purview of in-house employees, so assistance might be sought from someone (e.g., university faculty) who is specially trained in evaluation research.

Need for Training, Policy, Technology

Ongoing training is important to ensure that officers understand the contributing risk factors that can lead to an injury or death. First is training in the balancing of risks; for instance, they should understand the need to assess the potential hazards involved in foot pursuits: possibly being alone and without backup, and possibly chasing someone who may be armed, is in better physical condition, and while in unfamiliar areas. In sum, officer training should emphasize that sometimes the safety risks may not be worth pursuing a fleeing suspect.

Tactical training is also important, as it enables officers to keep their skills honed for emergency driving, handling violent encounters, and operating less-lethal and lethal weapons. Best practices can be demonstrated through classroom learning, range driving, use of firearms and driving simulators, and computer-based situations and scenarios. Such training is crucial in safeguarding officers' lives. It must also be borne in mind, however, that attention to safety and risk management also applies to training, which itself can be hazardous and even fatal, such as the case where a SWAT hostage rescue exercise on a commuter train resulted in one of the role players, a reserve officer, being killed with a supposedly unloaded firearm.[77]

For their part, police leaders should review tactical, pursuit, driving, and other related policies and procedures to ensure they are up-to-date for risk factor mitigation (e.g., high-speed vehicle pursuit policies should cover the types of pursuits permitted, who will supervise them, maneuvering/evasive driving, and mandatory training to ensure the implementation of best practices). And, given that officers do not always read updates of policies and procedures, agencies should post and ensure the reading of such materials and discuss them at roll call.

What Cities Are Doing: Selected Case Studies

Following are three brief descriptions of agency approaches to health and wellness—programs often being initiated due to demonstrated wellness and safety problems in their organizations:

- Fort Worth Police Alcohol Awareness

  After seeing an increase in the number of officers having problems with and being arrested for alcohol-related offenses, the Fort Worth, Texas, Police Department found that a culture of hard drinking and reluctance to seek help exacerbated the issue. In response, a mandatory alcohol awareness training program was initiated for all ranks; the program, emphasizing the seriousness of the problem, educated officers about the dangers of alcohol and abuse, fostered an environment in which officers are encouraged to seek help when needed, and de-emphasized the culture of hard drinking. Presentations featuring discussions on alcohol awareness and stress management were made available to all officers, and an outside mental health agency was hired to provide a confidential, in-house peer support program, eliminating the fear of reprisal. The agency realized a decline in both stress-related incidents and alcohol-related offenses.[78]

- Columbus Police Work to Prevent Injury

  Columbus, Ohio, police saw a substantial rise in injury reports resulting in thousands of lost and restricted workdays. Thinking many such injuries were preventable, a system called Non-Punitive Close Call Reporting was implemented in which officers share their mistakes in a group setting to prevent similar or more serious mishaps and to decrease officer injuries by increasing cooperative learning, heightening safety awareness, and preventing both new and repeated close calls. The nonpunitive nature of the program is paramount, and the agency also developed spreadsheet-based documentation and a reporting mechanism as a means to analyze results. Close call discussions occur at least once a week during roll call meetings, and the program is being expanded to include more shifts and officers. Preliminary results suggest injury rates either remained steady or slightly decreased.[79]

EXHIBIT 6.8

CITY OF BOCA RATON'S ON-DUTY TRAINING FACILITY[80]

The Police Department of the City of Boca Raton (BRPD), Florida, developed an on-duty exercise program, written directly into policy, as a part of a broader emphasis on health and wellness. Two exercise rooms are provided and maintained by the department and the city, and qualified instructors are available to assist in developing individualized exercise routines. Officers are permitted to exercise on duty within specified guidelines, specifically:

- officers working 10- or 12-hour shifts can exercise during their meal period provided they have supervisor approval
- officers working eight-hour shifts can exercise on duty for a maximum of three hours per week
- officers who wish to go jogging may use approved outdoor routes, but they must notify dispatch of their location while exercising and be available for immediate duty

The BRPD found that by implementing these kinds of programs within smaller units (e.g., a squad), they realized broader participation, generated subtle peer pressure to participate, created a supportive environment and friendly competition among officers, and promoted a group culture of fitness and health throughout the agency. Recruitment and retention were also positively impacted (the exercise program was advertised as a job "perk," and the people attracted to the agency were more fitness-minded).

- Sacramento Police Focus on Health and Wellness

  During a 4-year period, workers compensation claims for the Sacramento, California, Police Department averaged $2.1 million per year for sworn employees. To reduce these expenditures and the number of on-duty injuries, the agency contracted for a professional to give officers nutritional advice; provide customizable workout plans; and inform officers about exercise safety, healthy living, and creative ways to remain active. Later, an on-duty workout program was established, with twice weekly, hour-long workout sessions available to on-duty employees. Over the next 2 years, the number of employees participating in the program increased, and a corresponding 59 percent decrease in workers compensation claims was achieved.[81]

Summary

This chapter examined a number of issues that represent major challenges for today's law enforcement administrators: dealing with police shootings and managing the use of force, generally; the involvement of civilian review boards; fostering constitutional policing; new approaches to active shooters; and recognizing the hazards of police work and developing formal wellness programs to assist officers in need.

The nature and problems relating to this chapter's topics make clear that, perhaps more than any other time in the history of policing, there is a need for strong, capable guidance and leadership.

Key Terms and Concepts

Active shooter, p. 145
Body-worn camera, p. 134
Civilian review board, p. 143
Occupational hazards (of policing), p. 146
Proactive/reactive approaches to wellness, p. 147
Training, policy, technology, p. 149 (roles of, in police wellness), p. 149
Use-of-force continuum, p. 138
Vehicle (high speed) pursuits, p. 141
Wellness and safety plan, p. 147

Questions for Review

1. Why have police shootings gained considerable national concern?
2. How can a national database of police use of force inform policy and impact such practices?
3. What are the primary reasons for and against police use of body-worn cameras?
4. What is the central theme underlying de-escalation training for police?
5. How can police leaders better manage use of force, including the application of use-of-force continuums, techniques for dealing with persons having mental disorders, and vehicle pursuits?
6. What are some predominating reasons for and against the use of citizen review boards?
7. What are consent decrees, and how can they foster constitutional policing?
8. What is the "new approach" by police to active shooter situations?
9. What do the data tell us about the hazards of policing as an occupation?
10. How would you define officer wellness?
11. What are the steps for developing an agency wellness campaign?
12. How do police training, policies, and technologies relate to leadership and officer wellness?

Deliberate and Decide

Officer Callahan has been a member of your police agency for five years and is one of your subordinates for two years. Her productivity, both in terms of quality and quantity, as well as her interactions with the public, has generally been up to standard; her performance evaluations have been positive in nature. In the past month, however, there has been a significant decline in all aspects of her work; furthermore, there have been complaints from other officers about her not responding to calls for service in a timely manner resulting in their having to cover for her. You have also noted her investigations into routine crimes have been inadequate. In addition, Callahan's reports are often late, or submitted only after you have sent her several reminders. Today a citizen contacts you to complain about her rudeness while taking a burglary report yesterday. You have also noticed since the onset of her work-related problems, she seems more aloof and moody and was found crying in the briefing room a few days back. You decide it is time to call her into your office to discuss these matters.

Questions for Discussion

1. How would you approach this problem?
2. How would you try to determine why her performance has changed in the last month? Would your inquiries include asking personal questions?
3. If you found nothing significant (such as personal issues in her life) as a cause, how would you explain your expectations for improved performance? Would you document your conversation?
4. Assume she tells you that she has been severely affected, both physically and emotionally, by another male officer's unwelcome advances and seemingly stalking behavior toward her while she is off duty. What would you do?

Learn by Doing

1. An investigative report by the local media has revealed an unusually high number of incidents involving inappropriate use of force by the police during the past few years. One aspect of the public reaction to this revelation is that the agency's training, policies, and procedures are now being questioned. What training topics as well as policies and procedures concerning use of force do you believe should be examined (or, as necessary, added, clarified, or expanded) for the department? Defend your answers.

Case Study

Members of the Pineville County Sheriff's Department have been involved in several vehicle pursuits including one which resulted in the death of a 14-year-old juvenile who crashed trying to outrun the police in his parents' car. Due to lawsuits being filed against the department and public outcries of excessive force, the sheriff modified and tightened the department's policy regarding pursuits to where supervisors were to cancel any pursuit not involving violent felonies "*or in the absence of any other circumstance that would justify the danger and potential liability of such a pursuit*." All officers have been trained in the new policy. The policy includes a warning-shot provision whereby they can only be used safely and if the *circumstances warrant*.

At around 9:00 P.M. Deputy Ray Ripley is on a special detail patrolling an industrial park due to frequent reports of vandalism and building material theft. Ripley has been on the department for a little over a year, graduating from the police academy, finishing his field training program, and, about 3 months ago, completing his probationary period.

One day Ripley, while driving through the industrial area, observes a vehicle backed into one of the docking bays—an area that is normally vacant after hours. While about 50 yards from the vehicle, Ripley turns on his spotlight and begins slow approaching the car. Upon seeing the officer's spotlight, the driver of the vehicle leaves at a high rate of speed, driving directly at Ripley, wherein the officer stops his vehicle, exits, and yells "halt"; he then fires a warning shot from his duty weapon into the air in front of the car. The vehicle veers around his patrol car and exited the docking area. Ripley gets back into his car, immediately accelerates after the vehicle, and advises the dispatcher he is in "hot pursuit of a possible burglary suspect."

The shift commander—a patrol lieutenant—hears the radio transmission and begins driving in the direction of the pursuit while asking for more information; Ripley again states it's a possible burglary suspect and that he is driving over 100 mph. At about that same time, the driver of the vehicle, thinking he is still being pursed, crashes his car into a tree. When the sheriff's units arrive, it is determined that the man driving, married with children, is vice president of the business where he was originally seen parking and has a prostitute in the car with him.

Questions for Discussion

1. Do you see any issues or problems with the department's new pursuit policy or the firing of "warning shots? If so, what were they?
2. Do you think Ripley's approach to the vehicle in the docking bay was warranted? Good police procedure? What could he have done differently?
3. Was Ripley justified in firing the warning shot under these circumstances? Why or why not?
4. Do you believe any of Ripley's actions subjected the department to being deemed liable for damages if either passenger sued? Give which actions and why.
5. Is a departmental Internal Affairs investigation warranted concerning Ripley's actions?

Notes

1. Jon Swaine and Oliver Laughland, "Number of People Killed by US Police in 2015 at 1,000 after Oakland Shooting," *The Guardian,* U.S. Edition, November 16, 2015, http://www.theguardian.com/us-news/2015/nov/16/the-counted-killed-by-police-1000.
2. Kimberly Kindy, "Fatal Police Shootings in 2015 Approaching 400 Nationwide," *The Washington Post*, May 30, 2015, https://www.washingtonpost.com/national/fatal-police-shootings-in-2015-approaching-400-nationwide/2015/05/30/d322256a-058e-11e5-a428-c984eb077d4e_story.html.
3. "L.A. Police Corruption Case Continues to Grow," *The Washington Post*, February 13, 2000, p. 1A.
4. Human Rights Watch, *Shielded from Justice: Police Brutality and Accountability in the United States* (New York: Author, 1998).
5. The Cap Times (Madison, WI), February 19, 2013, http://host.madison.com/news/local/writers/pat_schneider/no-comprehensive-reliable-database-of-police-shootings-exists/article_9a0e40a2-7ac5-11e2-9f0d-001a4bcf887a.html
6. President's Task Force on 21st Century Policing, *Interim Report of the President's Task Force on 21st Century Policing*, Office of Community Oriented Policing Services, March 4, 2015, p. 21.
7. Kevin Johnson, "Feds to Begin Police Shooting Data Collection by 2017," *USA Today*, October 13, 2016, http://www.usatoday.com/story/news/politics/2016/10/13/police-shootings-data-justice-department/91997066/.
8. Police Executive Research Forum, in its publication *Guiding Principles on Use of Force,* March 2016, p. 6, http://www.policeforum.org/assets/30%20guiding%20principles.pdf.
9. Ibid., p. 15.
10. Adapted from Ibid., pp. 45–50.
11. See Dallas Police Department, http://dallaspolice.net/ois/docs/narrative/2013/OIS_2013_311475A.pdf.
12. Molly Hennessy-Fiske, "Nation's Largest Law Enforcement Agency Nixes Body Cameras," *Government Technology*, November 13, 2015, http://www.govtech.com/public-safety/Nations-Largest-Law-Enforcement-Agency-Nixes-Body-Cameras.html.
13. Cindy Shain, Personal Communication, October 11, 2015.
14. Adapted from Darren Smith, Police Departments Consider Discontinuing Use of Body Cameras Due to Expense of Public Disclosure Requirements, Jonathan Turley, http://jonathanturley.org/2014/11/22/police-departments-consider-discontinuing-use-of-body-cameras-due-to-expense-of-public-disclosure-requirements.
15. Richard N. Holden, "The Technology Cycle and Contemporary Policing," paper presented at the annual meeting of the Academy of Criminal Justice Sciences, March 5, 2015, Orlando, FL.
16. Bureau of Justice Assistance, "Body Worn Camera Toolkit: Training," https://www.bja.gov/bwc/Topics-Training.html.
17. Alan Gomez, "Who needs body cameras? Police testing cellphone cameras," *USA Today*, June 25, 2017, https://www.usatoday.com/story/news/world/2017/06/25/who-needs-body-cameras-police-testing-cellphone-cameras/426859001/.
18. Ibid.
19. Police Executive Research Forum, *Guiding Principles on Use of Force*, p. 5.
20. Ibid., p. 21.
21. Ibid., p. 22.
22. Ibid., p. 21.
23. Ibid., p. 22; also see John Wilkens, "Police Embrace 'De-escalation' to Reduce Shootings, But Some Officers Remain Skeptical," *Los Angeles Times,* October 1, 2016, http://www.latimes.com/local/california/la-me-elcajon-tactics-20161001-snap-story.html.
24. Police Executive Research Forum, *Guiding Principles on Use of Force*, p. 77.
25. International Association of Chiefs of Police, *Police Use of Force in America 2001*, p. 1, http://www.theiacp.org/Portals/0/pdfs/Publications/2001useofforce.pdf.
26. See, for example, Marisol Bello and Yamiche Alcindor, "Police in Ferguson Ignite Debate about Military Tactics," *USA Today*, August 19, 2014, http://feedblitz.com/f/?fblike=http%3a%2f%2fwww.usatoday.com%2fstory%2fnews%2fnation%2f2014%2f08%2f14%2fferguson-militarized-police%2f14064675%2f; also see Yamiche Alcindor and Brandi Piper, "National Guard Ordered to Ferguson after Curfew Brings More Clashes," *USA Today*, August 18, 2014, http://www.krem.com/video/featured-videos/Clashes-on-second-night-of-Ferguson-curfew-271632291.html.
27. *Graham v. Connor,* 490 U.S. 386 (1989), p. 397.
28. David Carter, "Theoretical Dimensions in the Abuse of Authority," in T. Barker and D. Carter (eds.), *Police Deviance* (Cincinnati, OH: Anderson, 1994), pp. 269–290.

29. *Tennessee v. Garner,* 471 U.S. 1, 105 S.Ct. 1694, 85 L.Ed.2d 1 (1985).
30. Based on Lorie A. Fridell, "Improving Use-of-Force Policy: Policy Enforcement and Training," in Joshua A. Ederheimer and Lorie A. Fridell (eds.), *Chief Concerns: Exploring the Challenges of Police Use of Force* (Washington, DC: Police Executive Research Forum, April 2005), p. 48.
31. International Association of Chiefs of Police, "Force Continuums: Three Questions," *The Police Chief,* October 2010, http://www.policechiefmagazine.org/magazine/index.cfm?fuseaction=display_arch&article_id=791&issue_id=12006.
32. Charles Joyner and Chad Basile, "The Dynamic Resistance Response Model," *FBI Law Enforcement Bulletin* (September 2007): 17.
33. Steven G. Brandl and Meghan S. Stroshine, "The Role of Officer Attributes, Job Characteristics, and Arrest Activity in Explaining Police Use of Force," *Criminal Justice Policy Review* 24(5) (September 2014): 551–572.
34. Kenneth Adams, "Measuring the Prevalence of Police Abuse of Force," in William A. Geller and Hans Toch (eds.), *And Justice for All: Understanding and Controlling Police Abuse of Force* (Washington, DC: Police Executive Research Forum, 1995), pp. 61–98; Hans Toch, "The 'Violence-Prone' Police Officer," in Ibid., pp. 99–112; also see Kenneth Adams, "What We Know about Police Use of Force," in Kenneth Adams (ed.), *Use of Force by Police: Overview of National and Local Data* (Washington, DC: National Institute of Justice, 1995), pp. 1–14.
35. Dragana Kesic, Stuart D. M. Thomas, and James R. P. Ogloff, "Use of Nonfatal Force on and by Persons with Apparent Mental Disorder in Encounters with Police," *Criminal Justice & Behavior* 40(3) (March 2014): 321–337.
36. Ibid.
37. National Highway Traffic Safety Administration, *National Highway Traffic Safety Administration Statistics* (Washington, DC: Author, 1995).
38. C. B. Eisenberg, "Pursuit Management," *Law and Order* (March 1999): 73–77; also see A. Belotto, "Supervisors Govern Pursuits," *Law and Order* (January 1999): 86.
39. G. T. Williams, "When Do We Keep Pursuing? Justifying High-Speed Pursuits," *The Police Chief* (March 1997): 24–27.
40. 118 S.Ct. 1708.
41. Ibid., p. 1720.
42. D. N. Falcone, M. T. Charles, and E. Wells, "A Study of Pursuits in Illinois," *The Police Chief* (March 1994): 59–64.
43. For a comprehensive overview of early intervention systems, see Samuel Walker, *Early Intervention Systems for Law Enforcement Agencies: A Planning and Management Guide* (Washington, DC: Office of Community Oriented Policing Services, 2003), http://www.cops.usdoj.gov/html/cd_rom/inaction1/pubs/EarlyInterventionSystemsLawEnforcement.pdf.
44. Gregg Zoroya, "After the Shooting Stops, Another Fear Sets In: PTSD," *USA Today*, June 13, 2016, http://www.usatoday.com/story/news/nation/2016/06/13/second-wave-hurt-after-shooting-ends-ptsd/85828138/?utm_source=feedblitz&utm_medium=FeedBlitzRss&utm_campaign=usatoday-newstopstories.
45. See National Association of Civilian Oversight of Law Enforcement, https://nacole.org/.
46. See Ibid. for a listing of jurisdictions with citizen review boards.
47. Martin Kaste, "Police Are Learning to Accept Civilian Oversight, But Distrust Lingers," *NPR*, February 21, 2015, http://www.npr.org/2015/02/21/387770044/police-are-learning-to-accept-civilian-oversight-but-distrust-lingers; also see Ben Brumfield, AnneClaire Stapleton, and Sara Sidner, "In Ferguson's Wake, Police and Citizens Scuffle at St. Louis Meeting," *CNN*, January 29, 2015, http://www.cnn.com/2015/01/28/us/st-louis-police-citizen-ferguson-outburst/.
48. Quoted in Kaste, "Police Are Learning to Accept Civilian Oversight, But Distrust Lingers," http://www.npr.org/2015/02/21/387770044/police-are-learning-to-accept-civilian-oversight-but-distrust-lingers.
49. Ibid.
50. President's Task Force on 21st Century Policing, *Interim Report of the President's Task Force on 21st Century Policing*, p. 26.
51. Office of Community Oriented Policing Services, "Boston Police Department: Enhancing Cultures of Integrity," April 2010, http://ric-zai-inc.com/Publications/cops-p184-pub.pdf.
52. Police Executive Research Forum, *Civil Rights Investigations of Local Police: Lessons Learned,* July 2013, p. 1, http://www.policeforum.org/assets/docs/Critical_Issues_Series/civil%20rights%20investigations%20of%20local%20police%20-%20lessons%20learned%202013.pdf
53. Ibid.
54. Joe Domanick, "Police Reform's Best Tool: A Federal Consent Decree, Center on Media and Crime and Justice, John Jay College," *The Crime Report*, July 2014, http://thecrimereport.org/2014/07/15/2014-07-police-reforms-best-tool-a-federal-consent-decree/.
55. Ibid.
56. Police Executive Research Forum, *Civil Rights Investigations of Local Police*, p. 31.
57. Ibid., p. 24.
58. Ibid., p. 34.
59. Ibid., pp. 3–4.
60. Ibid., p. 4.
61. Sharon LaFraniere, Sarah Cohen, and Richard A. Oppel, Jr., "How Often Do Mass Shootings Occur? On Average, Every Day, Records Show," *The New York Times*, December 2, 2015, https://www.nytimes.com/2015/12/03/us/how-often-do-mass-shootings-occur-on-average-every-day-records-show.html?_r=0.
62. "Shoot First: Columbine Tragedy Transformed Police Tactics," *USA Today*, April 19, 2009, http://usatoday30.usatoday.com/news/nation/2009-04-19-columbine-police-tactics_N.htm.

63. From the Gilbert and Sullivan opera "Pirates of Penzance" (1879).
64. William Westley, *Violence and the Police: A Sociological Study of Law, Custom, and Morality* (Cambridge, MA: MIT Press), 1970, p. 3.
65. University of Albany, *Sourcebook of Criminal Justice Statistics Online*, Table 3.154, http://www.albany.edu/sourcebook/pdf/xt31542012.pdf.
66. See Federal Bureau of Investigation, "Law Enforcement Officers Killed and Assaulted, 2001–2010," https://ucr.fbi.gov/leoka/leoka-2010/tables/table01-leok-feloniously-region-division-state-01-10.xls.
67. National Law Enforcement Officers Memorial, "Facts and Figures," January 2017, http://www.nleomf.org/facts/.
68. Center for the Study of Law Enforcement Officers Killed and Assaulted, January 2017, https://leoka.org/.
69. Bureau of Justice Assistance, BJA Fact Sheet, "Officer Safety Initiatives," September 2015, p. 1, https://www.bja.gov/Publications/OfficerSafetyFS.pdf.
70. Joseph B. Kuhns, Edward R. Maguire, and Nancy R. Leach, *Health, Safety, and Wellness Program: Case Studies in Law Enforcement* (Washington, DC: Office of Community Oriented Policing Services, 2015), p. 1.
71. Mora L. Fiedler, *Officer Safety and Wellness: An Overview of the Issues* (Washington, DC: Office of Community Oriented Policing Services, 2011), p. 9.
72. Kuhns et al., *Health, Safety, and Wellness Program*, p. 2.
73. Julia Hill, Sean Whitcomb, Paul Patterson, Darrel W. Stephens, and Brian Hill, *Making Officer Safety and Wellness Priority One: A Guide to Educational Campaigns* (Washington, DC: Office of Community Oriented Policing Services, 2014), pp. 15–17.
74. Ibid., pp. 15–16.
75. Adapted from Hill et al., *Making Officer Safety and Wellness Priority One*, pp. 18–34.
76. Adapted from Kuhns et al., *Health, Safety, and Wellness Program*, pp. 13–16.
77. Thomas Connelly, "Perspective: Risk Management and Police Training," *FBI Law Enforcement Bulletin*, March 2010, https://leb.fbi.gov/2010/march/perspective-risk-management-and-police-training.
78. Adapted from Hill et al., *Making Officer Safety and Wellness Priority One,* p. 17.
79. Ibid., p. 26.
80. Adapted from Kuhns et al., *Health, Safety, and Wellness Program*, pp. 7–8.
81. Ibid., p. 45.

PART 3

The Courts

This part consists of three chapters. Chapter 7 examines court organization and operation, Chapter 8 covers personnel roles and functions, and Chapter 9 discusses court issues and practices. The introductory section of each chapter previews the specific chapter content.

Konstantin L/Shutterstock

7 Court Organization and Operation

LEARNING OBJECTIVES

After reading this chapter, the student will be able to:

1. *understand the meaning and importance of court decor and decorum*
2. *describe the ramifications of the adversarial system*
3. *review the organization and administration of our dual (federal and state) court systems*
4. *delineate the roles and functions of the Judicial Conference of the United States and the Administrative Office of the U.S. Courts*
5. *list the four components of court unification, how a unified court is organized, and the functional and financial advantages of court unification*
6. *explain state courts and trial courts of general and limited jurisdictions*
7. *describe why the courts' caseloads have increased*
8. *review historical attempts to streamline the court systems in both England and the United States, as well as some reasons for and examples of doing so*
9. *describe the influence of courts on policymaking*

▶ Introduction

Courts have existed in some form for thousands of years. Indeed, the ancient trial court of Israel, and the most common tribunal throughout its biblical history, was the "court at the gate," where elders of each clan resolved controversies within the kin group. In the fourth century b.c.e., courts in Athens, Greece, dealt with all premeditated homicides and heard cases. The court system has survived the dark eras of the Inquisition and the Star Chamber (which, in England during the 1500s and 1600s, without a jury, enforced unpopular political policies and meted out severe punishment, including whipping, branding, and mutilation). The U.S. court system developed rapidly after the American Revolution and led to the establishment of law and justice on the Western frontier.

The two major frameworks for law structures in the world today are common law and civil law. In a simplistic explanation, civil law systems use legislation and code to determine legality. Common law, on the other hand, places the judiciary in a position of power: their interpretation of law and court decisions have legal "power." The United States is a common law system, and while common/civil laws are not mutually exclusive systems, common law is very much a minority practice in the world.[1]

This chapter opens by going inside the courts, considering their special nature in our country, as well as typical courtroom decor and decorum. Then we discuss how the courts attempt to get at the truth within the controversial adversary system of justice. The nature of our dual court system, comprising federal and state-level courts, is examined next; included are discussions of two entities (the Judicial Conference of the United States and the Administrative Office of the U.S. Courts [AO]) that administer those at the federal level. Our discussion of the federal court system focuses on the U.S. Supreme Court, appeals courts (with emphasis on the District of Columbia Circuit Court of Appeals), and district courts; our overview of state courts includes their courts of last resort, appeals courts, and trial courts (including the major trial courts having general jurisdiction and limited jurisdiction lower courts). Included in the discussion of state court systems is a look at the historical, functional, and financial advantages of statewide court unification/centralization. An underlying theme is that caseloads are generally burgeoning, and we consider some reasons for that trend. After discussing the role of courts as policymaking bodies, the chapter concludes with review questions and exercises in the Deliberate and Decide, Learn by Doing, and Case Study sections.

▶ Inside the Courts: Decor, Decorum, Citizens

Hallowed Places

Practically everything one sees and hears in an American courtroom is intended to convey the sense that the courtroom is a hallowed place in our society. Alexis de Tocqueville, in his study of the United States more than a century ago, observed the extent to which our legal system permeates our lives:

> Scarcely any political question arises in the United States that is not resolved, sooner or later, into a judicial question. Hence all parties are obliged to borrow, in their daily controversies, the ideas, and even the language, peculiar to judicial proceedings. [T]he spirit of the law, which is produced in the schools and courts of justice, gradually penetrates beyond their walls into the bosom of society, where it descends to the lowest classes, so that at last the whole people contract the habits and the tastes of the judicial magistrate.[2]

decor the physical or decorative style of a setting.

decorum correct or proper behavior indicating respect and politeness.

The physical decor—the physical or decorative style of a setting—one finds in many courts conveys this sense of importance. On their first visit, citizens often are struck by the court's high ceilings, ornate marble walls, and comparatively expensive furnishings.

An appropriate degree of decorum—correct or proper behavior indicating respect and politeness—is accorded to this institution. All people must stand up when the judge enters the courtroom, permission must be granted before a person can approach the elevated bench, and a general attitude of deference is granted to the judge. A vitriolic utterance that could lawfully be directed to the president of the United States could result in an individual being jailed for contempt of court when directed at a judge.

The design of the courtroom, although generally dignified in nature, also provides a safe, functional space that is conducive to efficient and effective court proceedings. The formal arrangement of the participants and furnishings reflects society's view of the appropriate relationships between the defendant and judicial authority. The courtroom must accommodate judges, court reporters, clerks, bailiffs, witnesses, plaintiffs, defendants, attorneys, juries, and spectators, as well as police officers, social workers, probation officers, guardians ad litem, interpreters, and the press. Space must also be allotted for evidence, exhibits, recording equipment, and computers.

Judges and court staff now may require high-technology audiovisual equipment and computer terminals to access automated information systems. Chapter 16 discusses the kinds of technologies that are now commonly used in the nation's courtrooms.

The growing ubiquitousness of technology and social media has influenced the decorum expected in courtrooms. In one instance, after securing an acquittal, a lawyer pulled out his phone and took a quick photo with his client, which was posted to social networks with the caption of "not guilty." The judge in this case did not notice this initially, but when it came to the judge's attention, the judge demanded that the lawyer appear before the court to explain himself. Naturally, with the formality and severity of criminal cases, it is easy to see how this could influence the level of credibility or perceived fairness for those who proceed through the justice system.[3]

Justice in the Eye of the Beholder

Whether or not justice is obtained in the courtrooms depends on the interests or viewpoints of the affected or interested parties. A victim may not agree with a jury's verdict; a winner in a civil case may not believe that he or she received an adequate sum of money for the suffering or damages involved. Thus, because the definition of *justice* is not always agreed on, the courts must *appear* to provide justice. The court's responsibility is to provide a fair hearing, with rights accorded to all parties to speak or not to speak, to have the assistance of counsel, to cross-examine the other side, to produce witnesses and relevant documents, and to argue their viewpoint. This process, embodied in the due process clause, must appear to result in justice.[4]

While an appearance-based judicial philosophy has its advantages, there are many who criticize the concept on the grounds that it represents too much concern being paid to the appearance, rather than actual enforcement of the law. However, a *Harvard Law Review* article found that many rulings which concern themselves with "apparent" impropriety often have concerns of real impropriety present as well.[5]

For an example of the criticism leveled at judges for overstepping what others feel are the Court's bounds, see a conservative Christian opinion of "judicial activism" from Southwestern Assemblies of God University president Kermit Bridges, who calls the Supreme Court the "highest governing authority in the nation" (p. 1). In this article, Bridges attacks the Court's more liberal opinions as evidence of the judiciary usurping the role of the legislation. Yet simultaneously, defenders of the Court's decision would argue that to not do so makes the judiciary subservient to the other branches.[6]

Seeking Truth in an Adversarial Atmosphere

Ralph Waldo Emerson stated that "every violation of truth is a stab at the health of human society."[7] Certainly, most people would agree that the traditional, primary purpose of our courts is to provide a forum for seeking and—through the adversarial system of justice—obtaining the truth. Indeed, the U.S. Supreme Court declared in 1966 in *Tehan v. United States ex rel. Shott*[8] that "the basic purpose of a trial is the determination of truth."

Today, however, increasing numbers of Americans have the impression that truth is being compromised and even violated with regularity in the trial, plea bargaining, and appellate apparatus of our justice system, thereby "stabbing at the health of human society."

High on their list of impediments is the **adversarial system** itself—the legal system whereby two opposing sides present their arguments in court. Because of cases that have included jury nullification (acquitting a defendant because the jury disagrees with a law or the evidence), lawyer grandstanding, improper and racist police procedures, and a general circus atmosphere allowed by the judge and engaged in by the media, the adversarial system has been questioned. Although many people would argue that such a system is vital to a free democratic society, under this system the courtroom becomes a battleground where participants often have little regard for guilt or innocence; rather, concern centers on whether the state is able to prove guilt beyond a reasonable doubt. To many people, this philosophy contradicts what courts were intended to accomplish. In the adversary system, the desire to win can become overpowering. As one state supreme court justice put it, prosecutors "are proud of the notches on their gun."[9] Defense counsel enjoys winning equally. The attention can shift from the goal of finding the truth to being effective game players.

adversarial system the legal system whereby two opposing sides present their arguments in court.

Criticism of the adversarial system has come concurrently with criticism of lawyers' ethics.[10] According to legal scholar Monroe Freedman, zealous advocacy and client-centeredness are at the root of the problem in the current adversarial process.[11] Should this system be modified or replaced? That is an important and difficult question. As one law professor observed, "Lawyers are simply not appropriate to correct the defects of our adversary system. Their hearts will never be in it; it is unfair to both their clients and themselves to require them to serve two masters."[12]

It would appear, however, that the adversarial system is here to stay. Indeed, several safeguards have been put in place to enable this system to reach the truth. First, evidence is tested under this approach through cross-examination of witnesses. Second, power is lodged with several different people; each courtroom actor is granted limited powers to counteract those of the others. If, for example, the judge is biased or unfair, the jury can disregard the judge and reach a fair verdict. If the judge believes the jury has acted improperly, he or she can set aside the jury's verdict and order a new trial. Furthermore, both the prosecuting and defense attorneys have certain rights and authority under each state's constitution. This series of checks and balances is aimed at curbing misuse of the criminal courts.

The adversarial system is in sharp contrast to the inquisitorial system, which was more common in the eighteenth and nineteenth centuries. Unlike the role of the judge in an adversarial system, as one might guess from the name "inquisitorial," the court or a part of it takes an active role in investigating and questioning during the trial stage. This has both advantages and disadvantages: judges are bound by precedent in adversarial systems more often than not, but in an inquisitorial setup, judges have greater leeway to decide cases on the circumstances of that incident alone. In both systems, the prosecution and defense are not always guaranteed to have equal resources, but in an adversarial system this can be a bigger problem, as the judge and jury are only triers of fact (rather than being able to supplement what they perceive to be lacking from one party).[13]

A Dual Court System

dual court system
an organizational distinction between courts, with a federal court system and 50 individual state court systems.

In order to better understand the court system of the United States, it is important to know that this country has a **dual court system**: essentially, an organizational distinction between courts, with one federal court system and a state court system (comprised of 50 individual state court systems plus the system of the District of Columbia). First, we will examine the federal court system; included are discussions of the entities responsible for overseeing the federal courts' operations: the Judicial Conference of the United States and the AO. Following that, we examine the state and local trial courts.

There are several types of appellate courts in the U.S. court system. Most frequently, they are distinguished by the number of levels. The Bureau of Justice Statistics divides them into courts of last resort (COLR) and intermediate appellate courts (IAC), whose cases are typically appealed to the state's supreme court. The most frequent type involves both COLRs and IACs, where COLRs hear cases by permission and IACs hear cases by right. Appellate courts are different from trial courts, in that they are more interested in determining whether the proper procedures and legal guidelines were followed, rather than actually retrying the case.[14]

▶ Federal Courts: Organization and Administration

The U.S. Supreme Court: Its Jurists, Traditions, and Work

Courtroom Participants: Judges and Advocates

Established in 1788, the U.S. Supreme Court is the highest and one of the oldest courts in the nation. It is comprised of nine justices: one chief justice and eight associate justices. Like other federal judges appointed under Article III of the Constitution, they are nominated to their post by the president and confirmed by the Senate, and they serve for life.[15] Each new term of the Supreme Court begins, by statute, on the first Monday in October.

Not just any lawyer may advocate a cause before the high court; all who wish to do so must first secure admission to the Supreme Court bar. Applicants must submit an application form that requires, under Supreme Court Rule 5, that applicants have been admitted to practice in the highest court of their state for a period of at least 3 years (during which time they must not have been the subject of any adverse disciplinary action), and they must appear to the Court to be of good moral and professional character. Each applicant must file with the clerk a certificate from the presiding judge or clerk of that court attesting that the applicant practices there and is in good standing, as well as the statements of two sponsors affirming that he or she is of good moral and professional character. Finally, applicants must swear or affirm to act "uprightly and according to law, and support the Constitution of the United States."[16]

Inside the Court: Revered Traditions and Practices

The Supreme Court Building, constructed in 1935, has 16 marble columns at the main west entrance that support the portico; on the architrave above is incised the words "Equal Justice Under Law." The building's chamber measures 82 feet wide by 99 feet long, rising 44 feet above the dark African marble floor. Gold leaf and red adorn the ceiling recesses. Twenty-four massive columns of silver gray Italian marble line walls of ivory mined in Spain. High on the walls, four 36-foot-long marble friezes depict the great classical and Christian lawgivers. A large clock is suspended high above the bench to remind the sometimes too verbose advocate that time marches on. Behind the bench are nine high-backed chairs and a flag.

The clerk's desk is at the left end of the bench, and counsel tables are in front of and below the bench. Squarely in the middle, facing the chief justice, is the lectern used by attorneys while addressing the Court. On the lectern are two lights—a white one comes on when the speaker has 5 minutes remaining and a red one is the signal to stop.[17] Millions of visitors to the U.S. Supreme Court have been struck by the sight and the power of the building and its primary occupants. Justice Robert Jackson once described the Court's uniqueness, saying, "We are not final because we are infallible, but we are infallible because we are final."[18]

In many respects, the Court is the same institution that first met in 1790. Since at least 1800, it has been traditional for justices to wear black robes while in session. White quills are placed on counsel tables each day that the Court sits, as was done at the earliest sessions of the Court. The "Conference handshake" has been a tradition since the late nineteenth century. When the justices assemble to go on the bench each day and at the beginning of the private conferences at which they discuss decisions, each justice shakes hands with each of the other eight—a reminder that differences of opinion on the Court do not preclude the overall harmony of purpose. When the Court is in session, the chief justice always sits in the middle, with four associate justices on either side. The justice who is senior in terms of service sits on the chief's immediate right as the justices face out; the justice who is second in seniority sits on the chief's left; thereafter, the justices are seated alternately right and left according to the amount of time served. The junior justice is always on the chief justice's extreme left.[19]

In 2017, Neil Gorsuch was confirmed as the 113th justice of the U.S. Supreme Court, filling the vacant seat of Justice Scalia, who passed away in early 2016. Gorsuch's confirmation was not without controversy as Republicans were able to facilitate the waiver of the required 60 U.S. Senate votes, which paved the way for the confirmation with a final vote tally of 54–45. While Gorsuch is now seated on the Supreme Court, there are over 400 other federal judge positions that can be filled over the next presidential term. This gives the president the ability to swing the courts back to a more conservative manner. Because judgeships in federal courts are nominated, rather than elected, this allows the president and Senate (both largely "elite" in the fiscal/power sense) to widely change the scope of legal reality, without the public's direct input into the process.

Caseload and Conferences

The Court does not meet continuously in formal sessions during its 9-month term. Instead, the Court divides its time into four separate but related activities. First, some period of time is allocated to reading through the thousands of petitions for review of cases that come annually to the Court—usually during the summer and when the Court is not sitting to hear cases. Second, the Court allocates blocks of time for oral arguments—the live discussion in which lawyers for both sides present their clients' positions to the justices, and where justices question lawyers. During the weeks of oral arguments, the Court sets aside its third allotment of time, for private discussions of how each justice will vote on the cases they have just heard. Time is also allowed for the justices to discuss which additional cases to hear. These private discussions are usually held on Wednesday afternoons and Fridays during the weeks of oral arguments. The justices set aside a fourth block of time to work on writing their opinions.[20]

The Court has complete discretion to control the nature and number of the cases it reviews by means of the writ (order) of *certiorari*—an order from a higher court directing a lower court to send the record of a case for review. The Court considers requests for writs of certiorari according to the *rule of four*; if four justices decide to "grant cert," the Court will agree to hear the case. Several criteria are used to decide whether a case requires action: First, does the case concern an issue of constitutional or legal importance? Does it fall within the Court's **jurisdiction**—which is, simply put, the power or authority given to a court by law to hear certain kinds of cases (the Supreme Court can only hear cases that

jurisdiction the power or authority given to a court by law to hear certain kinds of cases.

EXHIBIT 7.1

OYEZ! OYEZ! OYEZ!

Students of the U.S. Supreme Court are encouraged to check out Oyez.org, a free law project housed at the Illinois Institute of Technology Chicago-Kent College of Law. The objective of Oyez is to make the U.S. Supreme Court accessible by utilizing text, images, audio recordings, and video. The initial idea for such a project began in the 1980s, and the project has grown considerably through various grants. To date, Oyez.org has digitized the oral arguments of each U.S. Supreme Court case since audio recordings were first introduced in proceedings in 1955. The project provides information about cases, the justices, current news, and a 360-degree visual tour of the Court as described earlier in this chapter.

Interested in finding information about a landmark U.S. Supreme Court case, such as *Miranda v. Arizona*? Just go to Oyez.org and type in the case in the search bar. From there, you will have the ability to listen to the oral arguments from the case (with sentence-by-sentence transcription), the facts of the case and case summary, information about the case advocates, and a link to the full opinion of the Court.

Source: Data from https://www.oyez.org.

are mandated by Congress or the Constitution)? Does the party bringing the case have *standing*—a strong vested interest in the issues raised in the case and in its outcome?[21]

The Court hears only a tiny fraction of the thousands of cases it is petitioned to consider (approximately 1%). When it declines to hear a case, the decision of the lower court stands as the final word on the case. Adding to the Court's workload is a steady growth in congressional and state legislation that requires judicial interpretation and an increasing number of constitutional and other issues that can be reviewed in the federal courts.[22] After the Court decides to hear a case, a vote is taken, and the senior justice of the majority assigns the case to one of the other justices or him (or her)self. Justices write approximately 70 percent of their opinions on their own; the remainder is written by law clerks (each justice has four), typically top graduates from Ivy League law schools.[23] At times, the justice who writes the majority opinion will provide an oral summary at a public session of the court.

Administration

The chief justice orders the business of the Supreme Court and administers the oath of office to the president and vice president upon their inauguration. According to Article 1, Section 3, of the Constitution of the United States, the chief justice is also empowered to preside over the Senate in the event that it sits as a court to try an impeachment of the president. The duties of the chief justice are described more fully in Chapter 8.

The clerk of the Court serves as the Supreme Court's chief administrative officer, supervising a staff of 30 under the guidance of the chief justice. The marshal of the Court supervises all building operations. The reporter of decisions oversees the printing and publication of the Court's decisions. Other key personnel are the librarian, the public information officer, and the justices' law clerks.[24]

U.S. Courts of Appeals

Judges, Jurisdiction, Caseloads

The Evarts Act of 1891 created the structure and the original nine circuits of the U.S. Courts of Appeals; it also created the circuit judge positions. Today there are 13 courts of appeals (or circuit courts) for the federal court system. Eleven of the circuits are identified

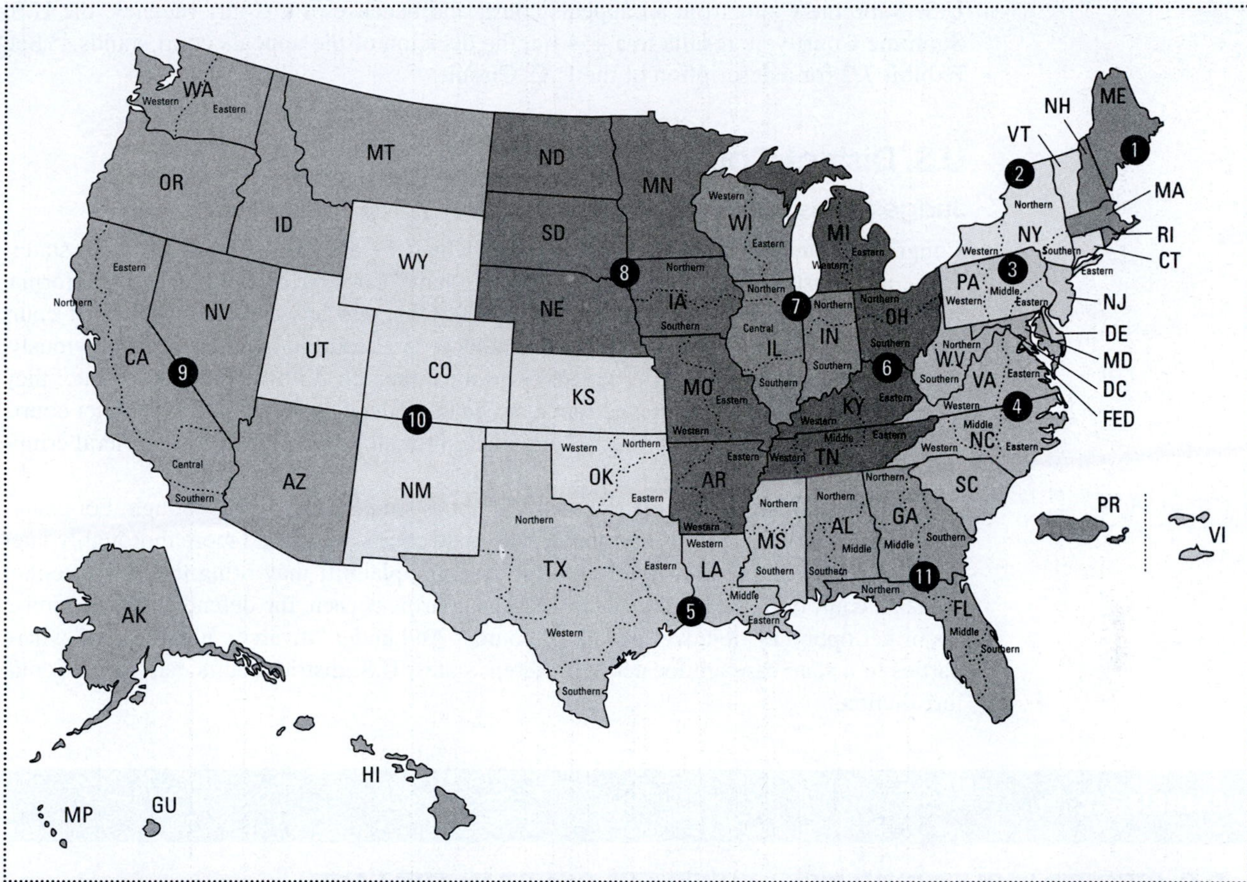

FIGURE 7-1 Geographic Boundaries of the U.S. Courts of Appeals and U.S. District Courts
Source: United States Courts of Appeals and United States District Courts, www.uscourts.gov/images/circuitmap.pdf.

by number, and another is called the D.C. Circuit. The U.S. Court of Appeals for the Federal Circuit, which hears cases across the country based on specific subject matter, is the thirteenth appeals court in the federal circuit (see Figure 7-1 ■). A court of appeals hears appeals from the district courts located within its circuit, as well as appeals from decisions of federal administrative agencies.

The courts of appeals are staffed with 179 judges nominated by the president and confirmed by the Senate. As with the U.S. district courts, discussed below, the number of judges in each circuit varies, from six in the First Circuit to 29 in the Ninth, depending on the volume and complexity of the caseload. Each circuit has a chief judge (chosen by seniority) who has supervisory responsibilities. Several staffers aid the judges in conducting the work of the courts of appeals. A circuit executive assists the chief judge in administering the circuit. The clerk's office maintains the records. Each judge is also allowed to hire three law clerks. In deciding cases, the courts of appeals may use rotating three-judge panels. Or, by majority vote, all the judges in the circuit may sit together to decide a case or reconsider a panel's decision; however, such *en banc* hearings are rare.[25] The caseload of the courts of appeals is about 52,700 per year, the lowest it has been in 20 years[26]—a little more than half being civil in nature, 20 percent being criminal, and the remainder originating from administrative agencies.[27] If the decision of one of the U.S. Courts of Appeals is denied review by the U.S. Supreme Court, the decision of the circuit court stands. And if a case is heard by the

U.S. Supreme Court from an appeals court, and because of a Court vacancy, the U.S. Supreme Court vote results in a 4–4 tie, the decision of the appeals court stands.[28] See Exhibit 7.2 for a description of the D.C. Circuit.

U.S. District Courts

Judges, Jurisdiction, Caseloads

Congress created 94 U.S. district courts, of which 89 are located within the 50 states. There is at least one district court in each state (some states have more, such as California, New York, and Texas, all of which have four). Congress has created 677 district court judgeships for the 94 districts. As with the other federal court judges discussed previously, the president nominates district judges, who must then be confirmed by the Senate; they then serve for life unless removed for cause. In the federal system, the U.S. district courts are the federal trial courts of original jurisdiction for all major violations of federal criminal law.[29]

The jurisdiction of U.S. district courts is not as simple as it sounds though. For example, some cases can have jurisdiction in both state courts (discussed more thoroughly later in this chapter) and federal courts. In this case, the plaintiff may bring the case to either the state court or federal court system. If state court is chosen, the defendant may exercise his or her option to "remove" to federal court.[30] And under "diversity jurisdiction," where parties to a state case are located in different states, U.S. district courts can have original jurisdiction.[31]

EXHIBIT 7.2

D.C. CIRCUIT: THE SECOND MOST POWERFUL COURT IN THE LAND

Any discussion of the federal court system would be incomplete without elaborating on the District of Columbia Circuit Court of Appeals (known as the D.C. Circuit). Often described (and widely regarded) as the second most powerful court in the United States (after the U.S. Supreme Court), the D.C. Circuit's reputation is well earned because it often decides cases having national implications, ranging from environmental regulations and national security policy to drinking water standards and clean air. It even has jurisdiction over the federal government's bureaucracy; indeed, a number of federal and administrative statutes and agencies designate the D.C. Circuit as the appropriate forum for challenging federal agency orders and rules. Trade associations, labor unions, and other such organizations often appear before this court's distinguished panel of one chief judge and eight associate judges.[32]

Finally, the D.C. Circuit is viewed as a springboard for one to be appointed to the highest court in the nation. Indeed, the bench of the D.C. Circuit once was the locus for Chief Justice John Roberts and Justices Ruth Bader Ginsburg, Antonin Scalia, and Clarence Thomas.[33]

District court judges are assisted by an elaborate supporting cast of clerks, secretaries, law clerks, court reporters, probation officers, pretrial services officers, and U.S. marshals. The larger districts also have a public defender. District judges also are assisted by federal magistrate judges, who are appointed by majority among the judges within the district. Federal magistrate judges have a variety of duties, including overseeing certain cases, issuing search and arrest warrants, setting bail, and so on[34] Another important actor at the district court level is the U.S. attorney; there is one U.S. attorney in each district, along with assistant U.S. attorneys. The work of district judges is significantly assisted by 352 bankruptcy judges, who are appointed for 14-year terms by the court of appeals in the district where it is located.[35] There are about 80,000 criminal cases filed per year over the last several years in the U.S. district courts, down from a high of over 100,000 in 2011.[36]

EXHIBIT 7.3

U.S. FOREIGN INTELLIGENCE SURVEILLANCE COURT: BEHIND CLOSED DOORS

While not a designated district court, when it comes to powerful courts, the FISC is certainly one of them. This court, in theory, hears and authorizes warrants for electronic surveillance of dangerous instigators or spies within the United States. While it is not entirely unusual for specific court hearings to be closed to the public, there have been concerns about the scope of what goes on behind the closed doors of the FISC. The government is the only party allowed to present cases to the FISC and since very few opinions are made public, criticisms have been leveled at the court for being a "rubber-stamp" for widespread, publicly unknown surveillance practices.[37]

Judicial Conference of the United States

The **Judicial Conference of the United States** is the administrative policymaking organization of the federal judicial system. Its membership consists of the chief justice, the chief judges of each of the courts of appeals, one district judge from each circuit, and the chief judge of the Court of International Trade. The conference meets semiannually for only 2-day sessions, generally at the U.S. Supreme Court building in Washington, DC, but most of the work is done by about 25 committees, such as the Space and Facilities Committee, the Committee on Audits and Administrative Office Accountability, and the Information Technology Committee.[38] The chief justice makes committee appointments, which are generally renewable 3-year, staggered terms to minimize the amount of turnover.[39]

Judicial Conference of the United States the administrative policymaking organization of the federal judicial system.

The Judicial Conference directs the Administrative Office of the U.S. Courts (discussed in the following section) in administering the judiciary budget and makes recommendations to Congress, concerning the creation of new judgeships, increase in judicial salaries, revising federal rules of procedure, and budgets for court operations. The Judicial Conference also plays a major role in the impeachment of federal judges.[40] And while impeachment seems to be the conventional wisdom for removing federal judges, others argue that nowhere is it stated that impeachment is the only method for removing federal judges.[41]

Administrative Office of the U.S. Courts

Since 1939, the day-to-day administrative tasks of the federal courts have been handled by the Administrative Office of the U.S. Courts (AO), a judicial agency. The director of the AO is appointed by the chief justice of the Supreme Court and reports to the Judicial Conference. The AO's lobbying and liaison responsibilities include presenting the annual budget request for the federal judiciary, arguing for the need for additional judgeships, and transmitting proposed changes in court rules. The AO is also the housekeeping agency of the judiciary, responsible for allotting authorized funds and supervising expenditures.[42]

In his recent Director's Message, AO director James C. Duff outlined a number of initiatives within the AO, including a space reduction effort that utilizes shared workstations for a more mobile workforce. Space reductions, according to Director Duff, are necessary to reduce rent and conserve more of the AO's authorized budget.[43] The message also articulated improvements to the judiciary's information technology program in the face of growing threats to cybersecurity.[44]

▶ Comparing Federal and State Court Systems

While approximately 1 million cases annually come before federal courts, this number is closer to 30 million for state courts, largely because state courts have the jurisdiction to handle most types of cases involving citizens.[45] Before we engage in a fuller discussion of state court systems and their variations, it's useful to generally compare the federal and state court systems in terms of structure, selection of judges, and types of cases heard, which can be found in Exhibit 7.4.

EXHIBIT 7.4

COMPARING FEDERAL AND STATE COURTS

COURT STRUCTURE

Federal Court System

Article III of the Constitution invests judicial power in the United States in the federal court system. Article III, Section 1, creates the U.S. Supreme Court and authorizes Congress to create the lower courts at the federal level.

Congress has used Article III, Section 1, to create 13 U.S. Courts of Appeals, 94 U.S. district courts, the U.S. Court of Claims, and the U.S. Court of International Trade. U.S. bankruptcy courts also were created. Magistrate judges handle some district court matters.

Parties dissatisfied with lower courts (U.S. district courts, U.S. Court of Claims, and the U.S. Court of International Trade) may appeal to the U.S. Court of Appeals.

Parties may ask the U.S. Supreme Court to review a decision of the U.S. Court of Appeals, but the Supreme Court can decide not to hear the case. The U.S. Supreme Court is the final arbiter on all federal constitutional matters.

State Court System

Constitution and laws of each state create state courts. A court of last resort, often termed the Supreme Court, is usually the highest court. Some states have an intermediate court of appeals. Below these courts are state trial courts, sometimes referred to as circuit or district courts.

States also usually have specialized courts, such as family court, juvenile court, drug court, or probate court.

Parties dissatisfied with the decision of a trial court may take their case to the intermediate court of appeals.

Parties have the option to ask the higher state court to hear the case.

Only certain cases are eligible for review by the U.S. Supreme Court.

SELECTION OF JUDGES

Federal Court System

Federal judges are nominated by the president and confirmed by the Senate.

Federal judges hold office for life, but can be removed from office through congressional impeachment proceedings.

State Court System

State court judges can be selected in a variety of ways, including:

Election

Appointment for a term of years

Appointment for life

Combination of appointment followed by election

TYPES OF CASES HEARD

Federal Court System

Cases dealing with constitutionality of a law

Cases involving the laws and treaties of the United States

Cases involving ambassadors and public ministers

Disputes between two or more states

Admiralty law

Bankruptcy

Habeas corpus issues

State Court System

Most criminal cases

Probate (wills and estates)

Most contract cases

Tort cases (personal injuries)

Family law (marriages, divorces, adoptions)

State courts are the final arbiters of state laws and constitutions. Their interpretation of federal law or the U.S. Constitution may be appealed to the U.S. Supreme Court. The Supreme Court may or may not choose to hear such cases.

Source: uscourts.gov, "Comparing Federal & State Courts"http://www.uscourts.gov/about-federal-courts/court-role-and-structure/comparing-federal-state-courts

▶ State Courts of Last Resort and Appeals

Courts of Last Resort

A **court of last resort**—that court in a given state that has its highest and final appellate authority—is usually referred to as the state supreme court; however, the specific names differ from state to state, as do their number of judges (from as few as five to as many as nine—see Figure 7-2 ■). Unlike the intermediate appellate courts (discussed in the "Intermediate Courts of Appeals" section), these courts do not use panels in making decisions; rather, the entire court sits to decide each case. All state supreme courts have a limited amount of original jurisdiction in dealing with matters such as disciplining lawyers and judges.[46]

court of last resort that court in a given state that has its highest and final appellate authority.

	Court of Last Resort		Intermediate Appellate Court	
	Court Name	**Place of Session**	**Court Name**	**No. of Chief Judges**
Alabama	Supreme Court	Montgomery	Court of Civil Appeals	1
			Court of Criminal Appeals	1
Alaska	Supreme Court	Anchorage, Fairbanks, and Juneau	Court of Appeals	1
Arizona	Supreme Court	Phoenix	Court of Appeals	1
Arkansas	Supreme Court	Little Rock	Court of Appeals	1
California	Supreme Court	Los Angeles, Sacramento, and San Francisco	Courts of Appeals	9
Colorado	Supreme Court	Denver	Court of Appeals	1
Connecticut	Supreme Court	Hartford	Appellate Court	1
Delaware	Supreme Court	Dover	~	~
District of Columbia	Court of Appeals	Washington, DC	~	~
Florida	Supreme Court	Tallahassee	District Courts of Appeal	5
Georgia	Supreme Court	Atlanta	Court of Appeals	1
Hawaii	Supreme Court	Honolulu	Intermediate Court of Appeals	1
Idaho	Supreme Court	7 locations	Court of Appeals	1
Illinois	Supreme Court	Springfield	Appellate Court	5
Indiana	Supreme Court	Indianapolis	Court of Appeals	1
			Tax Court	~
Iowa	Supreme Court	Des Moines	Court of Appeals	1
Kansas	Supreme Court	Topeka	Court of Appeals	1
Kentucky	Supreme Court	Frankfort	Court of Appeals	1
Louisiana	Supreme Court	New Orleans	Courts of Appeal	5
Maine	Supreme Judicial Court	Portland	~	~
Maryland	Court of Appeals	Annapolis	Court of Special Appeals	1
Massachusetts	Supreme Judicial Court	Boston	Appeals Court	1

FIGURE 7-2 Appellate Courts in the United States

	Court of Last Resort		Intermediate Appellate Court	
	Court Name	Place of Session	Court Name	No. of Chief Judges
Michigan	Supreme Court	Lansing	Court of Appeals	1
Minnesota	Supreme Court	St. Paul	Court of Appeals	1
Mississippi	Supreme Court	Jackson	Court of Appeals	1
Missouri	Supreme Court	Jefferson City Supreme	Court of Appeals	3
Montana	Supreme Court	Helena	~	~
Nebraska	Supreme Court	Lincoln	Court of Appeals	1
Nevada	Supreme Court	Carson City	~	~
New Hampshire	Supreme Court	Concord	~	~
New Jersey	Supreme Court	Trenton	Superior Court, Appellate Div.	1
New Mexico	Supreme Court	Santa Fe	Court of Appeals	1
New York	Court of Appeals	Albany	Supreme Court, Appellate Div.	4
North Carolina	Supreme Court	Raleigh	Court of Appeals	1
North Dakota	Supreme Court	Bismarck	~	~
Ohio	Supreme Court	Columbus	Courts of Appeal	12
Oklahoma	Supreme Court	Oklahoma City	Court of Civil Appeals	1
	Court of Criminal Appeals	Oklahoma City		
Oregon	Supreme Court	Salem	Court of Appeals	1
Pennsylvania	Supreme Court	Harrisburg, Philadelphia, and Pittsburgh	Superior Court	1
			Commonwealth Court	1
Puerto Rico	Supreme Court	San Juan	Court of Appeals	1
Rhode Island	Supreme Court	Providence	~	~
South Carolina	Supreme Court	Columbia	Court of Appeals	1
South Dakota	Supreme Court	Pierre	~	~
Tennessee	Supreme Court	Jackson, Knoxville, and Nashville	Court of Criminal Appeals	1
			Court of Appeals	
Texas	Supreme Court	Austin	Courts of Appeal	14
	Court of Criminal Appeals	Austin		
Utah	Supreme Court	Salt Lake City	Court of Appeals	1
Vermont	Supreme Court	Montpelier	~	~
Virginia	Supreme Court	Richmond	Court of Appeals	1
Washington	Supreme Court	Olympia	Courts of Appeal	3
West Virginia	Supreme Court of Appeals	Charleston	~	~
Wisconsin	Supreme Court	Madison	Court of Appeals	1
Wyoming	Supreme Court	Cheyenne	~	~

FIGURE 7-2 (continued)

In those 10 states that do not have an intermediate court of appeals, the state supreme court has no power to choose which cases will be placed on its docket; however, the ability of most state supreme courts to choose which cases to hear makes them important policymaking bodies. Although intermediate appellate courts review thousands of cases each year, looking for errors, state supreme courts handle 100 or so cases that present the most challenging legal issues arising in that state. Approximately 2 percent of all intermediate appellate court appeals are reviewed by the court of last resort.[47]

While state supreme courts are the ultimate review board for matters involving interpretation of state law,[48] nowhere is the policymaking role of state supreme courts more apparent than in deciding death penalty cases—which, in most states, are automatically appealed to the state's highest court, thus bypassing the ICAs. More than 100 death penalty appeals are resolved each year, most of those in states where death penalty convictions are the highest, including Florida, California, Texas, and Arizona.[49] The time to resolve death penalty cases on appeal is three times longer than in non-death penalty cases. And in 5 percent of death penalty appeals the length of time toward resolution is almost 14 years.[50]

Intermediate Courts of Appeals

Like their federal counterparts, state courts have experienced a significant growth in appellate cases that threatens to overwhelm the state supreme court; therefore, to alleviate the caseload burden on courts of last resort, state officials in 40 states have responded by creating an **intermediate court of appeals (ICA)**[51]—courts in both the federal and state court systems that hear appeals and are organizationally intermediate between the trial courts and the court of last resort. The states not having an ICA, such as New Hampshire, Vermont, Rhode Island, Delaware, and Maine, are typically sparsely populated and have low volumes of appeals. There are about 1,300 such judges in the nation today. The ICAs must hear all properly filed appeals.[52]

intermediate courts of appeals (ICAs) courts in the federal and state court systems that hear appeals, organizationally situated between the trial courts and the court of last resort.

The structure of the ICA varies; in most states, these bodies hear both civil and criminal appeals, and like their federal counterparts, these courts typically use rotating three-judge panels. Also, like the federal appellate courts, the state ICAs' workload is demanding: According to the National Center for State Courts, state ICAs hear about 280,000 cases annually.[53] ICAs engage primarily in error corrections; they review trials to make sure that the law was followed, and the overall standard is one of fairness. ICAs represent the final stage of the process for most litigants; very few cases make it to the appellate court in the first place, and of those cases, only a small proportion will be heard by the state's court of last resort.[54]

State appellate court systems—both courts of last resort and ICAs—are shown in Figure 7-2 ■. It was shown earlier that there is a widespread variation in terms of these courts' names and the number of judges for each.

In a report on the state of ICAs, there was considerable consistency in the stated goals and objectives, as one might expect. ICAs in every jurisdiction aim to dispense justice in the least controversial manner as possible. The report also articulated five general objectives that help ICAs achieve their goals. The institutional values and objectives are as follows:

1. Adopt and utilize effective resource management structures (ensure public resources are being used wisely);
2. Implement and continually review case disposition procedures that promote timeliness;
3. Increase public awareness about the court process and organization;
4. Develop an environment that promotes judges' and courts' integrity (within reason);
5. Make published opinions that are clearly understandable and apply specifically to the issue raised by the case.[55]

▶ Trial Courts

General Jurisdiction: Major Trial Courts

trial courts courts of original jurisdiction (or "first instance") where evidence and testimony are first introduced and findings of fact and law are made.

Trial courts are courts of original jurisdiction (or "first instance") where evidence and testimony are first introduced and findings of fact and law are made. There are an estimated 2,000 major trial courts in the 50 states and Washington, DC, staffed with more than 10,600 general jurisdiction judges, down about 1,000 judges from previous years. The term *general jurisdiction* means that these courts have the legal authority to decide all matters not specifically delegated to lower courts (limited jurisdiction courts); this division of jurisdiction is specified in law. Most often, trial courts of original jurisdiction hear more serious criminal cases as well as civil cases. Cases assigned to trial courts may be based on the severity of punishment for criminal cases or the dollar amount for civil cases.[56] The most common names for these courts are *district*, *circuit*, and *superior*.[57]

Each court has its own support staff consisting of a clerk of court, a sheriff, and others. In most states, the trial courts of general jurisdiction are also grouped into judicial districts or circuits. In rural areas, these districts or circuits encompass several adjoining counties, and the judges are true generalists who hear a wide variety of cases and literally ride the circuit; conversely, larger counties have only one circuit or district for the area, and the judges are often specialists assigned to hear only certain types of cases.[58]

The great majority of the nation's judicial business occurs at the state, not the federal, level. State courts decide primarily street crimes. The more serious criminal violations are heard in the trial courts of general jurisdiction. State courts must also process a rising volume of drug-related offenses. Incoming criminal cases to state courts comprise about 21 percent of the total number of cases. In 2015, 18.1 million criminal cases came into state courts, representing a steady decrease since 2006.[59] But as has been well documented, most criminal cases do not go to trial; thus, the dominant issue in the trial courts of general jurisdiction is not guilt or innocence, but what penalty to apply to the guilty.[60]

Figure 7-3 ■ shows the organizational structure of a county district court serving a population of 300,000. Note the variety of functions and programs that exist in addition to the basic court role of hearing trials and rendering dispositions.

It should also be noted that within the trial courts, a number of problem-solving or specialty courts have become more common.[61] These courts help offenders with drug and mental health issues, as well as military veterans experiencing problems (all of which is

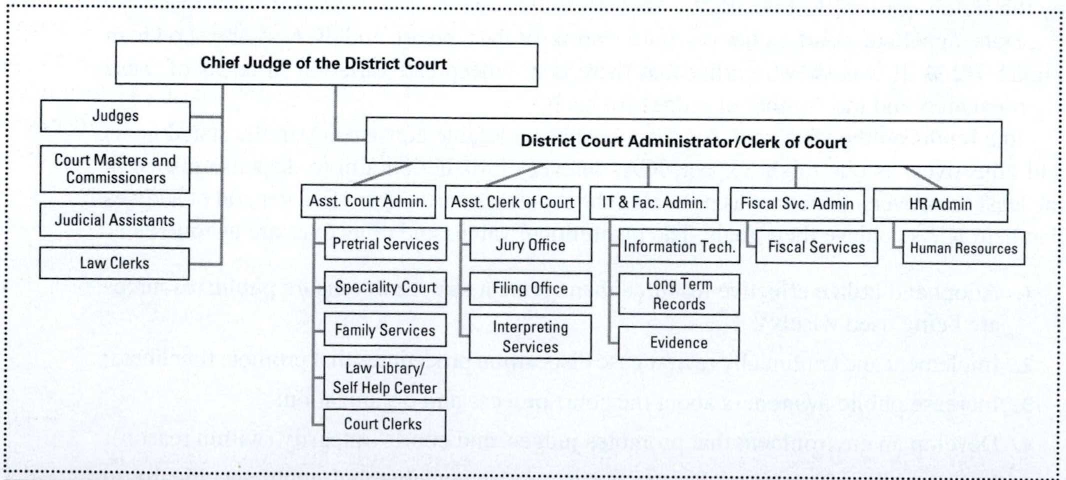

FIGURE 7-3 Org. Structure for a County District Court Serving a Pop. of 300,000

discussed in Chapter 9). Exhibit 7.5 speaks to those courts and several other aspects of court administration, looking at whether or not these courts have a culture of their own.

EXHIBIT 7.5

IS THERE A LEGAL CULTURE WITHIN THE TRIAL COURTS?

Do criminal trial courts have a legal culture, with distinctive norms, values, beliefs, and expectations? If so, what is the nature of local legal culture and how does it affect court performance? The National Institute of Justice funded a study that set out to answer that question. Data were obtained by surveying judges, senior court administrators, and prosecuting/defense attorneys in three states to gauge their views concerning how their courts handled cases, managed relationships between judges and court staff, and exercised courthouse leadership.

The study determined that there were four cultural orientations that can shape the conduct and performance of U.S. state trial courts: communal, networked, autonomous, and hierarchical.

1. ***Communal* courts emphasize *flexibility.*** General agreement on performance goals exists, but centralized judicial and administrative staff leadership is downplayed and creativity is encouraged. As a result, alternative and acceptable ways exist for individual judges to apply court rules, policies, and procedures. Here, judges and administrators emphasize the importance of getting along and acting collectively; group involvement, mutually agreed-upon goals, teamwork, and developing a humane work environment are emphasized.
2. ***Networked* courts emphasize *judicial consensus.*** Judicial expectations, creativity, innovation, and policymaking involve planning efforts of the entire bench. As innovators, these courts attempt to incorporate the latest thinking in specialty courts, problem-solving courts, and therapeutic justice. The networked court hopes to achieve both high solidarity and high sociability—judges, court administrators, and other court staff coordinate and work together to accomplish the work of the court.
3. ***Autonomous* courts emphasize *self-management.*** Limited discussion and agreement exist on the importance of court-wide performance goals. Judges and administrators emphasize the importance of allowing each judge to conduct business as he or she sees fit. Many judges in this type of court are most comfortable with the traditional adversarial model of dispute resolution, wherein the judge is relatively passive and essentially referees the cases presented by attorneys.
4. ***Hierarchical* courts emphasize *clear rules.*** Judges are committed to the use of case flow management (e.g., case coordination and firm trial dates), and written court rules and procedures are emphasized and applied uniformly by judges. These courts seek to achieve the advantages of order and efficiency, and the approach is to create a structured decision-making environment.

The survey also determined that every court surveyed exhibited a combination of cultures; that is, no court is wholly one type in its cultural nature. However, in every court, a particular culture tends to dominate each work area. Although there is no "correct" culture for a particular area of work, different cultural orientations do affect how work is accomplished. In sum, the conventional wisdom that U.S. courts are generally loosely run organizations dominated by autonomous judges who resist administrative controls is not supported. Instead, local legal culture prevails.

Source: Based on Brian J. Ostrom, Charles W. Ostrom, Roger A. Hanson, and Matthew Kleiman, *The Mosaic of Institutional Culture and Performance: Trial Courts as Organizations,* November 2005, pp. 51–52, http://www.ncjrs.gov/pdffiles1/nij/grants/212083.pdf.

Limited Jurisdiction: Lower Courts

inferior courts the lowest level of state courts, normally trial courts of limited jurisdiction.

At the lowest level of state courts are trial courts of limited jurisdiction, also known as **inferior courts** or *lower courts*. There are more than 13,500 trial courts of limited jurisdiction in the United States, staffed with about 16,800 judicial officers, comprising 61 percent of all trial court judges.[62] Because of court unification (discussed next in this chapter), the number of judicial officials serving limited jurisdiction courts has decreased over the years. For example, from 1980 to 2011, the number of limited jurisdiction court judges decreased by 12 percent.[63] The lower courts constitute 85 percent of all judicial bodies in the United States, and account for approximately 60 percent of all judicial proceedings in the United States.

Variously called *district, justice, justice of the peace, city, magistrate*, or *municipal courts*, the lower courts decide a restricted range of cases. These courts are created and maintained by city or county governments and, therefore, are not part of the state judiciary. You might say that these courts truly are the workhorses of the state court system. Of the 106 million cases in state court system, 70 million (66%) are cases in courts of limited jurisdiction.[64]

The workload of the lower courts can be divided into felony criminal cases, non-felony criminal cases, and civil cases. In the felony arena, lower court jurisdiction typically includes the preliminary stages of felony cases; therefore, after an arrest, a judge in a trial court of limited jurisdiction will hold the initial appearance, appoint counsel for indigents, and conduct the preliminary hearing. Later, the case is transferred to a trial court of general jurisdiction (discussed previously) for trial (or plea) and sentencing.[65]

Exhibit 7.6 provides a rather humorous take of what goes on at a lower court—all in a day's work.

EXHIBIT 7.6

ALL IN A DAY'S WORK AT A LOWER COURT

A lower court judge provided compelling realism and insight—as well as a bit of humor—on his court's website concerning the proper decorum and performance of lawyers who are about to litigate cases therein:

> We tend to be the fast-food operators of the court system—high volumes of traffic for short visits with a base of loyal repeat customers. Don't plan on having a private conversation with your client or a witness amid the throngs of other people trying to do the same thing. Prepared attorneys can be in and out in short order. Meeting your client for the first time after calling out his name in the lobby can take longer.
>
> Patience is a virtue and communication with the bailiffs and court staff will keep everyone happy. We coordinate the court's calendar, your calendar, and opposing counsel's calendar with the availability of the witnesses. Here are a few other "do's" and "don'ts" for successfully navigating this Court:
>
> - Everyone goes through the metal detector. Having to go back to your car to stow your Leatherman, linoleum cutting knife, stun gun, giant padlock, or sword-cane (all items caught by security) can be annoying.
> - I once ruled against a very sweet elderly lady who reminded me of my own grandmother. She simply didn't have a case and I thought I had ruled fairly and gently. As she slowly walked by the front of the bench on the way out of the courtroom, she looked up and said, "Aw, go—yourself," and walked out the door. My mouth was hanging open; I just didn't know what to do. I'm fairly sure that this is the first and last time someone will get away with this, so even if the judge rules against you, smile on the way out. You can mutter to yourself all you want on the way back to the office rather than the holding cell in the back of the courthouse.
> - I once watched a gentleman in the back row feed his parrot peanuts while it was sitting on his shoulder. I assumed I had a parrot case in the pile somewhere, but after the last case was called, the parrot left without testifying. I asked the security officer why he let the man with the parrot come into court. I was told that the man had been there to watch a friend's case and that his sick parrot needed to be fed every 15 minutes. While admiring the logic of his decision, I have advised our new court security officers that

unless an animal is actually a service animal, various beasts, fish, and fowl are not allowed in simply to watch court.

- Expect the unexpected. Recent interesting events include a live pipe bomb being left at the front door by a concerned citizen; a gentleman dancing on top of his motor home in the parking lot while his laundry hung from the trees and his morning coffee perked on the propane stove he had set up in the next space; and the occasional ammonia discharges into the holding cell by one of the neighboring businesses.

Source: Excerpt from *An Insider's View of a Lower Court* by Kevin Higgins. Copyright © 2008 by Kevin Higgins. Used by permission of Kevin Higgins.

▶ "Unification," "Consolidation," "Reform": By any Name, a Century's Attempts to Streamline the Courts

Imagine being a student of criminal justice—or one who has received a traffic citation—and finding yourself in a position of having to navigate your state and local court systems. You discover that you live in an area where the highest court of appeal is the court of appeals (not, as is commonly used, a "Supreme Court"), but the primary felony trial courts are called supreme courts and the county courts handle crimes occurring outside the city. There might also be city courts, county courts, municipal courts, and justice of the peace courts (still found in many states) that handle a variety of matters, such as traffic, small claims, and even some preliminary hearings. Then, say you move to another state and find that the state court system is yet another variation with different names attached to what you thought you learned from your previous state! And, what if you moved to the state of New York (see Figure 7.4 ■)?

Although this scenario might be a bit far-fetched, it really is not too different from what one might find in some states in the United States—a situation that has its roots in the early court systems of England. This section discusses how the courts became so confusing and convoluted over time, and what has been done through **court unification** to try to rectify the matter.

court unification reorganizing a trial court's structure, procedures, funding, and administration to streamline operations, better deploy personnel, and improve trial and appellate processes.

Court unification can be defined in several ways, but it typically includes an attempt to simplify a state trial court's structure, procedures, funding, and administration so as to eliminate or reduce overlapping and fragmented jurisdiction, better deploy and use judges and support staff, streamline and expedite trial and appellate processes, and generally make the system more understandable to the average citizen.[66]

Courts in Early England: A Desire to Unify

Beginning with the courts of the late 1800s in England, the need was demonstrated for "unified" state judicial systems, where the court system of any jurisdiction could be efficient, effective, and well understood by the people. But from their early beginnings, since the reign of Edward I in the late 1200s, this has been an elusive goal. Throughout most of the nineteenth century, according to William Raftery,[67] England's court system was a confusing patchwork, with courts for criminal proceedings, petty causes, and general civil matters. Towns, villages, and cities created their own courts or had them created for them by the legislature. Atop this myriad of courts sat, effectively, a jumble. State courts of last resort were just as convoluted as the trial courts. Legislators and governors were also invested with judicial authority, able to issue writs, grant divorces, and sit as appellate courts.

The United States: An Historical Hodgepodge

Although by the mid-1800s England had begun to discard this system of a-court-for-every-type-of-case,[68] the American states were continuing or expanding England's old system, and by 1900 the United States would see, in larger cities, numerous courts with various jurisdictions, overseen by a multitude of higher courts, and so the die was cast. Noted legal scholar and reformer Roscoe Pound was moved to comment on this situation in 1906, in what has become a classic essay entitled *The Causes of Population Dissatisfaction with the Administration of Justice*,[69] that this "multiplicity of courts" needed to come to an end.

In 1914, the American Judicature Society (AJS) began publishing bulletins spelling out what court systems should look like, arguing for a "single Court of Justice" comprised of three divisions: a court of appeal, a superior court, and a county court. It also took the position that one chief justice in each state should be given the same power as a governor and the "executive head" and administer the state's courts so as to reduce confusion and enhance cooperation.[70] A much more controversial recommendation by the AJS was that the judiciary be removed from any involvement from the other two branches of government in the selection of judges and clerks. Finally, the AJS recommended that, to be truly unified, state courts had to cease their legislatures' rule-making authority over the courts,[71] so that the state supreme court has the power to adopt uniform rules to be followed by all courts in the state, including procedures for disciplining attorneys and setting time standards for disposing of cases.

The U.S. court system's status as a mixed bag is in part a product of the political system under which it was established. The complex rules of federalism and division of power are partly responsible for the vast intricacy of the court system. However, this is not implying that the structure is "ideal" or should not be reformed. Unfortunately, it is difficult to compare these differences to other countries, given the relative independence and unique aspects of American government compared to many other first world nations. It would not be until the late 1930s that success in these areas was realized, with some state legislatures beginning to turn over rule-making authority to the state supreme courts and creating judicial councils to oversee the state systems. World War II intervened and halted progress, however, but in 1949 the American Bar Association reprised the idea with its publication of *Minimum Standards of Judicial Administration,*[72] setting forth what each individual state needed to do to implement a more effective procedural system. Thus began a movement focusing on centralization and unification that would last for three decades; between 1959 and 1978, 33 states amended their constitutions or statutes to provide that the chief justice was the administrative head of the court system; today 46 states have such provisions.[73]

As It Stands Today

Today, more than a century after the need was recognized to unify the courts in order to avoid duplication and waste of resources, the goal remains largely unmet. In order to be truly centralized or consolidated, a state's court system should have, at minimum: (1) consolidation into a single-tier trial court, (2) rule-making authority, and (3) centralization of administration. With unification would also come centralized budgeting by the state judicial administrator, a single budget would be prepared for the entire state judiciary and sent to the state legislature, the governor's power to recommend a judicial budget would be eliminated, and lower courts would be dependent on the Supreme Court for their monies. Today, many states claim to be "unified" and assert in their constitutions and statutes that they are so, but to this day such courts maintain up to eight or ten trial courts whose judges are not interchangeable.[74] Though the National Center for State Courts legally describes 26 of the 50 states as unified, the apparent standard for such definition is minimal—language in the state constitution that indicates a "centralized" approach to court dispensation. As such, barring a full-scale analysis of every state's court system, it is true that the goal of court unification is largely incomplete.

Two Examples at the Extremes

Looking at two systems—one that is unified on a statewide basis and one that is not—may assist in better comprehending the concept of unification; to do so, we examine the states of Illinois and New York (Figure 7-4 ■). In 1964, Illinois became the first state to become unified. All of its trial courts were consolidated into a unified circuit court with one chief judge overseeing the operations and procedures in each division. Today, Illinois's state court system includes one court of last resort, one intermediate appellate court divided into five districts, and one court of general jurisdiction sectioned into 22 trial court divisions.[75]

By contrast, New York's state court system, as depicted in Figure 7-4 ■, included one court of last resort, two intermediate appellate courts, two types of general jurisdiction trial courts divided into 69 divisions, and eight types of limited jurisdiction trial courts separated into 1,695 divisions.[76]

In February 2002, a governmental body examined the budgetary impact of trial court restructuring in New York State; first, it was observed that "no state in the nation has a more complex court system structure than New York's, which consists of 11 separate courts—the Supreme Court, the Court of Claims, the County Court, the Family Court, the Surrogate's Court, the New York City Civil and Criminal Courts, the District Courts on Long Island, the City Courts outside of New York City, and the Town and Village Justice Courts." The study noted the "numerous inefficiencies" of the arcane court structure while listing a number of benefits that would accrue to court unification—including an annual estimated net savings of $131.4 million over a 5-year period.[77]

And 15 years later, in January 2017, a report from the New York State Bar Association Committee on the New York State Constitution indicated that little had changed in New York from 2002.[78] The report noted that efforts to modernize the state court system have been unsuccessful. This has resulted in "an overly complex, unduly costly and unnecessarily inefficient court structure."

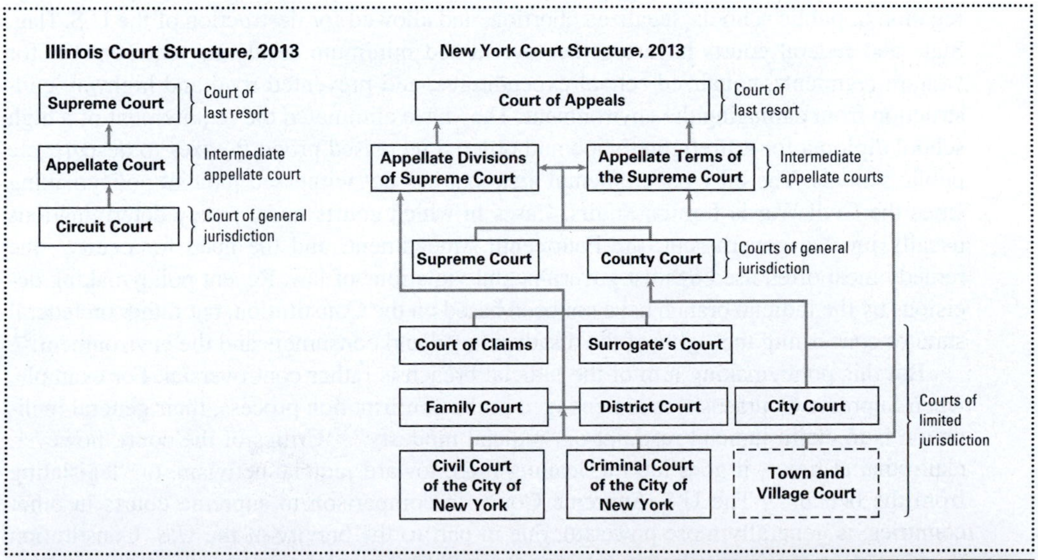

FIGURE 7-4 Illinois and New York Court Structures

But attempts at widespread state court system unification may ultimately be fruitless. Given the decentralized nature of our justice system, it may be unrealistic to truly centralize our state court systems in the way the AJS defines them. What's more, in other areas of the justice system (and in the private sector), we have seen a move away from centralization. Take, for example, the benefits of community policing and problem-solving described in an earlier chapter. Successes with this model of policing come from the ability of police and citizens to work together in a decentralized, neighborhood-based framework. And in the private sector, many for-profit companies are attempting to become flatter. As such, perhaps the next phase of court unification should focus on what Lipscher and Conti describe as "coordinated decentralization."[79] In this approach, much like in community policing and problem-solving, efforts would be made to develop collaborations among the courts and other service agencies.

▶ The Influence of Courts in Policymaking

The judicial branch has the responsibility to determine the legislative intent of the law and to provide public forums—the courts—for resolving disputes. This is accomplished by determining the facts and their legal significance in each case. If the court determines the legal significance of the facts by applying an existing rule of law, it is engaging in pure dispute resolution.[80] On the contrary, "if to resolve the dispute the court must create a new rule or modify an old one that is law creation."[81]

policymaking establishing rules, principles, or guidelines to govern actions by ordinary citizens and persons in positions of authority.

Determining what the law says and providing a public forum involve the courts in policymaking. **Policymaking** can be defined simply as "establishing rules, principles, or guidelines that govern actions by ordinary citizens as well as persons in positions of authority."[82] The policy decisions of the courts affect virtually all of us in our daily lives. In recent decades, the courts have been asked to deal with issues that previously were within the purview of the legislative and judicial branches. Because many of the Constitution's limitations on government are couched in vague language, the judicial branch must eventually deal with potentially volatile social issues, such as those involving prisons, abortion, and schools.[83]

U.S. Supreme Court decisions have dramatically changed race relations, resulted in the overhaul of juvenile courts, increased the rights of the accused, prohibited prayer and segregation in public schools, legalized abortion, and allowed for destruction of the U.S. flag. State and federal courts have together overturned minimum residency requirements for welfare recipients, equalized school expenditures, and prevented road and highway construction from damaging the environment. They have eliminated the requirement of a high school diploma for a firefighter's job and ordered increased property taxes to desegregate public schools. The only governmental area that has not witnessed judicial policymaking since the Civil War is foreign affairs. Cases in which courts make policy determinations usually involve government, the Fourteenth Amendment, and the need for equity—the remedy most often used against governmental violations of law. Recent policymaking decisions by the judicial branch have not been based on the Constitution, but rather on federal statutes concerning the rights of the disadvantaged and consumers and the environment.[84]

But this policymaking arm of the judicial branch is rather controversial. For example, when Supreme Court justices are engaged in the confirmation process, their general inclination is to claim judicial restraint or "judicial modesty."[85] Critics of the court, however, claim that at times, it goes too far, leaning more toward judicial activism, or "legislating from the bench."[86] The U.S. Supreme Court, in comparison to supreme courts in other countries, is generally more powerful, due in part to the brevity of the U.S. Constitution (compared to other countries) and the number of holes that have arisen. According to Tom Ginsburg, who has compared constitutions around the world, the U.S. Supreme Court is more likely to engage in policymaking than other high courts.[87] In fact, critics of judicial activism point to the landmark U.S. Supreme Court case of *Roe v. Wade*, where the court essentially legislated abortion by defining the amount of discretion a woman has to obtain an abortion based on what trimester she is in.[88]

But perhaps nowhere have the nation's courts had more of an impact than in the prisons—from which nearly 60,000 prisoner petitions are filed each year in the U.S. district courts.[89] Among the accomplishments of judicial intervention have been extending recognized constitutional rights of free speech, religion, and due process to prisoners; abolishing the South's plantation model of prisons; accelerating the professionalization of U.S. correctional managers; encouraging a new generation of correctional administrators more amenable to reform; reinforcing the adoption of national standards for prisons; and promoting increased accountability and efficiency of prisons. The only failure of judicial intervention has been its inability to prevent the explosion in prison populations and costs.[90]

The courts have become particularly involved in administrative policy because of public interest group litigation. For example, legislation was enacted allowing citizen lawsuits when certain federal regulatory agencies, such as the Environmental Protection Agency (EPA), failed to perform certain duties as required by statute. Thus, a citizens' environmental group was allowed to sue the EPA.

It may appear that the courts are too broad in their review of issues; however, it should be remembered that judges "cannot impose their views until someone brings a case to court, often as a last resort after complaints to unresponsive legislators and executives."[91] Plaintiffs must be truly aggrieved or have *standing*. The independence of the judicial branch, particularly at the federal court level, at which judges enjoy lifetime appointments, allows the courts to champion the causes of the underclasses: those with fewer financial resources or votes (by virtue of, say, being a minority group) or without a positive public profile.[92] It is also important to note that the judiciary is the "least dangerous branch," having no enforcement powers, but also, as some claim, the least democratic branch and, in the case of the U.S. Supreme Court, one of the most powerful in the world.[93] Moreover, the decisions of the courts can be overturned by legislative action. Even decisions based on the Constitution can be overruled by subsequent constitutional amendment. Thus, the judicial branch depends on a perception of legitimacy surrounding its decisions.[94]

Note: The "Deliberate and Decide" section at the end of this chapter concerns recent public policy areas where many people believe the courts have become too involved (judicial activism vs. judicial restraint); you are invited to voice your opinion concerning the handling and treatment of detainees at Guantánamo Bay, a U.S. naval base located at the southeast tip of Cuba.

Summary

This chapter reviewed the distinctive nature of the courts and their organization and some of their administration. Several areas were highlighted, including the nature of the courts in terms of the status they are accorded and their use of the adversarial system in trying to arrive at the truth; the dual system of courts in our country—the courts of last resort, appeals courts, and trial courts at the federal and state levels; and how the federal courts are administered and the growing movement toward court unification. We also discussed the role of courts in policymaking.

With regard to court unification, a need and an issue that is indicated in this chapter is that of court reform because of the often confusing way in which courts and judges are organized and utilized; many notable authorities believe changes are necessary to improve court efficiency and possibly to save large amounts of public money. It is clear, however, that until a number of political and tradition-based impediments are overcome, widespread court reform is unlikely. Alternatively, coordinated decentralization may be the answer.

Another issue raised in this chapter is the burgeoning caseloads of the courts; alternative dispute resolution, discussed in Chapter 9, is proposed as a means of helping in this area of court operation.

Key Terms and Concepts

Adversarial system, p. 161
Court of last resort, p. 169
Court unification, p. 175
Decor, p. 160
Decorum, p. 160
Dual court system, p. 162
Inferior courts, p. 173
Intermediate courts of appeals (ICAs), p. 171
Judicial Conference of the United States, p. 167
Jurisdiction, p. 163
Policymaking, p. 178
Trial courts, p. 172

Questions for Review

1. What is judicial activism? Provide an example of this.
2. How is the adversarial system of justice related to the truth-seeking function of the courts?
3. What is the organization of our dual court system, and what are the primary functions of each of the major types of courts that exist within the federal and state court systems?
4. Discuss the main differences between the federal and state court systems.
5. Describe the nature of limited jurisdiction courts. What types of cases do these courts hear? Why are they considered the "workhorses" of state judicial systems?
6. What are some perceived benefits of streamlining a state court system, and how would such a system be organized? What are examples of a highly unified system and a poorly unified state system?
7. What are the types of, and reasons for, court jurisdiction?
8. How do the courts influence public policymaking?

Deliberate and Decide

Courts, Policymaking, and the Guantánamo Detainees

What is the appropriate role for the judiciary in policymaking? While some people favor judicial restraint and believe the courts should have little or no role in policymaking—where judges play minimal policymaking roles and leave policy decisions to the legislatures—others argue for judicial activism, believing judges can make policy decisions that help those who are politically or economically disadvantaged. Prior to his death in 2016, U.S. Supreme Court justice Antonin Scalia was a proponent of the Court staying out of areas that would be best left to Congress or the people, citing the court's rulings in such areas as surveillance of phone records, a national health program (the Affordable Care Act), the right to bear arms, and "inventing" new classes of minorities such as the areas of gay marriage and benefits for same-sex couples.[95]

As another example, consider where the line should be drawn between protecting U.S. citizens from terrorists and individual rights and liberties. More specifically, what role should the courts play in determining how individuals be treated—both in terms of the rule of law and their confinement—when suspected of being "enemy combatants?" Furthermore, to what extent should the courts be involved in terms of crafting policy regarding law-of-war detention?

A specific example of policymaking in this arena is the detention of suspected enemy combatants at Guantánamo Bay, a 45-square-mile American naval base located at the southeast tip of Cuba. After the terrorist attacks of 9/11 and the war in Afghanistan, the United States moved about 600 captured prisoners to Guantánamo Bay, most of whom remained there for years without being charged with crimes or being given hearings.

In the wake of the September 11, 2001, attacks on the United States, the government authorized the use of "enhanced interrogation" techniques that were previously recognized as torture. The Bush administration contended that certain persons were dangerous enemy combatants who could be detained and interrogated legally and humanely during the ongoing war on terrorism. The detainees eventually challenged this policy, filing suits in federal courts and triggering policy discussions at the national level. In addition, the detainees engaged in hunger strikes (with many of them being force-fed); the Supreme Court issued several major decisions: first, the government should have the power to recognize and detain enemy combatants, including U.S. citizens, but the latter must be afforded due process rights[96]; the president could not create military commissions to try Guantánamo detainees, thereby invalidating the system established to try accused war criminals (this case was widely seen as the most important ruling on executive power in decades, or perhaps ever)[97]; and foreign nationals who are held at Guantánamo Bay have a right to *habeas corpus*.[98]

Questions for Discussion

As a preliminary question, should the court have remained detached from this entire matter—using restraint, as former justice Scalia suggested, and leaving it to Congress or the people to resolve?

1. Regarding the dilemma of protecting the public against terrorism versus individual rights, what do you believe are the major arguments for and against releasing the Guantánamo detainees? Should they ever be completely released, or at the very least committed to federal and state prisons?
2. What legal rights should these detainees possess? How do/should those rights differ from those of U.S. citizens who are accused of crimes?
3. Should such detainees who commit hunger strikes be force-fed, or left to either die or accept food on their own?[99]

Learn by Doing

1. You are a court administrator and have been invited to appear at a luncheon meeting of a local civic group of community and business leaders. While discussing your duties within the state court system, you are asked to explain the overall functions and interrelationship between the federal and state courts. How do you reply?
2. A county historical society has invited your criminal justice professor to speak at a meeting concerning the history and importance of the traditions within the U.S. Supreme Court. Your professor asks you, the graduate assistant, to draft an overview for this purpose. What will you write?
3. You are a teaching assistant in your university's criminal justice department and your instructor has fallen ill at the outset of the semester. As your instructor is a J.D./Ph.D., she often instructs courts courses. You are tasked to develop a one-hour lecture on how state trial courts of general jurisdiction (i.e., the major trial courts) differ in scope and function from the higher state courts of last resort as well as appellate courts. What will you include in your lecture?

Case Study

Court Unification and Systemic Complexity

You are a legislator who has been tasked with balancing the state's judicial budget, which has been significantly overspent for several years. The state's court structure is similar to that of New York State, with a plethora of distinctly separate courts: multiple courts of limited jurisdiction, a few courts of general jurisdiction, and several intermediate appellate courts. A proposal has been laid on your desk that suggests the court system should be consolidated/unified. On its face, this would seem to be a good solution to your problem: rather than having a labyrinth of different courts, staffs, and judges all with limited jurisdiction, your state would have a streamlined process for cases to proceed. However, you soon receive a letter from a group of several already-sitting judges who express their opposition to the idea. Not only would it potentially cost some judges and staff their jobs, but they also refer to a research article that calls into question the utility of court unification. The article suggests that the increase in case processing observed in consolidated court structures is likely due more to the additional resources brought on by such "experimentation." In addition, the judges from rural areas express skepticism that the infrastructure associated with centralized data storage will not be feasible in their areas due to the diminished tax bases of rural communities. Finally, the letter expresses doubt that such reforms will go smoothly with all judges: court unification will require a higher degree of judicial "cooperation" and personality mesh, which are not at all guaranteed to exist.

Questions for Discussion

1. What is your decision on court unification? How many levels of courts would it have? Where do specialty courts fit within your design, if at all?
2. How will you "defend" your decision to those who oppose it—for pro-unification, it is the judges; for the status quo, it is the proposal sponsors? What do you think will be the public's reaction to your decision?

Notes

1. The Common Law and Civil Law Traditions, October 24, 2016, https://www.law.berkeley.edu/library/robbins/CommonLawCivilLawTraditions.html.
2. Alexis de Tocqueville, *Democracy in America,* Vol. 1, trans. H. Reeve (New York: Daniel Appleton, 1904), pp. 283–284.
3. B. Vielmetti, "Attorney Flagged for Facebook Selfie with Client Cleared of Homicide," September 28, 2015, http://archive.jsonline.com/blogs/news/329539971.html
4. H. Ted Rubin, *The Courts: Fulcrum of the Justice System* (Santa Monica, CA: Goodyear, 1976), p. 3.
5. Satisfying the "Appearance of Justice": The Uses of Apparent Impropriety in Constitutional Adjudication, *Harvard Law Review,* 117(8) (2004): 2708. doi:10.2307/4093412
6. K. Bridges, "Judicial Activism and the U.S. Supreme Court—SAGU," May 25, 2016, http://www.sagu.edu/thoughthub/judicial-activism-supreme-court-decisions.
7. Stephen Whicher and R. Spiller (eds.), *The Early Lectures of Ralph Waldo Emerson* (Philadelphia, PA: University of Pennsylvania Press, 1953), p. 112.
8. 382 U.S. 406 (1966), 416.
9. Thomas L. Steffen, "Truth as Second Fiddle: Reevaluating the Place of Truth in the Adversarial Trial Ensemble," *Utah Law Review* 4 (1988): 821.
10. Monroe H. Freedman, Our Constitutionalized Adversary System, 1Chap. L. Review 57 (1998).
11. Ibid., p. 58.
12. W. Alschuler, "The Preservation of a Client's Confidences: One Value among Many or a Categorical Imperative?" *University of Colorado Law Review* 52 (1981): 349.
13. L. Nash, "Differences between an Adversarial and an Inquisitorial Legal System," October 1, 2015, http://www.ashfords.co.uk/article/differences-between-an-adversarial-and-an-inquisitorial-legal-system.
14. Nichole L. Waters, Anne Gallegos, and James Green, *Criminal Appeals in State Courts* (pp. 1–17) (United States Bureau of Justice Statistics, Office of Justice Programs, September 2015), https://www.bjs.gov/content/pub/pdf/casc.pdf.
15. David W. Neubauer, *America's Courts and the Criminal Justice System*, 9th ed. (Belmont, CA: Thomson Wadsworth, 2008), p. 63.
16. Supreme Court of the United States, "Instructions for Admission to the Bar," http://www.supremecourt.gov/bar/barinstructions.pdf.
17. Ibid., "Visitor's Guide to Oral Arguments," p. 1, http://www.supremecourt.gov/visiting/visitorsguidetooralargument.aspx.
18. Robert H. Jackson Center, "The Flags at Nuremberg," http://www.roberthjackson.org/the-man/speeches-articles/speeches/speeches-related-to-robert-h-jackson/the-flags-at-nuremberg/.
19. Supreme Court of the United States, "The Court and Its Traditions," http://www.supremecourt.gov/about/traditions.aspx.
20. United States Courts, "U.S. Supreme Court Procedures," http://www.uscourts.gov/EducationalResources/ConstitutionResources/SeparationOfPowers/USSupremeCourtProcedures.aspx.
21. Ibid., "Writs of Certiorari," http://www.uscourts.gov/educational-resources/get-informed/supreme-court/supreme-court-procedures.aspx.
22. See University of Missouri—Kansas City Law School, "Exploring Constitutional Conflict: The Supreme Court in the American System of Government," http://law2.umkc.edu/faculty/projects/ftrials/conlaw/supremecourtintro.html.
23. Brett Snider, "How Does the U.S. Supreme Court Work?" http;//blogs.findlaw.com/law_and_life/2013/10/how-does-the-us-supreme-court-work.html.
24. Supreme Court of the United States, "Members," http://www.supremecourt.gov/about/about_us.aspx.
25. Federal Judicial Center, "The U.S. Courts of Appeals and the Federal Judiciary," http://www.fjc.gov/history/home.nsf/page/courts_of_appeals.html.
26. U.S. Courts, "U.S. Courts of Appeals—Appeals Filed by Type of Appeal," http://www.uscourts.gov/sites/default/files/data_tables/Table2.03.pdf.
27. Ibid.
28. U.S. Courts, "U.S. Courts of Appeals and Their Impact of Your Life," http://www.uscourts.gov/educational-resources/educational-activities/us-courts-appeals-and-their-impact-your-life.
29. For more discussion about the court, see Eric Andreas, "Key Role of the DC Circuit," *Wiley Rein Winter 2007*, http://www.wileyrein.com/publications.cfm?sp=articles&newsletter=13&id=4074; also see Richard Wolf, "Senate Fights over Appeals Court Key to Obama Agenda," *USA Today*, November 21, 2013, http://www.usatoday.com/story/news/politics/2013/11/21/dc-circuit-judges-senate-obama-filibuster-nuclear/3663817/.
30. Office of the United States Attorneys, "Introduction to the Federal Court System," https://www.justice.gov/usao/justice-101/federal-courts.
31. Ibid.
32. More information about this court may be found at its websites at: http://www.cadc.uscourts.gov/internet/home.nsf and http://www.dccourts.gov/internet/appellate/main.jsf.
33. United States Courts, "Federal Judgeships," http://www.uscourts.gov/JudgesAndJudgeships/FederalJudgeships.aspx.
34. Office of the United States Attorneys, "Introduction to the Federal Court System."
35. Ibid.
36. "United States Courts, U.S. District Courts—Criminal Cases Commenced, Terminated, and Pending (Including Transfers) during the 12-Month Periods Ending March 31, 2011 and 2012," Table D, http://www.uscourts.gov/Viewer.aspx?doc=/uscourts/Statistics/FederalJudicialCaseloadStatistics/2012/tables/D00CMar12.pdf.

37. E. Lichtblau, In Secret, Court Vastly Broadens Powers of N.S.A., July 6, 2013, http://www.nytimes.com/2013/07/07/us/in-secret-court-vastly-broadens-powers-of-nsa.html.
38. U.S. Courts, "About the Judicial Conference," http://www.uscourts.gov/about-federal-courts/governance-judicial-conference/about-judicial-conference.
39. Ibid.
40. Neubauer, *America's Courts and the Criminal Justice System,* p. 68.
41. Saikrishna Prakash and Steven D. Smith, "Removing Federal Judges Without Impeachment," *The Yale Law Journal* 116 (October 2006), http://www.yalelawjournal.org/forum/removing-federal-judges-without-impeachment.
42. U.S. Courts, "The Federal Judiciary," http://www.uscourts.gov/adminoff.html.
43. U.S. Courts, "Annual Report 2015: Director's Message," http://www.uscourts.gov/statistics-reports/annual-reports/annual-report-2015.
44. Ibid.
45. Findlaw, "State Courts in Depth," http://files.findlaw.com/pdf/litigation.findlaw.com_legal-system_state-courts-in-depth.pdf.
46. Neubauer, *America's Courts and the Criminal Justice System,* p. 85.
47. Nicole L. Watters, Anne Gallegos, James Green, and Martha Rozsi, *Criminal Appeals in State Courts* (Washington, DC: Bureau of Justice Statistics, September 2015), p. 1.
48. Neubauer, *America's Courts and the Criminal Justice System*, p. 87.
49. Ibid., p. 8.
50. Ibid., p. 9.
51. See National Center for State Courts, *The Role of State Intermediate Appellate Courts: Principles for Adapting to Change* (November 2012), p. 3.
52. U.S. Department of Justice, Bureau of Justice Statistics, *State Court Organization, 2011* (Washington, DC: November 2013), p. 5.
53. National Center for State Courts, "Appellate Caseloads," http://www.courtstatistics.org/Appellate/2014Appellate.aspx.
54. Neubauer, *America's Courts and the Criminal Justice System*, p. 85.
55. J. P. Doerner and C. A. Markman, *The Role of State Intermediate Appellate Courts* (U.S. National Center for State Courts, November 2012).
56. U.S. Department of Justice, Bureau of Justice Statistics, *State Court Organization*, p. 2.
57. National Center for State Courts, "Court Statistics Project," http://www.courtstatistics.org.
58. Neubauer, *America's Courts and the Criminal Justice System*, p. 82.
59. Court Statistics Project, http://www.courtstatistics.org/~/media/Microsites/Files/CSP/EWSC%202015.ashx.
60. Neubauer, *America's Courts and the Criminal Justice System*, pp. 82–83.
61. U.S. Department of Justice, Bureau of Justice Statistics, *State Court Organization,* p. 3.
62. Ibid., p. 4.
63. Ibid., p. 4.
64. Janet G. Cornell, "Limited Jurisdiction Courts—Challenges, Opportunities, and Strategies for Action," Trends in State Courts, http://www.ncsc.org/sitecore/content/microsites/future-trends-2012/home/courts-and-the-community/3-6-limited-jurisdiction-courts.aspx.
65. Neubauer, *America's Courts and the Criminal Justice System*, pp. 402–403.
66. See, generally, William Raftery, "Unification and 'Bragency': A Century of Court Organization and Reorganization," *Judicature* 96(6) (May/June 2014): 338; also see National Center for State Courts, "Court Unification Resource Guide," http://www.ncsc.org/Topics/Court-Management/Court-Unification/Resource-Guide.aspx.
67. Ibid.
68. Ibid.
69. Roscoe Pound, "The Causes of Population Dissatisfaction with the Administration of Justice," *American Law Review* 40 (1926): 729.
70. American Judicature Society, "Model Judiciary Article," *Journal of the American Judicature Society* 6 (1922): 48–58.
71. Silas A. Harris, "The Extent and Use of Rule-making Authority," *Journal of the American Judicature Society* 22 (1938): 30.
72. See Louden L. Bomberger, "Minimum Standards of Judicial Administration, by Arthur T. Vanderbilt," *Indiana Law Journal* 26(1) (1950), http://www.repository.law.indiana.edu/ilj/vol26/iss1/13.
73. Raftery,"Unification and'Bragency,'"p. 342.
74. Ibid.
75. State of Illinois, "Illinois Court System," October 29, 2014, http://19thcircuitcourt.state.il.us/Organization/Pages/il_crts.aspx; also see Illinois State Courts, "The Illinois Judiciary," http://www.courts.us/state/il/courts.php.
76. NYCourts.gov, "Structure of the New York State Unified Court System," http://www.nycourts.gov/courts/8jd/structure.shtml.
77. New York State Unified Court System, "The Budgetary Impact of Trial Court Restructuring," http://www.nycourts.gov/reports/trialcourtrestructuring/ctmerger2802.pdf.
78. New York State Bar Association Committee on the New York State Constitution, The Judiciary Article of the New York State Constitution: Opportunities to Restructure and Modernize the New York Courts, January 27, 2017, http://www.nysba.org/judiciaryreport2017/.
79. Robert D. Lipscher and Samuel D. Conti, "A Postunification Approach to Court Organizational Design and Leadership," *Justice System Journal* 15(1991): 667.
80. Howard Abadinsky, *Law and Justice: An Introduction to the American Legal System,* 4th ed. (Chicago, IL: Nelson-Hall, 1999), p. 33.

81. Richard A. Posner, *The Federal Courts: Crisis and Reform* (Cambridge, MA: Harvard University Press, 1985), p. 3.
82. Wayne N. Welsh and Philip W. Harris, *Criminal Justice Policy & Planning*, 4th ed. (Boston, MA: Elsevier, 2013), p. 108; also see: Harold J. Spaeth, *Supreme Court Policy Making: Explanation and Prediction* (San Francisco, CA: William H. Freeman, 1979), p. 19.
83. Abadinsky, *Law and Justice,* p. 174.
84. Ibid., p. 170.
85. Eric Black, "How the Supreme Court Has Come to Play a Policymaking Role," *Minnpost*, November 20, 2012, https/www.minnpostg.com/eric-black-ink/2012/11/how-supreme-court-has-come-play-policymaking-role.
86. Ibid.
87. Ibid.
88. Ibid.
89. U.S. Department of Justice, *Sourcebook of Criminal Justice Statistics 2000* (Washington, DC: U.S. Government Printing Office, 2001), p. 467.
90. Malcolm M. Feeley and Edward L. Rubin, *Judicial Policy Making and the Modern State: How the Courts Reformed America's Prisons* (New York: Cambridge University Press, 1998).
91. Stephen L. Wasby, *The Supreme Court in the Federal System,* 3rd ed. (Chicago, IL: Nelson-Hall, 1989), p. 5.
92. Abadinsky, *Law and Justice,* p. 171.
93. Black, "How the Supreme Court Has Come to Play a Policymaking Role."
94. Abadinsky, *Law and Justice,* p. 166.
95. Matt Volz, "Antonin Scalia: Supreme Court Should Not Be Policymakers," *Huffington Post,* August 13, 2014, http://www.huffingtonpost.com/2014/08/19/antonin-scalia-supreme-court_n_3782297.html.
96. See *Hamdi v. Rumsfeld*, 542 U.S. 507 (2004).
97. See *Hamdan v. Rumsfeld,* 548 U.S. 557 (2006).
98. See *Boumediene v. Bush*, 553 U.S. 723 (2008).
99. George C. Edwards, III, Martin P. Wattenberg, and Robert L. Lineberry, "Government in America: People, Politics, and Policy," September 23, 2014, http://wps.ablongman.com/long_edwards_ga_12/33/8517/2180538.cw/; Susan Seligson, "The Legal Mess behind the Ethical Mess," Boston University "BU Today," May 28, 2014, http://www.bu.edu/today/2014/gitmo-the-legal-mess-behind-the-ethical-mess/; Dante Gatmaytan, "Crafting Policies for the Guantánamo Bay Detainees: An Interbranch Perspective," *DePaul Rule of Law Journal* (Fall 2010), http://www.academia.edu/3412061/Crafting_Policies_for_the_Guantanamo_Bay_Detainees_An_Interbranch_Perspective; see the U.S. Department of Defense Guantanamo website at: http://www.defense.gov/home/features/gitmo/.

Wavebreakmediamicro/123RF

8 Court Personnel Roles and Functions

LEARNING OBJECTIVES

After reading this chapter, the student will be able to:

1. *define and understand judicial administration and court administration*
2. *understand the methods of judicial selection: partisan elections, nonpartisan elections, merit selection, and appointment*
3. *discuss the benefits and problems encountered by judges, including the problems faced by newly appointed judges*
4. *describe how civility is maintained in the courtroom, the meaning of good judging, and a new model code of conduct for state and local judges*
5. *explain some issues surrounding judges' personal and professional use of electronic social media/networking sites*
6. *provide a description of the "appearance of impropriety" concept as it applies to judges (and other criminal justice employees), as well as its importance and how it functions*
7. *delineate the duties of judges who serve as court managers, including the chief justice of the U.S. Supreme Court*
8. *relate the importance of court clerks*

9. *define the six major duties of court administrators*
10. *review several strategies that judges follow in determining the quality of administrators' work*
11. *delineate the components of jury administration, including special considerations during notorious cases*

Introduction

Chapter 7 examined the "hallowed" nature of the courts and at how the courts and judges—with gavels, flowing robes, ornate surroundings, and other aspects of décor and decorum that are accorded their office—are enveloped in a mystique of importance and authority. This chapter expands that discussion, focusing more on judges and other key personnel who are involved in court administration.

The administration of the judicial process is probably the least understood area of justice administration and possibly all of criminal justice. This lack of understanding is compounded by the fact that, very often, even judges and court administrators are not formally trained in their roles. Furthermore, few judges would probably "like to spend all day or most of the day handling union grievances or making sure that employees know what their benefits are."[1] Opportunities to receive training and education are expanding, however, and this chapter addresses some of the means by which that can be accomplished. For example, with the proliferation of National Center for State Court (NCSC) resources and published works on court administration, more opportunities exist for judicial officers to be trained and prepared for the tasks associated with judicial administration. Even a cursory search of the term *judicial administration resources* will bring up the link to the NCSC page, where articles are linked and available for reference on a wide variety of topics relevant to judicial administration. But we're getting ahead of ourselves!

This chapter opens by defining and distinguishing the terms *judicial administration* and *court administration* and then considering judges: how they ascend to the bench, benefits and problems of the position, and some thoughts on good judging and courtroom civility; included here are discussions of a revised code of conduct for state and local judges, some ethical considerations concerning judges' use of social networking sites, and a definition and some examples of what is meant by the "appearance of impropriety." Then, we specifically examine the judge's role as the ultimate judicial administrator. The historically important role of court clerks is then reviewed, and next, we examine the relatively new position of the specially trained court administrator, including training and duties, judges' evaluation criteria, and conflict among judicial administrators. This is followed by an overview of the problems court administrators might confront in creating and maintaining juries, especially during sequestration and notorious trials. The chapter concludes with review questions and exercises in the Deliberate and Decide, Learn by Doing, and Case Study sections.

Note that Chapter 15, concerning financial administration, discusses a role of court administration that took on new significance with the onset of the recession about 10 years ago: grant writing.

judicial (court) administration the day-to-day and long-range activities of those persons who are responsible for the activities and functions of a court.

Defining Judicial Administration

The purpose of judicial independence is to mitigate arbitrariness in judging. But what is the definition and purpose of **judicial (or court) administration**. This relatively new criminal justice concept can be difficult to define. Consequently, as Russell Wheeler noted, "many court administrators today find themselves under the inevitable strain of not knowing for certain what their purpose is."[2]

Before we take a brief look back at some seminal works related to the administration of justice, it is important to note that court administration has considerably changed over time. This, in itself, can be a real challenge to the administrator, who finds himself or herself needing to work with others to plan strategically for growth and changes in technology. Take, for example, the technology boom and how this has been integrated into our court systems. It wasn't too long ago that "paper" drove our court processes. But as technology advanced, its incorporation into our court systems also has. Using computer software to track trial dates largely has replaced paper "dockets."[3] Administrators have taken the lead in integrating technology into our court systems. See "In Their Own Words" (discussed in the next section) as Chief Justice Jennifer Togliatti discusses electronic court filings and a CourtFinder app as some of her major accomplishments as an administrator.

Most works on judicial administration point to Roscoe Pound as the founder of the study of judicial administration because of his 1906 essay "The Causes of Popular Dissatisfaction with Administration of Justice."[4] Pound issued a call to improve judicial administration, by efficient and equitable practices, like others did around this time period in the fields of policing and corrections. Pound contended that the courts were archaic and did indeed need to be administered more effectively. He also noted that the adversary system often turned litigation into a game, irritating parties, jurors, and witnesses and giving the public a false notion of the purpose and end of law. Pound's lecture remains a treasure trove of ideas concerning the management of courts and has also led some states to unify their trial courts (discussed in Chapter 7).[5]

However, another major essay that influenced court administration was written by Woodrow Wilson 19 years earlier, in 1887, entitled "The Study of Administration." Wilson stressed that the vocation of administration was a noble calling and not a task for which every person was competent.[6] He emphasized that policy and administration are two different matters, and that judges are responsible for "establishing fundamental court policy," and that a "trained executive officer, working under the chief judge or presiding judge, [was needed to] relieve judges generally [of] the function of handling the numerous business and administrative affairs of the courts."[7] And, as we know from our discussion in Chapter 7, these administrative affairs have only become more diverse and complicated as our court systems have grown over time.

Wilson's essay certainly gives intellectual respectability to the field of administration; however, almost every administrator and policymaker knows that a court's policy decisions inevitably intertwine with administrative decisions. For example, today's court administrator must often set policy for dealing with issues, such as celebrity cases, evidence, case scheduling, and the use of cameras in the courtroom—the kinds of issues discussed here and in Chapter 9. Attention also should be paid to the importance of judicial policy. Judicial policy is the content that gives direction and guidance to judicial administration. It, in turn, is influenced by certain factors of the administration. It is no less important to define and understand policy when attempting to define administration. The difficulty of defining judicial administration became even more obvious during the 1970s when it became an attractive vocation. Various people and commissions tried to define it but seemed capable only of listing the duties of the office. For example, the National Advisory Commission on Criminal Justice Standards and Goals stated succinctly in 1973 that "the basic purpose of court administration is to relieve judges of some administrative chores and to help them perform those they retain."[8] Furthermore, in 1974, the American Bar Association (ABA) specified a variety of functions for the court administrator to perform "under the authority of the judicial council and the supervision of the chief justice."[9]

To help provide more clarity, a good working definition of judicial administration was advanced by Russell Wheeler and Howard Whitcomb in 1977:

> The direction of and influences on the activities of those who are expected to contribute to just and efficient case processing—except legal doctrinal considerations, insofar as they dispose of the particular factual and legal claims presented in a case.[10]

This definition also separates the judicial and nonjudicial functions of the court, and it implies that a *set* of people share a role norm and that judicial administration constitutes *all* of the factors that direct and influence those people.[11]

In sum, the term *court administration* might be conceived of as the day-to-day and long-range activities of those persons who are responsible for the activities and functions of the court system. This term is more commonly used in this chapter because of the development of the role and functions of the *individual trial court administrator*. This will become clearer as the chapter unfolds and the relationship between judge and court administrator is discussed.

▶ The Jurists

There are many facets involved with serving as a judge: getting educated and trained for the position, getting elected or appointed, overseeing the proper conduct of court proceedings, and administering the full range of services and resources pertaining to the court. This section discusses those elements.

IN THEIR OWN WORDS

ADMINISTRATIVE ADVICE FROM THE FIELD

Kenneth J. Peak

Name: Jennifer P. Togliatti

Current position/City/State: Chief Judge, Eighth Judicial District Court (EJDC), Las Vegas, NV

College attended/academic major/degree(s): Undergraduate: UNLV, Bachelor's degree in Business Administration

Graduate: California Western School of Law, Juris Doctorate degree

My primary duties and responsibilities in this position include: responsibility for performing duties as both an administrator and a judge. As an administrator, I conduct monthly meetings for all of the judges of the EJDC and attend meetings of the civil and criminal judges. I also lead a legislative committee that works with the judiciary statewide to monitor legislation for Nevada courts. I decide the vast majority of motions to disqualify judges filed in the EJDC, conduct settlement conferences, and handle criminal matters. I manage labor issues and deal with litigation matters for the Court. I conduct several monthly meetings with community partners in justice. I oversee the court executive officer and meet with him regularly to manage budgetary issues and all issues associated with the EJDC's functions. Finally, I am responsible for overseeing the management of 600 court employees, including the marshal force, 51 judges, and 17 hearing masters and commissioners, all while keeping costs within the Court's $54 million budget.

Personal attributes/characteristics that have proven to be most helpful to me in this position are: patience, diplomacy, and willingness to compromise.

My three greatest challenges in this administrative role include: providing consistent level of service in the face of historic budget cuts, managing the growth of the EJDC (namely the addition of 10 judges and 8 courtrooms), and dealing with problems regarding the separation of powers, which arise because the EJDC is funded by the legislative and executive branches.

Personal accomplishments during my administrative career about which I am most proud are: during my term as chief judge, focusing on major advances in technology. In order to expand the Court and provide greater access to justice, I instituted a new system of electronic filing, which resulted in a paperless filing system. This efficiency has aided the environment and has saved space at the courthouse. My administration also launched the EJDC's own app, CourtFinder (at: https://play.google.com/store/apps/details?id=gov.clarkcountynv.courts.docket.android). Next, I take pride in my work with the Court's marshal force. At this incredible time in our history, when we face threats ranging from basic criminal acts to domestic terrorism, our court system absolutely must focus on security while adhering to recent budget cuts. Our marshal force (consisting of 98 marshals and the head of court security, as well as 11 marshal support staff and court security administrators) has exploded in growth since I was sworn in as chief. Previously, the Court employed one marshal for each judge. As the Court grew, we became responsible for the security of a building that houses the municipal, district, and justice courts, as well as the Nevada Supreme Court. As chief, I am responsible for a marshal force that polices the facilities and keeps the building and its occupants safe. To accomplish this, I improved the EJDC's marshal training, developed new policies and procedures to manage a large administrative marshal pool, implemented an internal affairs bureau to increase integrity, and reorganized the Court to provide high-level management.

Advice for someone who is interested in occupying an administrative position such as mine would be: particularly in a large court, commit 100 percent of your time and attention to the duties of administration. While you may have the sense that you are first a judge, and therefore would enjoy maintaining a regular caseload, the policy matters, budgetary issues, personnel decisions, litigation, and necessary meetings with partners in the justice community require full attention at all times. Most importantly, start your term with several goals in mind, including the three to five most important changes to the policy or operations of your court you wish to make. Don't lose sight of these overarching goals, even when bogged down with daily problems and minutiae that seem to take up all your time.

Source: Used with permission from Jennifer P. Togliatti.

Methods of Judicial Selection

To a large extent, the quality of justice Americans receive depends on the quality of the judges who dispense it. Many factors have a bearing on the quality of judicial personnel: salary, length of term, prestige, independence, and personal satisfaction with the job. The most important factor considered by court reformers is judicial selection.[12]

In the federal system, as noted in Chapter 7, judges are nominated by the president and confirmed by the Senate; they then serve for life (unless they resign or are impeached). **Judicial selection**, or the method used to nominate, select, or elect and install judges into office, is quite varied in state courts. These methods include partisan elections, nonpartisan elections, merit selection, or appointment to select not only for a full term of office (see Figure 8-1 ■) but also to fill an unexpired term upon the death, retirement, or resignation of a judge, or at the end of a special term.[13]

judicial selection the method used to nominate, select, or elect and install judges into office.

Figure 8-1 demonstrates regional patterns in the methods of judicial selection. It shows that partisan elections are concentrated in the South, nonpartisan elections in the West and upper Midwest, legislative elections and executive appointments in the East, and merit selection west of the Mississippi River.[14]

We now turn to some brief discussions of each of the judicial selection methods, keeping in mind that there is no "perfect" method that provides the optimal balance between judicial independence and accountability.[15]

Merit selection has been favored by court reformers wanting to "remove the courts from politics!" They point to three problems with popular elections of judges: (1) Elections fail to encourage the ablest lawyers to seek judicial posts and discourage qualified persons who want to avoid the rigors (if not the ordeal) of a campaign, (2) elections may provide an incentive for judges to decide cases in a popular manner, and (3) the elective system is a contest in which the electorate is likely to be uninformed about the merits of the candidates.

merit selection/ Missouri Bar Plan a nonpartisan method of selecting judges; a nominating commission provides names of qualified persons to the governor, who chooses one person to serve.

Merit Selection (17)	Partisan Election (9)	Nonpartisan Election (17)	Gubernatorial (2) or Legislative (2) Appointment	Combined Methods (4)[1]
Alaska	Alabama	Arkansas	California (G)	Arizona
Colorado	Illinois	Georgia	New Jersey (G)	Florida
Connecticut	Louisiana	Idaho	South Carolina (L)	Indiana
Delaware[2]	New Mexico	Kentucky	Virginia (L)	Kansas
District of Columbia	Ohio[3]	Michigan		Missouri
Hawaii[4]	Pennsylvania	Minnesota		New York
Iowa	Texas	Mississippi		Oklahoma
Maine	West Virginia	Montana		South Dakota
Maryland[2]		Nevada		Tennessee
Massachusetts[2]		North Carolina		
Nebraska		North Dakota		
New Hampshire[2]		Oregon		
New Mexico		Washington		
Rhode Island		Wisconsin		
Utah				
Vermont				
Wyoming				

1. In these states, some judges are chosen through merit selection and some are chosen in competitive elections.
2. Merit selection is established by executive order.
3. Candidates appear on the general election ballot without party affiliation but are nominated in partisan primaries.
4. The chief justice makes appointments to the district court and family court.

FIGURE 8-1 Initial Selection Methods of State Judges

Source: Excerpt from *Judicial Selection in the States: Appellate and General Jurisdiction Courts.* Copyright © 2004 by American Judicature Society. Used by permission of American Judicature Society.

To solve these problems, reformers advocate merit selection, also known as the **Missouri Bar Plan**. Thirty-four states and the District of Columbia use the merit system, and a number of other states have considered it. Merit selection involves the creation of a nominating commission whenever a vacancy occurs for any reason; the commission is comprised of lawyers and laypersons; this group suggests a list of qualified nominees (usually three) to the governor, who chooses one person as the judge. After serving a period on the bench, the new judge stands uncontested before the voters. The sole question on the ballot is: "Should Judge X be retained in office?" If the incumbent wins a majority of the votes, then he or she earns a full term of office, and each subsequent term is secured through another uncontested *retention ballot*. Most judges are returned to office by a healthy margin.[16]

Note, however, that while the 1970s and 1980s marked the rise of merit selection for judges, the last 8 years have seen a trend whereby states have eliminated merit selection, modified its components, or returned judicial selection "to its roots." Several states seem to favor going to a quasi-federal system, where the executive appoints, the legislature (Senate or house and Senate) confirms, and judges are then subject to retention elections thereafter.[17]

A chief criticism of merit selection is that it merely obscures the influence of politics rather than eliminating it. Many selection committees include influential or powerful lawyers, which poses the risk of allowing this vested minority to wield too much power in the selection process. In addition, there is a risk of allowing the lawyers' politics to unduly influence what is intended to be an objective process. Because these meetings are often conducted in secret and lack an easy method for redress, abuses of lawyer authority can go essentially unpunished.[18]

Partisan and Nonpartisan Elections

In some states, judges are selected using partisan elections (the nominee's party is listed on the ballot). In other states, judges are selected using nonpartisan elections (no party affiliations are listed on the ballot). Nevertheless, even in these elections, partisan influences are often present: judicial candidates are endorsed or nominated by parties, receive party support during campaigns, and are identified with party labels. In either case, although campaigns for judgeships are normally low key and low visibility, in recent years, some contests—particularly for state supreme court seats—have been contentious and costly election battles that have involved millions of dollars.

The general lack of information about judges and the low levels of voter interest, however, give incumbent judges important advantages in running for reelection. As disinterested as the public may be in legislative/executive off-year elections (evidenced by low voter turnout), this apathy is even further magnified when it concerns the election of judges. Unless judges rule on notorious or heinous crimes in a manner that large numbers of community members disagree with, it is likely that their election race will be relatively free from competition or fanfare in most jurisdictions. The prestigious title of "judge" is often listed on the ballot in front of the judge's name or on political signs and billboards. Few sitting judges are even opposed for reelection.[19]

However, many experts—both individuals and groups—strongly believe that candidates for judgeships should not have to run for election to that office. For instance, retired U.S. Supreme Court justice Sandra Day O'Connor said in November 2007 that she would do away with such partisan elections because candidates for judgeships risk being compromised by the growing amount of campaign funds they must raise; she stated, "If I could wave a magic wand, I would wave it to secure some kind of merit selection of judges across the country."[20] After O'Connor's home state of Arizona switched from partisan elections of judges to an appointed system in the 1970s, she "watched the improvement of the judiciary in the state."[21]

Similarly, the American Judicature Society has supported limiting the role of politics in the selection of state judges, compiling comprehensive information on judicial selection processes in each of the 50 states and the District of Columbia and providing a website on the subject (at http://www.judicialselection.us/; topics covered include methods of selecting, retaining, and removing judges; successful and unsuccessful reform efforts; the roles of parties, interest groups, and professional organizations in selecting judges; and the diversity of the bench).[22]

Gubernatorial/Legislative Appointment

Gubernatorial/legislative appointment of judges is the earliest method of judicial selection and was characteristic of most states before the mid-nineteenth century.[23] This system generally included legislative confirmation, thereby mimicking the federal system of executive appointment with Senate confirmation. Today, only four states use the executive (gubernatorial/legislative) appointment method. Exhibit 8.1 shows the major pros and cons for each method of judicial selection we noted above.

Judicial Benefits and Problems

Judges enjoy several benefits of office, including life terms for federal positions and in some states. Ascending to the bench can be the capstone of a successful legal career for a lawyer, even though a judge's salary can be less than that of a lawyer in private practice. Judges certainly warrant a high degree of respect and prestige as well; from arrest to final disposition, the accused face judges at every juncture involving important decisions about their future: bail, pretrial motions, evidence presentation, trial, and punishment.

EXHIBIT 8.1

JUDICIAL SELECTION METHODS: MAIN PROS AND CONS

Selection Method	Pros	Cons
Merit Selection	• Protects judicial independence by insulating judges from partisan politics	• Voters should be given a voice in selecting judges • Merit selection is still a "political process"
Nonpartisan Election	• Does not attract as much funding as partisan elections, especially from interest groups	• Where there is campaigning, there are always interest groups hoping to "buy a vote"
Partisan Election	• Party affiliations communicate a candidate's values and ideologies	• Could give special interests the ability to manipulate the judiciary
Gubernatorial Appointment	• Protects the independence of the judiciary	• Voters don't have a direct voice and cannot hold judges accountable

Source: Data from *Ballotpedia, The Encyclopedia of American Politics,* https://ballotpedia.org/Judicial_selection_in_the_states.

Judicial decision making obviously spans a great deal of the justice system, but what are the legal qualifications for judges to ascend to the bench? As you might predict, there's considerable variation among states, and even within states there is variation between trial courts and lower courts.[24] For example, trial court judges in every state must have some type of legal requirement, which can include a law degree, state bar membership, attorney license, active legal practice, prior state judge service, or being learned in the law. By contrast, only 59 percent of judges in lower courts of limited jurisdiction were bound by a legal requirement.[25] But you might be surprised to know that only 79 percent of trial court judges and 27 percent of judicial officers in courts of limited jurisdiction were required to have a law degree to ascend to the bench.[26]

Yet another myth about judges is that they are always the primary decision makers in the court. But rather than acting alone in their decision making, judges often accept recommendations from others who are more familiar with the case—for example, bail recommendations from prosecutors, plea agreements struck by prosecuting and defense counsels, and sentence recommendations from the probation officer. These kinds of input are frequently accepted by judges in the informal courtroom network that exists. Although judges run the court, if they deviate from the consensus of the courtroom work group, they may be sanctioned: Attorneys can make court dockets go awry by requesting continuances or by not having witnesses appear on time. Occasionally, judges can be criticized by the public for deferring too much to these other members of the courtroom workgroup, though this is often done without understanding the influence of the group.

National Judicial College an institute of learning in Reno, Nevada, that trains lawyers on how to be judges as well as veteran judges on how to be better arbiters of justice and court administrators.

Other problems can await a new jurist-elect or appointee. Judges who are new to the bench commonly face three general problems:

1. ***Mastering the breadth of law they must know and apply.*** New judges would be wise, at least early in their career, to depend on other court staff, lawyers who appear before them, and experienced judges for invaluable information on procedural and substantive aspects of the law and local court procedures. Through informal discussions and formal meetings, judges learn how to deal with common problems. Judicial training schools and seminars have also been developed to ease the transition into the judiciary. For example, the **National Judicial College (NJC)**, located on the campus of

the University of Nevada, Reno, is a full-time institution offering nearly 100 educational sessions per year—including a number that are offered on the web as well as in 10 cities across the country—for more than 3,300 state judges, including judges from around the world (see Exhibit 8.2).

2. ***Administering the court and the docket while supervising court staff.*** One of the most frustrating aspects of being a judge is the heavy caseload and corresponding administrative problems. Instead of having time to reflect on challenging legal questions or to consider the proper sentence for a convicted felon, trial judges must move cases. They can seldom act like a judge in the "grand tradition" as we might see on television or in the movies. As Abraham Blumberg noted several years ago, the working judge must be a politician, administrator, bureaucrat, and lawyer in order to cope with the crushing calendar of cases.[27] Judges are required to be competent administrators, a fact of judicial life that comes as a surprise to many new judges. One survey of 30 federal judges found that 23 (77%) acknowledged having major administrative difficulties on first assuming the bench. Half complained of heavy caseloads, stating that their judgeship had accumulated backlogs and that other adverse conditions compounded the problem. A federal judge maintained that it takes about 4 years to "get a full feel of a docket."[28]

   Again, there are educational resources that can help judges (new or veteran) in balancing their various roles. The NJC offers both traditional and web-based courses that can assist judges in better administering their courts, including the following:

   - Court Management for Judges and Court Administrators (covering topics such as managing human resources, conflict resolution, team building, budgeting, data collection, public relations)
   - Leadership for Judges
   - Court Management for Tribal Judges and Personnel
   - Management Skills for Presiding Judges
   - Judges as Change Agents: Problem-Solving Courts

   The NCSC in Williamsburg, Virginia, also has a program designed specifically for management and leadership in the courts: the Institute for Court Management's Court Executive Development Program (CEDP).[29] We also note that state administrative offices of the courts typically have a number of functions, including judicial education. In fact, 45 states have administrative offices, which have either full or partial responsibility for judicial education.[30]

   The NCSC is an additional resource for judges to refer to. It is not the first such agency, as the federal courts have the very similar Federal Judicial Center (FJC). The purpose of both agencies is to provide research and information to judges and courts. The FJC was founded at the recommendation of then chief justice Earl Warren, who believed that regular, easy access to programs of education and research would help make the courts more efficient, as well as relieving some of the pressure imposed on judges by case overload. The NCSC is home to the largest library of materials on state court administration and is certainly a growing tool for judges and courts of any jurisdiction to use.[31]

3. ***Coping with the psychological discomfort that accompanies the new position.*** Most trial judges experience psychological discomfort upon assuming the bench. Seventy-seven percent of new federal judges acknowledged having psychological problems in at least one of five areas: maintaining a judicial bearing both on and off the bench, the loneliness of the judicial office, sentencing criminals, forgetting the adversary role, and local pressure. One aspect of the judicial role is that of assuming a proper

EXHIBIT 8.2

THE ROLE AND FUNCTION OF THE NATIONAL JUDICIAL COLLEGE

For over 50 years, the National Judicial College (NJC) has provided judicial education to judges around the nation and the world, being the first to offer programs toward improving the delivery of justice and the rule of law. After opening its doors in 1963 at the University of Colorado at Boulder, in 1964, the NJC moved its permanent academic home to the University of Nevada, Reno campus. With U.S. Supreme Court justice Tom C. Clark serving as one of its founders, since its inception the NJC has attracted a number of other Supreme Court justices as speakers and conference attendees. The ABA, State of Nevada, U.S. Department of Justice, the University of Nevada, Reno, and a variety of corporations and foundations provide ongoing financial support for the not-for-profit educational corporation.

The NJC offers an average of 100 courses/programs per year, with more than 8,000 judges attending from all 50 states and more than 150 countries. And as online education has advanced through the years, NJC is able to offer more courses to judges throughout the world. In fact, 10,000 judicial officers are accessing 30 to 50 web courses per year. The NJC also provides customized programs and technical assistance to judges, offering a broad range of specialized, practical, and advanced programs in administrative law, military and tribal justice systems, as well as for international countries seeking to enhance the rule of law. A professional certificate program allows judges to specialize in five areas: Administrative Law Adjudication Skills, Dispute Resolution Skills, General Jurisdiction Trial Skills, Special Court Trial Skills, and Tribal Judicial Skills. Furthermore, since 1986, the NJC has offered judges the opportunity to obtain advanced degrees, to include master's and doctoral degrees in judicial studies.

Source: Data from the National Judicial College, "A Legacy of Learning," http://www.judges.org/about/history.html.

mien, or "learning to act like a judge." One judge remembers his first day in court: "I'll never forget going into my courtroom for the first time with the robes and all, and the crier tells everyone to rise. You sit down and realize that it's all different, that everyone is looking at you and you're supposed to do something."[32] Like police officers and probation and parole workers, judges complain that they "can't go to the places you used to. You always have to be careful about what you talk about. When you go to a party, you have to be careful not to drink too much so you won't make a fool of yourself."[33] And the position can be a lonely one:

> After you become a … judge some people tend to avoid you. For instance, you lose all your lawyer friends and generally have to begin to make new friends. I guess the lawyers are afraid that they will someday have a case before you and it would be awkward for them if they were on too close terms with you.[34]

Judges frequently describe sentencing criminals as the most difficult aspect of their job: "This is the hardest part of being a judge. You see so many pathetic people and you're never sure of what is a right or a fair sentence."[35]

We end this section with another way to think about judicial "benefits." While nobody would dispute that judges are entitled to benefits and livable pensions for the service they perform for the community, even this is not without its issues. Relatively recently, critics have attacked the pension system in Illinois for its exceptionally large pension allotments toward retired judges. If they serve over 20 years, their first year's pension is fixed at 85 percent of their final year's salary, with their earning cap being whatever the payment scales for specific court judges. Because taxpayers fund most of, if not all of, the pension systems for public agents, this has created a very large burden that people are fairly correct to be upset with.[36]

EXHIBIT 8.3

THE GLOBAL NATURE OF JUDICIAL PENSION LITIGATION

In England, over 200 judges won a ruling very recently that challenged the government's rearrangement of the pension structure. Over 85 percent of all British judges were covered in part or in whole by the older, much more "generous" pension fund, which left about 270 judges (all of whom were younger and more recent additions to the bench) being forced to accept a much stricter arrangement. The complainants in this case argued that the government's rationale for its payment structure amounted to age discrimination. The appellate court ultimately ruled in their favor, stating that the government's organization and grandfathering in of older judges did not serve a compelling state interest in a ruling published in late January 2017.[37]

Good Judging, Courtroom Civility, and Judicial Misconduct

What Makes for "Good Judging"?

What traits make for good judging? Obviously, judges should treat each case and all parties before them in court with absolute impartiality and dignity while providing leadership as the steward of their organization in all of the court management areas described in the following section. In addition to those official duties, however, other issues and suggestions have been put forth.

For example, the Maryland State Bar Association formed a special committee that deliberated and articulated the qualities that should be sought after in judicial applicants.[38] These qualities included the following:

- Judicial temperament—the ability to communicate and to listen to all sides.
- Intelligence—knowledge of legal rules and to apply them to different circumstances.
- Ethics—maintaining a standard of conduct above the minimum.
- Experience and education—a variety of professional legal experience and education.
- Continuing legal education—a good indicator of attempts to remain current in the law.
- Ability to communicate—both orally and in writing.
- Civic and professional responsibility—service to civic and cultural organizations and volunteer efforts.
- Health—sufficient physical and mental health to perform duties of the office.
- Character—positive reputation, free of references to immorality or indiscretions, financial stability.[39]

Other writers believe that judges should remember that the robe does not confer omniscience or omnipotence; as one trial attorney put it, "Your name is now 'Your Honor,' but you are still the same person you used to be, warts and all."[40] Standards of judicial conduct exist in many nations, and while they may have slight differences between one another, they tend to be fairly consistent. For example, similar to what the Maryland State Bar Association recommended, Canada's superior court judges are expected to conduct their personal and professional lives with integrity, be knowledgeable about the law, be willing to undertake complex legal research on issues that come before them, and be capable of writing decisions that are understandable and will stand up to scrutiny. As will be discussed later in the text, this is where having a media/interpersonal relations course available for judges could be beneficial. Given the isolation identified as a facet of the job, it can be easy for newer and older judges alike to become "lost" in the status of their position.[41]

courtroom civility judges, litigants, and court actors conducting themselves appropriately so that all parties are afforded a fair opportunity to present their case.

As if it weren't difficult enough to strive for and maintain humility and balance in their personal lives, judges must also enforce **courtroom civility**—that is, a courtroom environment where litigants and all other court actors conduct themselves appropriately so that all parties are afforded a fair opportunity to present their case. Many persons have observed that we are becoming an increasingly uncivil society, and the courts are certainly not immune to acts involving misconduct (see the discussion of courthouse violence in Chapter 9).

Personal character attacks by lawyers, directed at judges, attorneys, interested parties, clerks, jurors, and witnesses, both inside and outside the courtroom, in criminal and civil actions have increased at an alarming rate over the years.[42] For example, in one case, an attorney stated that opposing counsel and other attorneys were "a bunch of starving slobs," "incompetents," and "stooges."[43] In another, the prosecutor called defense counsel "maggots" and "poor excuses for human beings"; defense counsel implied that the prosecutor was a "scumbag."[44]

Such invective clearly does not enhance the dignity or appearance of justice and propriety that is so important to the courts' public image and function. The Code of Judicial Conduct addresses these kinds of behaviors; Canon 3B(4) requires judges to be "patient, dignified, and courteous to litigants, jurors, witnesses, lawyers, and others with whom the judge deals in an official capacity" and requires judges to demand "similar conduct of lawyers, and of staff, court officials, and others subject to the judge's direction and control."[45]

At a minimum, judges need to attempt to prevent such vitriol and discipline offenders when it occurs. Some means that judges have at their disposal to control errant counsel include attorney disqualifications, new trials, and reporting of attorneys to disciplinary boards.[46] And in an ABA-sponsored program, entitled "Ethical Tools to Diffuse Incivility," that included judges and lawyers, participants were quick to point out the rising incivility in American courtrooms. Some participants called for lawyer self-regulation to deal with the problem, while others suggested that lawyers talk to their judges. Not taking any action to curb courtroom incivility could actually embolden those who engage in such behaviors.[47]

While ad hominem attacks may have increased in court, they do serve some purpose, even if technically impermissible. While the judicial process seeks to be as impartial as possible, this is not always achievable and a degree of emotional influence comes into play. Ad hominem and character attacks on witnesses certainly can create the emotional impact sought after by some lawyers in specific situations. For example, if the lawyer believes they can "bait" an individual (either an opposing witness or counsel) into improper action, they may be able to force the process to work or take a turn in a direction they desire.[48] Keeping our courtrooms civil is certainly no easy task.

Problems of Their Own: Types of Judicial Misconduct

What types of misconduct among judges themselves must the judiciary confront? Sometimes, medications may affect a judge's cognitive process or emotional temperament, causing him or her to treat parties, witnesses, jurors, lawyers, and staff poorly. Some stay on the bench too long; such judges will ideally have colleagues who can approach them, suggest retirement, and explain why this would be to their benefit. And sometimes, according to one author, judicial arrogance (sometimes termed *black robe disease* or *robe-itis*) is the primary problem. This is seen when judges "do not know when to close their mouths, do not treat people with dignity and compassion, do not arrive on time, or do not issue timely decisions."[49] In the federal system, the above examples may result in a complaint about a judge, as defined in Section 351 of Title 28 of the U.S. Code.[50]

Section 351 articulates that complaints may be made if the judge has engaged in behaviors that affect the expeditious administration of justice or if the judge is unable to perform his or her duties of the office because of a mental or physical disability.[51] State codes of judicial conduct have adopted similar language.

Some bar associations or judicial circuits perform an anonymous survey of a sample of local attorneys who have recently argued a case before a particular judge and then share the results with the judge. Sometimes, these surveys are popularity contests, but a pattern of negative responses can have a sobering effect on the judge and encourage him or her to correct bad habits. Many judges will be reluctant to acknowledge that they have problems such as those described earlier. In such cases, the chief judge may have to scold or correct a subordinate judge. Although this is difficult, it may be imperative to do so in trying to maintain good relations with bar associations, individual lawyers, and the public. A single judge's blunders and behaviors can affect the reputation of the entire judiciary as well as the workloads of the other judges in his or her judicial district. Chief judges must therefore step forward to address such problems formally or informally.[52] And sometimes these problems do not even occur in a judge's courtroom.

For example, Louisiana judge Mike Maggio was disbarred for judicial misconduct after making several derogatory comments involving the use of racist and sexist language at an LSU football forum. Maggio was investigated and later punished heavily for also unlawfully disclosing confidential details of actress Charlize Theron's 2012 adoption. In addition to forfeiture of his benefits and other sanctions, Maggio also agreed to never seek elected office again.[53] Actions such as those of Maggio can greatly erode the confidence that the public has in the justice system, which already struggles with legitimacy in some populations. As will be discussed later in the chapter, this sort of judicial misconduct has a grave impact on the perceptions and attitudes the public holds for the judiciary. The reader's attention is directed to the "Deliberate and Decide" section at the end of this chapter, discussing a New Jersey jurist's part-time job as a stand-up comedian; this situation certainly raised questions of judicial propriety, conflict of interest, and the *appearance* of justice (discussed in the "Appearance of Impropriety" section) on the part of this and other judicial officers. Related questions are included in this case study for your consideration. Then, Chapter 9 includes discussion of a related matter, gender bias in the courts, while Chapter 13 includes a broader discussion of ethics in the courts followed by a discussion of what is being done formally to address problems of sexual harassment within the judiciary.

A Revised Model Code of Conduct for State and Local Judges

The ABA adopted a **Model Code of Judicial Conduct** in 1990 (and last revised in 2011) that provides written standards concerning the ethical conduct of judges so as to guide and assist judges in maintaining the highest standards of judicial and personal conduct. It spelled out, for the first time, that they are to avoid "sexual advances," requests for sexual favors, and other such unwelcome behavior. The code is not binding, but it has long served as a model that individual states use in adopting rules for disciplining their judges. In fact, 35 states have approved a judicial code based on the revised Model Code of Judicial Conduct, while another 10 states have established committees to review their judicial code.[54]

> **Model Code of Judicial Conduct**
> standards written by the ABA to assist judges in maintaining the highest standards of judicial and personal conduct.

The Model Code covers a range of conduct, including ethical behavior for judicial candidates, when judges might accept gifts, and in what instances they should disqualify themselves from hearing cases. The ABA commission that prepared the revised code said that it adopted the language on sexual harassment after hearing from witnesses who were "emphatic about the need to single out sexual harassment for special mention, given the nature, extent, and history of the problem."[55] Exhibit 8.4 puts you in the shoes of a judge as you disclose your finances in an effort to maintain the integrity of the office.

EXHIBIT 8.4

YOU BE THE JUDGE

Judicial integrity is maintained, in part, by the requirement of financial disclosure, which allows the public to see the assets of judges and to be completely transparent regarding the appearance of impropriety (discussed in the next section). As a judge, you could be asked to disclose the following: organizational positions you hold, agreements you have made, your sources of income, your spouse's income, gifts you have received, liabilities you have, and investments you have made.

- Do you feel financial disclosure reports are necessary?
- Do you think the reports are asking you to reveal too many personal details about you and your family?
- Say, for example, that you own 50 shares of IBM stock valued at approximately $7,000. Should you recuse yourself from a case where IBM is a party? If you were to remain on the case, do you feel you could judge impartially? Why or why not?

A Thorny Issue: Judges' Use of Electronic Social Media Sites

Against the backdrop of widespread use of social media around the world, the Florida Supreme Court Judicial Ethics Advisory Committee concluded almost 10 years ago that judges and lawyers who interact in courtrooms should not "friend" one another on social media, citing perceptions of potential neutrality violations and influence.[56] Several years later, an appellate court in Florida was compelled to confront the following question: Where the presiding judge in a criminal case has accepted the prosecutor assigned to the case as a Facebook "friend," would a reasonably prudent person fear that he could not get a fair and impartial trial, so that the defendant's motion for disqualification should be granted? (The trial judge had denied the motion to be disqualified, as "legally insufficient.")

Using the test "whether or not the facts alleged … would prompt a reasonably prudent person to fear that he could not get a fair and impartial trial," the appellate court answered "yes" to the question, saying the judge should have disqualified himself and noting that

> [j]udges do not have the unfettered social freedom of teenagers. Central to the public's confidence in the courts is the belief that fair decisions are rendered by an impartial tribunal. Maintenance of the appearance of impartiality requires the avoidance of entanglements and relationships that compromise that appearance. Unlike face to face social interaction, an electronic blip on a social media site can become eternal in the electronic ether of the internet. Posts on a Facebook page might be of a type that a judge should not consider in a given case. The existence of a judge's Facebook page might exert pressure on lawyers or litigants to take direct or indirect action to curry favor with the judge.[57]

A number of other states have attempted to address the question concerning judges' use of electronic social media (ESM) sites. For example, Tennessee, citing the cautions of several other states (e.g., California, Maryland, Oklahoma), notes on its courts' website that

> [b]ecause of constant changes in social media, this committee cannot be specific as to allowable or prohibited activity, but our review, as set out in this opinion, of the various approaches taken by other states to this area makes clear that judges must be constantly aware of ethical implications as they participate in social media and whether disclosure must be made. In short, judges must decide whether the benefit and utility of participating in social media justify the attendant risks.[58]

The ABA has also offered guidelines on the matter. In February 2013, the ABA's Standing Committee on Ethics and Professional Responsibility stated that "a judge may participate in electronic social networking, but as with all social relationships and contacts, a judge must comply with relevant provisions of the Code of Judicial Conduct and avoid any conduct that would undermine the judge's independence, integrity, or impartiality, or create an **appearance of impropriety**."[59] The committee noted that judges should assume that comments posted using ESM "may be disseminated to thousands of people without the consent or knowledge of the original poster" and "have long, perhaps permanent, digital lives." The committee also cautioned judges to keep in mind the requirement that a judge act in a manner that promotes public confidence in the judiciary and stated that a judge should not form relationships with persons or organizations that may convey an impression that the persons or organizations are in a position to influence the judge. The committee concluded that judges who use ESM "do not necessarily compromise their duties under the Model Code any more than use of traditional and less public forms of social connection such as U.S. mail, telephone, e-mail or texting."[60]

appearance of impropriety where someone creates a circumstance or situation that appears to raise questions of ethics.

Certainly not all judges see problems with their use of ESM, however. A 2012 survey by the Conference of Court Public Information Officer found that nearly half (46.1%) of judges use social media sites. About the same number (44%) indicated a belief that judges can use social media sites in their personal lives without compromising professional conduct codes of ethics, much like what the ABA suggested above.

Nevertheless, accounts such as those mentioned earlier in the Florida case indicate that problems can and do arise. Another issue needing to be addressed, perhaps, concerns the basic definition of being "friends" on such websites—which in ESM terms does not necessarily mean being personal friends and is merely a means of connecting with other people. What about judges who "friend" attorneys who appear before them in court—or a related situation where a judge declines to be "friends" with an attorney on a social website?

These are key questions that go to the heart of the appearance of impropriety and impartiality; however, the "appearance of propriety" is not easily defined; there are not as yet any uniform, definitive rules in place; the ABA and state bar associations can only offer general guidelines.[61]

The NCSC has published a list of cases involving judicial misconduct, ranging from the relatively "minor" offense of having a lawyer as a Facebook "friend" to the severe misconduct of one judge sending illicit sexual messages to a woman who appeared before him. It is apparent that these sorts of problems may have to be monitored and responded to as we best understand them. Since social media is a recent phenomenon, judges and courts which rule on these matters will not have extensive precedent to rely on. Many of the "first wave" of social media court cases have rulings that advise judges to be cautious with their postings and friends. This is especially true when the postings contain, as one did in the NCSC's list, content related to the financial welfare of the judge's relatives and coworkers (p. 6).[62]

EXHIBIT 8.5

TWITTER WARS

While the president is certainly not part of the judiciary, President Trump has been criticized for his use of ESM, and in particular, Twitter. After the Supreme Court declined to uphold the controversial "refugee ban" executive order that was enacted shortly after his inauguration, President Trump took to Twitter to express his frustration. The content of the tweet was heavily satirized, as he indicated he would be taking the Supreme Court "to court" over its rulings. While judges do not have nearly the same public clout as the sitting U.S. president, it is clear from the antics and criticisms leveled at him for his Twitter "wars" that it has become an integral component of public office. The idea that judges are never truly "off duty" is even more true when social media is taken into account, and the necessity to conduct oneself accordingly is all the more important, in part to avoid the appearance of impropriety.

▶ What Does "Appearance of Impropriety" Mean? An Example

As indicated earlier, the appearance of impropriety—where someone creates a circumstance or situation that appears to raise questions of ethics—as a general concept may not be well understood; however, it takes on much more significance when judges, police officers, corrections personnel, and other criminal justice functionaries are involved. Indeed, it is a concept that wise public officials typically learn early in their careers. As Abraham Lincoln stated, in order to maintain credibility in his personal and professional lives, he had to "not only be chaste but above suspicion."[63] Lincoln even alluded to the appearance of propriety in his political appointments, saying, "Any man whom I may appoint to a [Cabinet] position, must be, as far as possible, like Caesar's wife, pure and above suspicion."[64] While it would be difficult to articulate all relevant scenarios that may result in appearance of judicial impropriety, in a commentary offered by the Texas Center of Legal Ethics regarding Canon 2A of the Texas Code of Judicial Conduct, appearance of impropriety occurs when "reasonable minds, with knowledge of all the relevant circumstances disclosed by a reasonable inquiry, would conclude that the judge's honesty, integrity, impartiality, temperament, or fitness to serve as a judge is impaired."[65] But as we saw earlier with regard to judges' use of ESM, states vary in their definitions of appearance of impropriety.

"Appearance of impropriety" is perhaps both shrouded in controversy and a lack of public awareness due to the roles of the people involved, as illustrated in the following example:

> Assume that a judge happens to be attending a public luncheon where new attorneys are being admitted to the county bar association. Upon entering, the judge observes that the room is nearly full, and takes the only vacant seat—which happens to be at a table occupied by an attorney who represents the plaintiff in a highly publicized trial currently before the judge. The judge mentions, and the attorney agrees, that they will not discuss the case during the luncheon festivities, and no such discussion takes place.

Now consider the other guests who observe these two sitting together. How will they perceive this situation? The answer depends on how much information the observers possess. One group of observers will be those who are unaware of the case involving the judge and attorney and probably think nothing of their sitting together. Another group will be those persons sitting at the table (or within hearing distance) who are fully informed of their agreement and would also not be concerned that any impropriety will occur—and perhaps even commending their ethical conduct. Third, however, are those attendees who are aware of neither the only-seat-available circumstance nor the agreement, and who may well perceive a serious problem with their sitting together; thus, the "appearance" problem.[66]

And so it is, as with gossip versus truth: The problem turns on how much information people possess. As an old saying goes, "perception is reality." The definition of the situation—different parties' knowledge of the facts and the situation—will determine for each whether or not there is a serious ethical problem involved. See Exhibit 8.6 for an example of a situation that can be perceived differently depending on the information people possess.

EXHIBIT 8.6

JUDGE CENSURED FOR DISCHARGING A FIREARM IN CHAMBERS[67]

In hindsight, an upstate New York judge admitted that a courthouse is probably not the best place to repair a revolver with a faulty firing mechanism. The gun discharged while the judge was alone in his chambers, striking a wall and injuring no one. The state's Commission on Judicial Conduct censured the judge for the mishap—and for having approved his own gun permit, which it termed *an obvious conflict.* Over a 4-year period the judge, who began carrying a weapon to court due to what he cited as several instances of threats on his life, made 14 amendments to his original gun permit, covering 17 other pistols. There were no administrative policies that prohibited judges from bringing firearms into their chambers.

Judges as Court Managers

The Administrative Office of the U.S. Courts coordinates and administers the operations of the federal courts. In the states, judges assume three types of administrative roles: (1) statewide jurisdiction for state supreme court chief justices, (2) local jurisdiction—a trial judge is responsible for administering the operations of his or her individual court, and (3) *presiding* or *chief* judge—supervising several courts within a judicial district.

The practice of having a judge preside over several courts within a district developed as early as 1940, when Dean Roscoe Pound recommended that a chief or presiding judge of a district or a region be responsible for case and judge assignment.[68] Today, these judges assume "general administrative duties over the court and its divisions" and are typically granted authority over all judicial personnel and court officials.[69] The duties of the presiding judge are numerous and include personnel and docket management and case and judge assignments; coordination and development of all judicial budgets; the convening of *en banc* (judges meeting as a whole) court meetings; coordination of judicial schedules; creation and use of appropriate court committees to investigate problems and handle court business; interaction with outside agencies and the media; the drafting of local court rules and policies; the maintenance of the courts' facilities; and the issuing of orders for keeping, destroying, and transferring records.[70]

A basic flaw in this system is that the chief or presiding judge is actually a "first among equals" with his or her peers. The title of chief judge is often assigned by seniority; therefore, there is no guarantee that the chief judge will be interested in management or will be effective at it.[71]

From a court administrator's standpoint, the office of presiding judge and the person serving in that capacity are of the utmost importance. As one judge put it, "the single most determinative factor of the extent of the administrator's role, aside from his personal attributes, is probably the rate of turnover in the office of the presiding judge."[72] And so while the public might view judges the way they see them on television or in the movies, the judge as court administrator must not only be an effective manager but also an effective leader. As we mentioned previously in this chapter, the NJC offers courses that can assist judges in their lesser known efforts as administrators. In addition, publications offered through the NJC and the Bureau of Justice Assistance (BJA) can assist judges in honing their administrative and leadership skills. One such publication, a joint effort between the NJC and BJA, focuses on "Effective Judging for Busy Judges."[73] Here, a problem-solving perspective is discussed, not only for individual cases and case-flow management but also for judges in their administrative role as a leader among court staff. A team approach is discussed, which focuses on partnership building.

While discussing the functions of the chief or presiding judges of this country, this is a good point at which to consider the varied duties of the chief justice of the United States; a few of those duties are listed in Exhibit 8.7.

EXHIBIT 8.7

DUTIES OF THE CHIEF JUSTICE OF THE UNITED STATES

Often incorrectly called the chief justice of the Supreme Court, the chief justice of the United States has 53 duties enumerated in the U.S. Code, the Constitution, and other sources. Following is a list of a few of those duties:

- Approve appointments and salaries of some court employees
- Direct the publication of Supreme Court opinions
- Approve rules for the Supreme Court library
- Select a company to handle the printing and binding of court opinions
- Send appeals back to lower courts if justices cannot agree on them
- Approve appointments of employees to care for the Supreme Court building and grounds as well as regulations for their protection
- Call and preside over an annual meeting of the Judicial Conference of the United States and report to Congress the conference's recommendations for legislation (the Judicial Conference is composed of 27 federal judges who represent all the levels and regions of the federal judiciary; the conference meets twice a year to discuss common problems and needed policies and to recommend to Congress measures for improving the operation of the federal courts)
- Report to Congress on changes in the Rules of Criminal Procedure
- Report to the president if certain judges have become unable to discharge their duties
- Designate a member of the Smithsonian Institution

Source: Based on The Federal Judicial Center, "History of the Federal Judiciary," http://www.fjc.gov/history/home.nsf/page/admin_04.html.

▶ Court Clerks

court clerk an officer of a court who is responsible for its clerical filings and recordkeeping, entering judgments and orders, and so on.

Not to be overlooked in the administration of the courts is the **court clerk**, an officer of the court who is responsible for its clerical filings and recordkeeping, entering judgments and orders, and so on. The court clerk is also referred to as a *prothonotary, registrar of deeds, circuit clerk, registrar of probate*, and even *auditor*. From the beginning of English settlement in North America, court clerks have been vital members of the society. "Clerks of writs" or "clerks of the assize" existed in early Massachusetts, where people were litigious primarily about land boundaries. Hostility toward lawyers carried over from England, and the clerk was the intermediary between the litigants and the justice of the peace. During the late seventeenth century, American courts became more structured and formalized. Books were available that imposed English court practices in the colonies, and clerks, judges, and attorneys were provided proper forms that had to be used. In fact, some of the forms used by clerks 200 years ago are similar to those that are currently used.[74]

Today, most courts have de facto court administrators in lieu of these clerks, even if they have appointed administrators. These are key individuals in the administration of local court systems. They also manage docket cases, collect fees and costs, oversee jury selection, and maintain court records. These local officials, elected in all but six states, can amass tremendous power.[75] But despite their power, the court clerk position is relatively unknown to most members of the public. Clerks have traditionally competed with judges for control over local judicial administration. In fact, one study found that the majority (58.9%) of elected clerks perceived themselves as colleagues of and equal to the judges,[76] even though clerks often are likened to an administrative assistant.

▶ Trained Court Administrators

Development and Training

One of the most recent and innovative approaches to solving the courts' management problems has been the creation of the position of court administrator. This relatively new criminal justice position began to develop in earnest during the 1960s; since that time, the number of practicing trial court administrators has increased tenfold and continues to expand. Actually, this concept has its roots in early England, where, historically, judges abstained from any involvement in court administration. This fact has not been lost on contemporary court administrators and proponents of this position: "It seems to be a very valuable characteristic of the English system that the judges expect to *judge* when they are in the courthouse ... it does not allow time for administrative distractions."[77]

Court administrators are trained specifically to provide the courts with the expertise and talent they have historically lacked. This point was powerfully made by Bernadine Meyer:

> Management—like law—is a profession today. Few judges or lawyers with severe chest pains would attempt to treat themselves. Congested dockets and long delays are symptoms that court systems need the help of professionals. Those professionals are managers. If court administration is to be effective, judicial recognition that managerial skill and knowledge are necessary to efficient performance is vital.[78]

But the development of the position of court administrator has been sporadic. In the early 1960s, probably only 30 people in the United States worked as court administrators. By 1970, there were fewer than 50 such specially trained employees.[79] Estimates differ concerning the expansion of the administrator's role during the 1980s. One expert maintained that by 1982 between 2,000 and 3,000 people were in the ranks of court managers;[80] another argued that there were only about 500.[81] At any rate, most agree that more than twice as many of these positions were created between 1970 and 1980 than in the preceding six decades.[82]

By the 1980s, every state had a statewide court administrator, normally reporting to the state supreme court or the chief justice of the state supreme court. The four primary functions of state court administrators are preparing annual reports, summarizing caseload data, preparing budgets, and troubleshooting.[83] Gregory Linhares, state court administrator in Missouri, further articulates the role of the position. Linhares suggests that today there is considerable communication among state court administrators to enhance the performance of one another.[84] Linhares states the court administrators are both strategists and project managers, number crunchers and budget managers, and communicators for multiple constituents in all branches of the government. Figure 8-2 ■ summarizes the means by which state court administrators are selected as well as their requirements.

Statewide court administrators are members of the Conference of State Court Administrators (COSCA), which was established in 1955 to increase efficiency and fairness in state courts.[85] COSCA's purposes are fourfold and formative, and attempt to improve state court administration: (1) to encourage policies, principles, and standards for court administration; (2) to facilitate cooperation and an exchange of ideas among those entities concerned with court administration; (3) to promote the use of modern techniques in judicial administration; and (4) to improve administrative practices with the goal of improving effectiveness and efficiency in state courts.[86]

Today, few, if any, metropolitan areas are without full-time court administrators[87] (the court organization chart shown in Figure 7-3 outlines the breadth of responsibilities held by

- State court administrator position established by state constitution only: Alaska, Arizona, Illinois, Nebraska, New York, Pennsylvania, South Carolina, and South Dakota.
- States that rely on statutes only: Arkansas, Connecticut, Delaware, Hawaii, Idaho, Indiana, Iowa, Kansas, Kentucky, Maine, Maryland, Massachusetts, Minnesota, Mississippi, Montana, Nevada, New Mexico, Oregon, Rhode Island, Tennessee, Texas, Vermont, Virginia, Washington, and the District of Columbia.
- States that use a mix of constitution and statute: Alabama, California, Colorado, Michigan, New Jersey, North Carolina, Ohio, Oklahoma, and West Virginia.
- States that rely on constitution and rule: Florida, Missouri, and North Dakota.
- Other permutations:
  - Georgia: statute and order
  - Louisiana: constitution, statute, and rule
  - Wisconsin: rule

Educational Requirements for State Court Administrators

- Bachelor's degree: 6 states
- Law degree: 13 states
- Law or graduate degree: 2 states
- Degree in business or public administration: 3 states
- None specified: 23 states and the District of Columbia

Figure 8-2 Establishing the Office of and Educational Requirements for State Court Administrators

Source: Excerpt from Creation of State Court Administrative Offices and Selection of State Court Administrators, from Technical Assistance Report by David C. Steelman and Anne E. Skove. Copyright © 2007 by National Center for State Courts. Used by permission of National Center for State Courts.

court administrators). An underlying premise and justification for this role is that by having a trained person performing the tasks of court management, judges are left free to do what they do best: decide cases. Indeed, since the first trial-court administrative positions began to appear, "there was little doubt or confusion about their exact purpose."[88] (As indicated above, however, there has been doubt and confusion concerning their proper role and functions.)

As court reformers have called for better-trained specialists (as opposed to political appointees) for administering court processes, the qualifications for this position have come under debate. The creation of the Institute for Court Management in 1970 was a landmark in the training for this role, legitimizing its standing in the legal profession. Many judges, however, still believe that a law degree is essential, whereas others prefer a background in business administration. There will probably never be complete agreement concerning the skills and background necessary for this position, but the specialized training that is offered by the Institute and a few graduate programs in judicial administration across the country seems ideal.

IN THEIR OWN WORDS

ADMINISTRATIVE ADVICE FROM THE FIELD

Kenneth J. Peak

Name: Maxine Cortes

Current position/City/State: Court Administrator, District Court and Justice/Municipal Court, Carson City, Nevada

College attended/academic major/degree(s): University of Phoenix, Masters in Organization Management, BS degree in Business Management

My primary duties and responsibilities in this position include: court management, project management, budgeting, grant writing, development of procedures/protocol and programs, review of legislation, court technology, and liaison between multiple agencies, the public, and vendors.

Personal attributes/characteristics that have proven to be most helpful to me in this position are: analytical abilities, conflict resolution, management, and communication and time management skills.

My three greatest challenges in this administrative role include: lack of adequate funding for programs, positions and training for staff development, constant change in local government leadership, and changing the culture of the organization to enhance public service.

Personal accomplishments during my administrative career about which I am most proud are: grant awards to implement and sustain court programs, advancement of staff to managerial levels through mentorship, and improving the courts through the use of technology.

Advice for someone who is interested in occupying an administrative position such as mine would be: take time to job shadow a court administrator. Possess a solid background in personnel and project management, budgeting, grant writing, understand technology trends in the court system, courthouse security, and learn about courts by researching the NCSC website.

Source: Used with permission from Maxine Cortes.

General Duties

Trial court administrators generally perform the following six major duties, with considerable overlap with state court administrators:

1. ***Reports.*** Administrators have primary responsibility for the preparation and submission to the judges of periodic reports on the activities and state of business of the court.
2. ***Personnel administration.*** Court administrators serve as personnel officers for the court's nonjudicial personnel.
3. ***Research and evaluation.*** This function is designed to improve court business methods.
4. ***Equipment management.*** Administrators are engaged in procurement, allocation, inventory control, and replacement of furniture and equipment.
5. ***Preparation of the court budget***
6. ***Training coordination.*** Court administrators provide training for nonjudicial personnel.[89]

Other duties that are assumed by the trained court administrator include jury management, case flow or calendar management, public information, and management of automated data processing operations.[90]

Evaluating Court Administrators

Judges must determine whether or not their court administrator is performing competently and effectively. According to John Greacen,[91] there are several basic strategies in determining the quality of the work performed by their administrators:

1. ***The judge looks for indications of good management.*** A well-managed organization will have a number of plans and procedures in place, including personnel policies, recruitment and selection procedures, an orientation program for new employees, performance evaluation procedures, a discipline and grievance process, case management policies, financial controls, and other administrative policies (such as for facilities and records management).
2. ***The judge should be receiving regular information.*** Critically important reports and data on the court's performance, plans, activities, and accomplishments should be provided to the judge on a routine basis. The judge should be notified of the number of case filings, terminations, and pending cases; financial information; staff performance; long- and short-range plans; and other statistical data.
3. ***Judges must often ask others about the performance of the administrator.*** This includes soliciting input from lawyers, other judges, and other court staff members.

Greacen's third point (above) indicates to a common evaluation practice in the private, public, and nonprofit sectors: the use of evaluation data to measure the performance of organizational employees. In colleges and universities, student feedback often is sought to measure the performance of professors in their classrooms. Similarly, administrators are often evaluated, at least in part, on feedback from other employees. These data can be either qualitative, quantitative, or both, and are valued because performance using these methods is measured using multiple perspectives. Combined with bottom line performance measures dealing with effectiveness and efficiencies, key stakeholder input can help transform a summative evaluation into one that is more formative.

jury administration ensuring that a jury is properly comprised and sustained prior to and during trials.

notorious cases local, regional, or national civil or criminal trials either involving celebrities or particularly egregious crimes, requiring special attention to jury selection and trial procedures.

Jury Administration

The jury system has been in the forefront of the public's mind in recent years, primarily as a result of the jury nullification concept (the right of juries to nullify or refuse to apply law in criminal cases despite facts that leave no reasonable doubt that the law was violated).[92] Here, however, we focus on the responsibilities of the court administrator in **jury administration**, ensuring that a jury is properly comprised and sustained prior to and during trials. Elements of the jury system that involve court administration include jury selection, sequestration, comfort, and dealing with notorious cases.

Regarding jury selection, the court administrator is responsible for compilation of a master jury list; this is a large pool of potential jurors compiled from voter registration, driver's license, or utility customer or telephone customer lists (which varies by state) to produce a representative cross-section of the community. From that master list, a randomly selected smaller venire (or jury pool) is drawn; a summons is mailed out to citizens, asking

EXHIBIT 8.8

SEQUESTRATION OR NO SEQUESTRATION? THAT IS THE QUESTION!

Without question, the trial of the surviving Boston Marathon bomber, Dzhokhar Tsarnaev, could have resulted in jury sequestration during the full length of the 10-week trial. Ultimately, the court decided not to use sequestration. Instead, the judge instructed jurors to shield themselves from news accounts of the case.[94] There are numerous reasons for not using sequestration these days, even for the most high-profile cases. First, it is very difficult to shield jurors from outside information about the case they are hearing in court, even while sequestered. Visits to sequestered jurors from family members and/or significant others can lead to unauthorized information getting to jurors. With this risk, even during jury sequestration, it may make more sense to instruct jurors to refrain from news accounts of the case, as was done in this case. Additionally, sequestration generally is not used these days given the extreme expense associated with it, particularly in high-profile, lengthy trials. **Notorious cases**—local, regional, or national civil or criminal trials either involving celebrities or particularly egregious crimes, requiring attention to jury selection and trial procedures—can cause problems for judges and court administrators. As examples, the trials of celebrities such as Martha Stewart and Michael Jackson, athletes like O. J. Simpson and Mike Tyson, mafia don John Gotti, and child star Robert Blake were clearly "notorious."[95] Court administrators and other court staff members must deal with media requests; courtroom and courthouse logistics for handling crowds, the media, and security; and the management of the court's docket of other cases. A notorious trial may also require that a larger courtroom be used and many attorneys accommodated.[96] A number of other issues must be considered: Are identification and press passes and entry screening devices needed? Do purses, briefcases, and other such items need to be searched? Perhaps the most important task in managing notorious cases is communication with the media, often by setting aside a certain time when reporters may discuss the case.[97]

them to appear at the courthouse for jury duty. There, they will be asked questions and either retained or removed as jury members.

Here is where juror comfort enters in. Unfortunately, many jurors experience great frustration in the process, being made to wait long hours, possibly in uncomfortable physical surroundings, while receiving minimal compensation and generally being inconvenienced. Courts in all states now have a juror call-in system, enabling jurors to dial a phone number to learn whether their attendance is needed on a particular day; in addition, acknowledging the burdens that "being selected" might create, many jurisdictions have reduced the number of days a juror remains in the pool.

Some trials involving extensive media coverage require jury sequestration—jurors remain in virtual quarantine, sometimes (but atypically) for many weeks, and are compelled to live in a hotel together. This can be a tiring experience for jurors and poses great logistical problems for jurors and court administrators alike. The court administrator must also consider security issues (protecting the jury from outside interference and providing for conjugal visits, room searches, transportation, and so on) as well as jurors' personal needs (such as entertainment and medical supplies).[93]

Summary

Today, the functions of judges and court administrators are quite different from those of earlier times and involve policymaking as well. It is clear that, as one New York judge put it, "The 'grand tradition' judge, the aloof brooding charismatic figure in the Old Testament tradition, is hardly a real figure."[98]

In addition, judicial administrators, the nonlawyers who help judges to run the courts, now possess a basic body of practical knowledge, a rudimentary theoretical perspective, and a concern for professional ethics.

It was also shown that there are still several obstacles to the total acceptance of court administration as an integral part of the judiciary. Court administration in many ways is still a developing field. Still, it has come far from its roots and is evolving into a bona fide, needed, element of the American justice system.

Above all, it is of great importance to recognize that any reforms do *not* mean the entire system is being scrapped. Changes will occur gradually, and while this may cause frustration from those who believe wholesale revolution is needed, it is far less dangerous than completely rewriting the legal process. It is advisable to include feedback from changes that may be taking place already: change a practice, review the effects of this change, make conclusions on its viability, and then adjust other practices as necessary.

Key Terms and Concepts

Appearance of impropriety, p. 199
Court clerk, p. 202
Courtroom civility, p. 196
Judicial (court) administration, p. 186
Judicial selection, p. 189
Jury administration, p. 206
Merit selection/Missouri Bar Plan, p. 189
Model Code of Judicial Conduct, p. 197
Notorious cases, p. 206
The National Judicial College (NJC), p. 192

Questions for Review

1. Why is the term *judicial administration* multifaceted? What would be a good working definition for this term? For *court administration*?
2. What are the elements of the newly revised Model Code of Judicial Conduct for state and local judges?

3. With the proliferation of social media and saturation of news sources, might we see a formal addition to the Model Code of Judicial Conduct regarding judges' use? What regulations/prohibitions would such an addition be likely to include?
4. How do you define the appearance of impropriety in our courts? What is an example of such an "appearance" dilemma?
5. How might judges and court administrators receive training for their roles?
6. How have court clerks traditionally assumed and performed the role of court administrator?
7. What criteria may be employed by judges to evaluate the effectiveness of their administrators?
8. What are the court administrator's duties in general? What issues must the court administrator address in composing or sequestering a jury? In dealing with notorious cases?

Deliberate and Decide

The Case of the Jocular Jurist

In early 2013, a part-time South Hackensack, New Jersey, municipal court judge held a unique part-time job—as a stand-up comedian on a major network's hidden-camera program. But the judge was told his part-time job—which is his primary source of income—conflicts with his judicial work and violates rules the state's judges are to follow. He pleaded his case to the state's supreme court.

One of the issues raised was whether or not the average person understands the difference between a character and an actor—as with movie actors, whether or not someone is seen as expressing their true selves or following a fictional script. A deputy attorney general argued that the judge's comedy program—which includes portraying racist and homophobic characters—may not know the judge is acting; in addition, the judge could meet defendants who are familiar with his comic routine and might not believe he is a serious judge. The state also argued that municipal court judges are the face of the judiciary for most citizens, and it is vital that such judges maintain the confidence of the public and the impartiality, dignity, and integrity of the court.[99] (The outcome of this matter is provided in the Notes section.)

Questions for Discussion

1. What do you think? If, as it is often said, judges must at all times "*appear* to do justice," should the judge be allowed to moonlight as a comedian on his own time?
2. Or, alternatively, do you agree with the state's arguments that judges are never actually "off-duty," and are thus obligated to avoid such activities?
3. What, if any, punishment do you believe would be appropriately meted out by the state bar association?

Learn by Doing

1. After many years of debate concerning its pros and cons, your state legislature appears to be edging closer to implementing the Missouri (or merit selection) Plan for judicial selection on the ballot. As a court administrator in your municipal court, you are asked by your local newspaper to prepare a position paper that presents both sides of the issues. What will you say are pros and cons, when compared with the current system of electing judges?
2. You are a court administrator and you are currently attending a workshop that includes a section on ethical considerations. You are given the following case involving actual impeachment hearings against a federal judge in Texas (see, e.g., http://www.vanityfair.com/online/daily/2009/06/a-real-case-of-judicial-misconduct.html) who had served in that position for 18 years. The judge had long lied concerning an "atrocious pattern of sexual misconduct" toward his subordinates. For years, two female staff members were assaulted by the judge, who was frequently intoxicated while on duty. After pleading guilty, the judge was convicted and sentenced to 3 years in prison. Then, he also asked that he
   - be allowed to retain his salary and benefits while he serves his sentence
   - be allowed to tender his resignation effective in about 1 year, so as to retain his medical insurance for a little bit longer
   - be shown mercy due to alcoholism and the death of his wife a few years earlier.

   Assume that you are one of the members of the panel that is considering whether or not the judge should be granted the earlier-mentioned concessions, as well as whether or not he should be impeached. How will you respond or vote, and why?

3. You are a member of the Senate when an impeachment proceeding is brought forth against a highly ranked and charismatic member of the House of Representatives on the basis of gross financial misconduct. Typical Senatorial deliberations on this matter would be kept private/confidential, but you and several other members (totaling 15) fear that the accused individual holds such sway over other Senators that closed-door proceedings present a danger for improper dismissal. With history and precedent not on your side, do you and the other Senators who agree with you attempt to fight to make the deliberations and proceedings public? What are the advantages and disadvantages of your decision?

Case Study

The Court Administrator and the Prudent Police Chief

You are the court administrator in a system that has the following procedure for handling traffic matters:

1. All persons who are given a traffic citation are to appear in court at 9:00 A.M. either on Monday or on Wednesday within 2 weeks of their citation date. They are given a specific date to appear.
2. Persons cited are not required to appear; they have the option of staying home and simply forfeiting their bond, which has been posted in advance of their initial appearance.
3. At the initial appearance, the arresting agency is represented by a court officer who has previously filed copies of all the citations with the clerk of the court.
4. The clerk, prior to the return date on the citation, prepares a file for each citation.
5. The clerk calls each case, and those persons appearing are requested by the court to enter a plea; if the plea is "not guilty," the matter is set for trial at a future date.
6. One case is scheduled per hour. On the trial date, the prosecutor and arresting officer are required to appear, ready for trial.
7. Statistics show that 75 percent of those persons pleading not guilty in this jurisdiction fail to appear for trial.

The chief of police in the court's jurisdiction is concerned about overtime for officers. He communicates with you, the court administrator, about this issue and explains that all police officers who appear in court for trial are entitled to the minimum 2 hours of overtime when they are not appearing during their regular shift. He views this as a tremendous and unnecessary expense to the city in view of the fact that most of the officers are not needed because the defendants do not appear and wishes to devise some system to save the city this high overtime cost.

Questions for Discussion

1. What system would you propose for solving the problem—within the existing law, with no changes in statutes or ordinances?
2. After you have finished designing a system, including how you would obtain the cooperation of the judges, prosecuting and defense attorneys, clerk's office, and other law enforcement agencies, discuss any proposed changes in the law that you think might improve the system further.
3. How would you go about making other significant, ongoing changes to improve the procedures and operation of this system?

Notes

1. Robert C. Harrall, "In Defense of Court Managers: The Critics Misconceive Our Role," *Court Management Journal* 14 (1982): 52.
2. Russell Wheeler, *Judicial Administration: Its Relation to Judicial Independence* (Williamsburg, VA: National Center for State Courts, 1988), p. 19.
3. West's Encyclopedia of American Law, 2nd ed., "Court Administrator," http://legal-dictionary.thefreedictionary.com/Court+Administrator.
4. See Roscoe Pound, "The Causes of Popular Dissatisfaction with the Administration of Justice," *Crime and Delinquency* 10 (1964): 355–371, for a discussion of Pound's discourse; see also Judith Resnik, "Roscoe Pound Round-Table Discussion," Yale Law School, *Faculty Scholarship Series.* Paper 695 (2007), http://digitalcommons.law.yale.edu/cgi/viewcontent.cgi?article=1696&context=fss_papers.
5. Pound, "The Causes of Popular Dissatisfaction with the Administration of Justice," p. 356.

6. Woodrow Wilson, "The Study of Administration," *Political Science Quarterly* 2 (1887): 197; reprinted in *Political Science Quarterly* 56 (1941): 481.
7. Quoted in Paul Nejelski and Russell Wheeler, *Wingspread Conference on Contemporary and Future Issues in the Field of Court Management* 4 (1980), Proceedings of the July 1979 Conference of the Institute for Court Management, July 9–11, 1979, Racine, Wisconsin.
8. National Advisory Commission on Criminal Justice Standards and Goals, *Courts* (Washington, DC: U.S. Government Printing Office, 1973), p. 171.
9. American Bar Association, Commission on Standards of Judicial Admission, *Standards Relating to Court Organization, Standard 1.41* (Chicago, IL: Author, 1974).
10. Russell R. Wheeler and Howard R. Whitcomb, *Judicial Administration: Text and Readings* (Upper Saddle River, NJ: Prentice Hall, 1977), p. 8.
11. Ibid.
12. David W. Neubauer, *America's Courts and the Criminal Justice System,* 9th ed. (Belmont, CA: Thomson/Wadsworth, 2008), pp. 170–176.
13. U.S. Department of Justice, Bureau of Justice Statistics, *State Court Organization, 2004* (Washington, DC: Author, October 2006), p. 23.
14. Barbara L. Graham, "Do Judicial Selection Systems Matter? A Study of Black Representation on State Courts," *American Politics Quarterly* 18 (1990): 316–336.
15. Charles G. Geyh, "Methods of Judicial Selection and Their Impact on Judicial Independence," Articles by Maurer Faculty. Paper 51 (2008), http://www.repository.law.indiana.edu/facpub/54.
16. Neubauer, *America's Courts and the Criminal Justice System,* p. 173.
17. William Raftery, "Judicial Selection in the States," National Center for State Courts, http://www.ncsc.org/sitecore/content/microsites/future-trends-2013/home/Monthly-Trends-Articles/Judicial-Selection-in-the-States.aspx.
18. Briant T. Fitzpatrick, "The Politics of Merit Selection." *Missouri Law Review*, 74(3) (Summer 2009), http://scholarship.law.missouri.edu/cgi/viewcontent.cgi?article=3840&context=mlr.
19. Neubauer, *America's Courts and the Criminal Justice System,* p. 172.
20. Law.com, "O'Connor Says Judges Shouldn't Be Elected," http://www.law.com/jsp/article.jsp?id=900005558371&OConnor_Says_Judges_Shouldnt_Be_Elected&slreturn=20140928164023.
21. Ibid.
22. American Judicature Society, "Judicial Selection in the States," http://www.judicialselection.us/.
23. Ballotpedia, "Judicial Selection in the States," https://ballotpedia.org/Judicial_selection_in_the_states.
24. Ron Malega and Thomas H. Cohen, *State Court Organization, 2011*, U.S. Department of Justice, Bureau of Justice Statistics (November 2013).
25. Ibid., p. 5.
26. Ibid.
27. Abraham Blumberg, *Criminal Justice* (Chicago, IL: Quadrangle Books, 1967).
28. Wheeler and Whitcomb, *Judicial Administration,* p. 370.
29. See, generally, the National Center for State Courts, "Education & Careers," http://www.ncsc.org/education-and-careers.aspx.
30. Malega and Cohen, *State Court Organization*, p. 9.
31. About Us | National Center for State Courts, August 31, 2016, http://www.ncsc.org/About-us.aspx
32. Wheeler and Whitcomb, *Judicial Administration,* p. 372.
33. Ibid.
34. Ibid.
35. Ibid., p. 373.
36. D. Byrne, Retired Illinois Judges Raking in Gluttonous Pensions, May 29, 2012, http://www.chicagonow.com/dennis-byrnes-barbershop
37. Judges Win Claim over Pension Scheme Changes, January 16, 2017, http://www.bbc.co.uk/news/business-38639818
38. A Pursuit of Justice, "The Qualities of a Good Judge," http://www.apursuitofjustice.com/the-qualitites -of-a-good-judge/.
39. Ibid.
40. Charles E. Patterson, "The Good Judge: A Trial Lawyer's Perspective," *The Judges Journal* 43(4) (Fall 2003): 14–15.
41. The Qualities Required of a Judge, 2006, http://cscja-acjcs.ca/qualities_required-en.asp?l=5
42. See, for example, Allen K. Harris, "The Professionalism Crisis—The 'Z' Words and Other Rambo Tactics: The Conference of Chief Justices' Solution," 53 S.C. L. Rev. 549, 589 (2002).
43. *In re First City Bancorp of Tex., Inc.*, 282 F.3d 864 (5th Cir. 2002).
44. *Landry v. State*, 620 So. 2d 1099, 1102 03 (Fla. Dist. Ct. App. 1993).
45. Marla N. Greenstein, "The Craft of Ethics," *The Judges Journal* 43(4) (Fall 2003): 17–18.
46. Ty Tasker, "Sticks and Stones: Judicial Handling of Invective in Advocacy," *The Judges Journal* 43(4) (Fall 2003): 17–18.
47. American Bar Association, "Tackling Incivility in the Legal Professor," http://www.americanbar.org/news/abanews/aba-news-archives/2013/08/tackling-incivility.htm.
48. The Qualities Required of a Judge.
49. Collins T. Fitzpatrick, "Building a Better Bench: Informally Addressing Instances of Judicial Misconduct," *The Judges Journal* 44 (Winter 2005): 16–20.
50. U.S. Legal, "Judicial Misconduct Law and Legal Definition," https://definitions.uslegal.com/j/judicial-misconduct/
51. Ibid.
52. Fitzpatrick, "Building a Better Bench," pp. 18–20.
53. M. Wagner, "Judge Fired for Leaking Charlize Theron Adoption Details," *New York Daily News* (September 13, 2014).
54. American Bar Association, "State Adoption of Revised Model Code of Judicial Conduct," http://www.americanbar.

org/groups/professional_responsibility/resources/judicial_ethics_regulation/map.html.
55. See American Bar Association, ABA Model Code of Judicial Conduct, "Preamble," p. 2, http://www.americanbar.org/content/dam/aba/migrated/judicialethics/ABA_MCJC_approved.authcheckdam.pdf.
56. Law360, "It's an Honor to Be Your Friend?: Social Media and Judges," https://www.law360.com/articiles/529874/it-s-an-honor-to-be-your-friend-social-media-and-judges.
57. See *Domville v. Florida*, No. 4D12-556 (2014).
58. Tennessee State Courts, "Judicial Ethics Committee Advisory Opinion No. 12-01," October 28, 2014, http://www.tncourts.gov/sites/default/files/docs/advisory_opinion_12-01.pdf.
59. Cynthia Gray, "ABA Social Media Advisory Opinion," *Judicature* 96 (5) (March/April 2014): 245.
60. American Bar Association, "Formal Opinion 462, Judge's Use of Electronic Social Networking Media," http://www.americanbar.org/content/dam/aba/administrative/professional_responsibility/formal_opinion_462.authcheckdam.pdf.
61. James Podgers, "ABA Opinion Cautions Judges to Avoid Ethics Pitfalls of Social Media," May 1, 2014, http://www.abajournal.com/magazine/article/aba_opinion_cautions_judges_to_avoid_ethics_pitfalls_of_social_media/; also see Cynthia Gray, "ABA Social Media Advisory Opinion," *Judicature* 96 (5) (March/April 2014), October 28, 2014, https://www.ajs.org/judicature-journal/editorial/surviving-storm-2/.
62. C. Gray, Social Media and Judicial Ethics, January 2017, https://www.ncsc.org.
63. Roy P. Basler (ed.), *The Collected Works of Abraham Lincoln* (Brunswick, NJ: Rutgers University Press, 1953), p. 41.
64. Ibid., remarks to a Pennsylvania Delegation (January 24, 1861), pp. 179–180.
65. Texas Center for Legal Ethics, "A Judge Should Avoid Impropriety and the Appearance of Impropriety in All Activities," https://www.legalethicstexas.com/Ethics-Resources/Rules/Code-of-Conduct-for-United-States-Judges/Canon-2/A-Judge-Should-Avoid-Impropriety-and-the-Appearanc.
66. For other examples of the appearance of impropriety, see Raymond J. McKoski, "Judicial Discipline and the Appearance of Impropriety: What the Public Sees Is What the Judge Gets," *Minnesota Law Review* 94(6) (2010): 1914–1996.
67. James Barron, "Upstate Judge Is Censured for Accidentally Firing Gun in Chambers," *The New York Times*, August 27, 2012, http://www.nytimes.com/2012/08/28/nyregion/judge-vincent-sgueglia-censured-after-gun-mishap-in-chambers.html?_r=0.
68. Roscoe Pound, "Principles and Outlines of a Modern Unified Court Organization," *Journal of the American Judicature Society* 23 (April 1940): 229.
69. See, for example, the Missouri Constitution, Article V, Sec. 15, paragraph 3.
70. Forest Hanna, "Delineating the Role of the Presiding Judge," *State Court Journal* 10 (Spring 1986): 17–22.
71. Neubauer, *America's Courts and the Criminal Justice System,* p. 102.
72. Robert A. Wenke, "The Administrator in the Court," *Court Management Journal* 14 (1982): 17–18, 29.
73. National Judicial College, *Effective Judging for Busy Judges* (Washington, DC: Bureau of Justice Assistance, 2006).
74. Robert B. Revere, "The Court Clerk in Early American History," *Court Management Journal* 10 (1978): 12–13.
75. Marc Gertz, "Influence in the Court Systems: The Clerk as Interface," *Justice System Journal* 2 (1977): 30–37
76. G. Larry Mays and William Taggart, "Court Clerks, Court Administrators, and Judges: Conflict in Managing the Courts," *Journal of Criminal Justice* 14 (1986): 1–7.
77. Ernest C. Friesen and I. R. Scott, *English Criminal Justice* (Birmingham: University of Birmingham Institute of Judicial Administration, 1977), p. 12.
78. Bernadine Meyer, "Court Administration: The Newest Profession," *Duquesne Law Review* 10 (Winter 1971): 220–235.
79. Harvey E. Solomon, "The Training of Court Managers," in Charles R. Swanson and Susette M. Talarico (eds.), *Court Administration: Issues and Responses* (Athens: University of Georgia Press, 1987), pp. 15–20.
80. Ernest C. Friesen, "Court Managers: Magnificently Successful or Merely Surviving?" *Court Management Journal* 14 (1982): 21.
81. Solomon, "The Training of Court Managers," p. 16.
82. Harrall, "In Defense of Court Managers," p. 51.
83. Neubauer, *America's Courts and the Criminal Justice System,* p. 104.
84. Gregory J. Linhares, "Vision, Function, and the Kitchen Sink: The Evolving Role of the State Court Administrator," *Trends in State Courts*, http://www.ncsc.org/sitecore/content/microsites/future-trends-2012/home/Leadership-and-the-Courts/4-2-Evolution-of-the-Court.aspx.
85. Conference of State Court Administrators, "Background," http://cosca.ncsc.org.
86. Ibid.
87. Neubauer, *America's Courts and the Criminal Justice System*, p. 104.
88. Geoffrey A. Mort and Michael D. Hall, "The Trial Court Administrator: Court Executive or Administrative Aide?" *Court Management Journal* 12 (1980): 12–16, 30.
89. Mort and Hall, "The Trial Court Administrator," p. 15.
90. Ibid.
91. John M. Greacen, "Has Your Court Administrator Retired? Without Telling You?" National Association for Court Management, Conference Papers from the Second National Conference on Court Management, Managing Courts in Changing Times, Phoenix, Ariz., September 9–14, 1990, pp. 1–20.

92. Darryl Brown, "Jury Nullification within the Rule of Law," *Minnesota Law Review* 81 (1997): 1149–1200.
93. Timothy R. Murphy, Genevra K. Loveland, and G. Thomas Munsterman, *A Manual for Managing Notorious Cases* (Washington, DC: National Center for State Courts, 1992), pp. 4–6. See also Timothy R. Murphy, Paul L. Hannaford, and Kay Genevra, *Managing Notorious Trials* (Williamsburg, VA: National Center for State Courts, 1998).
94. Katharine Q. Seelye, "Dzhokhar Tsarnaev Given Death Penalty in Boston Marathon Bombing," *The New York Times,* May 15, 2015, https://www.nytimes.com/2015/05/16/us/dzhokhar-tsarnaev-death-sentence.html?_r=0
95. See Murphy et al., *A Manual for Managing Notorious Cases,* pp. 53, 73, for other notable celebrity cases.
96. Ibid., p. 23.
97. Ibid., pp. 27–30.
98. Blumberg, *Criminal Justice*, p. 120.
99. "Comedian Resigns as Hackensack Judge after Losing Appeal," *CBS New York*, September 19, 2014, http://newyork.cbslocal.com/2014/09/19/nj-supreme-court-part-time-hackensack-judge-cant-also-be-comedian/.

Bikeriderlondon/Shutterstock

9 Court Issues and Practices

LEARNING OBJECTIVES

After reading this chapter, the student will be able to:

1. *distinguish the differences between the due process and crime control models*
2. *define the "CSI Effect" as it relates to court operations and actors*
3. *describe courthouse violence, both actual and potential, and what must be done to assess and deal with threats to court actors*
4. *describe the growing trend toward problem-solving courts*
5. *review the problems and consequences of, and solutions for, trial delays*
6. *diagram and explain the two systems used in scheduling cases*
7. *relate the importance of alternative dispute resolution (ADR) for decreasing litigation*
8. *describe a recent major U.S. Supreme Court decision concerning federal sentencing guidelines*
9. *explain the courts' role in media relations*
10. *discuss such issues as juveniles being waived into adult criminal court jurisdiction, the exclusionary rule, and the use of cameras in the courtroom*

▶ Introduction

This chapter, the last in our courts' section, examines some challenging areas that were mentioned in earlier chapters, as well as contemporary issues and practices.

The chapter begins with a consideration of the so-called "CSI Effect," and whether or not it has an impact on court operations and actors. Next, because history has shown that our courts—like the rest of our society—can be mean and brutish places, we review courthouse violence, its basic forms, and how to perform a threat assessment. We then discuss how problem-solving courts (focusing on drug, mental health, and veterans courts) are expanding and using their authority and innovative techniques. Then, we examine the dilemma of delay (including its consequences, suggested solutions, and two systems of scheduling cases) and review how the spreading concept of ADR is used to decrease litigation and court backlogs. In a related vein, we examine two recent U.S. Supreme Court decisions concerning federal sentencing guidelines. Next, after a look at media relations and the courts, we briefly consider how courts have become more successful at grant writing in difficult financial times. Then the following issues are considered: whether juveniles should be waived and tried as adults, the exclusionary rule should be banned, cameras should be used during trials, and plea bargaining should be kept. The chapter concludes with review questions and exercises in the Deliberate and Decide, Learn by Doing, and Case Study sections.

▶ Is There a "CSI Effect"?

"CSI Effect" the belief that a trial may be affected by television programming that creates inaccurate expectations by jurors regarding the power and use of forensic evidence.

Television programs focusing on criminal investigations and forensic techniques may not only be providing viewers with entertainment but also creating certain expectations about criminal cases in general and investigations in specific. This phenomenon—whereby television viewing influences peoples' perceptions, and is often referred to as cultivation theory—has been labeled the potential "**CSI Effect**": the possibility that the administration of justice is affected by television programming that creates inaccurate expectations in the minds of jurors regarding the power and use of forensic evidence. Indeed, the creator of *CSI*, Anthony E. Zuiker, observed, "'The CSI Effect' is, in my opinion, the most amazing thing that has ever come out of the series. For the first time in American history, you're not allowed to fool the jury anymore."[1]

Research findings on the CSI Effect, which began to appear in 2003, have been mixed. What is known, however, is as follows: Overall, a majority of citizens did not have knowledge of the CSI Effect, but when provided with a definition, believe it exists. Furthermore, people who are watching crime shows are more likely to think crime shows are accurate and educational. Viewing forensic and crime dramas, specifically, appears to be influencing people's views of social reality and can affect people's perceptions of crime investigation in the real world, which then affects their behavior during trial.[2] Studies of the legal field primarily indicate that many legal professionals believe it exists.[3] Some prosecutors and defense attorneys argue that the shows aid their opponents: prosecutors believe that juries want to see all evidence subjected to substantial forensic examination, whether warranted in a specific case or not, while defense attorneys have indicated that juries believe that scientific evidence is perfect and thus trustworthy in establishing guilt. Finally, a recent study of 104 persons who had served as jurors supported the pro-defense argument, which states that if forensic evidence is absent, the jury who watches *CSI*-type shows will be less likely to convict than the jury that does not watch *CSI*-type shows.[4]

However, Donald Shelton, a chief judge in the state of Michigan, and his colleagues conducted their own study of over 1,000 jurors to determine if there was support for the

CSI Effect. Shelton found that *CSI* viewers had higher expectations for the use of scientific evidence at trial, unlike the previous study; however, Sheldon found that this had very little to do with their decision to convict.[5] In other words, there were differences in expectations between *CSI* watchers and non-*CSI* watchers, but neither group was more likely than the other to convict based on their expectations of scientific evidence. Instead of a CSI Effect, Shelton found a broader issue at play: a "tech effect."[6] "The more sophisticated technological devices jurors had, the higher their expectations for the prosecutors to present evidence."[7] Not surprisingly, it appears that the CSI Effect can extend beyond expectations regarding forensics. In a 2016 review, forensic/DNA-centric fictional shows such as *CSI* and *SVU* and more FBI/psychology-based shows such as *Criminal Minds* and *Without a Trace* were differentiated. Depending on the shows that some people watch or know of, expectations in the courtroom may be altered, including the expectation of more psychological analysis for viewers of such shows as *Criminal Minds* and *Without a Trace*. The lesson here, of course, revolves around better education of the television viewing public concerning television reality and actual reality.[8]

So, given the somewhat conflicting evidence presented about the CSI Effect, it is safe to say that the "jury is still out" on this issue. To the extent the CSI Effect exists, it may well be changing the manner in which many people in the criminal justice system approach their duties. Prosecutors might be using more PowerPoint and video presentations and might take pains to explain to jurors that forensic evidence is not always collectible—or at the very least use experts to explain to jurors why they did not logically collect forensic evidence in a particular case. The *voir dire* process may also be altered to ensure that those jurors who are unduly influenced by shows like *CSI* are screened from jury service. In addition, some judges during their instructions are now warning jurors about their expectations regarding scientific evidence.[9] Such adaptations might be resulting in longer trials and an increased use of expert witnesses to aid the jury in understanding the presence or absence of physical evidence.[10]

So, in this technological age, it appears at the very least that jurors might expect more scientific evidence at trial, especially for murder and rape cases. But accommodating such expectations can substantially affect the criminal justice system. Here, resources would be needed to better equip law enforcement with necessary forensics equipment. Bigger crime labs would be needed, and more specially trained personnel would need to be hired. Without the increased capacity in labs, the ability to process scientific evidence would be diminished.[11] See Exhibit 9.1 for more information.

EXHIBIT 9.1

THE CSI EFFECT: "NOW PLAYING IN A COURTROOM NEAR YOU"

In a Delaware trial,[12] the defendant, having been indicted for murder, filed motions to exclude several pieces of state's evidence, including footwear impressions, voice identification, handwriting, fiber, DNA, fabric impressions, hair, video, and tool marks. The defendant argued that tests for each piece of evidence were all inconclusive, exculpatory, or irrelevant.

In its response, the prosecution stated that the tests were necessary to show the jury that it had conducted a thorough criminal investigation. Noting the extent of crime show viewing by the public, the prosecution believed that it needed to produce such an amount of evidence in order to address jurors' heightened expectations of the prosecution to meet the burden of proof.

The judge admitted that, after reviewing the literature on the CSI Effect, it would be naive to not believe the effect exists—especially having witnessed defendants taking advantage of the concept. The court also acknowledged that the defendant's objection had put the prosecution in a "Catch-22" position: On the one hand, the prosecution could be criticized for presenting

(continued)

too much irrelevant evidence, while on the other hand, it could be criticized for not presenting enough.

In the end, the court opted to not limit the prosecution's ability to thoroughly state its case and found little harm in allowing the presentation of inconclusive evidence.

This is obviously an area of criminal justice that must continue to be monitored and examined to determine whether or not knowledge of the CSI Effect affects juror expectations and decision making (either pro-prosecution or pro-defense), and if so, whether or not steps can be taken to correct for that bias.

The "Deliberate and Decide" section at the end of this chapter elaborates on this phenomenon, presenting related problems and approaches taken in two states and posing some questions for consideration.

▶ Courthouse Violence

Shooters in the Courthouses

It has been said that judges deal with "a segment of society that most people don't have to deal with—people who are violent, might be mentally unstable, are desperate because they don't have much more to lose."[13] That assessment is becoming increasingly true, especially when one considers some of the recent violent acts committed in and around courthouses against the judiciary and other courtroom participants:

- A family court judge in Reno, Nevada, standing at a window in his chambers, is shot by a sniper.[14]
- A prisoner in Atlanta steals a deputy's gun and fatally shoots a judge, his court reporter, and a deputy sheriff.[15]
- A Michigan man facing kidnapping and sexual assault charges steals a bailiff's gun, kills two other bailiffs, takes hostages, and then is shot by police officers.[16]
- The May 2016 trial of a woman and her daughter accused of stabbing a juvenile to death resulted in a fight breaking out just outside of a Chicago courthouse, which went on for several minutes before police officers were able to break it up.[17]

And while several fatalities resulted from the above courthouse shootings, such was not the case for the family court judge in Reno, who survived his attack. He is still on the bench and he now helps other jurists learn the signs of courthouse violence. As he tells it, the judge noticed one very telling signal in the shooter's behavior that day: excessive anger directed at specific "targets." This is just one example of how one might begin to conduct a threat assessment, which we discuss later in this chapter.[18]

courthouse violence where individuals perpetrate violent incidents against others in courthouses, both targeted and nontargeted in nature.

Recently, Etter and Swymeler conducted a study of **courthouse violence**, particularly shootings,[19] and determined that the problem of violent acts in courts has escalated in recent years. Selected findings from their study follow:

- Victims of the shootings were judges (8%), police officers (about one-third), and litigants or other court officials (including plaintiffs, defendants, witnesses, and lawyers [59%]).
- About 40 percent of the shooters were shot either by the court's security forces or by their own hand (with 87% of the shooters dying as a result).
- The majority (61%) of the 114 courthouse shooting incidents that were identified occurred in about the past 25 years.
- The firearms used were brought in by the shooter (77% of the time), taken from a deputy (19% of the time), or smuggled into a defendant or prisoner (4% of the time).

- Domestic violence or domestic problems were the motive in one-third of the shootings; escape was the motive in one-fourth; and assassination or another reason was the motive in 35 percent of the cases.
- The vast majority of the shooters were captured.

General Types of Court Violence

Data from the Center for Judicial and Executive Security (CJES) show that violent incidents and threats have steadily increased in both the federal and state court systems.[20] For example, shootings, bombings, and arson attacks in state courts have increased from 20 during the 1970s to 102 from 2000 to 2011.[21] The CJES also recently has tracked other violent incidents in our nation's state courts, such as knifings, bomb plots, and other assaults. Not surprisingly, these incidents have increased as well, from 10 in 2005 to 67 in 2011.[22] Two types of courthouse violence can occur:

- Nontargeted courthouse violence involves an individual who has no specific preexisting intention of engaging in violence but who, either during, at the conclusion of, or sometime shortly after the court proceeding becomes incensed and defiant at some procedure or outcome and acts out in the courtroom or public corridors. If this person also has a weapon, it might be used against the source of the grievance—a judge, attorney, witness, court employee, defendant or plaintiff, or bystander. If there are no judicial security screening devices or patrols on the premises, the person may proceed to attack people within the courthouse.
- Targeted courthouse violence involves an individual who expressly intends to engage in courthouse violence. These persons often simmer and stew for long periods of time so there is often some delay in responding to real or perceived affronts and insults. During this time, these people may or may not make threats and often create plans to circumvent security measures. They deliberately focus on specific individuals or the judiciary itself.[23]

With proper security precautions, many of these acts can be prevented or thwarted. This is a daunting task, however; each year, 106 million cases come into the state court system with 10,600 judges presiding over 2,000 major trial courts in 50 states and in Washington, DC.[24] And of the 106 million cases, 70 million are cases in courts of limited jurisdiction with approximately 16,800 judicial officers.[25] Because each filed case is potentially contentious, violence is also a potential outcome.

Other disturbing behaviors can affect the courts' functions as well. For example, judges can be sent inappropriate communications containing threats. Bombings of state and local government buildings have occurred as well.[26] Concerns about such acts of violence have spurred the implementation of enhanced security measures in many of our nation's courthouses, most of which have focused on the courts' physical environment to detect weapons, including the installation of metal detectors, which can be costly. Duress alarms and video surveillance cameras have been installed and separate prisoner, court staff, and public areas created. Without a doubt, a threat or perception of a threat can influence the decision-making processes of judges. Any extrajudicial factor that impacts or alters the mind-set of a judge is worthy of investigation, as the problem of threats affecting judges is obvious: it weakens the integrity of the entire justice process.[27]

One problem with enhancing courthouse security is its cost. In 1997, the cost to install 35 bullet-resistant windows in a Tacoma, Washington, federal courthouse following a shooting through a judge's window was $550,000. Today, the cost is still quite high: To install a bullet-resistant glass would cost over $1,500 for the window frame and as much as $100 per square foot for the glass.[28] Another problem is that such glass can weigh several hundred pounds a square foot, depending on thickness and type; not all buildings can handle such weight.

Following the sniper shooting of the judge in Reno,[29] mentioned earlier, several U.S. senators introduced a bill, The Court Security Improvement Act of 2006, which would have provided funds for both federal and state court security measures, but the bill was not passed before Congress adjourned.[30] However, a very similar bill was passed in 2007, receiving broad bipartisan support in Congress. It had essentially the same goals: increasing courthouse safety and providing additional resources to keep judges and system participants safe. From 2007 to 2011, the Court Security Improvement Act granted additional federal funding for the purposes of hiring additional U.S. marshals, increasing the security of courthouse computers, and allowing the redaction of certain types of information pertaining to judges in official reports.[31]

Conducting a Threat Assessment

threat assessment a process of identifying, assessing, investigating, and managing a courthouse threat.

A good beginning point for enhancing courthouse security is to conduct a **threat assessment**, which involves, at a minimum, the following steps:[32]

1. ***Identifying the threat.*** First, determine if in fact there is a threat—an expression of intent to injure someone or damage something. Also, the suspect and who represents the potential target of the threat must be identified so as to understand the relationship, if any, between the two.
2. ***Assessing the threat.*** If a threat is identified, assess how serious the threat appears to be. Consider the suspect's commitment—intent, motive, opportunity, and ability—individually and in combination. For example, a suspect may be highly motivated but incapable of instigating an attack himself due to being incarcerated or some other limitation.
3. ***Investigating the threat.*** If a suspect does pose a serious threat, next, attempt to conduct an interview with the suspect at his home (by two trained investigators), observing the contents of the house, the suspect's demeanor, level of agitation, and so on. The presence of weapons and any other such items can indicate the suspect's resolve and ability to conduct the violence.
4. ***Managing the threat.*** When a suspect represents a bona fide risk, then put in place such measures as a simple warning to court personnel (so they may take precautions), placing the subject under surveillance, or even incarcerating him if warranted. Also, use of a mental health commitment and/or a temporary restraining order might be considered.

Obviously, the circumstances of the individual case will determine the strategies to be used. Such strategies can be derived from a comprehensive courthouse security analysis, which judges or court administrators might consider facilitating with independent third parties.[33] One benefit of a third party analysis is the legitimacy that comes from it when used as a vehicle to apply for grant funding to seek security enhancements—enhancements that can be costly, as mentioned earlier in this chapter.[34] Court administrators also can request assistance from the National Center for State Courts (NCSC), which can conduct its own security analysis of individual jurisdictions.

When it comes to conducting threat assessments, Hall published a recent report on best practices for increasing courthouse security. Among the many suggestions proposed is the necessity of preparedness and procedure. Each member of the courthouse "workgroup" should have a clear understanding of what to do if a threat has been identified and reasonably probable. Evacuation routes should be delineated and practiced to ensure that in panic situations, they do not present a danger in themselves.[35] See Exhibit 9.2 for effective threat management techniques to protect judicial officers.

EXHIBIT 9.2

GOLDEN RULES FOR EFFECTIVE THREAT MANAGEMENT

The Bureau of Justice Assistance has articulated a threat management process to protect judicial officials. This process is comprised of the 10 Golden Rules for Effective Threat Management:

Rule 1: Recognize the need for a threat management process

Rule 2: Assign responsibility of managing cases to trained threat managers

Rule 3: Provide training for and establish liaison with protectees and court staff

Rule 4: Create an incident-tracking system with well-documented files

Rule 5: Establish liaison with other agencies

Rule 6: Use consistent and valid threat-assessment methods

Rule 7: Conduct thorough fact-finding

Rule 8: Apply threat-management strategies flexibly and intelligently

Rule 9: Communicate with protectees in a professional, confident, and competent manner

Rule 10: Manage cases appropriately

Source: "Protecting Judicial Officials: Implementing an Effective Threat Management Process," Bureau of Justice Assistance, Office of Justice Programs, U.S. Department of Justice, Washington, DC: June 2006.

▶ Problem-Solving Courts

Origin, Functions, and Rationale

The 1990s saw a wave of court reform across the United States as judges and other court actors experimented with new ways to deliver justice: Drug courts (discussed later) expanded into every state, and new mental health and veterans courts began targeting different kinds of problems in different places, all with a desire to improve the results for victims, litigants, defendants, and communities.

Although **problem-solving courts**—special courts created to accommodate persons with specific needs and problems, such as drug, veteran, and mentally ill offenders—are still very much a work in progress, according to Robert V. Wolf[36] they share five principal aspects:

1. The proactive, problem-solving orientation of the judge
2. The integration of social services
3. The team-based, nonadversarial approach
4. Their interaction with the defendant/litigant and
5. Their ongoing judicial supervision.

These courts use their authority to forge new responses to chronic social, human, and legal problems, such as family dysfunction, addiction, delinquency, and domestic violence that have proven resistant to conventional solutions. But problem-solving courts are expensive given the extensive treatment and evaluation associated with them. Today, problem-solving courts continue to thrive, but a constant battle is acquiring the funding needed to operate them.[37]

Community courts, like those in New York City, target misdemeanor "quality-of-life" crimes (e.g., prostitution, shoplifting, and low-level drug possession) and have offenders

problem-solving courts special courts created to accommodate persons with specific needs and problems, such as drug, veteran, and mentally ill offenders.

pay back the community by performing service functions. Similar stories can be told about the genesis and spread of domestic violence courts, mental health courts (MHCs), and others.[38] There are also courts that cater specifically to family issues, where one judge sees a case through from beginning to end.[39]

A New Role for the Courtroom Work Group

Problem-solving courts are presented as a judge-led and judge-centered movement; however, although it is true that judges are the public face of such courts, other members of the courtroom work group take on central roles as well. For example, probation officers (POs) spend the most time with problem-solving court participants and are charged with keeping other courtroom work group actors informed about the participant's progress and recommending incentives or sanctions for participants. POs may be said to act as the gatekeepers to the courts—recommending who should participate in these newly designed programs. POs maintain their traditional supervisory roles, overseeing the participants' progress in drug treatment, employment training, and prosocial skill development.[40]

Judges, who traditionally adjudicate the guilt or innocence of the defendants, still maintain a leadership role in the courtroom, but now lead a team focused on rehabilitative goals through collaborative processes. Judges in these courts base their interactions and decisions on information provided by other courtroom actors, often increasing their frequency of contact with participants while also limiting their contact with the criminal justice system. The presentation of information in problem-solving courts takes place behind closed doors in pre-court sessions. Participants no longer have a legally trained attorney to guide their decision making; instead, they now have a whole courtroom workgroup team (again, led by the judge) that is dedicated to their progress in a rehabilitative process. The team shares information as a whole before they interact with the participant.[41] Of course, there are variations in this model depending upon the jurisdiction. Integral to the operation of the problem-solving courts in some jurisdictions are drug court coordinators as well as compliance officers, in addition to the actors mentioned above.

Drug, Mental Health, and Veterans Courts

Extent and Effectiveness of Drug Courts

Despite their costs and a recent recession, drug courts continue to proliferate. As of mid-2015, there were 3,142 drug court programs operating in the United States.[42] Over half of these are adult drug courts. Still others include juvenile drug courts, family drug courts, veterans drug courts, DWI courts, tribal drug courts, co-occurring courts, and others.[43] Drug court participants undergo long-term treatment and counseling, are given sanctions and incentives, and make frequent court appearances. Successful completion of the program results in dismissal of charges, reduced or set-aside sentences, lesser penalties, or a combination of these. Most important, graduating participants gain the necessary tools to rebuild their lives. The drug court model includes the following key components:

- Offender screening and assessment of risks, needs, and responsivity
- Judicial interaction
- Monitoring (e.g., drug testing) and supervision
- Graduated sanctions and incentives
- Treatment and rehabilitative services[44]

The NCSC has articulated performance measures for drug courts, which include recidivism (post-program), accountability, retention and graduation rates, interaction and collaboration with other agencies and community partners, and costs.[45] So, do drug courts work? The National Institute of Justice has sponsored a number of research projects examining drug court outcomes and costs. Here, we briefly review two of these outcomes: recidivism and cost.

1. ***Impact on recidivism.*** Several studies have found that drug courts reduced recidivism among program participants as compared to comparable probationers. For example, one study found that within a 2-year follow-up period, the felony rearrest rate decreased from 40 percent before the drug court to 12 percent after the drug court began in one county. Rearrests were lower 5 years later when compared with rearrests for similar drug offenders within the same county. In Oregon, using data from 6,500 Oregon offenders, participation in a drug court treatment program also reduced recidivism.
2. ***Impact on cost.*** In a longitudinal study (over 10 years), the National Institute of Justice researchers found that, using data from the same 6,500 Oregon offenders, costs averaged $1,392 lower per drug court participant and resulted in public savings of $6,744 on average per participant (or $12,218 if victimization costs are included).[46]

Additionally, a 2016 report by the National Association of Drug Court Professionals (NADCP) finds support for all three types of problem-solving courts discussed in this section: they have better success rates across the board, but the shift in political philosophy in the Trump era could affect the allotment of resources to agencies, which can effectively control their quality.[47]

IN THEIR OWN WORDS

ADMINISTRATIVE ADVICE FROM THE FIELD

Kenneth J. Peak

Name: Norma Jaeger

Current and former positions/City/State: While I never would have imagined that my career path would end up at the Idaho Supreme Court, my background provided the perfect grounding for my most recent position as the statewide director of problem-solving courts. Prior to working for the courts, my work was managing public systems of drug and alcohol programs, and, in later years, systems that we now refer to as behavioral health. I began my career in mental health services, became involved in drug and alcohol programs in north Idaho in 1979, and then worked in Portland, Oregon, and Seattle, Washington, for 14 years as county administrator of those systems. This work inevitably connected me to criminal justice programs, as well, so when I returned to Idaho in 2000, I was recruited to oversee rehabilitation programs for the Idaho Department of Correction. In 2002, I accepted the position with the Supreme Court to guide a major expansion of problem-solving courts, now numbering 68 courts throughout Idaho.

Primary duties and responsibilities in your position as problem-solving courts' administrator: In general, I was responsible for guiding the operations of the state's problem-solving courts toward stronger and more consistent use of evidence-based practices and expanding the system beyond drug courts, to include mental health courts, DUI courts, family dependency courts, juvenile drug and mental health courts, and most recently, veterans courts. I led the initial development of statewide standards of operation for several of our court types and the development of court rules specific to problem-solving courts. I provided training to court teams, both new and established. I was able to expand the statewide staff to include positions to encourage alternative sentencing practices, effective misdemeanor probation services, behavioral health management, and outcome evaluation efforts. I wrote and administered several grants to expand services and to improve the effectiveness of problem-solving court operations.

Personal attributes/characteristics that have proven to be most helpful in my position: One characteristic that has been particularly useful to me is emotional maturity—the ability to not overreact to the disagreements and conflicts that come up in multidisciplinary and multiagency collaborations. It has been important to be able to be flexible in managing multiple priorities and to tolerate schedule interruptions and sudden, emerging priorities. I think a sense of humor and real respect for, and an enjoyment in, working with my colleagues across the state has also smoothed my path. Beyond these, I would add that strong verbal and written communication skills, an interest in continued learning (in October 2016, I completed the course work requirements for a Ph.D.), creativity, and good problem-solving skills have all been important in my work with these courts. Finally, I would have to add that the willingness to put in extra hours, when necessary, has been a major part of whatever success I have achieved. That is why I believe you must really love what you do or you just won't put in that extra time.

My three greatest challenges in the role of problem-solving courts' administrator: The first and ongoing challenge has been gaining the necessary financial resources to meet the demand for problem-solving court access and to provide for the scope of services needed. During my years of managing this program, we have experienced two significant financial downturns. These have constrained our ability to add capacity and to improve our mix of therapeutic services. Secondly, it is a major challenge to achieve the desired level of consistency of practice across 68 courts throughout the state. It is amazing how practices, once established, can wander, over the months, or years, and sometimes teams are very attached to such practice variations. I think the third greatest challenge has been achieving the necessary level of data collection and process documentation that is necessary to be able to conduct strong outcome evaluations. Data entry is not at the top of any practitioner's priority list. Our court colleagues have generally tried to do the best they could, with limited staff and hours in the day, but it remains a constant challenge to have complete and timely data in our system.

Personal accomplishments during my administrative career about which I am most proud: I was elected to the Board of Directors of the National Association of Drug Court Professionals for three terms and have given presentations at their national conferences for 15 years. I led the state of Idaho in establishing its system of mental health courts and in carrying out strategic planning projects in justice/mental health collaboration. I developed a system of peer review that continues to be a national model. I facilitated the establishment of Idaho's newest problem-solving courts, the veterans courts, and I now work nationally, conducting planning and training sessions for new veterans courts. A closely related task has been helping to establish the Idaho Military Legal Alliance, which provides free legal clinics to veterans, and Joining Forces for Treasure Valley Veterans, a monthly networking organization that is beginning to expand to other communities in Idaho and even to neighboring states.

Advice for someone who is interested in occupying an administrative position in problem-solving courts: Develop excellent written and oral communications skills and the ability to facilitate multidisciplinary working groups. Develop an understanding of the multiple elements of the justice and correctional systems including courts, probation and parole systems, behavioral health treatment programs, and the work of prosecutorial and defense agencies. Understand and respect the multiple sets of ethics and cultures within each of these differing systems. Develop patience—patience for extended process work and for achieving system changes. These are systems that change slowly. Listen more than you talk and laugh more than you cry. Become knowledgeable of both well-established and emerging evidence-based practices. Develop a deep understanding of the people who find themselves caught up in the justice system and hold on to both a sincere compassion and a healthy skepticism. And above all, believe in the ability of people and systems to change, and a deep appreciation of the commitment to "liberty and justice for all."

July 11, 2017, marked the 50th anniversary of starting my first job in public service. I believe I enjoy it as much today, in my semi-retirement, as I did when I began. It has been a privilege to do work that has always seemed to me to be meaningful and to have had many opportunities for creativity and collaboration.

Source: Used with permission from Norma Jaeger.

Rationales and Methods of Mental Health Courts (MHCs)

Against the backdrop of initial evidence in the 1990s that the drug court model was effective, the first MHC—based on a similar model—opened its doors in Broward County, Florida, in 1997. Prior to the establishment of MHCs, the criminal justice system tended to deal with mental illness in a rather formal, legalistic way, primarily based on competency to stand trial—for cases that got to that point. For example, a defendant must be able to understand the proceedings against him, and assist in his defense. In *Dusky v. United States* (1960),[48] the U.S. Supreme Court, in essence, affirmed this standard, as well as a defendant's right to have a competency evaluation prior to trial.

It is estimated that courts order 60,000 mental competency hearings per year; about 20 percent of such defendants are found unfit to stand trial.[49] In addition, the prevalence of serious mental illness among the jail population is 16.9 percent,[50] and there are more than one million inmates with mental illness in prisons or jails.[51] As a result, MHCs continue to grow as alternatives to traditional criminal court proceedings, and are in use for juveniles as well adults. Since the late 1990s, just under 400 such courts have been established and dozens more are being planned.[52] Eligible participants typically have a misdemeanor or low-level felony charge and a diagnosis of schizophrenia, bipolar disorder, or major depression. In some jurisdictions, defendants receive a suspended sentence after pleading guilty to a crime; in other jurisdictions, charges are suspended and eventually dropped upon successful completion of the program.[53] Judges hold participants accountable to take their psychotropic medications, avoid taking illegal drugs, and attend hearings. In a review of the MHC literature, Lauren Almquist and Elizabeth Dodd found the following common characteristics of MHCs:

- MHC teams generally include judges, representatives from the defense bar and district attorney's office, probation/parole, cases managers and/or representatives for treatment from the mental health system.
- Referrals to MHC generally are made by judges, family members, jail staff, or defense attorneys.
- MHCs use graduated incentives and sanctions to ensure that clients are motivated and stay in treatment programs.
- Many MHC clients have serious mental health problems and co-occurring substance abuse problems.
- MHCs are increasingly accepting individuals with more serious felonies—and in some areas—violent crimes.[54]

The basic premise of these courts is that they increase public safety, facilitate participation in effective mental health and substance abuse treatment, improve the quality of life for people with mental illnesses charged with crimes, and make more effective use of limited criminal justice and mental health resources.[55] And while evaluation research on MHCs is still in its early, formative stage, research findings suggest that at least in some MHCs, recidivism rates among MHC participants are lower than for those who go through the traditional court process. In addition, MHCs seem to be better than the traditional court system in connecting those with mental illness to treatment services.[56]

While mental health courts are not the "easy way" out of punishment that some members of the public think, some criticize such courts for increasing the justice system's involvement in the sphere of mental health, an area where there was considerable issue already. Because of variation in structure and programming, some mental health courts have even come under fire for being too punitive in comparison to traditional court, the opposite of its original intent.[57] Exhibit 9.3 provides an example of a unique approach now associated with these courts.

EXHIBIT 9.3

MOCK HEARINGS AND TRIALS PREPARE MENTALLY ILL PATIENTS

Some mental health hospitals are using psychiatrists, treatment, and mock trials to prepare criminal defendants for actual trial. Mentally ill patients participate in make-believe hearings, assuming key courtroom roles, sitting on a "bench" and looking down at a fictitious courtroom (with tables marked as "prosecution" and "defense" and people sitting in a box marked "jury," while making "rulings") all of which is geared toward helping them to better understand real court proceedings. As a result, it is hoped that recidivism and public safety will be improved.[58]

Juvenile MHC services are being developed as well. Often, juveniles demonstrate mental health issues and behavioral problems because their families are going through a period of dysfunction, and are perhaps desperate due to multiple crises, including unemployment, a serious accident, death of a close friend or family member, drug abuse, and so on. Most states provide expanded Medicaid services to all children under age 18 from low-income families. As with adult MHCs, juvenile MHCs have defined goals, such as weeks of sobriety, days of school attendance, and negative drug tests, in order to provide structure for moving through the program's various phases.[59]

Diverting Veterans into Treatment

Since the first veteran's court opened in Buffalo, New York, in 2008, veterans courts have also been spreading across the United States, with 113 veterans courts now classified as veterans treatment courts (VTCs). Certainly, the wars in Iraq and Afghanistan have created a nationwide push to help veterans who have trouble reintegrating into civilian life—20 percent of whom suffer from post-traumatic stress disorder (PTSD) and traumatic brain injuries (that percentage increases with the number of tours served).[60] These courts are diversion programs where, in exchange for a guilty plea to crimes charged, the veteran consents to regular court visits, counseling, and random drug testing. Then, if successful in completing the treatment program, the criminal record is expunged (meaning it is erased or stricken from the record). This allows for better access to employment, housing, and educational opportunities while also avoiding the pains of prison and having a criminal record.[61] As with mental health and drug courts, veterans courts serve a particular classification of individuals. Their overall purpose and structure is in many jurisdictions essentially identical to other problem-solving courts: an alternative route for processing individuals whose military service and subsequent psychological problems make them uniquely challenging to dispense with fairly. Recently, the federal Veterans Administration became involved in veterans courts as well, teaming with state and county organizations as well as the U.S. Department of Justice, Bureau of Justice Assistance (BJA), and the U.S. Department of Health and Human Services Substance Abuse and Mental Health Services Administration (SAMHSA). Veteran Justice Outreach (VJO) specialists work in veterans courts in 168 veterans courts, dockets, and tracks, serving nearly 8,000 veterans who had been admitted to these courts by late 2012. The length of involvement with the courts ranges from 15 to 18 months, and data indicate that more than two-thirds of the veterans completed the court and healthcare treatment regime successfully.[62] On the heels of initial positive outcomes for VTCs, the Justice Department recently expanded the funding available to facilitate such efforts, providing over $4 million in grants to expand jurisdictional aid to veterans. This money not only goes to the courts themselves, but it also goes to research to determine best practices for treating and rehabilitating veterans. One of the major focal points of this grant program will be substance abuse treatment agencies, given that one in six veterans who served in either the Iraq War or Operation Enduring Freedom suffers from substance abuse.[63] See Exhibit 9.4 for a description of a veterans treatment court in Oklahoma.

EXHIBIT 9.4

HOW VETERANS COURTS WORK[64]

When someone is arrested in Tulsa, Oklahoma, officers ask if they are a military veteran. If so, those veterans who face criminal charges and are in need of mental health or substance use treatment may be eligible for the veterans treatment court (VTC). VTCs were developed to help veterans avoid unnecessary incarceration if they have developed mental health problems. Although most courts work with veterans of all decades and wars, many such courts were initiated out of concern for veterans returning from Afghanistan and Iraq and encountering legal trouble.

VTCs connect vets with services at the earliest possible time and provide volunteer veteran mentors to provide nonclinical support. Their participation is voluntary, and those who choose to participate are first assessed by a mental health professional and their treatment needs are determined.

While the veteran remains in the community while undergoing treatment, a judge regularly checks on his or her progress. If not meeting the requirements of the program (e.g., failing a drug screening or disobeying court orders), the court will impose sanctions that may include community service, fines, jail time, or transfer out of veterans court and back into a traditional criminal court. Judges provide ongoing encouragement to participants as long as they continue on the path of recovery.

▶ The Dilemma of Delay

"Justice Delayed—"

There is no consensus on how long is too long with respect to bringing a criminal case to trial. Still, the principle that "justice delayed is justice denied" says much about the longstanding goal of processing court cases with due dispatch. Charles Dickens condemned the practice of slow litigation in nineteenth-century England, and Shakespeare mentioned "the law's delay" in *Hamlet*. Delay in processing cases is one of the oldest problems of U.S. courts. The public often hears of cases that have languished on court dockets for years. This can only erode public confidence in the judicial process.[65]

Case backlog and trial delay affect many of our country's courts. The magnitude of the backlog and the length of the delay vary greatly, however, depending on the court involved. It is best to view delay not as a problem, but as a symptom of a problem.[66] Yet, some time is needed to prepare a case. What is a concern is *unnecessary* delay; however, there seems to be no agreed-on definition of unnecessary delay.

The Consequences

The consequences of delay can be severe. It can jeopardize the values and guarantees inherent in our justice system, and deprive defendants of their Sixth Amendment right to a speedy trial. Lengthy pretrial incarceration pressures can cause a defendant to plead guilty.[67] The reverse is also true: delay can strengthen a defendant's bargaining position; prosecutors are more apt to accept pleas to a lesser charge when dockets are crowded. Delays cause pretrial detainees to clog the jails, police officers to appear in court on numerous occasions, and attorneys to spend unproductive time appearing on the same case. In sum, **case delay** in the courts is generally considered to be bad for multiple reasons. It deprives defendants of a timely (speedy) trial. It may result in loss or deterioration of evidence, cause severe hardship to some parties (victims, witnesses), and bring about a loss of public confidence in the court system.

case delay an excessive amount of time passing prior to bringing a criminal case to trial.

One factor contributing to court delay is the lack of incentive to process cases speedily. Although at least 10 states require cases to be dismissed and defendants to be released if they are denied a speedy trial,[68] the U.S. Supreme Court has refused to give the rather vague concept of a "speedy trial" any precise time frame.[69] The problem with time frames, however, is twofold: first, more complex cases legitimately take a longer time to prepare, and second, these time limits may be waived due to congested court dockets. In sum, there is no legally binding mechanism that works. Exhibit 9.5 discusses delay in executing sentences after conviction, specifically in death penalty cases.

EXHIBIT 9.5

DELAYED JUSTICE AND CAPITAL PUNISHMENT

The phenomenon of delayed justice is most apparent in capital cases. Death row inmates are far more likely to die on death row than actually be executed. This is often a point of contention for those who support the practice: "Why bother keeping them alive?" among other similar rhetoric. However, even for death row inmates who waive their right to appeals, by statute there are often a number of appeals that *must* be heard before the sentence can be carried out. Given the extreme backlog of cases on many judges' dockets, these mandatory appeals can take years to be heard. The passage of time can also complicate the appeals process: witnesses may move away or forget details, and may simply tire of dealing with the case and wish to move on.[70] Capital punishment itself is also a point of contention. The United States is one of the only Western countries that still employs the penalty, and the most frequent method—lethal injection—is becoming increasingly difficult to perform without issue. Many of the companies that produce the drugs used in the procedure are refusing to allow the United States to purchase any because of its use in executions. Public opinion was historically in favor of the practice, but is increasingly divided. The fallacy that it is somehow less expensive to execute an individual as opposed to imprisonment for life is still a fairly common defense when the question of cost is raised. This is demonstrably false, even in the "speedier" cases where the defendant waives his or her rights to appeals.[71] However, in extreme cases, those awaiting the execution of the sentence of death are still waiting, even after nearly three decades, while the family members of victims continue to suffer.[72]

Suggested Solutions and Performance Standards

The best-known legislation addressing the problem of delay is the Speedy Trial Act of 1974, amended in 1979. It provides firm time limits: 30 days from the time of arrest to indictment and 70 days from indictment to trial. Thus, federal prosecutors have a total of 100 days from the time of arrest until trial. This speedy trial law has proven effective over the years, although individual districts can create exceptions in their implementation rules. For example, in the district of Kansas, if the defendant is charged with a felony, but there is no grand jury in session during the time of the defendant's arrest, another 30 days may be tacked on to the original 30-day requirement from arrest to indictment.[73]

Unfortunately, however, laws that attempt to speed up trials at the state level have had less success than this federal law because most state laws fail to provide the courts with adequate and effective enforcement mechanisms. As a result, the time limits specified by speedy trial laws are seldom followed in practice.[74]

A number of proposals have emerged to alleviate state and local courts' logjams, ranging from judicial jury selection and limits on criminal appeals to six-person juries. The latter was actually suggested more than two decades ago as a means of relieving the congestion of court calendars and reducing court costs for jurors.[75] Thirty-three states have specifically authorized juries of fewer than 12, but most allow smaller juries only in misdemeanor cases. In federal courts, defendants are entitled to a 12-person jury unless the prosecuting and defense attorneys agree in writing to a smaller one.[76] Furthermore, the

National Center for State Courts has developed a listing of *CourTools*,[77] which together provide a set of trial court performance measures that offer court administrators a perspective on their court's operations.

The Speedy Trial Act does *not*, however, extend to sentencing. A Montana man waited in jail for 14 months after his trial for jumping bail to hear what his sentence was, and after his incarceration, he appealed on the grounds that such a delay was in violation of this act. The U.S. Supreme Court disagreed, remarking that the protections owed to individuals before a sentence is passed are invalidated once they are formally convicted. The typical response to a finding of inappropriate delay is often dismissal of the case, which the Court held would be an inappropriate response in the event of post-conviction relief. It is unlikely that this changes any time soon.[78]

Case Scheduling: Two Systems

A key part of addressing case delay concerns the ability of the court administrator to set a date for trial. Scheduling trials is problematic because of forces outside the administrator's control: slow or inaccurate mail delivery, which can result in notices of court appearances arriving after the scheduled hearing; an illegible address that prevents a key witness or defendant from ever being contacted about a hearing or trial; or a jailer's inadvertent failure to include a defendant on a list for transportation. If just one key person fails to appear, the matter must be rescheduled. Furthermore, judges have limited ability to control the actions of personnel from law enforcement, probation, or the court reporter's offices, all of whom have scheduling problems of their own.[79]

The two primary methods by which cases are scheduled by the courts are the individual calendar and the master calendar.

Individual Calendar System

The simpler procedure for scheduling cases is the **individual calendar system**. A case is assigned to a single judge, who oversees all aspects of it from arraignment to pretrial motions and trial. The primary advantage is continuity; all parties to the case know that a single judge is responsible for its conclusion. There are other important advantages as well. Judge shopping (in which attorneys try to get their client's case on a particular judge's docket) is minimal, and administrative responsibility for each case is fixed. In addition, it is easier to pinpoint delays because one can easily compare judges' dockets to determine where cases are moving along and where they are not.

individual calendar system a system whereby cases are assigned to a single judge, who oversees all aspects of it from arraignment to pretrial motions and trial.

This system, however, is often affected by major differences in *case stacking* because judges work at different speeds. In addition, if a judge draws a difficult case, others must wait. Because most cases will be pleaded, however, case stacking is not normally a major problem unless a judge schedules too many cases for adjudication on a given day. Conversely, if a judge stacks too few cases for hearing or adjudication each day, delay will also result. If all cases settle, the judge has downtime from the courtroom.

Master Calendar System

The **master calendar system** is a more recent development. Here, judges oversee (usually on a rotating basis) all stages of a case: preliminary hearings, arraignments, motions, bargaining, or trials. A judge is assigned a case from a central or master pool; once he or she has completed a specific phase of it, the case is returned to the pool. The primary advantage of this system is that judges who are good in one particular aspect of litigation (such as preliminary hearings) can be assigned to the job they do best. The disadvantage is that it is more difficult to pinpoint the location of or responsibility for delays. Judges also have less incentive to keep their docket current because when they dispose of one case, another appears. In addition, the distribution of work can be quite uneven. If, for example, three

master calendar system a system whereby judges are assigned to oversee all stages of a case (arraignment, preliminary hearing, trial).

judges are responsible for preliminary hearings and one is much slower than the others, an unequal shifting of the workload will ensue; in other words, the two quicker judges will be penalized by having to handle more cases.

Which System Is Better?

Each calendar system has its advantages and disadvantages, and a debate has developed over which is better. The answer probably depends on the nature of the court. Smaller courts, such as U.S. district courts, use the individual calendar system more successfully. Largely because of their complex dockets, however, metropolitan and state courts almost uniformly use the master calendar system. Research indicates that courts using the master calendar experience greater difficulty. Typical problems include the following: (1) Some judges refuse to take their fair share of cases; (2) the administrative burden on the chief judge is often great; and (3) as a result of these two factors, a significant backlog of cases may develop. In those courts where the master calendar system was discontinued in favor of the individual system, delay was greatly reduced.[80]

In this technological era, we also note the voluminous court scheduling software systems now available to judges and judicial assistants that attempt to keep cases moving in our nation's courthouses. Whether they are used as an individual calendar or a master calendar, these software systems have become not only sophisticated but also flexible, allowing judicial officers to create their own rules for calendaring and reporting. In a recent search for court management software, more than 50 different systems were considered "top court management software products," some of which are browser-based, allowing access with an internet connection.[81]

▶ Decreasing Litigation: Alternative Dispute Resolution

Chapter 7 included information concerning annual caseloads of some of the nation's courts. Although these lawsuits—both criminal and civil—have arguably resulted in greater safety and a better quality of life in the United States, the fact remains that the weight of this litigation has imposed a tremendous workload on the nation's courts.

Several methods are now being proposed to reduce the number of lawsuits in this country. One is to limit punitive damages, with only the judge being allowed to levy them. Another is to force losers to pay the winners' legal fees. This, however, has the potential problem of placing additional financial burdens on individuals who are already sinking considerable quantities of their own money into the legal process. The process of discovery also warrants examination. This process involves exchange of information between prosecutors and defense attorneys to ensure that the adversary system does not give one side an unfair advantage over the other. Many knowledgeable people believe that the process of discovery wastes much time and could be revamped.[82]

alternative dispute resolution (ADR) settling disputes outside of court, typically by negotiation, conciliation, mediation, and arbitration.

Another procedure that is already in relatively widespread use is **alternative dispute resolution (ADR)**, or any means of settling disputes outside of court (and typically involving negotiation, conciliation, mediation, and arbitration). Realizing that the exploding backlog of both criminal and civil cases pushes business cases to the back of the queue, many private corporations are attempting to avoid courts and lawyers by using alternative means of resolving their legal conflicts. Some corporations have even opted out of litigation altogether; top corporations have signed pledges with other companies to consider negotiation and other forms of ADR prior to suing other corporate signers.[83]

ADR, which some courts introduced already in the 1960s, is appropriate when new law is not being created. ADR can provide the parties with a forum to reach a resolution that may benefit both sides. Litigation is adversarial; ADR can resolve disputes in a collaborative manner that allows parties' relationship to be maintained. Furthermore, ADR proceedings are normally confidential, with only the final agreement being made public. ADR is also much more expedient and less costly than a trial.[84] Interestingly enough, ADR may also reduce courtroom violence (discussed earlier in this chapter). By allowing participants to be part of a collaborative process where they feel they are heard, and where an authority figure is responding to concerns on both sides, the outcome is less likely to be construed as unfair—a problem that may precipitate violence in courtrooms.[85]

The two most common forms of ADR used today are arbitration and mediation. Arbitration is similar to a trial, though less formal, and in some civil cases is mandated in order to keep a court's docket clear for cases with higher dollar amounts. An arbitrator is selected or appointed to a case; civil court rules generally apply. Parties are usually represented by counsel. The arbitrator listens to testimony by witnesses for both sides; then, after hearing closing remarks by counsel, the arbitrator renders a verdict. Arbitration may be mandatory and binding, meaning that the parties abandon their right to go to court once they agree to arbitrate. The arbitration award is usually appealable. In nonbinding arbitration, the loser in the case can request a trial in civil court. Types of disputes commonly resolved through arbitration include collective bargaining agreements, construction and trademark disputes, sales contracts, warranties, and leases.[86]

Mediation is considerably less formal and friendlier than arbitration. Parties agree to negotiate with the aid of an impartial person who facilitates the settlement negotiations. A mediation session includes the mediator and both parties; each side presents his or her position and identifies the issues and areas of dispute. The mediator works with the parties until a settlement is reached or the negotiations become deadlocked; in the latter case, the matter may be continued in court. Mediation is not binding or adversarial; instead, it encourages the parties to resolve the dispute themselves. Mediation is commonly used when the parties in dispute have a continuing relationship, as in landlord–tenant disputes, long-term employment/labor disputes, and disputes between businesses.[87] We note as well that mediation is central to the ideals of restorative justice, where some offenders (both juveniles and adults) are brought together with victims so that offenders better understand the harm done. Accountability agreements also are forged in mediation so that offenders and victims see a more peaceful future.[88]

Exhibit 9.6 takes a closer look at mediation.

EXHIBIT 9.6

THE QUESTIONS MEDIATORS ASK

The American Bar Association has published a list of frequent questions and background knowledge that mediators should have in order for the practice to be successful.[89]

- What is the case about from each point of view?
- What does each party perceive to be the issue in contention?
- Are there any hidden issues that need to be discovered and addressed?
- What are the goals of each party?
- How do the circumstances fit in a legal context (i.e., what events occur and what is their legal significance)?
- What is the plan if no settlement can be reached?
- Are there practical arrangements for drafting a settlement? How are settlement terms going to be circulated?

Given the increasing number of lawsuits in this country, it appears that ADR is the wave of the future; as one law professor noted, "In the future, instead of walking into a building called a courthouse, you might walk into the Dispute Resolution Center."[90]

▶ Supreme Court Decisions on Federal Sentencing Guidelines

Congress passed the Sentencing Reform Act of 1984[91] to achieve three main objectives: (1) to allow the criminal justice system to combat crime through a fair sentencing system, (2) to reduce sentence disparity that existed in the federal system, and (3) to create proportional sentences in relation to the severity of the crime.[92] To achieve these objectives, the act provided instructions to create sentences based on both offenses and offender characteristics.[93] The act also created the U.S. Sentencing Commission, which in turn established **federal sentencing guidelines**—rules for computing uniform sentencing policy that also provide classifications of offenses and offenders, severity of crimes, and suggested punishments for the federal criminal justice system. These guidelines took effect on November 1, 1987. Since that time, two notable U.S. Supreme Court decisions have been rendered concerning federal sentencing guidelines and federal judges' sentences using them.

federal sentencing guidelines rules for computing uniform sentencing policy; they also provide classifications of offenses and offenders, severity of crimes, and suggested punishments.

First, in January 2005, the Supreme Court in *U.S. v. Booker*[94] reaffirmed the importance of sentencing guidelines when determining the appropriate sentence for a crime to ensure that similarly situated defendants were treated more or less alike rather than depending on the judge to whom their case happened to be assigned.[95] The case involved a crack cocaine possession conviction where the guidelines required a possible 210- to 262-month sentence; the trial judge, however, believed the defendant possessed a much larger amount of cocaine, and rendered a sentence that was almost 10 years longer than the one the guidelines prescribed.[96] By a 5–4 vote, the U.S. Supreme Court found that the U.S. Sentencing Guidelines violated the Sixth Amendment by allowing judicial, rather than jury, fact-finding to form the basis for the sentence; in other words, letting in these judge-made facts is unconstitutional.[97] The Court did not discard the guidelines entirely, however, saying the guidelines are meant to be advisory and not mandatory. Thus, this advisory guideline system is a resource a judge can consider but may choose to ignore. In other words, courts still must consider the guidelines, but they need not follow them. In addition, sentences for federal crimes became subject to appellate review for "unreasonableness," allowing appeals courts to reduce particular sentences that seem far too harsh.

Then, in late 2007, the Supreme Court went further and explained what it meant in 2005 by "advisory" and "reasonableness," deciding two cases that together restored federal judges to their traditional central role in criminal sentencing. The Court found that district court judges do not have to justify their deviations from the federal sentencing guidelines and have broad discretion to disagree with the guidelines and to impose what they believe are reasonable sentences—even if the guidelines call for different sentences. Both cases—*Gall v. U.S.* and *Kimbrough v. U.S.*—were decided by the same 7–2 margin, and the Supreme Court chided federal appeals courts for failing to give district judges sufficient leeway.[98] A related subject—the effect of the Prison Litigation Reform Act of 1996 on the filing of petitions by state prisoners—is discussed in Chapter 10.

▶ Courts' Media Relations

The lawyer defending singer Michael Jackson at his child molestation trial in 2005 caused a furor among the popular media when he asked the judge for a gag order in the case. The lawyer said he was not thinking about the First Amendment when he requested the order, but rather about his client's best interests. The media, conversely, felt that the public had a right to know what was occurring in the case. This issue brings to light the importance of good relations between the media and courts. In fact, the National Center for State Courts suggests that courts should promote effective relationships between the two entities to ensure that cases are handled fairly and efficiently.[99]

A debate between journalists and key players in high-profile legal cases occurred recently at one of many conferences sponsored by an organization that is a corollary to the National Judicial College, discussed in Chapter 8; this organization, the National Center for Courts and Media, also located in Reno, Nevada, was established to foster better communication and understanding between judges and lawyers on the one hand and between judges and journalists who serve the public on the other hand. The goal is to eliminate unnecessary friction between courts and the media, and bridge the gap between the two through workshops and conferences. The center helps judges to understand what a reporter is seeking and why; conversely, the workshops help journalists learn what records are open to the public, how the legal system works, who to go to for court information, how to gain access to documents, and what restrictions a judge works under.[100]

EXHIBIT 9.7

TOP 10 SUGGESTIONS FOR ESTABLISHING RELATIONS WITH THE MEDIA

The National Judicial College now offers a course in High Media Interest Cases. Below is a list of 10 tips, developed by Gary Hengstler, for enhancing relationships between the media and judiciary.[101]

1. Take advantage of educational opportunities so that judges, lawyers, and the media can better understand each other's roles.
2. Assume public access of all court proceedings; the burden of proof for closure rests with the entity seeking secrecy.
3. Gag orders should be used only in extraordinary cases.
4. Support interdisciplinary committees comprised of the bench, bar, and media to discuss issues of mutual concern.
5. Establish guidelines for trial-media management in high-profile cases.
6. Consider nonbinding professional standards for journalists.
7. Assume that courtrooms are open to media cameras unless there is a strong case for barring them.
8. Encourage judges to explain their rulings on the record.
9. Determine under what circumstances it is appropriate to compel the media to testify in court or to produce tapes and other materials to the court.
10. Encourage media organizations to develop an ombuds system to listen to recommendations from the publics and the courts.

▶ Other Issues and Practices

Are "851 Notices" Being Overused and Abused?

There is growing criticism about a section of the **United States Code 21 U.S.C. §851** that triggers enhanced penalties against drug dealers and is said to be the reason why "thousands of prisoners are serving life without parole for nonviolent crimes."[102]

***United States Code* 21 U.S.C. §851** a federal law allowing federal prosecutors to more heavily punish hard-core drug traffickers who have prior drug felony convictions.

Enacted by Congress in 1970, the original purpose of the law was straightforward and rational enough: to allow federal prosecutors to identify and more heavily punish (with sentencing enhancements, such as doubling the mandatory minimum sentences) those hard-core drug traffickers having prior drug felony convictions. However, many people now argue that the law is being used by prosecutors to coerce guilty pleas by routinely threatening, as one federal judge put it, "ultra-harsh, enhanced mandatory sentences that no one ... thinks are appropriate."[103]

Writing "statements of reason" in October 2013—a means by which judges may express their views—Judge John Gleeson of the Eastern District of New York took strong issue with the use of "851 notices," citing one case in specific that had come before him.[104] Lulzim Kupa was convicted of distributing marijuana in 1999 and again in 2007. Kupa was paroled in 2010 but was soon caught trafficking cocaine, which carried a possible sentence of 10 years to life. Prosecutors offered Kupa 24 hours to accept or reject an offer—plead guilty and be sentenced to 110–137 months. Kupa rejected the offer, so prosecutors filed an "851 notice," citing his two prior marijuana convictions and threatening him with life without parole. Then, however, prosecutors gave Kupa 1 day to consider another proposal—plead guilty and receive a sentence of about 9 years (or, again, face a sentence of life without parole). After taking too long to decide, prosecutors again increased their recommended sentence. At this point, Kupa gave in, telling Judge Gleeson, "I want to plead guilty, your honor, before things get worse."[105]

Alternatively, assume that Kupa—being 37 years of age in October 2013—had received the 851 notice and again declined to accept the prosecutors' offer and was later convicted at trial. He would thus have died in prison for committing a nonviolent drug offense. Judge Gleeson added that because there is no judicial oversight of the enhanced mandatory minimums prosecutors can inject into a case, they can put enormous pressure on defendants to plead guilty—using the threat of a life sentence as a "sledgehammer" to extort guilty pleas and in effect waive their right to trial.[106] Furthermore, because 97 percent of all federal convictions come without trials, the government is thus spared of the burden of proving guilt beyond a reasonable doubt—meaning that in 97 of 100 cases, the conviction is obtained with mere probable cause, which is all that is required of a grand jury indictment.[107]

Critics note that 851 notices can be a form of overcharging, a prosecutorial tactic that induces defendants to plead guilty to lesser offenses. Overcharging, in a general sense, occurs when prosecutors charge with more serious crimes than they know they can prove. There are two general types of overcharging: vertical and horizontal. Vertical overcharging is the practice of charging the offense at a much higher severity level than is actually warranted (e.g., charging possession of .01 ounces of a drug as intent to distribute). Horizontal overcharging occurs when prosecutors tack on far more additional charges than the case actually merits. Both are permitted and have been in legal practice long before the 851 notice was codified.[108]

However, former attorney general Eric Holder in late October 2014 issued a memo to federal prosecutors limiting their ability to use section 851 enhancements as a threat to encourage plea bargaining. The memo stated that a defendant's willingness to enter into a plea negotiation is not a factor in the 851 charging policy, and therefore cannot be used by prosecutors as a bargaining chip. According to Holder, this practice is inappropriate.[109]

Time to Rethink Juvenile Waivers?

Although crime in the United States peaked in the mid-1990s, there are yet about 650,000 arrests of juveniles under age 18 each year for Part I and Part II offenses, about 36,000 of which are arrests for murder and nonnegligent manslaughter, forcible rape, robbery, and aggravated assault.[110]

Certainly there are some crimes committed by juveniles in our society that are so heinous or otherwise indicative that the youth is not amenable to the rehabilitative philosophy and protective shroud of the juvenile justice system. In such cases, nearly all states (45) have discretionary **juvenile waiver** provisions, allowing juvenile court judges to waive (transfer) jurisdiction over individual juvenile cases to *adult* criminal court for prosecution.[111]

juvenile waiver a provision for juvenile court judges to transfer jurisdiction over individual juvenile cases to an adult criminal court for prosecution.

There are three ways that a juvenile can be waived to adult criminal court: judicial, prosecutorial, and legislative:

- *Judicial waivers* allow the juvenile court judge to determine if the juvenile meets minimum waiver criteria, including such variables as age, type of offense, previous criminal record, or a combination of the three. In some states, waivers are mandatory given certain specified criteria (age, offense, prior record).

- A *prosecutorial waiver* (also called concurrent jurisdiction) gives the decision making to the prosecutor who can decide whether to try a case in juvenile or adult court, depending on his or her assessment of the facts.
- A *legislative waiver* (also called statutory exclusion) occurs when state laws require that certain offenses (such as murder) be automatically turned over to the adult criminal justice system—sometimes regardless of the youth's age.[112]

In 23 states, a *reverse waiver* authorizes a criminal court judge to decide whether it is appropriate for a juvenile case to be handled in the criminal justice system or "reversed" back to the juvenile justice system. In some states, the reverse waiver can be used for all three of the reasons we stated above that the juvenile case came into the jurisdiction of the criminal courts to begin with. Here, if a juvenile objects to the case being heard in a criminal court and if a judge determines that the "best interests" of the juvenile are served in the juvenile justice system, the case may be transferred (back) there.[113]

Statistically, juvenile waivers do not occur often, and the number of waivers has declined significantly since 1994 (when there were 13,800 such cases). Today, of about 1.2 million juvenile delinquency cases handled by the courts, about half (54%) are handled formally (i.e., a petition is filed requesting an adjudication or waiver hearing). Of those, an estimated 5,400 cases, or about 1 percent, results in judicial waiver. Most waivers involve crimes against persons (47%), property offenses (31%), drug offenses (13%), and public order offenses (8%).[114]

Some researchers now argue that in recent years a movement has developed that militates against juvenile waivers and toward a less punitive philosophy. At the core of this argument are three U.S. Supreme Court decisions of the 2000s:

1. *Roper v. Simmons*,[115] in which the Court held that it is unconstitutional to impose a death sentence for a capital crime committed when one was under the age of 18;
2. *Graham v. Florida*,[116] where the Court decided that juvenile offenders cannot be sentenced to life imprisonment without parole (LWOP) for non-homicide offenses; and
3. *Miller v. Alabama*,[117] which extended Graham and held that the Eighth Amendment forbids sentencing juvenile homicide offenders to LWOP.

In these cases, the Court relied heavily on social-science rationales to draw their conclusions: the tendency of juveniles toward immature and irresponsible behavior, juveniles being more susceptible to peer pressures and outside influences, and the fact that their personality or identity is not as well formed as an adult's. In sum, the young are very immature, impulsive, and easily manipulated or influenced. As a result, some authors have even questioned whether or not, under *Roper*, juvenile waiver is even constitutional.[118]

It is also argued that for extralegal reasons, juveniles should not be waived: such transfers discriminate against males, minorities, and the poor, and doing so does not reduce violent crime once juvenile offenders are released into the community as adults. Finally, it has been argued that the original purpose of the juvenile justice system was to operate with the juvenile's best interest in mind, to rehabilitate rather than employ retribution, and to view each juvenile offender on a case-by-case basis.[119]

There is a distinct lack of study on what actually happens to juveniles who are waived into the adult system. The underlying philosophy of waiver is that of deterrence: that harsher punishments permitted in adult court are intended to "scare" those who might otherwise offend into a life of compliance, clearly directly contradicting the original rationale of the juvenile court system of parens patriae. However, the effectiveness of deterrence has long been questioned. Research into the adult court system has found little evidence that adults are deterred from crime by harsh punishments. Even for crimes that carry the risk of a death sentence, its deterrent effect is very weak, if present at all. Juveniles who come into contact with the justice system typically have higher rates of re-offense. The recidivism rates for those waived into adult court are even higher.[120] See Exhibit 9.8 for an example of a juvenile waiver.

EXHIBIT 9.8

AN EXAMPLE OF JUVENILE WAIVER

An example of juvenile waiver into adult court is a Florida case involving Lionel Tate, who, at age 12, was charged with first-degree murder of a 6-year-old girl. Tate declined a plea negotiation offer for second-degree murder that would have had him serving a term of 3 years in a juvenile facility, and then 10 years on probation. Under a prosecutorial waiver system, his case was then transferred to adult criminal court.

Over the defense's argument that Tate did not intend to harm the girl, and in view of medical reports showing the victim had suffered repeated violent blows, Tate was convicted of first-degree murder charge and sentenced to life in prison without parole (this case was decided in 2001, prior to the *Graham* or *Miller* decisions).

Both prosecuting and defense attorneys expressed the view that sentencing Tate to life in prison was not appropriate punishment for the 12-year-old Tate; however, the sentencing judge refused to overturn the conviction, believing that to do so would be disrespectful to the jury's discretion, and doing so would also have required him to disregard the evidence presented in the case.

In December 2003, Florida's appellate court granted Tate a retrial on the ground that his competency had not been evaluated prior to the conviction. In the end, after serving 3 years in prison, Tate finally agreed to accept the original plea offer that he had turned down earlier and was released from prison.[121]

Other critics suggest that the juvenile justice system is becoming too similar to the adult criminal justice system, pointing to specific cases, including a 14-year-old boy who was charged with two felonies after throwing rocks at police officers during a political rally. The juvenile's attorneys disagreed with the charging decision and pointed out that charging a juvenile (particularly a young one) with two felonies over such a case poses a very significant risk of tainting him criminogenically, given the negative impact of justice system contact on juveniles. The American Bar Association also agreed, suggesting that reforms and analysis are needed in the juvenile system so that it does not become a punitive parallel to the adult system.[122]

Given the aforementioned Supreme Court decisions and their rationales, do you disagree that juveniles should be waived and tried/punished as adults? Or, conversely, do some crimes (particularly those against the person) committed by juveniles indicate such youths are beyond rehabilitation and thus warrant transfer to adult courts? Should the traditional rehabilitative philosophies and functions of the juvenile justice system be taken into account? These questions must be addressed not only in light of the hardened nature of today's violent juvenile offenders but also in terms of what the future holds for juvenile violence.

Should the Exclusionary Rule Be Banned?

exclusionary rule the constitutional principle holding that evidence obtained illegally by law enforcement officers cannot be used against the suspect in a criminal prosecution.

The **exclusionary rule**—the constitutional principle holding that evidence obtained illegally by law enforcement officers cannot be used against the suspect in a criminal prosecution—quickly became controversial for both crime control and due process advocates when it was adopted in 1961 by the U.S. Supreme Court in *Mapp v. Ohio*.[123] The view of the due process model—as expressed by President Ronald Reagan in 1981—was, and is, that the rule "rests on the absurd proposition that a law enforcement error, no matter how technical, can be used to justify throwing an entire case out of court. The plain consequence is a grievous miscarriage of justice: the criminal goes free."[124]

For many legal experts who are inclined toward the due process model, however, illegal conduct by the police cannot be ignored. They believe that a court that admits tainted evidence tolerates the unconstitutional conduct that produced it and demonstrates an "insufficient commitment to the guarantee against unreasonable search and seizure."[125] In the same vein, others believe the exclusionary rule is an important check against police misconduct that is harder to control in this country given its decentralized and fragmented nature as compared to more centralized law enforcement models in other countries.[126]

Although the exclusionary rule remains controversial, the nature of the debate has changed. Initially, critics called for complete abolition of the rule; now, they suggest modifications. Former chief justice Warren Burger urged an "egregious violation standard," whereby the police could be liable to civil suits when they were believed to be in error. Others support an exception for reasonable mistakes by the police. In fact, the U.S. Supreme Court recognized an "honest mistake" or "good faith" exception to the rule only in extremely narrow and limited circumstances.[127] Furthermore, the Rehnquist Court included six justices who publicly criticized *Mapp*. This majority, however, was not able to fashion a means of replacing *Mapp* while prohibiting truly bad-faith searches by the police. And some have argued that the current Roberts Court may try to further erode the exclusionary rule. In a 2009 decision, for example, Chief Justice Roberts wrote that evidence should not be excluded on account of errors in police databases, as this was not the main concern of the exclusionary rule.[128] As a result, predicting the future of the exclusionary rule is difficult at best.

Should the exclusionary rule be abolished outright? Modified? Kept in its present form? These are compelling questions that our society and its courts may continue to ponder for many years to come.

Cameras in the Courtroom

As the trial of actor Robert Blake (charged with murdering his wife, Bonny Lee Bakley) was being prepared in 2002, the controversy over whether cameras should be allowed in court—with a well-known actor playing himself in a real-life courtroom drama—was rekindled. The widely televised trial of O.J. Simpson clearly caused a reconsideration of this issue.

Perceptions that Simpson's lawyers played to the cameras apparently had an impact in several highly publicized cases that followed: A judge refused to allow broadcasts in the trial of Susan Smith, a South Carolina woman accused of drowning her two young sons in 1995,[129] and a California judge barred cameras in the trial of Richard Allen Davis, who kidnapped and killed Polly Klaas in 1993.

By the late 1990s, however, despite the Simpson trial backlash, opposition had cooled; a study found that four of every five television requests were approved by judges in California in 1998 and 1999.[130] Indeed, a judge allowed coverage of the trial of four police officers accused (and acquitted) of murdering Amadou Diallo in New York City in 2000, and in the 2011 case of Casey Anthony in Florida who was accused murdering her 2-year-old daughter.

The Blake trial once again put the spotlight on all of the concerns about televising high-publicity trials. Opponents of cameras in court—including due process advocates—complain that televising trials distorts the process by encouraging participants to play to the cameras, and that by covering only sensational trials and presenting only dramatic moments of testimony, television does not portray the trial process accurately.[131] They argue that in celebrity cases, even the witnesses "exaggerate things to give themselves a bigger role."[132] Supporters of the practice, conversely, maintain that televising trials has educational value, providing the public with a firsthand view of how courts operate. Indeed, studies have found that viewers of a television trial of moderate interest became more knowledgeable about the judicial process.[133]

The question of publicizing high-profile cases is not new. Cameras or recording devices were forbidden in the courthouse following the excessive press coverage of the trial of German immigrant Bruno Hauptman, who was accused of kidnapping and murdering the son of the famous aviator Charles Lindbergh in the 1930s. This case is the reason that television stations began to hire artists to provide sketches of courtroom participants.

Restrictions on cameras in the courtroom are changing, however. The Supreme Court unanimously held that electronic media and still photographic coverage of public judicial proceedings does not violate a defendant's right to a fair trial; states are therefore free to set their own guidelines. Only 2 states prohibit all forms of electronic coverage of criminal trial proceedings; 35 states allow it.[134] The remaining states are still undecided.

To prevent disruption of the proceedings and to prohibit camera operators from moving about the courtroom while the trial is in session, states have limitations on electronic coverage. In fact, recently, an Indiana court experimented with a wall-mounted camera to provide streaming coverage of cases—without any negative impacts.[135] Furthermore, some states require the consent of the parties, meaning that either side can veto it. In others, the news media need only receive permission from the trial judge to broadcast the proceedings.[136]

Cameras continue to be banned in federal courts, including the U.S. Supreme Court, based on Federal Rule 53, which states that the taking of photographs and the broadcasting of proceedings is not permitted. Despite this rule, the debate regarding cameras in federal courts continues along the lines we articulated above for state courts. In 2006, Chief Justice John Roberts stated, "There's a concern [among justices] about the impact of television on the functioning of the institution. We're going to be very careful before we do anything that might have an adverse impact."[137]

The lingering question is whether cameras are an asset or a liability in the courtroom. To answer it, one must determine whether their education and publicity value exceeds their potential liabilities.

Summary

This chapter discussed several challenges involving the courts, generated from both internal and external sources, for today and for the future.

It is obvious that contemporary and future court issues and operations carry tremendous challenges for administrators. Those who serve as court leaders must be innovative, open to new ideas, accountable, well trained, and educated for the challenges that lie ahead. Legislators and policymakers must also become more aware of the difficulties confronting the courts and be prepared to provide additional resources for meeting the increasing caseloads, issues, and problems of the future.

Key Terms and Concepts

Alternative dispute resolution (ADR), p. 228
Case delay, p. 225
Courthouse violence, p. 216
"CSI Effect", p. 214
Exclusionary rule, p. 234
Federal sentencing guidelines, p. 230
Individual calendar system, p. 227
Juvenile waiver, p. 232
Master calendar system, p. 227
Problem-solving courts, p. 219
Threat assessment, p. 218
United States Code 21 U.S.C. §851, p. 231

Questions for Review

1. What is the "CSI Effect," and in what ways does research indicate it has affected court operations and court actors?
2. What are the characteristics of courthouse shootings, the differences between courthouse violence that is targeted and nontargeted, and means by which a threat assessment helps to determine whether someone poses a serious risk to court safety?
3. What is the underlying philosophy of problem-solving courts? Are problem-solving courts soft on crime? Explain?
4. What are the possible consequences of delay in the courts, and what are some possible solutions to this problem?
5. What are the two primary methods of case scheduling employed by the courts? What are the advantages and disadvantages of each?
6. In what ways does ADR hold promise for reducing the current avalanche of lawsuits?
7. What did the U.S. Supreme Court recently decide concerning the application of federal sentencing guidelines?
8. What are the major considerations regarding the courts' relations with the media?
9. How have courts been successful in becoming grant writers in recent hard times?
10. What was the original purpose of juvenile courts? To what extent has this "purpose" changed with juvenile waiver?
11. Should the exclusionary rule be banned? Why or why not?
12. Should courtroom cameras be kept or barred from our legal system? Why or why not?

Deliberate and Decide

The CSI Effect

Although the debate rages on concerning the "CSI Effect," most "evidence" of this effect has been anecdotal in nature. But the fact remains that tens of millions of viewers watch television crime dramas each week, spawning a national obsession with forensic science.

A fundamental question is, "Should prosecutors be permitted to question potential jurors concerning their views of forensics and to pose CSI-related questions to them—specifically, whether they would expect prosecutors to produce scientific evidence to prove their case beyond a reasonable doubt?"

States differ in this regard. For example, the Massachusetts Supreme Judicial Court recently ruled[138] that it was not an abuse of discretion for trial judges to pose CSI-related questions to potential jurors. The court gave judges wide discretion in jury selection and concluded that the trial judge had not abused his discretion and tilted the case toward the prosecution in attempting to seat jurors who were capable of deciding the case without bias and based on the evidence.

Conversely, Maryland's highest court[139] recently overturned two murder convictions because, during *voir dire* jury questioning, the trial judge asked people to stand up if they were "currently of the opinion or belief that you cannot convict a defendant without 'scientific evidence,' regardless of the other evidence in the case and regardless of the instructions that I will give you as to the law." The court, in ordering a new trial for the defendants, held that "the trial judge abused his discretion by essentially instructing the jury to convict the defendants 'on the non-scientific evidence of the case' … suggesting that the jury's only option was to convict, regardless of whether scientific evidence was adduced."

Questions for Discussion

1. Should trial judges be allowed to question potential jurors concerning their views of forensics and to pose CSI-related questions to them?
2. If you were a member of the jury, could you render a guilty verdict if there was no forensic evidence presented and yet it appeared from other evidence that the prosecutors proved their case beyond a reasonable doubt?
3. Do you believe, the lack of compelling evidence notwithstanding, there does in fact exist such an effect?

Learn by Doing

1. You are enrolled in a criminal justice internship with the district attorney's Victim Assistance Program. Recently there has been so much violence in the district court's courtrooms directed toward members of the district attorney's staff that the level of concern has been greatly elevated—even more so because a

high-profile case is scheduled for trial next week. The defendant has a lengthy criminal history, and the media have been full of phone calls and letters from citizens expressing outrage about the defendant and concerns about his being acquitted and eventually paroled back into the community. A reporter has also heard rumors of a planned attack against the defendant by some citizen-observers in court. What sort of threat assessment would be in order prior to the start of this trial?

2. Your criminal justice professor has been contacted by the local district court administrator seeking information concerning the methods and pitfalls involved in creating a veterans court. You are to delineate what experts say are "do's and don'ts," relying on such resources as the Hamilton County, Ohio, Municipal Court's Veterans Treatment Court experience (see http://www.hamilton-co.org/municipalcourt/Veterans/Veteran%20Project%20Handbook%20Final%20Municipal.htm). What will you write?

Case Study

Justice Delayed, Justice Denied?

Though it is highly unlikely that the Supreme Court ever gives a flat mandate for what constitutes a "speedy" trial, this has not stopped some states and jurisdictions from requiring certain timelines to be met. For example, some states require that arraignments are held within the first 48 hours, but others do not have such standards. The only federal-level mandate is the 1974 Speedy Trial Act, which requires that indictment occur within 30 days of arrest, and 70 days from indictment to trial. However, this does not and has not stopped defendants from requesting continuances for multiple reasons, which create delays. There is no consensus on what constitutes a "speedy" trial with these additional delays factored in, leading some to conclude, "justice delayed, justice denied."

Questions for Discussion

1. If you were to designate or enforce certain ranges and deadlines to avoid unnecessary delay, what would they be? Would they vary by crime? By offender? Any extrajudicial factors?
2. Should courts be incentivized to process cases more quickly? What advantages would this have? What would such a process look like?

Notes

1. Brian Dakss, "The CSI Effect: Does the TV Crime Drama Influence How Jurors Think?" March 21, 2005, http://www.cbsnews.com/stories/2005/03/21/earlyshow/main681949.shtml.
2. Rebecca Hayes-Smith and Lora M. Levett, "Community Members' Perceptions of the CSI Effect," *American Journal of Criminal Justice* 38(2) (June 2014): 216–235.
3. Rebecca Hayes-Smith and Lora M. Levett, "Jury's Still Out: How Television and Crime Show Viewing Influences Jurors' Evaluations of Evidence," *Applied Psychology in Criminal Justice* 7(1) (2011): 29–46.
4. Hayes-Smith and Levett, "Community Members' Perceptions of the CSI Effect," p. 216.
5. Donald E. Shelton, "The 'CSI Effect': Does It Really Exist?" U.S. Department of Justice, National Institute of Justice, https://www.nij.gov/journals/259/pages/csi-effect.aspx.
6. Ibid.
7. Arun Rath, "Is the 'CSI Effect' Influencing Courtrooms?" *National Public Radio*, February 5, 2011, http://www.npr.org/2011/02/06/133497896/Is-the-csi-effect-influencing-courtrooms.
8. Gayle Rhineberger-Dunn, Steven J. Briggs, and Nichole E. Rader, "The CSI Effect, DNA Discourse, and Popular Crime Dramas," *Social Science Quarterly* 98(2) (2016): 532–547. DOI:10.1111/ssqu.12289.
9. Ibid.
10. Thomas Hughes and Megan Magers, "The Perceived Impact of Crime Scene Investigation Shows on the Administration of Justice," *Journal of Criminal Justice and Popular Culture* 14(3) (2007); 259–276, http://www.albany.edu/scj/jcjpc/vol14is3/HughesMagers.pdf.
11. Shelton, "The 'CSI Effect': Does It Really Exist?"
12. See *State v. Cooke*, 914 A.2d 1078 (2007).
13. Herbert L. Packer, *The Limits of the Criminal Sanction* (Stanford, CA: Stanford University Press, 1968).
14. Lee Sinclair, "Judicial Violence: Tipping the Scales," in Gary Hengstler (ed.), *Case in Point* (Reno, NV: The National Judicial College, 2006), p. 5.
15. Gary Hengstler, "Judicial Violence: Tipping the Scales," ibid., pp. 3–5.
16. Robert Allen, Gina Damron, and Tresa Baldas, T. Berrien County Court Shooter's Past: Pipe Bombs, Guns, Teen Sex Tapes, July 13, 2016, http://www.freep.com/story/news/local/michigan/2016/07/12/larry-gordon-bailiff-shooting-berrien/87008852/.
17. W. Lee, "'I Killed Her, I Killed Her,' 13-Year-Old Cried after Stabbing Another Girl: Prosecutor." *Chicago Tribune* (May 18, 2016).

18. M. Neil, Judge who survived courthouse shooting now educates others about domestic-violence case risks, June 13, 2016, http://www.abajournal.com.
19. Gregg W. Etter and Warren G. Swymeler, "Research Note: Courthouse Shootings, 1907–2007," *Homicide Studies* 14(1) (2009): 90–100, November 1, 2014, http://0-hsx.sagepub.com.innopac.library.unr.edu/content/14/1/90.full.pdf+html.
20. Timm Fautsko, Steve Berson, and Steve Swensen, "Courthouse Security Incidents Trending Upward: The Challenges Facing State Courts Today," *National Center for State Courts*, 2012.
21. Ibid., p. 102.
22. Ibid., p. 103.
23. Etter and Swymeler, "Research Note."
24. U.S. Department of Justice, Bureau of Justice Statistics, State Court Organization 2011, p. 2.
25. Ibid., p. 4.
26. David W. Neubauer, *America's Courts and the Criminal Justice System*, 9th ed. (Belmont, CA: Wadsworth, 2008), p. 82.
27. American Bar Association, "A Judge Reflects on How to Reduce Courtroom Violence," December 2014, http://www.americanbar.org/publications/youraba/2014/december-2014/a-judge-reflects-on-how-to-reduce-courtroom-violence.html.
28. See, for example, Installations, Inc., "Bullet Proof Glass vs. Bullet Resistant Glass," http://www.installations.org/bullet-proof-glass-vs-bullet-resistant-glass/; for a description of the eight levels of security glass, see http://cdn2.hubspot.net/hub/211952/file-213902473-pdf/docs/tss_the_8_levels_of_resistance.pdf?hsCtaTracking=d64e25a0-a93d-4163-9dd5-8b05f78cfcff%7Ceb640bd0-b869-45f4-9b13-f901a22d9601.
29. Susan Voyles, "Shooting Sparks Worries about Safety," *Reno Gazette-Journal* (June 14, 2006); p. 1C.
30. See GovTrack.US, "H.R. 1751 [109th]: Court Security Improvement Act of 2006," November 1, 2014, http://www.govtrack.us/congress/bill.xpd?bill=h109-1751.
31. The Court Security Improvement Act of 2007 (2008), https://ballotpedia.org/.
32. Conference of Chief Judges/Conference of State Court Administrators, *Court Security Handbook: Ten Essential Elements for Court Security and Emergency Preparedness* (September 2012), 5-1-5-5, November 4, 2014, http://ncsc.contentdm.oclc.org/cdm/singleitem/collection/facilities/id/165/rec/12.
33. Fautsko et al., "Courthouse Security Incidents Trending Upward."
34. Ibid.
35. Nathan W. Hall, Steven V. Berson, Timothy F. Fautsko, James F. O'Neil, Kevin W. Sheehan, and Hon. V. Lee Sinclair, Jr., "Steps to Best Practices for Court Building Security," 2016, http://ncsc.contentdm.oclc.org/cdm/ref/collection/facilities/id/170.
36. Robert V. Wolf, "Breaking with Tradition: Introducing Problem Solving in Conventional Courts," *International Review of Law Computers & Technology* 22(1–2) (2008): 77–93.
37. Gordon M. Griller, "The Quiet Battle for Problem-Solving Courts," *National Center for State Courts*, http://www.ncsc.org/sitecore/content/microsites/future-trends-2011/home/specialized-courts-services/3-1-the-quiet-battle-for-problem-solving-courts.
38. Greg Berman and John Feinblatt, "Problem-Solving Courts: A Brief Primer," *Law & Policy* 23(2) (2001): 125–140.
39. National Council of Juvenile and Family Court Judges, "One Family, One Judge: Evaluating a Resource Guidelines 'Best Practice,'" *Research Snapshot*, December 2013, https://www.ncjfcj.org/sites/default/files/One%20Family%20One%20Judge%20Snapshot.pdf.
40. Shannon Portillo, Danielle S. Rudes, Jill Viglione, and Matthew Nelson, "Front-Stage Stars and Backstage Producers: The Role of Judges in Problem-Solving Courts," *Victims & Offenders: An International Journal of Evidence-based Research, Policy, and Practice* 8(1) (2014), DOI: 10.1080/15564886.2012.685220.
41. Ibid.
42. U.S. Department of Justice, National Institute of Justice, "Drug Courts," https://www.nij.gov/topics/courts/drug-courts/Pages/welcome.aspx.
43. Ibid.
44. Ibid.
45. National Center for State Courts, "Performance Measures for Problem Solving Courts," http://www.ncsc.org/Services-and-Experts/Areas-of-expertise/Problem-solvving-courts/Performance-measures-for-PSC.aspx.
46. National Institute of Justice, *Do Drug Courts Work? Findings from Drug Court Research,* November 1, 2014, http://www.nij.gov/topics/courts/drug-courts/work.htm; many drug court evaluations may be found at *NIJ's Multisite Adult Drug Court Evaluation*, http://www.nij.gov/nij/topics/courts/drug-courts/madce.htm.
47. "The Verdict Is In: Drug Courts Work," 2016, http://www.nadcp.org/learn/what-are-drug-courts.
48. *Dusky v. United States*, 362 U.S. 402 (1960).
49. Michael Brick, "Making Mentally Ill Defendants Ready for Trial," *Associated Press*, May 19, 2014, http://bigstory.ap.org/article/making-mentally-ill-defendants-ready-trial.
50. Lauren Almquist and Elizabeth Dodd, *Mental Health Courts: A Guide to Research-Informed Policy and Practice* (New York, NY: Council of State Governments Justice Center, 2009).
51. Maia Szalavitz, "Five Studies: Mental Health Courts Are Finding Their Footing," *Pacific Standard*, November 25, 2015, https://psmag.com/five-studies-mental-healt-courts-are-finding-thier-footing-a5c297e80c76#.ln45eq71v.
52. Ibid.
53. Ibid.
54. Almquist and Dodd, *Mental Health Courts,* p. vi.
55. Brick, "Making Mentally Ill Defendants Ready for Trial."
56. Almquist and Dodd, *Mental Health Courts,* p. vi.
57. Carol Fisler, "Building Trust and Managing Risk: A Look at a Felony Mental Health Court," *Psychology, Public Policy, and Law* 11(4) (2016): 587–604.
58. Brick, "Making Mentally Ill Defendants Ready for Trial," p. 1.
59. Lisa Callahan, Ph.D., Henry J. Steadman, Ph.D., and Lindsay Gerus, "7 Common Characteristics of Juvenile

Mental Health Courts," *Substance Abuse and Mental Health Services Administration*, http://gainscenter.samhsa.gov/cms-assets/documents/122718-887312.common-characteristics-jmhcs.pdf.

60. Nicholas Riccardi, "These Courts Give Wayward Veterans a Chance," *Los Angeles Times*, March 30, 2009, http://articles.latimes.com/2009/mar/10/nation/na-veterans-court10.
61. Disabled World, "Veterans Courts: A Second Chance for Those Who Have Served," http://www.disabled-world.com/disability/legal/veterans-court.php.
62. Jim McGuire, Sean Clark, Jessica Blue-Howells, and Cedric Coe, "An Inventory of VA Involvement in Veterans Courts, Dockets and Tracks," VA Veterans Justice Programs, February 7, 2014, http://www.justiceforvets.org/sites/default/files/files/An%20Inventory%20of%20VA%20involvement%20in%20Veterans%20Courts.pdf.
63. Justice Department Announces over $4 Million in Grants to Rehabilitate and Reduce Recidivism among Military Veterans, September 20, 2016, https://www.justice.gov.
64. Adapted from Veterans Health Administration, "Vets in Crisis Get a Chance, Not a Cell," http://www.va.gov/health/NewsFeatures/20120216a.asp.
65. Neubauer, *America's Courts and the Criminal Justice System,* pp. 112–114.
66. Ibid.
67. Ibid.
68. See *Barker v. Wingo,* 407 U.S. 514 (1972).
69. Ibid., p. 522.
70. Bureau of Justice Statistics, "Capital Punishment, 2010-Statistical Tables," December 20, 2011, https://www.bjs.gov/index.cfm?ty=pbdetail&iid=2236.
71. Ibid.
72. Paul Cassell, "Do Crime Victims Have an Interest in Avoiding Unreasonable Delay in Criminal Appeals?," *The Washington Post*, February 3, 2017, https://www.washingtonpost.com/news/volokh-conspiracy/wp/2017/02/03/do-crime-victims-have-an-interest-in-avoiding-unreasonable-delay-in-criminal-appeals/?utm_term=.b7fd36e11a97.
73. District of Kansas, "Rule CR50.1 Implementation of the Speedy Trial Act," http://www.ksd.uscourts.gov/rule-cr50-1-implementation-of-the-speedy-trial-act/.
74. Neubauer, *America's Courts and the Criminal Justice System,* pp. 114–116.
75. National Advisory Commission on Criminal Justice Standards and Goals, *Courts* (Washington, DC: U.S. Government Printing Office, 1973), p. 12.
76. Neubauer, *America's Courts and the Criminal Justice System,* pp. 293–295.
77. Adapted from the National Center for State Courts, "CourTools: Trial Court Performance Standards," http://www.ncsconline.org/D_Research/CourTools/Images/CourToolsOnlineBrochure.pdf.
78. Adam Liptak, "Supreme Court Rules Right to Speedy Trial Ends at Guilty Verdict," *The New York Times*, May 19, 2016, https://www.nytimes.com/2016/05/20/us/politics/supreme-court-sentencing-speedy-trial.html?_r=0.
79. Steven Flanders, *Case Management and Court Management in the United States District Courts* (Washington, DC: Federal Judicial Center, 1977).
80. David W. Neubauer, Maria Lipetz, Mary Luskin, and John P. Ryan, *Managing the Pace of Justice: An Evaluation of LEAA's Court Delay Reduction Programs* (Washington, DC: U.S. Government Printing Office, 1981).
81. Best Court Management Software, "Top Court Management Software Products," http://www.capterra.com/court-management-software/.
82. Bob Cohn, "The Lawsuit Cha-Cha," *Newsweek* (August 26, 1991): 59.
83. Michele Galen, Alice Cuneo, and David Greising, "Guilty!" *Business Week* (April 13, 1992): 63.
84. American Bar Association, *Dispute Resolution: A 60-Minute Primer* (Washington, DC: Author, 1994), pp. 1–2.
85. American Bar Association, "A Judge Reflects on How to Reduce Courtroom Violence," December 2014, http://www.americanbar.org/publications/youraba/2014/december-2014/a-judge-reflects-on-how-to-reduce-courtroom-violence.html.
86. Ibid., p. 3.
87. Ibid., p. 4.
88. See, for example, Restorative Justice Mediation Program, http://www.sdrjmp.org/index.php?page=about-rjmp.
89. Edmund J. Sikorski, Jr., "Multiparty Mediation," December 5, 2016, http://www.americanbar.org.
90. ABA, *Dispute Resolution*, p. 64.
91. 18 U.S.C. Secs. 3551–3626 and 28 U.S.C. Secs. 991–998 (October 12, 1984).
92. United States Sentencing Commission, Guidelines Manual, §3E1.1 (November 2016).
93. Ibid, p. 2.
94. *U.S. v. Booker,* 543 U.S.125 S.Ct. 738 (2005).
95. Mark Allenbaugh, "The Supreme Court's New Blockbuster U.S. Sentencing Guidelines Decision," http://writ.news.findlaw.com/allenbaugh/20050114.html.
96. FindLaw Legal News, "*United States v. Booker,*" January 17, 2005, http://caselaw.lp.findlaw.com/scripts/printer_friendly.pl?page=us/000/04-104.html.
97. Allenbaugh, "The Supreme Court's New Blockbuster U.S. Sentencing Guidelines Decision," p. 2.
98. *San Francisco Chronicle*, SFGate.com, "High Court Gives U.S. Judges More Freedom in Sentencing," http://www.sfgate.com/cgi-bin/article.cgi?f=/c/a/2007/12/11/MNE3TRS7O.DTL. See *Gall v. U.S.*, 446 F3d 884 (cert. granted 6/11/2007), and *Kimbrough v. U.S*, 174 Fed. Appx. 798 (cert. granted 6/11/2007).
99. National Center for State Courts, "Media Relations Resource Guide," http://www.ncsc.org/Topics/Media/Media-Relations/Resource-Guide.aspx.
100. Martha Bellisle, "Bridging the Gap: Judges, Lawyers, and Members of the Media Learn to Understand One Another," *Reno Magazine* (September–October 2006): 74.
101. Gary Hengstler, "Top Ten Tips for Establishing Relationships with the Media," *The National Judicial College*,

http://www.nvcourts.gov/Conferences/Leadership/Documents/Public_Trust_and_Confidence_(2)/.

102. George F. Will, "The Sledgehammer Justice of Mandatory Minimum Sentences," *The Washington Post*, December 25, 2013, http://www.washingtonpost.com/opinions/george-will-the-sledgehammer-justice-of-mandatory-minimum-sentences/2013/12/25/959e39de-6cb2-11e3-a523-fe73f0ff6b8d_story.html.
103. Doug Berman, "Double Your Pleasure, Double Your Fun, with 21 U.S.C. § 851," *Simple Justice*, http://blog.simplejustice.us/2013/10/12/double-your-pleasure-double-your-fun-with-21-u-s-c-%C2%A7-851/; also see Drug Enforcement Administration, Office of Diversion Control, "Title 21 United States Code, Controlled Substances Act, Subchapter 1, Control and Enforcement, Proceedings to Establish Prior Convictions," http://www.deadiversion.usdoj.gov/21cfr/21usc/851.htm.
104. *U.S. v. Kupa*, No. 11-CR-345 (E.D.N.Y. October 9, 2013).
105. John Gleeson, *U.S. v. Kupa*, Statement of Reason, 11-CR345, p. 23, http://sentencing.typepad.com/files/us-v-kupa-statement-of-reasons-final.pdf.
106. Ibid., p. 32.
107. Will, "The Sledgehammer Justice of Mandatory Minimum Sentences."
108. Kyle Graham, "Overcharging," *Santa Clara Law Digital Commons*, 2013, http://digitalcommons.law.scu.edu/facpubs/608/.
109. FAMM (Families Against Mandatory Minimums), "AG Eric Holder: No More Super Mandatory Minimums to Punish Defendants Who Want a Trial," October 1, 2014, http://famm.org/ag-eric-holder-no-more-super-mandatory-minimums-to-punish-defendants-who-want-atrial/.
110. FBI, "Crime in the United States, 2015," https://ucr.fbi.gov/crime-in-the-u.s/2015/crime-in-the-u.s.-2015/persons-arrested/persons-arrested.
111. Sarah Hockenberry and Charles Puzzanchera, *Delinquency Cases Waived to Criminal Court, 2011* (Washington, DC: U.S. Department of Justice, Office of Juvenile Justice and Delinquency Prevention, December 2014), p. 1.
112. Maisha N. Cooper and Lynn S. Urban, "Factors Affecting Juvenile Waiver to Adult Court in a Large Midwestern Jurisdiction," *Journal of the Institute of Justice & International Studies* 12 (2012): 43–61.
113. Office of Juvenile Justice and Delinquency Prevention, "Reverse Waiver," http://www.ojjdp.gov/pubs/tryingjuveasadult/transfer4.html.
114. Hockenberry and Puzzanchera, *Delinquency Cases Waived to Criminal Court, 2011*, p. 2.
115. *Roper v. Simmons*, 543 U.S. 551 (2005).
116. *Graham v. Florida* 130 S.Ct. 2011 (2010).
117. *Miller v. Alabama*, 567 U.S. ____ (2012).
118. John M. Fabian, "Applying Roper v. Simmons in Juvenile Transfer and Waiver Proceedings: A Legal and Neuroscientific Inquiry," *International Journal of Offender Therapy and Comparative Criminology* 55 (August 2011): 732–755.
119. Cooper and Urban, "Factors Affecting Juvenile Waiver to Adult Court in a Large Midwestern Jurisdiction," p. 60.
120. United States Public Broadcasting Service. "Juvenile Justice."
121. Adapted from Daniel Mole and Dodd White, *Transfer and Waiver in the Juvenile Justice System* (Washington, DC: Child Welfare League of America, 2005), pp. 25–26, November 2, 2014, http://www.cwla.org/programs/juvenilejustice/jjtransfer.pdf.
122. Nicole Scialabba, "Should Juveniles Be Charged as Adults in the Criminal Justice System?" *American Bar Association*, October 3, 2016, http://www.americanbar.org/publications/litigation-committees/childrens-rights/articles/2016/should-juveniles-be-charged-as-adults.html.
123. 367 U.S. 643.
124. Quoted in Neubauer, *America's Courts and the Criminal Justice System*, p. 265.
125. Yale Kamisar, "Is the Exclusionary Rule an 'Illogical' or 'Unnatural' Interpretation of the Fourth Amendment?," *Judicature* 78 (1994): 83–84.
126. Adam Liptak, "U.S. Is Alone in Rejecting All Evidence If Police Err," *The New York Times*, July 19, 2008, http://www.nytimes.com/2008/07/19/us/19exclude.html.
127. See, for example, *U.S. v. Leon,* 486 U.S. 897 (1984), and *Illinois v. Krull,* 480 U.S. 340 (1987).
128. Adam Cohen, "Is the Supreme Court About to Kill Off the Exclusionary Rule?," *The New York Times*, February 15, 2009, http://www.nytimes.com/2009/02/16/opinion/16mon4.html.
129. Jesse Holland, "Susan Smith Judge Bars TV Cameras from Murder Trial," *Times-Picayune,* June 25, 1995, p. 1A.
130. Zanto Peabody, "Blake Case Revives Issue of Cameras in Court," *Los Angeles Times,* May 27, 2002, p. 1A.
131. Paul Thaler, *The Watchful Eye: American Justice in the Age of the Television Trial* (Westport, CT: Praeger, 1994).
132. Peabody, "Blake Case Revives Issue of Cameras in Court," p. 1A.
133. S. L. Alexander, "Cameras in the Courtroom: A Case Study," *Judicature* 74 (1991): 307–313; Paul Raymond, "The Impact of a Televised Trial on Individuals' Information and Attitudes," *Judicature* 57 (1992): 204–209.
134. Alexander, "Cameras in the Courtroom."
135. Kate Wheeling, "Should There Be Cameras in Courtrooms?" *Pacific Standard Magazine*, March 6, 2015, https://psmag.com/should-there-be-cameras-in-courtrooms-14ad60f374a2#.nbf3eebiz.
136. Neubauer, *America's Courts and the Criminal Justice System*, pp. 312–313.
137. Robert Kessler, "Why Aren't Cameras Allowed at the Supreme Court Again?," *The Atlantic*, March 28, 2013, https://www.theatlantic.com/national/archive/2013/03/case-allowing-cameras-supreme-court-proceedings/316876.
138. See *Commonwealth v. Perez*, 460 Mass. 683 (2011).
139. *Jamal Charles and Dwayne Drake v. Maryland*, 411 Md. 355, 983 A.2d 431 (2009).

PART 4

Corrections

This part includes three chapters that address corrections administration. Chapter 10 examines corrections organization and operation, including prisons, jails, and probation and parole agencies. Chapter 11 covers personnel roles and functions. Chapter 12 reviews corrections issues and practices. Specific chapter content is previewed in the introductory section of each chapter.

Georgios Tsichlis/Shutterstock

10 Corrections Organization and Operation

LEARNING OBJECTIVES

After reading this chapter, the student will be able to:

1. *describe the general features of a correctional organization in the United States, including the levels of correctional incarceration, employment, expenditures, and several factors affecting prison and jail populations*
2. *delineate the personnel and divisions found in the state's central office as well as in individual prisons*
3. *describe supermax prisons, including their method of operation, alleged effects on inmates, constitutionality, and implications for corrections policy*
4. *explain the early hands-off era of the courts toward prisons and selected constitutional rights afforded jail and prison inmates*
5. *describe what civil rights are held by institutionalized persons, under federal law*

6 *relate the nature and extent of litigation by prison and jail inmates, including the rationale, provisions, and impact of the Prison Litigation Reform Act (PLRA)*

7 *describe how direct supervision jails differ from the traditional model in design and functions*

8 *explain the U.S. Supreme Court's view of warrantless collection of DNA from pretrial arrestees*

9 *explain the means and rationale for accreditation of corrections facilities*

10 *generally describe how adult and juvenile probation and parole agencies are organizationally structured within their states, and whether or not their officers are armed and granted peace officer powers*

11 *relate the systems theory of probation and the six categories of probation systems, including their resources, activities, and outcomes*

12 *articulate the three services of parole agencies and the two models used for administering them*

13 *review the advantages of the independent and consolidated models of parole*

Introduction

The organization and operation of prisons, jails, and probation and parole functions in our society are largely unknown and misunderstood. Indeed, most of what the public "knows" about the inner workings of these organizations is obtained through Hollywood's eyes and depictions—*The Shawshank Redemption, The Green Mile, The Longest Yard, Escape from Alcatraz,* and *Cool Hand Luke* are a few examples of such popular depictions that are frequently shown on the big screen and on television.

Unfortunately, however, because the movie industry is more concerned with box office sales than with depicting reality, liberties are taken and the portrayal of prisons in film is generally inaccurate. Furthermore, although problems certainly can and do arise in correctional institutions, movies often accentuate and exaggerate their negative aspects; therefore, it should be remembered that the reality of prison operations, and prison life for that matter, is often at considerable variance with what is projected on the big screen. For example, among individuals who have not been incarcerated, there is an exaggerated fear of being raped in jails or prisons. In reality, only 4 percent of state and federal prison inmates and 3.2 percent of jail inmates reported some form of sexual victimization in a recent survey. While each case is certainly unacceptable in its own right, the degree of fear among the general public does not match the actual risk.[1]

This chapter begins by demonstrating that corrections is yet a booming industry in terms of both expenditures and employment, although correctional populations have been declining over the past few years. We look at some reasons for the decline. Then we focus on correctional agencies as organizations, including their mission and a view of the statewide central offices overseeing prison systems and their related functions as well as individual prisons. Next is a discussion of supermax prisons, including their unique method of operation, alleged effects on inmates, constitutionality, and implications for corrections policy. After that is a consideration of selected constitutional and civil rights that federal courts and Congress have granted to jail and prison inmates; then we review prison litigation generally, including the rationale and impact of the Prison Litigation Reform Act (PLRA).

Next, we examine local jails, including their organization, the unique structure and function of podular direct supervision jails, and, after briefly considering the accreditation of corrections facilities, we review probation and parole organizations, to include the organizational structure, arming, and peace officer status of adult and juvenile probation and parole agencies and their officers. The chapter concludes with review questions and exercises in the Deliberate and Decide, Learn by Doing, and Case Study sections.

▶ Correctional Organizations

Employment and Expenditures

Today, prisons and jails at the federal, state, and local levels employ about 785,000 people (one-third of them at the local level and about 60% for state governments), and cost about $36 billion in annual payrolls.[2] This figure excludes another $5.4 billion in annual prison costs arising from such expenditures as retiree health care, employee benefits, and taxes; capital costs; underfunded employee pensions; and health and hospital care for the prison population.[3] For just the federal system (which is barely a fraction of the population of the state system), it costs taxpayers $31,977.65 per year, or an average of $87.61 per day to incarcerate offenders.[4]

Declining Prison Populations: Reasons and Some Caveats

As shown in Table 10-1 ■, U.S. prisons now hold about 1,526,800 adult prisoners—a number that has been generally declining since 2010, when there was approximately 100,000 more prison inmates than there are today (while the table shows the number of jail inmates has remained fairly stable, averaging about 753,000 since 2005).[5]

Why a decline in prison populations? According to experts, the hard-nosed, punitive crime policies that began in the early 1980s—which included mass incarceration of nonviolent drug addicts, mandatory sentencing laws, and stiff sentences for repeat offenders, all of which brought a prison construction boom—are now being relaxed in many states. Some argue that declaring "war" on social issues now amounts to little more than a shout in the crowded public sphere. This initially may have worked for the Drug War: individuals

TABLE 10-1 Prison Populations in the United States

Year	Total Correctional Population	Community Supervision			Incarcerated		
		Total	Probation	Parole	Total	Jail	Prison
2000	6,467,800	4,564,900	3,839,400	725,500	1,945,400	621,100	1,394,200
2005	7,055,600	4,946,600	4,162,300	784,400	2,200,400	747,500	1,525,900
2010	7,089,000	4,888,500	4,055,900	840,800	2,279,000	748,700	1,613,800
2011	6,994,500	4,818,300	3,973,800	855,500	2,252,500	735,600	1,599,00
2012	6,949,800	4,790,700	3,944,900	858,400	2,231,300	744,500	1,570,400
2013	6,899,700	4,749,800	3,912,900	849,500	2,222,500	731,200	1,577,000
2014	6,856,900	4,713,200	3,868,400	857,700	2,225,100	744,600	1,562,300
2015	6,741,400	4,650,900	3,789,900	870,500	2,173,800	728,200	1,526,800
Average annual percent change, 2007-2015	-1.1%	-1.2%	-1.6%	0.7%	-0.7%	-0.9%	-0.6%
Percent change, 2014-2015	-1.7%	-1.3%	-2.0%	1.5%	-2.3%	-2.2%	-2.3%

Source: U.S. Department of Justice, Bureau of Justice Statistics, *Correctional Populations in the United States, 2015* (December 2016).

were asked to sacrifice some measure of privacy and judicial forgiveness in the battle to get drugs off the streets and keep our kids safe. However, the secondary consequences of this militaristic approach are now understood to be ineffective in preventing cycles of crime.[6] Indeed, marijuana is being increasingly decriminalized, and stiff sentences for repeat offenders that were in effect in a number of states are being eased. Another telling development is that 13 states have abolished the death penalty since 2007.[7]

Why this philosophical shift? Certainly dwindling public resources are a major reason: it costs all units of government about $80 billion per year to house close to 2.2 million inmates in their jails and prisons. Also, experts increasingly see the fundamental question of fairness being raised; as David Kennedy of New York's John Jay College of Criminal Justice put it, the movement to ease mandatory minimum sentences and to reduce the use of solitary confinement is a result of "the basic recognition that the application of power without justice is brutal."[8] Not surprisingly, then, there is even a measure of growing public support for alternative sanctions for drug offenders. In a recent survey in Florida, slightly over half of the respondents (51.1%) agreed that drug treatment is needed to best fight the war on drugs.[9]

Even some conservative politicians are admitting that the extreme punishment policies of the past several decades have largely failed. And this philosophical shift is literally paying off for the states. Since 2011, New York has closed 24 of its 93 adult and juvenile corrections facilities (thus saving about $221 million per year), and 16 other states have either closed or proposed prison closings of their own in a bid to slice about 30,000 beds.[10] More recently, New York governor Andrew Cuomo spoke of further intentions to continue this trend of prison closures, citing a desire to find alternatives to incarceration.[11] And California voters in 2014 passed Proposition 47, which reduced some possession charges and other nonviolent offenses from felonies to misdemeanors, allowing prison inmates to petition a reduction in their sentences.[12] See Exhibit 10.1 for a description of further reductions to California's prison system.

EXHIBIT 10.1

AS CALIFORNIA GOES, SO GOES THE NATION...

It would probably not be inaccurate to say "As California goes, so too goes the nation" with respect to U.S. prison populations. In May 2011, the U.S. Supreme Court (in *Brown v. Plata*) upheld a lower court ruling mandating that within 2 years the state reduce its prison population to alleviate overcrowding (built to house approximately 85,000 inmates, at that time the prison system housed nearly twice that number, approximately 156,000 inmates).[13] Known as the Public Safety Realignment (PSR) policy, this approach "realigned" almost 30,000 inmates—some of whom were kept in county jails, others paroled, and still others put on probation. The policy pertained to those inmates who were convicted of nonviolent, nonserious, and non–sex related crimes.[14]

Another problem is that today's former prison inmates are less likely to have participated in prison rehabilitation and work programs, which also militates against their succeeding in the free world. At least a part of this lack of involvement in programming may be due to Robert Martinson's well-publicized finding of the mid-1970s that "almost nothing works"[15] in correctional treatment programs served to ignite a firestorm of debate that has lasted more than two decades.[16] Legislators and corrections administrators became unwilling to fund treatment programs from dwindling budgets, and academics such as Paul Louis and Jerry Sparger noted that "perhaps the most lasting effect of the 'nothing works' philosophy is the spread of cynicism and hopelessness" among prison administrators and staff members.[17]

Interestingly enough, despite the mass decarceration in California due to the Supreme Court ruling and the ensuing legislation noted above, two recent studies suggest that it has not had a negative effect on California's crime rates as some had feared.[18] Only automobile thefts in California increased in 2012, followed by another slight increase in 2013, then no increase by 2014. And in terms of violent crime, prisoner realignment was associated with a decrease from 2013 to 2014.[19] Additionally, cost savings from the reduced prison populations have been estimated at over $450 million.[20]

General Mission and Features

Correctional organizations are complex hybrid organizations that utilize two distinct yet related management subsystems to achieve their goals: One is concerned primarily with managing correctional employees and the other is concerned primarily with delivering correctional services to a designated offender population. The correctional organization, therefore, employs one group of people (correctional personnel) to work with and control another group (offenders).

The mission of corrections agencies has changed little over time. It is as follows: to protect the citizens from crime by safely and securely handling criminal offenders while providing offenders some opportunities for self-improvement and increasing the chance that they will become productive and law-abiding citizens.[21]

An interesting feature of the correctional organization is that *every* correctional employee who exercises legal authority over offenders is a supervisor, even if the person is the lowest-ranking member in the agency or institution. Another feature of the correctional organization is that—as with the police—everything a correctional supervisor does may have civil or criminal ramifications, both for himself or herself and for the agency or institution. Therefore, the legal and ethical responsibility for the correctional (and police) supervisor is greater than it is for supervisors in other types of organizations.

EXHIBIT 10.2

PRISON MISSIONS: A COMPARATIVE ANALYSIS

While the idea would certainly be unpopular with some American voters, the fact is that Swedish and other Scandinavian prisons have lower rates of recidivism—in part because they focus on treatment of criminogenic issues for each inmate. It would be foolish to suggest that these lower crime levels are due solely to the increased role of treatment in correctional facilities, but it would be equally foolish to think that the findings do not have any relation to fundamental philosophical differences. Justice leadership is slowly realizing that solely focusing on punishment and incarceration of offenders ultimately does very little to stop the cycle of crime.[22]

Finland, similar to the United States, dealt with an increase in illegal drug use in the late 1980s into the 1990s. However, they did not respond in nearly the same fashion as the United States. Instead of focusing on harsh punishments and punitive sanctions, the ultimate goal in Finnish courts and corrections is to decrease recidivism, even if this involves a degree of what is called "penal welfarism."[23] Compare penal welfarism in Finland, for example, with the mission of the Michigan Department of Corrections: "We create a safer Michigan by holding offenders accountable while promoting their success."[24] The goal of rehabilitation is not mentioned in the Michigan mission, but is implied in its vision.

▶ Prisons as Organizations

As noted earlier in this chapter, the mission of most prisons is to provide a safe and secure environment for staff and inmates, as well as programs for offenders that can assist them after release.[25] This section describes how prisons are organized to accomplish this mission. First, we examine the larger picture—the typical organization of the central office within the state government that oversees *all* prisons within its jurisdiction. Then, we review the characteristic organization of an individual prison.

The Central Office

The state's central organization that oversees its prison system is often called the **central office**. Some of the personnel and functions typically found in a central office are discussed in the following subsections.

central office the state's central organization that oversees its prison system.

Office of the Director

Each state normally has a central department of corrections that is headed by a director (or someone with a similar title); in turn, the director appoints a person to direct the operation of all of the prisons in the state. The **prison director** sets policy for all wardens (discussed more thoroughly in Chapter 11) and prisons in terms of how the institutions should be managed and inmates cared for (with regard to both custody and treatment). In addition to the director, the staff within the office of the director typically includes public or media affairs coordinators, legislative liaisons, legal advisers, and internal affairs representatives.

prison director the person who sets policy for all wardens and prisons to follow in terms of management and inmate treatment.

As they are one of the largest state agencies, a tremendous demand for public information is made on correctional agencies. If a policy issue or a major incident is involved, the media will contact the director for a response. The office of public affairs also oversees the preparation of standard reports, such as an annual review of the department and its status or information on a high-profile program or project. In addition, because state correctional agencies use a large percentage of the state budget, the legislature is always interested in their operations. Therefore, there is usually within the department of corrections an office of legislative affairs, which responds to legislative requests and tries to build support for resources and programs.[26]

Legal divisions, typically comprised of four to six attorneys, often report to the director as well. The work of the legal division includes responding to inmate lawsuits, reviewing policy for its legal impact, and offering general advice regarding the implementation of programs in terms of past legal decisions. These attorneys will predict how the courts are likely to respond to a new program in light of legal precedents.

Finally, the director's office usually has an inspector or internal affairs division. Ethics in government is a major priority; corrections staff may be enticed to bring contraband into a prison or may be physically abusive to inmates. Whenever there is a complaint of staff misconduct by anyone, the allegation needs to be investigated.

Administrative Division

Two major areas of the administrative division of a corrections central office are budget development/auditing and new prison construction. The administrative division collects information from all of the state's prisons, other divisions, and the governor's office to create a budget that represents ongoing operations and desired programs and growth. Once it is approved by the governor's office, this division begins to explain the budget to the legislative budget committee, which reviews the request and makes a recommendation for funding to the full legislature. After a budget is approved, this division maintains accountability of funds and oversees the design and construction of new and renovated facilities.[27]

Correctional Programs Division

A central office will usually have a division that oversees the operation of correctional programs, such as security, education, religious services, mental health, and unit management. It is clear that

> Offenders enter prison with a variety of deficits. Some are socially or morally inept, others are intellectually or vocationally handicapped, some have emotional hangups that stem from psychological problems, still others have a mixture of varying proportions of some or even all of these.[28]

Having to deal with inmates suffering from such serious and varied problems is a daunting task for correctional organizations. Prison culture makes the environment inhospitable to programs designed to rehabilitate or reform.

A major contemporary problem among persons entering prison is drug addiction. To put this into perspective, a recent report from the Center on Addiction and Substance Abuse (CASA) indicated that more than 60 percent of those in jails and prisons met the medical standards for addiction.[29] Drug-addicted offenders are subjected to one of three types of treatment programming that attempt to address the problem: punitive (largely involving withdrawal and punishment), medical (consisting of detoxification, rebuilding physical health, counseling, and social services), and the communal approach (using group encounters and seminars conducted by former addicts who serve as positive role models).[30] Chapter 12 discusses what prison administrators can do to interdict drugs coming into prisons and the kinds of treatment programs that are maintained in them.

Medical or Health Care Division

One of the most complicated and expensive functions within a prison is health care. As a result, this division develops policy, performs quality assurance, and looks for ways to make health care more efficient for inmates and less expensive for the prison. One of the best outcomes for a corrections health care program involved HIV/AIDS. A widespread epidemic of HIV/AIDS cases was initially feared in prisons (through homosexual acts and prior drug use) but such an outbreak never happened. Today, the problem persists, with about 20,100 prison inmates having HIV or AIDS, but the overall number has declined about 3 percent per year, from 194 cases per 10,000 inmates in 2001 to 146 per 10,000 at present.[31]

Human Resource Management Division

The usual personnel functions of recruitment, hiring, training, evaluation, and retirement are accomplished in the human resource management division. Affirmative action and labor relations (discussed in Chapter 14) may also be included. Workplace diversity is important for corrections agencies, particularly with the growing number of African American and Hispanic inmates. Most states have a unionized workforce, and negotiating and managing labor issues are time-consuming; therefore, this division has staff with expertise in labor relations.

It's important to note that states differ in terms of the organization of their central offices. In one Midwestern state, for example, its budget and operations administration are housed together within the central office. In addition, many states' central offices also have research and planning units, training units, probation and parole services, prison industries division, and emergency response teams.

Figure 10-1 ■ shows an example of the organizational structure of a central office in a state of 3 million people.

Individual Prisons

Over time, prison organizational structure (see Figure 10-2 ■) has changed considerably to respond to external needs. Until the beginning of the twentieth century, prisons were administered by state boards of charities, boards comprised of citizens, boards of inspectors, state prison commissions, or individual prison keepers. Most prisons were individual provinces; wardens who were given absolute control over their domain were appointed by governors through a system of political patronage. Individuals were attracted to the position of warden because it carried many fringe benefits, such as a lavish residence, unlimited inmate servants, food and supplies from institutional farms and warehouses, furnishings, and a personal automobile. Now most wardens or superintendents are civil service employees who have earned their position through seniority and merit.[32]

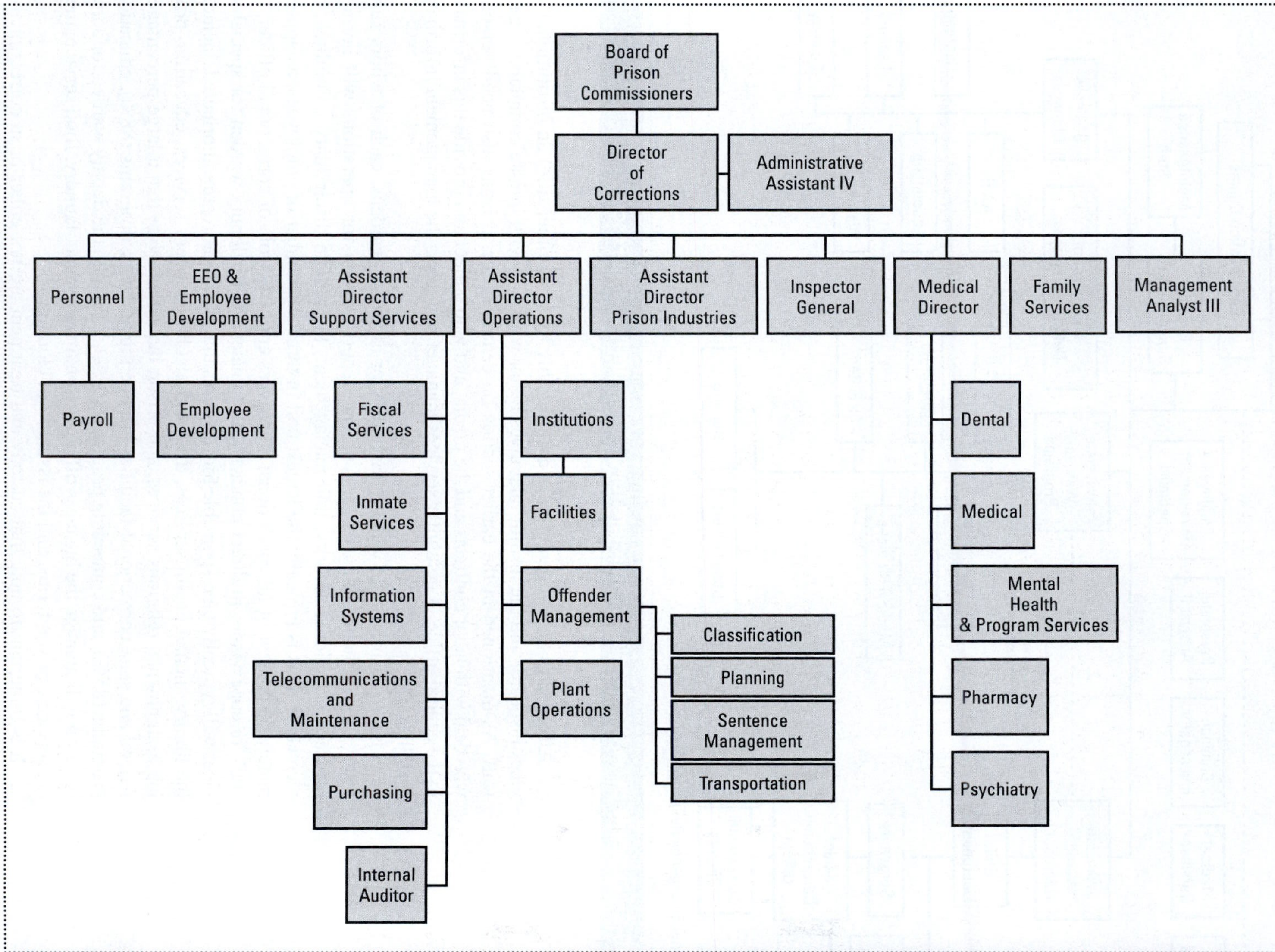

FIGURE 10-1 Example of an Organizational Structure for a Correctional Central Office

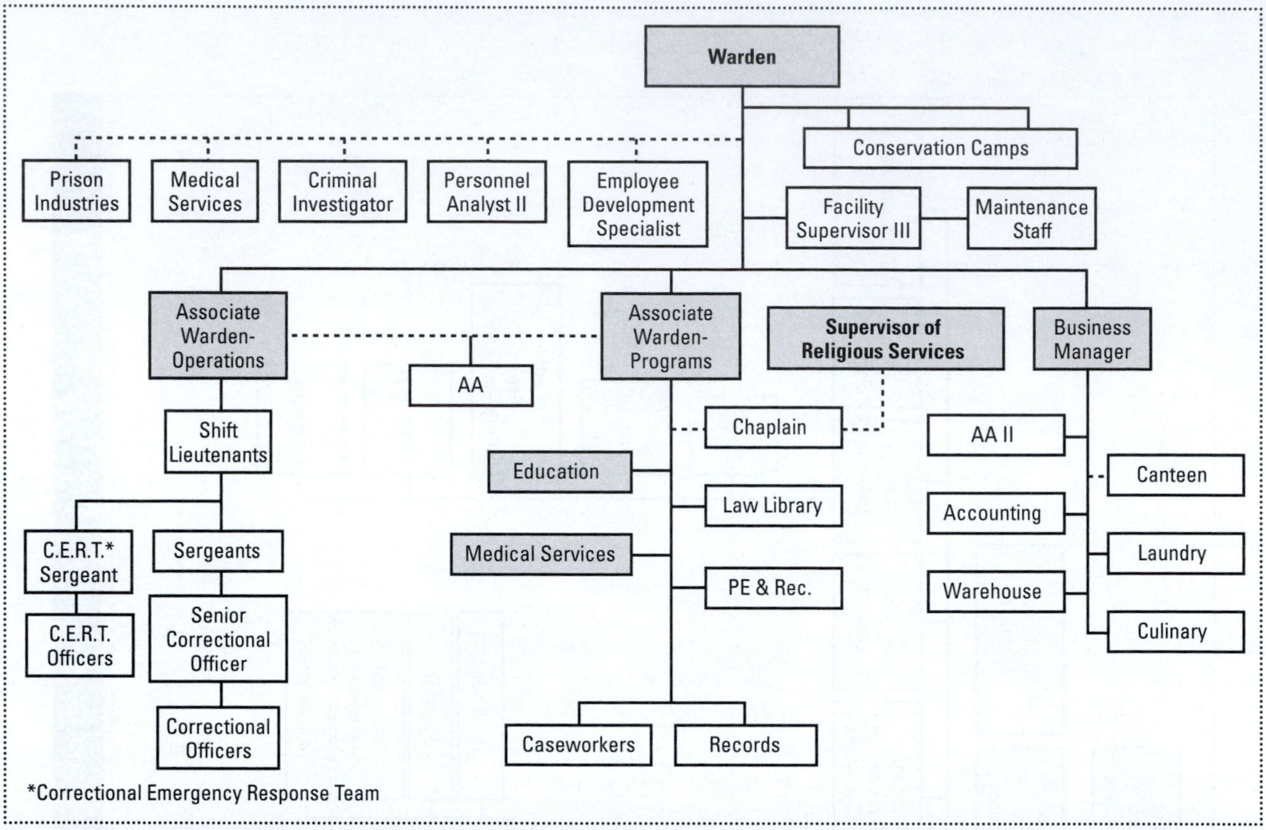

FIGURE 10-2 Example of an Organizational Structure for a Maximum-Security Prison

Attached to the warden's office are (possibly by some other title) an institutional services inspector and the institutional investigator who deal with inmate complaints against staff. As mentioned in the earlier section on central office, prisons also need personnel who deal with labor contracts and the media, and who collect and provide this information to the central office. A computer services manager maintains the management information systems.

Also reporting to the warden are deputy or associate wardens, each of whom supervises a department within the prison. The deputy warden for operations will normally oversee correctional security, unit management, the inmate disciplinary committee, and recreation. This is typically the largest unit in terms of number of employees, as approximately 66 percent of all correctional employees are in the role of correctional officer, line staff, or supervisors in direct contact with inmates.[33] The deputy warden for special services will typically be responsible for functions that are more treatment oriented, including the library, mental health services, drug and alcohol recovery services, education, prison job assignments, religious services, and prison industries. Note that a large percentage of federal and state correctional facilities provide inmate work programs (88%), educational programs (85%), and counseling programs (92%).[34] Finally, the deputy warden for administration will manage the business office, prison maintenance, laundry, food service, medical services, prison farms, and the issuance of clothing.[35]

It is important to note that custody and treatment are not either-or in correctional organizations; rather, they are complementary. Although custody overshadows treatment in terms of operational priorities—treatment programs are unable to flourish if security is weak and staff and inmates work and live in chronic fear and danger—prisons without programming options for offenders are nothing more than warehouses, being amenable to violence, disruption, and the continuation of criminally deviant behavior. Correctional staff, regardless of their job function, does not support such volatile conditions. Most often, the overriding concern in a prison or jail is and should be security. Security must be maintained so that programs can be implemented. Programs are generally supported by staff, especially those that address inmate deficiencies such as lack of education and job skills as well as substance abuse. Keep in mind that according to a recent report, only a low percentage of offenders actually receive treatment: just 11 percent of all jail and prison inmates receive the proper level of treatment prescribed by the judiciary.[36] Prison administrators must decide which programs they will allow to be introduced into their facility; this is not often an easy task, especially when much of the public perceives that programs only "coddle" inmates.[37]

Next, we discuss several related aspects—correctional security, unit management, education, and penal industries—in more detail.

- The correctional security department supervises all of the security activities within a prison, including any special housing units, inmate transportation, and the inmate disciplinary process. Security staff wear military-style uniforms, a captain normally runs each 8-hour shift, lieutenants often are responsible for an area of the prison, and sergeants oversee the rank-and-file correctional staff. Missteps by this department, in particular, can have dire consequences for officer and prisoner safety and institutional integrity, such as recently when a group of inmates at a Delaware maximum-security prison took several officers hostage and engaged in a standoff with police that lasted several hours.[38]
- The *unit management* concept originated in the federal prison system in the 1970s and now is used in nearly every state to control prisons by providing a "small, self-contained, inmate living and staff office area that operates semiautonomously within the larger institution."[39] The purpose of unit management is twofold: to decentralize the administration of the prison and to enhance communication among staff and between staff and inmates. Unit management breaks the prison into more manageable sections based on housing assignments; assignment of staff to a particular unit; and staff authority to make decisions, manage the unit, and deal directly with inmates. Units are usually comprised of 200 to 300 inmates; staff are not only assigned to units, but their offices are also located in the housing area, making them more accessible to inmates and better able to monitor inmate activities and behavior. Directly reporting to the unit manager are *case managers*, or social workers, who develop the program of work and rehabilitation for each inmate and write progress reports for parole authorities, inmate classifications (discussed in Chapter 12), or inmate transfers to another prison. Correctional counselors also work with inmates in the units on daily issues, such as finding a prison job, working with their prison finances, and creating a visiting and telephone list.[40]
- The education department operates the academic teaching, vocational training, library services, and sometimes recreation programs for inmates. An education department is managed similarly to a conventional elementary or high school, with certified teachers for all subjects that are required by the state department of education or are part of the General Education Degree (GED) test. In federal and state prisons, 90 percent of facilities offer formal educational programs, the most common of which is a secondary education or a GED program.[41] Vocational training can include carpentry, landscaping or horticulture, food service, and office skills.

Prison industries also exist—programs intended to provide productive work and skill development opportunities for offenders, to reduce recidivism and prepare offenders for reentry into society.[42] They are typically legislatively chartered as separate government corporations

prison industries
prison programs intended to provide productive work and skill development opportunities for offenders, to reduce recidivism and prepare offenders for reentry into society.

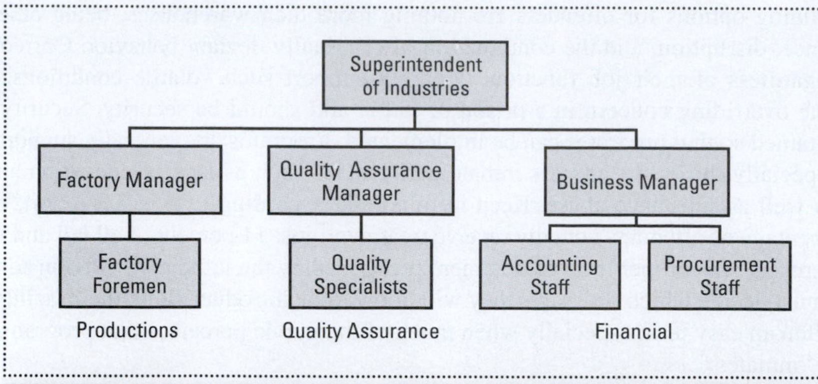

FIGURE 10-3 Organizational Structure for a Prison Industry

Source: Seiter, Richard P., *Correctional Administration: Integrating Theory and Practice,* 1st Ed., © 2002, p. 199. Reprinted and Electronically reproduced by permission of Pearson Education, Inc., Upper Saddle River, New Jersey.

and report directly to the warden because there is often a requirement that the industry be self-supporting or operate from funds generated from the sale of products. Generally, no tax dollars are used to run the programs, and there is strict accountability of funds.

Correctional administrators report that joint ventures provide meaningful, productive employment that helps to reduce inmate idleness and supplies companies with a readily available and dependable source of labor, as well as the partial return to society of inmate earnings to pay state and federal taxes, offset incarceration costs, contribute to the support of inmates' families, and compensate victims.

Several different types of business relationships exist—the personnel model, the employer model, and the customer model. In the personnel model, prisoners are employed by the state division of correctional industries, which in turn charges the companies a fixed rate for their labor. In the employer model, the company employs the inmates, and private companies own and operate their prison-based businesses, with prison officials providing the space in which the companies operate as well as a qualified labor pool from which the companies hire employees. In the customer model, the company contracts with the prison to provide a finished product at an agreed-on price. The correctional institution owns and operates the business that employs the inmates. These joint ventures provide challenges and problems: absenteeism and rapid turnover of employees, limited opportunities for training, and logistical concerns. Still, many inmates who participate in these programs show up for their jobs on time, work hard during their shifts, and have been hired by companies after their release.[43] A typical prison industry organizational structure is presented in Figure 10-3 ■.

▶ The Controversy of Supermax

Definition and Operation

supermax prison institutions providing the most secure levels of custody in prisons, with long-term, segregated housing for inmates who represent the highest security risks.

There are **supermax prisons** or their equivalent in more than 40 U.S. states; these institutions provide the most secure levels of custody in prisons, with long-term, segregated housing for inmates who represent the highest security risks.[44] Their method of operations and, as will be seen, the degree of controversy about them among academics and others justify some discussion about them specifically. To understand what supermax prisons are and how they operate, one can look at the Administrative Maximum prison, or ADX, located in Florence, Colorado.

ADX is the only federal supermax prison in the country (the others are state prisons). It is home to a Who's Who of criminals: "Unabomber" Ted Kaczynski; "Shoe Bomber" Richard Reid; Ramzi Yousef, who plotted the 1993 World Trade Center attack; "Oklahoma City Bomber" Terry Nichols; "Olympic Park Bomber" Eric Rudolph, and "Boston Marathon Bomber" Dzhokhar Tsarnaev. ADX is known as the "Alcatraz of the Rockies"; 95 percent of its prisoners are the most violent, disruptive, and escape-prone inmates from other federal prisons. Upon viewing its external aspect for the first time, one immediately sees that this is not the usual prison: large cables are strung above the basketball courts and track; they are helicopter deterrents.[45]

The supermax prison is known variously in different states as a *special management unit, security housing unit (SHU), high-security unit, intensive management unit*, or *special control unit*; its operations are quite different inside as well. In a recent study, 95 percent of state wardens agreed that the defining characteristics of supermax are the following: (1) a stand-alone facility or part of another facility designated for violent or disruptive inmates; (2) supermax facilities typically adhere to a 23-hour per day, single-cell confinement regimen for an indefinite period of time; and (3) supermax inmates have little contact with other inmates or staff.[46] In addition, inmates are generally denied access to vocational or educational training programs.[47]

EXHIBIT 10.3

MIMICKING SUPERMAX IN LOWER SECURITY INSTITUTIONS

While only a small number of supermax facilities exist in the country, lower security institutions are mimicking some of the distinctive features of supermax facilities. Communication management units, or CMUs, severely restrict inmates' ability to communicate with the outside world. Rather than two calls per week (the normal standard), inmates may be restricted to only three 15-minute calls per month, with calls being able to be cut down to as little as 3 minutes at the discretion of the warden. Furthermore, while all inmate mail is screened for contraband, those in CMUs typically have their mail opened, read, analyzed, and independently evaluated before it is sent or received, which causes delays. The sole exception is for correspondence with lawyers and the courts.[48]

Effects on Inmates

While research indicates a high degree of public support for supermax prisons,[49] since their early existence and given their nature of confinement, researchers have been interested in determining the effects of supermax prisons on inmates—specifically, whether or not their treatment is cruel and inhumane. Given the high degree of isolation and lack of activities, a major concern voiced by critics of supermax facilities is their *social pathology* and potential effect on inmates' mental health. Although there is very little research to date concerning the effects of supermax prison confinement,[50] some authors point to previous isolation research showing that greater levels of deprivation lead to psychological, emotional, and physical problems: as inmates face greater restrictions and social deprivations, their level of social withdrawal increases; limiting human contact, autonomy, goods, or services is detrimental to inmates' health and rehabilitative prognoses, and tends to result in depression, hostility, severe anger, sleep disturbances, and anxiety. Women living in a high-security unit have been found to experience claustrophobia, chronic rage reactions, depression, hallucinatory symptoms, withdrawal, and apathy.[51] In addition, increased mental illness is a very real danger to inmates in supermax facilities.[52]

In a recent essay, Travis Dusenbury describes his 10-year stint at the ADX Florence. Dusenbury explains that at the so-called "Alcatraz of the Rockies," inmates are unable to see virtually any semblance of nature. Supermax cells are solid concrete and induce, in Dusenbury's opinion, a measure of claustrophobia that can result in eventual insomnia. In fact, Dusenbury claims that his insomnia lasted his entire 10-month stint at the ADX. When Dusenbury was not in his cell, he was in a recreation cage for an hour a day. To communicate with a neighbor in the cell below him, Dusenbury would take a toilet paper roll and blow water down a sink or shower drain, just far enough so that the pipes between him and his neighbor were clear. He could then speak through the toilet paper roll.[53]

Constitutionality

Because of their relatively recent origin, the constitutionality of supermax prisons—whether or not the conditions of confinement constitute cruel and unusual punishment (i.e., that the punishment either inflicts unnecessary or wanton pain or is grossly disproportionate to the severity of the crime)—has been tested in only a few cases. Not surprisingly, most of these challenges assess the harms done by extreme social isolation. The first, *Madrid v. Gomez,*[54] in 1995, addressed conditions of confinement in California's Pelican Bay Special Housing Unit (SHU). The judge pointed to the "stark sterility and unremitting monotony" of the interior of the prison and noted that its image was "hauntingly similar to that of caged felines pacing in a zoo" (p. 1229; however, the judge concluded that he lacked any constitutional basis to close the prison).

In 1999, a federal district court in *Ruiz v. Johnson*[55] examined Texas's high-security units and concluded that prisoners there "suffer actual psychological harm from the almost total deprivation of human contact, personal property, and human dignity" (p. 913). This judge also opined that such units are virtual incubators of psychoses and that long-term supermax confinement could result in mental illness.

In *Jones 'El v. Berge,*[56] in 2004, a federal district court in Wisconsin concluded that "extremely isolating conditions cause SHU syndrome in relatively healthy prisoners, as well as prisoners who have never suffered a breakdown; supermax is not appropriate for seriously mentally ill inmates." The judge ordered several prisoners to be removed from the supermax facility.

Finally, *Cunningham v. Federal Bureau of Prisons* is an ongoing class action lawsuit filed in 2012 by 12 inmates at ADX Florence. The suit contends that BOP and certain personnel at the facility have failed to adhere to federal policy and the Eighth Amendment by not properly treating inmates with serious mental illness.[57] The suit requests reform at the ADX by providing appropriate mental health treatment. In late 2016, an initial settlement was reached between the two parties, which remedied some of the major contentions by the plaintiffs, including the following: (1) ADX will screen all inmates for mental illness and ensure access to treatment; (2) ADX will improve conditions of confinement so as to reduce the risk for mental illness or its exacerbation, including enhancing recreation programs, creating private counseling areas, group therapy facilities; and (3) mental health units will be developed at several other BOP locations.

A Boon to Public Safety?

Pizarro et al.[58] examined whether supermax prisons, by housing the worst of the worst inmates, actually enhance public and prison safety. This claim, Pizarro et al. argue, has not been proven; they believe that the potential long-term, negative effects of supermax institutions (as discussed earlier) on inmates will contribute to future violence because the inmates begin to lose touch with reality and exhibit symptoms of psychiatric decomposition. Consequently, they believe that supermax prisons potentially endanger society, beyond regular imprisonment. They also bemoan that although most supermax inmates will one day return to society or to the general prison population, only a few supermax prisons provide inmates with a transitional program (e.g., moving inmates from supermax prison into a maximum-security prison, allowing inmates to participate in group activities, and placing inmates in institutional jobs).[59] Gordon[60] found similar trends in the long-term recidivism rates among former supermax inmates: the isolation and lack of contact tends more often than not to worsen the psychological problems present in many inmates.

Policy Implications

Given the negative psychological effects of many forms of long-term supermax confinement, researchers such as Craig Haney[61] believe that there is a strong argument for limiting the use of supermax prisons:

> We should take steps to ensure that all such facilities implement the best and most humane of the available practices. Far more careful screening, monitoring, and removal policies should be implemented to ensure that psychologically vulnerable prisoners do not end up there in the first place, and that those who deteriorate once they are immediately identified and transferred. Strict time limits should be placed on the length of time that prisoners are housed in supermax. [T]here are very serious psychological, correctional, legal, and even moral issues at the core that are worthy of serious, continued debate.

What's the future of the supermax? While many believe that there is a need for supermax prisons for the most dangerous and violent inmates,[62] others point to the unintended, negative consequences to inmates noted above, including increased mental illness among inmates who spend long periods of time in solitary confinement. Brutal conditions and high costs have led to the closing of some supermax prisons, including the Tamms Correctional Center in Illinois in 2013.[63] In Chapter 12, we discuss the related issue of solitary confinement and movements to limit its use across correctional systems in the United States. Suffice it to say, additional research is warranted to determine whether supermax prisons can be effective.

▶ Constitutional Rights of Inmates

From Hands Off to Hands On: A Shift in Prisoners' Rights, Law, and Philosophy

Historically, the courts followed a **hands-off policy** regarding prisons, and prisoners' rights were virtually nonexistent as prisoners were deemed as "slaves of the state." Hands-off meant that the judiciary, believing it was neither trained in nor knowledgeable about penology, allowed wardens the freedom and discretion to operate their institutions without outside interference while being fearful of undermining the structure and discipline of the prison.

hands-off policy a practice by judges, in a pre mid-1960s era when they believed they had neither training nor knowledge concerning penology, allowing wardens the freedom to operate prisons as they saw fit.

All that has changed, and the hands-on policy, beginning in the mid-1960s, brought about a change of philosophy in the courts regarding **prisoners' rights**—the collective body of constitutional rights afforded jail and prison inmates relating to the fundamental human rights and civil liberties, to include the right to acceptable prison conditions and treatment. In sum, prison inmates now retain all the rights of free citizens except those restrictions necessary for their orderly confinement or to provide safety in the prison community.

prisoners' rights the collective body of constitutional rights afforded jail and prison inmates relating to the fundamental human rights and civil liberties.

In subsequent sections, we discuss several U.S. Supreme Court decisions that spelled the demise of the hands-off era, in which it was established that no "iron curtain" was erected between inmates and the Constitution and that they were not "wholly stripped of constitutional protections" (see the discussion of *Wolff v. McDonnell*). These decisions improved the everyday lives of prison and jail inmates and reformed correctional administration. Specifically, basic rights extended to inmates included greater access to the courts, to appeal their convictions and conditions of confinement; greater freedom of religious expression; restricting mail censorship by prison officials; and granting them due process for the purpose of inmate disciplinary proceedings.

A "Slave of the State"

Ruffin v. Commonwealth (1871)

An excellent beginning point for this overview of significant court decisions concerning inmates' rights is the 1871 case of *Ruffin v. Commonwealth*.[64] There, the Virginia Supreme Court held that a prisoner "had, as a consequence of his crime, not only forfeited his liberty, but also all his personal rights except those that the law in its humanity accords to him." The Court in *Ruffin* even declared inmates to be "slaves of the state," mentioned earlier, losing all their citizenship rights, including the right to complain about living conditions.

This view certainly does not reflect the law at present and may never have been entirely accurate. For example, in 1948, in *Price v. Johnston*,[65] the Supreme Court declared that "lawful incarceration brings about the necessary withdrawal or limitation of many privileges and rights," which indicated a much softer view than that stated in *Ruffin*; furthermore, "many" privileges indicate less than "all," and it was clear that the due process and equal protection clauses did apply to prisoners to some extent.

Prison Regulations and Laws vis-à-vis Inmates' Constitutional Rights

Turner v. Safley[66] (1987)

Prison inmates brought a class action suit challenging the reasonableness of certain regulations of the Missouri Division of Corrections. Here, the Supreme Court took the opportunity to modify previous standards—such as "compelling state interest," "least restrictive means," and "rational relationship"—used to determine whether prison regulations and laws violate constitutional rights of inmates. In *Turner v. Safley*, the Court said that a prison regulation that impinges on inmates' constitutional rights is valid if it is reasonably related to *legitimate penological interests* (emphasis added). This decision gave prison authorities more power; all they must do is prove that a prison regulation is reasonably related to a legitimate penological interest in order for that regulation to be valid, even if a constitutional right is infringed. The policies challenged in this case were then-present prison regulations that forbade inmates from corresponding with inmates in other institutions, as well as requiring warden approval for inmates to marry. The Supreme Court upheld the former, determining that it served a valid penological interest, but struck down the latter, opining that an inmate's right to marriage does not fall under the purview of the institution.

Legal Remedy and Access to the Courts

Cooper v. Pate[67] (1964)

One of the earliest prison cases, it is significant because the Supreme Court first recognized the use of Title 42 of the U.S. Code Section 1983 as a legal remedy for inmates. (Section 1983, discussed thoroughly in Chapter 14, concerns a public officer's violation of a prisoner's constitutional rights while acting under "color of law.") Cooper, an inmate at the Illinois State Penitentiary, sued prison officials under Section 1983, alleging that he was unconstitutionally punished (i.e., placed in solitary confinement) and denied permission to purchase certain Muslim religious publications. Both the federal district court and the circuit court of appeals upheld Cooper's punishment but the Supreme Court reversed their ruling, finding that he was entitled to relief—and that he could use Section 1983, thereby mandating that prison administrators treat religions equally unless there is a compelling reason not to do so.

Johnson v. Avery[68] (1969)

This was one of the first prison decisions that involved an alleged violation of a constitutional right—here, the right of access to the courts. Johnson, a Tennessee prisoner, was disciplined for violating a prison regulation that prohibited inmates from assisting other prisoners in preparing writs. The Supreme Court acknowledged that "writ writers" like Johnson are sometimes a menace to prison discipline, and their petitions are often so unskillful as to be a burden on the courts receiving them. However, because the State of Tennessee provided no "reasonable alternative" to assist illiterate or poorly educated inmates in preparing petitions for postconviction relief, the Supreme Court held that the state could not bar inmates from furnishing such assistance to other prisoners. However, what constituted "reasonable alternatives" to writ writers was not explained.

Bounds v. Smith[69] (1977)

This was another court-access decision, clarifying *Johnson v. Avery*. In *Bounds*—where North Carolina inmates alleged denial of reasonable access by having only one library in the North Carolina prison system (which was inadequate in nature)—the Court went further, saying that prisoners have a constitutional right to adequate law libraries or assistance from persons trained in the law, guaranteed by the First and Fourteenth Amendments. This case also listed several possible alternatives that prisons could use for providing inmates such access, including training inmates as paralegals to work under lawyers' supervision; using paraprofessionals and law students to advise inmates; hiring lawyers on a part-time consultant basis; and having voluntary programs through bar associations, whereby lawyers visit the prisons to consult with inmates.

Lewis v. Casey[70] (1996)

In the same year that the Prison Litigation Reform Act was signed (discussed later in this chapter), the Supreme Court ruled on a case that took issue with the ruling in *Bounds v. Smith*. In *Lewis*, inmates contended that the law library provided to them in the Arizona corrections system was inadequate and called for mandated access to translators for inmates who did not speak English. The Supreme Court ruled in favor of the state, rejecting the prisoners' claims and directly stating that in order for a prison law library to be deemed unacceptable, prisoners must prove not only that it is inadequate in a theoretical sense (i.e., fails to provide the needed breadth of topics and laws) but also that the library's inadequacy disadvantaged their case specifically.

First Amendment

Cruz v. Beto[71] (1972) (Religious Practices)

This landmark case clarified the right of inmates to exercise their religious beliefs, even if they did not belong to what are considered mainstream or traditional religions. Cruz, a Buddhist, was not allowed to use the prison chapel and was placed in solitary confinement on a diet of bread and water for sharing his religious material with other prisoners. He sued under Section 1983, alleging violations of the First Amendment right to freedom of religion. The Supreme Court held that inmates with unconventional religious beliefs must be given a reasonable opportunity to exercise those beliefs. In January 2012, the U.S. Department of Justice issued a consent injunction with a South Carolina county based on the concerns raised in the Federal District Court of South Carolina case of *Prison Legal News et al. v. DeWitt et al.* (2011), affirming the reasonable right for inmates to exercise certain religious practices.[72]

Procunier v. Martinez[73] (1974) (Mail Censorship)

Here, the Supreme Court invalidated prison mail censorship regulations that permitted authorities to hold back or to censor mail to and from prisoners whenever they thought that the letters "unduly complain[ed]," "express[ed] inflammatory views or beliefs," or were "defamatory" or "otherwise inappropriate." The Court based its ruling not on the rights of the prisoner, but instead on the free-world recipient's right to communicate with the prisoner, either by sending or by receiving mail, and in this case law students who were attempting to communicate with prisoners. The Court held that the regulation of mail must further an important interest unrelated to the suppression of expression; regulation must be shown to further the substantial interest of security, order, and rehabilitation; and it must not be utilized simply to censor opinions or other expressions. Furthermore, a prison's restriction on mail must be no greater than is necessary to the protection of the security interest involved.

Fourth Amendment

Bell v. Wolfish[74] (1979) (Searches of Body Cavities and Cells, Other Conditions of Confinement)

This is one of the few cases decided by the Supreme Court concerning the rights of *pretrial* detainees housed in local jails. Here, the Court in effect said that jail officials may run their institutions the same way prisons are managed. New York City's Metropolitan Correctional Center, within a short time of opening, experienced overcrowding and began double bunking inmates in rooms built for single occupancy (later). Guards also conducted searches of inmates' cells in their absence, prohibited inmates from receiving hardcover books that were not mailed directly by publishers or bookstores, prohibited inmates' receipt of personal items from visitors, and employed body cavity searches of inmates following contact visits. Inmates sued and alleged several constitutional violations based on the First, Fourth, Fifth, and Fourteenth Amendments, but the Supreme Court held none of these practices to be unconstitutional "punishment," saying that these restrictions and practices were reasonable responses to legitimate security concerns and noting that they were of only limited duration. (Note that in a 1981 case specifically challenging the use of double bunking, *Rhodes v. Chapman*,[75] the Court held that double bunking of prisoners does not constitute cruel and unusual punishment as long as the conditions of confinement do not constitute the wanton infliction of pain.)

Eighth Amendment

Estelle v. Gamble[76] (1976) (Medical Care)

Although Gamble lost in this case, it was the first major prison medical treatment case decided by the Supreme Court and set the standards by which such cases are determined. Here, the Court coined the term *deliberate indifference*, which occurs when the serious medical needs of prisoners involve the unnecessary and wanton infliction of pain. Examples the Court gave are injecting penicillin with the knowledge that the prisoner is allergic to it, refusing to administer a prescribed painkiller, and requiring a prisoner to stand despite the contrary instructions of a surgeon. Gamble, an inmate of the Texas Department of Corrections, claimed that he received cruel and unusual punishment because of inadequate treatment of a back injury sustained while he was engaged in prison work. The Court did not find a constitutional violation in his case, however, because medical personnel saw him on 17 occasions during a 3-month period, and treated his injury and other problems. Justice Thurgood Marshall, who wrote the opinion of the court, indicated that medical attention that does not result in adequate medical care does not constitute medical mistreatment under the Constitution, so long as it is inadvertent.[77]

Overton v. Bazzetta[78] (2003) (Visitation)

The Michigan Department of Corrections (MDOC) prohibited younger siblings, nieces, nephews, and other minors from visiting inmates. A group of prisoners sued MDOC, contending that the ban violated both their First Amendment's right to association and the Eighth Amendment's ban on cruel and unusual punishment. The Sixth Court of Appeals unanimously ruled in favor of the district court's official dismissal of the case before it went to the Supreme Court. The Supreme Court, in a unanimous decision, ruled that the MDOC's regulations were within constitutional bounds. Justice Anthony Kennedy delivered the Court's opinion, which reasoned that the restrictions on visitation served a legitimate penological interest in ensuring institutional security.

Fourteenth Amendment

Wolff v. McDonnell[79] (1974) (Due Process)

This case is significant because, for the first time, the Supreme Court acknowledged that inmates are entitled to certain due process rights—"fundamental fairness"—during prison disciplinary proceedings. McDonnell and other inmates at a Nebraska prison alleged, among other things, that disciplinary proceedings at the prison violated their due process rights. To establish misconduct, prison officials required a preliminary conference, where the prisoner was orally informed of the charge; a conduct report was prepared and a hearing was held before the prison's disciplinary body; and the inmate could ask questions of the charging party. The Court said, now rather famously, "There is no iron curtain drawn between the Constitution and the prisons of this country, a prisoner is not wholly stripped of constitutional protections, and prisoners must be given the following due process rights":

- Advance written notice of charges no less than 24 hours before appearing before the hearing committee.
- A written statement by the fact finders as to the evidence relied on and reasons for the disciplinary action.
- Ability to call witnesses and to present documentary evidence in the inmate's defense (if this did not jeopardize institutional safety or correctional goals).
- Use of counsel substitutes (e.g., a friend or staff member) when the inmate is illiterate or when complex issues require such assistance.
- An impartial prison disciplinary board.

The Court, however, did not go so far as to say that prisoners have full due process protections, especially when prison safety would be at stake.

Wilkinson v. Austin[80] (2005) (Due Process)

When Ohio opened its first supermax prison in Youngstown, there were no standards or guidelines to help judges and corrections professionals to determine when an inmate should be classified for placement to this facility or to a lower-security type. This was obviously unacceptable, and after a short time the state devised a new policy for practitioners to refer to. The guidelines included, but were not limited to, formalized definitions for crimes meriting supermax assignment, a tiered review process after a supermax assignment was made, and opportunity for the inmate to rebut the placement at a hearing. Prisoners sued the state, complaining that the policies violated the Fourteenth Amendment's right to due process. The district court agreed and initially ordered far-reaching modifications to the policy. The U.S. Court of Appeals for the Sixth Circuit affirmed, in part, but dismissed the modifications on the grounds that they exceeded the court's authority. The Supreme Court unanimously reversed it, opining that prisoners' constitutional rights are needfully limited and that the procedures in Ohio's new policy met the standards for due process.

See Exhibit 10.4 for a description of the world's worst prisons.

EXHIBIT 10.4

THE WORLD'S WORST PRISONS[81]

Certainly any attempt to catalogue the worst prisons in the world will be open to serious debate, and the following list of such prisons is no exception; however, as will be seen, these are included (in no particular order) for very good reasons:

- ***La Sant, France:*** This, the last remaining prison in Paris, was established in 1867. Its mattresses are infested with lice; because prisoners can only take two cold showers per week, skin diseases are common. Overcrowded cells, infestation of vermin, and inmate rape are also common. Its rate of suicide attempts each year is estimated to be almost five times higher than that of California's prison system. Its conditions have been condemned by the U.N. Human Rights Committee and the country's own minister of justice.
- ***Black Beach Prison, Equatorial Guinea:*** Amnesty International has described life in this prison as a slow, lingering death sentence. Torture, burning, beatings, and rape are systematic and brutal. Because food rations are minimal, with prisoners sometimes going up to 6 days without food, starving to death is common. Amnesty also reports that inmates are routinely denied access to medical treatment.
- ***Vladimir Central Prison, Russia:*** Constructed by Catherine the Great to house political prisoners during the Soviet era, the prison became synonymous with persecution of political dissidents. Today the prison also functions as a museum for the public. Visitors are not allowed into the penitentiary, where cells often contain six prisoners and reports of abuse by guards are common. HIV and tuberculosis are also rampant.
- ***Camp 1391, Israel:*** Officially, this prison does not exist, but descriptions of its conditions have been validated. Even the Red Cross is banned from visiting, and prisoners typically have no idea where they are being kept or when they might be released—a fact that former inmates say is the worst torture of all. Sexual humiliation and even rape are reportedly used as interrogation techniques.
- ***The North Korean Gulag:*** Up to 200,000 prisoners are held in these detention centers, and one houses more than 50,000 inmates. Entire families and even neighborhoods are sent here as punishment for the infraction of one member. In some camps, up to 25 percent of the prisoners die every year, only to be replaced by new inmates. Most of the camps are located along the North Korean border with China and Russia, and thus prisoners are forced to endure harsh weather conditions as well as inhumane treatment.
- ***Petak Island, Russia:*** Comparisons to Alcatraz are common when speaking of Petak Island. It is not officially a supermax prison, but it's geographically isolated in a similar manner to Alcatraz and ADX Florence. Inmates in this institution often stay in their cells for at least 22 hours a day. On top of the virtually unending sense of isolation just within the cell, prisoners are only allowed to have two visitors per year. If prisoners do not follow the rules, they are punished by being sent to an even smaller cell, devoid of natural light. The minimum term for this punishment is 15 days.

Again, any such list is debatable given harsh prison conditions in many places around the world; prisons and/or labor camps in China, Thailand, Cuba, Venezuela, Syria, Africa, and other foreign venues could easily have been included.[82]

▶ Civil Rights of Institutionalized Persons

The **Civil Rights of Institutionalized Persons Act** (CRIPA) of 1980 is a federal law[83] broadly enacted to protect the rights of people in state or local facilities who are mentally ill, disabled, or chronically ill or handicapped, and are residing in a jail, prison, or other correctional facility or pretrial detention facility. Juveniles are also covered, to be free from violent residents and abusive staff members and not be excessively isolated or unreasonably restrained. They must also receive medical and mental health care; be educated, and be granted access to legal counsel, family communication, recreation, and exercise. Private institutions are not covered under CRIPA.

Civil Rights of Institutionalized Persons Act a federal law protecting the rights of people in state or local correctional facilities who are mentally ill, disabled, or handicapped.

The U.S. Department of Justice claims to now have open CRIPA matters in more than half the states.[84] Potential CRIPA law violations are investigated and prosecuted by the U.S. Department of Justice Civil Rights Division (CRD). If a pattern of civil violations is uncovered, the facility will be informed of the alleged violations and the evidence supporting the findings, as well as what must minimally be done to correct the violations. Under CRIPA, there's an emphasis on remedying conditions through the process of negotiation; lawsuits under CRIPA are a last resort and cannot award money. If suggested remedies are not fulfilled by a stated deadline, the Department of Justice has the option of bringing a lawsuit against the institution.

The following are four examples of jail- and treatment-related CRIPA investigations:[85]

- ***Erie County, New York (agreement reached, June 2010):*** A complaint was filed regarding conditions at several correctional facilities, alleging unconstitutional conditions that included the following: staff-on-inmate violence, inmate-on-inmate violence, sexual misconduct between staff and inmates, sexual misconduct among inmates, inadequate systems to prevent suicide and self-injurious behavior, inadequate medical and mental health care, and serious deficiencies in environmental health and safety. The agreement also addressed the county's inadequate system of suicide prevention and self-injurious behavior of holding center inmates, requiring officials to implement measures to ensure that holding center inmates are protected from suicide hazards.
- ***Lake County, Indiana (agreement reached, December 2010):*** Unlawful conditions of confinement were corrected after an investigation of the jail uncovered systemic deficiencies, including a suicide rate that was more than five times the national average. Conditions violated the constitutional rights of approximately 1,000 male and female inmates confined there, including failure to protect individuals from harm (particularly involving suicide risk); failure to identify and treat individuals' psychiatric disabilities; failure to provide adequate medical services and fire safety; and failure to adequately maintain the physical plant of the facility, thereby endangering both staff and inmates.
- ***Delaware Mental Health (agreement reached, July 2011):*** An investigation concluded that the state's mental health services system failed to provide services to individuals with serious mental illness in the most integrated setting appropriate to their needs, as required by the ADA. These failures were needlessly prolonging institutionalization of many individuals who could have been adequately served in community settings. Delaware will prevent unnecessary hospitalization by expanding and deepening its crisis intervention system and providing intensive community supports, such as assertive community treatment and intensive case management, rehabilitation services, and improved family and peer support systems.
- ***Rikers Island (CRIPA investigation ongoing):*** Rikers Island is one of the more notorious facilities in the New York corrections system. Founded in 1932, the jail facility takes in more than 100,000 inmates per year, with a daily population of approximately 10,000.

The budget for this institution alone is $860 million. In the last 10 to 15 years especially, the facility has come under intense scrutiny and criticism for numerous instances of violence. *Mother Jones* ranked Rikers Island as one of the ten worst correctional institutions in the United States. Abuse and neglect of prisoners is reportedly commonplace.

▶ Inmate Litigation

Prior to the Twenty-First Century: "Hair-trigger" Suing

The volume of inmate litigation increased significantly following the aforementioned *Cooper v. Pate* decision in 1964. In 1980, inmates in state and federal correctional institutions filed 23,287 petitions alleging both civil and criminal violations of their rights and seeking compensatory damages, injunctions, and property claims.[86] By 1990, the number of such petitions had swollen to nearly 43,000, and more than 64,000 petitions were filed in 1996[87] (a more contemporary view of inmate filings, since the passage of the PLRA of 1995, is provided in the "Has PLRA Served Its Purpose" section later in this chapter).

Prisoners sued primarily because they were either unwilling to accept their conviction or wished to harass their keepers.[88] Inmate litigants tend to fall into one of two categories. First are those who file a single suit during their entire period of incarceration (usually requiring the assistance of others to do it); one study found that 71 percent of all litigants filed only one action but accounted for about half of all litigation.[89] The other group is comprised of inmates who make law a prison career—the so-called jailhouse lawyers or writ writers.[90]

frivolous lawsuit an action filed by a party or attorney who is aware it is without merit, due to a lack of legal basis or argument for the alleged claim.

Although in past decades the media brought to light many abuses inside prisons, in the 1980s and 1990s media attention began turning in another direction: reports of trivial and **frivolous lawsuits**—those actions filed by parties or attorneys who are aware they are without merit, due to a lack of legal basis or argument for the alleged claim—by inmates. The following are some examples:

- A death row inmate sued correction officials for taking away his Gameboy electronic game.
- A prisoner sued demanding L.A. Gear or Reebok "Pumps" instead of Converse.
- An inmate sued because he was served chunky instead of smooth peanut butter.
- An inmate claimed it was cruel and unusual punishment that he was forced to listen to his unit manager's country and Western music.
- An inmate claimed $1 million in damages because his ice cream melted (the judge ruled that the "right to eat ice cream was clearly not within the contemplation" of our nation's forefathers).[91]
- A now-released Pennsylvania inmate filed over 2,600 different lawsuits in various jurisdictions, sometimes against defendants who did not exist.[92]

Such examples of litigation caused an uproar over frivolous civil right lawsuits brought by inmates. Furthermore, the expense of defending against such lawsuits, coupled with the fact that the United States has the world's largest and costliest prison system,[93] combined to foster public resentment against prisons and prisoners.

Of course, not all lawsuits against prison administrators concerning inmate living conditions and treatment are frivolous. For example, in August 2006 Timothy Joe Souders, a 21-year-old mentally ill young man held in the Southern Michigan Correctional Facility in Jackson, died after 5 days of horrific abuse and neglect. He was held for 5 days in isolation, naked, shackled by his arms and legs to a concrete slab in temperatures exceeding 100 degrees, and forced to lie in his own urine. His family settled for $3.25 million.[94] A federal judge called Souders' death "predictable and preventable," and cited numerous documented and appalling instances of nontreatment, including an inmate who died of untreated cancer. He was found lying in excrement in his cell, after having lost 60 pounds from a "hunger strike."[95]

The Prison Litigation Reform Act

Four Main Parts

By the late 1980s, the courts were displaying more tolerance for minor violations of prisoners' constitutional rights, as exemplified by the following three cases:

1. *Turner v. Safley* (1987),[96] discussed earlier, in which the Supreme Court stated that when a prison regulation impinges on inmates' constitutional rights, "the regulation is valid if it is reasonably related to legitimate penological interests."
2. *Wilson v. Seiter* (1991),[97] which stated that when an inmate claims that the conditions of his or her confinement violate the Eighth Amendment, he or she must show a culpable state of mind on the part of prison officials.
3. *Sandin v. Conner* (1995),[98] which emphasized the Supreme Court's desire to give "deference and flexibility to state officials trying to maintain a volatile environment." This decision made it "more difficult to bring constitutional suits challenging prison management."[99]

Then, in April 1996, the **Prison Litigation Reform Act** (PLRA) of 1995 was enacted.[100] The PLRA has been praised by proponents as necessary "to provide for appropriate remedies for prison condition lawsuits, to discourage frivolous and abusive prison lawsuits, and for other purposes."[101]

Prison Litigation Reform Act a law providing remedies for prison condition lawsuits and to discourage frivolous and abusive prison lawsuits.

The PLRA has four main parts:[102]

- ***Exhaustion of administrative remedies.*** Before inmates can file a lawsuit, they must try to resolve their complaint through the prison's grievance procedure, which usually includes giving a written description of their complaint to a prison official; if the prison requires additional steps, such as appealing to the warden, then the inmate must also follow those steps. The PLRA, however, does not mandate specific procedures for grievances, only that the inmate must follow the procedure set forth by the state. Finally, the one exception to the exhaustion requirement is when no formal grievance procedures exist or when a formal grievance is lost.[103]
- ***Filing fees.*** All prisoners must pay court filing fees in full. If they do not have the money up front, they can pay the fee over time through monthly deductions from their prison commissary account. A complex statutory formula requires the indigent prisoner to pay an initial fee of 20 percent of the greater of the prisoner's average balance or the average deposits to the account for the preceding 6 months.
- ***Three-strikes provision.*** Each lawsuit or appeal that an inmate files that is dismissed for being frivolous, malicious, or not stating a proper claim counts as a *strike.* After an inmate receives three strikes, he or she cannot file another lawsuit *in forma pauperis*; that is, he or she cannot file another lawsuit unless he or she pays the entire court filing fee up front (an exception is made if the inmate is at risk of suffering serious physical injury in the immediate future, described in the next point). An appeal of a dismissed action that is dismissed is a separate strike, and even dismissals that occurred prior to the effective date of the PLRA count as strikes.

- ***Physical injury requirement.*** An inmate cannot file a lawsuit for mental or emotional injury unless he or she can also show physical injury. (The courts differ in their evaluation of what constitutes sufficient harm to qualify as physical injury.)

Has PLRA Served Its Purpose?

According to a recent study, in 1995—the year before the implementation of the act—there were 24.6 prisoner civil rights filings in federal district court per 1,000 inmates; in 1997, the first year following the implementation of the act, there were 15.1 filings per 1,000 inmates. By 2012, the number of filings had gone down to 10.2 per 1,000.[104] Clearly, prisoner petitions to the U.S. district courts have significantly diminished in number. We also note that the PLRA has been criticized on the grounds that it has contributed to the over-incarceration and crowding present in many corrections facilities: inmates who bring even legitimate cases against the prison are all but guaranteed to have their cases viewed with extreme skepticism. The burden of proof still rests on the plaintiff, but given the other hurdles that inmates face in cases (they may have access to law libraries, but are unlikely to have the same intricate understanding that a lawyer will), it can be questioned as to whether the process is fair.[105]

▶ Jails as Organizations

Across the United States, approximately 3,280 jails are administered,[106] which together have an average daily population of approximately 721,000 inmates. This number, however, does not represent the total number of inmates admitted into jails in a given year at 10.9 million.[107] The organization and hierarchical levels of jails are determined by several factors: size, budget, level of crowding, local views on punishment and treatment, and even the levels of training and education of the jail administrator. An organizational structure for a jail serving a population of about 250,000 is suggested in Figure 10-4 ■.

The administration of jails is frequently one of the major tasks of county sheriffs. Several writers have concluded that sheriffs and police personnel see themselves primarily as law enforcers first and view the responsibility of organizing and operating a jail as an unwelcome task.[108] Therefore, their approach is often said to be at odds with advanced corrections philosophy and trends.

Podular/Direct Supervision Jails

Rationale and Expanding Use

As noted previously, in the past, the federal courts have at times become more willing to hear inmate allegations of constitutional violations ranging from inadequate heating, lighting, and ventilation to the censorship of mail. One of every five cases filed in federal courts was on behalf of prisoners,[109] and 20 percent of all jails were a party in a pending lawsuit.[110]

podular direct supervision jail a type of jail design where cells are arranged in podular fashion, have an open dayroom area, and correctional officers are close to and interact with the inmates.

Court-ordered pressures to improve jail conditions afforded an opportunity for administrators to explore new ideas and designs; therefore, over the past several decades and in response to the deluge of lawsuits concerning jail conditions, many local jurisdictions constructed what is now known as the podular **direct supervision (PDS) jail**, where inmates' cells are arranged around a common area—in podular fashion, with no physical barriers between the officer and the inmates, having an open dayroom area—and inmate management style is direct in nature, with officers moving about the pod and interacting with the inmates to manage their behavior. PDS jails also typically offer more amenities in the living areas, including visiting areas, books, and telephones.[111] The PDS jail (formerly

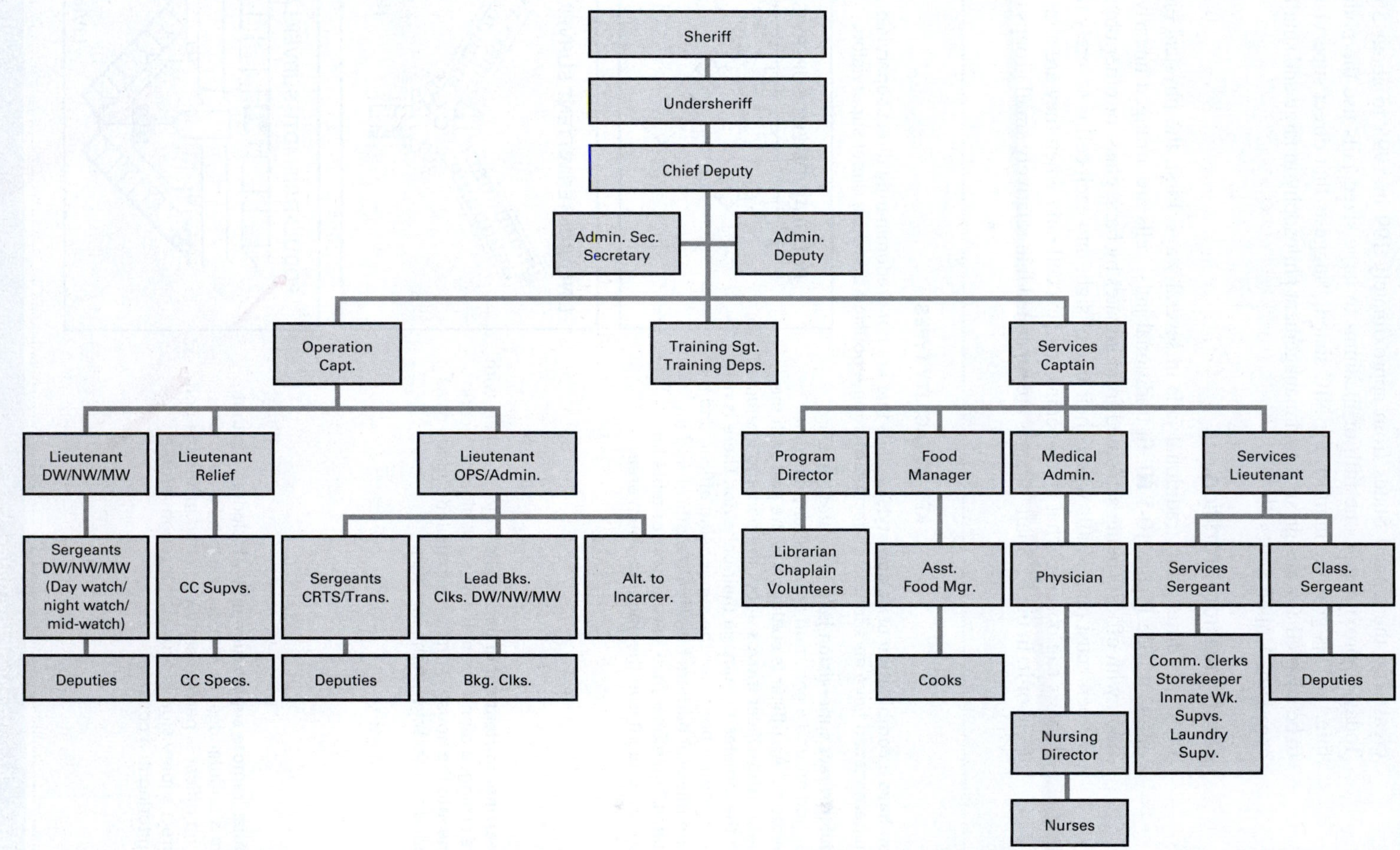

FIGURE 10-4 Organizational Structure of a Jail Serving a Population of 250,000

known as "new-generation" jail) represents a comparatively new approach for addressing many of the earlier problems found in local jails.[112]

According to the National Institute of Corrections (NIC), the number of PDS jails increased in the United States from approximately 199 in 1995 to about 350 at present. Today, approximately one-fifth of medium- to large-sized jails use the podular architecture.[113] This growing number, the NIC stated, "suggests that direct supervision continues to be adopted as a design style and management philosophy in large and small jurisdictions across the United States."[114]

Departing from Tradition

PDS jails differ from traditional jails in several ways. First, the physical environment is different (See Figure 10-5 ■). In traditional jails, cells are arranged linearly along a corridor, with officers being separated from inmates by bars, glass, or other physical barriers. Officers must patrol halls where their line of sight into each cell is severely restricted, and officers can observe what is happening inside a cell only when they are almost directly in front of it. In the PDS jail, inmates are separated into relatively small groups (usually 50 or

KEY TO FACILITY TYPES

Jails can have a combination of design styles – Jails that are not predominantly direct supervision in design or management can have an addition or section of inmate housing that uses direct supervision.

- **Podular/direct supervision jails** – Inmates' cells are arranged around a common area, usually called a "dayroom." An officer is stationed in the pod with the inmates. The officer moves about the pod and interacts with the inmates to manage their behavior. There is no secure control booth for the supervising officer, and there are no physical barriers between the officer and the inmates. The officer may have a desk or table for paperwork, but it is in the open dayroom area.

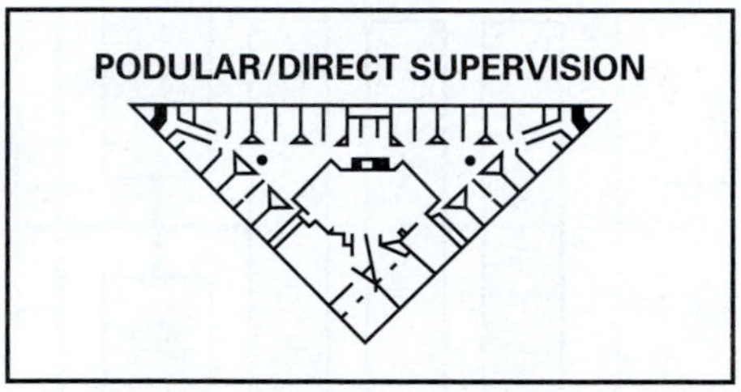

- **Linear/intermittent supervision jails** – Includes jails with cells arranged along the sides of a cell block. Officers come into the housing unit on scheduled rounds or as needed to interact with the inmates.

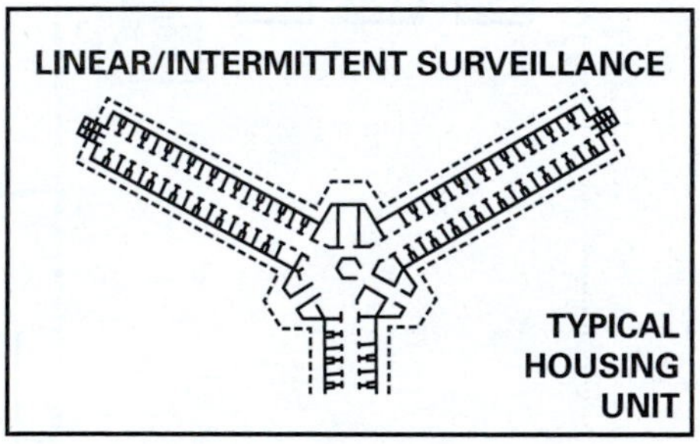

- **Podular/remote supervision jails** – Includes jails that have a podular design with cells around a dayroom, but no officer is permanently stationed inside the pod. Indirect supervision is provided through remote monitoring at a console.

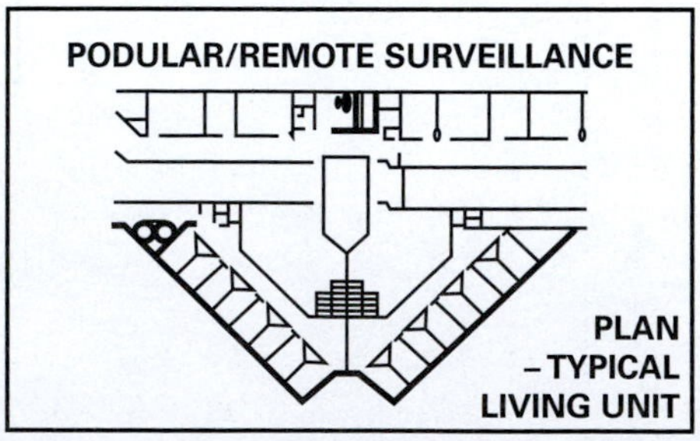

FIGURE 10-5 Architectural Jail Types
Source: United States Department of Justice.

fewer), housed in self-contained living units including several one- to two-person cells, a day room, and recreation space. These units, or "pods," usually are triangular or wedge shaped so that jail officers have a direct line of sight into all areas of the pod at all times. The furnishings in the living units also differ and generally include carpeting, porcelain lavatories, moveable furniture that may be padded or plastic, and other "soft" fixtures. The direct supervision philosophy has officers stationed within the living area with no physical barriers to separate them from inmates. In these units, officers maintain a constant physical presence, but they also interact extensively with inmates.[115]

Because of their constant physical and close presence, correctional officers (COs) in PDS jails (unlike in linear or podular/remote supervision jails pictured in Figure 10-5 ■) must use active observation in order to gather information about what is occurring in the module, to gauge sources of conflict or tension, and to identify and react to situations before they escalate into serious problems. They must also develop a higher degree of interpersonal skills and creativity in managing inmates. Even minor conflicts and problems must be proactively addressed within the pod. The COs must also be fair with their discipline, and treat inmates with respect and dignity. Both formal and informal sanctions should be used so that punishment meted out is commensurate with the gravity of the infraction. Inmates should also be told the reason for their punishment.[116]

Most evaluations of direct supervision jails have been encouraging. Researchers and practitioners have reported reductions in inmate–inmate violence and assaults against jail officers and staff members;[117] inmates have also reported having more positive attitudes about the officers than inmates in more traditional facilities, and direct supervision officers have reported feeling less hostile toward the inmates.[118] In addition, there appear to be fewer lawsuits arising out of PDS jails, which reduce overall costs, and officers tend to have a more enriched worklife (as discussed in Chapter 2).[119]

Community Jails

Beyond jail design and supervision type, with almost 11 million inmates admitted into our local jails each year, jail administrators undoubtedly must be concerned with the provision of treatment services for inmates both within the jail and in the community once an inmate is released. The community jail concept is akin to a system of care that recognizes that some inmates admitted into jail are already receiving treatment in the form of mental health services, drug and alcohol treatment, and/or educational programming. Community jails continue to provide these treatment services while the inmate is incarcerated, and ensure that services continue when the inmate is released—whether that's days, weeks, or months later.[120]

What's unique about community jails are the intentional efforts to view the jail as part of the larger community where treatment services are provided. Ideally, the same service providers in the community provide the services to inmates upon entry into the jail, and again once released. While the concept is appealing on many fronts, including from the perspective of a continuity of care, implementation of community jails is easier said than done. For example, jails must create space for treatment to occur. In addition, with scarce resources available for treatment services, providing these services to jail inmates may be a tough sell.[121]

Along the lines of the community jail concept, the National Institute of Corrections and the Urban Institute has launched the Transition from Jail to Community (TJC) initiative, which focuses on offender reentry into the community. The goal of this initiative is to improve long-term integration for those returning to the community from jail.[122] Under this program, NIC provides technical assistance to selected jurisdictions to support collaborative planning, continuity of care, and systems change processes.[123]

▶ A New Supreme Court Decree: Collecting DNA at Point of Arrest

After the U.S. Supreme Court decision in *Maryland v. King* (2013), employees of local jails have been kept somewhat busier and have had more responsibility. The Court ruled that a DNA swab may be taken from anyone arrested for a crime of violence. The Court's majority rationalized the decision on the grounds that, like fingerprinting and photographing, taking and analyzing a cheek swab of the arrestee's DNA is a legitimate police booking procedure, akin to fingerprinting, under the Fourth Amendment. The majority also maintained that a DNA swab serves legitimate state interests and is not invasive enough to require a warrant.[124] The dissenting minority, however, suggested that the Fourth Amendment protections against unreasonable searches and seizures prohibit DNA swabs when there is no evidence linking an arrestee to a specific DNA-related crime.[125]

Getting DNA swabs from arrestees was already a common practice in all 50 states; however, what set this decision apart was the Court's allowing DNA collection before conviction and without a judge issuing a warrant.[126]

▶ Corrections Accreditation

Like police organizations (discussed in Chapter 4), corrections organizations may be accredited by meeting national standards through a series of reviews, evaluations, audits, and hearings. Since 1978, the American Correctional Association (ACA) has promulgated standards generally covering administrative and fiscal controls, staff training and development, physical plant, safety and emergency procedures, sanitation, food service, and rules and discipline. The ACA utilizes a 28-member private, nonprofit body, the Commission on Accreditation for Corrections, to render accreditation decisions. Today, approximately 1,300 facilities and agencies are accredited through the ACA.[127]

There are 22 different sets or manuals of accreditation standards covering all types of correctional facilities and programs, including state and federal adult institutions, juvenile facilities, probation and parole agencies, and health care and electronic monitoring programs. In order for a state or federal adult corrections institution to be accredited, it must meet 100 percent of 62 mandatory standards as well as 90 percent of 468 nonmandatory standards.[128] Because of differences among facilities, not all standards apply to all facilities. When this occurs, these standards are deducted from the overall compliance score.

As with the police, there are several benefits to be realized for corrections agencies wishing to become accredited: determining the facility or program's strengths and weaknesses, identifying obtainable goals, implementing state-of-the-art policies and procedures, establishing specific guidelines for daily operations, aiding in defending against frivolous lawsuits, and ensuring a higher level of staff professionalism and morale.[129]

▶ Probation and Parole Agencies as Organizations

Community corrections originated in the years following World War II, when returning veterans encountered adjustment problems as they attempted to reenter civilian life.[130] It has also been stated that community corrections is "the last bastion of discretion in the criminal justice system."[131] Community corrections are typically viewed as a humane, logical, and effective approach for working with and changing criminal offenders.[132]

Today there are about 4.65 million adults under community supervision in the United States, a 6 percent decline from 2005. Of the 4.65 million, 3.8 million are on probation (the lowest number since 2005) and about 870,500 on parole. While probationers have steadily decreased, parolees have increased by 11 percent since 2005.[133]

Agency Organization, Armed and Sworn Status of Officers

What follows is a secondary analysis of a national survey by the American Probation and Parole Association. Specifically, the survey included questions concerning how adult/juvenile probation and parole agencies in the 50 states are organizationally structured (e.g., under which branch of government they function, to whom the administrators report), and whether or not the probation and parole officers are armed and possess **peace officer** powers. (Note: The definition of a "peace officer" can be quite broad, but normally includes those persons having arrest authority either with a warrant or based on probable cause.)[134]

peace officer those persons having arrest authority either with a warrant or based on probable cause.

- ***Adult probation:*** 32 (64%) of the state agencies are under the executive branch, and 13 (26%) are under the judicial branch; 5 (10%) are organized under an agency that is either a combination of these or a state or county agency.
- ***Juvenile probation:*** 21 (42%) of the state agencies are organized under the executive branch, and 19 (38%) are under the judicial branch; 10 (20%) are either a combination of these or under a state or county agency.
- ***Adult parole:*** 43 (86%) of the state agencies are organized under the executive branch, and 2 (4%) are under the judicial branch; 4 (8%) are either a combination of these or under a state or county agency; one state has abolished parole. We note here that parole rates tend to be quite low in states where parole is administered. For example, only 116 of 3,156 cases that came before the Virginian parole board actually resulted in parole being granted.[135]
- ***Juvenile parole*** (generally, aftercare plans and activities for institutionalized juvenile offenders assist them to transition back into the community): 39 (78%) of the state agencies are organized under the executive branch, and 6 (12%) are under the judicial branch; 5 (10%) are either a combination of these or under a state or county agency.

Regarding the arming of these officers, 18 states (36%) do not authorize their officers to carry arms, while 19 (38%) authorize it; the remainder of the states are optional or allow being armed if approved by the governing body or supervisor. In the federal system, U.S. probation officers have statutory authority to carry firearms. With so much variation among states, the carrying of firearms among probation/parole officers is an often debated topic in corrections. The American Probation and Parole Association's official position on the issue is that they neither support nor oppose the carrying of firearms. Its statement reads, in part, "should the decision be made by an agency to authorize officers to carry weapons, that decision must be made within the framework of actual need, officer safety demands, and must be consistent with the laws and policies which guide that agency."[136]

Traditionalists believe that carrying a firearm contributes to an atmosphere of distrust between the client and the officer; enforcement-oriented officers, conversely, view a firearm as an additional tool to protect themselves from the risk associated with violent, serious, or high-risk offenders.[137] The latter view is understandable, given that officers must make home and employment visits in the neighborhoods in which offenders live (some of which are very unsafe), and officers must often revoke offenders' freedom.

Some states classify probation and parole officers as peace officers and grant them the authority to carry a firearm both on and off duty.[138] Some believe that officers should not be required to carry a firearm if they are opposed to arming, and that providing an option allows for a better officer/assignment match.[139] In sum, it would seem that the administrator's decision concerning arming should focus on need, officer safety, and local laws and policies.

Probation and parole officers do not possess peace officer authority in 24 (48%) of the states, while they are authorized such powers in 26 (52%) states. Note, however, that in 8 (16%) of those states that grant officers such powers, it is granted only to *adult* probation and parole officers, not to those who work with juveniles.[140]

Probation Systems

Types of Systems

probation where a court places an offender on supervision in the community, generally in lieu of incarceration.

Figure 10-6 ■ depicts an organizational structure for a regional probation and parole organization. **Probation**—where a court places a person on supervision in the community, generally in lieu of incarceration—is the most frequently used sanction; it costs offenders their privacy and self-determination and usually includes some element of the other

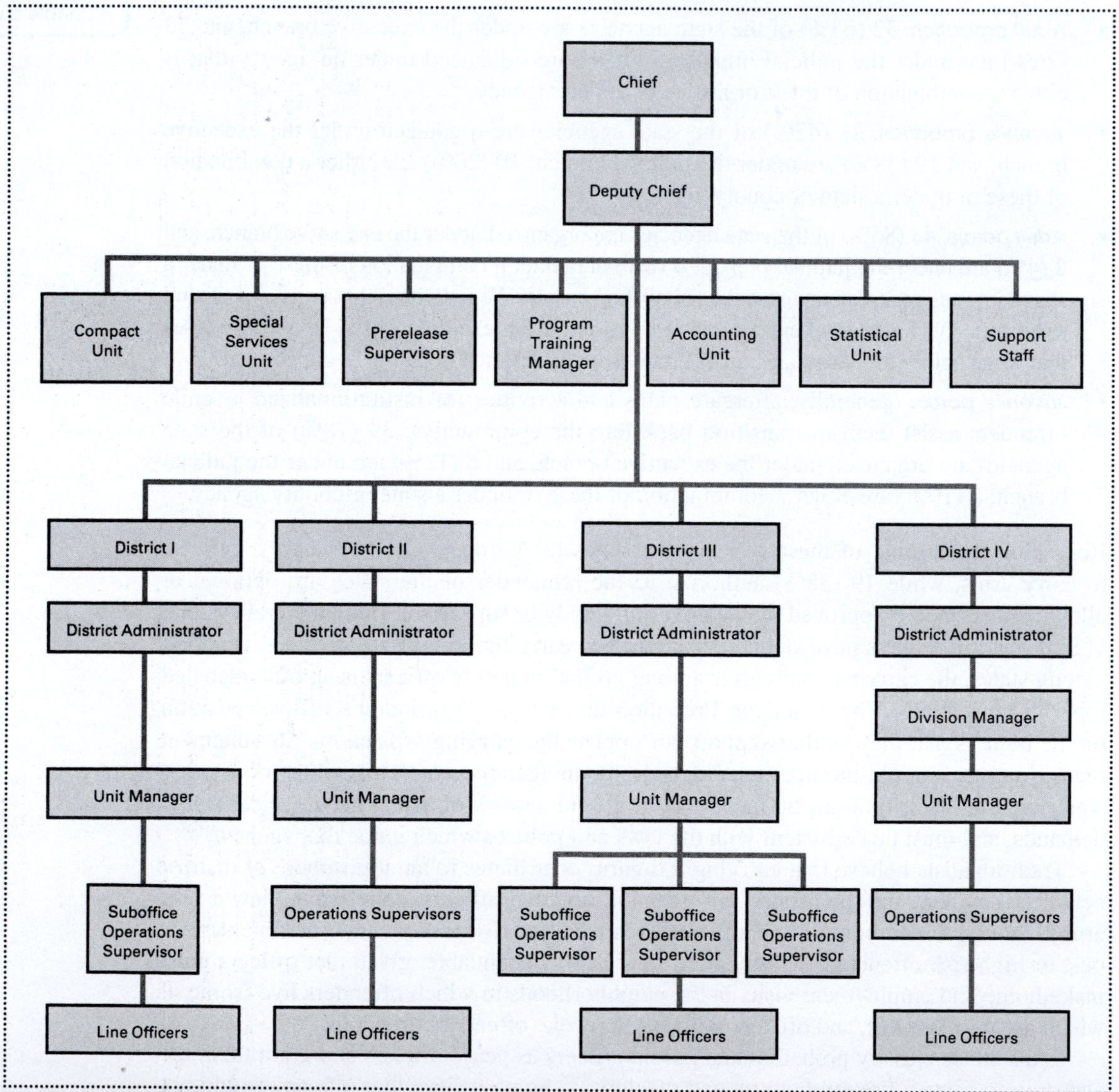

FIGURE 10-6 Organizational Structure for a Regional Probation and Parole Organization

sanctions: jail time, fines, restitution, or community service.[141] Probation in the United States is administered by more than 2,000 different agencies. Its organization is a patchwork that defies simple explanation. In about three-fourths of the states, adult probation is part of the executive branch of state government.[142] By contrast, more than half of the agencies providing juvenile probation services are administered in juvenile courts on the local level.[143]

According to Howard Abadinsky, the administration of probation systems can be separated into six categories:[144]

1. ***Juvenile.*** Separate probation services for juveniles are administered on a county, municipal, or state level.
2. ***Municipal.*** Independent probation units are administered by the lower courts under state laws and guidelines.
3. ***County.*** Under laws and guidelines established by the state, a county operates its own probation agency.
4. ***State.*** One agency administers a central probation system, which provides services throughout the state.
5. ***State combined.*** Probation and parole services are administered on a statewide basis by one agency.
6. ***Federal.*** Probation is administered as an arm of the federal courts.

This patchwork nature of probation systems has raised two central organizational questions concerning the administration of probation services: Should probation be part of the judicial or the executive branch of government? Does the lack of uniformity in administering probation make justice less equitable statewide?[145] These important and lingering issues were first considered nearly 50 years ago by the President's Commission.[146]

Although it was shown previously that few probation/parole agencies are organized and governed at the county level, Abadinsky argued that probation administered by the judiciary on a county level promotes diversity:

> Innovative programming can be implemented more easily in a county agency because it has a shorter line of bureaucratic control than would a statewide agency. A county agency can more easily adapt to change, and the successful programs of one agency can more easily be adopted by other probation departments and unsuccessful programs avoided. Although the judiciary is nominally responsible for administering probation, the day-to-day operations are in the hands of a professional administrator—the chief probation officer.[147]

Systems Theory

As with the administration of police, court, or prison organizations, the probation department administrator's goals may affect the services provided to the client, which in turn may have an impact on the client's request for services. This systematic interaction between an organization's resources and structure and the community has been referred to as its "sociotechnical environment,"[148] meaning that the principles of the system are organized to execute the basic production technologies of the organization.

Each probation administrator needs to recognize that the organization is a system of inputs, processes, and outputs (discussed in Chapter 2). For probation, inputs are clients coming into the office for counseling and supervision (the processes); outputs are the probationer's obtaining employment, acquiring a skill, observing a curfew, and so on. This understanding of probation, using systems theory, provides a means of learning how probation departments function and interact with their environment and of examining the resources, activities, and outcomes in a way that can identify the goals, describe the day-to-day activities, and link the department's activities to resources and outcomes.

According to systems theory, probation may be conceptualized as a network of interwoven resources, activities, and outcomes.[149] According to Hardyman, resources include the probation department's funding level, goals, policies and procedures, organizational structure, and caseload; the probation staff's characteristics; the services available to probationers; and the rates of unemployment, poverty, and crime in the county. Activities are supervision techniques, rewards, leadership style, contacts, and direct and indirect services provided by the probation department. Outcomes, according to systems theory, are the number of probationers who were arrested, incarcerated, and/or cited for a technical violation during the follow-up period, as well as the needs of probationers that were considered.[150] See Exhibit 10.5 for a description of Hawaii's Project HOPE.

EXHIBIT 10.5

A "BEST PRACTICE" IN PROBATION: HAWAII'S PROJECT HOPE

A probation reform program developed in 2004 in Hawaii has resulted in an 80 percent drop in positive drug tests and in recidivism. The backbone of the program is simple: Rather than let small problems pile up, closely monitored probationers receive immediate punishment, usually a brief stint in jail. The Hawaii model, known as HOPE, or Hawaii's Opportunity Probation Enforcement, has now been implemented in five states while also being established in cities in four states. The U.S. Department of Justice also is experimenting with HOPE.

According to program founder Judge Steve Alm, "This is Parenting 101, Personal Responsibility 101. One reason it works is because even the offenders think it's fair. They used to go along with infraction piling on top of infraction, over and over with no consequences. Now there is some jail every time, though it's brief—it is swift, certain and proportionate. They get it."

HOPE's stated goals are reductions in drug use, new crimes, and incarceration. The National Institute of Justice commissioned a study to determine whether or not those goals were met. According to the study's authors:

> Those goals have been achieved. Probationers assigned to HOPE had large reductions in positive drug tests and missed appointments, and were significantly less likely to be arrested during follow-up at 3 months, 6 months, and 12 months. They averaged approximately the same number of days in jail for probation violations, serving more but shorter terms. They spent about one-third as many days in prison on revocations or new convictions.[151]

In the state of Washington, where HOPE's model is being replicated under the name Swift and Certain (SAC) throughout its community supervision system, initial results are promising across multiple measures, including recidivism. But with many programs of this type, it remains to be seen whether long-term success (beyond one year) can be realized.

Parole Systems

Models for Providing Services

parole where an offender is conditionally released from prison to serve the remaining portion of a criminal sentence in the community.

Unlike the general trend in probation, offenders on parole have increased over the last 10 years. From an organizational perspective, the administration of **parole**—for offenders who are conditionally released from prison to serve the remaining portion of their sentence in the community—is much less complex than that of probation because parole services are administered centrally on a statewide basis.[152] (It should also be noted that in about 20 states, probation officers also serve as parole officers; thus, much of the information presented in the previous section applies to parole as well.) One state agency administers the parole function on a statewide basis, except that in a number of states, parolees from a local jail come under the supervision of a county probation and parole department.[153]

A parole agency can provide three basic services: parole release, parole supervision, and executive clemency. In a number of states that have abolished discretionary parole release (such as California), parole officers continue to supervise offenders released by the prison through mandatory parole, based on good time (reduction of sentence through good behavior).

The National Advisory Commission on Criminal Justice Standards and Goals delineated two basic models for administering parole services:

1. ***The independent model.*** A parole board is responsible for making release (parole) determinations as well as supervising persons released on parole (or good time). It is independent of any other state agency and reports directly to the governor.
2. ***The consolidated model.*** The parole board is a semiautonomous agency within a large department that also administers correctional institutions. Supervision of persons released on parole (or good time) is under the direction of the commissioner of corrections, not the parole board.[154]

Both models sometimes combine probation services with parole services in a single statewide agency.

The President's Commission summarized the advantages of the *independent* model:[155]

1. The parole board is in the best position to promote the idea of parole and to generate public support and acceptance of it. Because the board is accountable for parole failures, it should be responsible for supervising parolees.
2. The parole board that is in direct control of administering parole services can evaluate and adjust the system more effectively.
3. Supervision by the parole board and its officers properly divorces parole release and parolees from the correctional institution.
4. An independent parole board in charge of its own services is in the best position to present its own budget request to the legislature.

Conversely, the commission summarized the advantages of including both parole services and institutions in a *consolidated* department of corrections as follows:[156]

1. The correctional process is a continuum; all staff, both institutional and parole, are under a single administration rather than divided, which avoids competition for public funds and friction in policies.
2. A consolidated correctional department has consistent administration, including staff selection and supervision.
3. Parole boards are ineffective in performing administrative functions; their major focus should be on case decision, not on day-to-day field operations.
4. Community-based programs that fall between institutions and parole, such as work release, can best be handled by a single centralized administration.

Clearly, the trend in this country, beginning in the late 1960s, has been in the direction of consolidation. With the number of parolees on discretionary parole increasing and mandatory parolees decreasing (resulting in an overall increase in the parolee population), further research is warranted as to the effectiveness of independent and consolidated models across significant parole outcomes, including efficiency and effectiveness.

Summary

This chapter presented an overview of corrections as a booming industry; it discussed prison and jail organization; the rise of, and controversies surrounding, supermax prisons; selected inmate rights under the First, Fourth, Eighth, and Fourteenth Amendments as set forth by the U.S. Supreme Court; inmate litigation; and the organization of probation and parole agencies.

The chapter also demonstrated how times have changed with respect to the manner in which correctional facilities are organized while providing a glimpse into some of the issues and problems that challenge administrators, some of which are further examined in the following chapter.

Key Terms and Concepts

Central office, p. 249
Civil Rights of Institutionalized Persons Act, p. 263
Direct supervision jail, p. 266
Frivolous lawsuits, p. 264
Hands-off policy, p. 257
Parole, p. 274
Peace officer, p. 271
Prison director, p. 249
Prison industries, p. 253
Prison Litigation Reform Act (PLRA), p. 265
Prisoners' rights, p. 257
Probation, p. 272
Supermax prison, p. 254

Questions for Review

1. What factors contribute to the recent decline in correctional populations? What impact do drug laws have on them? How do California's prison populations affect that of the nation?
2. What does the available research suggest regarding the effects of California's decarceration?
3. What are some of the major administrative positions within a prison system?
4. How do supermax prisons differ from other prisons? What concerns have been raised concerning their alleged effects on inmates, constitutionality, and public safety?
5. What are at least five of the major U.S. Supreme Court decisions affording rights to prisoners? When and how did such decisions serve to end the hands-off doctrine?
6. What is a direct supervision jail, and how does it differ in design and function from traditional jails?
7. Why was the Prison Litigation Reform Act enacted, and has it made an impact? Why do critics say that the PLRA is punitive to inmates?
8. In what major ways do jails differ from prisons in their organization and administration?
9. What did the U.S. Supreme Court hold recently concerning the warrantless collection of DNA from pretrial arrestees?
10. What advantages accrue to a corrections facility if it is accredited?
11. What is the profile of state adult and juvenile probation and parole agencies in terms of their organizational structure as well as the arming and peace officer status of their officers?
12. What are the various types of probation systems administered in the United States? Describe each.
13. Should probation services be placed within the judicial or the executive branch of government? Defend your answer.
14. What are the two basic models of parole administration?

Deliberate and Decide

Prison Policy Options

Your state's prison population has risen dramatically since the early 1990s, with much of the growth being attributable to changes in criminal justice policy during the previous three decades. As a result, your state is now experiencing a rapid rise in per capita cost of incarceration, making it very expensive to operate and maintain the prison system; increasingly crowded conditions (which can negatively affect inmate misconduct) have resulted, and there has been an increase in the inmate-to-staff ratio (increasing from

4.1 to 5.2 inmates per staff member in the past few years). Furthermore, crowding takes a toll on the prison system's infrastructure, further exacerbating maintenance costs. Your governor has chosen to consider a variety of policy options to address the issues resulting from this growth.

Consider what types of data and program information you would need if asked to investigate the following policy options, as well as how you might measure any outcomes. Where possible, determine which, if any, policy options you would endorse, and *why* or *why not.*

Questions for Discussion

1. Expanding the capacity of your prison system (to include construction of new facilities and adding staffing): Can you "sell" the construction costs to relevant politicians and the public?
2. Investing in more in rehabilitative programs: Can academic and vocational education, work programs, and substance abuse treatment programs reduce recidivism?
3. Placing some inmates in private prisons: Can private facilities incarcerate inmates at a lower cost and provide adequate services?
4. Changing the state's existing sentencing policies: Will some or all mandatory minimum penalties be repealed?
5. Greater use of alternatives to incarceration: Do house arrest, electronic monitoring, intensive supervision, boot camps, day reporting centers, fines, and community service work?
6. Expanding use of residential reentry centers: Can more inmates with short sentences who are deemed to be low security risks be placed into such transitional halfway houses?
7. Expanding good time credits: To slow or reduce prison growth, can you use such approaches as reducing a nonviolent inmate's sentence by up to 1 year if the inmate participates in residential substance abuse treatment and other rehabilitative programs? What do current laws allow?[157]

Learn by Doing

1. As part of a criminal justice honor society paper to be presented at a national conference, you are examining the role of local jails. Considering the diagram of the flow of the justice system process in the front matter of this book, as well as this chapter's discussion about jails, at which point(s) would you argue that jails become involved and contribute to the overall functions of the criminal justice system? How does the direct supervision jail concept apply to these functions?
2. Your criminal justice professor has assigned a class debate wherein class members are to determine which court decision within *each* of three amendments—the Fourth, Fifth, and Sixth—is the most important right therein granted to inmates. You are to analyze those three amendments and explain and defend your decision.
3. Your criminal justice professor is concerned because it seems that students know relatively little about the general functions and organizational attributes of probation and parole agencies. As an upper-division criminal justice student, she asks you to prepare a short presentation on that topic for the coming "Career Day" program offered each year by the faculty. What will you say?
4. You are a criminal justice professor teaching a course on corrections. The week you are planning to discuss the prisoner issues associated with supermax and other high-security institutions, a significant escape occurs from the state's maximum-security institution. The public is furious and you recognize that your students may have very strong opinions especially given the circumstances. Do you still follow through with the scheduled topic? Does the recent escape affect how you would discuss the issues of supermax prisons and inmate health? How so?

Case Study

From Jail Redesign to Prison Redesign

A corrections advisor and architect has been asked to assist a state in designing a new prison, as the current facilities are presently suffering from overcrowding and are falling into disrepair. Most are arranged in the traditional correctional layout: long horizontal corridors with bars in front of each cell. Problems with this design include poor sightlines for supervising officers, inability to monitor inmates effectively, and the potential for unwitnessed abuse. Legislators and corrections administrators want to address these shortcomings in the new facility by building off of currently popular ideas regarding the design of county jails, namely direct supervision jails and community jails. Benefits of a nontraditional design for prisons include community building, better supervision capabilities by staff, and better spaces for treatment services.

Questions for Discussion

1. Which of the three types of facility layouts, if any, discussed in this chapter should be chosen for this prison? Would it depend on the type of institution (minimum vs. medium vs. maximum security prison)? How will the type of jurisdiction that the facility will serve influence your decision?
2. Are some types of layouts better suited to certain types of offenders? Which are those, and why are they uniquely beneficial for COs in those situations?
3. What is it about community jails that could benefit prison inmates? How should this be incorporated into prison design?

Notes

1. Allen J. Beck, Marcus Berzofsky, Rachel Kaspar, and Christopher Krebs, "Sexual Victimization in Prisons and Jails Reported by Inmates, 2011–12" Bureau of Justice Statistics, December 9, 2014, https://www.bjs.gov/content/pub/pdf/svpjri1112.pdf.
2. Bureau of Justice Statistics, "Percent Distribution of Employment and Payrolls for the Justice System by Level of Government," Table 2, jeeus1002.csv, July 1, 2014, http://www.bjs.gov/index.cfm?ty=pbdetail&iid=4679.
3. For a cost breakdown, see Vera Institute of Justice, *The Price of Prisons: What Incarceration Costs Taxpayers*, January 2012, p. 6, http://www.vera.org/sites/default/files/resources/downloads/Price_of_Prisons_updated_version_072512.pdf.
4. United States Bureau of Prisons. *Annual Determination of Average Cost of Incarceration,* July 19, 2016, https://www.federalregister.gov/
5. Bureau of Justice Statistics, *Correctional Populations in the United States, 2015* (December 2016), p. 2.
6. Andrew D. Leipold, "The Collateral Benefits of Declaring War on Social Issues," *The Journal of Gender, Race, and Justice* 15(2) (2012): 231–255.
7. Kevin Johnson, "Toughness on Crime Gives Way to Fairness, Cost Reality," *USA Today,* March 30, 2014, http://www.usatoday.com/story/news/nation/2014/03/30/tough-crime-fairness-cost/6836605/.
8. Ibid.
9. Vincent A. Giordano, "Public Acceptance for Drug Treatment in Lieu of Incarceration for Drug Offenders in Florida," *Journal of Drug Issues* 44(4) (2014): 414–429.
10. Johnson, "Toughness on Crime Gives Way to Fairness, Cost Reality."
11. Brian Mann, "Governor Cuomo Says He Will Close More State Prisons," *North County Public Radio*, January 11, 2016, https://www.northcountrypublicradio.org/news/story/30633/20160111/governor-cuomo-says-he-will-close-more-state-prisons.
12. Lydia O'Connor, "Landmark California Law Has Released Nearly 3,000 Inmates," *Huffington Post*, March 6, 2016, http://www.huffingtonpost.com/2015/03/06/california-prop-47-releases_n_6819242.html.
13. See William J. Newman and Charles L. Scott, "*Brown v. Plata*: Prison Overcrowding in California," *Journal of the American Academy of Psychiatry Law* 40(4) (December 2012): 547–552, http://www.jaapl.org/content/40/4/547.full.
14. Tom Jackman, "Mass Reduction of California Prison Population Didn't Cause Rise in Crime, Two Studies Find," *The Washington Post*, May 18, 2016, https://www.washingtonpost.com/news/true-crime/wp/2016/05/18/mass-release-of-california-prisoners-didnt-cause-rise-in-crime-two-studies-find/?utm_term=.806886593499.
15. Robert Martinson, "What Works? Questions and Answers about Prison Reform," *The Public Interest* 35 (1974): 22–54.
16. T. Paul Louis and Jerry R. Sparger, "Treatment Modalities within Prison," in John W. Murphy and Jack E. Dison (eds.), *Are Prisons Any Better? Twenty Years of Correctional Reform* (Newbury Park, CA: Sage, 1990), p. 148.
17. Ibid., p. 149.
18. Jackman, "Mass Reduction of California Prison Population Didn't Cause Rise in Crime, Two Studies Find."
19. Ibid.
20. Ibid.
21. Richard P. Seiter, *Correctional Administration: Integrating Theory and Practice* (Upper Saddle River, NJ: Prentice Hall, 2002), p. 11.
22. Per Ake Nylander, Claes Holm, Elma Jukic, and Odd Lindberg, "Drug Treatment in Swedish Prisons—Moving Towards Evidence-Based Interventions?" *Nordic Studies on Alcohol and Drugs* 29(6) (2012): 561–574.
23. Jouni Tourunen, Antti Weckroth, and Teemu Kaskela, "Prison-Based Drug Treatment in Finland: History, Shifts in Policy Making and Current Status," *Nordic Studies on Alcohol and Drugs* 29(6) (2012): 575–588.
24. Michigan Department of Corrections, "Mission, Vision, Values," http://www.michigan.gov/corrections/0,4551,7-119-62761_62788-5428–,00.html.
25. Seiter, *Correctional Administration*, p. 192.
26. Ibid., p. 189.
27. Ibid., pp. 190–191.
28. Robert Levinson, "Try Softer," in Robert Johnson and Hans Toch (eds.), *The Pains of Imprisonment* (Beverly Hills, CA: Sage, 1982), p. 246.
29. New CASA* Report Finds 65% of All U.S. Inmates Meet Medical Criteria for Substance Abuse Addiction, Only 11% Receive Any Treatment, February 26, 2010, http://www.centeronaddiction.org.

30. Louis and Sparger, "Treatment Modalities within Prison," pp. 147–162.
31. Bureau of Justice Statistics, *HIV in Prisons, 2001–2010* (September 2012), pp. 1–2, http://www.bjs.gov/content/pub/pdf/hivp10.pdf.
32. James A. Inciardi, *Criminal Justice,* 7th ed. (Fort Worth, TX: Harcourt Brace, 2001), p. 454.
33. James J. Stephan, "Census of State and Federal Correctional Facilities, 2005," U.S. Department of Justice, Bureau of Justice Statistics (October 2008), p. 4.
34. Ibid., p. 5.
35. Ibid., p. 194.
36. CASA Report, Ibid.
37. Mary E. Mastrorilli, Personal Communication, September 1, 2010.
38. Chris Boyette and Darran Simon, "Delaware Corrections Officers Held Hostage at Prison," February 2, 2017, http://www.cnn.com/2017/02/01/us/delaware-prison-standoff/.
39. United States Bureau of Prisons, *Unit Management Manual* (Washington, DC: Author, 1977), p. 6.
40. Seiter, *Correctional Administration,* p. 196.
41. Stephan, "Census of State and Federal Correctional Facilities, 2005," p. 6.
42. See, for example, a description of prison industries as operated by the California Prison Industry Authority, http://pia.ca.gov/About_PIA/mission.aspx.
43. U.S. Department of Justice, National Institute of Justice, *Work in American Prisons: Joint Ventures with the Private Sector* (Washington, DC: U.S. Government Printing Office, 1995), pp. 2–3.
44. ABCNews.go.com, "How to Survive a Supermax Prison," http://abcnews.go.com/TheLaw/Story?id=3435989&page=1.
45. CNN.com/U.S., "Reporters Get First Look inside Mysterious Supermax Prison," http://www.cnn.com/2007/US/09/13/supermax.btsc/index.html.
46. Daniel P. Mears, *Evaluating the Effectiveness of Supermax Prisons*, Urban Institute, Justice Policy Center (June 2005).
47. Craig Haney, "Mental Health Issues in Long-term Solitary and 'Supermax' Confinement," *Crime & Delinquency* 49(1) (January 2003): 124–156.
48. Christie Thompson, "Another Kind of Isolation," *The Marshall Project*, January 28, 2015, https://www.themarshallproject.org/2015/01/28/another-kind-of-isolation#.4sX8SodY5.
49. See Daniel P. Mears, Christina Mancini, Kevin M. Beaver, and Marc Gertz, "Housing for the 'Worst of the Worst' Inmates: Public Support for Supermax Prisons," *Crime & Delinquency* 59(4) (June 2014): 587–615. This survey of about 1,300 adults in Florida found that more than 80 percent of respondents supported supermax prisons; however, the support declined to 60 percent when there was no expectation of public-safety benefit; furthermore, 70 percent did not believe supermaxes are inhumane.
50. See, however, Ibid.
51. Sharon Shalev, "Solitary Confinement and Supermax Prisons: A Human Rights and Ethical Analysis," *Journal of Forensic Psychology Practice* 11(2/3) (2011): 151–183; also see Jesenia Pizarro and Vanja M. K. Stenius, "Supermax Prisons: Their Rise, Current Practices, and Effect on Inmates," *The Prison Journal* 84(2) (June 2004): 248–264.
52. Mears et al., "Housing for the 'Worst of the Worst' Inmates."
53. Hager, "My Life in the Supermax | The Marshall Project."
54. *Madrid v. Gomez,* 889 F. Supp. 1146 (1995).
55. 37. F. Supp. 1265 (1980).
56. 374. F.3d 541 (7th Cir. 2004), p. 1118.
57. *Cunningham v. Federal Bureau of Prisons*, Civil Rights Litigation Clearinghouse, University of Michigan, https://www.clearinghouse.net/detail.php?id=12177.
58. Jesenia M. Pizarro, Vanja M. K. Stenius, and Travis C. Pratt, "Supermax Prisons: Myths, Realities, and the Politics of Punishment in American Society," *Criminal Justice Policy Review* 17(1) (March 2006): 6–21.
59. Ibid.
60. Shira E. Gordon, "Solitary Confinement, Public Safety, and Recidivism," *University of Michigan Journal of Law Reform*, 47(2) (2014): 495–528.
61. Haney, "Mental Health Issues in Long-term Solitary and 'Supermax' Confinement," p. 150.
62. See, for example, Mears et al., "Housing for the 'Worst of the Worst' Inmates."
63. Jacob McCleland, "The High Costs of High Security at Supermax Prisons," *National Public Radio*, June 19, 2012, http://www.npr.org/2012/06/19/155359553/the-high-costs-of-high-security-at-supermax-prisons.
64. *Ruffin v. Commonwealth*, 62 Va. 790 (1871).
65. *Price v. Johnston*, 334 U.S. 266, 144 F.2d 260 (1948).
66. *Turner v. Safley*, 482 U.S. 78 (1987).
67. *Cooper v. Pate*, 378 U.S. 546, 384 S. Ct. 1733 (1964).
68. *Johnson v. Avery*, 393 U.S. 483, 89 S. Ct. 747 (1969).
69. *Bounds v. Smith*, 430 U.S. 817, 97 S. Ct. 1491 (1977).
70. *Lewis v. Casey*, (94-1511), 516 U.S. 804 (1996).
71. *Cruz v. Beto*, 405 U.S. 319, 92 S. Ct. 1079 (1972).
72. Religion Clause, January 15, 2012, http://religionclause.blogspot.com/2012/01/recent-prisoner-free-exercise-cases_15.html.
73. *Procunier v. Martinez*, 416 U.S. 396, 94 S. Ct. 1800 (1974).
74. *Bell v. Wolfish*, 441 US 520, 99 S. Ct. 1861 (1979).
75. *Rhodes v. Chapman,* 452 U.S. 337 (1981).
76. *Estelle v. Gamble*, 429 U.S. 974, 97 S. Ct. 285 (1976).
77. "*Estelle v. Gamble*," *Oyez*, https://www.oyez.org/cases/1976/75-929.
78. *Overton v. Bazzetta*, 539 U.S. 126 S. Ct 02-94 (2003)
79. *Wolff v. McDonnell*, 418 U.S. 539, 394 S. Ct. 296 (1974).
80. *Wilkinson v. Austin*, 543 US 1032, S. Ct. 04-495 (2005)
81. Greg Shtraks, "The List: The World's Most Notorious Prisons," *Foreign Policy*, January 21, 2009, http://www.foreignpolicy.com/articles/2009/01/20/the_list_the_worlds_most_notorious_prisons.
82. "The Ten Worst Prisons in the World," http://www.thetoptenworld.com/violent_prisons.html.
83. See 42 U.S.C. § (1997).

84. U.S. Department of Justice Office, "Rights of Persons Confined to Jails and Prisons: Overview," http://www.justice.gov/crt/about/spl/corrections.php.
85. U.S. Department of Justice Office of Legislative Affairs, *Department of Justice Activities Under the Civil Rights of Institutionalized Persons Act, Fiscal Year 2011* (March 28, 2012), pp. 4–9, November 2, 2014, http://www.justice.gov/crt/about/spl/documents/split_cripa11.pdf.
86. Timothy J. Flanagan and Kathleen Maguire (eds.), *Sourcebook of Criminal Justice Statistics 1991* (Washington, DC: U.S. Government Printing Office, 1992), p. 555.
87. Ibid. Also see Kathleen Maguire and Ann L. Pastore (eds.), *Sourcebook of Criminal Justice Statistics 1995* (Washington, DC: U.S. Government Printing Office, 1996), p. 177.
88. Jim Thomas, Kathy Harris, and Devin Keeler, "Issues and Misconceptions in Prisoner Litigation," *Criminology* 24 (1987): 901–919.
89. Jim Thomas, "Repackaging the Data: The 'Reality' of Prisoner Litigation," *New England Journal of Criminal and Civil Confinement* 15 (1989): 195–230.
90. Ibid., p. 50.
91. Jennifer A. Puplava, "Peanut Butter and the Prison Litigation Reform Act," http://www.law.indiana.edu/ilj.v73/no1/puplava.html.
92. Faces of Lawsuit Abuse, "Former Inmate Alleges Kardashians, Rapper Kanye West Conspired with Terrorists (June 26, 2012), http://www.facesoflawsuitabuse.org/2012/06/former-inmate-alleges-kardashians-rapper-kanye-west-conspired-with-terrorists/.
93. Francis X. Cline, "Prisons Run Out of Cells, Money and Choices," *New York Times,* May 28, 1993, p. B7.
94. Associated Press, "Lawsuit over Michigan Inmate Death Settled for $3.25 Million," November 20, 2010, http://blog.mlive.com/grpress/2008/07/lawsuit_over_michigan_inmate_d.html.
95. Libby Sander, "Inmate's Death in Solitary Cell Prompts Judge to Ban Restraints," *The New York Times,* November 20, 2014, http://www.nytimes.com/2006/11/15/us/15prison.html.
96. 107 S. Ct. 2254 (1987), at 2254.
97. 111 S. Ct. 2321 (1991).
98. 115 S. Ct. 2321 (1995), at 2293.
99. Linda Greenhouse, "High Court Makes It Harder for Prisoners to Sue," *New York Times,* June 20, 1995, p. A11.
100. Public Law No. 104–134, 110 Stat. 1321 [codified as amended in scattered sections of 18 U.S.C., 28 U.S.C., and 42 U.S.C.] (1996).
101. See 141 *Congressional Record* S14,413 (daily ed., September 27, 1995), Senator Robert Dole's statement in his introduction of the PLRA as a bill to the Senate. Senator Dole provided other examples of the frivolous litigation that he felt the PLRA was needed to cure: "insufficient storage locker space, a defective haircut by a prison barber, [and] the failure of prison officials to invite a prisoner to a pizza party for a departing prison employee."
102. American Civil Liberties Union, "The Prison Litigation Reform Act (PLRA)," http://www.aclu.org/Prisons/Prisons.cfm?ID=14379&=26.
103. FindLaw, "Prison Litigation Reform Act," http://criminal.findlaw.com/criminal-rights/prison-litigation-reform-act.html.
104. Margo Schlanger, "Trends in Prisoner Litigation, as the PLRA Enters Adulthood," September 28, 2015, https://www.prisonlegalnews.org/.
105. Ibid.
106. Peter Wagner and Bernadette Rabuy, "Mass Incarceration: The Whole Pie 2016," *Prison Policy Initiative*, May 14, 2016, https://www.prisonpolicy.org/reports/pie2016.html.
107. Todd D. Minton and Zhen Zeng, *Jail Inmates in 2015* (Bureau of Justice Statistics, December 2016), p. 1.
108. For example, see James M. Moynahan and Earle K. Stewart, *The American Jail: Its Development and Growth* (Chicago, IL: Nelson-Hall, 1980), p. 100; Clemens Bartollas, Stuart J. Miller, and Paul B. Wice, *Participants in American Criminal Justice: The Promise and the Performance* (Upper Saddle River, NJ: Prentice Hall, 1983), p. 59.
109. J. Moore, "Prison Litigation and the States: A Case Law Review," *State Legislative Report* 8 (1981):1.
110. National Sheriffs' Association, *The State of Our Nation's Jails, 1982* (Washington, DC: Author, 1982), p. 55.
111. Mary K. Stohr and Anthony Walsh, *Corrections: The Essentials*, 2nd ed. (Thousand Oaks, CA: Sage, 2016), p.110.
112. Linda L. Zupan, *Jails: Reform and the New Generation Philosophy* (Cincinnati, OH: Anderson, 1991), p. 71.
113. Christine Tartaro, "Examining Implementation Issues with New Generation Jails," *Criminal Justice Policy Review* 13 (2002): 219–237.
114. U.S. Department of Justice, National Institute of Justice, *Direct Supervision Jails: 2006 Yearbook* (Longmont, CO: National Institute of Corrections Information Center, 2006), p. viii.
115. Gerald J. Bayens, Jimmy J. Williams, and John O. Smykla, "Jail Type Makes a Difference: Evaluating the Transition from a Traditional to a Podular, Direct Supervision Jail across Ten Years," *American Jails* 11(2) (1997): 32–39.
116. Ibid.
117. Ibid.
118. R. Yocum, J. Anderson, T. DaVigo, and S. Lee, "Direct-supervision and Remote-supervision Jails: A Comparative Study of Psychosocial Factors," *Journal of Applied Social Psychology* 36(7) (2006): 1790–1812.
119. Stohr and Walsh, *Corrections*, p. 111.
120. Ibid.
121. Ibid.
122. National Institute of Corrections, "Transition to Jail to Community (TJC)," https://nicic.gov/jailttransition.
123. Ibid.

124. *Maryland v. King, Oyez*, https://www.oyez.org/cases/2012/12-207.
125. Ibid.
126. See *Maryland v. King*, 12–207 (2013).
127. American Correctional Association, "Standards & Accreditation," http://www.aca.org/standards.faq.asp.
128. Ibid.
129. Ibid.
130. Belinda McCarthy and Bernard McCarthy, quoted in Howard Abadinsky, *Probation and Parole: Theory and Practice,* 7th ed. (Upper Saddle River, NJ: Prentice Hall, 2000), p. 196.
131. Todd R. Clear, "Punishment and Control in Community Supervision," in Clayton A. Hartjen and Edward E. Rhine (eds.), *Correctional Theory and Practice* (Chicago, IL: Nelson-Hall, 1992), pp. 31–42.
132. See the President's Commission on Law Enforcement and Administration of Justice, *Task Force Report: Corrections* (Washington, DC: U.S. Government Printing Office, 1967), p. 7
133. Bureau of Justice Statistics, *Probation and Parole in the United States, 2015* (December 2016), pp. 1–2, http://www.bjs.gov/content/pub/pdf/ppus15.pdf.
134. See, for example, the state of California Model Penal Code Section 830–832.17, which defines the following persons as peace officers: the office of attorney general special agents and investigators, deputy sheriffs, certain corrections employees (e.g., jail, prison, probation and parole), highway patrol troopers, campus police, fish and game employees, forestry and alcoholic beverage control agents, and state fair marshals; at: http://www.leginfo.ca.gov/cgi-bin/displaycode?section=pen&group=00001-01000&file=830-832.17.
135. Sarah Scarborough, "Parole Abolition—Did It Work?" March 14, 2015, http://sarahscarbrough.com/news/parole-abolition-did-it-work/.
136. American Probation and Parole Association, "Position Statement: Weapons," https://www.appa-net.org/eweb/Dynamicpage.aspx?site=APPA_2&webcode=IB_PositionStatement&wps_key=e2e80331-3bed-4d64-a044-ea98ee53bd17.
137. Shawn E. Small and Sam Torres, "Arming Probation Officers: Enhancing Public Confidence and Officer Safety," *Federal Probation* 65(3) (2001): 24–28.
138. Seiter, *Correctional Administration,* p. 387.
139. Small and Torres, "Arming Probation Officers," p. 27.
140. American Probation and Parole Association, *Adult and Juvenile Probation and Parole National Firearm Survey,* 2nd ed., October 2006, http://www.appanet.org/eweb/Resources/Surveys/National_Firearms/docs/NFS_2006.pdf.
141. Barry J. Nidorf, "Community Corrections: Turning the Crowding Crisis into Opportunities," *Corrections Today* (October 1989): 82–88.
142. Howard Abadinsky, *Probation and Parole: Theory and Practice*, 5th ed. (Englewood Cliffs, NJ: Prentice Hall, 1994), p. 104.
143. Ibid., p. 57.
144. Ibid., pp. 104–105.
145. Ibid., pp. 106–107.
146. See President's Commission, *Task Force Report,* pp. 35–37.
147. Abadinsky, *Probation and Parole,* p. 107.
148.. Eric Trist, "On Socio-Technical Systems," in Kenneth Benne and Robert Chin (eds.), *The Planning of Change,* 2nd ed. (New York: Holt, Rinehart and Winston, 1969), pp. 269–281.
149. Daniel Katz and Robert I. Kahn, *The Social Psychology of Organizations* (New York: John Wiley & Sons, 1966).
150. Patricia L. Hardyman, "Management Styles in Probation: Policy Implications Derived from Systems Theory," in Clayton A. Hartjen and Edward E. Rhine (eds.), *Correctional Theory and Practice* (Chicago, IL: Nelson-Hall, 1992), p. 68.
151. Angela Hawken and Mark Kleiman, "Managing Drug Involved Probationers with Swift and Certain Sanctions: Evaluating Hawaii's HOPE National Institute of Justice," December 2, 2009, p. 4, https://www.ncjrs.gov/pdffiles1/nij/grants/229023.pdf; also see Steve Lopez, "Hawaii Finds Success with Tough-Love Approach to Repeat Offenders," *Los Angeles Times*, December 1, 2012, http://hopehawaii.net/assets/la-times-total.pdf (accessed December 4, 2014).
152. Abadinsky, *Probation and Parole,* p. 223.
153. Ibid.
154. National Advisory Commission on Criminal Justice Standards and Goals, *Corrections* (Washington, DC: U.S. Government Printing Office, 1973), pp. 396–397.
155. President's Commission, *Task Force Report,* p. 71.
156. Ibid.
157. Adapted from Nathan James, *The Federal Prison Population Buildup: Overview, Policy Changes, Issues, and Options*, Congressional Research Service, January 22, 2014 (accessed October 2, 2014), https://digital.library.unt.edu/ark:/67531/metadc287931/m1/1/high_res_d/R42937_2014Apr15.pdf.

Egd/Shutterstock

11 Corrections Personnel Roles and Functions

LEARNING OBJECTIVES

After reading this chapter, the student will be able to:

1. *describe in general the duties of prison, jail, and probation and parole administrators and their employees*
2. *review the type of training that is available to new wardens to help them be successful and the principles of good prison leadership*
3. *review the basic responsibilities of prison wardens in carrying out executions*
4. *describe the responsibilities of middle managers and supervisors*
5. *relate the duties and types of correctional officers*
6. *delineate and describe several key issues for, and practices of, prison administrators, to include achieving racial balance, managing staff deviance, and maintaining appropriate staff–inmate relationships*
7. *explain how jail administrators can motivate and retain jail employees*

8 *review probation administrators' management styles*

9 *discuss the kinds of organizational stressors that can occur and cause depression, low job satisfaction, and high attrition among corrections employees, and some measures to be taken to deal with it*

Introduction

The 1994 movie *Shawshank Redemption* depicts prison life during a 20-year period beginning in 1947 and centers around its title character, Andy Dufresne, who is convicted of murdering his wife and her lover. The film features multiple transgressions among inmates, as well as those of prison administrators and correctional officers (COs). Warden Samuel Norton eventually takes his own life, but prior to this appears to have little control over Shawshank Prison, a facility that he supposedly runs. During the course of the movie, we see contraband running through the prison by an inmate, Red; a particularly brutal CO, Hadley; and Warden Norton himself, engaged in a money-making scheme, as well as facilitating the murder of another inmate, Tommy. Prison administration at Shawshank is at its worst. But as we shall cover in this chapter, Hollywood's depiction of prison management (or lack thereof) is unlikely to be anywhere near reality.

This chapter focuses on the role and functions of personnel who work within correctional institutions and in probation and parole agencies. Presented first is a profile of prison wardens, including means of preparing new wardens for the position, principles of good prison leadership, and the administrator's role in carrying out death sentences. Next, we cover the roles of correctional middle managers and supervisors, and following that we examine the front-line personnel in prisons: COs. This section includes a typology of the types of COs in terms of their overall job performance. Then, we consider the "cousins" of prisons, the local jails: the functions of the jail administrator, motivating and retaining jail personnel, and some problems in selecting and keeping people who will want detention work to be their career. Next, we consider administrative functions and management styles as they relate to probation and parole. The chapter concludes with review questions and exercises in the Deliberate and Decide, Learn by Doing, and Case Study sections.

Before examining these personnel who work within corrections, it is important to bear in mind that correctional facilities constitute a society within a society; as such, a wide range of personnel are employed therein. As examples, a typical prison employs food service workers, skilled tradesmen (e.g., carpenters and electricians), teachers, secretaries, chaplains, nurses, mental health clinicians, computer technicians, and recreation personnel.

Even more importantly, as mentioned in Chapter 10, remember that whether or not one wears a correction officer's uniform, *everyone's* job is to be security oriented. As former corrections administrator Mary Ellen Mastrorilli puts it:

> Nurses must double and triple check their syringe counts to ensure that syringes do not end up in the hands of an inmate. Catholic priests must substitute grape juice for wine when saying Mass, as alcohol is prohibited inside prison walls. Carpenters must carefully account for each and every one of their tools during the work day. A hacksaw in the hands of an inmate can mean a future escape or a deadly assault. Every secretary's desk is home to a pair of scissors or a letter opener, but not so in a prison. A prison chef must keep track of all kitchen utensils, especially cutlery, because metal objects can be easily fashioned into shanks (homemade prison knives).[1]

Finally, before discussing corrections administration, we need to mention two basic principles that undergird corrections administration: First, whatever the reasons for which a person is incarcerated, he or she is not to suffer pains beyond the deprivation of liberty—confinement itself is the punishment. Second, regardless of the crime, the prisoner must be treated humanely and in accordance with his or her behavior. Even the most heinous offender is to be treated with respect and dignity and given privileges if institutional behavior warrants it.[2] Our analysis of institutional management is predicated on these two principles.

▶ Prisons

The Warden: A Profile

warden the person responsible for all activities, safety, and security of the staff and inmates within a prison.

Several guest corrections speakers in one of the author's criminal justice administration classes have argued that the prison **warden**—that person who is responsible for all activities, safety, and security of the staff and inmates within the prison, to include establishing prison policies and carrying out financial and programming goals—has the most difficult position of all in the corrections field.[3] This assessment is arguably true because the warden must also take the central office and prison director's general policies and put them into effect throughout the prison, while being responsible for the smooth day-to-day operation of the institution. These correctional executives also oversee the fastest-growing agencies in state government; administer increasingly visible operations; and are held accountable by politicians, auditors, the press, organized labor, and numerous other stakeholders.[4] Wardens work within a field that has become more demanding, consumes an increasing share of public funds, and involves responsibility for the lives and safety of others.

IN THEIR OWN WORDS

ADMINISTRATIVE ADVICE FROM THE FIELD

Name: Robert Bayer, Ph.D.

Current position/City/State: Former director of Corrections/Warden/Inspector General, other related positions, State of Nevada

College attended/academic major/degree(s): University of Nevada, Reno: Ph.D., political science/public administration; master of public administration (MPA); master of arts, English literature. University of New York, College at Oswego, bachelor of arts in liberal arts.

My primary duties and responsibilities in this position include: functioning as the CEO of a very large public organization. Unlike a warden, who administers departmental policy, the director is responsible for the actual promulgation and oversight of the department's policies and procedures. It is important to operate a constitutional prison within the budget provided by the legislature and the policies and procedures are the lynchpin to accomplish this duty. The director is responsible for the overall departmental budget development, legislative passage, and ongoing implementation throughout the budget calendar. The director also provides testimony during the legislative session, presents to the Board of Prison Commissioners, and provides key testimony on policies, procedures, and actions of the department in state and federal court as required. As one of the senior cabinet members for the governor, an essential responsibility is to function as part of the governor's cabinet and ensure that there is an efficient and effective flow of information between the governor and the department. The director must be an effective communicator and this takes up much of the average working day at every level including inmates, inmate families, victims and victim groups, interested stakeholder groups, legislators, staff and staff organizations, the courts, and the media. One of the key divisions reporting directly to the director is the human resources division, which recognizes the critical importance of every level of staff recruitment, hiring, training, and benefits. The inspector general of the system reports directly to the director to ensure that all levels of staff and inmate investigations are being properly conducted and brought to a timely conclusion. It is important to develop a span of control that is practical and provides you with the proper level of control and oversight over the entire system in order to accomplish all of these duties and responsibilities.

Personal attributes/characteristics that have proven to be most helpful to me in this position are:

Top Ten:

1. Intelligence. It may be a trait we are born with, but it is essential at this level because of the constant multitasking and complexity of decisions that must be made.
2. Integrity. Demonstrate a strong moral ethic. Always do the right thing, even when no one is looking. Staff looks to you as true north on their compass even though they may not say it.
3. A sense of fairness to everyone, the public, legislators, staff, and inmates alike.
4. Commitment to the position. Demonstrate a strong work ethic that includes reliability, willingness to take on more important assignments, and the stamina to work long hours.
5. Develop a reputation for loyalty and trust.
6. Assertiveness and tenacity while remaining open to criticism and new ideas.
7. An absolute passion for the field of corrections. This attitude is infectious with staff. Love every assignment and learn as much as you can from every position you work. It all goes into a valuable database in your brain that you will rely on during critical times and emergency situations.
8. Be honest, approachable, and always tell the truth to staff, politicians, and even the inmate population. Your reputation for diligence and honesty will really help develop a solid rapport with the inmate population, which is always important.
9. Cooperate with all stakeholders in this field. Ensure that they all feel welcomed at the discussion table, even if their constituency holds opposite opinions.
10. A sense of humor is critical in a field like this that is rife with tensions and life-altering decisions.

My three greatest challenges in this administrative role include: (1) the operation of a constitutional prison system in the face of dwindling and scarce fiscal resources; (2) the nurturing, maintaining, and developing good political relationships with all legislative and executive branch stakeholders; (3) the hiring, training, and retention of sufficient professional and law enforcement staff to ensure the seamless operation of a state prison system.

Personal accomplishments during my administrative career about which I am most proud are:

- The first privatization of a prison in Nevada: the women's correctional center in Las Vegas. It stood for years as one of the best examples of a privatization contract in the nation.
- The appointment by first a Democratic governor and then a Republican governor.
- The first director of corrections ever promoted from within the Nevada system and subsequent to retirement, three of my top level staff were appointed to director in succession. Nevada has not had to look outside the system for talented, well-trained, and well-qualified administrative appointments.
- No staff ever died or sustained serious life-altering injury while on duty during my watch. Staff safety was always a paramount concern. The department experienced a steady decline in industrial injury claims and expenditures from the first year to the last year of my employment as director.
- The longest serving director in Nevada's 150-year history.

Advice for someone who is interested in occupying an administrative position such as mine would be: to take a long-term view of a position such as this. Corrections is a field that takes a lot of actual experience in a wide variety of positions, to gain the necessary experience to make good decisions, especially in emergency situations. I would urge anyone interested in becoming a director or commissioner of corrections to become a "triple threat" in these areas: operations, programming, and budget. In addition, here are some milestones to accomplish:

- Develop a mentor relationship with a top-level role model who will take an active interest in your education and advancement through the system.
- Obtain an advanced education, because that is a characteristic that is found in most current directors. A master's degree should be considered a minimal criterion. Never forget, however, that

this is an experience-based field and it is critical to develop a thorough operational knowledge of the laws, policies, and procedures of the system. Remember that when you attain the position of director, "the buck stops here," and it is important to make final decisions with the confidence of a complete experience-based background.

- Study the budget and learn in great detail how to build and execute a budget within appropriations.
- Develop excellent written and verbal skills. Again, be a good communicator.
- Be a student of politics and develop the political connections needed for support when a governor begins to search for the next director of corrections.
- Develop your leadership skills throughout your career. They should improve with every promotion that you receive. Although there are certain characteristics of leadership that a person is born with, leadership is a skill that can be learned and one should read and study management and leadership throughout their career.

Source: Used with permission from Robert Bayer.

Of course, both staff and inmates are sensitive to the warden's granting of what each side perceives to be a strengthened position for the other side. For example, if a policy is enacted that gives the staff more power over inmates, the inmates will be unhappy, perhaps even rebellious; conversely, if a policy is put into practice that the staff thinks affords too much additional freedom to inmates, the staff will feel sold out. Furthermore, the prison director, typically appointed by and serving at the pleasure of the state's governor, can exert on the warden all manner of political influences at any time.

Who are prison wardens? A national survey of wardens was commissioned by the National Institute of Corrections (NIC) in 2013, which sheds some light on who wardens are. A total of 326 wardens responded to the survey representing a total of 43 states.[5] Of the surveyed wardens, the mean number of years they have been working in the corrections field was 26.65, indicating considerable, relevant experience among the top leaders in correctional institutions. Seventy-eight percent of the wardens indicated they were male, while 22 percent were female. The average age of the surveyed wardens was 51.72 years. The minority of wardens possessed an earned associate's degree or less (28%), while the majority of wardens possessed a bachelor's degree (51%) or higher (21%).[6] Seventy-seven percent of wardens identified as Caucasian, another 18 percent as black, and 4 percent as Hispanic.

A national survey by Kim et al.[7] of more than 600 male and female prison wardens at adult state prisons suggested some interesting differences between male and female wardens. Regarding the goals of imprisonment, male wardens ranked their four preferred goals as follows: incapacitation, deterrence, rehabilitation, and retribution. Female wardens, however, ranked them thus: incapacitation, rehabilitation, deterrence, and retribution. A greater proportion of female wardens (89.9%) than male wardens (83.3%) strongly or very strongly agreed that rehabilitation programs had an important place in their institutions. A majority of the wardens thought that the following amenities should be reduced or eliminated in prisons: martial arts instruction, conjugal visitation, cosmetic surgery and dentistry, condom distribution, disability benefits, sexually oriented reading material, and nonregulation clothing. Male wardens were more likely than female wardens to support the reduction of college education, copy privileges, condom distribution, a full-time recreation director, musical instruments, and special diets. By contrast, female wardens were more likely to support reduction of organ transplants, weight lifting, boxing, and tobacco smoking. Generally, data support the findings that female wardens seem more likely to reduce amenities that can potentially promote violence in prison and are more interested than male wardens in the health conditions of inmates. Overall, Kim et al. concluded that although the differences between male and female wardens are somewhat noticeable, the roles of corrections administrators are becoming more gender neutral.[8]

Preparing New Wardens for Success

The nature of, and issues posed by today's incarcerated population, discussed in Chapter 12, has increased the need for competent correctional administrators to ensure public safety, ensure that staff and inmates are safe, and spend tax dollars effectively. They must also understand and appreciate the importance of culture (the sum total of the organization's history, staff, inmates, community, and past leadership) as they begin their tenure at an institution. Today's correctional administrator must excel in more than just correctional operations and not rely on the all-powerful, autocratic working style and strong paramilitary organization of decades past.[9]

In fact, in the 2013 national survey of wardens, there was widespread agreement regarding a variety of necessary skills and abilities to be a successful warden.[10] These include the following: capability of identifying emerging trends in correction; capability to assure organizational accountability; capability to assure compliance with legal mandates; capability to assure ethical decision making; capability to assess/manage organizational culture; capability to resolve organizational conflicts; capability to guide organizational change; capability to manage human resources; capability to plan for future leadership/management needs; capability to take disciplinary action; capability to mentor subordinates; capability to develop a positive rapport with stakeholder organizations; capability to develop positive rapport with the community; and capability to balance work and personal life. Of interest to note is that while 95 percent of the surveyed wardens noted that balancing work and personal life was either "very necessary" or "completely necessary," only 67 percent indicated that they were either "very capable" or "completely capable" of doing so.

New wardens who were surveyed by McCampbell indicated that they would have been better prepared for the challenges of the job had they had job experience or skills in business administration/fiscal management, personnel and labor relations, legislative issues, and media and public relations.[11] Unfortunately, however, a large majority (90%) of new wardens also reported in this survey that they did not receive any special training or orientation for their new responsibilities prior to, or just after, they received their assignment. Since 1994, there has been a 36-hour training program for new wardens, as well as related publications and other resources, available through the NIC. Participants of **NIC Executive Training Program for New Wardens** enhance their understanding in such areas as institutional culture, central office relationships, budget management strategies, decision making, and media relations.[12]

NIC Executive Training Program for New Wardens training for new wardens to help grasp such areas as institutional culture, budget management, decision making, and media relations.

Principles of Good Prison Leadership

Throughout the nineteenth century and the early twentieth century, studies of prisons generally focused on the administrators rather than the inmates. Beginning in the 1940s, however, an ideological shift from studying prison administrators to studying inmates occurred. The central reason for the shift seems to have been that prisons were poorly managed or were what prison researcher John J. DiIulio Jr. referred to as "ineffective prisons."[13] Many writers expressed grave doubts about the efficacy of correctional administrators and stated that prison managers could do nothing to improve conditions behind bars.

It is not surprising that when contemporary researchers attempt to relate prison management practices to the quality of life behind bars, the results are normally quite negative: Prisons that are managed in a tight, authoritarian fashion are plagued with disorder and inadequate programs; those that are managed in a loose, participative fashion are equally troubled; and those with a mixture of these two styles are no better.[14]

In a 3-year study of prison management in Texas, Michigan, and California, however, DiIulio found that levels of disorder (rates of individual and collective violence and other forms of misconduct), amenities (availability of clean cells, decent food, and so on), and service (availability of work opportunities and educational programs) did not vary with any of the following factors: a higher socioeconomic class of inmates, higher per capita spending, lower levels of crowding, lower inmate–staff ratios, greater officer training, more modern plant and equipment, and more routine use of repressive measures. DiIulio concluded that "all roads, it seemed, led to the conclusion that the quality of prison life depended mainly on the quality of prison management."[15]

DiIulio also found that prisons managed by a stable team of like-minded executives, structured in a paramilitary, security-driven, bureaucratic fashion, had better order, amenities, and service than those managed in other ways *even when* the former institutions were more crowded, spent less per capita, and had higher inmate–staff ratios: "The only finding of this study that, to me at least, seems indispensable is that *prison management matters*" (emphasis in the original).[16]

Studies analyzing the causes of major prison riots found that they were the result of a breakdown in security procedures—the daily routine of numbering, counting, frisking, locking, contraband control, and cell searches—that are the heart of administration in most prisons.[17] Problems such as crowding, underfunding, festering inmate–staff relations, and racial animosities may make a riot more *likely*, but poor security management will make a riot *inevitable*.[18]

principles of good prison leadership
DiIulio's six principles for success in corrections management.

DiIulio offered six general **principles of good prison leadership**:[19]

1. Successful leaders focus, and inspire their subordinates to focus, on results rather than process, on performance rather than procedures, on ends rather than means. In short, managers are judged on results, not excuses.
2. Professional staff members—doctors, psychiatrists, accountants, nurses, and other nonuniformed staff—receive some basic prison training and come to think of themselves as COs first.
3. Leaders of successful institutions follow the *management by walking around* principle. These managers are not strangers to the cellblocks and are always on the scene when trouble erupts.
4. Successful leaders make close alliances with key politicians, judges, journalists, reformers, and other outsiders.
5. Successful leaders rarely innovate, but the innovations they implement are far reaching and the reasons for them are explained to staff and inmates well in advance. Line staff is notoriously sensitive to what administrators do "for inmates" versus "what they do for us." Thus, leaders must be careful not to upset the balance and erode staff loyalty.
6. Successful leaders are in office long enough to understand and, as necessary, modify the organization's internal operations and external relations. DiIulio used the terms *flies, fatalists, foot soldiers,* and *founders.* The flies come and go unnoticed and are inconsequential. Fatalists also serve brief terms, always complaining about the futility of incarceration and the hopelessness of correctional reform. The foot soldiers serve long terms, often inheriting their job from a fly or fatalist, and make consequential improvements whenever they can. Founders either create an agency or reorganize it in a major and positive way.

new old penology
DiIulio's term for a shift of attention from the society of captives to the government of keepers.

To summarize, to "old" penologists, prison administrators were admirable public servants, inmates were to be restricted, and any form of self-government was eschewed. To "new" penologists, prison administrators are loathsome and evil, inmates are responsible victims, and complete self-government is the ideal. DiIulio called for a **new old penology**, or a shift of attention from the society of captives to the government of keepers. He asserted that tight administrative control is more conducive than loose administrative control to decent prison conditions. This approach, he added, will "push administrators back to the bar of attention," treating them at least as well as their charges.[20]

Stan Stojkovic adds to DiIulio's notions of good prison leadership by articulating that prison leaders must adapt to increasing prison oversight.[21] He notes, "Prison oversight, in its varied forms, will be the norm for prison leadership and management in the 21st century prison."[22] Stojkovic suggests that prison leaders will need to demonstrate greater transparency, which can improve effectiveness of prisons in the long run. Because of increased prison oversight in the twenty-first century, prison leaders will be held more accountable to democratic values.[23]

Administering the Death Penalty

One of the major responsibilities of prison administrators, in 32 states (three states abolishing capital punishment since 2009) and in federal prisons, is to carry out the death penalty. By law, the warden or a representative presides over the execution.

To minimize the possibility of error, executions are carried out by highly trained teams. The mechanics of the process have been broken down into several discrete tasks and are practiced repeatedly. During the actual death watch—the 24-hour period that ends with the prisoner's execution—a member of the execution team is with the prisoner at all times. During the last 5 or 6 hours, two officers are assigned to guard the prisoner. The prisoner then showers, dons a fresh set of clothes, and is placed in an empty tomb-like death cell. The warden reads the court order or death warrant. Meanwhile, official witnesses—normally 6 to 12 citizens—are prepared for their role. The steps that are taken from this point to perform the execution depend on the method of execution that is used.[24]

Today state prisons and the Federal Bureau of Prisons hold about 3,000 inmates under sentence of death; lethal injection is the predominant method of execution in use; it is employed in all death-penalty states and in the federal system. In addition to lethal injection, 16 states authorize an alternative method of execution: Eight states also use electrocution; three states, lethal gas; three states, hanging; and two states, firing squad. California has the most number of prisoners under the sentence of death (735), followed by Florida (398) and Texas (273)[25] See Exhibit 11.1 for a recent notorious case.

EXHIBIT 11.1

THE FEDERAL GOVERNMENT AND CAPITAL PUNISHMENT: COMPLICATED AND CONTROVERSIAL

Dzhokhar Tsarnaev was convicted in 2015 for the Boston Marathon attack that killed three people and injured hundreds of others. Tsarnaev was also convicted of killing an MIT police officer in a gun battle after the attack. In May 2015, Dzhokhar was sentenced to death and currently resides in the United States Penitentiary in Florence, Colorado, also known as the Supermax. Should Tsarnaev ultimately be executed, he will be moved beforehand to Terre Haute, Indiana, where federal executions are carried out.[26] Prior to the sentencing decision, there was considerable speculation as to whether Tsarnaev's sentence would be life in prison or death. A majority of Americans favor capital punishment and have little or no sympathy toward terrorists since 9/11; furthermore, the case against him was strong, and he was ultimately convicted of all 30 counts in the indictment.[27]

In Tsarnaev's case, a litany of factors could have militated against his execution. First, although a poll conducted in May 2013 by the *Washington Post* found that 70 percent of respondents favored Tsarnaev's execution, Massachusetts jurors have long opposed the death penalty[28]; then there was Tsarnaev's youthfulness—and the question of whether or not Tsarnaev's participation may have been the result of duress or influence by his older brother, Tamerlan (who was killed during the incident by police). Finally, the federal government has an extensive appeals process and, at the time, was also coping with challenges to its lethal injection protocol.[29]

Despite his sentence of death, it likely will be years (if ever) before Tsarnaev is actually executed.

In the new millennium, the U.S. Supreme Court has rendered a number of significant decisions concerning the administration of the death penalty: In *Roper v. Simmons* (March 2005), the Court abolished the death penalty for convicted murderers who were less than 18 years of age when they committed their crimes; this decision ended a practice used in 19 states and affected about 70 death row inmates who were juveniles when they committed murder. In *Atkins v. Virginia* (June 2002), the Court held that the execution of mentally retarded persons—which was permissible in 20 states—constituted cruel and unusual punishment.[30] And in 2015 in a 5–4 decision, the Court upheld the use of midazolam, the first drug sedative in a three-drug protocol for administering the death penalty via lethal injection.[31]

Achieving Racial Balance

The rapid growth of the inmate population, increased oversight by the federal courts, increased demands from the public, and a change in the demographic composition of the inmate population (more African American and Hispanic prisoners) all have presented wardens with a new set of challenges. As a result, half of all wardens in maximum-security prisons now have a policy on racially integrating male inmates within prison cells to try to achieve racial balance. Similarly, about 40 percent of these wardens do not allow their inmates to object to their cell assignments.[32] In a national survey of wardens conducted by Martha Henderson and her colleagues,[33] wardens reported that even in the absence of specific policies on racial integration, they attempted to work toward racial balance. This represents a major shift from arguments by wardens beginning in the 1960s that integration could lead to a loss of control. In Henderson and colleagues' study, the majority of wardens reported that there had been no instances of inmate violence in racially balanced prison cells.[34]

Middle Managers and Supervisors

Chapter 5 examined in detail the roles of *police* supervisors and managers. It would be repetitious to dwell at length here on those roles and functions because most of them apply to *corrections* supervisors and managers as well.

Custodial staff at most prisons is typically divided into four ranks: captain, lieutenant, sergeant, and officer. Captains typically work closely with the prison administration in policymaking and disciplinary matters, lieutenants are even more closely involved with the security and disciplinary aspects of the institution, and sergeants oversee a specified number of rank-and-file COs who work in their assigned cellblocks or workplaces.

Middle managers, although not on the front lines, are also in challenging and important positions. They are responsible for organizing their departments, planning and developing goals and objectives, overseeing the efficient use of resources, and developing effective communication networks throughout the organization.

Clearly, supervisors have one of the most demanding positions in correctional institutions. They must direct work activities, assign tasks, provide employee feedback, and serve as technical experts for the staff reporting to them. They serve as boss, adviser, counselor, mentor, coach, trainer, and motivator.

Carl ToersBijns, who served in the corrections field for over 25 years, notes that corrections supervisors must correct potential "bad traits" in order to be successful with today's generation of COs and inmates.[35] According to ToersBijns, these bad traits include the following: (1) Arrogance, which can create an us versus them mentality between supervisors and officers; (2) Being Opaque, which does not convey a sense of transparency; (3) Being Undisciplined, which can result in over delegation, something officers tend to resent; (4) Being Detached, which conveys a disinterest in officers and the role they play in the institution; and (5) Exhibiting a Lack of Self-Awareness, which can lead to a lack of understanding of one's own strengths and weaknesses.[36]

"Thy Brother's Keeper": Evolving Roles and Types of COs

Subordinate to the institutional administrator, middle managers, and supervisors is the correctional staff itself—those who, in the words of Gordon Hawkins, are "the other prisoners."[37] Their role is particularly important and challenging, given that they provide the front-line supervision and control of inmates and constitute the level from which correctional administrators may be chosen. Recall, for example, that in the 2013 National Survey of Prison Wardens, they worked an average of nearly 27 years in the field of corrections, many of whom likely rose through the ranks.[38] Certainly one of the most challenging positions in prisons is that of the front-line **correctional officer** (CO), who is generally responsible for the following: the custody, safety, security, and supervision of inmates; ensuring that inmates adhere to the relevant rules, regulations, and policies; maintaining discipline, peace, and order in prison; conducting searches for contraband; transporting inmates as needed; and tactically responding to riots and other emergency situations.

correctional officer the person responsible for the custody, safety, security, and supervision of inmates in a prison or other correctional facility.

According to Harriet Fox, a CO in California, successful COs exhibit eight traits that will carry COs far in their profession.[39] These traits include the following: (1) excellent communication skills—both in written reports and oral communication; (2) teamwork promoter—rather than working solo; (3) practical problem-solving—evaluate, assess, and work toward problem resolution; (4) decisiveness—take action in a timely manner after processing information; (5) resilience—learning from mistakes strengthens leaders; (6) selflessness—do not lead out of ego; (7) open-mindedness—in order to adapt to changes in the environment; and (8) dedication—a must to earn the respect of coworkers.

Correctional officer duties may be categorized as follows:

1. ***Work detail supervisors:*** Many prisons have inmates working in various positions, such as the prison cafeteria, laundry, and other such locations; officers must supervise them during such activities.
2. ***Industrial shop and educational programs:*** Prison industries have inmates producing everything from license plates, state-use paint, and mattresses to computer parts; COs must ensure that inmates do not create any problems during their workday and do not misappropriate any related tools that may be fashioned into weapons.
3. ***Yard officers:*** While inmates are outdoors and engaged in physical exercise and socialization, there is the potential for problems, such as fights between different racial or ethnic groups; officers must be alert for breaches of security and order.
4. ***Tower guards:*** Officers observe inmates who are in the prison yard while encased in an isolated, silent post high above the prison property and being vigilant for any outbreaks of violence or attempts to escape while inmates are outdoors.
5. ***Administrative building assignments:*** Officers are responsible for providing security at all prison gates, places where inmates' families come to visit, clerical work that involves inmate transfer, and so on.[40]

Mary Ann Farkas[41] also categorized COs into five types based on their approach to, and philosophy regarding, their role, as follows:

1. *Rule enforcers* (about 43% of COs) are the most common type in Farkas' sample. They are characterized as rule bound and inflexible in discipline. They are likely to

be less than 25 years old and to have a baccalaureate degree; they tend to have less work experience and to work the evening or night shift. They are more likely to have entered corrections for extrinsic reasons, including job security, benefits, and job availability, and to have a militaristic approach to inmates, expecting deference to their authority and obedience to their orders. Generally, they are not willing to negotiate or use exchange as a strategy to gain inmate compliance.[42]

2. *The hard-liners* (14%) are actually an extreme version of the rule enforcers, being hard, aggressive, power hungry, and inflexible in applying rules. These officers are also more likely to be men, with a high school education or GED, and between the ages of 26 and 36 years. They also tend to work in maximum-security or segregation units, and to endorse militaristic values and distinction and deference to rank and the chain of command. At times, they may become abusive and aggressive toward inmates and perceive acting tough as the way a CO is supposed to act to maintain control and order.[43]
3. *People workers* (22% of COs) have a more comfortable style with inmates, are more flexible in rule enforcement and disciplinary measures, use their own informal reward and punishment system, and believe that the way to gain inmate compliance is through interpersonal communication and personalized relations. They regard overreliance on conduct reports as an indication of one's inability to resolve difficult situations. They often discuss issues privately with inmates instead of embarrassing them in front of peers. They often rely on verbal skills in defusing situations, enjoy the challenge of working with inmates, and prefer the posts with more inmate contact.[44]
4. *The synthetic officers* (14% of COs), according to Farkas, are essentially a synthesis of the rule enforcer and the people worker types. They are typically older (37 years of age or older), more experienced officers who work in regular inmate housing units on the day shift. These officers follow rules and regulations closely, yet they try to consider the circumstances. They are careful not to deviate too far from procedure, however, which might cause sanctions for themselves. Strict enforcement of rules and flexibility in enforcement are juggled in their interactions with inmates.[45]
5. *Loners* (about 8% of COs) are also similar to rule enforcers but differ in the motivation behind their policy of strict enforcement. Loners closely follow rules and regulations because they fear criticism of their performance. Farkas believes that female and black officers are more likely to be of this type. Loners are likely to be between the ages of 26 and 36 years, to be less experienced COs, and to work on solitary posts. They feel a need to constantly prove themselves, and neither feel accepted by other officers nor identify with them. They are wary of inmates. There is a basic mistrust, even fear, of working with inmates.[46]

To summarize, age and seniority are associated with officer types. Rule enforcers and hard-liners tend to be younger, less experienced COs, whereas older, more experienced officers belong to the people worker or synthetic officer categories. Generally, as officers mature, they become more interested in service delivery. Educational attainment is also a factor as Farkas found that rule enforcers were more likely to hold baccalaureate or master's degrees.[47] Considerable evidence also suggests that higher education may lead to lower job satisfaction.[48] Other studies have determined that as officers' educational level increases, the less likely they are to feel a sense of accomplishment working as COs, or to want to make a career of corrections, and the less willing they are to engage in rehabilitation activities.[49]

Managing Staff Deviance

In Chapter 14, we will discuss examples of deviant behavior and ethical misconduct in corrections. Here we focus more on what to do to manage it.

Certainly most COs are honest, hard-working people; however, as with any occupation, there will be a few individuals who come into this work and engage in deviant behavior. Such behavior may simply be defined as that CO conduct performed while on duty that violates either statutory law or agency policies and procedures.

Prison and jail corruption differs from other forms of public corruption because of the uniqueness of the environment, function, opportunities, and patterns of relationships of correctional institutions. Prison and jail personnel must control a reluctant, resistant, and sometimes hostile inmate population whose welfare—and comfortable lifestyle, by their standards—may seem better served by corruption than by honest compliance with prison rules; a culture of manipulation and violence may ensue.

To counter the existence of such acts, there are three types of approaches that administrators can take in terms of one's career phase: preservice, in-service, and continuous. Following are activities relating to all three phases that, per criminal justice ethicist Sam Souryal, correctional administrators can implement:

1. ***Upgrade the quality of correctional personnel.*** The entry-level pay for COs must be competitive. Correctional administrators should ensure that their hiring standards are competitive enough to attract qualified applicants yet high enough to keep high-risk applicants away from employment. Certainly included are thorough background investigations and certification. Psychological testing should also be used to check the character of those who are selected, and interviews should be conducted by a hiring board prior to appointment.
2. ***Establish quality-based supervisory techniques.*** Supervisors should realize that loyalty to moral principles is more durable than loyalty to individuals, and understand that although trivial and insignificant policy violations can be justified, serious transgressions must be earnestly reported. Quality-based supervisors are expected to possess the professional wisdom to be able to know which matter is trivial and which is serious, without being told. They should also see that employees are properly evaluated, subjected to random drug tests, and credit checks.
3. ***Strengthen fiscal controls.*** Most acts of prison corruption involve the illegal acquisition of money; therefore, establishing financial controls is an effective tool for checking corruption in correctional institutions and involves the proper conduct of preaudit and postaudit controls. Experienced internal auditors can determine whether bidding procedures are followed, expenditure ceilings are observed, and purchase vouchers are issued for the exact objects.
4. ***Emphasize true ethical training.*** If correctional leaders truly want their subordinates to act professionally, to pursue integrity, fidelity, and obligation and to shun corruption, they should support and increase such training—to include cultural awareness, diversity, and gender sensitivity training. Doing otherwise would signal that the subject is unimportant.[50]

Staff–Inmate Relationships

Despite formal policies prohibiting familiarity between inmates and prison staff employees, infractions occur that range from serious (e.g., romantic affairs—sometimes leading to childbearing) to minor (e.g., giving or receiving candy or soft drinks to/from an inmate). Many contemporary prisons are no longer sexually segregated, with female security officers working in male institutions. Such situations—and adding as well the fact that many inmates are quite manipulative—can foment different types of **inappropriate staff-inmate relationships** to develop. These relationships can involve behavior that is not only sexual in nature but also other transgressions, such as staff performing special favors for inmates or

inappropriate staff-inmate relationships such correctional staff behaviors as sexual relations with inmates, providing special favors for inmates, or smuggling in contraband.

smuggling in contraband. Such wrongdoing by staff typically results in both staff and inmates being placed at risk and undermining the overall safety of the prison.

Worley et al.[51] found three types of "turners"—offenders identified as developing inappropriate relationships with staff members:

1. ***Heartbreakers.*** They seek to form an emotional bond with a staff member, which can even lead to marriage; they generally act alone and may spend several months courting a staff member.
2. ***Exploiters.*** They use an employee as a means of obtaining contraband or fun and excitement; they usually act with the help of other inmates, are very manipulative, and are likely to use a "lever" (intimidation) on prison employees.
3. ***Hell raisers.*** These inmates engage in a unique kind of psychological warfare, and simply want to cause trouble and create hell for the prison system. They often have a long history of personal involvement and form relationships as a way to create problems or disruptions. They thrive on putting staff members in situations wherein their jobs are compromised and enjoy the notoriety that follows the exposure of their relationship. They focus on staff members (e.g., secretaries; trustees have even become involved with staff members' spouses) rather than security officers.

Worley et al. point out that such behaviors are not the norm in penal environments; nevertheless, prison administrators must understand that offenders are very persistent in initiating interactions with employees for a variety of reasons.[52]

▶ Jail Personnel

About 721,000 individuals are incarcerated in local jails on an average day in the United States, either awaiting trial or serving a sentence.[53] The jail incarceration rate of 230 inmates per 100,000 is the lowest since mid-year 2000 when the rate was 220 per 100,000.[54] Furthermore, about 161,000 people are employed in local jails.[55] Jails represent the point of entry into the criminal justice system. Although prisons hold persons who have committed felonies and have been sentenced to at least 1 year in prison, jails hold persons who are arrested and booked for criminal activity or are waiting for a court appearance if they cannot arrange bail, as well as those who are serving sentences of up to 1 year for misdemeanors. Jails also temporarily hold felons whose convictions are on appeal or are awaiting transfer to a state prison.

Perhaps one of the most neglected areas in criminal justice research concerns individuals who are employed in local jails; what limited studies have been performed generally focus on the conditions of confinement. Jail personnel—such as police and prison employees—must often work in an environment that is potentially unstable, uncertain, and unsafe. Therefore, it would be beneficial for jail administrators to become knowledgeable about why people choose to work in local jails, as well as jail employee job satisfaction and turnover, discussed later.

Jail Administrators' Functions

Because of their responsibilities, changes in structure and function, and shifts in inmate populations (as discussed in Chapter 10), today's jails warrant being recognized and operated as professional institutions—rather than an adjunct to, or an *ad hoc* appendage (most of them being administered by a county sheriff, in the sheriff's department). The jail administrator should be a full-time professional, capable of handling multiple roles internal and external to the jail; therefore, according to a federal report, jail administrators must function as the jail's *leader*, as the *manager* of its operations and resources, and as its *supervisor*.[56] Exhibit 11.2 discusses these three roles in more depth, and "In Their Own Words" (next page) lets you hear from a former jail administrator.

EXHIBIT 11.2

THE SHERIFF'S ROLES IN EFFECTIVE JAIL OPERATIONS

As a *leader,* the sheriff:

- helps define the jail's mission and the goals that must be met to achieve that mission.
- creates a sheriff's office executive management team that includes the jail administrator as an equal member.
- builds a culture within the jail division that supports the attainment of desired outcomes.
- serves as liaison to the external environment (i.e., the local criminal justice system, special interest groups, stakeholders, the community, and the media).
- influences and develops public policy supporting the agency mission.
- creates and maintains a competent and diverse workforce.

As a *manager,* the sheriff:

- mentors and coaches the jail administrator and other staff to elicit desired behaviors and develop talent.
- ensures that policies and procedures that meet professional standards are established to guide the staff and the organization in day-to-day operations.
- motivates the jail administrator and other staff to align their personal goals with those of the jail.
- provides thorough written directives and training on those directives.
- monitors activities and assesses results by collecting and analyzing performance data on a regular basis.
- manages and allocates budgets, staff, and other resources.
- manages the organization's preparation for and response to crisis situations and emergencies.

As a *supervisor*, the sheriff:

- stays informed about day-to-day operations in the jail and is visible and available to assist when necessary.
- monitors compliance with policies, standards, and legal requirements through the establishment of a systematic internal inspection and review process.
- supports and facilitates the jail administrator's efforts to redirect underperformers and address misconduct of jail staff.
- monitors the jail administrator's performance through regular reviews and quality assessment.

Source: Based on Mark D. Martin and Paul Katsampes, *Sheriff's Guide to Effective Jail Operations* (Washington, DC: U.S. Department of Justice, National Institute of Corrections, 2006), pp. 5–6.

A Few Comments on "Jail First" Policies and Detention as a Career Path

A "jail first" policy is where sheriffs' offices require that recruits first work in the jail—often for several years—before they can become eligible for patrol duties. Such policies can result in jail administrators having considerable difficulty in recruiting and keeping people for jail duties, and can also result in high employee attrition due to low job satisfaction (deputies going elsewhere to do "real" police work out on patrol). Jail administrators may wish to reexamine this policy and try to create a culture that values detention work. In addition to thus establishing *detention as a career path*—where one can choose to remain in detention, be promoted within it, and, it is hoped, eventually retire from it—jail administrators can encourage their recruiters to emphasize the "big picture," for example, that only about 20 percent of a deputy's 20-year career would be spent working in detention, with the remaining 80 percent being spent as a road deputy.

Employee Training

Jail administrators and employees need to be thoroughly trained in all aspects of their job. Jail workers have been criticized for being untrained and apathetic, although most are highly effective and dedicated. One observer wrote that:

> [p]ersonnel is still the number one problem of jails. Start paying decent salaries and developing decent training and you can start to attract bright young people to jobs in jails. If you don't do this, you'll continue to see the issue of personnel as the number one problem for the next 100 years.[57]

Training should be provided on the booking process; inmate management and security; general liability issues; policies related to AIDS; problems of inmates addicted to alcohol and other drugs; communication and security technology; and issues concerning suicide, mental health problems, and medication. In-house training can be supplemented by trainings offered through the NIC. A brief review of NIC's training catalog for 2017 revealed a number of topical sessions, including direct supervision training, planning and implementing effective mental health services in jails, managing restrictive housing, and inmate behavior management.[58]

IN THEIR OWN WORDS

ADMINISTRATIVE ADVICE FROM THE FIELD

Name: Gary Raney

Current and former positions/City/State: I started with the Ada County, Idaho, Sheriff's Office in 1983 as a jail deputy and rose through the ranks and was elected sheriff in 2004. The Sheriff's Office is a full-service agency with a large jail, a consolidated emergency communications center, and policing duties that include three contract city police departments. I have also held the positions of vice-chair of the Idaho Criminal Justice Commission, the chair of the Peace Officers Standards and Training Council, the chair of the Idaho Criminal Justice Grants Council, the president of the Idaho Sheriffs' Association, and a US attorney general appointment to the board of the NIC.

Primary duties and responsibilities in your position as sheriff: While the county commissioners are statutorily bound to provide funding for the jail, as sheriff I am solely responsible for the operation of it. As we all know, there are many different philosophies about what that should look like, but mine is that it should be a positive and safe place for staff and inmates and that we have an obligation to help inmates improve their lives and reduce the likelihood they will reoffend. The Ada County Jail has been recognized as a model jail by the U.S. Department of Justice, jail experts, and others since about 2008. Our jail and its related services include:

- A 1,300-bed facility that has housing areas that range from maximum-security single cells to large dormitory settings. Every housing unit built since 2004 has been built for direct supervision, where the staff is directly interacting with the inmates 24/7/365.
- An 80-bed specialized area for medical and mental health treatment for inmates.
- Evidence-based recidivism reduction programs and a comprehensive inmate behavior management system that incentivizes inmates to be active in their success and learn good decision-making skills that translate to better decisions after they reenter the community.
- Pretrial release services that rely upon research and science to guide the judiciary in their release decisions. The research is clear that low risk offenders are harmed by being held in jail and high risk offenders are too often released simply because they have access to bail money.
- Alternative sentencing programs that allow offenders to serve their sentence through community contribution and reinvestment rather than sitting in jail.

Personal attributes/characteristics that have proven to be most helpful in my position as sheriff: While my experience has been invaluable, it is my education and personal reliance upon research and data that has helped me make the best decisions. I returned to college and earned my master's degree near the time I became sheriff and it was during that coursework that I came to appreciate the vast amount of research that is available to help us make better criminal justice decisions. There are many myths around jails like, "Let them sit there a couple days and that'll teach them a lesson." We made smarter decisions based on reliable research and that has lowered the incarceration rate, lowered the recidivism rate, and made the community better.

Along with my education, my curiosity has been a great asset. I try to be a life-long learner and I love discussions that bring forth new ideas and new ways of doing things. I have always had an open mind and I listen to people even though I may disagree with them. When you model that as a leader, others follow and I have always tried to create a collaborative learning organization.

My three greatest challenges in the role of sheriff:

- Hiring and retaining the absolute best people. Even if you're the greatest organization in the world, you should always try to be better. All law enforcement and corrections agencies are service organizations because our success depends upon the quality of people we hire and the way they interact with others, including inmates. The difference between a deputy who takes the opportunity to talk to an inmate and the one who avoids talking to an inmate is all the difference in the world. Agencies that don't develop hiring and promotional processes to put the best people in the right position are destined to be average at best.
- Leadership requires constant and iterative communication and it's easy to forget that when you're the one who is responsible to do it. Whether changing public attitudes about jails or helping employees understand the direction of the agency, success comes by not only having a vision but by being able to explain it in a way that people buy into. Then, you have to repeat those messages over and over and over. Sometimes it seems like you've beaten a subject to death, just to then see someone new "get it."
- Changing attitudes and perceptions about jails. Even today some people think the right way to deal with crime is to make more arrests. We know crime and criminal behavior are complex problems that require complex solutions. Forward thinking people now recognize the critical role jails play in criminal justice and that they are the pivot point where we can intercept offenders early in their lifestyles and redirect them to be healthy, positive members of our community. We need to be prescriptive about the way we deal with offenders. Some need locked up. Others need enough education to get a job that pays enough to live on. Still others need help dealing with the physical and sexual abuse they experienced as a child. Many need to overcome substance abuse and mental health issues. We are learning more all the time, but right now we are at an exciting time when we are seeing change come at an exponential pace.

Personal accomplishments during my administrative career about which I am most proud:

- Having a consistently high rate of employee satisfaction. Happy people are productive people. Just before I became sheriff, I initiated an annual employee satisfaction survey as a report card on our leadership. We consistently had about a 94 percent satisfaction rating across all employees that work in the jail. There are few organizations that could exceed that, regardless of who they are.
- Changing the jail from one that was probably better than average to one that was nationally recognized as a model. We have had people come from all over the nation to watch and learn how we run our jail. That makes the jail staff and me proud and reminds us of the importance of what we do.
- I have been fortunate to meet and learn from many criminal justice leaders from across the country who are changing the nation, if not the world. Those opportunities came because I was involved. I count that as an accomplishment because I controlled my destiny. Over time, I moved from being more of a listener to being someone people wanted to listen to. It's a good feeling to contribute.

Advice for someone who is interested in occupying an administrative position such as sheriff:

1. You must be educated. This is the information age and just like the CEO of a business, the modern criminal justice leader has to be knowledgeable in many areas. You must not only know how to do the job but how to do it differently, in a better way and in the right way. We have moved from corrections

being a high-school educated blue-collar job to one where advanced degrees are common and the modern CO is an educated professional. The future will only further that trend and leaders must be the example of the educated professional.

2. Good leaders are passionate. Leadership is hard because it takes a lot of time and effort. It's not for those people who want to send e-mails and then go home at 5:00 (or the end of shift). Leaders need knowledge, but they also need to be committed to the success of the organization and willing to put in the time and effort to make it better. One of the most common failures of leadership is not having the courage to do the right thing rather than the easy thing.

Source: Used with permission from Gary Raney.

You need to be a communicator and that also means being a listener. First, you need to be open-minded. It's the only way you can hear all the potential answers to a problem. It also creates buy-in from those involved in creating the solution. People who think they know all the answers lead by ego, and they eventually fail. Listeners succeed. But also, once you know the right answer, the real job becomes communicating it. You must know your people and you must know their concerns and perceptions. Change will be hard for some of them but effective leaders are effective communicators and they help everyone understand their role in the future of the organization.

▶ Probation and Parole Officers

How many probation and parole officers are employed in the United States today? Unfortunately, that question is impossible to answer, due to the diverse nature of organization and functions of the community corrections field. For example, does one count only those officers who supervise a caseload? What about supervisory staff, with no direct supervisory duties? Furthermore, some staff members only write presentencing reports or work in an agency's pretrial division, and larger agencies may also have treatment staff. The problem of "headcounts" thus becomes obvious, so even the national American Probation and Parole Association does not venture to estimate the numbers of officers.[59] What is known, however, is that these persons directly or indirectly supervise 4.7 million adults who are either on parole or probationary status.[60] This section discusses their primary duties, supervisory styles (over their probationers and parolees), and sources of stress.

IN THEIR OWN WORDS

ADMINISTRATIVE ADVICE FROM THE FIELD

Kenneth J. Peak

Name: Jolene R. Whitten

Current position/City/State: Chief United States Probation and Pretrial Services Officer, Northern District of Texas, Dallas, Texas

College attended/academic major/degree(s): Bachelor of Science in Education (major in Political Science, minor in English), Midwestern State University, Wichita Falls, Texas; Master of Arts, Humanities (coursework in history, literature, art, music, and philosophy), California State University at Dominguez Hills.

My primary duties and responsibilities in this position include: serving as the court unit executive for the United States Probation and Pretrial Services Office in the Northern District of Texas, which covers a geographical area that includes 100 counties. I am responsible for the oversight of our mission and staff, as well as for the budgetary and personnel decisions, implementation of policy, and communicating with our judges, including the Chief U.S. District Judge. I also represent our office when meeting with leaders of other agencies and community organizations. As the chief probation and pretrial services officer, I am also a law enforcement officer.

Personal attributes/characteristics that have proven to be most helpful to me in this position are: optimism, resilience, innovation, integrity, the ability and desire to interact with people from diverse backgrounds, written and verbal communications skills, organizational skills, confidence, compassion, a high energy level, and knowledge about and a strong belief in our mission. A sense of humor also helps!

My three greatest challenges in this administrative role include:

1. **Budgeting:** Over the past 2 years, the federal courts have not been funded adequately to achieve our mission. Sequestration has hit us hard. Our work does not decrease when we have limited resources, so we've had to be very innovative in order to be effective and also protect our employees' jobs.
2. **Communication:** Because our district is so large, it's not possible to communicate face-to-face with all employees. Learning how and when to communicate information has been challenging but is critical. Effective communication can prevent problems and ensure success.
3. **Personnel issues:** Even in the best of organizations, personnel issues will arise. Learning how to respond appropriately for all concerned can be challenging.

Personal accomplishments during my administrative career about which I am most proud are: managing our limited resources innovatively so our agency did not have to furlough staff during sequestration while maintaining our ability to meet our mission. Working with others to implement strengths-based leadership and evidence-based practices in our district. Having the first mobile officer team in the system and expanding the mobile concept in order to greatly reduce rental costs for the judiciary by closing three field offices. Ensuring quality to serve our courts, protect our communities, and assist clients in making positive changes in their lives.

Advice for someone who is interested in occupying an administrative position such as mine would be: first—work hard! If you are successful in your current position, others will recognize your efforts. Furthermore, developing a strong work ethic will serve you well, regardless of your position. Be willing to take on additional responsibilities and volunteer for projects and initiatives that will benefit your organization. Be a "servant leader," in whatever position you occupy. You don't have to have a title to be a leader. Be innovative and always continue learning. Learn to work with others, rather than trying to do it all yourself. Find good mentors, and be a mentor to others. Take care of your health and don't forget your personal priorities, such as family. In this type of position, one never really escapes the responsibilities of the job. During vacations, I've responded to e-mails, taken calls, and made some difficult work-related decisions. Over time, it can be draining. So, it's important to find ways to make time for yourself and to live a healthy, balanced lifestyle. Have a few people you can trust and call for advice or just to listen. Always remember the "why" of what you do—I can't imagine doing this job if I didn't believe in the purpose of the organization.

Source: Used with permission from Jolene R. Whitten.

Duties and Orientation

Probation officers supervise convicted offenders whom the courts have allowed to remain at liberty in the community, while being subject to certain conditions and restrictions on their activities. Parole officers, conversely, supervise inmates who have been conditionally released from prison and returned to their community. These officers report violations of the conditions of offenders' release to the body that authorized their community placement and placed conditions on their behavior (the court for probation and the parole board for parole).[61]

Because a number of agencies are often organized under a state's department of public safety umbrella—probation and parole, state police/highway patrol, capitol police, state bureau of investigations, and even fire marshals—probation and parole officer recruits often go through the same background, physical, polygraph, drug testing, and psychiatric exam regardless of which division they wish to work in.

Probation and parole officers must possess important skills similar to those of a prison caseworker, such as good interpersonal communication, decision making, and writing skills. They operate independently, with less supervision than most prison staff. These officers are trained in the techniques for supervising offenders and then assigned a caseload. Probation and parole officers supervise inmates at the two ends of the sentencing continuum (incarceration being in the middle).

Whom do we want to be supervising probationers and parolees—officers who are more grounded in enforcement or treatment in their orientation? In some jurisdictions, probation and parole officers are given, to the extent possible, a far different role or job description from those agencies having much more of an enforcement-oriented mission. As one Western probation and parole administrator put it:

> Although we arrest people, conduct investigations, conduct surveillance, and so on, a huge part of our job is trying to help people. The biggest hat we wear here is social worker. The law enforcement officer hat is much smaller for the most part. I think that is the most unique situation P&P has to offer. Our officers find themselves being social workers, disciplinarians, officers, mentors, coaches, etc. given the offender and his/her specific set of needs.[62]

In fact, official job duties of and postings for probation and parole officers tend to articulate both the enforcement-oriented approach and the treatment approach. For example, the Florida Department of Corrections posts the following about the duties and responsibilities of its correctional probation officers:

- Maintains an awareness of offenders' daily activities and evaluates desirability to remain at liberty;
- Counsels and refers offenders to specialized treatment services at guidance clinics, mental health clinics, and related organizations;
- Assists offenders in securing jobs;
- Evaluates offender progress and recommends intensity of supervision.[63]

The relative influence of one approach over the other is likely dependent on a variety of factors, including offender caseload type, supervisory orientation, and agency culture. For agencies wishing to screen for applicants' orientation, there are means for determining this.[64] One approach to determining such orientation—although no doubt considerably more costly, time-intensive, and laborious—is for the agency to hire a for-profit human resources firm that has developed a reliable and valid survey instrument for this purpose. Such questions as the following might be included in such a survey: "Most offenders should receive strict and harsh discipline," "Most offenders are lazy and do not wish to work," "Most offenders cannot be trusted," "Most offenders want to better themselves," "Most offenders are not better or worse than other people," "Most offenders are victims of unfortunate circumstances," and "In general, rehabilitation of criminal offenders is not possible."

In reality, most probation and parole agencies probably cannot afford to employ an outside entity to test prospective officers in terms of their attitudes; however, once an extensive background investigation has been completed, applicants can then be sent to a contracted psychiatrist for an evaluation. In addition, as indicated above, because some parole and probation agencies are part of their state's larger department of public safety or corrections, all prospective officers can be subjected to the same hiring process as other state employees.

Research has shown, not surprisingly, that probation and parole officers' attitudes will largely influence and can even predict their supervisory practices toward their offender clients. The message for parole and probation administrators is that they may wish to consider applicants' attitudes when making hiring decisions. See Exhibit 11.3 for a parole decision-making exercise.

EXHIBIT 11.3

PAROLE DECISION MAKING FOR A NOTORIOUS KILLER[65]

Assume that you are a parole officer who is to make a recommendation to your state's parole board in the following matter: Charles Manson, age 83, is serving a life sentence for a 1969 killing spree in Los Angeles (his "family" brutally murdered seven people). Manson has not been a model inmate, recently caught possessing a weapon, threatening a peace officer, and being caught twice with contraband cell phones. Given his age, this could be Manson's final appearance before the state parole board. Debra Tate, a victim's sister (murdered actress Sharon Tate), is attending the hearing, and attorneys from both sides are prepared to give presentations, read documents by victims' relatives or other interested parties, and examine Manson's prison records. Manson, as is his custom, is not attending the parole hearing.

- Will you recommend that the board grant or deny Manson's parole at this time?
- If not, do you believe there are programs or redeeming actions or qualities Manson might undertake or possess to secure his freedom in the future?

(The outcome of Manson's 2012 parole hearing is provided in the Notes section.)

Probation Management Styles

Patricia Hardyman's study of probation administrators focused on their *probation management style*—this style being the fundamental determinant of the nature of the probation organization—and was instructive in describing the impact of this style on the department's operation. Few departments, even those with a hierarchical organizational structure, had a pure management style; administrators vacillated among a variety of styles, including laissez faire, democratic, and authoritarian. The degree to which administrators included the probation officers in the decision-making process and communicated with officers varied. Authoritarian administrators created emotional and physical distance between the officers and themselves. Surprisingly, the most common management style used by probation administrators was laissez faire.[66]

Hardyman found that many probation administrators simply did not participate in the day-to-day activities and supervision strategies of the staff. They remained remote but made final decisions on critical policies and procedures.[67] Hardyman also found that few probation administrators across the country operated with the democratic style. Those who did, of course, listened more to the concerns and suggestions of the line supervisors and officers, which, as you might recall from Chapter 2, can be likened to operating in an open system where employee contributions are valued. The administrator still made the final decisions, but information was generally sought from the line staff and their opinions were considered. Officers working under administrators with this style had a greater sense that their opinions mattered and that the administrator valued their input. An additional benefit of the democratic style was that the administrators had power by virtue of both their position and their charisma, which inspired teamwork and task accomplishment.[68]

▶ Addressing Stress, Burnout, and Attrition

As with the other components of the criminal justice system, anyone working in corrections—either with clients behind bars or in an office, often in antiquated facilities, and surrounded by clients who possess all forms of social and behavioral problems—can find themselves to be severely stressed. Certainly, administrators must realize that such stress can have a direct bearing on the quality of one's work productivity, job satisfaction, and even retention on the job; therefore, this is a topic that merits closer examination.

Stressful Prisons

Concerning COs in prisons, one recent study of 500 officers in a Southern prison system found that while race, marital status, and education did not appear to significantly affect CO's job stress or satisfaction, their gender and generation did. Specifically, female COs often feel that some characteristics they can bring to the job—compassion and a family orientation, for example—might be undervalued in a correctional environment that emphasizes toughness and physical strength. Furthermore, individuals who are part of the younger X and Y generations were found to be far more likely to be dissatisfied with their job as COs than older generations. As indicated in Chapter 2, as younger people enter the correctional workforce, it is important to understand what motivates them, and for correctional administrators to consider the needs of workers of every generation, for developing retention strategies and increasing job satisfaction. Allowing for individual preferences in such areas as compressed work schedules and a more participatory style of leadership and management, to the extent that doing so is viable, may help to improve generation X and Y workers' needs and job satisfaction.[69]

Prison crowding has also been correlated with stress, fear of inmates, and health issues. Although, as was shown in Chapter 10, U.S. prison populations have declined a bit in the past few years, many if not most remain crowded due to the tough sentencing policies and War on Drugs of past decades. A study of three Alabama prisons for men found that *all* responding officers identified crowding as negatively affecting officer safety, job performance, and health while leading to violence at their facility. Specifically, crowding foments mental and physical health problems among officers, causing chronic health problems involving headaches, alcoholism, hypertension, obesity, heart attacks, diabetes, and weak immune systems. The study concluded that such issues will likely persist unless state and federal policymakers begin to address prison crowding, especially with regard to greater use of diversion programs (e.g., drug courts) and alternative sentencing (discussed in Chapter 12), as well as U.S. crime and sentencing laws.[70]

The effects of job stress can permeate throughout the institution. For example, in a study conducted at a Midwestern correctional facility, job stress was related to lower levels of organizational commitment and job satisfaction among correctional staff.[71] While little research has been conducted on organizational commitment in correctional institutions, low levels of commitment likely result in low levels of organizational pride and a decreased willingness to go the extra mile for the sake of organizational goals. What's more, job satisfaction and organizational commitment have a positive relationship to one another, underscoring the importance for correctional administrators to work toward creating a favorable work environment, including low levels of job stress.[72]

Stressors in Jails

Stress among COs in jails is an understudied area in the field of corrections. In one of the few studies on this topic in the twenty-first century in a Northeastern jail, Tammy Castle and Jamie Martin found that a number of factors predicted occupational and general stress.[73] Occupational stress was operationalized as job-related stress, and general stress was defined as stress from the workplace that affected officers outside of work. In this study of 373 COs, individual factors such as perceptions of danger and ambiguous expectations resulted in both occupational and general stress, while correctional experience affected general stress. Organizational factors also affected levels of stress. Here, if an officer believed that the organization was running well, he or she was more likely to have less occupational and general stress. Those more satisfied with their salary (likely because of higher positions with more responsibilities) were more likely to have higher levels of occupational stress. And lower job satisfaction resulted in an increase in both occupational and general stress. Finally, jail factors such as the number of training hours pre-employment affected general stress and the daily population of the jail affected occupational stress (lower population, higher stress).[74]

More recent studies have also examined generational differences in jails in order to assess job satisfaction and hopefully stem turnover rates. Jail administrators also need to realize that, like in prison, when employees from different generations come together in the same workplace, they are not likely to be motivated or rewarded in the same manner, or responsive to the same supervisory techniques. And, as Abraham Maslow taught us in the 1950s in his hierarchy of needs (see Chapter 2), what satisfies employees' needs can also vary depending on one's priorities and even location in the organizational hierarchy: Extrinsic motivators as paychecks, fringe benefits, and other economic incentives are generally sufficient only at the lowest levels, where salaries are lower and working conditions possibly more demanding; conversely, individuals functioning at higher levels are more likely to be motivated intrinsically, deriving satisfaction from receiving respect and appreciation from subordinates, and given more and more responsibility. As was also indicated in Chapter 2, the younger generations are more positively influenced by having input into decisions that affect them, control over how they complete their assignments, engaging in leadership mentoring programs, and a say in how things are done. They are more motivated by being recognized for good work and feeling appreciated by the community for the work they do, and seek opportunities for personal development and upward advancement. They also value such extrinsic benefits as college tuition, child care, and a fitness center. Although there will always be some aspects of the workplace that agency officials can do nothing about—for example, civil service rules and bargaining contracts regarding tenure and seniority, legislative control over compensation and retirement plans—there are a number of intrinsic types of rewards that administrators can attempt to use to positively influence job satisfaction and reduce turnover—for example, reducing paperwork, treating people fairly, maintaining a positive work climate, and allowing employees to have input and to be recognized and appreciated.[75]

But keeping people happily working in the nation's jails may not be as daunting as it might appear: A national survey by Jeanne Stinchcomb of more than 2,000 line staff and nearly 600 administrators[76] found, for example, that:

- Jail employment was not the job of "last resort"—only 13 percent of staff said they had no other employment options when they accepted the jail's offer.
- Most staff rated their jail as a good (45%) or an excellent (20%) place to work.
- Fifty-nine percent of jail staff described themselves as "very committed" to the agency where they work, and this finding held among various generations of employees.
- Nearly 7 in 10 (69%) staff members felt appreciated by their supervisor, and believed that they are recognized when they do good work (64%).[77]

Still, Stinchcomb's survey underscored the need for jail administrators to strengthen the jail as a workplace by providing some of the intrinsic and extrinsic rewards that are discussed above.

Stress in Probation and Parole

Finally, with regard to probation and parole officers, studies indicate that their job stress and clinical depression are closely related to organizational climate. In specific, a study of nearly 900 probation and parole officers found that they tend to characterize their work environments as having high levels of role ambiguity (i.e., they are unclear about the objectives and goals of their position—see the discussion of enforcement versus assistance orientations, above), role conflict (i.e., having a general feeling that one cannot satisfy the conflicting demands of their administrators, managers, and supervisors), role overload (e.g., feeling under heavy job pressure at all times), and emotional exhaustion/burnout. Of particular note, researchers found that emotional exhaustion/burnout and role conflict contribute to, and can even predict, depression. And in another study of 300 probation officers in three states, researchers found that challenging elements of some caseloads resulted in higher levels of traumatic stress and burnout.[78] Many challenging caseload events also resulted in mistrust, family issues, anger, and social/emotional isolation.[79] Challenging caseload events included such things as a personal or family threat made by the offender; offender suicide while on the officer's caseload; a violent offense involving a child; and sex offense recidivism.

This is obviously a complex undertaking for probation and parole administrators—that is, untangling the web of complex work roles and organizational environment in order to identify those aspects of work that contribute to stress, burnout, and depression. Clearly, administrators must do what they can to investigate and identify such stressors (perhaps being manifested by employees' resignations, interpersonal problems, poor work productivity, etc.), and then develop strategies for ameliorating their negative effects. Such strategies may include knowing how and when to refer such officers to professional counseling, given that many officers may well lack adequate coping skills with high levels of stress, role conflict, and burnout associated with their jobs.[80]

Summary

This chapter examined the criminal justice employees who work in correctional institutions and probation and parole agencies, with particular emphasis placed on administrators. Certainly, as noted in this chapter, substantial pressures are now placed on these administrators by the external and internal environments. They must maintain a secure environment while attempting to offer some treatment to their clients, who should not leave incarceration or probation/parole in a much worse condition than when they entered. At the same time, another increasingly difficult challenge is that these administrators must constantly strive to maintain a competent, dedicated, noncorrupt workforce—as well as an organizational climate that will maintain a desirable level of job satisfaction for employees and minimize attrition—that will also uphold the primary tenets of incarceration: providing a secure environment while ensuring that inmates are treated with respect and dignity.

Key Terms and Concepts

Correctional officer, p. 291
Inappropriate staff–inmate relationships, p. 293
New old penology, p. 288
NIC Executive Training Program for New Wardens, p. 287
Principles of good prison leadership, p. 288
Stressors, p. 302
Warden, p. 284

Questions for Review

1. What is meant by the term *new old penology*?
2. What are some of the main characteristics of wardens, according to the National Survey of Wardens?
3. According to DiIulio, what are some major principles of successful prison administration?
4. What are some of the major problems encountered by prison or jail employees?

5. What are the types of COs, per Farkas? How do age, length of service, type of assignment, and education affect where one fits in this typology?
6. What factors can lead to stress when working in a jail?
7. What are the three types of inmates who engage in inappropriate relationships with correctional staff members?
8. What are the functions of middle managers and supervisors in jails and prisons (see Chapter 3 if necessary)?
9. How would you describe the prison warden and his or her role? What kinds of training and education are necessary for a new warden to succeed?
10. What are the primary roles of the jail administrator?
11. What are the advantages and disadvantages of having, in effect, two career tracks in jails: a detention track and a patrol track? What can jail administrators do to foster careers and improve job satisfaction in the jail or detention side?
12. What are the primary duties and orientation of probation and parole officers, and what are the arguments for and against their carrying firearms?
13. What are some organizational stressors that can occur and cause depression, low job satisfaction, and high attrition among corrections employees, and what kinds of measures can be taken to minimize it?
14. What factors could have been taken into consideration at the time of the Boston Marathon Bomber's sentencing?

Deliberate and Decide

Parole Decision Making

O. J. Simpson—whose widely publicized trial resulted in his acquittal in 1995 after being charged with murdering his ex-wife Nicole Brown Simpson and her friend Ron Goldman—would again run afoul of the law in Las Vegas in September 2007. He and six other men forcibly entered the hotel room of a sports memorabilia collector and robbed him at gunpoint of several pieces of Simpson's sports memorabilia. In 2008, a predominantly white, predominantly female jury found the former NFL Hall of Fame player and actor guilty of 12 robbery, kidnapping, and weapons charges. By July 2017, he had served almost nine years of a 9- to 33-year sentence he received for his role in the incident, and in that month he attended a pivotal and widely publicized parole hearing Simpson fit the profile of an inmate who is typically paroled on his or her initial attempt. Specifically, under the Nevada point system, a person with a score of 0–5 points is deemed low risk; 6–11 points, medium risk; and 12 or more, high risk. The following factors were in Simpson's favor at the time of the parole hearing: Simpson was 70 and retired; he had never been denied parole or had parole or probation revoked; he had no known gang ties; and he was a model prisoner in a medium custody institution (all 0 points). Factors working against him, however, were the following: his property crime conviction in the 2007 incident (2 points); a history of "frequent abuse" in the drugs/alcohol category (2 points), and one point for his gender (men being statistically more likely than women to commit crimes). The severity of the Las Vegas crime (i.e., armed kidnapping) was another factor, and he scored the highest level of offense severity. "Substantial financial loss" experienced by one of the memorabilia dealers was also a factor that made the crime more serious.[81] After the unusually long hearing, and with Simpson ultimately remorseful for the 2007 crimes, Nevada parole commissioners voted unanimously to grant Simpson parole. Simpson will be under the supervision of a parole officer until 2022, at which point he will have served approximately 50 percent of his original maximum sentence.

Questions for Discussion

1. If you had been a member of the parole board, how would you have voted in this case, and why?
2. As you read this chapter, explain why you believe justice was or was not served in Simpson's cases, whether he poses a risk to the community upon being paroled, and if parole and probation generally serve the purpose of rehabilitation.
3. At his parole hearing, Simpson requested permission to move from Nevada to Florida, where some of his family members reside. What are the benefits and drawbacks to allowing Simpson to leave Nevada?

Learn by Doing

1. Most, if not all, of us have had to work in a position where we were supervised. Using DiIulio's "Six Principles of Good Prison Leadership," identify a supervisor you either worked for directly or were able to observe and discuss how this person measured up in his or her leadership skills. Also, discuss one of

DiIulio's traits of leadership you would implement were you in a leadership position.

2. Your criminal justice honor society is planning a noon forum/debate concerning capital punishment. Your role will be to discuss the problems that exist with prison wardens administering the death penalty, as well as whether or not the recruitment of wardens is limited if one of their position requirements is the ability to supervise use of the death penalty.
3. You are a well-known jail consultant and have been hired by a medium-sized county to examine its jail operations. One observation you quickly make concerns its pattern of recruitment and hiring of personnel: A newly hired deputy, upon completion of required academy training, is automatically assigned to work in the jail. Then, perhaps several years later, as he or she gains seniority and a position becomes available, application may be made for a transfer to the patrol division. What would seem to be the advantages of such an arrangement? Disadvantages? What would you recommend is needed in order to establish a career path for correctional workers in the jail?
4. As part of your criminal justice department's annual "Career Day" program, you are to discuss the general roles of prison COs and jailers as well as the primary differences between probation and parole officers. What will be in your oral report?

Case Study

The Wright Way

Lieutenant Bea Wright has been in her current position in the state prison for 1 year and is the shift supervisor on the swing (evening) shift, which consists of 20 officers. There is also a recreation and development lieutenant who oversees the yard, commissary, and other high-use areas during the shift. Wright begins at 4:00 P.M. by holding a roll call for officers, briefing them on the activities of the day, any unusual inmate problems or tensions in progress, and special functions (such as Bible study groups) that will be happening during the evening. Soon after roll call, Wright has the staff conduct the very important evening count—important because inmates have not been counted since the morning. At about 5:00 P.M., Wright determines that there are only four COs in the dining room with 1,000 inmates, so she contacts other units (such as education, library, and recreation) and asks them to send available staff to the dining hall for support. After dinner, Wright finds a memo from the warden asking her to recommend ways of improving procedures for having violent inmates in the Special Housing Unit (SHU) taken to the recreation area in the evening. Wright asks two of her top COs who work in the SHU to provide her with some preliminary information concerning the system in place and any recommendations they might have. While walking the yard, Wright observes what appears to be an unusual amount of clustering and whispering by inmates by race; she asks a sergeant to quietly survey the COs to determine whether there have also been unusual periods of loud music or large amounts of long-lasting foodstuffs purchased in the commissary (together, these activities by inmates might indicate that a race war is brewing or an escape plan is being developed). Furthermore, as she is on the way to her office, an inmate stops her, saying that a group of inmates is pressuring him to arrange to have drugs brought into the prison and he fears for his safety. Wright arranges for him to be called out of the general population the next day under the guise of being transported to a prison law library, at which time he can meet privately with an investigator and thus not draw suspicion to himself for talking to the staff. At about 9:00 P.M., Anderson, a CO, comes to her office to report that he overheard another CO, Jones, making disparaging remarks to other staff members concerning Anderson's desire to go to graduate school and to become a warden some day. Anderson acknowledges that he does not get along with Jones and is tired of his "sniping," and he asks Wright to intercede. She also knows that Jones has been argumentative with other staff members and inmates of late and makes a mental note to visit with him later in the shift to see if he is having personal problems.

Questions for Discussion

1. Does it appear that Lieutenant Wright, although fairly new in her position, has a firm grasp of her role and performs well in it?
2. In what ways is it shown that Wright seeks input from her subordinates?
3. How does she delegate to and empower her subordinates?
4. Is there any indication that Wright is interested in her COs' training and professional development?
5. In which instances does Wright engage in mediation? In management by walking around?

Notes

1. Mary E. Mastrorilli, Personal Communication, September 11, 2010.
2. John J. DiIulio, Jr., *Governing Prisons: A Comparative Study of Correctional Management* (New York: Free Press, 1987), p. 167.
3. Personal Communication, Ron Angelone, Director, Nevada Department of Prisons, April 27, 1992.
4. Francis T. Cullen, Edward J. Latessa, R. Kopache, Lucien X. Lombardo, and Velmer S. Burton, Jr., "Prison Wardens' Job Satisfaction," *The Prison Journal* 73 (1993): 141–161.
5. Center for Innovative Public Policies, "Methodology and Results: 2013 National Survey of Prison Wardens, Conducted in Conjunction with Updating the *Resource Guide for Newly Appointed Wardens*," http://www.cipp.ort/pdf/Attachment%202%20NIC%20Survey%20Summary%20%20for%20web.pdf.
6. Ibid.
7. Ahn-Shik Kim, Michael DeValve, Elizabeth Q. DeValve, and W. Wesley Johnson, "Female Wardens: Results from a National Survey of State Correctional Executives," *The Prison Journal* 83(4) (December 2003): 406–425.
8. Ibid.
9. Susan W. McCampbell, "Making Successful New Wardens," *Corrections Today* 64(6) (October 2002): 130–134. Also see the National Institute of Corrections website, http://nicic.org.
10. Center for Innovative Public Policies.
11. Ibid.
12. Ibid.
13. John J. DiIulio, Jr., "Well Governed Prisons Are Possible," in George F. Cole, Marc C. Gertz, and Amy Bunger (eds.), *The Criminal Justice System: Politics and Policies,* 8th ed. (Belmont, CA: Wadsworth, 2002), pp. 411–420.
14. Ibid., p. 449.
15. DiIulio, *Governing Prisons,* p. 256.
16. Ibid.
17. Bert Useem, *States of Siege: U.S. Prison Riots, 1971–1986* (New York: Oxford University Press, 1988).
18. DiIulio, "Well Governed Prisons Are Possible," p. 413.
19. John J. DiIulio, Jr., *No Escape: The Future of American Corrections* (New York: Basic Books, 1991), Chapter 1.
20. DiIulio, "Well Governed Prisons Are Possible," p. 456.
21. Stan Stojkovic, "Prison Oversight and Prison Leadership," *Pace Law Review* 30(5) (Fall 2010): 1476–1489.
22. Ibid., p. 1489.
23. Ibid.
24. See Robert Johnson, *Death Work: A Study of the Modern Execution Process,* 2nd ed. (Belmont, CA: West/Wadsworth, 1998); Robert Johnson, "This Man Has Expired," *Commonweal* (January 13, 1989): 9–15.
25. Tracy L. Snell, *Capital Punishment, 2011: Statistical Tables* (U.S. Department of Justice, *Bureau of Justice Statistics,* July 2014), http://www.bjs.gov/content/pub/pdf/cp11st.pdf, pp. 1–4.
26. Allison Sonfist, "What's Life in Prison Like for Boston Marathon Bomber Dzhokhar Tsarnaev?" *New England Cable News*, October 27, 2015, http://www.necn.com/news/new-england/Whats-Life-in-Prison-Like-for-Boston-Marathon-Bober-Dzhokhar-Tsarnaev–337449791.html.
27. See, for example, Kevin Johnson, "Death Penalty for Boston Bomber a Complicated Question," *USA Today,* December 1, 2014, http://www.usatoday.com/story/news/nation/2014/12/01/boston-marathon-bomber-tsarnaev/3760253/.
28. Sebastian Murdock, "Dzhokhar Tsarnaev, Boston Bombing Suspect, Has Life or Death Resting in Attorney General," *Huffington Post*, December 1, 2014, http://www.huffingtonpost.com/2014/12/01/boston-bombing-death-penalty_n_4367908.html.
29. Johnson, "Death Penalty for Boston Bomber a Complicated Question."
30. *Roper v. Simmons,* No. 03-633 (2005); *Atkins v. Virginia,* 536 U.S. 304 (2002).
31. *Glossip v. Gross*, No. 14-7955 (2015).
32. Barbara Sims, "Surveying the Correctional Environment: A Review of the Literature," *Corrections Management Quarterly* 5(2) (Spring 2001): 1–12.
33. Martha L. Henderson, Francis T. Cullen, Leo Carroll, and William Feinberg, "Race, Rights, and Order in Prison: A National Survey of Wardens on the Racial Integration of Prison Cells," *The Prison Journal* 80(3) (September 2000): 295–308.
34. Ibid.
35. Carl ToersBijns, "Correctional Supervisors with Bad Traits," Corrections.com, April 22, 2013, http://www.corrections.com/news/article/32825-correctional-supervisors-with-bad-traits-.
36. Ibid.
37. Gordon Hawkins, *The Prison* (Chicago: University of Chicago Press, 1976).
38. Center for Innovative Public Policies.
39. Harriet Fox, "8 Skills of Successful Correctional Officers," CorrectionsOne.com, July 21, 2015, http://www.correctionsone.com/column/articles/8685690-8-skills-of-successful-correctional-officers/.
40. Adapted from Lucien X. Lombardo, *Guards Imprisoned: Correctional Officers at Work* (Cincinnati, OH: Anderson, 1989), pp. 51–71.
41. Mary A. Farkas, "A Typology of Correctional Officers," *International Journal of Offender Therapy and Comparative Criminology* 44 (2000): 431–449.
42. Ibid., pp. 438–439.
43. Ibid., pp. 439–440.
44. Ibid., pp. 440–441.
45. Ibid., p. 442.
46. Ibid., pp. 442–443.
47. Ibid.
48. Susan Philliber, "Thy Brother's Keeper: A Review of the Literature on Correctional Officers," *Justice Quarterly* 4 (1987): 9–37.

49. David Robinson, Frank J. Porporino, and Linda Simourd, "The Influence of Educational Attainment on the Attitudes and Job Performance of Correctional Officers," *Crime and Delinquency* 43 (1997): 60–77.
50. Adapted from Ibid., pp. 41–43.
51. Robert Worley, James W. Marquart, and Janet L. Mullings, "Prison Guard Predators: An Analysis of Inmates Who Established Inappropriate Relationships with Prison Staff, 1995–1998," *Deviant Behavior: An Interdisciplinary Journal* 24 (2003): 175–194.
52. Ibid., p. 93.
53. U.S. Department of Justice, Bureau of Justice Statistics, *Jail Inmates in 2015: Summary* (December 2016), p. 1.
54. Ibid.
55. U.S. Department of Labor, Bureau of Labor Statistics, "Occupational Employment and Wages, May 2016, 33-3012 Correctional Officers and Jailers," https://www.bls.gov/oes/current/oes333012.htm.
56. Mark D. Martin and Paul Katsampes, *Sheriff's Guide to Effective Jail Operations* (Washington, DC: U.S. Department of Justice, National Institute of Corrections, 2006), pp. 5–6.
57. Quoted in Advisory Commission on Intergovernmental Relations, *Jails: Intergovernmental Dimensions of a Local Problem* (Washington, DC: Author, 1984), p. 1.
58. National Institute of Corrections, "Training Catalog," http://nicic.gov/training/.
59. Personal communication, Diane Kincaid, Deputy Director/Information Specialist, American Probation and Parole Association, November 21, 2014.
60. Bureau of Justice Statistics, *Probation and Parole in the United States, 2014* (November 2015), pp. 1–2, http://www.bjs.gov/content/pub/pdf/ppus15.pdf.
61. Richard P. Seiter, *Correctional Administration: Integrating Theory and Practice* (Upper Saddle River, NJ: Prentice Hall, 2002), pp. 387–388.
62. Anonymous personal communication, November 12, 2014.
63. Florida Department of Corrections, "Correctional Probation Officer Careers: Examples of Duties and Responsibilities," http://www.fldocjobs.com/paths/cpo/duties.html.
64. See Benjamin Steiner, Lawrence F. Travis III, Matthew D. Makarios, and Taylor Brickley, "The Influence of Parole Officers' Attitudes on Supervision Practices," *Justice Quarterly* 28(6) (December 2011): 903–930.
65. Manson was denied parole for the 12th time in April 2012. He is next eligible for parole in 2027 when he will be 92 years old. The parole board duly noted that he had recently bragged to a prison psychologist, "I'm special. I'm not like the average inmate. I have spent my life in prison. I have put five people in the grave. I am a very dangerous man." The board stated: "This panel can find nothing good as far as suitability factors go." See Christina Ng, "Charles Manson Denied Parole after Saying He Is a 'Very Dangerous Man,'" *ABC News*, April 11, 2012, http://abcnews.go.com/US/charles-manson-denied-parole-dangerous-man/story?id=16111128.
66. Patricia L. Hardyman, "Management Styles in Probation: Policy Implications Derived from Systems Theory," in Clayton A. Hartjen and Edward E. Rhine (eds.), *Correctional Theory and Practice* (Chicago, IL: Nelson-Hall, 1992), pp. 61–81.
67. Ibid.
68. Ibid., p. 71.
69. Kelly A. Cheeseman and Ragan A. Downey, "Talking 'Bout My Generation: The Effect of 'Generation' on Correctional Employee Perceptions of Work Stress and Job Satisfaction," *The Prison Journal* 92(1) (2011): 24–44.
70. Joseph L. Martin, Bronwen Lichtenstein, Robert B. Jenkot, and David R. Forde, "'They Can Take Us Over Any Time They Want': Correctional Officers' Responses to Prison Crowding," *The Prison Journal* 92(1) (2012): 88–105.
71. Eric Lambert, "The Impact of Job Characteristics on Correctional Staff Members," *The Prison Journal* 84(2) (June 2004): 208–227.
72. Ibid.
73. Tammy Castle and Jamie Martin, "Occupational Hazard: Predictors of Stress Among Jail Correctional Officers," *American Journal of Criminal Justice* 31(1) (September 2016): 65–80.
74. Ibid.
75. Jeanne B. Stinchcomb and Leslie A. Leip, "Turning Off Jail Turnover: Do Generational Differences Matter?" *Criminal Justice Studies* 26(26) (March 2014): 67–83; also see Jeanne B. Stinchcomb and Leslie A. Leip, "Retaining Desirable Workers in a Less-Than-Desirable Workplace: Perspectives of Line Staff and Jail Administrators," *Corrections Compendium* 37(2) (Summer 2014): 1–8. Matthew D. Gayman and Mindy S. Bradley, "Organizational Climate, Work Stress, and Depressive Symptoms among Probation and Parole Officers," *Criminal Justice Review* 26(3) (September 2014): 326–346.
76. See Jeanne B. Stinchcomb, *The National Jail Workforce Survey: Methodological Challenges,* April 1, 2010, http://www.faqs.org/periodicals/201004/2041517401.html.
77. Ibid.
78. Kristen R. Lewis, Ladonna S. Lewis, and Tina M. Garby, "Surviving the Trenches: The Personal Impact of the Job on Probation Officers," *American Journal of Criminal Justice* 38(1) (March 2013): 67–84.
79. Ibid.
80. Jeanne B. Stinchcomb and Leslie A. Leip, "Turning Off Jail Turnover: Do Generational Differences Matter?" *Criminal Justice Studies* 26(26) (March 2014): 67–83; also see Jeanne B. Stinchcomb and Leslie A. Leip, "Retaining Desirable Workers in a Less-Than-Desirable Workplace: Perspectives of Line Staff and Jail Administrators," *Corrections Compendium* 37(2) (Summer 2014): 1–8.
81. See Paul Vercammen, "O.J. Simpson Could Be Released as Early as October," *CNN*, March 8, 2017, http://www.cnn.com/2017/03/07/us/oj-simpson-parole-hearing/; also see Melissa Arseniuk, "Simpson Guiltyon All Counts," *Las Vegas Sun*, October 3, 2008, https://lasvegassun.com/news/2008/oct/03/jury-still-out-oj-simpson-trial/.

Rudall30/Shutterstock

12 Corrections Issues and Practices

LEARNING OBJECTIVES

After reading this chapter, the student will be able to:

1. *explain the Supreme Court's rationales for ending juvenile life without parole sentences*
2. *delineate several issues and problems concerning inmate populations: sexual and physical violence, issuing condoms to inmates, hostage taking, and dealing with mentally ill and geriatric inmates*
3. *discuss the rationale and major administrative considerations regarding inmate classification*
4. *describe the problem and possible solutions of drugs in prisons and jails*
5. *articulate the general approach used to treat drug abuse by a therapeutic community, and the kinds of approaches that seem to work best*
6. *discuss the pros, cons, and efficacy of privatizing correctional operations and programs*
7. *explain the types and effects of intermediate sanctions that stop short of incarceration*

▶ Introduction

The preceding two chapters in this part addressed some of the organizational and personnel issues and functions related to correctional institutions (i.e., prisons and jails) and community corrections (probation and parole). This chapter discusses additional issues related to correctional administrators regarding their operations.

First, we briefly examine several selected issues in the institutional setting that concern certain offender populations: new developments concerning juvenile offenders and life sentences, sexual and physical violence in prisons (and the Prison Rape Elimination Act of 2003 or PREA), whether or not inmates should be issued condoms, hostage taking in detention facilities, mentally ill and geriatric inmates, the rationale and methods for using inmate classification, and an overview of the drug problem in prisons (to include some treatment efforts). The move to privatize prisons is then examined, including purported advantages, disadvantages, and evaluations of such attempts. After discussions of several intermediate sanctions—punishments that are more severe than mere probation but less than prison—including intensive probation/parole, house arrest (HA), electronic monitoring (EM), shock probation and parole, shock incarceration, and day reporting—the chapter concludes with review questions and exercises in the Deliberate and Decide, Learn by Doing, and Case Study sections.

▶ Issues Concerning Inmate Populations

Correctional administrators must not only deal with issues such as institutional population and design, budgets, politics, and the Eighth Amendment's proscription against cruel and unusual punishment, but also cope with problems relating to the types of inmates who are under their supervision. Here, we consider several selected administrative issues and problems.

Juvenile Justice: An End to Death and Life without Parole Sentences

Over the past 10–15 years, juvenile offenders have received considerable attention from the U.S. Supreme Court, and have seen a more benevolent justice system as a result. First, having ruled in 2005 that it is unconstitutional to execute a person who committed a capital crime while younger than 18 years (see *Roper v. Simmons*, 543 U.S. 551), in May 2010, the U.S. Supreme Court decided *Graham v. Florida*,[1] which held that the Eighth Amendment's ban on cruel and unusual punishment prohibits juveniles who commit nonhomicide crimes from being sentenced to **life without parole (LWOP)** (however, this type of sentence can still be applied to convicted adult offenders, who must spend the remainder of their natural life in prison). Although 37 states, the District of Columbia, and the federal government had laws allowing LWOP sentences for youthful offenders, the justices stated that such sentences had been "rejected the world over," and that only the United States and perhaps Israel had imposed such punishment even for *homicides* committed by juveniles.

life without parole (LWOP) a type of sentence that can be applied to convicted adult (not juvenile) offenders, requiring that they spend the remainder of their natural life in prison.

Then, in 2012 the Court, combining two cases, ruled that the Eighth Amendment also prohibits sentencing any juvenile offender who commits a murder to serve a term of LWOP sentence (see *Miller v. Alabama* and *Jackson v. Hobbs*).[2] The Court noted that such sentences do not take into account the possibility that an adolescent's personality and judgment are still developing, and that criminal tendencies can be outgrown. And in a Supreme Court ruling in 2016, Justice Anthony Kennedy, who wrote the majority decision, expanded the 2012 decision of the Court by applying the ruling retroactively to those serving the LWOP sentence when they were convicted as a juvenile.[3] Essentially, the 2016 decision allows the 1,200 to 1,500 inmates who were previously sentenced to LWOP to argue for a favorable parole decision, despite their life sentence.[4] Justice Kennedy noted in the majority option that the 2012 decision was a "substantive change in the law," and therefore should be applied to LWOP cases retrospectively.[5]

Sexual and Physical Violence: Facts of Institutional Life

Physical violence is a constant possibility in correctional institutions, and **sexual violence**—termed *the plague that persists*[6]—must also be addressed. Sexual violence is defined by the World Health Organization as

> any sexual act, attempt to obtain a sexual act, unwanted sexual comments or advances, or acts to traffic, or otherwise directed, against a person's sexuality using coercion, by any person regardless of their relationship to the victim, in any setting, including but not limited to home and work.[7]

sexual violence any sexual act or attempted sexual act, unwanted sexual comments or advances, or acts to traffic, against a person's sexuality using coercion.

Persons entering prisons and jails express their sexuality in many forms: solitary or mutual masturbation, consensual homosexual behavior, and gang rapes. Factors that appear to increase sexual coercion rates include large population size (more than 1,000 inmates), understaffed workforces, racial conflict, barracks-type housing, inadequate security, and a high percentage of inmates incarcerated for crimes against persons.[8] Furthermore, inmates who are young, physically small or weak, suffering from mental illness, known to be "snitches," not gang affiliated, or convicted of sexual crimes are at increased risk of sexual victimization.[9]

Wolff and Shi[10] examined physical and sexual victimizations that were reported by nearly 7,000 male inmates. They found that during the study period, nearly one-third (32%) of inmates had been *physically* assaulted at least once, and approximately 3 percent reported at least one *sexual* assault. On average, regardless of the type of assault, victims were typically in their early 30s, African American, had spent 2 years at their prison, had 4 to 5 years left on their current sentences, and had spent roughly 8 years in prison since turning 18. Mental health problems were more frequently reported by victims of sexual assault. The most common forms of physical assault reported were being threatened with a weapon and being hit. Inmate-on-inmate sexual assault most often involved forced, attempted, or coerced anal or oral sex. Physical assaults were most likely to occur between noon and midnight (primarily between noon and 6 P.M.) and in an inmate's cell or yard. For sexual assaults, the inmate's cell was also the most likely place of occurrence, and inmates were at greatest risk of sexual assault by other inmates between 6 P.M. and midnight.[11]

Wolff and Shi also found that inmate-on-inmate physical and sexual assault incidents most often involved attackers with a gang affiliation and with whom the victim was acquainted, and roughly half of the incidents involved the use of a weapon, typically a knife or shank. Victims typically did not know why they were attacked. Episodes of inmate-on-inmate sexual assault were more likely to be committed by a repeat perpetrator, and physical injuries were more likely from inmate-on-inmate sexual assaults; injuries typically involved bruises, cuts, and scratches. One-third of the physical and sexual assaults resulted in medical attention, and about one-fifth of the incidents involving medical attention required hospitalization outside the prison.[12]

Alarid conducted a content analysis of sexual assault and coercion based on 5 years of letters from a female inmate in multiple institutions. She found that sexual coercion (pressuring and harassment) in female institutions was much more prevalent than sexual assaults, particularly among those who were in the masculine "stud" role in homosexual relationships.[13] Alarid also found that later instances of physical and sexual violence were related to sexual pressure tactics. Sexually aggressive, heterosexual femmes saw few constraints to their behavior by correctional officers (COs).[14]

Several policy issues arise from these findings. Wolff and Shi[15] suggest that, at a minimum, an intervention plan be employed that is selectively targeted to prison areas and times of day, and to inmates who are most at risk (e.g., those with mental illness; mental disabilities; or bisexual, transsexual, or homosexual orientations); these at-risk individuals should be placed in single cells or protective units. Prison administrators must attempt to prevent and prosecute sexual assaults, as well as increase surveillance in vulnerable areas, such as transportation vans, holding tanks, shower rooms, stairways, and storage areas. In addition, Alarid suggests that prison administrators make efforts to identify those who engage in sexual coercion, a factor related to later physical and sexual assault. Finally, new inmates should be informed of the potential for being sexually assaulted while incarcerated and be told about prevention and what medical, legal, and psychological help is available if they are targeted.[16]

The Urban Institute's report on addressing sexual violence in prisons provides a number of strategies for administrators and others to prevent and respond to sexual violence in prisons.[17] Among the recommendations are the following: (1) Department of Corrections (DOCs) should engage in multipronged approaches to deal with sexual violence, including specific policies, prevention programs, staff training, investigation, prosecution, victim services, and documenting incidents;[18] (2) DOCs should include outside experts in the area of prison sexual violence and use them to help develop appropriate response strategies; (3) policymakers should authorize funding for community organizations to assist DOCs with prison sexual violence; (4) DOCs should forge partnerships with prosecutors in an effort to facilitate successful prosecutions; and (5) DOCs should thoroughly document instances of sexual violence to identify hot spots and to improve problem-solving.[19]

The Prison Rape Elimination Act of 2003

Prison Rape Elimination Act of 2003 a law mandating national data collection on the incidence and prevalence of sexual assault in correctional facilities.

Until recently, there were very little current data on the extent of sexual coercion in prisons. Fortunately, however, federal legislation has indirectly provided some enlightenment. As part of the **Prison Rape Elimination Act of 2003 (PREA)** (P.L. 108-79), the U.S. DOJ's Bureau of Justice Statistics (BJS) was mandated to develop a new national data collection effort on the incidence and prevalence of sexual assault in correctional facilities. The law also required that public hearings be held concerning the prisons having the highest and lowest rates in order to determine what they are doing, that is, right and wrong; ultimately, a commission is to develop national standards for preventing prison rape.[20]

A BJS survey of federal and state prisons and local jails found that the number of allegations of sexual violence actually *increased* by 21 percent following enactment of the PREA; some of this increase, BJS states, may be the result of new definitions that were adopted, as well as improved reporting by correctional authorities. In fact, a more recent BJS survey found that, while the problem of sexual violence still exists, it is at least consistent with patterns over the previous 6 years.[21] Following are some of the BJS findings:

- An estimated 4 percent of state and federal prison inmates and 3.2 percent of jail inmates experienced one or more incidents of sexual victimization in the past 12 months.
- Among state and federal prison inmates, 2 percent reported an incident involving another inmate, 2.4 percent reported an incident involving facility staff, and 0.4 percent reported both an incident by another inmate and staff.
- About 1.6 percent of jail inmates reported an incident with another inmate, 1.8 percent reported an incident with staff, and 0.2 percent reported both an incident by another inmate and staff.[22]

In 2016, the BJS published a report dealing with sexual victimization in juvenile facilities, as reported by juvenile correctional authorities. Among the findings were the following:

- 865 allegations of sexual victimization were made in juvenile correctional facilities in 2012, up from 690 in 2010.
- Within state juvenile systems, the rate of sexual victimization allegations more than doubled from 2006 to 2012, from 19 per 1,000 youth to 47 per 1,000.
- From 2007 to 2009, 55 percent of allegations of sexual victimization of youth involved youth-on-youth victimization; 45 percent involved staff-on-youth victimization.[23]

A Dilemma: Should Inmates Be Issued Condoms?

An issue related to the earlier discussion of sexual violence in prisons is whether or not inmates should be given condoms. Given that prison inmates have unprotected sexual contact, both forced and consensual—and at times leading to the spread of HIV and other sexually transmitted diseases in the prisons as well as in communities where felons are paroled—the question is raised about the possible wisdom of offering inmates condoms.

Recently, California passed a law requiring that condoms be made available in all of its state prisons by 2020.[24] Prior to this, only the Vermont Department of Corrections had made condoms available throughout its prison system; it has been doing so since 1987, and the state's 2,200 inmates can request one condom at a time from a nurse. Canada, most of the European Union, Australia, Brazil, Indonesia, and South Africa already offer condoms to inmates. Mississippi has provided condoms to inmates for at least 20 years, but only to the few (about 10%) of inmates who are married and qualify for conjugal visits.[25]

Public health officials have found few problems and recommended the program be expanded. Similarly, the Center for Health Justice has found no related security problems in cities where condoms are being issued.[26] On the other hand, critics believe that handing out condoms would result in increased levels of voluntary or forced sexual activity, and that the condoms could be used to smuggle or hide drugs and other contraband.

From a policy standpoint, what must be recognized is that illicit relations by inmates have always been, and will likely always be an ongoing problem, and no state law barring inmate sex alone will solve the problem. Perhaps what might serve to convince both camps—those pros and cons—is an estimate by the University of California, San Francisco, that the rate of HIV infection among state prison inmates is 10 times higher than in the population at large (the main reason why Vermont issued its prison directive in the 1980s); in addition, California's prison officials estimate that more than 1,000 prisoners are HIV-infected, or about 1 percent of the state's inmate population.[27]

But prison and jail administrators take another tack: Issuing condoms sends the wrong message; it encourages consensual or coercive sex (and prison rapists might use condoms to avoid leaving DNA evidence after their assaults), and condoms can be used to conceal drugs. Others suggest that the issuing of condoms, which might send the message that consensual sex is condoned, can create disharmony in the institution, which could create security risks.[28] Nonetheless, the dilemma of issuing condoms to prisoners remains a hotly debated topic. Despite the Vermont directive and the recent California law, the fact is that few institutions make condoms available to its inmates. What do you think?

Hostage Taking in Detention Facilities: An Overview

Nature of the Problem

Riots and hostage taking are probably as old as corrections itself, and are the jail and prison administrator's worst nightmare. They can occur at any time; even the most safety-concerned staff cannot always avoid such crises. Inmates will be inmates, and they do not

hostage taking when any person—staff, visitor, or inmate—is held against his or her will by an inmate seeking to escape, gain concessions, or achieve other goals.

want to be where they are.[29] A corrections **hostage-taking** event occurs when any person—staff, visitor, or inmate—is held against his or her will by an inmate seeking to escape, gain concessions, or achieve other goals such as publicizing a particular cause. It may also be a planned or an impulsive act. When they occur, jail and prison rioting and hostage taking are potentially explosive and perilous situations from beginning to end; hostages are always directly in harm's way.[30] The following are some examples of such incidents:

- At the Morey Unit of the Lewis Prison Complex in Buckeye, Arizona, two inmates took two COs hostage and seized the unit's tower, triggering a 15-day standoff—the longest prison hostage situation in the nation's history.[31]
- Approximately 450 prisoners rioted in the Southern Ohio Correctional Facility, in Lucasville, Ohio; nine inmates and one officer were murdered and six officers taken hostage during the 10-day siege.[32]
- Jail inmates in a Louisiana parish held the warden and two corrections officers hostage at knifepoint, demanding a helicopter to escape to Cuba or anywhere else.[33]
- One female correctional staff member was rescued and a male CO was killed in a day-long standoff at the James T. Vaughn Correctional Center in Smyrna, Delaware[34] (see Exhibit 12.1).

EXHIBIT 12.1

THE 2017 SMYRNA, DELAWARE, STANDOFF: AN EXAMPLE OF A HOSTAGE RESCUE PROTOCOL

An early February 2017 standoff at the James T. Vaughn Correctional Center near Wilmington, Delaware, ended with the rescue of a correctional staff member and the death of a 16-year veteran correctional officer, Sergeant Steven Floyd. The standoff, which began on February 1 and ended 18 hours later, involved irate inmates in the C Building and four hostages. Within the first 10 hours, two of the four hostages were freed. In contacting a local newspaper, hostage takers noted that their rebellion was due to the then newly elected President Trump's policies and their concerns about the future of the correctional facility. The hostage takers demanded education, a rehabilitation program, and disclosure of the prison's budget and spending. Negotiations with the hostage takers were constant, and at one point, the water was turned on, conceding to one demand while developing a tactical plan to rescue the hostages. During their negotiations, officials believed that inmates were involved in stalling tactics to allow them more time to build a barricade. The tactical plan eventually included using a backhoe at the prison to knock down a make-shift wall inmates had built using containers that were filled with water once it had been turned back on. Once the plan was implemented, the rescue of the last hostages took place—a female staff member as well as Sergeant Floyd, who was later pronounced dead. None of the inmates were harmed during the standoff. An after-incident investigation would be conducted and would focus on how the standoff occurred in the first place and steps to prevent such an incident in the future.

Source: Max Berman and Katie Mettler, Mark Berman and Katie Mettler, "Hostage standoff in Delaware prison ends with one corrections officer dead," *The Washington Post,* February 2, 2017, https://www.washingtonpost.com/news/morning-mix/wp/2017/02/02/inmates-demanding-education-protesting-trump-take-hostages-at-delaware-prison/?utm_term=.47fdccfeb27a.

Also permanently seared in the annals of corrections rioting are the horrific incidents at the Attica Correctional Facility in Attica, New York, in 1971 (39 inmates and staff killed), and at the New Mexico State Prison in Santa Fe, in 1980 (33 inmates dead), where inmates took over most of these institutions.[35]

Local jails are included in this discussion because such incidents certainly occur in them, and are even more common in jails in foreign venues. U.S. jails—such as prisons—can become quite dangerous because of their overcrowded conditions and the nature of their clientele, which include arrestees awaiting trial for felony offenses, mentally ill persons awaiting movement to health facilities, convicted felons awaiting transport to a state or federal institution, military offenders, and many violent, often mentally unstable or sociopathic offenders with histories of substance abuse; certainly such individuals are capable of hostage taking. Indeed, about 7 of 10 jail inmates are being held for a felony offense.[36] Because 85 percent of local jails are operated by sheriff's offices or municipal police departments,[37] local sheriffs and police chiefs with lockup responsibilities must shoulder the burden of preparing for such emergencies.

Administrative Considerations: Using Force and Negotiation

Before correctional administrators can begin to plan for emergencies within their facilities, the following three broad elements are especially important: command, planning, and training (subsequently). Successful resolution also requires a controlled, measured response, clear lines of authority, and effective communication. Unity of command—the principle that members of an organization are accountable to a single superior—is also a paramount consideration.[38] Also, staffing levels must be established—traditional crisis response teams (CRTs), armed CRTs, and tactical teams—all of which can employ less lethal intervention options and even the use of deadly force:

1. ***Traditional CRTs.*** The first, primary level of response is the traditional CRT, which is comprised of staff from all job specialties who train in riot control formations and use of defensive equipment (e.g., batons, stun guns, chemical agents, control, and containment).
2. ***Armed CRTs.*** This level of response provides managers with an option for dealing with the emergency situation if it escalates to the point where staff members' or inmates' lives are in imminent danger; it involves a specially trained team that can respond with deadly force when necessary.
3. ***Tactical teams.*** These are the most highly trained and skilled emergency response staff. They must be trained in advanced skills, such as barricade breaching; hostage rescue; and precision marksmanship with pistols, rifles, and assault rifles.[39]

Another critical element of emergency planning is a use-of-force policy. Which staff members are authorized to order the use of force, and what weapons and less lethal munitions are appropriate? The riot plan should also include contact names and phone numbers and an outline of existing agreements between agencies.[40] Training is another indispensable facet of emergency planning. It does little good to have an emergency plan if staff and supervisors are not trained to activate it; people must clearly understand their own functions as well as those of people in other components; indeed, negotiators and personnel from tactical teams should train together regularly.[41]

The goals of hostage negotiation are to open communication lines, reduce stress and tension, build rapport, obtain intelligence, stall for time, allow hostage takers to express emotion and ventilate, and establish a problem-solving atmosphere.[42] Jail/prison records will provide valuable intelligence information on the hostage taker, including prior criminal, educational, work, psychological, and family history. Studies of hostage negotiations indicate that they tend to follow a common cycle: Initially, both parties make exaggerated demands. This is followed by a period of withdrawal and a return to negotiations with more moderate demands.

The passage of time can be a very important ally during such incidents and is a major element of the negotiator's role. Often, the preferred strategy for negotiating is to wait it out. The advantages of time's passing include that hostage takers may develop sympathy for their hostages, develop rapport with negotiators, or just get tired of doing what they are doing.[43] The question "How long is too long?" cannot be easily answered because every incident is different. Generally, negotiations may continue if no one is being injured and if no major damage or destruction to the facility is occurring.

Certain demands by hostage takers are nonnegotiable: Allowing release or escape, weapons, an exchange of hostages, and pardon or parole are not on the table. A number of other demands are open to negotiation. A maxim of negotiations is "Always get something for something." Negotiators should never cede to a demand without obtaining a concession in return.[44] Nor should they engage in trickery such as trying to drug hostage takers' food or drink (it might backfire) or have face-to-face contact (unless, as in rare instances, the decision is made that it is advantageous to do so).[45]

When negotiations deadlock, commanders may decide to employ ultimatums regarding use of force and issues. A *use-of-force ultimatum* can be given in the expectation that inmates, given a clear choice between surrender and an armed assault, will choose surrender.[46]

Aftermath: A Return to Normalcy

In the aftermath of hostage incidents, it is critical to learn whether or not there were contributing factors such as lax inmate search activities, contraband, contractors and visitors coming and going, inmate familiarity with staff work routines, unlocked doors or gates, or other contributing factors; if so, new policies and procedures must be enacted covering those exigencies. The administration must also consider any damages, renovations, repairs, and remodeling that need to be addressed, and continuing control of the inmates while these are attended to.[47]

Mentally Ill Offenders

While in solitary confinement in a Massachusetts prison, an inmate cut his legs and arms, tried to hang himself with tubing from a breathing machine, smashed the machine to get a sharp fragment to slice his neck, and ate pieces of it, hoping to cause internal bleeding; he eventually hanged himself. Such inmates, with histories of mental illness and depression, often try suicide. In fact, this was one of 18 suicides or attempted suicides in Massachusetts during a three-year period. A federal lawsuit filed by advocates for inmates and the mentally ill is seeking to prevent the state from placing mentally ill inmates in such segregated cells.[48] But, correctional administrators certainly are in a pinch as to what to do with mentally ill inmates at a time when "prisons and jails have become America's 'new asylums'."[49]

mentally ill inmate one who meets the definition and has a significant mental disorder(s), which can include schizophrenia, bipolar disorders, and major depression, among others.

Several other states have faced similar lawsuits and other challenges in attempting to address the problem of **mentally ill inmates**. These are prisoners who meet a specified definition based on the diagnostic system of the American Psychiatric Association and can include schizophrenia, bipolar disorders, and major depression, among others.[50]

To provide some perspective on the issue of mental illness among the incarcerated population, the BJS noted the following:[51]

- Fifty-six percent of state prisoners, 45 percent of federal prisoners, and 64 percent of jail inmates had a mental health problem.
- State prisoners who had a mental health problem were twice as likely as those who did not to have been homeless in the year before their arrest.
- An estimated two-thirds of state prisoners with a mental health problem used drugs the month prior to their arrest (compared to less than half who did not have a mental health problem).
- About three-fourths of state prisoners and jail inmates who had a mental health problem also fit the criteria for substance dependence or abuse.

Owing to several causes—the closing or downsizing of state psychiatric hospitals, the lack of adequate community support programs, chronic underfunding of public services, the poverty and transient lifestyles of many people with serious mental illness, and substance abuse disorders—the number of criminal offenders and inmates suffering from mental illness has been increasing.[52] In 2017, the BJS reported that 26 percent of jail inmates and 14 percent of state and federal prisoners met the threshold for serious psychological distress.[53] In prison, these individuals pose a dual dilemma for administrators. They are often violent and may be serving a long sentence; therefore, they require a high level of security and are housed with other offenders who have committed equally serious offenses and who are serving equally long sentences. The presence of potentially violent, mentally ill prisoners in high-security and probably overcrowded institutions is a dangerous situation. Mental illness must be treated while inmates are incarcerated.

A related problem concerns the release of mentally ill convicts back into the community. These inmates must be tracked and supervised to ensure that they receive proper case management and stay on their medications. This approach goes far beyond the traditional "$25 in gate money and a bus ticket" for the inmate, and not only protects the public but also helps to hold the prison population down. To provide these follow-up services, many states have developed written agreements between the state and local correctional agencies and between the state and local mental health services agencies. Local mental health agencies can be used to provide counseling and support to probationers. The challenge for correctional administrators is to maintain a viable program to treat and control a difficult group of offenders, some of whom have both serious mental health issues and the co-occurring disorder of substance abuse. The treatment of this group requires resources, trained staff, and appropriate facilities. BJS also reports that of those incarcerated persons afflicted with a mental health problem, 49 percent of prison inmates and 24 percent of jail inmates are receiving counseling or therapy.[54]

According to the Treatment Advocacy Center's 2014 report, prison and jail administrators have few options when it comes to the treatment of inmates with serious mental health issues. Administrators are neither trained nor equipped to handle such inmates, often do not have the medications to treat their conditions, and sometimes rely on solitary confinement as a way to protect mentally ill inmates, other inmates, and correctional staff.[55] Among the solutions offered by the Treatment Advocacy Center are the following: (1) eliminate barriers to treatment in the community; (2) reform laws so that inmates can receive adequate mental health services while behind bars; (3) promote diversion programs such as mental health courts; and (4) develop release planning to increase the odds of recovery.[56]

The Problem with Solitary Confinement

Earlier in this section, we discussed the need for correctional officials to use solitary confinement for inmates with severe mental health problems, as well as other inmates in special groups, namely some of the most violent inmates. Solitary confinement is known by various names, including administrative segregation, restrictive housing, or the box.[57] Recently, however, the use of solitary confinement in prisons and jail has come under scrutiny, and reform movements to ban or significantly reduce it have surfaced. In fact, in 2016, President Barack Obama adopted a list of recommendations limiting the use of solitary confinement in federal prisons.[58] President Obama's action stemmed from the potential detrimental effects of long-term solitary confinement, the lack of data concerning its effects, how segregation policies were written, and whether solitary confinement achieves its goals.[59]

A study in 2014 sheds some light on the detrimental effects of solitary confinement in jails, which indicated that it was strongly associated with instances of self-harm.[60] The researchers also found that with the mentally ill population in solitary confinement, they often commit new infractions, which lead to more time in solitary confinement.[61] In Colorado, the practice and use of solitary confinement is now rare throughout the state's prison system, due in large part to a state statute that prohibits its use for those with severe mental illness.[62] Given growing research on the negative effects of solitary confinement, the challenge for administrators is to find ways to deal with violent inmates and those with mental illness in a way that keeps them and others safe. In this regard, Colorado has experimented with de-escalation rooms, where inmates are provided stress balls, chalkboards to write down their thoughts, and music.[63]

Finally, in the summer of 2016, President Obama directed the DOJ (DOJ) to review the use of solitary confinement for 100,000 prisons then being held in federal prisons. Although finding certain circumstances when solitary is a necessary tool (e.g., to protect themselves, staff, and other inmates), the DOJ put forth a number of recommendations to reform the federal prison system, which the president adopted: banning solitary confinement for juveniles, expanding treatment for the mentally ill, and increasing the amount of time inmates in solitary can spend outside of their cells.[64]

The Aging of Inmates: Problems and Approaches

James "Whitey" Bulger, Boston's most notorious gangster, was convicted in 2013 at age 84 for 11 murders and 31 counts of racketeering, extortion, money laundering, trafficking in cocaine and marijuana, and weapons possession; he was sentenced to 2 life sentences plus 5 years after evading capture for 16 years.[65]

This example, while unusual given Bulger's age at the time of conviction, is symbolic of a significant national problem that the U.S. DOJ has also termed a top management problem: the aging of the inmate population and the special needs of **geriatric inmates**.[66] According to the Vera Institute of Justice, there is no national consensus or definition concerning when an inmate qualifies as "old" or "elderly." While the U.S. Census Bureau defines the general "elderly" population as those 65 and older, the 27 states that have definitions for who is an "older prisoner" include 15 states that used age 50 as the cutoff, five states age 55, four states 60, two states 65, and one used age 70.[67]

geriatric inmates
while there is no standard definition concerning what age an inmate becomes "elderly," it is known that the aging inmate population is growing rapidly, raising medical costs and requiring special needs be met.

What is known, however, is that prisoners older than 55 make up the single fastest-growing segment of the U.S. prison community—indeed, approximately 124,000 inmates are now age 55 or older (a 282% increase from 1995) and are raising medical costs dramatically (see Exhibit 12.2).[68] Unforeseen consequences of legislative enactments—tougher mandatory sentencing laws, "truth in sentencing" laws, three-strikes laws, the abolition of parole for certain violent offenders (with concurrent reductions in early release), and the elimination of parole in the federal system—have combined to put people in prison longer and create this situation.[69]

Certainly, prison administrators are already confronted with an aging inmate population, seeing increasing numbers of prisoners who need wheelchairs, walkers, canes, a supply of oxygen, and hearing aids; many cannot even dress or go to the bathroom by themselves and are incontinent, suffering from dementia and chronic illnesses, extremely ill, or dying. They also see the high costs of caring for these inmates: it costs approximately $24,000 per year for younger prisoners, but costs associated with older prisoners can be as high as $72,000 per year; this gap is largely due to higher health care costs.[70]

Some states now contract with private providers to establish and operate skilled nursing facilities to incarcerate and care for inmates who (1) have limited ability to perform activities of daily living and (2) need skilled nursing services. Others contract with physicians to assess and diagnose all inmates who are limited in performing activities of daily living; the physicians then develop a service plan to meet the individual inmate's medical and mental health needs, and to see they are housed consistent with their custody level and medical status. Other states have developed special units to work with the cognitively impaired (dementia).[71] Finally, one state has a dedicated structured living program just for such inmates (see Exhibit 12.2).

There are some relatively easy, short-term responses and accommodations that can be adopted for this growing population: assigning them to a bottom bunk, installing grab bars near the toilets and in showers, housing them closer to the dining hall, and giving them more time to report to prison counts.[72] However, policy decisions and recommendations for a more long-term time frame are more challenging; in short, the policy question that requires more thought and attention concerns what to do, as a society, with inmates who suffer from dementia or have become nearly or totally paralyzed—in short, how to make society safe but also be as humanitarian as possible. Compassionate release is one option that we may see more of in the future, given the continued increases in the elderly prison population. But such programs require lengthy application and evaluation processes, and some deem their release as simply unfair.[73] Despite this, former attorney general Eric Holder announced in 2013 an early release program for elderly inmates who had served at least one-half of their sentence and did not pose a threat to society. As we have seen, however, the aging of the inmate population is a complex problem with no easy solutions.

EXHIBIT 12.2

NEVADA'S PROGRAM FOR GERIATRIC INMATES

Only about 5.8 percent of Nevada's 13,000 prison inmates are age 60 and older, but they consume 20 percent of the medical budget. The state now has 14 inmates in their 80s, and until recently, one inmate was in his 90s.[74]

A unique—and increasingly publicized—program at the Northern Nevada Correctional Center in Carson City, Nevada, called the Senior Structured Living Program, is designed to work with such inmates. The program provides physical fitness, diversion therapy (arts, crafts, games, reading, poetry), music (a choir and band), wellness and life skills training, individual and group therapy, and community involvement (involving area social services, veterans, Alcoholics Anonymous, and other groups). Volunteers also provide psychological, spiritual, and social support to the men. To enter the program, inmates must sign a contract obligating them to maintain certain standards of conduct, be at least 60 years of age, and not be engaged in a full-time job or educational program. Today, 170 men are enrolled in the program (with a waiting list of 50). The prison medical department has witnessed a significant reduction in the men's overall medical complaints, overutilization of medical care, and the use of psychotropic medications.[75] As such, this program is an innovative example of rehabilitation, constructive care for elderly inmates, and a novel way to prepare for reentry into the community.

Inmate Classification: Cornerstone of Security and Treatment

Although it may not seem to be so on its face, the **classification** of inmates into proper levels of security, housing, programming, and other aspects of their incarceration is of utmost importance. Classification decisions will have a major influence on their behavior, treatment, and progress while in custody, as well as the general safety of inmates and staff.

classification the placing of inmates into the proper levels of security, housing, programming, and other aspects of their incarceration.

Corrections staff must make classification decisions in at least two areas: the inmate's level of *physical restraint* or "security level" and the inmate's level of supervision or *custody grade*. These two concepts are not well understood and are often confused, but they significantly impact a prisoner's housing and program assignments[76] as well as an institution's overall security level.

unit management a corrections management approach with the larger prison population being subdivided into smaller units, felt to be more effective and to improve inmate classification.

The most recent development in classification is **unit management**, in which a large prison population is subdivided into several mini-institutions analogous to a city and its neighborhoods.

Unit management is felt to be a more humane, effective, and efficient approach than the former, centralized approach. A unit can include a unit manager, case manager(s), counselor(s), full- or part-time psychologist(s), an education representative, and COs whose offices are in the living unit; this approach also enables classification decisions to be made by personnel who are in daily contact with their inmates and know them fairly well.[77]

Robert Levinson delineated four categories into which corrections agencies classify new inmates: security, custody, housing, and programs:[78]

1. *Security* needs are classified in terms of the number and types of architectural barriers that must be placed between the inmates and the outside world to ensure that they will not escape and can be controlled. Most correctional systems have four security levels: supermax (highest), maximum (high), medium (low), and minimum (lowest).
2. *Custody* assignments determine the level of supervision and types of privileges an inmate will have. A basic consideration is whether or not an inmate will be allowed to go outside the facility's secure perimeter, so some systems have adopted four custody grades—two inside the fence (one more restrictive than the other) and two outside the fence (one more closely supervised than the other).
3. *Housing* needs were historically determined by an "assign to the next empty bed" system, which could place the new, weak inmate in the same cell with the most hardened inmate; a more sophisticated approach is known as *internal classification*, in which inmates are assigned to live with prisoners who are similar to themselves. This approach can involve the grouping of inmates into three broad categories: heavy (victimizers), light (victims), and moderate (neither intimidated by the first group nor abusers of the second).
4. *Program* classification involves using interview and testing data to determine where the newly arrived inmate should be placed in work, training, and treatment programs; these are designed to help the prisoner make a successful return to society.

In the past, most prison systems used a highly subjective system of classifying inmates that involved a review of records pertaining to the inmate's prior social and criminal history, test scores, school and work performance, and staff impressions developed from interviews. Today, however, administrators employ a much-preferred objective system that is more rational, efficient, and equitable. Factors used in making classification decisions are measurable and valid and are applied to all inmates in the same way. Criteria most often used are escape history, detainers, prior commitments, criminal history, prior institutional adjustment, history of violence, and length of sentence.[79]

Prison administrators also should facilitate systematic evaluations of their inmate classification systems to ensure that the system being used is achieving its goals. Here, administrators may want to partner with trained social scientists to conduct both process and outcome evaluations. According to the National Institute of Corrections (NIC), an objective classification system should be evaluated in terms of implementation (process evaluation) and goals (outcome evaluation).[80] The NIC also recommends the following: (1) evaluations should be based on objective data; (2) evaluations should be timely and useful; (3) evaluations should be fair; and (4) evaluations should be clearly written.

Drug Use in Prisons: Interdiction and Treatment

More than half of all adult arrestees test positive for drug use at the time of their apprehension; their drug use prior to incarceration is typically chronic. Indeed, 50 percent of federal prisoners and 56 percent of state prison inmates used drugs during the month before the arrest for which they were incarcerated.[81] Furthermore, offenders still manage to obtain illicit drugs during their incarceration, threatening the safety of inmates and staff while undermining the authority of correctional administrators, contradicting rehabilitative goals, and reducing public confidence.[82]

Some jail and prison administrators have aimed to reduce the number of visitors to an institution by switching to a video visitation system. The advantages to such a system, in part, is that there is less worry about contraband coming into the institution, fewer inmate searches, and reductions in staff time.[83] More than 500 correctional facilities use some form of video visitation, although it's used mostly in county jails. Indeed, a multipronged effort is needed to deal with inmates who not only are addicted to substances but who also *use* drugs in our prisons and jails.

We first discuss Pennsylvania's approach to **drug interdiction**, which may be defined as a continuum of efforts to reduce the supply and demand for drugs in the prison, and includes focusing on visitors, staff, mail, warehouses, gates, volunteers, and contractors. Next, we examine what can be done to treat offenders' substance abuse problems inside the institution.

drug interdiction efforts to reduce the supply and demand for drugs in prison, to include focusing on visitors, staff, mail, warehouses, gates, volunteers, and contractors.

The Pennsylvania Plan

The state of Pennsylvania was compelled to acknowledge that drug use was pervasive in several of its prisons. Six inmates had died from overdoses in a 2-year period, and assaults on COs and inmates had increased. To combat the problem, the state first adopted a zero-tolerance drug policy, the so-called Pennsylvania Plan for drug interdiction. Inmates caught with drugs were to be criminally prosecuted, and those who tested positive (using hair testing) were to serve disciplinary custody time. Highly sensitive drug detection equipment was employed to detect drugs that visitors might try to smuggle into the prison, to inspect packages arriving in the mail, and to detect drugs that correctional staff might try to bring in. New policies were issued for inmate movement and visitation, and a new phone system was installed to randomly monitor inmates' calls.[84]

The results were impressive. The state's 24 prisons became 99 percent drug free. The number of drug finds during cell searches dropped 41 percent, assaults on staff decreased 57 percent, inmate-on-inmate assaults declined 70 percent, and the number of weapons seized during searches dropped from 220 to 76. Marijuana use dropped from 6.5 percent before interdiction to 0.3 percent, and there was a significant decline in the use of other types of drugs. Pennsylvania now believes that the foundation has been laid for inmates to abstain from drug use while serving their sentences—a necessary first step toward long-term abstinence and becoming a better citizen for their families and communities.[85] However, despite the apparent effectiveness of the Pennsylvania Plan, there are no simple solutions to the complex problem of drug dependency among many inmates.

Treating the Problem

During the past several years, a number of aggressive federal and state initiatives have been undertaken to expand substance abuse treatment within correctional settings. These initiatives have been fueled by the high rates of substance abuse among offenders. In Ohio in 2014, for example, 1,900 inmates in the state prison system did not pass random drug screens, a 41 percent increase over previous years.[86] Intensive prison-based treatment efforts can significantly reduce postprison substance use and recidivism.[87]

Several barriers remain for correctional administrators in implementing substance abuse treatment programs, however. First, institutions tend to use limited criteria (such as any lifetime drug use, possession, drug sales, or trafficking) to determine the need for treatment, leading to a lack of treatment of a large portion of the prison population that has abused substances; conversely, many inmates who legitimately need treatment may be excluded for reasons unrelated to their substance abuse problems (e.g., because of gang affiliation or the commission of a sexual or violent offense). Kathryn Nowotny, in her recent study, found that less than 50 percent of more than 5,000 inmates received any kind of treatment in prison.[88] What's more, she found that Hispanic inmates (vs. white or black inmates) were least likely to use treatment services in prison. The explanation, at least in part, may have to do with the differences between white inmates and Hispanic inmates when it comes to court-ordered treatment in prison; whites were more likely than Hispanics to have mandated treatment as part of their sentence. Nowotny also suggests that language barriers may make a difference.[89] Treatment staff should be involved in the selection of candidates for treatment to ensure the appropriateness of the program population.[90]

Second, it is difficult to find and recruit qualified and experienced staff in the remote areas where prisons are often located. In addition, counselors who are well suited for community-based treatment programs will not necessarily be effective in the prison setting. They often resist the rigid custody regulations that are common in institutional settings. For these reasons, limited human resources and high turnover rates for drug abuse treatment counselors make staffing an ongoing problem for prison administrators.[91]

Possible solutions to this staffing problem include offering sufficient wages and other amenities to induce counselors to move to and stay with the prison, recruiting and training "lifers" as inmate counselors and mentors, and professionalizing treatment positions for COs. With the use of counselors, certification and financial incentives would help to retain staff, as well as enhance their professional development for the treatment setting.[92]

Can a "Therapeutic Community" Work?

As indicated earlier, drug use is not unknown to most prison inmates, with more than half of all adult arrestees testing positive for drug use at the time of their apprehension and using drugs during the month before the arrest for which they were incarcerated. Several treatment modalities have been attempted in the past to deal with such offenders, including individual and group counseling, methadone maintenance, Vivitrol injections,[93] shock incarceration (or boot camp), drug education, and 12-step programs.[94]

therapeutic community drug-free residential programs relying heavily on peer influence and group processes to promote drug-free behavior.

One of the most widely used treatment models, however, is the **therapeutic community** (TC). Existing for more than a half-century, contemporary TCs have evolved over the years and are typically drug-free residential programs relying heavily on peer influence and group processes to promote drug-free behavior. At the root of TCs is the provision of an environment in which drug abusers seek and receive support from individuals with similar problems. Also extremely important for drug-abusing inmates' success is aftercare upon release. Contemporary TCs use a social learning theoretical framework and stress the importance of community. It is within a community that an individual can best realize the impact of TC.

Evaluations of TCs with prison inmates have been mostly positive, finding that TCs that include aftercare are both effective in reducing drug use and recidivism, and cost effective. However, the use of boot camps (or shock incarceration discussed later in this chapter) and group counseling have not been found to be effective in these regards. Most studies of TCs have been based on short-term outcomes, typically one to two years following release.[95]

A more long-term study, using 5 years of data with about 400 California inmates, contradicted these studies; it found that TCs as implemented there failed to reduce reincarceration and rearrest rates over time. Researchers believed that this was a result of the prison TC program failing to optimize its aftercare-phase treatment. Furthermore, because most aftercare programs are voluntary, it appears that inmates there fell short of the levels of participation needed and thus successful reintegration into the community.[96] Other evaluations of TCs suggest that there is a relationship between duration of treatment, aftercare participation, and ultimately recovery. Participating in a TC for at least 3 months was associated with positive outcomes; participation for at least 6 months was even better, with 5-year outcomes indicating reduced drug use and criminal activity as well as increased employment rates.[97]

The implications are obvious: Because few prison drug programs are available, and yet the demand for such programs remains high, there needs to be rigorous research into what seems to work best for the TC as a treatment strategy, along with appropriate community-based aftercare treatment.

▶ The Controversy of Private Prisons

Emergence of the Concept

Perhaps one of the most controversial and rapidly growing aspects of corrections has been the outsourcing or **privatization** of prisons, a term that includes either the operation of existing prison facilities by a private company or the building and operation of new prisons by for-profit companies. In 1995, there were fewer than 30 adult facilities operated by private contractors. Within 5 years, private prisons had increased to more than 100.[98] Now, the BJS reports that about 7 percent of state prison inmates (91,300) and 18 percent of federal prisoners (34,900, including federal immigration detainees) are in private correctional facilities.[99] Currently, six states (Hawaii, Mississippi, Montana, New Mexico, North Dakota, and Oklahoma) house 20 percent or more of their state inmates in private facilities.[100]

privatization either the operation of existing prison facilities or the building and operation of new prisons by for-profit companies.

The two largest companies, CoreCivic (formerly Corrections Corporation of America) and the Geo Group, reported combined revenues of $2.9 billion in 2010. CoreCivic houses about 80,000 prisoners; of the more than 60 facilities it operates, it owns 44.[101]

Historically, strong arguments have been put forth, both pro and con, regarding the privatizing of prisons; and today there is no dearth of differing viewpoints on the matter. Proponents, such as the Reason Foundation, argue that private prisons

> provide an effective, cost-saving alternative for governments seeking to address significant capacity needs while taking pressure off their corrections budgets. Studies have consistently shown that privately run correctional facilities typically save a conservative range of 5 to 15% over staterun prisons while offering the same level of security and service and easing overcrowding in staterun prisons.[102]

Opponents, on the other hand, maintain that there is no guarantee that standards will be upheld, no one will maintain security if employees go on strike, the public will have regular access to the facility, there will be different inmate disciplinary procedures, the company will be able to refuse certain inmates or could go bankrupt, and the company can increase its fees to the state.[103]

Comparing Public versus Private Prisons

Which is better—public or private prisons? There is a tendency to compare public and private institutions in terms of their inmates' recidivism rates; however, some observers[104] argue that this is an unfair comparison, as prison administrators are not responsible for what occurs outside of their prison's walls.

What might stand as a much better and comprehensive standard to use for comparison is what was developed originally in 1992 by Charles H. Logan,[105] and refined in 2003 by Dina Perrone and Travis C. Pratt,[106] which are termed the *seven domains* of prison quality and include the following:

- *Condition*, which refers to the physical environment in which the inmates are held. Indications of a poorly kept prison such as crowding, noise, food, and sanitation have been used as measures.

- *Management,* which refers to the ability of the prison administrators to effectively and efficiently run their institution; it can be measured by comparing staff turnover and stress rates.
- *Activity,* which refers to the ability of prison administrators to keep their inmate population involved and active in prison life; this domain is commonly measured in terms of the number of educational, treatment, and work programs available to and used by inmates.
- *Care* refers to the extent and quality of medical care afforded to inmates.
- *Security* measures how well the prison is able to keep its inmates securely incapacitated from the outside world; it can be evaluated by measuring the number of escapes, while some studies have also taken into account the amount of contraband entering the prison.
- *Safety* refers to the ability to keep both inmates and prison staff from being assaulted or killed; and
- *Order* refers to the overall ability of an institution to control its population; often considered is the number of disciplinary actions and disturbances that occur.

No single study has examined all seven domains; however, a number of studies have examined the quality of private prisons by examining some of the domains. The results have tended to be mixed in all such studies, with most comparing only a small number of private institutions (usually one or two) to a public institution(s); therefore, generalizing these findings to other institutions is problematic. Another shortcoming is that custody level, size, crowding, age, and architecture all can have a strong influence on such measures of quality.

Makarios and Maahs sought, in 2012, to address these shortcomings by examining a larger sample of private and public prisons. Specifically, they examined 1,129 institutions—105 private, 80 federal, and 944 state-operated.[107] They found a significant difference in one regard: state prisons were much more likely to be under a court order for the conditions of confinement than private prisons. Therefore, private prisons are less crowded than those that are publicly operated. Given the negative effects of crowding, this is a significant finding and most likely a result of public facilities having much less control over the level and nature of new admissions.

Overall, however, Makarios and Maahs generally found a fair degree of similarity between private and public prisons. Consistent with prior research, they found that "the differences between private and public prisons become relatively small."[108] Despite this, private prisons have come under considerable scrutiny of late for problems discovered across many of the seven domains.

In fact, in 2016 prior to President Donald Trump's election, the U.S. DOJ announced its plans to discontinue the use of private prisons in the federal system, affecting 13 federal prisons and 22,000 inmates.[109] The plan called for a nonrenewal of private prison contracts over the next 5 years. The inspector general's report, which preceded the announcement, articulated more safety and security violations in private prisons than in prisons run by the Federal Bureau of Prisons. The report noted property damage in private prisons, personal injuries, and the death of a CO.[110] The report also noted that private prisons in the federal system were expensive and ineffective at reducing recidivism.[111]

However, during the Trump presidency, we may see a reversal of sorts from the Justice Department's announcement. First, it is well known that President Trump is a fan of privatization and he has gone on record saying that private prisons work better than government-operated prisons.[112] In addition, immigrant detention could increase markedly under President Trump. Currently, the U.S. Immigration and Customs Enforcement agency holds 60 percent of its detainees in private prisons, and an increase in the numbers of detainees may result in the need for more bed space in prisons.[113] In 2016, just when it appeared that prison privatization was beginning to show a downturn, private prisons may be making a resurgence.

Alternatives to Incarceration: Intermediate Sanctions

Because prisons are not in a position to effect great change,[114] the search for solutions must include correctional programs in the community. The demand for prison space has created a reaction throughout the corrections industry.[115] With the cost of prison construction now exceeding $250,000 per cell in maximum-security institutions, cost-saving alternatives are not only becoming more attractive but also essential.

An **alternative to incarceration** can be any form of punishment or treatment other than prison or jail time given to a convicted person. It must have three elements to be effective—it must incapacitate offenders enough so that it is possible to interfere with their lives and activities to make committing a new offense extremely difficult, it must be unpleasant enough to deter offenders from wanting to commit new crimes, and it has to provide real and credible protection for the community.[116]

alternatives to incarceration any form of punishment or treatment other than prison or jail time given to a convicted person.

The aforementioned realities of prison construction and crowding have led to a search for an intermediate range of punishments.[117] This, in turn, has brought about the emergence of a new generation of programs, making community-based corrections, according to Barry Nidorf, a "strong, full partner in the fight against crime and a leader in confronting the crowding crisis."[118] Economic reality dictates that cost-effective measures be developed, and this is motivating the development of **intermediate sanctions**:[119] a range of sentencing options designed to fill the gap between probation and confinement, reduce institutional crowding, and reduce correctional costs. They have included such sanctions as intensive supervision probation (ISP), problem-solving courts, fines, community service, day reporting centers (DRC), home detention/EM, and boot camps.

intermediate sanctions a range of sentencing options designed to fill the gap between probation and confinement, reduce institutional crowding, and reduce correctional costs.

A recent survey by the BJS found that of all persons being supervised outside a jail facility, 23 percent were engaged in some form of community service and 22 percent were involved in EM; fewer than one percent were undergoing home detention only.[120] Table 12-1 ■ shows these findings as well as the number of persons under jail supervision and involved with other types of programs.

Intensive Supervision in the Community

Intensive supervision—tight control and supervision of offenders in the community through strict enforcement of conditions and frequent reporting to a probation officer—has become a popular program in probation and parole. Early versions were based on the premise that increased client contact would enhance rehabilitation while affording greater client control. Current programs are simply a means of easing the burden of prison crowding.[121]

intensive supervision tight control and supervision of offenders in the community through strict enforcement of conditions and frequent reporting to a probation officer.

Intensive supervision can be classified into two types: those stressing diversion and those stressing enhancement. A diversion program is commonly known as a *front door* program because its goal is to limit the number of generally low-risk offenders who enter prison. Enhancement programs generally select already sentenced probationers and parolees and subject them to closer supervision in the community than they receive under regular probation or parole.[122]

Intensive supervision units generally are in charge of intensive supervision in a given jurisdiction—for those who are deemed high risks in the community. Commonly, these

TABLE 12-1 Persons Under Jail Supervision, by Confinement Status and Type of Program, Midyear 2000 and 2006–2014

Confinement status and type of program	2000	2006	2007	2008	2009	2010	2011	2012	2013	2014
Total	687,033	826,041	848,419	858,385	837,647	809,360	798,417	808,622	790,649	808,070
Held in jail	621,149	765,819	780,174	785,533	767,434	748,728	735,601	744,524	731,208	744,592
Supervised outside of a jail facility	65,884	60,222	68,245	72,852	70,213	60,632	62,816	64,098	59,441	63,478
Weekend programs	14,523	11,421	10,473	12,325	11,212	9,871	11,369	10,351	10,950	9,698
Electronic monitoring	10,782	10,999	13,121	13,539	11,834	12,319	11,950	13,779	12,023	14,223
Home detention	332	807	512	498	738	736	809	2,129	1,337	646
Day reporting	3,969	4,841	6,163	5,758	6,492	5,552	5,200	3,890	3,683	4,413
Community service	13,592	14,667	15,327	18,475	17,738	14,646	11,680	14,761	13,877	14,331
Other pretrial supervision	6,279	6,409	11,148	12,452	12,439	9,375	10,464	7,738	7,542	8,634
Other work programs	8,011	8,319	7,369	5,808	5,912	4,351	7,165	7,137	5,341	7,003
Treatment programs	5,714	1,486	2,276	2,259	2,082	1,799	2,449	2,164	2,002	2,100
Other	2,682	1,273	1,857	1,739	1,766	1,983	1,731	2,149	2,687	2,430

offenders have either committed violent crimes, are gang members, sex offenders, or serious substance abusers. ISP officers have a dual role of both law enforcement officers and brokers of treatment, and conduct their jobs by building relationships not only with offenders but also with the offenders' social networks, as well as law enforcement agencies, employers, treatment providers, and school officials (in the case of juveniles).

As of 1990, jurisdictions in all 50 states had instituted intensive supervision programs (ISP). Persons placed on ISP are supposedly those offenders who, in the absence of intensive supervision, would have been sentenced to imprisonment. In parole, intensive supervision is viewed as risk management—allowing a high-risk inmate to be paroled but under the most restrictive circumstances. In either case, intensive supervision is a response to crowding; although ISP is invariably more costly than regular supervision, the costs "are compared not with the costs of normal supervision but rather with the costs of incarceration."[123] However, the cost savings from ISP and its potential to reduce prison overcrowding only come when ISP is used as an alternative to incarceration. When it's used as an alternative to a less restrictive sanction, widening of the criminal justice net occurs.

ISP is demanding for probationers and parolees, and while they are not incarcerated, ISP does not represent freedom; in fact, it may stress and isolate repeat offenders more than imprisonment does. Given the option of serving prison terms or participating in ISPs, many offenders have chosen prison.[124] Many offenders may prefer to serve a short prison term rather than spend five times that in ISP. Consider the alternatives now facing offenders in one Western state:

> ISP. The offender serves two years under this alternative. During that time, a probation officer visits the offender two or three times per week and phones on the other days. The offender is subject to unannounced searches of his or her home for drugs and has his or her urine tested regularly for alcohol and drugs. The offender must strictly abide by other conditions set by the court: not carrying a weapon, not socializing with certain persons, performing community service, and being employed or participating in training or education. In addition, he or she is strongly encouraged to attend counseling and/or other treatment, particularly if he or she is a drug offender.
>
> Prison. The alternative is a sentence of two to four years, of which the offender will serve only about three to six months. During this term, the offender is not required to work or

to participate in any training or treatment but may do so voluntarily. Once released, the offender is placed on two-year routine parole supervision and must visit his or her parole officer about once a month.[125]

This point also can be illustrated with a recent case in Colorado, where a convicted felon (sexual exploitation of a child) asked the court to send him to prison, rather than serving out 20 years on ISP.[126] The court agreed to revoke his probation, and he was sentenced to 12 years in prison. At the hearing, the offender argued that he did not want to be in the "probation/treatment" trap any longer.[127]

Although compelling evidence of the effectiveness of ISP is lacking, it has been deemed a public relations success.[128] Intensive supervision is usually accomplished by greatly reducing the caseload size per probation or parole officer, leading to increased contact between officers and clients or their significant others (such as the client's spouse or parents). It is hoped that this increased contact will improve service delivery and control and thus reduce recidivism.[129]

House Arrest/Electronic Monitoring

house arrest/electronic monitoring court-ordered punishment where a convicted or accused offender must remain in his or her home, usually while being remotely monitored electronically.

House arrest (or home detention) is typically a court-ordered punishment where convicted or accused offenders must remain in their home, usually while being monitored electronically, and can leave only for work, community service, or medical attention. Although it has become increasingly common, BJS data provided in Table 12-1 ■ show that few offenders are sentenced to home detention only. Many more (about 14,000, or about 22% of those sentenced in the community) were being monitored electronically—many of them monitored in their homes. The primary motivation for using this intermediate sanction is a financial one: the conservation of scarce resources. It is also hoped, of course, that HA is more effective in preventing recidivism than traditional probation alone or incarceration.

But does HA work? In a study of public perceptions of HA and its potential goals, many people feel that HA is not effective or punitive enough; nearly half (44%) of the public feels that HA is not very effective or not effective at all.[130] In terms of recidivism as an outcome measure, Jeffery Ulmer[131] found that the sentencing combination associated with the least likelihood of rearrest was HA/probation. The combinations of HA/work release and HA/incarceration were also significantly associated with decreased chances of rearrest compared with traditional probation. Furthermore, whenever any other sentencing option was paired with HA, that sentence combination significantly reduced the chances and frequency of rearrest.[132] Clearly, HA works when used in tandem with other forms of sentencing options and when rearrest is used as the outcome variable.

What is it about HA that might explain its success? First, it's not all about punishment. Rather, it puts the offender in touch with opportunities and resources for rehabilitative services (such as substance abuse or sex offender counseling and anger management classes), which supports the contention that for intermediate sanctions of any type to reduce recidivism, they must include a rehabilitative emphasis.[133] Other studies have sought to determine the effectiveness of HA paired with EM, the more usual form of HA according to the BJS data provided in Table 12-1 ■. For example, Martin et al.[134] examined offenders' perceptions of HA/EM. The typical respondent in their survey spent approximately one month on HA/EM, paid $3,578.00 in fines, and provided 17 hours of community service. Respondents indicated that while being sentenced to HA was preferable to being incarcerated, it is a punitive sanction. These punitive aspects are manifested in at least two ways:

- The restrictive nature of personal freedoms: Offenders reported that this was the most troublesome aspect of their experience with EM. Although employed offenders were permitted to go to and from work, they are generally prohibited from leaving their homes to run errands or to complete outdoor tasks without permission from their probation officer.

- The degree to which this sanction causes embarrassment/shame for the offender: Respondents reported that EM had a shaming effect for them or their family members, and that the supervision associated with EM was intrusive. Wearing a visible ankle bracelet and having a device attached to their telephone caused embarrassment, as well as having to tell other people that they could not leave the house.

Despite the loss of freedom and embarrassment of serving time on EM, the survey respondents indicated that they preferred EM to incarceration. The majority (about 70%) of the respondents in this study indicated that they would rather be sentenced to HA than to jail.[135]

Finally, other studies have examined the cost estimates of HA/EM as compared to incarceration. It is far cheaper to keep an offender at home on EM than to incarcerate him or her in prison—which runs about $62 per day compared with EM's cost of about $5.00 per day. Even a higher-level system where an e-mail is sent or a beep goes off if an offender goes past set boundaries or active monitoring (an offender's movement is tracked on a computer screen) costs only about $12 a day.[136] Of course, cost savings are only realized if HA/EM is used as an alternative to incarceration rather than an alternative to a less restrictive community alternative. Critics suggest that with the growing technology, HA/EM is being used for an expanded array of individuals and dispositions, including those awaiting trial, those on probation or parole, and simply as its own punishment.[137] The question being asked, then, is whether some of these individuals really would have been incarcerated prior to the growth of HA/EM.

Shock Probation/Parole

shock probation/parole where a judge sends a convicted offender to prison for a short time and then suspends the remainder of the sentence, granting probation.

Shock probation/parole—where a judge sends a convicted offender to prison for a short time and then suspends the remainder of the sentence by granting probation—has as its goal the hope that the "shock" of a short stay in prison will give the offender a taste of institutional life and make such an indelible impression that he or she will be deterred from future crime and thus avoid the negative effects (and costs) of lengthy confinement.[138] Typically, the sentencing judge will reconsider the original sentence to prison and, upon a motion, recall the inmate after a few months in prison and place him or her on probation under conditions deemed appropriate.

Shock probation is typically used for first-time or early career lower-level offenders. Offense categories typically eligible for shock probation include drug crimes, larceny/theft, and forgery crimes. Shock probation is not used with violent offenders. From the perspective of the offender, and perhaps from that of correctional officials, the major advantage to shock incarceration is that the offender spends only a short time incarcerated (usually a period of months) and then returns to the community under supervision. Like other alternatives to incarceration, shock probation can result in a cost savings (compared to longer-term incarceration), and can provide the offender with community resources once on supervised probation. But like other alternatives to incarceration, the cost savings are only real when it's used as an alternative to longer-term incarceration.

In many states, each candidate for shock probation/parole must obtain a community sponsor who will be responsible for the applicant's actions while in the community. The sponsor serves as an adjunct to and a resource for the probation officer. Specific activities for the sponsor can include providing transportation to work, checking on compliance with curfew and other restrictions, assisting with housing and employment problems, and maintaining contact with the probation officer. The offender may also be required to perform community service, usually physical labor.[139]

Boot Camps/Shock Incarceration

Correctional **boot camps**, also called **shock incarceration**, were first implemented as an intermediate sanction in 1983.[140] This approach is usually a few months' duration, where (typically) young, nonviolent offenders experience rigorous military drill and ceremony, strenuous physical training and labor, and treatment and education to promote their reintegration into the community as law-abiding citizens and the development of personal responsibility. The goal is to reduce recidivism, prison and jail populations, and operating costs. Eligible inmates are young, nonviolent offenders.

shock incarceration/boot camp a short-term program where offenders experience rigorous military drill and ceremony, physical training and labor, and treatment and education to reduce recidivism and develop personal responsibility.

However, the effectiveness of boot camps has been called into question. Early evaluations of boot camps generally found that participants did no better than other offenders without this experience.[141] For example, California's juvenile boot camp, LEAD (leadership, esteem, ability, and discipline), which was established in 1992, was subject to an evaluation, which indicated that LEAD was no more effective than other custodial sanctions at reducing recidivism or saving money.[142] Only boot camps that were carefully designed, targeted the right offenders, and provided rehabilitative services and aftercare were deemed likely to save the state money and reduce recidivism.[143] As a result of these findings, the number of boot camps declined; by the year 2000, only 51 prison boot camps remained out of the more than 100 that had been in operation by the mid-1990s.[144]

Boot camps have evolved over time, however, and are now in their third generation. The first-generation camps were those just discussed, which stressed military discipline and physical training. Second-generation camps emphasized rehabilitation by adding components such as alcohol and drug treatment and social skills training (some even including postrelease EM, HA, and random urine tests). Recently, in the third generation, some boot camps have replaced the military components with an emphasis on educational and vocational skills.[145] In an evaluation of the Pennsylvania State Motivational Boot Camp—a program that combined militaristic exercise with multilayered treatment (much like the second-generation programs)—overall results related to recidivism were disappointing when comparing boot camp participants to those released from prison. More encouraging results were noted regarding recidivism for boot camp participants who were employed and those who were repeat offenders. On average, a boot camp sentence reduced a prison stay by 1 year.[146]

A U.S. DOJ report, coauthored by former U.S. attorney general John Ashcroft, stated that correctional administrators and planners might learn from boot camps' failures to reduce recidivism or prison populations by considering the following:[147]

1. Building reintegration into the community into an inmate's program may improve the likelihood that he or she will not recidivate.
2. Programs that offer substantial reductions in time served to boot camp "graduates" and that choose for participation inmates with longer sentences are the most successful in reducing prison populations.
3. The chances of reducing recidivism increase when boot camps last longer and offer more intensive treatment and postrelease supervision.

Day Reporting Centers

Another intermediate sanction is the **day reporting center** (DRC)—a site where selected offenders report while under probation or parole supervision to receive an array of educational, vocational, treatment, and other services in order to reduce the risk factors that are linked with recidivism. The needs of each offender are assessed so that case workers and employment specialists may provide positive problem-solving, coping, and social skills. Also used for offenders returning from incarceration, the centers also assist in their reintegration back into society.[148] Table 12-1 ■ shows about 7 percent (roughly 4,400 of 63,500) of persons being

day reporting center a site where offenders report to receive an array of educational, vocational, treatment, and other services, to reduce the risk factors associated with recidivism.

supervised outside of jail were involved with day reporting. The goals of DRCs are twofold: to provided needed treatment to offenders and to reduce jail and prison crowding.[149]

DRCs tend to operate using a phased approach, where offenders move through phases from higher to lower levels of control based on their ability to successfully complete treatment and their compliance with rules of supervision.[150] Exhibit 12.3 discusses some of the benefits one jurisdiction has realized by opening DRCs—rather than by expanding their existing jails.

EXHIBIT 12.3

FIVE YEARS OF SUCCESS FOR WAUKESHA COUNTY DAY REPORT CENTER

In 2012, Waukesha County, Wisconsin, officials celebrated 5 years of successes for its day report center. Praise for the program's contribution to public safety and prisoner rehabilitation came with the realization that many offenders don't need to be locked up; they can be held accountable in other ways while being given a chance and support to change their behavior.

A Waukesha County circuit judge called its establishment and success his proudest accomplishment in 6 years with the council. According to program statistics, the day report center has had nearly 1,000 participants since opening in April 2007. Of those, 85 percent have successfully completed requirements that may include drug and alcohol testing, EM, job searches, community service, and regular meetings with case managers (who connect with, monitor, advise, encourage, and support the clients).

The program, first established in an open hallway area of a jail, now has several offices and a group meeting room, so participants can meet with staff. The caseload is 55 participants—many of whom have been convicted of drunken driving, but also include those convicted of other nonviolent misdemeanors and felonies.

Judges order center reporting as an addition to or condition of sentences, while the sheriff uses it to supplement some Huber inmates released on EM. Officials say it appears to be reducing crowding in jails and changing clients' behavior. The day report center saved 13,739 jail bed days in 2011—each the equivalent of one prisoner a day—and 38,969 days over 5 years.[151]

The Waukesha County example notwithstanding, studies of DRCs generally indicate success, but there are few of them. A 2011 study of day centers in Pennsylvania found that 95 percent of offenders completed the treatment programs without recidivating and the results translated to cost savings for the county—about $970,000 over 3 years.[152] But without additional evidence, administrators are left with numerous questions about the effectiveness of DRCs. What's the correct mix of surveillance and treatment, for example?[153] Until we have more studies on the effectiveness of DRCs, administrators will need to operate with incomplete information on impact and potential cost savings.[154]

Source: Excerpt from Laurel Walker (2012). Officials Laud Success of Waukesha County Day Report Center.

Summary

This chapter has examined several major contemporary and future issues confronting correctional administrators. It is clear that many, if not all, of these issues do not have easy or quick solutions and will continue to pose challenges to correctional administrators for many years. Included in this discussion were several new forms of *intermediate sanctions*, which if used as alternatives to incarceration offer the best hope at reducing prison overcrowding. But questions of effectiveness in terms of recidivism rates and public safety should continue to be monitored.

Corrections agencies bear the brunt of the combined effects of increases in some crimes, tough mandatory sentencing laws leading to increased incarceration of offenders, a get-tough public and justice system attitude toward crime that permeates the country, overcrowded prisons, and large probation and parole caseloads. As a result, and as this chapter has shown, they must develop new ways to deal with offenders.

Key Terms and Concepts

Alternatives to incarceration, p. 319
Classification, p. 319
Day reporting center, p. 329
Drug interdiction, p. 321
Geriatric inmates, p. 318
Hostage taking, p. 314
House arrest/Electronic monitoring, p. 327
Intensive supervision, p. 325
Intermediate sanctions, p. 325
Life without parole (LWOP), p. 310
Mentally ill inmate, p. 316
Prison Rape Elimination Act of 2003, p. 312
Privatization, p. 323
Sexual violence, p. 311
Shock incarceration/boot camp, p. 329
Shock probation/parole, p. 328
Therapeutic community, p. 322
Unit management, p. 320

Questions for Review

1. What was the Supreme Court's decision concerning capital punishment for someone who committed a capital crime while younger than the age of 18 years? Life without parole sentences? What was the Court's reasoning in both?
2. What do studies show concerning the nature and extent of physical and sexual victimizations in prisons? What policy issues arise from those findings?
3. What options do corrections' administrators have when it comes to the treatment of inmates with serious mental health issues?
4. How would you delineate the major arguments for and against inmates being issued condoms?
5. What administrative considerations apply to the potential problem of hostage taking in detention facilities?
6. What unique problems are involved with mentally ill and geriatric inmates?
7. What are the major arguments for and against the use of solitary confinement?
8. Discuss some of the emerging options for elderly inmates for reentry into the community.
9. What are some stated advantages and disadvantages of privatization, what criteria can be used to evaluate them, and what do available studies report concerning their efficacy?
10. How would you define and describe the underlying philosophy of intermediate sanctions? Why are they so widely used, and what does research tell us about their efficacy?
11. How can shock probation further the goals of corrections? Boot camps/shock incarceration? What successes and problems have been found with these practices?

Deliberate and Decide

The Controlling Convict

You are the warden at a medium-security prison of approximately 1,000 inmates. One of your inmates is serving a life sentence for killing a highway patrol trooper in your state.

The determined inmate wants to take control of his life and situation either by escaping or by ending his life—and thus, either way, "leaving" prison. He has, therefore, hatched a plot: He plans to take a hostage, and then either use that person to escape or die trying. Another major component of his plan is for it to occur on his own terms—either to escape or to die *tomorrow*, on the tenth anniversary of his killing the state trooper.

At 4:00 P.M. today, he manages to feign illness and is escorted to the infirmary to see the prison doctor, a female around age 40. Once inside the small room serving as an infirmary, he manages to obtain a sharp instrument, and does in fact take the doctor hostage. (*Note*: This real-life scenario, occurring in a Western prison, was resolved without use of a highly trained CRT. However, you may assume you have such a team in your institution and can also request that another institution—with probably 12 hours' delay in travel and preparation time—send you its team.)

Question for Discussion

1. The walls of the infirmary are solid concrete block; there is only one door leading in and out. What will you do to attempt to safely defuse this situation, and what other trained teams of experts might you call in to assist?

Learn by Doing

1. As a state criminal justice agency employee, your duties include working as a legislative liaison for your agency. You have been contacted by a state senator and asked to summarize the problem of sexual assaults in correctional institutions, and specifically what the Prison Rape Elimination Act has added to our knowledge of sexual assaults—and whether it has contributed to its diminution—in correctional institutions. What will be the content of your report?
2. You are engaging in a class discussion about the potential problem of hostage taking in correctional institutions. Your criminal justice professor asks that after reading the accounts of two such incidents in the 1970s and 1980s in which hostages were taken, you consider whether, in the long run, these tragedies had positive or negative effects for the administration of prisons. What is your response, and why?
3. While your criminal justice professor is away from campus attending a conference, you, her teaching assistant, are assigned to present a lecture on privatization of prisons in her introductory corrections course. You are to focus on what "domains" were used to evaluate them, and what studies do in fact reveal about their efficacy. What will you say?
4. You have been invited to appear at a luncheon meeting of a local civic group. During your luncheon speech, the topic of discussion turns to the high cost of incarceration, and then questions segue to using alternatives to incarceration. What will you say concerning the types—and the efficacy—of these intermediate sanctions?

Case Study

Private Prisons in Context

While corrections has been a publicly run endeavor since its inception, it is not without its detractors. Proponents of private prisons say that they are an option that provides a cost-effective alternative for governments that are dealing with budget issues or overcrowding in their public facilities. Opponents of private prisons argue that there are lower standards for security and proper conduct, lack of safeguards in the event of an employee strike, and different procedures for inmate sanctions. Some states have flatly prohibited private prisons; others ban such facilities from "importing" prisoners from outside the jurisdiction, and many areas require very similar or identical standards to those of public facilities. A 2016 report from the U.S. DOJ illustrates that private prisons perform demonstrably poorer than public prisons, and indicates the department's intent to terminate for-profit prison contracts.

Questions for Discussion

1. Do you agree or disagree with the Justice Department's decision to terminate for-profit prison contracts? Why or why not?
2. What are the practical problems with closing private prisons? Given the possibility of overcrowding in public prisons when closing private ones, which is the "lesser evil"?

Notes

1. *Graham v. Florida,* No. 08-7412 (May 17, 2010); also see Adam Liptak, "Justices Limit Life Sentences for Juveniles," *The New York Times*, May 17, 2010, http://www.nytimes.com/2010/05/18/us/politics/18court.html?pagewanted=print
2. *Miller v. Alabama*, 132 S. Ct. 2455 (2012); *Jackson v. Hobbs*, No. 10–9647 (2012).
3. *Montgomery v. Louisiana*, 577 US (2016).
4. Robert Barnes, "Supreme Court: Life Sentences of Juveniles Open for Later Reviews," *The Washington Post*, January 25, 2016, https://www.washingtonpost.com/politics/courts_law/supreme-court-juveniles-sentenced-to-life-have-option-for-new-reviews/2016/01/25/06e3dfc2-c378-11e5-8965-0607e0e265ce_story.html?utm_term=.d0c6bfd10f60
5. Ibid.
6. Robert W. Dumond, "Inmate Sexual Assault: The Plague That Persists," *The Prison Journal* 80 (December 2000): 407–414; see also Human Rights Watch, *No Escape: Male Rape in U.S. Prisons* (New York: Author, 2001).
7. World Health Organization, *World Report on Violence and Health*, 2002, p. 149, http://www.who.int/violence_injury_prevention/violence/world_report/chapters/en/
8. Cindy Struckman-Johnson and David Struckman-Johnson, "Sexual Coercion Rates in Seven Midwestern Prison Facilities for Men," *The Prison Journal* 80 (December

2000): 379–390. See also Christopher Hensley, Robert W. Dumond, Richard Tewksbury, and Doris A. Dumond, "Possible Solutions for Preventing Inmate Sexual Assault: Examining Wardens' Beliefs," *American Journal of Criminal Justice* 27(1) (2002): 19–33.

9. Dumond, "Inmate Sexual Assault," p. 408.
10. N. Wolff and J. Shi, "Contextualization of Physical and Sexual Assault in Male Prisons: Incidents and Their Aftermath," *Journal of Correctional Health Care* 15(1) (2009), http://www.ncbi.nlm.nih.gov/pmc/articles/PMC2811042/.
11. Ibid.
12. Ibid.
13. Leanne F. Alarid, "Sexual Assault and Coercion Among Incarcerated Women Prisoners: Excerpts from Prison Letters," *The Prison Journal 80* (December 2000): 391–406.
14. Ibid., p. 403.
15. Wolff and Shi, "Contextualization of Physical and Sexual Assault in Male Prisons."
16. Alarid, "Sexual Assault and Coercion Among Incarcerated Women Prisoners."
17. Janine M. Zweig, Rebecca L. Naser, John Blackmore, and Megan Schaffer, *Addressing Sexual Violence in Prisons: A National Snapshot of Approaches and Highlights of Innovative Strategies* (Washington, DC: Urban Institute, 2006).
18. Ibid., p. viii.
19. Ibid., p. ix.
20. U.S. DOJ, *Bureau of Justice Statistics Status Report, Data Collections for the Prison Rape Elimination Act of 2003* (Washington, DC: Author, 2004), pp. 1–2.
21. Bureau of Justice Statistics, *Sexual Victimization in Prisons and Jails Reported by Inmates, 2011–12* (May 2014), p. 6, http://www.bjs.gov/content/pub/pdf/svpjri1112.pdf.
22. Bureau of Justice Statistics, *PREA Data Collection Activities*, June 2014, p. 1, http://www.bjs.gov/content/pub/pdf/pdca13.pdf
23. Bureau of Justice Statistics, *PREA Data Collection Activities*, June 2016, p. 1, https://www.bjs.gov/content/pub/pdf/pdca16.pdf.
24. George Lavender, "California Prisons Aim to Keep Sex Between Inmates Safe, If Illegal," *National Public Radio*, January 21, 2015, http://www.npr.org/2015/01/21/378678167/california-prisons-aim-to-keep-sex-between-inmates-safe-if-illegal.
25. CBS Los Angeles, "To Cut STD Rate, Calif. Considers Condoms in Prison," July 17, 2014, http://losangeles.cbslocal.com/2014/07/07/to-cut-std-rate-calif-considers-condoms-in-prison/.
26. *Chicago Tribune News*, "Condom Debate Targets Prisons," March 18, 2007, http://articles.chicagotribune.com/2007-03-18/news/0703180058_1_prisons-state-inmates-condoms.
27. CBS Los Angeles, "To Cut STD Rate, Calif. Considers Condoms in Prison."
28. Lavender, "California Prisons Aim to Keep Sex Between Inmates Safe, If Illegal."
29. Earnest A. Stepp, "Preparing for Chaos: Emergency Management," in Peter M. Carlson and Judith S. Garrett (eds.), *Prison and Jail Administration: Practice and Theory* (Boston, MA: Jones and Barlett Publishers, 2006), p. 367.
30. Thomas A. Zlaket, Personal Communication to Hon. Janet Napolitano, governor of Arizona, October 25, 2004, p. 2.
31. State of Arizona, Office of the Governor, *The Morey Unit Hostage Incident: Preliminary Findings and Recommendations* (Phoenix, AZ: Author, 2004), p. 1.
32. Ohio History Central, "Lucasville Prison Riot," http://www.ohiohistorycentral.org/entry.php?rec=1634.
33. "Meet Captors' Demands, Hostages Urge," *Chicago Tribune News*, December 7, 1999, http://articles.chicagotribune.com/1999-12-17/news/9912170075_1_warden-todd-louvierre-jolie-sonnier-female-guard.
34. Mark Berman and Katie Mettler, "Hostage Standoff in Delaware Prison Ends with One Corrections Officer Dead," *The Washington Post*, February 2, 2017, https://www.washingtonpost.com/news/morning-mix/wp/2017/02/02/inmates-demanding-education-protesting-trump-take-hostages-at-delaware-prison/?utm_term=.18b48bdc8d07.
35. For an excellent examination and comparison of these two extremely violent prison riots, see Sue Mahan, "An 'Orgy of Brutality' at Attica and the 'Killing Ground' at Santa Fe: A Comparison of Prison Riots," in Michael C. Braswell, Reid H. Montgomery, Jr., and Lucien X. Lombardo (eds.), *Prison Violence in America*, 2nd ed. (Cincinnati, OH: Anderson, 1994), pp. 253–264.
36. U.S. DOJ, Bureau of Justice Statistics, Jail Inmates in *2015* (Washington, DC: December 2016).
37. U.S. DOJ, Bureau of Justice Statistics, *Local Police Departments, 2003* (Washington, DC: Author, 2006), p. iii; U.S. DOJ, Bureau of Justice Statistics, *Sheriff's Offices, 2003* (Washington, DC: Author, 2006), p. iii.
38. U.S. DOJ, National Institute of Justice, *Resolution of Prison Riots* (Washington, DC: Author, October 1995), pp. 2–5.
39. Adapted from Stepp, "Preparing for Chaos: Emergency Management," pp. 367–368.
40. U.S. DOJ, *Resolution of Prison Riots*, pp. 2–5.
41. B. Wind, "A Guide to Crisis Negotiations," *FBI Law Enforcement Bulletin* (October 1995): 1–7.
42. Gabriel Lafleur, Louis Stender, and Jim Lyons, "Hostage Situations in Correctional Facilities," in Peter M. Carlson and Judith S. Garrett (eds.), *Prison and Jail Administration: Practice and Theory* (Boston, MA: Jones and Bartlett, 2006), p. 376.
43. U.S. DOJ, *Resolution of Prison Riots*, p. 13.
44. Ibid., p. 292.
45. National Institute of Justice Information Center, *Prison Hostage Situations* (Boulder, CO: Author, 1983), pp. 16–17.

46. U.S. DOJ, *Resolution of Prison Riots*, p. 14.
47. Ibid., p. 21.
48. Pam Belluck, "Mentally Ill Inmates Are at Risk Isolated, Suit Says," *The New York Times*, March 9, 2007, p. A10.
49. Treatment Advocacy Center, *The Treatment of Persons with Mental Illness in Prisons and Jails: A State Survey*, April 8, 2014, p. 6.
50. Steven C. Norton, "Successfully Managing Mentally Ill Offenders: Thoughts and Recommendations," *Corrections Today* 67(1) (February 2005): 28–29, 37.
51. Doris J. James and Lauren E. Glaze, "Mental Health Problems of Prison and Jail Inmates," *Bureau of Justice Statistics Special Report* (September 2006): 1.
52. U.S. DOJ, National Institute of Corrections, *Effective Prison Mental Health Services* (Washington, DC: Author, May 2004), p. 1.
53. Bureau of Justice Statistics, Indicators of Mental Health Problems Reported by Prisoners and Jail Inmates, 2011-12, June 2017, p. 1, https://www.bjs.gov/content/pub/pdf/imhprpji1112.pdf.
54. Ibid.
55. Treatment Advocacy Center, "*The Treatment of Persons with Mental Illness in Prisons and Jails*," p. 8.
56. Ibid.
57. Juleyka Lantigua-Williams, "More Prisons Are Phasing Out the 'Box,'" *The Atlantic*, December 1, 2016, https://www.theatlantic.com/politics/archive/2016/12/more-prisons-are-phasing-out-the-box/509225/.
58. Denis-Marie Ordway and John Wihbey, "Solitary Confinement in Prisons: Key Data and Research Findings," *Journalist's Resource*, January 26, 2016, https://journalistsresource.org/studies/government/criminal-justice/solitary-confinement-prisons-key-data-research-findings.
59. Ibid.
60. Fatos Kaba, Andrea Lewis, Sarah Glowa-Kollish, James Hadler, David Lee, Howard Alper, Daniel Selling, Ross MacDonald, Angela Solimo, Amanda Parsons, and Homer Venters, "Solitary Confinement and Risk of Self-Harm Among Jail Inmates," *American Journal of Public Health* 104(3) (March 2014): 442–447.
61. Ibid.
62. Juleyka Lantigua-Williams, "More Prisons Are Phasing Out the 'Box,'" p. 5.
63. Ibid.
64. See U.S. DOJ Archives, Report and Recommendations Concerning the Use of Restrictive Housing, updated March 13, 2017, https://www.justice.gov/archives/dag/report-and-recommendations-concerning-use-restrictive-housing.
65. Katherine Q. Seelye, "Crime Boss Bulger Gets 2 Life Terms and Is Assailed by Judge for His 'Depravity,'" *The New York Times*, November 14, 2014, http://www.nytimes.com/2014/11/15/us/bulger-sentenced-to-life-in-prison.html?_r=0.
66. Valeriya Metla, "Aging Inmates: A Prison Crisis," *Law Street Media*, February 15, 2015, https://lawstreetmedia.com/issues/law-and-politics/aging-inmates-prison-crisis/.
67. Vera Institute of Justice, *It's About Time Aging Prisoners, Increasing Costs, and Geriatric Release* (New York: Author, 2010), p. 4.
68. Ibid., p. 2.
69. Kevin E. McCarthy and Carrie Rose, "State Initiatives to Address Aging Prisoners," *Connecticut General Assembly*, March 4, 2014, http://www.cga.ct.gov/2014/rpt/2014-R-0166.htm.
70. Ibid.
71. Ibid.
72. Brie Williams, "Geriatric Inmates Face Challenges Unique to Prison," March 10, 2006, http://www.ucsf.edu/news/2006/03/5398/geriatric-inmates-face-challenges-unique-prison.
73. Valeriya Metla, *It's About Time Aging Prisoners, Increasing Costs, and Geriatric Release*.
74. Geoff Dornan, "Aging Prisoners Boost Costs," *NevadaAppeal.com*, October 13, 2014, http://www.nevadaappeal.com/news/8481490-113/inmates-population-medical-older.
75. Mary Harrison, *True Grit Notes* 5(3) (Summer 2009); Terence P. Hubert, Mary T. Harrison, and William O. Harrison, *True Grit: An Innovative Humanistic Living Program for a Geriatric Population* (Carson City, NV: Nevada Department of Corrections, n.d.)
76. Robert B. Levinson, "Classification: The Cornerstone of Corrections," in Peter M. Carlson and Judith S. Garrett (eds.), *Prison and Jail Administration: Practice and Theory* (Boston, MA: Jones and Bartlett, 2006), pp. 261–267.
77. Ibid., p. 262.
78. Ibid., pp. 262–263.
79. James Austin and Patricia L. Hardyman, *Objective Prison Classification: A Guide for Correctional Agencies* (Washington, DC: National Institute of Corrections, July 2004); also see R. Buchanan, "National Evaluation of Objective Prison Classification Systems: The Current State of the Art," *Crime and Delinquency* 32(3) (1986): 272–290.
80. U.S. DOJ, National Institute of Corrections, *Handbook for Evaluating Objective Prison Classification Systems* (Washington, DC, U.S. DOJ, June 1992), p. 9.
81. U.S. DOJ, Bureau of Justice Statistics, *Drug Use and Dependence, State and Federal Prisoners, 2004* (Washington, DC, U.S. DOJ, January 2007), p. 3, http://www.bjs.gov/content/dcf/duc.cfm.
82. Thomas E. Feucht and Andrew Keyser, *Reducing Drug Use in Prisons: Pennsylvania's Approach* (Washington, DC: National Institute of Justice Journal, October 1999), p. 11.
83. Natasha Haverty, "Video Calls Replace In-Person Visits in Some Jails," *National Public Radio*, December 5, 2014, http://www.npr.org/2016/12/05/504458311/video-calls-replace-in-person-visits-in-some-jails.

84. Feucht and Keyser, *Reducing Drug Use in Prisons*, pp. 11–12.
85. Ibid., pp. 14–15.
86. Lauren Kirchner, "Who Does, and Who Doesn't, Get Drug Treatment in Prison," *Pacific Standard*, August 20, 2015, https://psmag.com/who-does-and-who-doesn-t-get-drug-treatment-in-prison-dc1bbb579b45#.rx8ecgwpj.
87. David Farabee, Michael Prendergast, Jerome Cartier, Harry Wexler, Kevin Knight, and M. Douglas Anglin, "Barriers to Implementing Effective Correctional Drug Treatment Programs," *The Prison Journal* 79 (June 1999): 150–162.
88. Kathryn M. Nowotny, "Race/Ethnic Disparities in the Utilization of Treatment for Drug Dependent Inmates in U.S. Correctional Facilities," *Addictive Behaviors* 40 (January 2015): 148–153.
89. Ibid.
90. Farabee et al., "Barriers to Implementing Effective Correctional Drug Treatment Programs," p. 152.
91. Ibid., p. 153.
92. Ibid., pp. 154–155.
93. Jim Axelrod, "Kentucky Jail Using New Drug Treatment for Inmates Addicted to Opioids," *CBS News*, October 19, 2016, http://www,cbsnews.com/news/kentucky-jail-pioneering-treatment-for-inmates-addicted-to-opioids.
94. Sheldon X. Zhang, Robert E. L. Roberts, and Kathryn E. McCollister, "Therapeutic Community in a California Prison: Treatment Outcomes after 5 Years," *Crime & Delinquency* 57(1) (2011): 82–101.
95. Ibid.
96. Ibid.
97. National Institute on Drug Abuse, "Are Therapeutic Communities Effective?" July 2015, https://www.drugabuse.gov/publications/research-reports/therapeutic-communities/are-therapeutic-communities-effective.
98. J. J. Stephan and J. C. Karlberg, *Census of State and Federal Correctional Facilities, 2000* (Washington, DC: U.S. DOJ, Bureau of Justice Statistics, 2003), http://www.bjs.gov/index.cfm?ty=pbdetail&iid=53.
99. Bureau of Justice Statistics, *Prisoners in 2015*, December 2016, https://www.bjs.gov/content/pub/pdf/p15_sum.pdf.
100. Ibid., p. 1.
101. Matthew D. Makarios and Jeff Maahs, "Is Private Time Quality Time? A National Private–Public Comparison of Prison Quality," *Prison Journal* 92(3) (September 2012): 336–357.
102. Leonard C. Gilroy, Adam B. Summers, Anthony Randazzo, and Harris Kenny, *Public-Private Partnerships for Corrections in California: Bridging the Gap between Crisis and Reform*, Reason Foundation, April 2011, p. 3, http://reason.org/files/private_prisons_california.pdf.
103. O'Connor, "The Debate over Prison Privatization," p. 1.
104. C. Thomas, "Recidivism of Public and Private State Prison Inmates in Florida: Issues and Unanswered Questions," *Criminology and Public Policy* 4 (2005): 89–100.
105. Charles H. Logan "Well Kept: Comparing Quality of Confinement of Private and Public Prisons," *Journal of Criminal Law and Criminology 83* (1992): 577–603.
106. Dina Perrone and Travis C. Pratt, "Comparing the Quality of Confinement and Cost Effectiveness of Public versus Private Prisons: What We Know, Why We Do Not Know More, and Where to Go from Here," *The Prison Journal* 83 (2003): 301–322.
107. Makarios and Maahs, "Is Private Time Quality Time?," p. 336.
108. Ibid.
109. Matt Zapotosky and Chico Harlan, "Justice Department Says It Will End Use of Private Prisons," *The Washington Post*, August 18, 2016, https://www.washingtonpost.com/news/post-nation/wp/2016/08/18/justice-department-says-it-will-end-use-of-private-prisons/?utm_term=.a5882d4b01ef.
110. Ibid.
111. Juleyka Lantigua-Williams, "Feds End Use of Private Prisons, But Questions Remain," *The Atlantic*, August 18, 2016, https://www.theatlantic.com/politics/archive/2016/08/end-of-private-prison-contracts-with-federal-government-496469.
112. James Surowiecki, "Trump Sets Private Prisons Free," *The New Yorker*, December 5, 2016, http://www.newyorker.com/magazine/2016/trump-sets-private-prisons-free.
113. Chico Harlan, "The Private Prison Industry was Crashing—Until Donald Trump's Victory," *The Washington Post*, November 10, 2016, https://www.washingtonpost.com/news/wonk/wp/2016/11/10/the-private-prison-industry-was-crashing-until-donald-trumps-victory/?utm_term=.01cd947bef8e.
114. John P. Conrad, "The Redefinition of Probation: Drastic Proposals to Solve an Urgent Problem," in Patrick McAnany, Doug Thomson, and David Fogel (eds.), *Probation and Justice: Reconsideration of Mission* (Cambridge, MA: Oelgeschlager, Gunn, and Hain, 1984), p. 258.
115. Peter J. Benekos, "Beyond Reintegration: Community Corrections in a Retributive Era," *Federal Probation* 54 (March 1990): 53.
116. Ibid.
117. Belinda R. McCarthy, *Intermediate Punishments: Intensive Supervision, Home Confinement, and Electronic Surveillance* (Monsey, NY: Criminal Justice Press, 1987), p. 3.
118. Barry J. Nidorf, "Community Corrections: Turning the Crowding Crisis into Opportunities," *Corrections Today* (October 1989):85.
119. Benekos, "Beyond Reintegration," p. 54.
120. U.S. DOJ, Bureau of Justice Statistics, *Jail Inmates at Midyear-2014: Statistical Tables*, June 2015, p. 9, https://www.bjs.gov/content/pub/pdf/jim14.pdf.
121. Howard Abadinsky, *Probation and Parole: Theory and Practice,* 7th ed. (Upper Saddle River, NJ: Prentice Hall, 2000), p. 410.

122. Joan Petersilia and Susan Turner, *Evaluating Intensive Supervision Probation/Parole: Results of a Nationwide Experiment* (Washington, DC: National Institute of Justice, 1993).
123. Lawrence A. Bennett, "Practice in Search of a Theory: The Case of Intensive Supervision—An Extension of an Old Practice," *American Journal of Criminal Justice* 12 (1988): 293–310.
124. Ibid., p. 293.
125. This information was compiled from ISP brochures and information from the Oregon Department of Correction by Joan Petersilia.
126. Brittany Anas, "Boulder Sex Offender Balks at 'Intensive' Probation, Asks to be Sent to Prison," *Daily Camera*, August 19, 2012, http:www.dailycamera.com/boulder-.
127. Ibid.
128. Todd R. Clear and Patricia R. Hardyman, "The New Intensive Supervision Movement," *Crime and Delinquency* 36 (January 1990): 42–60.
129. Ibid., p. 44.
130. Barbara A. Sims, "Questions of Corrections: Public Attitudes toward Prison and Community-Based Programs," *Corrections Management Quarterly* 1(1) (1997): 54.
131. Jeffery T. Ulner, "Intermediate Sanctions: A Comparative Analysis of the Probability and Severity of Recidivism," *Sociological Inquiry* 71(2) (Spring 2001): 164–193.
132. Ibid., p. 184.
133. Ibid., p. 185.
134. Jamie S. Martin, Kate Hanrahan, and James H. Bowers, Jr., "Offenders' Perceptions of House Arrest and Electronic Monitoring," *Journal of Offender Rehabilitation* 48 (2009): 547–570.
135. Ibid.
136. Sandra Norman-Eady, "Electronic Monitoring of Probationers and Parolees," OLR Research Report, January 2007, http://www.cga.ct.gov/2007/rpt/2007-R-0096.htm.
137. Maya Schenwar, "The Quiet Horrors of House Arrest, Electronic Monitoring, and Other Alternative Forms of Incarceration," *Mother Jones*, January 22, 2015, http://www.motherjones.com/politics/2015/01/house-arrest-surveillance-state-prisons.
138. Jeanne B. Stinchcomb and Vernon B. Fox, *Introduction to Corrections*, 5th ed. (Upper Saddle River, NJ: Prentice Hall, 1999), p. 165.
139. Abadinsky, *Probation and Parole,* p. 434.
140. Gaylene S. Armstrong, Angela R. Gover, and Doris L. MacKenzie, "The Development and Diversity of Correctional Boot Camps," in Rosemary L. Gido and Ted Alleman (eds.), *Turnstile Justice: Issues in American Corrections* (Upper Saddle River, NJ: Prentice Hall, 2002), pp. 115–130.
141. Doris L. MacKenzie, "Boot Camp Prisons and Recidivism in Eight States," *Criminology* 33(3) (1995): 327–358.
142. Joshua A. Jones, "A Multi-State Analysis of Correctional Boot Camp Outcomes: Identifying Vocational Rehabilitation as a Complement to Shock Incarceration," *Inquiries* 4(9) (2012): 1–3.
143. Doris L. MacKenzie and Alex Piquero, "The Impact of Shock Incarceration Programs on Prison Crowding," *Crime and Delinquency* 40(2) (April 1994): 222–249.
144. John Ashcroft, Deborah J. Daniels, and Sarah V. Hart, *Correctional Boot Camps: Lessons from a Decade of Research* (Washington, DC: U.S. DOJ, Office of Justice Programs, June 2003), p. 2.
145. Ibid.
146. Joshua A. Jones, "A Multi-State Analysis of Correctional Boot Camp Outcomes."
147. John Ashcroft, Deborah J. Daniels, and Sarah V. Hart, *Correctional Boot Camps: Lessons from a Decade of Research*, p. 9.
148. Dale G. Parent, "Day Reporting Centers: An Evolving Intermediate Sanction," *Federal Probation* 60 (December 1996): 51–54.
149. Dale Parent, Jim Byrne, Vered Tsarfaty, Laura Valade, and Julie Esselman, "Day Reporting Centers, Volume 1," *National Institute of Justice: Issues and Practices* (Washington, DC: U.S. DOJ, Office of Justice Programs, September 1995).
150. Ibid.
151. Excerpt from "Officials Laud Success of Waukesha County Day Report Center" by Laurel Walker. Copyright © 2012 by Journal Sentinel. Used by permission of Journal Sentinel.
152. David R. Champion, Patrick J. Harvey, and Youngyol Y. Schanz, "Day Reporting Center and Recidivism: Comparing Offender Groups in a Western Pennsylvania County Study," *Journal of Offender Rehabilitation* 50(7) (October 2011): 433–446.
153. Parent et al., "Day Reporting Centers, Volume 1."
154. Ibid.

PART **5**

Issues Spanning the Justice System

Administrative Challenges and Practices

The five chapters in this part focus on administrative problems or methods spanning the entire justice system. Chapter 13 examines ethical considerations that relate to police, courts, and corrections administration. Chapter 14 discusses several challenges involving human resources (employee discipline, labor relations, and liability). Chapter 15 discusses financial administration. Chapter 16 examines terrorism and the challenges posed at present to law enforcement agencies and executives. Finally, Chapter 17 reviews the latest technological hardware and software now in use in criminal justice agencies.

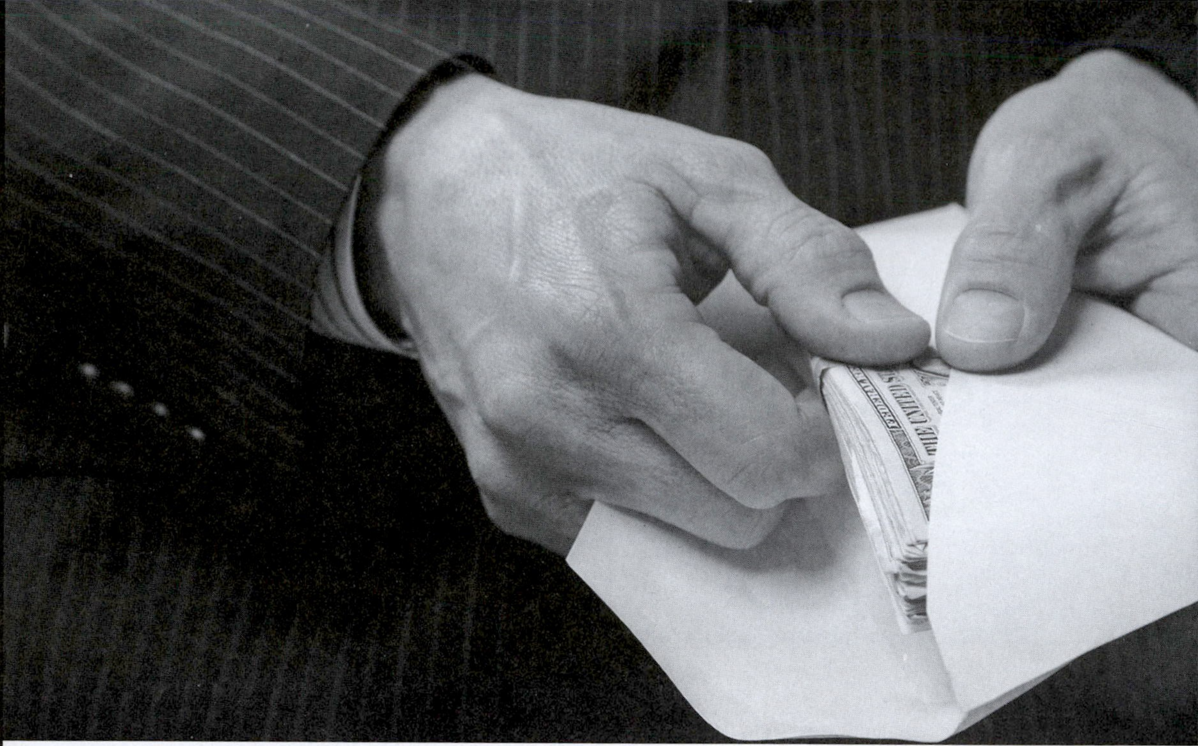

Njgphoto/E+/Getty Images

13 Ethical Considerations

LEARNING OBJECTIVES

After reading this chapter, the student will be able to:

1. *explain absolute and relative ethics, the utilitarian approach to ethics, and the meaning of noble cause corruption*
2. *identify the issues surrounding the acceptance of gratuities and a proposed model for determining whether or not such acceptance is corrupt*
3. *describe ethics among criminal justice employees, including potentially career-ending Brady materials*
4. *review employees' role in the ethics of the court system*
5. *review the different tests for the justice system recruitment*
6. *explain the types of workplace loyalties, and why loyalty to one's superiors can be problematic*
7. *explain how the concept of ethics applies in corrections agencies*
8. *delineate some helpful guidelines for making ethical decisions*

▶ Introduction

As the late U.S. attorney general and U.S. Senator Robert Kennedy once informed a law school class where he was guest lecturing, by the time one reaches the point of being a college or university student, hopefully he or she (and, it might be added, everyone who is studying the field of criminal justice) will have a deeply ingrained desire to practice exemplary and ethical behavior. Ethical behavior is often emphasized in postsecondary education in the form of instructors explaining the need for academic honesty. Later, at some point in your life, it will likely be emphasized in terms of how you are to conduct yourself in terms of dealing with others as well as perhaps with the property and responsibility that has been entrusted to you.

"Character," it might be said, "is who we are when no one is watching." Unfortunately, character cannot be trained at the police or corrections academy, or in law school, or given to someone intravenously, or in a pill. Character and ethical conduct, for criminal justice personnel, means that they would never betray their oath of office, their public trust, or their badge. Indeed, as is indicated by several practitioners in boxed exhibits throughout this book, character and ethics are *sine qua non* for these persons—without those attributes, nothing else matters. These qualities constitute the foundation of their occupation and will certainly affect the manner in which they carry out their public safety duties.

At its root, then, criminal justice administration is about people and activities; in the end, the primary responsibilities of administrators involve monitoring subordinates' activities to ensure that they act correctly relative to their tasks and responsibilities and that these duties and responsibilities are carried out in an acceptable and effective manner. Therefore, this chapter is essentially concerned with what constitutes correct behavior in the administration of criminal justice. Individuals and organizations have standards of conduct. To understand organizations, it is important to comprehend these standards and their etiology.

The chapter opens with a glimpse into the kinds of ethical situations criminal justice employees experience, providing three scenarios based on actual cases. Then, we discuss ethics in general, reviewing philosophical foundations and types of ethics. Next, we examine ethics in policing. Because of the nature of their contacts with the public and the unique kinds of vices, crimes, and temptations to which they are directly exposed, the police are given a high degree of attention; included here are problems such as the "slippery slope," lying and deception, the receipt of gratuities, and greed and temptation. Also emphasized and examined here is a relatively new and powerful—and possibly career-ending—area of police ethics, which is an outgrowth of the U.S. Supreme Court's decision in *Brady v. Maryland*.[1] We then also examine ethical considerations as they apply to courts and corrections organizations.

This chapter contains more than a dozen case studies and ethical dilemmas to challenge the reader as well as a consideration of the value of organizational loyalty. The chapter concludes with review questions and exercises in the Deliberate and Decide, Learn by Doing, and Case Study sections.

▶ Food for Thought: Six Ethical Dilemmas

There is probably no limit to the kinds of ethical dilemmas that can confront criminal justice practitioners; the number of potential situations, temptations, and financial awards to which they can be exposed are simply unbounded. Following are examples (most are factual) of the kinds of such situations that can arise; remember, too, that criminal justice practitioners must always give the *appearance* of ethics and probity as well as actually practicing it:

- You, a night shift police officer, are about to leave a restaurant at 1 A.M. when a slightly intoxicated local gentleman offers to pay for your meal. This individual is well known in the area, as he owns and operates a nightclub (where it is also fairly well known that there are illegal gambling devices on the premises). You decline his offer, but he then loudly broadcasts to all patrons his intention to follow through; he gives the waiter the money for your meal.
- You are an off-duty police officer and receive a phone call from Smith, an on-duty officer, saying that a few hours ago your sister, while driving her car and accompanied with two girlfriends, rammed into and damaged a parked car belonging to a man who has been bothering her; the man has a prior record of stalking women. As a courtesy, Smith asks you how he should handle the matter.
- While performing a patrol deployment study at a neighboring police agency, you learn that the night shift captain, Hill, continually hounds his officers to make more DUI arrests. When doing so, officers must transport the arrestee 10 miles to the county jail and, while performing required tests and paperwork, leave his or her beat unprotected for 2–3 hours. You discover that a number of burglaries are occurring on those very beats while officers are away and busy with their DUI arrests. You suspect there might be a connection.
- A part-time New Jersey municipal court judge holds a unique part-time job as a stand-up comedian at a club. You, his chief judge, learn that the judge's comedy program includes portraying racist and homophobic characters. You inform him that he must give up his part-time job—which has become his primary source of income—as it conflicts with his judicial work and violates ethics rules. You are also concerned about his ability to maintain the confidence of the public and the impartiality, dignity, and integrity of the court. He refuses to resign from the bench and pleads his case to the state's supreme court[2] (see Note 2 for outcome).
- The code of ethics of the American Corrections Association states that "Members shall refrain from allowing personal interest to impair objectivity in the performance of duty while acting in an official capacity." You are associate warden for programs at your state prison, and have just learned that your brother-in-law is being sent to your institution for drug trafficking. Your wife informs you that he plans to continue his college courses while incarcerated. What, if any, ethical issues will you face?
- Pregnant women in correctional institutions are typically transferred to medical facilities for delivery. In 27 states, these inmates may be shackled with handcuffs, leg irons and/or waist chains during transport, labor, delivery and postdelivery, to prevent escape attempts and to protect correctional officers (COs) and medical personnel. You, a CO, agree with the 17 states that do not believe the physical and emotional stress of labor and delivery—and very low risk of escape—justifies such treatment. This evening one of your inmates goes into labor and you and she are en route to the hospital in a prison van. Your captain radios you and says to restrain her in shackles now and throughout delivery, as she is an escape risk. What will you do? Assume you are accompanied by a new CO, is your decision any different? What if your prisoner lost a child previously during childbirth?[3]

Each of these scenarios poses an ethical dilemma for the criminal justice employee involved. In each case, the officer or agent had to determine the best course of action. In making this determination, the employee had to draw on his or her ethical foundation and training and even on the organization's subculture.

These scenarios should be kept in mind as this chapter examines ethics and many related dilemmas.

▶ Ethics, Generally

Philosophical Foundations

The term **ethics** is rooted in the ancient Greek idea of *character*. Ethics involves moral principles and behavior, based on ideas about what is morally good and bad, doing what is right or correct, and how people should behave in their professional capacity.

ethics moral principles governing individual and group behavior, based on ideas concerning what is morally good and bad.

A central problem with understanding ethics is the question of "whose ethics" or "which right." This becomes evident when one examines controversial issues, such as the death penalty, abortion, use of deadly force, and gun control. How individuals view a particular controversy largely depends on their values, character, or ethics. Both sides on controversies such as these believe that they are morally right. These issues demonstrate that to understand behavior, the most basic values must be examined and understood.

Another area for examination is that of **deontological ethics**, which does not consider consequences, but instead examines one's duty to act. The word *deontology* comes from two Greek roots: *deos*, meaning duty, and *logos*, meaning study. Thus, deontology means the study of duty. When police officers observe a violation of law, they have a duty to act. Officers frequently use this as an excuse when they issue traffic citations that appear to have little utility and do not produce any great benefit for the rest of society. For example, when an officer writes a traffic citation for a prohibited left turn made at 2 o'clock in the morning when no traffic is around, the officer is fulfilling a departmental duty to enforce the law. From a utilitarian standpoint (where we judge an action by its consequences), however, little, if any, good was achieved. Here, duty, and not good consequence, was the primary motivator.

deontological ethics a branch of ethics that focuses on the duty to act and the rightness or wrongness of actions, rather than rightness or wrongness of the consequences of those actions.

Immanuel Kant, an eighteenth-century philosopher, expanded the ethics of duty by including the idea of *good will*. People's actions must be guided by good intent. In the previous example, the officer who wrote the traffic citation for an improper left turn would be acting unethically if the ticket was a response to a quota or some irrelevant motive. On the contrary, if the citation was issued because the officer truly believed that it would result in something good, it would have been an ethical action.

Some people have expanded this argument even further. Richard Kania[4] argued that police officers should be allowed to accept gratuities because such actions would constitute the building blocks of positive social relationships between the police and the public. In this case, duty is used to justify what under normal circumstances would be considered unethical. Conversely, if officers take gratuities for self-gratification rather than to form positive community relationships, then the action would be considered unethical by many.

Types of Ethics

Ethics usually involves standards of fair and honest conduct—what we call conscience, the ability to recognize right from wrong—and actions that are good and proper. There are absolute ethics and relative ethics. **Absolute ethics** has only two sides: something is good or bad, black or white; in other words, certain acts are inherently right or wrong in themselves, irrespective of one's culture. Some examples in police ethics would be unethical behaviors such as bribery, extortion, excessive force, and perjury, which nearly everyone would agree are unacceptable behaviors by the police.

absolute ethics a belief that something is good or bad, black or white, and that certain acts are inherently right or wrong in themselves, irrespective of one's culture.

relative ethics a belief that determining what is good or bad is relative to the individual or culture and can depend on the end or outcome of an action.

Relative ethics is more complicated because here judgments of what acts are good and bad are relative to the individual or culture and thus can depend on the end or outcome of an action or one's culture; here, what is considered ethical behavior by one person or culture may be deemed highly unethical by someone else. Not all ethical issues are clear-cut, however, and communities *do* seem willing at times to tolerate extralegal behavior if a greater public good is served, especially in dealing with problems such as gangs and the homeless. This willingness on the part of the community can be conveyed to the police. A community's acceptance of relative ethics as part of criminal justice may send the wrong message: that there are few boundaries placed on justice system employees' behaviors and that, at times, "anything goes" in their fight against crime. As John Kleinig[5] pointed out, giving false testimony to ensure that a public menace is "put away" or the illegal wiretapping of an organized crime figure's telephone might sometimes be viewed as necessary and justified, though illegal. Another example is that many police officers believe they are compelled to skirt the edges of the law—or even violate it—to arrest drug traffickers. The ethical problem here is that even if the action could be justified as morally proper, it remains illegal. For many persons, however, the protection of society overrides other concerns.

This viewpoint—the *principle of double effect*—holds that when one commits an act to achieve a good end and an inevitable but intended effect is negative, the act might be justified. A long-standing debate has raged about balancing the rights of individuals against the community's interest in calm and order.

These special areas of ethics can become problematic and controversial when police officers use deadly force or lie and deceive others in their work. Police can justify a whole range of activities that others may deem unethical simply because the consequences result in the greatest good for the greatest number—the *utilitarian* approach. If the ends justified the means, perjury would be ethical when committed to prevent a serial killer from being set free to prey on society. In a democratic society, however, the means are just as important as, if not more important than, the desired end.

The community—and criminal justice administrators—cannot tolerate completely unethical behavior, but they may seemingly tolerate extralegal behavior if it serves a greater public good.

It is no less important today than in the past for criminal justice employees to appreciate and come to grips with ethical considerations. Indeed, ethical issues in policing have been affected by three critical factors:[6] (1) growing level of temptation stemming from illicit drug trade, (2) potentially compromising nature of the organizational culture—a culture that can exalt loyalty over integrity, with a "code of silence" that protects unethical employees, and (3) challenges posed by decentralization (flattening the organization and pushing decision making downward) through the advent of community-oriented policing and problem-solving (discussed in Chapter 4).

Noble Cause Corruption

Bending the Rules

noble cause corruption corruption committed in the name of good ends; when an act is committed to achieve a good end, it might still be justified.

When relative ethics and the principle of double effect, described above, are given life and practiced in overt fashion by the police, the situation is known as **noble cause corruption**—what Thomas Martinelli[7] defined as "corruption committed in the name of good ends, corruption that happens when police officers care too much about their work." This viewpoint is also known as the principle of double effect. As noted above, it holds that when an act is committed to achieve a good end (such as an illegal search) and an inevitable but intended effect is negative (the person who is searched eventually goes to prison), the act might still be justified.

Although noble cause corruption can occur anywhere in the criminal justice system, we might look at the police for examples. Officers might bend the rules, such as not reading a drunk person his rights or performing a field sobriety test; planting evidence; issuing "sewer" tickets—writing a ticket but not giving it to the person, resulting in a warrant issued for failure to appear in court; "testilying"; or "using the magic pencil," where police officers write up an incident in a way that criminalizes a suspect (this is a powerful tool for punishment). Noble cause corruption involves a different way of thinking about the police relationship with the law; here, officers operate on a standard that places personal morality above the law, become legislators *of* the law, and act as if they *are* the law.[8]

Such activities can be rationalized by some officers; however, as a Philadelphia police officer put it, "When you are shoveling society's garbage, you gotta be indulged a little bit."[9]

Nonetheless, when officers participate in such activities and believe that the ends justify the means, they corrupt their own system.

Challenges for Administrators, Managers, and Supervisors

Obviously, the kinds of ends-justify-means noble cause behaviors that are mentioned above often involve arrogance on the part of the police and ignore the basic constitutional guidelines their occupation demands. Administrators and middle managers must be careful to take a hard-line view that their subordinates always tell the truth and follow the law. For their part, when red flags surface, supervisors must look deep for reasons behind this sudden turn of events and make reasonable inquiries into the cause.[10] They must not fail to act, lest noble cause corruption be reinforced and entrenched; their inability to make the tough decisions that relate to subordinate misconduct can be catastrophic.

A supervisory philosophy of discipline based on due process, fairness, and equity, combined with intelligent, informed, and comprehensive decision making, is best for the department, its employees, and the community. This supervisory philosophy demonstrates the moral commitment employees look for in their leaders and the type that is expected in police service.[11]

Having defined the types of ethics and some dilemmas, we will now discuss in greater detail some of the ethical issues faced by police leaders and their subordinates.

▶ Ethics in Policing

The Root of the Problem: Greed and Temptation

Edward Tully[12] underscored a vast amount of temptation that confronts today's police officers and what police leaders must do to combat it:

> Socrates, Mother Teresa, or other revered individuals in our society never had to face the constant stream of ethical problems of a busy cop on the beat. One of the roles of police leaders is to create an environment that will help an officer resist the temptations that may lead to misconduct, corruption, or abuse of power. The executive cannot construct a work environment that will completely insulate the officers from the forces that lead to misconduct. The ultimate responsibility for an officer's ethical and moral welfare rests squarely with the officer.

Most citizens have no way of comprehending the amount of temptation that confronts today's police officers. They frequently find themselves alone inside retail business stores after normal business hours, clearing the building after finding an open door or window. A swing or graveyard shift officer can easily obtain considerable plunder on these occasions, acquiring everything from clothing to tires for his or her personal vehicle. At the other end of the spectrum is the potential for huge payoffs from drug traffickers or other big-money offenders who will gladly pay the officer to look away from their crimes. Some officers, of course, find this temptation impossible to overcome.

EXHIBIT 13.1

MISFORTUNE IN FERGUSON: THE JUSTICE DEPARTMENT FINDINGS

The U.S. Department of Justice investigation of the city of Ferguson, Missouri, found a policing strategy built around writing tickets and assessing fines and fees in order to feed the city budget. The police chief was routinely urged to generate more revenue through enforcement. Officers sometimes wrote six, eight, as many as fourteen citations for a single encounter. In one four-year span of time, approximately 90,000 citations and summonses were issued for municipal violations (the city had a population of about 21,000, about 25% of whom were African American). Indeed, there were outstanding warrants for more than two-thirds of the city's citizens. Citations were written with abandon and racial discrimination abounded; African Americans accounted for 95 percent of "Manner of Walking in Roadway" and 94 percent of "Failure to Comply" charges. One charge, "Making a False Declaration," was issued to a man for giving his first name as "Mike" instead of "Michael," while another was charged for not wearing a seat belt even though he was seated in a parked car. The city's municipal court was actually run by the chief of police, and thus did not act as a neutral arbiter of the law or a check on unlawful police conduct.[13]

1. What factors contributed to this state of affairs?
2. If you were hired as the city's new police chief, what would you do in terms of training, policies, and changing agency culture to right this ship? (Referring Chapters 4–6 will be helpful.)

A Primer: The Oral Interview

During oral interviews for a position in policing, applicants are often placed in a hypothetical situation that tests their ethical beliefs and character. For example, they are asked to assume the role of a police officer who is checking on foot an office supplies retail store that was found to have an unlocked door during early morning hours. On leaving the building, the officer observes another officer, Smith, removing a $300 writing pen from a display case and placing it in his uniform pocket. What should the officer do?

This kind of question commonly befuddles the applicant: "Should I 'rat' on my fellow officer? Overlook the matter? Merely tell Smith never to do that again?" Unfortunately, applicants may do a lot of "how am I *supposed* to respond" soul-searching and second-guessing with these kinds of questions.

Bear in mind that criminal justice agencies do not wish to hire someone who possesses ethical shortcomings; it is simply too potentially dangerous and expensive, from both the perspectives of potential litigation and morality, to take the chance of bringing someone who is corrupt into an agency. That is the reason for such questioning and a thorough background investigation of applicants.

Before responding to a scenario like the one concerning Officer Smith, the applicant should consider the following issues: Is this likely to be the first time that Smith has stolen something? Don't the police arrest and jail people for this same kind of behavior?

In short, police administrators should *never* want an applicant to respond that it is acceptable for an officer to steal. Furthermore, it would be incorrect for an applicant to believe that police do not want an officer to "rat out" another officer. Applicants should never acknowledge that stealing or other such activities are to be overlooked.

Accepted and Deviant Lying

In many cases, no clear line separates acceptable and unacceptable behavior. The two are separated by an expansive gray area that comes under relative ethics. Some observers have referred to such illegal behavior as a *slippery slope*. People tread on solid or legal ground, but at some point slip beyond the acceptable into illegal or unacceptable behavior.

Criminal justice employees lie or deceive for different purposes and under varying circumstances. In some cases, their misrepresentations are accepted as an integral part of a criminal investigation; in other cases, they are viewed as violations of law. David Carter[14] examined police **lying** and perjury and developed a taxonomy that centered on a distinction between accepted lying and deviant lying. *Accepted lying* includes police activities intended to apprehend or entrap suspects. This type of lying is generally considered to be trickery. *Deviant lying*, on the contrary, refers to officers committing perjury to convict suspects or being deceptive about some activity that is illegal or unacceptable to the department or the public in general.

lying (accepted/deviant) lying that serves legitimate purposes and lying that conceals or promotes crimes or illegitimate ends.

Deception has long been practiced by the police to ensnare violators and suspects. For many years, it was the principal method used by detectives and police officers to secure confessions and convictions. Accepted lying is that allowed by law and, to a great extent, is expected by the public. Gary Marx[15] identified three methods used by police to trick a suspect: (1) performing an illegal action as part of a larger, socially acceptable, and legal goal; (2) disguising the illegal action so that the suspect does not know it is illegal; and (3) morally weakening the suspect so that the suspect voluntarily becomes involved. The courts have long accepted deception as an investigative tool. For example, in *Illinois v. Perkins*,[16] the U.S. Supreme Court ruled that police undercover agents are not required to administer the *Miranda* warning to incarcerated inmates when investigating crimes. Lying, although acceptable by the courts and the public in certain circumstances, results in an ethical dilemma. It is a dirty means to accomplish a good end; the police use untruths to gain the truth relative to some event.

In their taxonomy of lying, Barker and Carter[17] identified two types of deviant lying: lying that serves legitimate purposes and lying that conceals or promotes crimes or illegitimate ends. Lying that serves legitimate goals occurs when officers lie to secure a conviction, obtain a search warrant, or conceal omissions during an investigation. Barker[18] found that police officers believe that almost one-fourth of their agency would commit perjury to secure a conviction or to obtain a search warrant. Lying becomes an effective, routine way to sidestep legal impediments. When left unchecked by supervisors, managers, and administrators, lying can become organizationally accepted as an effective means to nullify legal entanglements and remove obstacles that stand in the way of convictions. Examples include using the services of nonexistent confidential informants to secure search warrants, concealing that an interrogator went too far, coercing a confession, or perjuring oneself to gain a conviction.

Lying to conceal or promote criminality is the most distressing form of deception. Examples range from lying by the police to conceal their use of excessive force when arresting a suspect to obscuring the commission of a criminal act.

"*Brady* Material"

Consider the following scenario:

> At the end of his duty shift, Officer Jones acknowledges a dispatch to assist an animal control unit that is struggling to pick up a large, vicious dog. Because he has social plans after work and believes the incident to be minor in nature, Jones opts instead to drive to the police station and leave for home. The animal control officer, thus acting alone, incurs a number of severe dog bites, $10,000 in medical costs (she has medical insurance), the loss of 2 weeks' work, and potential long-term injuries. As a result, Jones is contacted by his supervisor to justify his lack of response; he explains that he was en route to the call, but was diverted by seeing what he felt was a robbery in progress that needed "checking out"

(no robberies were reported). Largely owing to the animal control officer's injuries, the matter is referred to the department's Internal Affairs (IA) office for investigation. Upon being questioned, Jones initially lies to IA investigators, but when pressed for specifics concerning the alleged robbery, Jones finally admits that he thought the dog call was a minor problem and opted to ignore it. He is given 2 weeks' leave without pay, and placed on a performance review for 6 months.

To Officer Jones, this matter may seem to be ended, a lesson learned for the future. In truth, however, Jones has possibly opened a can of worms from which his career may never recover. Jones lied to both his supervisor and the IA investigators. Police officers are first and foremost required to tell the truth; to do any less can be career-ending. An officer with credibility issues is unable to make cases because he or she can no longer testify effectively in court from that point forward. His or her department is required to advise the prosecutor's office of this issue—and the prosecutor is required to disclose it to the defense—in every criminal case in which Jones will testify during the remainder of his career. Furthermore, Jones may well have to endure the following type of cross-examination and/or closing argument by the defense attorney:

> Ladies and gentlemen of the jury, as you consider the testimony of Officer Jones, whom the prosecution has called as its witness, it is my duty to inform you that you are being asked to believe the testimony of an officer who will lie in his reports.

To further sully Jones' reputation, the prosecutor's office may also inform the chief of police or sheriff that they will not take any future cases in which Jones was a witness.[19]

Questions for you to consider:

1. What *internal* (department level, per agency policies and procedures) punishment, if any, would you deem appropriate for Jones in this incident?
2. (Looking at information presented in Chapter 9, on civil liability): Assume the animal control officer files a civil suit against the city and Jones for his negligence, seeking (1) compensatory damages (medical costs, pain and suffering, loss of wages, etc.) and (2) punitive damages (money due to Jones' acting in a wanton, malicious, vindictive, or oppressive manner). How much is the animal control officer due?

Such is the current status of policing, a result of *Brady v. Maryland* (1963),[20] with one large Western police agency recently discovering more than 135 of its officers having potential *Brady* problems in a disciplinary case.[21] Brady was convicted of first-degree murder and sentenced to death. He testified at trial about his participation in the crime, but also stated that his companion, Boblit, was the actual murderer. Before trial, Brady's attorney had requested to see Boblit's statements. The government provided some of his statements, but did not turn over those in which Boblit actually admitted to the murder. Brady was convicted, and later his attorney, then knowing of Boblit's statement admitting guilt, filed an appeal. The U.S. Supreme Court stated that Brady was entitled to obtain and use Boblit's statement, and that the government's failure to provide the statement amounted to a denial of his right to due process.

***Brady* material** evidence in the government's possession that is favorable to the accused, material to either guilt or punishment, and must, therefore, be disclosed to the defense.

Brady thus established that in a criminal case the accused has a right to any exculpatory evidence (sometimes termed "***Brady* material**," i.e., any evidence in the government's possession that is favorable to the accused and is material to either guilt or punishment). Prosecutors must, therefore, disclose to the defense all exculpatory evidence.[22]

Today many police agencies take the "Brady officer" matter quite seriously, training officers about its existence, sanctions, and ramifications. They are generating policies and procedures that address this issue, explaining that the agency may be placed in a position where the officer's termination is the only appropriate outcome.

Finally, agencies are encouraged to review all officers' personnel files to determine if any of them has a disciplinary history that would seriously impeach his or her credibility as a witness. Any such information should also be made available to the prosecutor before such officers are allowed to testify in a criminal prosecution.[23]

Gratuities: A Model for Gauging Degrees of Corruption

gratuities complimentary gifts of money, services, or something of other value.

Gratuities are complimentary gifts of money, services, or something of other value given by one party to another. In policing, on-duty officers are often provided free or reduced-price meals and drinks by restaurants and convenience stores, and some businesses offer officers discounts on services or merchandise. While some agencies consider the offer of gratuities to be simple gestures to reward officers for their (often thankless) tasks, other departments prohibit all such gifts and discounts. In either case, agencies must spell out clearly—and enforce—what its views and practices will be regarding the receipt of gratuities.

There are two basic arguments *against* police acceptance of gratuities. First is the slippery slope argument, discussed earlier, which proposes that gratuities are the first step in police corruption. This argument holds that once gratuities are received, police officers' ethics are subverted and they are open to additional breaches of their integrity. In addition, officers who accept minor gifts or gratuities are then obligated to provide the donors with some special service or accommodation. Furthermore, some propose that receiving a gratuity is wrong because officers are receiving rewards for services that, as a result of their employment, they are obligated to provide. That is, officers have no legitimate right to accept compensation in the form of a gratuity. If the police ever hope to be accepted as members of a full-fledged profession, then they must decide whether accepting gratuities is a professional behavior or not.

Police officers who solicit and receive free gifts were categorized by the Knapp Commission in New York City as either "grass-eaters" or "meat-eaters."[24] *Grass-eaters* are officers who freely accept gratuities and sometimes solicit minor payments and gifts. *Meat-eaters*, on the contrary, spend a significant portion of the workday aggressively seeking out situations that can be exploited for financial gain. These officers are corrupt and are involved in thefts, drugs, gambling, prostitution, and other criminal activities.

At least in some cases, it seems that taking gratuities may be the first step toward corruption. Gratuities do indeed provide a slippery slope from which officers can easily slide into corruption. The problem is that many officers fail to understand when and where to draw the line. In a different light, one writer[25] argues that retail store and restaurant owners often feel indebted to the police and that gratuities provide an avenue of repayment. Thus, gratuities result in social cohesion between the police and business owners, and the acceptance of gratuities does not necessarily lead to the solicitation of additional gratuities and gifts or corruption.

model of circumstantial corruptibility a view regarding acceptance of gratuities, holding that the exchange of a gift is influenced by two elements: the roles of the giver and the receiver.

Withrow and Dailey[26] recently offered a uniquely different viewpoint on gratuities. They propose a **model of circumstantial corruptibility**, stating that the exchange of a gift is influenced by two elements: the role of the giver and the role of the receiver. The role of the giver determines the level of corruptibility; in this model, the giver is either taking a position as a

- *presenter*, who offers a gift voluntarily without any expectation of a return from the receiver;
- *contributor*, who furnishes something and expects something in return;
- *capitulator*, who involuntarily responds to the demands of the receiver.

The role of the receiver of the gift is obviously very important as well in the model; the receiver can act as

- an *acceptor*, who receives the gift humbly and without any residual feelings of reciprocity;
- an *expector*, who looks forward to the gift and regards it as likely to be given, and will be annoyed by the absence of the gift;
- a *conqueror*, who assumes total control over the exchange and influence over the giver.

The function of the model, Withrow and Dailey argue, is centered on the intersection of the giver and the receiver; for example, when the giver assumes the role of the presenter and the receiver is the acceptor, the result is a giving exchange and corruption does not occur. However, if the giver and the receiver occupy other roles, corruptibility can progress to higher levels of social harm, which they term *hierarchy of wickedness*. Bribery results when something of value is given and the giver expects something in return, while the receiver agrees to make his or her behavior conform to the desires of the giver. This model is not clear-cut, however, because the confusion of roles between givers and receivers is inevitable.[27]

Withrow and Dailey's model is distinguishable from Kania's view, discussed above, that the police should be encouraged to accept minor gratuities to foster good relations; rather, Withrow and Dailey encourage the police to consider the role of the giver as well as their own intentions when deciding whether or not to accept a gratuity. In certain circumstances, the exchange of *any* gratuity is ethical or unethical regardless of its value.[28]

Figure 13-1 ■ is an example by the U.S. Department of Justice concerning gratuities.

Training, Supervision, and Values

Another key element of ethics in policing is the recruitment and training of police personnel. Formal training programs in ethics can help to ensure that officers understand their department's

U.S. Dept. of Justice Policy on Gifts and Entertainment

An employee may not solicit or accept a gift given because of his official position or from a prohibited source to include anyone who:

- Has or seeks official action or business with the Department;
- Is regulated by the Department;
- Has interests that may be substantially affected by the performance of an employee's official duties; or
- Is an organization composed mainly of persons described above.

An employee may accept:

- Gifts based on a personal relationship when it is clear that the motivation is not his official position.
- Gifts of $20 or less per occasion, not to exceed $50 in a year from one source.
- Discounts and similar benefits offered.
- Most genuine awards and honorary degrees.
- Free attendance, food, refreshments and materials provided at a conference or widely attended gathering which an employee attends in his official capacity, with approval.
- Gifts based on an outside business relationship, such as travel expenses related to a job interview.

—U.S. Department of Justice.

Figure 13-1 U.S. Department of Justice Gratuities Policy

Source: Adapted from U.S. Department of Justice, "Gifts and Entertainment," https://www.justice.gov/jmd/gifts-and-entertainment#outside.

code of ethics, elevate the importance of ethics throughout the agency, and underscore top management's support. It is imperative that police administrators see that applicants are thoroughly tested, trained, and exposed to an anticorruption environment by proper role modeling.

No supervision of police officers, no matter how thorough and conscientious, can keep bad cops from doing bad things. There are simply too many police officers and too few supervisors. If there is not enough supervision, then the bad cop will not be afraid. As Marcus Aurelius said, "A man should be upright, not be kept upright." There must be leadership at every level. Line officers are sincere and hard-working; their leaders need to ensure that core values are part of the department's operations and become the basis of the subordinates' behavior.

The organization's culture is also important in this regard. The police culture often exalts loyalty over integrity. Given the stress usually generated more from within the organization than from outside and the nature of life-and-death decisions they must make daily, even the best officers who simply want to catch criminals may become frustrated and vulnerable to bending the rules for what they view as the greater good of society.

Police agencies must also attempt to shape the standards of professional behavior. Many begin to do so by articulating their values such as "we believe in the sanctity of life" and "we believe that providing superior service to the citizens is our primary responsibility." Other rules try to guide officers' behavior such as not lying or drinking in excess in a public place.

▶ Ethics in the Courts

Evolution of Standards of Conduct

The first call during the twentieth century for formalized standards of conduct in the legal profession came in 1906 with Roscoe Pound's speech "The Causes of Popular Dissatisfaction with the Administration of Justice,"[29] discussed in Chapter 7. The American Bar Association (ABA) quickly responded by formulating and approving the Canons of Professional Ethics in 1908 governing lawyers. No separate rules were provided for judges, however.

The first Canons of Judicial Ethics probably grew out of baseball's 1919 scandal, in which the World Series was "thrown" by the Chicago White Sox to the Cincinnati Reds. Baseball officials turned to the judiciary for leadership and hired U.S. district court Judge Kenesaw Mountain Landis as baseball commissioner—a position for which Landis was paid $42,500 compared with his $7,500 earnings per year as a judge. This affair prompted the 1921 ABA convention to pass a resolution of censure against the judge and appoint a committee to propose standards of judicial ethics.[30]

In 1924, the ABA approved the Canons of Judicial Ethics under the leadership of Chief Justice William Howard Taft, and in 1972 the ABA approved a new **Model Code of Judicial Conduct**—rules governing the conduct of judges while acting in their professional capacity; in 1990, the same body adopted a revised Model Code. Nearly all states and the District of Columbia have promulgated standards based on the code. In 1974, the U.S. Judicial Conference adopted a Code of Conduct for Federal Judges, and Congress has, over the years, enacted legislation regulating judicial conduct, including the Ethics Reform Act of 1989. Finally, in October 1977, the American Judicature Society (AJS) established the Center for Judicial Conduct Organizations. The Center compiles materials involving judicial discipline, advisory opinions, disciplinary procedures, codes of judicial conduct, and related court decisions, and is probably best known in judicial circles for its publication, *Judicial Conduct Reporter*.[31]

Model Code of Judicial Conduct rules governing the conduct of judges while acting in their professional capacity.

The Judge

Ideally, our judges are flawless. They do not allow emotion or personal biases to creep into their work, treat all cases and individual litigants with an even hand, and employ "justice tempered with mercy." The perfect judge would be like the one described by the eminent Italian legal philosopher Pierro Calamandrei:

> The good judge takes equal pains with every case, no matter how humble; he knows that important cases and unimportant cases do not exist, for injustice is not one of those poisons, which when taken in small doses may produce a salutary effect. Injustice is a dangerous poison even in doses of homeopathic proportions.[32]

Not all judges, of course, can attain this lofty status. Recognizing this fact, nearly 800 years ago, King John of England met with his barons on the field of Runnymede and, in the Magna Carta, promised that henceforth he would not "make men justices, unless they are such as know the law of the realm and are minded to observe it rightly."[33] See Exhibit 13.2 for information about the "Cash for Kids" Scandal.

EXHIBIT 13.2

THE "CASH FOR KIDS" SCANDAL

A former county juvenile court judge in Pennsylvania was sentenced to prison for 28 years after being convicted on federal racketeering charges—specifically, sentencing juveniles to a detention facility for minor crimes while accepting more than $1 million in kickbacks from the private company that built and maintained the facility.[34]

One-fourth of this judge's juvenile defendants were sentenced to detention centers, as he routinely ignored requests for leniency made by prosecutors and probation officers. Some of the nearly 5,000 sentenced juveniles were as young as 10. One girl, who described the experience as a "surreal nightmare," was sentenced to 3 months of "hard time" for posting spoofs about an assistant school principal on the Internet. Some juveniles even committed suicide following their commitment.[35]

The judge was said to have maintained a culture of intimidation in which no one was willing to speak up about the sentences he was handing down. Although he pleaded guilty to the charges, he denied sentencing juveniles who did not deserve it or receiving remuneration from the detention centers.[36]

The matter—termed *Cash for Kids*[37]—also raised concerns about whether juveniles should be required to have counsel either before or during their appearances in court: It was revealed that more than 500 juveniles had appeared before the judge without representation. Although juveniles have long had a right to counsel,[38] Pennsylvania, like at least 20 other states, allows children to waive counsel, and about half of these Pennsylvania youths had chosen to do so.[39]

The subject of judicial ethics seemed to arouse little interest until relatively recently. Indeed, from 1890 to 1904, an era of trusts and political corruption, only a few articles were published on the subject of judicial ethics. By contrast, since 1975, more than 900 articles have appeared in magazines and newspapers on the topic of judges and judicial ethics.

Judges can engage in improper conduct or overstep their bounds in many ways: abuse of judicial power (against attorneys or litigants), inappropriate sanctions and dispositions (including showing favoritism or bias), not meeting the standards of impartiality and competence (discourteous behavior, gender bias and harassment, and incompetence), conflict of interest (bias, conflicting financial interests or business, social, or family relationships), and personal conduct (criminal or sexual misconduct, prejudice, or statements of opinion).[40]

Following are examples of some true-to-life ethical dilemmas involving the courts:[41]

1. A judge convinces jailers to release his son on a nonbondable offense.
2. A judge is indicted on charges that he used his office for a racketeering enterprise.
3. Two judges attend the governor's $500-per-person inaugural ball.

4. A judge's allegedly intemperate treatment of lawyers in the courtroom is spurred by a lawyer's earlier complaints against the judge.
5. A judge is accused of acting with bias in giving a convicted murderer a less severe sentence because the victims were homosexual.
6. A judge whose car bears a bumper sticker reading "I am a pro-life democrat" acquits six pro-life demonstrators of trespassing at an abortion clinic on the ground of necessity to protect human life.

These incidents do little to bolster public confidence in the justice system. People expect more from judges, who are "the most highly visible symbol of justice."[42] The quality of the judges determines the quality of justice.

Many judges recoil at the need for a code of judicial conduct or an independent commission to investigate complaints. They dislike being considered suspect and put under regulation. No one likes to be watched, but judges must heed Thomas Jefferson's admonition that everyone in public life should be answerable to someone.[43]

Unfortunately, codes of ethical conduct have not served to eradicate the problems or allay the concerns about judges' behavior. Indeed, as three professors of law put it, "The public and the bar appear at times to be more interested in judicial ethics and accountability than the judges are."[44] One judge who teaches judicial ethics at the National Judicial College in Reno, Nevada, stated that most judges attending the college admit never having read the ABA's Model Code of Judicial Conduct before seeking judicial office.[45] Some judges also dismiss the need for a judicial conduct code because they believe that it governs aberrant behavior, which, they also believe, is rare among the judiciary. According to the AJS, however, during one year, 25 judges were suspended from office and more than 80 judges resigned or retired either before or after formal charges were filed against them; 120 judges also received private censure, admonition, or reprimand.[46]

The Code of Judicial Conduct strives to strike a balance between allowing judges to participate in social and public discourse and prohibiting conduct that would threaten a judge's independence. The essence of judicial independence is that judges' minds, according to John Adams, "should not be distracted with jarring interests; they should not be dependent upon any man, or body of men."[47]

Living by the code is challenging; the key to judicial ethics is to identify the troublesome issues and to sharpen one's sensitivity to them, that is, to create an "ethical alarm system" that responds.[48] Perhaps the most important tenet in the code, and the one that is most difficult to apply, is that judges should avoid the appearance of impropriety.

By adhering to ethical principles, judges can maintain their independence and follow the ancient charge Moses gave to his judges in Deuteronomy:

> Hear the causes between your brethren, and judge righteously. Ye shall not respect persons in judgment; but ye shall hear the small as well as the great; ye shall not be afraid of the face of man; for the judgment is God's; and for the cause that is too hard for you, bring it unto me, and I will hear it.[49]

See Exhibit 13.3 for information about ethics training for federal judges.

Lawyers for the Defense

Defense attorneys, too, must be legally and morally bound to ethical principles as agents of the courts. Elliot Cohen[50] suggested the following moral principles for defense attorneys:

1. Treat others as ends in themselves and not as mere means to winning cases.
2. Treat clients and other professional relations in a similar fashion.

EXHIBIT 13.3

ETHICS TRAINING FOR FEDERAL JUDGES

According to the Code of Conduct for U.S. Judges, Canon 1, commentary, "Deference to the judgments and rulings of courts depends upon public confidence in the integrity and independence of judges."

To further those goals, the Federal Judicial Center—the education agency for the federal courts—works closely with the Judicial Conference to provide orientation programs for new judges. By regularly covering ethics, the goal is to heighten judges' sensitivity to ethical issues and to interpret the sources of ethical rules: statutes and the *Code of Conduct for United States Judges*. Together they have developed curricula for in-class programs, online formats, and television programs.

An overview is provided of the seven canons of the Code of Conduct. Other specific ethical areas that are covered include conflicts of interest, relationships with a former law firm, and outside activities such as teaching, membership in legal or social organizations, fund-raising prohibitions, and political activities. Greatest attention is devoted to conflicts of interest—particularly financial conflicts—because mistakes seem to occur more commonly here. There is also a detailed discussion of how to fill out the financial-disclosure report. Examples are provided concerning judges who did not, or allegedly did not, follow the rules.

Source: Based on John S. Cooke, "Judicial Ethics in the Federal Courts," *Justice System Journal* 28(3) (2007): 385–393.

3. Do not deliberately engage in a behavior apt to deceive the court as to truth.
4. Be willing, if necessary, to make reasonable personal sacrifices of time, money, and popularity for what you believe to be a morally good cause.
5. Do not give money to, or accept money from, clients for wrongful purposes or in wrongful amounts.
6. Avoid harming others in the course of representing your client.
7. Be loyal to your client and do not betray his or her confidence.

Prosecutors

Prosecutors can also improve their ethical behavior. Contrary, perhaps, to what is popularly believed, it was decided over a half century ago that the primary duty of a prosecutor is "not that he shall win a case, but that justice shall be done."[51]

Instances of prosecutorial misconduct were reported as early as 1897[52] and are still reported today. One of the leading examples of unethical conduct by a prosecutor was *Miller v. Pate*,[53] in which the prosecutor concealed from the jury in a murder trial the fact that a pair of undershorts with red stains on it were stained not by blood but by paint.

If similar (though not so egregious) kinds of misconduct occur today, one must ask why. According to Cohen,[54] the answer is simple: Misconduct works. Oral advocacy is important in the courtroom and can have a powerful effect. Another significant reason for such conduct is the *harmless error doctrine*, in which an appellate court can affirm a conviction despite the presence of serious misconduct during the trial. Only when appellate courts take a stricter, more consistent approach to this problem, will it end.[55]

Other Court Employees

Other court employees have ethical responsibilities as well. Primarily known as *confidential employees*, these are justice-system functionaries who have a special role in the court system and work closely with a judge or judges. These individuals have a special responsibility to maintain the confidentiality of the court system and, thus, have a high standard of trust. For example, an appellate court judge's secretary is asked by a good friend, who is a lawyer, whether the judge will be writing the opinion in a certain case. The lawyer may wish to attempt to influence the judge through his secretary, renegotiate with an opposing party, or engage in some other improper activity designed to alter the case outcome.[56] Bailiffs, court administrators, court reporters, courtroom clerks, and law clerks all fit into this category. The judge's secretary, of course, must use his or her own ethical standard in deciding whether to answer the lawyer's question.

It would be improper for a bailiff who is accompanying jurors back from a break in a criminal trial to mention that the judge "sure seems annoyed at the defense attorney" or for a law clerk to tell an attorney friend that the judge she works for prefers reading short bench memos.[57]

▶ Ethics in Corrections

By virtue of their association with offenders, corrections personnel confront many of the same ethical dilemmas as police personnel. Thus, prison and jail administrators, like their counterparts in the police realm, would do well to understand their occupational subculture and its effect on ethical decision making.

Worley and Worley studied CO misconduct and deviance (which they defined as "behavior that is either against policy or illegal, performed during a CO's employment")[58] using surveys administered to COs in the Texas prison system. They found that an overwhelming number of COs perceived that their fellow staff members were involved in inappropriate and, in some cases, illegal types of behavior. One of the most often-reported types of deviance was that "some employees have inappropriate relationships with inmates." Also heavily reported was that "some employees allow inmates to break the rules."[59] The researchers also observed that "every year there are some correctional officers who end their careers in disgrace by engaging in activities that are deemed illegal and/or at the very least highly unethical."[60]

According to noted criminal justice ethicist Sam Souryal,[61] public corruption is ostensibly a learned behavior—no one is born corrupt, and assuming correctional applicants are carefully scrutinized prior to employment, the logical explanation must be that COs learn corruption in the course of performing their job. Ensuring a work environment that is conducive to an ethical work culture is essential.

misfeasance illegitimate acts likely committed by high-ranking officials who knowingly allow indiscretions that undermine the public interest and benefit them personally.

In very broad terms, there are two major types of CO deviance: the abuse of power and corruption.[62] More specifically, Souryal described the following three general categories of prison corruption:

1. *Acts of* **misfeasance**. These acts are illegitimate acts more likely committed by high-ranking officials who knowingly allow contractual indiscretions that would undermine the public interest and benefit them personally. Misfeasance can also involve outsiders—a building firm, a group of consultants, a planning and research agency, and a law firm hired to defend the agency—who are associated with the correctional facility through a political or professional appointment.
2. *Acts of* **malfeasance**. These acts involve crimes or misconduct that officials knowingly commit in violation of state laws and/or agency rules and regulations. Acts of malfeasance are usually committed by officials at the lower or middle management levels. Acts that might fall in this category include theft; embezzlement; trafficking in contraband; extortion; official oppression; and the exploitation of inmates or their families for money, goods, or services.
3. *Acts of* **nonfeasance**. These are acts of omission or avoidance knowingly committed by officials who are responsible for carrying out such acts. Examples of

malfeasance crimes or misconduct that officials knowingly commit in violation of state laws and/or agency rules and regulations.

nonfeasance acts of omission or avoidance knowingly committed by officials who are responsible for carrying out such acts.

nonfeasance would include looking the other way when narcotics are smuggled into a prison by inmates or visitors, and failure to report misconduct by other officers out of personal loyalty.[63]

The strength of the corrections subculture is correlated with the security level of a correctional facility and is strongest in maximum-security institutions. Powerful forces within the correctional system have a stronger influence over the behavior of COs than the administrators of the institution, legislative decrees, or agency policies.[64] Indeed, it has been known for several decades that exposure to external danger in the workplace creates a remarkable increase in group solidarity.[65]

Some of the job-related stressors for COs are similar to those the police face: the ever-present potential for physical danger, hostility directed at officers by inmates and even by the public, unreasonable role demands, a tedious and unrewarding work environment, and dependence on one another to work effectively and safely in their environment.[66] For these reasons, several norms of corrections work have been identified—always go to the aid of an officer in distress, do not "rat," never make another officer look bad in front of inmates, always support an officer in a dispute with an inmate, always support officer sanctions against inmates, and do not wear a "white hat" (participate in behavior that suggests sympathy or identification with inmates).[67]

Security issues and the way in which COs have to rely on each other for their safety make loyalty to one another a key norm. The proscription against ratting out a colleague is strong. In one documented instance, two officers in the Corcoran, California, State Prison blew the whistle on what they considered to be unethical conduct by their colleagues: Officers were alleged to have staged a gladiator-style fight among inmates from different groups in a small exercise yard. The two officers claimed that their colleagues would even place bets on the outcome of the fights, and when the fights got out of hand, the officers would fire shots at the inmates. Since the institution had opened in 1988, eight inmates had been shot dead by officers and numerous others had been wounded. The two officers who reported these activities were labeled by colleagues as "rats" and "no-goods" and had their lives threatened; even though they were transferred to other institutions, the labels traveled with them. Four COs were indicted for their alleged involvement in these activities, and all were acquitted in a state prosecution in 2001.[68]

In another case, a female CO at a medium-security institution reported some of her colleagues for sleeping during the night shift. She had first approached them and expressed concern for her safety when they were asleep, and told them that if they did not refrain from sleeping, she would have to report them to the superintendent. They continued sleeping and she reported them. The consequences were severe: Graffiti was written about her on the walls, she received harassing phone calls and letters, her car was vandalized, and bricks were thrown through the windows of her home.[69]

It would be unfair to suggest that the kind of behavior depicted here reflects the behavior of COs in all places and at all times. The case studies demonstrate, however, the power and loyalty of the group, and correctional administrators must be cognizant of that power. It is also noteworthy that the corrections subculture, like its police counterpart, has several positive qualities, particularly in crisis situations, including mutual support and protection, which is essential to the emotional and psychological health of the officers involved; the "family" is always there to support you.

Guiding Decision Making

One of the primary purposes of ethics is to guide decision making.[70] Ethics provides more comprehensive guidelines than law and operational procedures, and answers questions that might otherwise go unanswered. When in doubt, justice administrators and employees should be able to consider the ethical consequences of their actions or potential actions to determine how they should proceed. Guidelines must be in place to assist employees in making operational decisions. Criminal justice leaders obviously play a key role in ethics. Not only must they enforce and uphold ethical standards, they must also set an example and see that employees are instructed in the ethical conduct of police business.

Some experts in police ethics lay problems involving employees' ethics, and their lapses in good conduct, squarely at the feet of their leaders; for example, Edward Tully[71] stated the following:

> Show me an agency with a serious problem of officer misconduct and I will show you a department staffed with too many sergeants not doing their job. Leaders must recognize the vital and influential role sergeants play within an organization. They should be selected with care, given as much supervisory training as possible, and included in the decision-making process. Sergeants are the custodians of the culture, the leaders and informal disciplinarians of the department, and the individual most officers look to for advice.

Stephen Vicchio[72] added another caveat. Even in communities where all seems to be going well with respect to ethical behavior, trouble may be lurking beneath the surface:

> In departments where corruption appears to be low and citizen complaints are minimal, we assume that the officers are people of integrity. Sometimes this is a faulty assumption, particularly if the motivation to do the right thing comes from fear of punishment.

Most efforts to control justice system employees' behavior are rooted in statutes and departmental orders and policies. These written directives spell out inappropriate behavior and, in some cases, behavior or actions that are expected in specific situations. Written directives cannot address every contingency, however, and employees must often use their discretion. These discretionary decisions should be guided by ethics and values. When there is an ethics or policy failure, the resulting behavior is generally considered to be illegal or inappropriate.

▶ Ethics Tests for Justice Professionals

Following are some tests to help guide the criminal justice employee in deciding what is and is not an ethical behavior:[73]

- ***Test of common sense.*** Does the act make sense, or would someone look askance at it?
- ***Test of publicity.*** Would you be willing to see what you did highlighted on the front page of the local newspaper?
- ***Test of one's best self.*** Will the act fit the concept of oneself at one's best?
- ***Test of one's most admired personality.*** What would one's parents or minister do in this situation?
- ***Test of hurting someone else.*** Will it cause pain for someone?
- ***Test of foresight.*** What is the long-term likely result?

Other questions that the criminal justice professional might ask are: Is it worth my job and career? Is my decision legal?

Another tool is that of "the bell, the book, and the candle": Do bells or warning buzzers go off as I consider my choice of actions? Does it violate any laws or codes in the statute or ordinance books? Will my decision withstand the light of day or the spotlight of publicity (the candle)?[74]

In sum, all we can do is try to make the best decisions we can and be good persons and good justice system employees, who are consistent and fair. We need to apply the law, the policy, the guidelines, or whatever it is we dispense in our occupation without bias or fear and to the best of our ability, be mindful along the way that others around us may have lost their moral compass and attempt to drag us down with them. To paraphrase Franklin Delano Roosevelt, "Be the best you can, wherever you are, with what you have."

Is Workplace Loyalty Always Good?

> *Loyalty*
>
> *If you work for someone, in heaven's name, work for him!*
>
> *Speak well of him and stand by the institution he represents.*
>
> *Remember, an ounce of loyalty is worth a pound of cleverness.*
>
> *If you must growl, condemn, and eternally find fault, resign your position. And when you are on the outside, damn to your heart's content; but as long as you are part of the institution, do not condemn it. If you do, the first high wind that comes along will blow you away, and probably you will never know why.*
>
> —Author Unknown

This quote leaves no doubt that loyalty to the organization, and to one's superior, is highly desired. But is such unequivocal loyalty always a good thing, especially in criminal justice organizations? Certainly, one would think that justice system administrators would view loyalty as a very positive attribute for their employees. There are some, however, who have serious doubts about whether loyalty is indeed an asset.

personal loyalty syndrome loyalty that can be given to unworthy peers or superiors, even when resulting in violations of constitutional provisions, legal requirements, or the public good.

Sam S. Souryal and Deanna L. Diamond, for example, believe that criminal justice employees often suffer from a "**personal loyalty syndrome**," which can be defined as loyalty that is given by subordinates to their unworthy peers or superiors—even when resulting in violations of constitutional provisions, legal requirements, or the public good.

They are often compelled to offer unwavering personal loyalty to their superiors and, as a result, can violate constitutional provisions, legal requirements, or the public good; therefore, in extreme cases, practitioners may find themselves justifying untruth, impeding justice, supporting cover-ups, and lying under oath.[75]

Souryal and Diamond argued that there are several paradoxes involving the expectation and practice of personal loyalty to superiors in criminal justice agencies:

- Despite the emotional support for the practice, there is no mention of it in agency rules and regulations. If loyalty is such a great virtue, why are agency rules and regulations silent about it?
- Superiors usually make demands for loyalty when the agency is under attack, not when the agency is stable and business is conducted "as usual."
- Personal loyalty to superiors ignores the fact that some superiors are not worthy of loyalty; hundreds of supervisors and administrators are fired or disciplined each year for violating agency rules.
- Loyalty is a one-way street (superiors need not return the loyalty).[76]

In sum, there are three types of loyalty for justice practitioners to follow and to think about before offering their loyalties unconditionally; ranked from most important to least important, they are as follows:

First is *integrated* loyalty, the highest and most virtuous level of loyalty at the workplace. It is the genuine concern of each worker for the values and ideals of the profession, honoring the ideals of accountability, rationality, fairness, and good will. This is the cornerstone of all workplace loyalties and is pursued before any institutional loyalty.

Second is *institutional* loyalty; it is the obligation of each agency member, including subordinates and superiors, to support the agency's mission. Examples include the obligation of police, court, and probation and parole officers to be loyal to agency policies, rules, and regulations. This form of loyalty is the most supportive and durable, and should be positioned ahead of loyalty to superiors.

Finally, there is *personal* loyalty, the lowest level of loyalty in the workplace because it is mechanical in nature. Examples include the obligation of deputy sheriffs to be loyal to their sheriff. This form of loyalty is the most volatile and temporal, and should never replace institutional loyalty.[77]

In the final analysis, criminal justice administrators need to educate themselves in the exercise of workplace loyalties—both as an asset and as a detriment—as it relates to ethics, public service, and public good. They must act in good faith and, at a minimum, must be certain that the loyalties of their subordinates are legally and morally justified.

Summary

This chapter has examined criminal justice employee behavior from an ethical standpoint. Ethics form the foundation for behavior. It is important that police, courts, and corrections administrators and subordinates understand ethics and the role ethics plays in the performance of their duties. It is also important that these leaders understand the incipient and dangerous nature of noble cause corruption, in which their employees (and the community) may support unethical actions if they are deemed worthwhile to accomplish a good end.

Corruption has few easy remedies. Although not discussed, given civil service regulations, union rules, and other forms of job protection, it can be very difficult to remove even the worst employees. To avoid rotten apples, criminal justice administrators need to maintain high standards for recruitment and training. And to avoid rotten structures, these kinds of agencies need leaders who will not tolerate corruption, institutional procedures for accountability, and systematic investigation of complaints and of suspicious circumstances.[78]

Key Terms and Concepts

Absolute ethics, p. 341
Brady material, p. 346
Deontological ethics, p. 341
Ethics, p. 341
Gratuities, p. 347
Lying (accepted/deviant), p. 345
Malfeasance, p. 353
Misfeasance, p. 353
Model Code of Judicial Conduct, p. 349
Model of circumstantial corruptibility, p. 347
Noble cause corruption, p. 342
Nonfeasance, p. 353
Personal loyalty syndrome, p. 356
Relative ethics, p. 341

Questions for Review

1. How would you define *ethics*? What are examples of relative and absolute ethics?
2. What is the meaning of *noble cause corruption*, and how does it apply to policing?
3. Should police accept minor gratuities? Explain why doing so might be permitted, per Withrow and Dailey's model of circumstantial corruptibility.
4. How has *Brady v. Maryland* affected both police and prosecutors, and how might one's career be ruined if *Brady's* provisions are violated?
5. In what ways can judges, defense attorneys, and prosecutors engage in unethical behavior?
6. In what substantive ways do the police and corrections subcultures resemble each other?
7. How may corrections officers in prisons be unethical?

Deliberate and Decide

Confronting Ethical Dilemmas

Like most of the scenarios presented at the chapter's beginning, the following scenarios are based on actual cases and pose a possible ethical dilemma for the criminal justice employee (and, by extension, the agency's leadership or governing body). After reading each scenario, address the question for discussion provided at the end.

1. A deputy sheriff has been using a variety of problem-solving approaches to address problems at a shopping mall where juveniles have been loitering, engaging in acts of vandalism, dumping trash, and generally causing traffic problems after hours in the parking lot. Now the mall manager, Mr. Chang, feels morally obligated to express his appreciation to the deputy. Mr. Chang has made arrangements for the deputy and family to receive a 15 percent discount while shopping at any store in the mall. Also, as part-owner of a children's toy store in the mall, Mr. Chang offers the deputy a bicycle for his young daughter. Knowing that the agency policy requires that such offers be declined, the deputy is also aware that Mr. Chang will be very hurt or upset if the proffered gifts are refused.
2. A municipal court judge borrows money from court employees, publicly endorses and campaigns for a candidate for judicial office, conducts personal business from chambers (displaying and selling antiques), directs other court employees to perform personal errands for him during court hours, suggests that persons appearing before him contribute to certain charities in lieu of paying fines, and uses court employees to perform translating services at his mother's nursery business.
3. A. An associate warden and "rising star" in a state's prison system has just been stopped and arrested for driving while intoxicated while off-duty and in his personal vehicle. There are no damages or injuries involved, he is very remorseful, and he has just been released from jail. You, as warden, must determine whether or not the individual should receive agency discipline for this action.

   B. One week later, this same associate warden stops at a local convenience store after work; as he leaves the store, a clerk stops him and summons the police—the individual has just been caught shoplifting a package of cigarettes. You have just been informed of this latest arrest.

Question for Discussion

For each scenario, determine the available options and select what you believe is the best course of action, drawing on information presented in this chapter as well as from your own moral compass.

Learn by Doing

1. As a criminal justice student and friend of the president of your local Citizens' Police Academy, you are asked to speak at the group's training session concerning police ethics. Specifically, you are to discuss ethical dilemmas in policing—providing several examples—and explain how the police must deal with such dilemmas. What would your presentation address?
2. You are a court administrator in a county district court, supervised by Chief Judge Williams. While walking through staff office area today, you believe you overhear a court reporter say that on two occasions that week, Judge Williams smelled like he had alcohol on his breath. They stifle their conversation when they see you walk by. Later that day, you send your administrative assistant to Judge Williams' chambers to borrow a budget sheet. When he returns, he tells you that the judge appeared to smell of alcohol. A week later, while working late, the judge summons you to his office. There he explains that he is awaiting a jury verdict, and while casually chatting, he makes himself a cocktail. In fact, he eventually consumes several of these drinks (and appears to be more than "tipsy"). When word comes that the jury has returned with its verdict, he quickly leaves his office to return to the bench.
   a. What, if anything, are you ethically bound to do regarding Judge Williams?
   b. Do you draw a distinction between his drinking which occurred while he was in his office versus while he is in the court chamber and sitting on the bench?
   c. Do you draw a distinction between someone merely smelling alcohol versus actually seeing him drink alcohol? The number of occasions people have smelled alcohol on his breath? Whether

he only smelled of alcohol, as opposed to appearing to be intoxicated? Whether he acted inappropriately, unprofessionally, or incompetently while in the observed condition or after drinking alcohol?

d. Would you feel any differently if, instead of a judge, the same situation involved a prosecutor or defense attorney? Why or why not?

3. You are a final candidate for a staff position at a newly constructed state prison in your community. An oral board member asks you the following questions: You discover that a fellow staff member routinely accepts free food, candy, and other gifts of small value from inmates/clients. These items are not solicited from inmates, nor is special treatment given to the gift-givers. (1) How serious do you consider this behavior to be? (2) Do you believe such behavior should be prohibited under official policy in your organization? (3) What, if any, disciplinary measures do you believe to be appropriate in this case? (4) Would you report a fellow staff member to a supervisor for engaging in this behavior? How do you respond to each?

Case Study

Late one night Officer Nichols is involved in a massive, late-night drug bust of several residences, during which time she absentmindedly placed a bag of drugs on the hood of her car. Approximately an hour later when leaving for another call, she remembered that she had forgotten to mark and secure the bag of drugs from the previous call. She immediately returned to the scene and discovered the bag of drugs had apparently slid off the car hood and landed in a bush on the side of the road. In her report, she does not mention this disregard of evidentiary procedures. Later, at the preliminary hearing at which time the defense counsel asks Nichols if she ever left this piece of evidence unattended (and thus breaking the chain of custody), she testifies that she did not (she is quite certain that no one saw her leave the bag unattended, and knows that if she admits to her inattention to the evidence, the guilty party will go free).

Questions for Discussion

1. Assume that someone did in fact make a videotape of the bag being left unattended and posted it on YouTube. What actions, if any, may be taken against her by the courts as a result of her testimony in trial? How might her lying bear on the case after the fact?
2. How should Nichols' department respond to this revelation and what potential discipline may be imposed? Could/should she later be charged with perjury?

Notes

1. 373 U.S. 83
2. The judge soon resigned from the bench. In a unanimous 7–0 decision, the Supreme Court ruled that his acting and comedy career was "incompatible" with judicial conduct codes. See "Comedian Resigns as Hackensack Judge after Losing Appeal," *CBS New York*, September 19, 2014, http://newyork.cbslocal.com/2014/09/19/nj-supreme-court-part-time-hackensack-judge-cant-also-be-comedian/.
3. For more information, see Jennifer G. Clarke and Rachel E. Simon, "Shackling and Separation: Motherhood in Prison," *American Medical Association Journal of Ethics*, http://journalofethics.ama-assn.org/2013/09/pfor2-1309.html.
4. Richard Kania, "Police Acceptance of Gratuities," *Criminal Justice Ethics* 7 (1988): 37–49.
5. John Kleinig, *The Ethics of Policing* (New York: Cambridge University Press, 1996).
6. Timothy J. O'Malley, "Managing for Ethics: A Mandate for Administrators," *FBI Law Enforcement Bulletin* (April 1997): 20–25.
7. Thomas J. Martinelli, "Unconstitutional Policing: The Ethical Challenges in Dealing with Noble Cause Corruption," *The Police Chief* (October 2006): 150.
8. John P. Crank and Michael A. Caldero, *Police Ethics: The Corruption of Noble Cause* (Cincinnati, OH: Anderson, 2000), p. 75.
9. U.S. Department of Justice, National Institute of Justice, Office of Community Oriented Policing Services, *Police Integrity: Public Service with Honor* (Washington, DC: U.S. Government Printing Office, 1997), p. 62.
10. Ibid.
11. Ibid.
12. Edward Tully, "Misconduct, Corruption, Abuse of Power: What Can the Chief Do?" http://www.neiassociates.org/-misconduct-corruption-abuse-i/
13. U.S. Department of Justice, Civil Rights Division, *Investigation of the Ferguson Police Department*, March 4, 2015, https://www.justice.gov/sites/default/files/opa/press-releases/attachments/2015/03/04/ferguson_police_department_report_1.pdf.
14. David Carter, "Theoretical Dimensions in the Abuse of Authority," in Thomas Barker and David Carter (eds.), *Police Deviance* (Cincinnati, OH: Anderson, 1994), pp. 269–290; also see Thomas Barker and David Carter, "Fluffing Up the Evidence and 'Covering Your Ass': Some

Conceptual Notes on Police Lying," *Deviant Behavior* 11 (1990): 61–73.
15. Gary T. Marx, "Who Really Gets Stung? Some Issues Raised by the New Police Undercover Work," *Crime & Delinquency* 28 (2) (1982): 165–193.
16. *Illinois v. Perkins,* 110 S.Ct. 2394 (1990).
17. Barker and Carter, *Police Deviance*.
18. Thomas Barker, "An Empirical Study of Police Deviance Other Than Corruption," in Thomas Barker and David L. Carter (eds.), *Police Deviance* (Cincinnati, OH: Anderson, 1994), pp. 123–138.
19. Jaxon V. Derbeken, "Police with Problems Are a Problem for the D.A.," *San Francisco Chronicle*, May 16, 2010, http://www.sfgate.com/cgi-bin/article.cgi?f=/c/a/2010/05/15/MNKC1DB57E.DTL.
20. *Brady v. Maryland*, 373 U.S. 83 (1963).
21. See Richard Lisko, "Agency Policies Imperative to Disclose *Brady v. Maryland* Material to Prosecutors," *The Police Chief* 77(3) (March 2011), http://www.policechiefmagazine.org/magazine/index.cfm?fuseaction=display_arch&article_id=2329&issue_id=32011.
22. Lisko, "Agency Policies Imperative to Disclose *Brady v. Maryland* Material to Prosecutors," also see Val V. Brocklin, "Brady v. Md Can Get You Fired," *Officer.com*, August 16, 2010, http://www.officer.com/article/10232477/brady-v-md-can-get-you-fired.
23. Jack Ryan, "Police Officers May Be Liable for Failure to Disclose Exculpatory Information under the Brady Rule Managing Risks," *Policelink* (n.d.), http://policelink.monster.com/training/articles/2123-police-officers-may-be-liable-for-failure-to-disclose-exculpatory-information-under-the-brady-rulemanaging-risks-.
24. New York City Commission to Investigate Allegations of Police Corruption and the City's Anti-Corruption Procedures, *The Knapp Commission Report on Police Corruption* (New York: George Braziller, 1972), p. 4.
25. Kania, "Police Acceptance of Gratuities," p. 40. For an excellent analysis of how the acceptance of gratuities can become endemic to an organization and pose ethical dilemmas for new officers, see Jim Ruiz and Christine Bono, "At What Price a 'Freebie'? The Real Cost of Police Gratuities," *Criminal Justice Ethics* (Winter–Spring 2004): 44–54. The authors also demonstrate through detailed calculations how the amount of gratuities accepted can reach up to 40 percent of an annual officer's income—and therefore no minor or inconsequential infraction of rules that can be left ignored or unenforced.
26. Brian L. Withrow and Jeffrey D. Dailey, "When Strings Are Attached," in Quint C. Thurman and Jihong Zhao (eds.), *Contemporary Policing: Controversies, Challenges, and Solutions* (Los Angeles, CA: Roxbury, 2004), pp. 319–326.
27. Ibid.
28. Ibid.
29. See *Crime Delinquency* 10 (1964): 355–371; American Bar Association, 29 *A.B.A. Report* 29, part I (1906): 395–417.
30. John P. MacKenzie, *The Appearance of Justice* (New York: Scribner's, 1974). See also Eliot Asimof, *Eight Men Out: The Black Sox and the 1919 World Series* (New York: Henry Holt, 1963); a movie by the same name was released in 1988.
31. Cynthia Gray, "The Center for Judicial Ethics," *Judicature* 96(6) (May/June 2014): 305–313. https://www.ajs.org/index.php/judicial-ethics/judicial-conduct-reporter For more information about Judicial Conduct Reporter, see its website at https://www.ajs.org/index.php/judicial-ethics/judicial-conduct-reporter.
32. Quoted in Frank Greenberg, "The Task of Judging the Judges," *Judicature* 59 (May 1976): 464.
33. Ibid., p. 460; direct quote from the original.
34. Walter Pavlo, "Pennsylvania Judge Gets 'Life Sentence' for Prison Kickback Scheme," http://www.forbes.com/sites/walterpavlo/2011/08/12/pennsylvania-judge-gets-life-sentence-for-prison-kickback-scheme/.
35. Ian Urbina and Sean D. Hamill, "Judges Plead Guilty in Scheme to Jail Youths for Profit," *The New York Times*, February 12, 2009, http://www.nytimes.com/2009/02/13/us/13judge.html?pagewanted=all&_r=0.
36. Ibid.
37. Cynthia Gray, "Top Judicial Ethics Stories of 2010," *Judicature* 94(4) (January/February 2011): 187–191.
38. See *In re Gault,* 387 U.S. 1 (1967).
39. Urbina and Hamill, "Judges Plead Guilty in Scheme to Jail Youths for Profit."
40. For thorough discussions and examples of these areas of potential ethical shortcomings, see Jeffrey M. Shaman, Steven Lubet, and James J. Alfini, *Judicial Conduct and Ethics,* 3rd ed. (San Francisco, CA: Matthew Bender & Co., 2000).
41. Ibid.
42. Ibid., p. vi.
43. Ibid.
44. Ibid., p. vi.
45. Tim Murphy, "Test Your Ethical Acumen," *Judges' Journal* 8 (1998): 34.
46. American Judicature Society, *Judicial Conduct Reporter* 16 (1994): 2–3.
47. John Adams, "On Government," quoted in Russell Wheeler, *Judicial Administration: Its Relation to Judicial Independence* (Alexandria, VA: National Center for State Courts, 1988), p. 112.
48. Shaman et al., *Judicial Conduct and Ethics,* p. viii.
49. Deut. 1:16–17.
50. Elliot D. Cohen, "Pure Legal Advocates and Moral Agents: Two Concepts of a Lawyer in an Adversary System," in Michael C. Braswell, Belinda R. McCarthy, and Bernard J. McCarthy (eds.), *Justice, Crime and Ethics,* 2nd ed. (Cincinnati, OH: Anderson, 1996), pp. 131–167.
51. *Berger v. United States*, 295 U.S. 78 (1935).
52. See *Dunlop v. United States,* 165 U.S. 486 (1897), involving a prosecutor's inflammatory statements to the jury.

53. 386 U.S. 1 (1967). In this case, the Supreme Court overturned the defendant's conviction after determining that the prosecutor "deliberately misrepresented the truth."
54. Cohen, "Pure Legal Advocates and Moral Agents," p. 168.
55. Ibid.
56. Cynthia K. Conlon and Lisa L. Milord, *The Ethics Fieldbook: Tools for Trainers* (Chicago, MA: American Judicature Society, n.d.), pp. 23–25.
57. Ibid., p. 28.
58. Robert M. Worley and Vidisha B. Worley, "Guards Gone Wild: A Self-report Study of Correctional Officer Misconduct and the Effect of Institutional Deviance on 'Care' Within the Texas Prison System," *Deviant Behavior* 32(4) (April 2011): 293–319.
59. Ibid.
60. Ibid.
61. Sam Souryal, "Deterring Corruption by Prison Personnel: A Principle-Based Perspective," *The Prison Journal* 89(1) (March 2009): 21–45.
62. Jeffrey I. Ross, "Deconstructing Correctional Officer Deviance: Toward Typologies of Actions and Controls," *Criminal Justice Review* 38(1) (March 2014): 110–126.
63. Ibid., p. 36.
64. Elizabeth L. Grossi and Bruce L. Berg, "Stress and Job Dissatisfaction Among Correctional Officers: An Unexpected Finding," *International Journal of Offender Therapy and Comparative Criminology* 35 (1991): 79.
65. Irving L. Janis, "Group Dynamics under Conditions of External Danger," in Darwin Cartwright and Alvin Zander (eds.), *Group Dynamics: Research and Theory* (New York: Harper & Row, 1968), pp. 80–90.
66. Ibid.
67. Ibid., p. 85.
68. *CBS News*, March 30, 1977; also see Jones and Carlson, *Reputable Conduct: Ethical Issues in Policing and Corrections* (Upper Saddle River, NJ: Prentice Hall, 2000), p. 76.
69. Ibid, p. 77.
70. Frank K. Fair and Wayland D. Pilcher, "Morality on the Line: The Role of Ethics in Police Decision-Making," *American Journal of Police* 10(2) (1991): 23–38.
71. Tully, "Misconduct, Corruption, Abuse of Power."
72. Stephen J. Vicchio, "Ethics and Police Integrity," *FBI Law Enforcement Bulletin* (July 1997): 8–12.
73. Kleinig, *The Ethics of Policing*.
74. Ibid.
75. Sam S. Souryal and Deanna L. Diamond, "The Rhetoric of Personal Loyalty to Superiors in Criminal Justice Agencies," *Journal of Criminal Justice* 29 (2001): 543–554.
76. Ibid., p. 548.
77. Ibid., p. 549
78. Delattre, *Character and Cops,* p. 84.

Mediaphotos/Shutterstock

14 Special Challenges

Labor Relations, Liability, and Discipline

LEARNING OBJECTIVES

After reading this chapter, the student will be able to:

1. *define collective bargaining and the three models of collective bargaining*
2. *delineate the four types of job actions in which employees can engage*
3. *define civil liability, which actions can lead to a finding of negligence, and types of lawsuits filed against criminal justice practitioners*
4. *describe the due process and disciplinary actions and approaches (e.g., the positive discipline approach) that may be used with criminal justice employees*
5. *delineate the steps taken when a citizen's complaint is filed*
6. *review the grievance process*
7. *explain how one can appeal a disciplinary action as well as the system for identifying problem employees*
8. *describe some of the issues arising with the spread of legal, recreational marijuana use, and how administrators will likely deal with them*

▶ Introduction

Those who administer criminal justice agencies are confronted with, and must successfully address, countless challenges in the course of performing their daily duties; therefore, because they provide criminal justice administrators with nearly endless challenges—as well as trials, tribulations, and often a very large proportion of their workload—we discuss three broad topics concerning personnel.

This chapter opens by discussing labor relations/collective bargaining. In the past 50 years, probably no factor has had a greater impact on the administration of criminal justice agencies, with the possible exception of civil liability (which is also discussed in this chapter). Indeed, the decade of the 2010s witnesses unprecedented battles between politicians (who are trying to address huge budget deficits, union powers, and what they perceive to be runaway wages and benefits packages) and labor unions (who are trying to protect their members' wages and benefits). This chapter discusses how the unionization movement developed in criminal justice as well as contemporary collective bargaining practices.

Then we examine criminal justice employees vis-à-vis potential civil liability. This discussion includes several legal concepts (such as negligence and torts), court decisions, and legislation that serve to hold criminal justice practitioners accountable, both civilly and criminally, for acts of misconduct and negligence.

Next is a look at employee discipline, including the tradition of problems in policing, due process requirements that must be afforded such employees, what is being done to identify and deal with problem officers, how a positive discipline program functions, some proper means of dealing with citizen complaints, and the need to account for violations of *internal* departmental standards. Then, after discussing the conundrum of legalized recreational marijuana for criminal justice employees, the chapter concludes with review questions and exercises in the Deliberate and Decide, Learn by Doing, and Case Study sections. Four exhibits and five figures will provide further information and food for thought concerning liability, corruption, and discipline.

▶ Collective Bargaining, Generally

The Nature and Principles of Shared Governance

Three Models

Each state is free to decide whether and which public sector employees will have **collective bargaining** rights and under what terms; therefore, there is considerable variety in collective bargaining arrangements across the nation. In states with comprehensive public sector bargaining laws, the administration of the statute is the responsibility of a state agency such as a public employee relations board (PERB) or a public employee relations commission (PERC). There are three basic models used in the states: binding arbitration, meet-and-confer, and bargaining-not-required.[1]

collective bargaining a term referring to the process of negotiation between employers and employees for arriving at agreements concerning salaries, working conditions, benefits, and so on.

The binding arbitration model is used in 25 states and the District of Columbia. Public employees are given the right to bargain with their employers.[2] If the bargaining reaches an impasse, the matter is submitted to a neutral arbitrator who decides what the terms and conditions of the new collective bargaining agreement will be.[3] Here, the arbitrator hears the case and makes a decision, acting in place of a trial before a judge or jury. The arbitrator should therefore be unbiased and attempt to pursue an outcome that is fair and reasonable to all parties.

Only eleven states use the **meet-and-confer** model, which grants very few rights to public employees. As with the binding arbitration model, criminal justice employees

meet-and-confer a comparatively weak bargaining system where employees may organize and select bargaining representatives; but if an impasse occurs, their options are limited.

in meet-and-confer states have the right to organize and to select their own bargaining representatives.[4] When an impasse is reached, however, employees are at a distinct disadvantage. Their only legal choices are to accept the employer's best offer, try to influence the offer through political tactics (such as appeals for public support), or take some permissible job action.[5]

The 15 states that follow the *bargaining-not-required* model either do not statutorily require or do not allow collective bargaining by public employees.[6] In the majority of these states, laws permitting public employees to engage in collective bargaining have not been passed.

States with collective bargaining must also address the issue of whether an individual employee must be a member of a union that represents his or her class of employees in a particular organization. In a "closed shop," employees must be dues-paying members or they will be terminated by the employer. "Open" shops, conversely, allow employees a choice of whether to join, even though the union has an obligation to represent them.

Organizing for Collective Bargaining

If collective bargaining is legally established, the process of setting up a bargaining relationship is as follows: First, a union will begin an organizing drive seeking to get a majority of the class(es) of employees it wants to represent to sign authorization cards. At this point, agency administrators may attempt to convince employees that they are better off without the union. Questions may also arise, such as whether certain employees (e.g., police or prison lieutenants) are part of management and therefore ineligible for union representation.

Once a majority ("50% plus 1" of the eligible employees) have signed cards, the union notifies the criminal justice agency. If management believes that the union has obtained a majority legitimately, it will recognize the union as the bargaining agent of the employees it has sought to represent. Once recognized by the employer, the union will petition the PERB or other body responsible for administering the legislation for certification.

Negotiation

negotiation a dialogue between labor and management for developing a written agreement concerning such issues as working conditions, salaries, and benefits.

Labor **negotiation** typically involves a dialogue between labor and management that is intended to develop a written agreement that will bind both parties during the life of the agreement concerning such issues as working conditions, salaries, and benefits. Negotiations at times are also used to prevent or to resolve disputes concerning same.

Management normally prefers a narrow scope of negotiations because it means less shared power; conversely, the union will opt for the widest possible scope. The number of negotiating sessions may run from one to several dozen, lasting from a few minutes to 10 or more hours, depending on how close or far apart union and management are when they begin to meet face to face.

Figure 14-1 ■ depicts a typical configuration of the union and management bargaining teams. Positions shown in the broken-line boxes typically serve in a support role and may or may not actually partake in the bargaining. Management's labor relations manager (lead negotiator) is often an attorney assigned to the human resources department, reporting to the city manager or assistant city manager and representing the city in grievances and arbitration matters; management's chief negotiator may also be the director of labor relations or human resources director for the unit of government involved or a professional labor relations specialist. Similarly, the union's chief negotiator normally is not a member of the organization involved; rather, he or she will be a specialist who is brought in to represent the union's position and to provide greater experience, expertise, objectivity, and autonomy. The union's chief negotiator may be accompanied by some people who have conducted surveys on wages and benefits, trends in the consumer price index, and so on.[7]

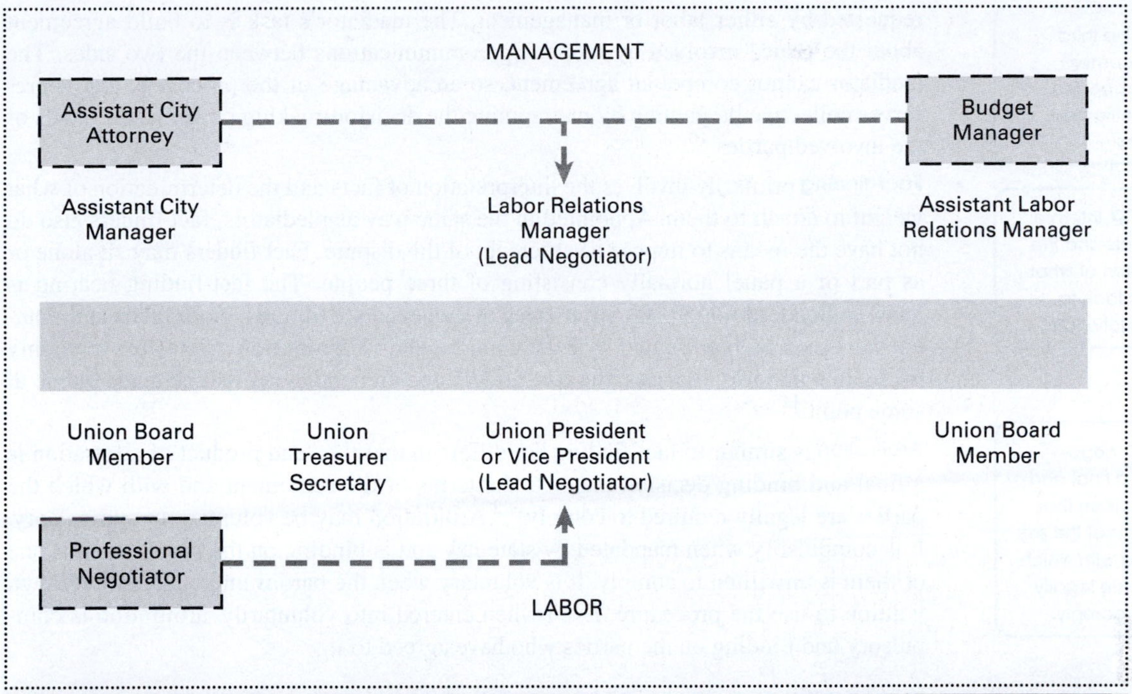

FIGURE 14-1 Union and Management Collective Bargaining Teams
Source: Union and Management Bargaining Teams by Jerry Hoover. Used by permission of Jerry Hoover.

In the minds of many chief executives, the agency administrator should NOT appear at the bargaining table; it is difficult for the chief executive to represent management one day and then return to work among the employees the next. Rather, management is represented by a key member of the command staff having the executive's confidence.

The issues, and the way in which they are presented, will impact how the negotiations will go. In the initial session, the chief negotiator for each party will make an opening statement. Management's representative will often go first, touching on general themes such as the need for patience and the obligation to bargain in good faith. The union's negotiator will generally follow, outlining what the union seeks to achieve under the terms of the new contract. Ground rules for the bargaining may then be reviewed, modified, or developed. The attention then shifts to the terms of the contract that the union is proposing. Both sides need to understand what it is they are attempting to commit each other to. Ultimately, unless a total impasse is reached, agreement will be obtained on the terms of a new contract. The union's membership will vote on the contract as whole. If approved by the membership, the contract then goes before the necessary government officials and bodies for approval.[8]

In the Event of an Impasse. . .

Even parties bargaining in good faith may not be able to resolve their differences by themselves, and an impasse may result. In such cases, a neutral third party may be introduced to facilitate, suggest, or compel an agreement. Three major forms of impasse resolution are mediation, fact-finding, and arbitration.

- **Mediation** occurs when a third party, called the mediator, comes in to help the opposing parties to settle their negotiations.[9] This person may be a professional mediator or someone else in whom both parties have confidence. In most states, mediation may be

mediation a third party who comes in to help opposing parties to settle their negotiations.

fact-finding interpretation of facts and the determination of what weight to attach to them in negotiations.

arbitration negotiation with a final and binding decision that sets the terms of the settlement and with which the parties are legally required to comply.

requested by either labor or management. The mediator's task is to build agreement about the issues involved by reopening communications between the two sides. The mediator cannot compel an agreement, so an advantage of the process is that it preserves collective bargaining by maintaining the decision-making power in the hands of the involved parties.[10]

- **Fact-finding** primarily involves the interpretation of facts and the determination of what weight to attach to them. Appointed in the same way as mediators, fact finders also do not have the means to impose a settlement of the dispute. Fact finders may sit alone or as part of a panel normally consisting of three people. The fact-finding hearing is quasi-judicial, although less strict rules of evidence are applied. Both labor and management may be represented by legal counsel, and verbatim transcripts are commonly made. In a majority of cases, the fact finder's recommendations will be made public at some point.[11]
- **Arbitration** is similar to fact-finding but differs in that the "end product of arbitration is a final and binding decision that sets the terms of the settlement and with which the parties are legally required to comply."[12] Arbitration may be voluntary or compulsory. It is compulsory when mandated by state law and is binding on the parties even if one of them is unwilling to comply. It is voluntary when the parties undertake of their own volition to use the procedure. Even when entered into voluntarily, arbitration is compulsory and binding on the parties who have agreed to it.

The establishment of a working agreement between labor and management can also become the basis for strife. Questions can arise concerning the interpretation and application of the document and its various clauses, and grievances (discussed earlier) may arise. The sequence of grievance steps will be spelled out in the collective bargaining agreement and typically include the following five steps: (1) The employee presents the grievance to the immediate supervisor, and if satisfaction is not achieved, (2) a written grievance is presented to the division commander, then (3) to the chief executive officer, then (4) to the city or county manager, and, finally, (5) to an arbiter, selected according to the rules of the American Arbitration Association.[13]

The burden of proof is on the grieving party, except in disciplinary cases, when it is always on the employer. The parties may be represented by counsel at the hearing, and the format will include opening statements by each side, examination and cross-examination of any witnesses, and closing arguments in the reverse order of which opening arguments were made.[14]

Job Actions

job action an activity by employees to express their dissatisfaction with a particular person, event, or condition relating to their work.

A **job action** is an activity by employees to express their dissatisfaction with a particular person, event, or condition or to attempt to influence the outcome of some matter pending before decision makers. Employees seek to create pressure that may shift the course of events to a position more favorable or acceptable to them.[15] Job actions are of four types: the vote of confidence, work slowdowns, work speedups, and work stoppages.

- ***Vote of confidence.*** This job action is used sparingly; a vote of no confidence signals employees' collective displeasure with the chief administrator of the agency. Although such votes have no legal standing, they may have high impact as a result of the resulting publicity.
- ***Work slowdowns.*** Employees continue to work during a slowdown, but they do so at a leisurely pace, causing productivity to fall. As productivity declines, the unit of government is pressured to resume normal work production; for example, a police department may urge officers to issue more citations so that revenues are not lost. Citizens may complain to politicians to "get this thing settled."[16]

- ***Work speedups.*** These involve accelerated activity in the level of services and can foster considerable public resentment. For example, a police department may conduct a "ticket blizzard" to protest a low pay increase, pressure governmental leaders to make more concessions at the bargaining table, or abandon some policy change that affects their working conditions.
- ***Work stoppages.*** When a bargaining impasse occurs, a work stoppage—or strike—can constitute the most severe job action employees can undertake. Because it involves the withholding of all employees' services in an attempt to force management back to the bargaining table, public employees are generally forbidden by state law to strike. Therefore, work stoppages involving public employees are rare, but they do occur and often involve educational systems (such as the 2012 strike involving the Chicago Public Schools and the Chicago Teachers Union, with 26,500 workers accounting for 185,500 days idle).[17] In criminal justice agencies, what is seen more often is what is termed in policing the "blue flu," where a high number of officers claim to be too sick to work (an example of this tactic is the 2014 case in Memphis, Tennessee, where 550 officers (one-fourth of the agency's total staff) called in sick; the "epidemic" was a response to the city council making deep cuts to city employee benefits.[18]

▶ Labor Relations in Criminal Justice

In 1971, Tucson police legal advisor John H. Burpo authored a book entitled *The Police Labor Movement: Problems and Perspectives*.[19] In the book's Preface, Burpo stated, "Police labor problems, of which unionization is but one facet, will be the major administrative headache facing the police service during the next decade."[20]

Burpo was possibly correct in his assessment. However, many of today's police, courts, and corrections administrators would argue that he was off by nearly a half century in his view of unionization as posing an "administrative headache" for a decade. Unions obviously are here to stay—and have become involved in all manner of issues, including not only wages and benefits but also working conditions, promotions, staffing levels, bans on smoking in public, even the kinds of vehicles officers drive. And they have contributed much to the rights and privileges that criminal justice employees enjoy and were discussed in Chapter 13.

In this section, we discuss the history, nature, and principles of collective bargaining in criminal justice organizations. Included is a discussion of how criminal justice administrators must "navigate the waters" of unionization in order to coexist with them in today's criminal justice environment.

The Movement Begins: Policing Then and Now

Early Campaigns

The early development of police unions was met with considerable opposition. For example, in 1919 the Boston police commissioner refused to recognize the union or allow officers to join it, and filed charges against several union officials. Shortly thereafter, on September 9, the Boston police initiated their now-famous (or infamous) 3-day strike, leading to major riots and a furor against the police all across the nation; 9 rioters were killed and 23 were seriously injured. During the strike, Massachusetts governor Calvin Coolidge stated, "There is no right to strike against the public safety by anybody, anywhere, anytime."

During and after World War II, however, the police unions began to burgeon as charters were issued to a few dozen locals all over the country and organizers began to help enlist the rank and file. Most police chiefs continued speaking out against unionization, but their subordinates were moved by the thousands to join, sensing the advantage in having unions press for higher wages and benefits.[21] In a series of rulings, however, the courts upheld the right of police authorities to ban police unions.

The unions were survived in the early 1950s by many benevolent and fraternal organizations of police. Some were patrolmen's benevolent associations (PBAs), like those formed in New York City, Chicago, and Washington, DC; others were fraternal orders of police (FOPs). Today labor relations remain a critical topic in policing, and a virtual maze of affiliations dots the police labor landscape, with the two largest unions—the Fraternal Order of Police and the National Association of Police Organizations—reporting a combined membership of nearly 570,000 sworn officers in more than 3,300 lodges and agencies.[22] Police unions are strongest in the Northeast, Midwest, and West and tend to play a greater role in larger departments. Unions or associations in larger departments tend to have offices with full-time staff members working to advance union causes as well as lobbyists who work the political system for union purposes. Thus, police unions in many jurisdictions are a formidable force with which to be reckoned.

Once unions are recognized in a jurisdiction, the relationship between the department and the governmental entity is codified in a contract or memorandum of understanding. The contract specifies the rights and privileges of employees, and it places restrictions on the political entity and police administrators. In effect, the contract has the force of law. The contract can only be changed via renegotiations, which occur generally on a 3-year cycle or by mutual agreement on the part of the union and police management. When there is a dispute over the interpretation of the contract or its administration, the question is sorted out by an arbitrator or sometimes in the courts.[23]

As noted above, unions can obviously have a major impact on police departments. Their activities and the contract not only affect police administrators but also place limitations or restrictions on supervisors and managers. Thus, it is important for supervisors and managers to understand the collective bargaining process, the implications of the contract, and how supervisors and managers negotiate tasks and responsibilities within the confines of the contract.

Corrections Follows the Precedent

Correctional officers (COs) were probably the last group of public workers to organize. After authorization of collective bargaining in the 1960s and 1970s, correctional administrators feared that unionization would diminish management authority and undermine staff discipline and prison security. Over the years that collective bargaining has been in place for correctional agencies, however, the early fears have not materialized, and the benefits of shared governance by line staff and management have led to better decisions and higher morale. As with the police, negotiations usually involve pay and benefits for correctional employees, including seniority rights, how staff members are selected for overtime, the type of clothing provided to staff by the agency, educational programs, and so on. After a contract is negotiated, each prison or community corrections office must implement and administer it. When disputes about the true meaning of a contract arise, management can make a decision, and the union can file a grievance to argue against it.[24]

Collective bargaining is now well entrenched in prison and other correctional agency operations, and it will continue to have an impact on policy and practice. There remains some disagreement, however, concerning its implications. Some argue that sharing of power in a correctional setting benefits all parties, and that unions are a powerful voice to the legislature for increases in staffing and budgets. Others maintain that collective bargaining has resulted in a clear distinction between line staff and management, with managers no longer looking out for subordinates because union leadership promotes an adversarial relationship. As James Jacobs and Norma Crotty suggested, collective bargaining "has redefined the prison organization in adversary terms so that wardens are bosses and complaints are grievances."[25]

A major issue with corrections unions involves the right to strike. One can only imagine the chaos that would occur if COs strike. Such unlawful strikes have occurred. The most infamous strike action was in New York State in 1979, when 7,000 correctional workers simultaneously struck the state's 33 prisons. A court found the union in violation of the law, heavily fined the union for the failure of its members to return to work, and jailed union leaders for contempt of court.[26] The strike ended 17 days after it began; the corrections officers gained very few concessions, and the salary gains did not offset the fines imposed on the strikers.[27]

Unionization in the Courts

The movement to exercise the right to bargain collectively, especially when compared with law enforcement and corrections, has been rare in the courts, occurring on a random, localized basis; however, unified court systems exist in which court personnel are organized statewide, as in Hawaii. Many states adhere generally to model legislation on public employee relation commissions, which provide mediation and fact-finding services and make determinations of unfair labor practices. On occasion, these commissions make decisions that greatly affect the management authority of the judiciary over its personnel.

When a collective bargaining unit exists in a court system, the process has all the basic elements found in other systems: (1) recognition (the employing court recognizes that henceforth employees will be represented by their chosen agent); (2) negotiation (there are established methods for arriving at collective bargaining agreements, breaking deadlocks, ratifying contracts, and so on); and (3) contract administration (the day-to-day management of a court is accomplished within the framework of the labor contract).[28]

▶ Civil Liability: A Primer

Definitions and Legal Foundation

Criminal justice administrators, particularly those working in law enforcement and corrections, certainly understand the potential and actual existence of **civil liability**—that is, blame assigned to a person or organization because its employees committed negligent or other acts resulting in some type of harm. These administrators very likely reflect their experiences and concerns with litigation in their training, policies and procedures, general orders, and so on.

civil liability blame assigned to a person or organization because its employees committed negligent or other acts resulting in some type of harm.

They also understand that, with the possible exception of professionals working in the medical field, no group of workers is more susceptible to litigation and liability than police and corrections employees. Frequently thrust into confrontational situations, and given the complex nature of their work and its requisite training needs, they will from time to time act in a manner that evokes public scrutiny and complaints. As we will see, the price of failure among public servants can be quite high in both human and financial terms. In addition, some police officers and COs are overzealous and even brutal in their work; they may intentionally or otherwise violate the rights of the citizens they are sworn to protect, detain, or supervise. For these inappropriate actions, the public has become quick to file suit for damages for what are perceived to be egregious actions.

Next, we examine the kinds of inappropriate and negligent behaviors that can lead to civil liability and even incarceration for police and corrections personnel in the justice system; included is a discussion of a major legislative tool that citizens use to seek redress when such activities occur: Title 42, *U.S. Code*, Section 1983.

Torts and Negligence

tort the infliction of some injury on one person by another.

negligence when someone's conduct creates a danger to others, often by subjecting others to a risk of harm and resulting in some form of injury.

It is important to have a basic understanding of tort liability. A **tort** is the infliction of some injury on one person by another. Three categories of torts generally cover most of the lawsuits filed against criminal justice practitioners: negligence, intentional torts, and constitutional torts.

Negligence can arise when a criminal justice employee's conduct creates a danger to others. In other words, the employee did not conduct his or her affairs in a manner that avoids subjecting others to a risk of harm and may be held liable for the injuries caused to others.[29]

Intentional torts occur when an employee engages in a voluntary act that is quite likely to result in injury to another; examples are assault and battery, false arrest and imprisonment, malicious prosecution, and abuse of process.

Constitutional torts involve employees' duty to recognize and uphold the constitutional rights, privileges, and immunities of others; violations of these guarantees may subject the employee to a civil suit, most frequently brought in federal court under 42 *U.S. Code* Section 1983, discussed in the next section.[30]

Assault, battery, false imprisonment, false arrest, invasion of privacy, negligence, defamation, and malicious prosecution are examples of torts that are commonly brought against police officers.[31] False arrest is the arrest of a person without probable cause. False imprisonment is the intentional illegal detention of a person not only in jail but also in any confinement to a specified area. For example, the police may fail to release an arrested person after a proper bail or bond has been posted, may delay the arraignment of an arrested person unreasonably, or may fail to release a prisoner after they no longer have authority to hold him or her.[32]

A single act may also be a crime as well as a tort. If Officer Smith, in an unprovoked attack, injures Jones, the state will attempt to punish Smith in a *criminal* action by sending him to jail or prison, fining him, or both. The state would have the burden of proof at a criminal trial, having to prove Smith guilty "beyond a reasonable doubt." Furthermore, Jones may sue Smith for money damages in a *civil* action for the personal injury he suffered. In this civil suit, Jones would have the burden of proving that Smith's acts were tortious by a "preponderance of the evidence"—a lower standard than that in a criminal court and thus easier to satisfy.

Section 1983 Legislation

Title 42, *U.S. Code*, Section 1983 a law making it a civil offense for any person acting under color of law to violate another person's civil rights.

Following the Civil War and in reaction to the activities of the Ku Klux Klan, Congress enacted the Ku Klux Klan Act of 1871, later codified as **Title 42, *U.S. Code*, Section 1983**. It states:

> Every person who, under color of any statute, ordinance, regulation, custom, or usage of any State or Territory, subjects, or causes to be subjected, any citizen of the United States or any other person within the jurisdiction thereof to the deprivation of any rights, privileges, or immunities secured by the Constitution and laws, shall be liable to the party injured in an action at law, suit in equity, or other proper proceeding for redress.

This legislation was intended to provide civil rights protection to all "persons" protected under the act when a defendant acted "under color of law" (misused power of office) and provided an avenue to the federal courts for relief of alleged civil rights violations. We will see how Section 1983 can be used against the police.

Lawsuits Against the Police Generally

A police executive once commented to one of the authors, "The decision-making process is not directed so much by the question 'Is it right or wrong?' but rather 'How much will it cost us if we're sued?'" While that viewpoint may be overstated by quite a lot, nonetheless, the specter of lawsuits certainly looms large over police executives, their supervisors and officers, and their unit of government; and errors in judgment or misbehaviors can be costly.

No one knows for certain how much money is paid by local police agencies each year to settle lawsuits. What is known, however, is that some cities have seen lawsuits against their city's police force soar. From 2010 through 2014, the 10 cities with the largest police agencies in the United States paid out over $1.4 billion in settlements and court judgments due to lawsuits against police.[33] Those same departments were responsible for almost $250 million in payouts due to misconduct cases alone in the year 2014—an increase of nearly 50 percent from 2010.[34]

Settlements that concern controversial cases involving the use of deadly force by police are particularly costly. The City Council of Chicago recently approved a settlement with the family of Laquan McDonald for $5 million after he was shot and killed by Chicago PD officer Jason Van Dyke in 2014;[35] in a recent case in New York City, the city agreed to pay $5.9 million to the family of Eric Garner to settle a wrongful-death claim (Garner had been killed by NYPD officers after an altercation).[36] Although obviously very expensive to settle, these outcomes are often preferred to taking the case to court in a long and expensive legal battle—and one in which the jury might award much more money to the plaintiffs.

A relatively new concern about liability among police administrators concerns body-worn cameras (BWCs) for officers. These cameras, which are discussed more in Chapters 6 and 16, are designed to record interactions between police and citizens in the belief that they can help to guard against false allegations of misconduct or abuse. Agency administrators, however, are scrambling to develop policies for the use of such recording devices, in order to address a number of legal issues, including potential privacy concerns.[37]

Liability of Police Leadership

Another trend is for such litigants to cast a wide net in their lawsuits, suing not only the principal actors in the incident but also agency administrators and supervisors; this breadth of suing represents the notion of *vicarious liability* or the doctrine of *respondeat superior*, an old legal maxim meaning "let the master answer." In sum, an employer can be found liable in certain instances for wrongful acts of the employee.

Using Section 1983, litigants often allege inadequate hiring and/or training of personnel by police leadership, or that they knew, or should have known, of the misconduct of their officers yet failed to take corrective action and prevent future harm. An example is the case of *Brandon v. Allen*,[38] in which two teenagers parked in a lovers' lane were approached by an off-duty police officer, Allen, who showed his police identification and demanded that the male exit the car. Allen struck the young man with his fist, stabbed him with a knife, and then attempted to break into the car where the young woman was seated. The young man was able to reenter the car and manage an escape. As the two teenagers sped off, Allen fired a shot at them with his revolver. The shattered windshield glass severely injured the youths to the point that they required plastic surgery. Allen was convicted of criminal charges, and the police chief was also sued under Section 1983. The plaintiffs charged that the chief and others knew of Allen's reputation as an unstable officer; none of the other police officers wished to ride in a patrol car with him. At least two formal charges of misconduct had been filed previously, yet the chief failed to take any remedial action or even to review the disciplinary records of officers when he became chief. The court called this behavior "unjustified inaction," held the police department liable, and allowed the plaintiffs damages. The U.S. Supreme Court upheld this judgment.[39]

Police supervisors have also been found liable for injuries arising out of an official policy or custom of their department. Injuries resulting from a chief's verbal or written support of heavy-handed behavior resulting in the use of excessive force by officers have resulted in such liability.[40]

Title 18, *U.S. Code*, Section 242 a law making it a criminal offense for any person acting under color of law to violate another person's civil rights.

Title 18, *U.S. Code*, Section 242, makes it a *criminal* offense for any person acting under color of law to violate another person's civil rights. An example of the use of Section 242 with law enforcement officers is the murder of a drug courier by two U.S. customs agents while the agents were assigned to the San Juan International Airport. The courier flew to Puerto Rico to deposit approximately $700,000 in cash and checks. He was last seen being interviewed by the two customs agents in the airport; 10 days later, his body was discovered in a Puerto Rican rain forest. An investigation revealed that the agents had lured the victim away from the airport and had murdered him for his money, later disposing of the body. They were convicted under Section 242 and related federal statutes, and each agent was sentenced to a prison term of 120 years.[41] Section 242 prosecutions remain relatively rare, however (one source indicating that of 13,233 civil rights complaints against police between 1995 and 2015, federal prosecutors only brought charges 4% of the time).[42] Prosecutors must prove beyond a reasonable doubt that the officer violated an individual's civil rights *and* that he or she had done so "willfully." Proving intent to juries is often difficult in these cases, and prosecutors are generally reluctant to bring charges against an officer when faced with such high standards of proof.

Duty of Care and Failure to Protect

The *public duty doctrine* is derived from common law and holds that police have a duty to protect the general public where they have a "special relationship"; this exists, for example, where the officer knows or has reason to know the likelihood of harm to someone if he or she fails to do his or her duty, and is thus defined by the circumstances surrounding an injury or damage. A special relationship can be based on:

1. whether the officer could have foreseen that he or she was expected to take action in a given situation to prevent injury[43] (such as where a police officer released from his custody an intoxicated pedestrian near a busy highway)
2. departmental policy or guidelines that prohibit a certain course of action[44] (such as a case where an officer released a drunk driver who then killed another driver, and the police department had a standard operating procedure manual that mandated that an intoxicated individual likely to do physical injury to himself or others "*will* be taken into protective custody")
3. the spatial and temporal proximity of the defendant–officer behavior to the injury damage[45] (an example is where an individual was arrested for drunk driving, taken into custody, found to have a high blood alcohol level, was released 3 hours later, and then had a fatal car accident).

duty of care a doctrine holding that police have a duty to protect the general public where a "special relationship" exists.

proximate cause due to someone's conduct, a person sustained injury or damage.

Under the general heading of **duty of care** are three related concepts: proximate cause, persons in custody, and safe facilities.

a. **Proximate cause** is established by asking the question "But for the officer's conduct, would the plaintiff have sustained the injury or damage?" If the answer to this question is no, then proximate cause is established, and the officer can be held liable for the damage or injury. An example is where an officer is involved in a high-speed chase and the offending driver strikes an innocent third party. Generally, if the officer was not acting in a negligent fashion and did not cause the injury, there would be no liability on the officer's part.[46] Proximate cause may also be found in such cases as one where an officer leaves the scene of an accident aware of dangerous conditions (e.g., spilled oil, smoke, vehicle debris, stray animals) without giving proper warning to motorists.[47]

b. Courts generally confer on police executives a duty of care for *persons in their custody*[48] to ensure that reasonable precautions are taken to keep detainees free from harm, to render medical assistance when necessary, and to treat detainees humanely.[49] A duty is also owed to persons in custody and while outside a jail setting, such as when arresting or transporting prisoners and mental patients, as well as in booking or interrogation areas.[50] Courts have also held that if a prisoner's suicide is "reasonably foreseeable," the jailer owes the prisoner a duty of care to help prevent that suicide.

c. A related area concerns administrators' *need to provide safe facilities*. For example, a Detroit jail's holding cell was constructed so that it did not allow officers to observe detainees' movements; there were no electronic monitoring devices for observing detainees or detoxification cells, as required under state policy. Therefore, following a suicide in this facility, the court concluded that these conditions constituted building defects and were the proximate cause of the decedent's death.[51]

Failure to protect as a form of negligence may occur if a police officer fails to protect a person from a known and foreseeable danger. These claims most often involve battered women, but other circumstances can also create a duty to protect people from crime. Informants, witnesses, and other people who are dependent on the police can be a source of police liability if officers fail to take reasonable action to prevent victimization. The officer's conduct cannot place a person in peril or demonstrate deliberate indifference to his or her safety. An example is where the Green Bay, Wisconsin, Police Department released the tape of a phone call from an informant, which led to the informant's death.[52] See Exhibit 14.1 for an exercise on failure to protect.

failure to protect a form of negligence where a police officer fails to protect a person from a known and foreseeable danger.

EXHIBIT 14.1

LIABILITY FOR FAILURE TO PROTECT

What, if any, legal obligation is held by the police to protect someone from their estranged spouse who has been served with a legal restraining order? That question was at the crux of a lawsuit from Castle Rock, Colorado, which was ultimately heard by the U.S. Supreme Court. Jessica Gonzales' restraining order required her husband to remain at least 100 yards from her and their three daughters except during specified visitation times. One evening the husband took possession of the three children in violation of the order; Mrs. Gonzalez repeatedly urged the police to search for and arrest her husband, but they took no immediate action (due to Jessica's allowing her husband to take the children at various hours). At approximately 3:20 A.M., the husband appeared at the city police station and instigated a shoot-out with the police (he died). A search of his vehicle revealed the corpses of the three daughters, whom the husband had killed. U.S. cities are generally immune from lawsuits, so in this case the Supreme Court was asked to decide whether Jessica Gonzales could sue the city because of inaction by its police officers.[53]

Questions for Discussion

1. Were the police *morally* responsible for the deaths of the three girls?
2. Were the police *legally* responsible for their deaths?
3. If you believe Jessica should be allowed to sue the city, and the police were liable, how much financial compensation should Jessica receive?

(See the Notes section for the outcome.)

Vehicle Pursuits

Basically, with regard to operation of their vehicles, officers are afforded *no* special privileges or immunities.[54] While driving in nonemergency situations, officers do not have immunity for their negligence or recklessness and are held to the same standard of conduct as private citizens. When responding to emergency situations, however, officers are governed by statutes covering emergency vehicles.[55] In such circumstances, most jurisdictions afford the police limited immunity for violations of traffic laws; in other words, they are accorded some protections and privileges not given to private citizens, and are permitted to take greater risks that would amount to negligence if taken by citizens.[56]

vehicle pursuit where one or more law enforcement officers is attempting to apprehend a suspect who is evading arrest while operating a motor vehicle, usually at high speed or using other elusive means.

In 2007, the U.S. Supreme Court issued a major decision concerning the proper amount of force the police may use during a high-speed **vehicle pursuit**—when one or more law enforcement officers attempting to apprehend a suspect who is evading arrest while operating a motor vehicle, usually at high speed or using other elusive means. The issue was whether or not the serious danger created by the fleeing motorist and high-speed pursuers justifies the use of deadly force to eliminate the threat; in other words, was the level of force used proportionate to the threat of reckless and dangerous driving? Victor Harris, a 19-year-old Georgia youth, drove at speeds of up to 90 miles per hour and covered 9 miles in 6 minutes with a deputy sheriff in pursuit. The chase ended in a violent crash that left Harris a quadriplegic; his lawyers argued that the Fourth Amendment protects against the use of such excessive force and high-speed drivers having their cars rammed by police (by intentionally stopping a fleeing vehicle in such a manner, a "seizure" occurs for Fourth Amendment purposes). Conversely, the deputy sheriff's lawyers argued that such drivers pose an escalating danger to the public and must be stopped to defuse the danger (the deputy's supervisor had authorized the use of the Precision Immobilization Technique [PIT], whereby the officer uses the patrol vehicle to cause the speeder's car to spin out. PIT was not used in the Harris chase, however). The Court's 8–1 opinion held that "A police officer's attempt to terminate a dangerous high-speed car chase that threatens the lives of innocent bystanders does not violate the Fourth Amendment, even when it places the fleeing motorist at risk of serious injury or death."[57]

IN THEIR OWN WORDS

ADMINISTRATIVE ADVICE FROM THE FIELD

Name: Samuel G. Chapman

Degrees: Bachelor's and master's, criminology, University of California, Berkeley

What CJ-related jobs have you held? Consultant on police functions and use of police dogs; professor emeritus, University of Oklahoma; assistant director, President's Commission on Law Enforcement and the Administration of Justice, Washington, DC; chief, Multnomah County Sheriff's Office, Portland, Oregon; police officer, Berkeley, California.

What advice do you have concerning police liability? Police departments must take civil rights litigation seriously. Actually, civil rights lawsuits are seen by many as an occupational hazard in policing. When a lawsuit has been filed, the allegations should be evaluated by the government's attorneys. Fact-finding may disclose that the allegations appear to have little merit. It could be that the lawsuit is of dubious substance, really seeking what is called a "convenience settlement"—a defendant's paying the plaintiff a dollar amount less than what the defendant's costs would be to prepare for trial. But if after fact-finding it appears that the department and its officers are culpable, the defense team should start settlement negotiations early. The defense should make a meaningful offer, keeping it in the range of settlements for cases of a similar sort elsewhere. At the same time, the defense (both the government and the officer) must commence their discovery, with the goal of minimizing loss should the case eventually go to trial. Settlements that occur just before trial are invariably costly. The defense team should also evaluate the courtroom record of the plaintiff's law firm and opposing attorneys, since some firms are more competent than others. Fact-finding will often indicate that a case is realistically defensible. If so, the defense team may decide to reject a convenience settlement and prepare for trial. This will cause the plaintiffs to evaluate whether to expend resources and time in pursuing a case that they are not likely to win. When the defense decides to stand up and fight, it establishes the jurisdiction as a "hard target" and sends a message that lawsuits with little merit are going to be forcefully defended. Whoever is named to defend officers and police agencies must be skilled in handling civil rights cases. It is a grave mistake for the government to take a "bargain basement" approach by assigning staff attorneys who have little or no experience working with these highly technical types of litigation. The police can fight back by suing those who sue them, but this means hiring counsel, which is expensive. And even if the lawsuit is successful and brings a dollar judgment against the defendant, such a defendant is usually poor and thus unable to meet any financial judgment levied against him or her. The government's best defense against an adverse judgment in a civil rights lawsuit is to thoroughly train and regularly retrain its police personnel, and to supervise them well. Also, the police department's rules, regulations, policies, and procedures must be kept current. Then, if officers perform as trained and properly under departmental guidelines, a persuasive defense can be mounted against any allegations of misconduct.

Source: Used with permission from Samuel G. Chapman.

Liability of Corrections Personnel

The liability of corrections workers often centers on their lack of due care for persons in their custody. This responsibility concerns primarily police officers and civilians responsible for inmates in local jails.

When an inmate commits suicide while in custody, police agencies are frequently—and often successfully—sued in state court under negligence and wrongful death claims. The standard used by the courts is whether the agency's act or failure to act created an unusual risk to an inmate. A "special duty" of care exists for police officers to protect inmates suffering from mental disorders and those who are impaired by drugs or alcohol. Foreseeability—the reasonable anticipation that injury or damage may occur—may be found when inmates make statements of intent to commit suicide, have a history of mental illness, are in a vulnerable emotional state, or are at a high level of intoxication or drug dependence.[58]

Suicides are not uncommon among jail inmates; each year, more than 300 jail inmates take their own lives.[59] Inmate suicide rates have also been found to be higher in small jails and highest in small jails with lower population densities.[60] State courts generally recognize that police officials have a duty of care for persons in their custody.[61] Thus, jail administrators are ultimately responsible for taking reasonable precautions to ensure the health and safety of persons in their custody; they must protect inmates from harm, render medical assistance when necessary, and treat inmates humanely.[62]

Several court decisions have helped to establish the duties and guidelines for jail employees concerning the care of their charges. An intoxicated inmate in possession of cigarettes and matches started a fire that resulted in his death; the court stated that "the prisoner may have been voluntarily drunk, but he was not in the cell voluntarily … [he] was helpless and the officer knew there was a means of harm on his person." The court concluded that the police administration owed a greater duty of care to such an arrestee.[63] Emotionally disturbed arrestees can also create a greater duty for jail personnel. In an Alaskan case, a woman had been arrested for intoxication in a hotel and had trouble talking, standing, and walking; her blood alcohol content was 0.26 percent. Two and a half hours after her incarceration, officers found her hanging by her sweater from mesh wiring in the cell. The Alaska Supreme Court said that the officers knew she was depressed and that in the past few months, one of her sons had been burned to death, another son had been stabbed to death, and her mother had died. Thus, the court believed that the officers should have anticipated her suicide.[64]

In New Mexico, a 17-year-old boy was arrested for armed robbery; he later told his mother that he would kill himself rather than go to prison and subsequently tried to cut his wrists with an aluminum can top. The assistant chief executive ordered the officers to watch him, but he was found dead by hanging the following morning. The state supreme court held that the knowledge officers possess is an important factor in determining liability and negligence in such cases.[65] In a New Jersey case in which a young man arrested for intoxication was put in a holding cell but officers failed to remove the leather belt that he used to take his life, the court found that the officers' conduct could have been a "substantial" factor in his death.[66]

As mentioned earlier, courts have also found the design of detention facilities to be a source of negligence—where a Detroit holding cell limited officers' ability to observe inmates' movements, and no detoxification cell or electronic monitoring devices were used; a suicide in such circumstances may constitute a "building defect" and a finding of proximate cause.[67] In another incident, an intoxicated college student was placed in a holding cell at the school's public safety building. Forty minutes later, officers found him hanging from an overhead heating device by a noose fashioned from his socks and belt. The court found the university liable for operating a defective building and awarded his parents $650,000.[68]

The behavior of jail personnel *after* a suicide or attempted suicide may also indicate a breach of duty. Officers are expected to give all possible aid to an inmate who is injured or has attempted suicide. Thus, when officers found an inmate slumped in a chair with his belt around his neck and left him in that position instead of trying to revive him or call for medical assistance, the court ruled that this behavior established a causal link between the officers' inaction and the boy's death.[69]

It is clear that correctional administrators must ensure that their organizations are cognizant of their legal responsibilities and their expanded custodial role in dealing with their detainees.

▶ Disciplinary Policies and Practices

By virtue of their relatively high numbers and frequent contacts with the general public, a great majority of complaints and disciplinary actions in criminal justice will involve law enforcement personnel, and thus the following discussion centers on police behaviors. However, occasionally, as seen in Exhibit 14.2, the taint of corruption and abuse can also involve corrections personnel.

EXHIBIT 14.2

DEPUTIES INDICTED IN CORRUPTION PROBE

Nearly 20 current and former Los Angeles County sheriff's deputies were arrested recently following a 2-year federal probe into corruption and inmate abuse in the county jail system. Several grand jury indictments and criminal complaints alleged the unjustified beating of inmates, unjustified detention, and a conspiracy to obstruct a federal investigation. Included were civil rights violations that included excessive force and unlawful arrests.

The investigation revealed that the jailers' behavior had become institutionalized to the point that some employees of the Sheriff's Department considered themselves to be above the law. Deputies also attempted to conceal an informant who was providing photos and information to the FBI while locked up, leading to additional charges of conspiracy to obstruct justice. Two sergeants also allegedly confronted an FBI agent at her home in an attempt to intimidate her into revealing details concerning the investigation.[70]

The public's trust and respect are precious commodities and can be quickly lost with improper behavior by criminal justice employees and the improper handling of an allegation of misconduct. The public expects that criminal justice agencies will have sound disciplinary policies, and make every effort to respond to citizens' complaints in a judicious, consistent, fair, and equitable manner.

Employee misconduct and violations of departmental policy are the two principal areas in which discipline is involved (see Exhibit 14.3).[71] Employee misconduct includes those acts that harm the public, including corruption, harassment, brutality, and civil rights violations. Violations of policy may involve a broad range of issues, including substance abuse and insubordination, as well as minor violations of dress and lack of punctuality.

EXHIBIT 14.3

EXAMPLE OF AGENCY POLICY GOVERNING OFFICER CONDUCT

Following is a section of the Pine Bluff, Arkansas, Police Department Policy & Procedures Manual as it pertains to officers' conduct:

IV. PROCEDURES

A. GENERAL CONDUCT

1. OBEDIENCE TO LAWS, REGULATIONS, AND ORDERS
   a. Officers shall obey the constitutional, civil and criminal laws of the city, state, and federal government.
   b. Officers shall obey all lawful orders.
   c. VIOLATIONS INCLUDE, BUT ARE NOT LIMITED TO:
      i. Committing a willful violation of constitutional civil rights that demonstrates reckless disregard.
      ii. Committing non-exempted infractions of traffic codes (e.g., driving over the speed limit, failing to observe traffic control devices, parking in unauthorized locations, failing to wear seat belts, etc.)
      iii. Inflicting punishment or mistreatment (includes both physical as well as mental) upon a prisoner or person in custody or detention or any other member of the public.
      iv. Non-exempted violations of any local, state or federal criminal or civil codes or ordinances.
      v. Refusing or failing to protect a prisoner's civil rights when such need is made known or should have been known by a competent officer.
      vi. Unprivileged publication of a false statement intending to harm the reputation of another member of this agency or any person in general (slander if done verbally and libel if put in written form).
      vii. Using excessive force to hold, affect an apprehension, arrest or detain any person.
      viii. Using prohibited devices, procedures, tactics or techniques to affect a holding, apprehension, arrest or detention of another.
2. CONDUCT UNBECOMING AN OFFICER
   a. Honesty, efficiency, and integrity are the first guidelines for a law enforcement officer's conduct. All law enforcement officers must remember that they are employed to serve the citizens of this jurisdiction. The public is entitled to courteous efficient response to requests for law enforcement services.
   b. Law enforcement officers, whether on or off duty, shall be governed by ordinary and reasonable rules of good conduct and behavior and shall not commit any act which could adversely affect the department.

c. Officers shall not make known to any person any order or information which they have knowledge of or have received, unless it is in the performance of official duty and given to a person entitled to have the information.

d. All officers when off duty, but in uniform, shall conduct themselves as though they were on duty.

e. Members shall conduct themselves (on duty as well as off duty) in a manner that does not damage or have the probable expectations of damaging or bringing the public image, integrity or reputation of the Pine Bluff Police Department into discredit, disrepute or impair its efficient and effective operation.[72]

Source: Adapted from Pine Bluff, Arkansas, Police Department, Pine Bluff Police Department Policy & Procedures Manual, Policy. Used with permission.

Due Process Requirements

The well-established, minimum due process requirements for discharging public employees include that employees must:

1. Be afforded a public hearing.
2. Be present during the presentation of evidence against them and have an opportunity to cross-examine their superiors.
3. Have an opportunity to present witnesses and other evidence concerning their side of the controversy.
4. Be permitted to be represented by counsel.
5. Have an impartial referee or hearing officer presiding.
6. Have a decision made based on the weight of the evidence introduced during the hearing.

Such protections apply to any disciplinary action that can significantly affect a criminal justice employee's reputation and/or future chances for special assignment or promotion. A disciplinary hearing that might result in only a reprimand or short suspension may involve fewer procedural protections than one that could result in more severe sanctions.[73]

An example is a Chicago case involving a patrol officer who was transferred to what he deemed a less desirable work area. The court determined that the transfer was in retaliation for his political activities, in this case also involving his First Amendment free speech rights being violated, and that he was thus entitled to civil damages. The court stated, "Certainly a demotion can be as detrimental to an employee as denial of a promotion."[74]

On the contrary, however, no due process protection may be required when the property interest (one's job) was fraudulently obtained. Thus, a deputy sheriff was not deprived of due process when he was summarily discharged for lying on his application about a juvenile felony charge, which would have barred him from employment in the first place.[75]

In sum, agency rules and policies should state which due process procedures will be utilized under certain disciplinary situations; the key questions regarding due process are whether the employer follows established agency guidelines and, if not, whether the employer has a compelling reason not to do so.

At times, the administrator will determine that an employee must be disciplined or terminated. What are adequate grounds for discipline or discharge? Grounds can vary widely from agency to agency. Certainly, the agency's formal policies and procedures should specify and control what constitutes proper and improper behavior. Normally, agency practice and custom enter into these decisions. Sometimes administrators will "wink" at the formal policies and procedures, overlooking or only occasionally enforcing certain provisions contained in them. But the failure of the agency to enforce a rule or policy for a long period of time may provide "implied consent" by the employer that such behavior, although officially prohibited, is permissible. (In other words, don't allow an employee to violate the agency's lateness policy for 3 months and then decide one day to summarily fire him.) Attempts to fire employees for behavior that has been ignored or enforced only infrequently at best may give rise to a defense by the employee.

Generally, violations of an employee's rights in discharge and discipline occur (1) in violation of a protected interest, (2) in retaliation for the exercise of protected conduct, (3) with a discriminatory motive, and (4) with malice.[76]

A Tradition of Problems in Policing

Throughout its history, policing has experienced problems involving misconduct and corruption. Recent incidents such as the shooting deaths of unarmed, young, African American males as well as major corruption scandals (e.g., officers ripping off drug dealers and even dealing drugs themselves; attempting to cover up their acts of violence; see the following for recent examples: http://www.alternet.org/drugs/5-outrageous-cases-drug-war-police-corruption-week) have led many people to believe that police misbehavior is greater today than ever before.

Without question, police administrators need to pay close attention to signs of police misconduct, respond quickly, and enact policies to guide supervisors in handling disciplinary issues. Such policies should ensure that there is certainty, swiftness, fairness, and consistency of punishment when it is warranted.

Automated Records Systems

A number of police agencies have automated their personnel processes in an effort to establish a better system for tracking and sanctioning personnel actions.[77] Specifically, an **automated records system** involves use of technologies to assist police administrators to more equitably receive, investigate, and arrive at proper dispositions concerning employee complaints and commendations. Within minutes, the database provides supervisors with 5 years of history about standards of discipline for any category of violation. A variety of reports can be produced, showing patterns of incidents for the supervisor.

automated records system technologies that assist police administrators in receiving, investigating, and arriving at proper dispositions concerning employee complaints and commendations.

Determining the Level and Nature of Action

When an investigation against an employee is sustained, the sanctions and level of discipline must be decided. Management must be careful when recommending and imposing discipline because of its impact on the morale of the agency's employees. If the recommended discipline is viewed by employees as too lenient, it may send the wrong message that the misconduct was insignificant. On the other hand, discipline that is viewed as too harsh may have a demoralizing effect on the officer(s) involved and other agency employees and result in allegations that the leadership is unfair. This alone can have significant impact on the esprit de corps or morale of the agency.

In addition to having a disciplinary process that is viewed by employees as fair and consistent, it is important that discipline be progressive and that more serious sanctions be invoked when repeated violations occur. For example, a third substantiated instance of rude behavior may result in a recommendation for a 1-day suspension without pay, but a first offense may be handled by documented oral counseling or a letter of reprimand. The following list shows disciplinary actions commonly used by agencies in increasing order of severity.

Counseling. This is usually a conversation between the supervisor and employee about a specific aspect of the employee's performance or conduct; it is warranted when an employee has committed a relatively minor infraction or the nature of the offense is such that oral counseling is all that is necessary. For example, an employee who is usually punctual but arrives at a briefing 10 minutes late 2 days in a row may require nothing more than a reminder and a warning to correct the problem.

Documented oral counseling. This is usually the first step in a progressive disciplinary process and is intended to address relatively minor infractions. It occurs when there are no previous reprimands or more severe disciplinary action of the same or a similar nature.

Letter of reprimand. This is a formal written notice regarding significant misconduct, more serious performance violations, or repeated offenses. It is usually the second step in the formal disciplinary process and is intended to provide the employee and agency with a written record of the violation of behavior; it identifies what specific corrective action must be taken to avoid subsequent, more serious disciplinary steps.

Suspension. This is a severe disciplinary action that results in an employee being relieved of duty, often without pay. It is usually administered when an employee commits a serious violation of established rules or after written reprimands have been given and no change in behavior or performance has resulted.

Demotion. In this situation, an employee is placed in a position of lower responsibility and pay. It is normally used when an otherwise capable employee is unable to meet the standards required for the higher position, or when the employee has committed a serious act requiring that he or she be removed from a position of management or supervision.

Transfer. Many agencies use the disciplinary transfer to deal with problem employees; they can be transferred to a different location or assignment, and this action is often seen as an effective disciplinary tool.

Termination. This is the most severe disciplinary action that can be taken. It usually occurs when previous serious discipline has been imposed and there has been inadequate or no improvement in behavior or performance. It may also occur when an employee commits an offense so serious that continued employment would be inappropriate.

Positive and Negative Discipline

When policies and procedures are violated, positive or negative disciplinary measures may be imposed. Although different in their philosophy, both seek to accomplish the same purpose: to correct negative behavior and promote the employee's voluntary compliance with departmental policies and procedures.

positive discipline a formal program that attempts to change poor employee behavior without invoking punishment.

A **positive discipline** program (also known as *positive counseling*) attempts to change poor employee behavior without invoking punishment. An example of positive discipline or counseling is when an employee ("John") has been nonproductive and nonpunctual, has caused interpersonal problems with coworkers, and/or has other problems on the job. To this point, John has been in control of the situation—on the offensive, one might say—whereas the supervisor ("Jane") and his coworkers have been on the defensive. John is jeopardizing the morale and productivity of the workplace, but the preferred approach is to try to salvage him because of the agency's investment in time, funds, and training.

Finally, Jane calls John into her office. She might begin with a compliment to him (if indeed she can find one) and then proceed to outline all of his workplace shortcomings; this demonstrates to John that Jane "has his number" and is aware of his various problems. Jane explains to him why it is important that he improve (for reasons related to productivity, morale, and so on) and the benefits he might realize from improvement (promotions, pay raises, bonuses). She also outlines what can happen if he does *not* show adequate improvement (demotion, transfer, termination). Now having gained John's attention, she gives him a certain time period (say, 30, 60, or 90 days) in which to improve; she emphasizes, however, that she will be constantly monitoring his progress. She might even ask John to sign a counseling statement form that sets forth all they have discussed, indicating that John has received counseling and understands the situation.

Note that Jane is now on the offensive, thereby putting John on the defensive and in control of his destiny; if he fails to perform, Jane would probably give him a warning, and if the situation continues, he will be terminated. If he sues or files a grievance, Jane has proof that every effort was made to allow John to salvage his position. This is an effective means of giving subordinates an incentive to improve their behavior while also making the department less vulnerable to successful lawsuits.

Negative discipline is some form of punishment. It is generally used when positive efforts fail or the violation is so serious that punishment is required. Negative discipline varies in its severity and involves documented oral counseling, a letter of reprimand, demotion, days off without pay, or even termination.

negative discipline that which involves some form of punishment.

Types and Causes

Complaints may be handled informally or formally, depending on the seriousness of the allegation and the preference of the complainant. A formal complaint occurs when a written and signed and/or tape-recorded statement of the allegation is made and the complainant asks to be informed of the investigation's disposition. Figure 14-2 ■ provides an example of a complaint form used to initiate a personnel investigation.

An informal complaint is an allegation of minor misconduct made for informational purposes that can usually be resolved without the need for more formal processes. When a citizen calls the watch commander to complain about the rude behavior of a dispatcher but does not wish to make a formal complaint, the supervisor may simply discuss the incident with the dispatcher and resolve it through informal counseling as long as more serious problems are not discovered and the dispatcher does not have a history of similar complaints.

Studies show that the majority of complaints involve verbal abuse, discourtesy, harassment, improper attitude, and ethnic slurs.[78] It is also known that minority citizens are more likely to file complaints of misconduct and to allege more serious forms of misconduct.[79]

Receipt and Referral

Administrators should have in place a process for receiving complaints that is clearly delineated by departmental policy and procedures. Generally, a complaint will be made at a police facility and referred to a senior officer in charge to determine its seriousness and the need for immediate intervention.

In most cases, the senior officer will determine the nature of the complaint and the employee involved; the matter will be referred to the employee's supervisor to conduct an initial investigation. The supervisor completes the investigation, recommends any discipline, and sends the matter to the Internal Affairs Unit (IAU) and the agency head for finalization of the disciplinary process. This method of review ensures that consistent and fair standards of discipline are applied.

The Investigative Process

D. W. Perez[80] indicated that all but a small percentage of the 17,000 police agencies in the United States have a process for investigation of police misconduct. Generally, the employee's supervisor will conduct a preliminary inquiry of the complaint, commonly known

****

Control Number______

Date & Time Reported — Location of Interview — Interview

______ ______ ______Verbal ______Written ______Taped

Type of Complaint: ______Force ______Procedural ______Conduct
______Other (Specify)

Source of Complaint: ______In Person ______Mail ______Telephone
______Other (Specify)

Complaint originally Received by: ______Supervisor ______On Duty Watch Commander ______Chief
______IAU ______Other (Specify)

Notifications made: Received by: ______Division Commander ______Chief of Police
______On-Call Command Personnel
______Watch Commander ______Other (Specify)

Copy of formal personnel complaint given to complainant? ______Yes ______No

****

Complainant's name: ______ Address: ______ Zip______

Residence Phone: ______ Business Phone: ______

DOB: ______ Race: ______ Sex: ______ Occupation: ______

****

Location of Occurrence: ______ Date & Time of Occurrence: ______

Member(s) Involved:
(1)______ (2)______
(3)______ (4)______

Witness(es) Involved:
(1)______ (2)______
(3)______ (4)______

****

(1)______ Complainant wishes to make a formal statement and has requested an investigation into the matter with a report back to him/her on the findings and actions.

(2)______ Complainant wishes to advise the Police Department of a problem, understand that some type of action will be taken, but does not request a report back to him/her on the findings and actions.

****

CITIZEN ADVISEMENTS

(1) If you have not yet provided the department with a signed written statement or a videotaped or tape-recorded statement, one may be required in order to pursue the investigation of this matter.

(2) The complainant(s) and/or witness(es) may be required to take a polygraph examination in order to determine the credibility concerning the allegations made.

(3) Should the allegations prove to be false, the complainant(s) and/or witness(es) may be liable for criminal and/or civil prosecution.

______ Signature of Complainant ______ Date & Time

______ Signature of Member Receiving Complaint

FIGURE 14-2 Police Department Formal Personnel Complaint Report Form

as fact-finding. Once it is determined that further investigation is necessary, the supervisor may conduct additional questioning of employees and witnesses, obtain written statements from those persons immediately involved in the incident, and gather any evidence that may be necessary for the case, including photographs. Care must be taken to ensure that the accused employee's rights are not violated. The initial investigation is sent to an appropriate division commander and forwarded to IAU for review.

Making a Determination and Disposition

Categories

Once an investigation is completed, the supervisor or IAU officer must make a determination as to the culpability of the accused employee and report this to the administrator. Each allegation should receive a separate adjudication. Following are the categories of dispositions that are commonly used:

- ***Unfounded.*** The alleged act(s) did not occur.
- ***Exonerated.*** The act occurred, but it is lawful, proper, justified, and/or in accordance with departmental policies, procedures, rules, and regulations.
- ***Not sustained.*** There is insufficient evidence to prove or disprove the allegations made.
- ***Misconduct not based on the complaint.*** Sustainable misconduct was determined but is not a part of the original complaint. For example, a supervisor investigating an allegation of excessive force against an officer may find that the force used was within departmental policy but that the officer made an unlawful arrest.
- ***Closed.*** An investigation may be halted if the complainant fails to cooperate or if it is determined that the action does not fall within the administrative jurisdiction of the police agency.
- ***Sustained.*** The act did occur, and it was a violation of departmental rules and procedures. Sustained allegations include misconduct that falls within the broad outlines of the original allegation(s).

Once a determination of culpability has been made, the complainant should be notified of the department's findings. Details of the investigation or recommended punishment will not be included in the correspondence. As shown in Figure 14-3 ■, the complainant will normally receive only information concerning the outcome of the complaint, including a short explanation of the finding along with an invitation to call the agency if further information is needed.

Grievances

Criminal justice employees may complain—have a **grievance**, which is a real or imagined wrong or other cause for complaint about job-related matters. Following is an overview of the general process that exists for handling grievances.

Grievance procedures establish a fair and expeditious process for handling employee disputes that are not disciplinary in nature. Grievance procedures involve collective bargaining issues, conditions of employment, and employer–employee relations. More specifically, grievances may cover a broad range of issues, including salaries, overtime, leave, hours of work, allowances, retirement, opportunities for advancement, performance evaluations, workplace conditions, tenure, disciplinary actions, supervisory methods, and administrative practices. Grievance procedures are often established as a part of the collective bargaining process.

grievance a real or imagined wrong or other cause for complaint by an employee concerning job-related matters.

Police Department
3300 Main Street
Downtown Plaza
Anywhere, USA. 99999
June 20, 2000

Mr. John Doe
2200 Main Avenue
Anywhere, USA.

Re: Internal affairs #000666-98
Case Closure

Dear Mr. Doe:

Our investigation into your allegations against Officer Smith has been completed. It has been determined that your complaint is SUSTAINED and the appropriate disciplinary action has been taken.

Our department appreciates your bringing this matter to our attention. It is our position that when a problem is identified, it should be corrected as soon as possible. It is our goal to be responsive to the concerns expressed by citizens so as to provide more efficient and effective services.

Your information regarding this incident was helpful and of value in our efforts to attain that goal. Should you have any further questions about this matter, please contact Sergeant Jane Alexander, Internal Affairs, at 555-9999.

Sincerely,

I.M. Boss
Lieutenant
Internal Affairs Unit

FIGURE 14-3 Citizens' Notification-of-Discipline Letter

As indicated above, the preferred method for settling employees' grievances is through informal discussion, in which the employee explains his or her grievance to the immediate supervisor. Most complaints can be handled through this process. Complaints that cannot be dealt with informally are usually handled through a more formal grievance process, as described next. A formal grievance begins with the employee submitting the grievance in writing to the immediate supervisor, as illustrated in Figure 14-4 ■.

The process for formally handling grievances will vary among agencies and may involve as many as three to six different levels of action. Following is an example of how a grievance may proceed:

Level I. An employee's grievance is submitted in writing to a supervisor. The supervisor will be given 5 days to respond. If the employee is dissatisfied with the response, the grievance moves to the next level.

Level II. At this level, the grievance proceeds to the chief executive, who will be given a specified time (usually 5 days) to render a decision.

Police Department
Formal Grievance Form

Grievance #______________

Employee Name: ______________________ Work Phone: ______________________
Department Assigned: ______________________
Date of Occurrence: ______________________
Location of Occurrence: ______________________

Name of: 1. Department Head: ______________________
2. Division Head: ______________________
3. Immediate Supervisor: ______________________

Statement of Grievance: ______________________

Witnesses: ______________________

What article(s) and or section(s) of the labor agreement of rules and regulations do you believe have been violated? ______________________

What remedy are you requesting? ______________________

______________________ ______________________
Employee signature Signature of labor representative

FIGURE 14-4 Employee Grievance Form

Level III. If the employee is not satisfied with the chief's decision, the grievance may proceed to the city or county manager, as appropriate. The manager will usually meet with the employee and/or representatives from the bargaining association and attempt to resolve the matter. An additional 5–10 days is usually allowed for the manager to render a decision.

Level IV. If the grievance is still not resolved, either party may request that the matter be submitted to arbitration. Arbitration involves a neutral outside person, often selected from a list of arbitrators from the Federal Mediation and Conciliation Service. An arbitrator will conduct a hearing, listen to both parties, and usually render a decision within 20–30 days. The decision of the arbitrator can be final and binding. This does not prohibit the employee from appealing the decision to a state court.

Failure to act on grievances quickly may result in serious morale problems within an agency.

Appealing Disciplinary Measures

Appeals processes—frequently outlined in civil service rules and regulations, labor agreements, and departmental policies and procedures—normally follow an officer's chain of command. For example, if an officer disagrees with a supervisor's recommendation for discipline, the first step of an appeal may involve a hearing before the division commander, usually of the rank of captain or deputy chief. The accused employee may be allowed labor representation or an attorney to assist in asking questions of the investigating supervisor, clarifying issues, and presenting new or mitigating evidence. The division commander often has 5 days to review the recommendation and respond in writing to the employee.

If the employee is still not satisfied, an appeal hearing before the chief executive is granted. This is usually the final step in appeals within the agency. The chief or sheriff communicates a decision in writing to the employee within 5 to 10 days. Depending on labor agreements and civil service rules and regulations, some agencies extend their appeals of discipline beyond the department. For example, employees may bring their issue before the civil service commission or city or county manager for a final review. Employees may also have the right to an independent arbitrator's review of the discipline. The arbitrator's decision is usually binding.

Alerting to Problems: The Early Intervention System

It has become a truism among police leadership that about 10 percent of their officers cause 90 percent of the problems. Indeed, some research has indicated that as little as 2 percent of all officers are responsible for 50 percent of all citizen complaints. However, there might also be times, for various reasons, when officers who are normally stellar performers act in ways that are uncharacteristically inappropriate. Therefore, the early identification of and intervention with employees engaging in misconduct or performance problems can be vital to preventing ongoing and repeated incidents—and possibly leading to personal injuries with citizens and lawsuits. A mechanism exists to assist police leaders in these tasks.

Early intervention systems (EIS) are a tool being adopted at an increasing rate by law enforcement agencies of all sizes and types. These systems are usually in the form of an electronic database, although some agencies find paper files are effective.

Information collected in EIS concerning officers' behaviors will help to identify problematic behaviors early on. Some of the more common kinds of information collected by EIS are use of sick leave, the number and type of community complaints, and the number and type of use-of-force incidents.[81] EIS, therefore, functions most effectively when used to help identify and address problems before officers get into serious trouble (e.g., before formal complaints or lawsuits arise and before an officer's well-being is compromised).

It is important to note that first-line supervisors are really the key to successful use of EIS. They are typically the first to observe potentially problematic behavior among their officers and are typically involved in the intervention process when required. For that reason, the chief executive also has a major role within EIS, ensuring that those first-line supervisors are prepared for this major aspect of their role (i.e., being able to analyze system data—see Figure 14-5 ■), willing to formally approach officers about personal or other problems that may be affecting their work, and following up with appropriate intervention options).[82]

Not to Be Overlooked: Internal Complaints and Problems

Generally when looking to identify problem police and corrections officers, their administrators and supervisors focus on citizens' excessive force complaints and related actions. However, there are some officers who might interact well with citizens but fail to meet internal departmental standards, generating internal complaints—as indicated earlier, those complaints filed against employees by persons within the organization, either peers or supervisors. Or, there may be officers who are rude to citizens and generate the most use-of-force

Report Criteria: Complaints Occurred Between: 01/01/2016 AND 06/30/2017

Officer Complaints Summary Rpt #C-8

Your Agency Name Will Print Here

Number Of Complaints / Violations Alleged By Officer

The totals below represent that number of different types of Complaints / Violations alleged against each Officer, Not the number of incidents.

Officer - ID Number		Complaints	Citizen	Internal	Racial	Off Duty	Body Camera	Priority	Still Active
Auburn, Steven	#22013	9	8 88.9%	1 11.1%	2 22.2%	2 22.2%	6 66.7%	3 33.3%	2 22.2%
Beige, Matt	#29861	8	7 87.5%	1 12.5%	2 25.0%	0 0.0%	7 87.5%	6 75.0%	0 0.0%
Black, Steve	#12647	7	7 100.0%	0 0.0%	2 28.6%	2 28.6%	4 57.1%	4 57.1%	0 0.0%
Bronze, Jennifer	#30042	3	2 66.7%	1 33.3%	1 33.3%	0 0.0%	2 66.7%	1 33.3%	0 0.0%
Brown, Alan	#22413	1	1 100.0%	0 0.0%	0 0.0%	0 0.0%	0 0.0%	0 0.0%	1 100.0%
Gold, Danny	#06744	3	2 66.7%	1 33.3%	1 33.3%	0 0.0%	2 66.7%	0 0.0%	0 0.0%
Gray, Michael	#6547	3	3 100.0%	0 0.0%	1 33.3%	0 0.0%	1 33.3%	2 66.7%	0 0.0%
Green, Tony	#22560	2	1 50.0%	1 50.0%	0 0.0%	0 0.0%	1 50.0%	0 0.0%	0 0.0%
Maroon, Patrick	#17765	5	3 60.0%	2 40.0%	2 40.0%	2 40.0%	4 80.0%	0 0.0%	0 0.0%
Orange, John	#29445	2	2 100.0%	0 0.0%	1 50.0%	0 0.0%	0 0.0%	0 0.0%	0 0.0%
Pink, John	#15484	3	3 100.0%	0 0.0%	0 0.0%	0 0.0%	2 66.7%	2 66.7%	0 0.0%
Purple, Jeff	#18032	4	3 75.0%	1 25.0%	2 50.0%	1 25.0%	1 25.0%	2 50.0%	0 0.0%
Red, Jeff	#19280	6	6 100.0%	0 0.0%	1 16.7%	0 0.0%	5 83.3%	3 50.0%	0 0.0%
Red, Mark	#18649	6	4 66.7%	2 33.3%	0 0.0%	0 0.0%	4 66.7%	3 50.0%	1 16.7%
Silver, Jon	#32663	3	3 100.0%	0 0.0%	1 33.3%	0 0.0%	0 0.0%	1 33.3%	1 33.3%
Tan, Julie	#18927	3	2 66.7%	1 33.3%	1 33.3%	0 0.0%	0 0.0%	0 0.0%	0 0.0%
Turquoise, John D.	#12345	3	2 66.7%	1 33.3%	0 0.0%	0 0.0%	1 33.3%	1 33.3%	1 33.3%
White, Ron	#00705	5	5 100.0%	0 0.0%	0 0.0%	0 0.0%	3 60.0%	2 40.0%	2 40.0%
	Totals:	76	64 84.2%	12 15.8%	17 22.4%	7 9.2%	43 56.6%	30 39.5%	8 10.5%

39 Total Number Of Incidents

13 Different Types Of Complaints

18 Different Officers Involved

76 Totals Entries (Officers "Plus" Complaint Violations Alleged)

L.E.A. Data Technologies *ADMINISTRATIVE Database* *08/02/2017 12:05:49 PM* *Page 1 of 1*

FIGURE 14-5 A sample administrative database, taken from actual records, from L.E.A. Data Technologies, http://www.leadatatech.com/reports/admin/Complaint-Summary-Totals.pdf. Used with permission.

complaints—and who also generate internal complaints by neglecting their duties, being insubordinate to their supervisors, failing to be at work punctually, and so on. Therefore, agency administrators and supervisors should also seek to determine the extent of *internal* complaints and the relationship between internal complaints and citizen complaints.[83]

Indeed, research indicates that officers demonstrating behavioral problems with citizens are also those officers who are identified by their peers or supervisors. In addition, while complaints generated by citizens generally peak early in one's career and then decline thereafter, internal complaints (although at lower rates than citizen complaints) quickly peak but then maintain a steady level across one's career[84]—indicating that misbehavior that involves internal departmental standards can be a problem that lasts many years.

▶ The Recreational Marijuana Conundrum: To Smoke or Not to Smoke?

With the spread of legalized marijuana use—both for medical and recreational purposes—across the United States, a question that is already being posed is whether or not criminal justice employees—particularly the police (who, from 2000 to 2014 alone, made from 600,000 to 775,000 marijuana arrests per year)[85] should or will be permitted to use it when off-duty. This is a thorny issue, especially given that marijuana use has been one of the primary disqualifiers of police applicants for many years—some agencies in the past disqualifying would-be officers for using marijuana within the past 5 years (it is still common for agencies to bar applicants who have used marijuana over the past 3 years).

How should police leaders view this matter, in general? How should agency policy be drafted? Following are some points to consider. First, although officers might reside in a state where marijuana use is legal, marijuana remains a Schedule 1 substance under the Controlled Substances Act (which means it is determined by the Food and Drug Administration to have no medical use). Therefore, until its legal status is changed, officers would be violating federal law by using it.

Another viewpoint is that while officers could use marijuana without being in violation of their state law, they would still be subject to their agencies' conduct policies, which generally prohibit the use of certain drugs. Therefore, if the officers' use of marijuana was discovered, they could be disciplined or terminated.[86]

Finally, a potential hurdle is drug testing that cannot distinguish between past and current use. Police officers must of course be able to prove at any time that they are not under the influence of any substance. However, today's marijuana tests do not discriminate between current and past intoxication—tests of hair, urine, blood, and saliva indicate ingestion days, weeks, even months after usage; so even if an agency allowed its officers to use cannabis recreationally while off-duty, contemporary testing protocol probably still makes it difficult if not impossible to prove they were not intoxicated while on-duty.[87]

In sum, police leaders probably will continue taking a hard-line approach against in-service officers' use of cannabis at any time; however, agencies can always ease their requirements for applicants. Such was the case in Seattle, Washington: the police department formerly required that applicants not have used marijuana for 3 years. Now the rule is no use with at least 1 year before joining the force.[88] The option of relaxing standards of past marijuana use may soon be spreading, as recruiting pools and positions become more difficult to fill and agencies begin to realize that societal attitudes are also relaxing. As examples, the U.S. Drug Enforcement Administration bars those who have experimented with or used narcotics from becoming agents, but it can make exceptions "for applicants who admit to limited youthful and experimental use of marijuana."[89]

EXHIBIT 14.4

TO SPEAK OR NOT TO SPEAK—THAT IS THE QUESTION (WITH MARIJUANA)

Recently a young Border Patrol agent learned that certain utterances concerning marijuana and immigration can be career-ending in nature.

Stationed in Deming, New Mexico, the agent and a coworker were parked in their patrol vehicles next to each other, when one began expressing the frustrations of the job. If marijuana were legalized, he opined, drug violence in Mexico would cease. In addition, he indicated support for ending the war on drugs and expressed sympathy for illegal immigrants. His remarks were sent to Border Patrol headquarters in Washington, DC, where, following an investigation, the agent was terminated for holding "personal views that were contrary to core characteristics of Border Patrol Agents, which are patriotism, dedication and esprit de corps."[90]

Questions for Discussion

1. Do you agree with the agent's termination? Explain.
2. Should *any* form of disciplinary action have been taken in this case, given the agent's comments? If so, what other disciplinary options do you believe might have been considered or more appropriate than termination?

Summary

This chapter has examined three aspects of criminal justice administration that pose exceptionally serious challenges for administrators: discipline, liability, and labor relations. It is clear from this triad of issues that administrators need to understand the current and developing laws that serve to make criminal justice practitioners legally accountable; this need cannot be overstated. It is far better to learn the proper means of discipline, areas of liability, and effective collective bargaining methods through education and training than to learn about these issues by virtue of serving in the role of a defendant in a lawsuit—indeed, it is far better to learn the law "in house," rather than to learn it "in the courthouse."

Key Terms and Concepts

Arbitration, p. 366
Automated records system, p. 379
Civil liability, p. 369
Collective bargaining, p. 363
Duty of care, p. 372
Early intervention system (EIS), p. 386
Fact-finding, p. 366
Failure to protect, p. 373
Grievance, p. 383
Internal complaints, p. 386
Job action, p. 366
Marijuana (recreational use of), p. 387
Mediation, p. 365
Meet-and-confer, p. 363
Negative discipline, p. 381
Negligence, p. 370
Negotiation, p. 364
Positive discipline, p. 380
Proximate cause, p. 372
Title 18, *U.S. Code*, Section 242, p. 372
Title 42, *U.S. Code*, Section 1983, p. 370
Tort, p. 370
Vehicle pursuit, p. 374

Questions for Review

1. How and why did unionization begin, what is its contemporary status in policing, and how does it influence courts and corrections organizations?
2. What are the three models of collective bargaining, as well as the process that comes into play when an impasse is reached?
3. What are the seven forms of disciplinary action that may be taken against police officers?
4. How would you define the following: *tort, Section 1983*, and *respondeat superior*?
5. How can the doctrines of duty of care and failure to protect, as well as laws covering vehicle pursuits, lead to police liability?
6. For what kinds of actions (and lack of action) can corrections agencies be held liable?
7. How would you delineate the minimum due process requirements for discharging public employees?
8. How would you explain the differences between positive and negative discipline?
9. What are the categories of dispositions that are commonly used with complaints?
10. What is an example of how a grievance may proceed through its various levels?
11. What are the benefits and functions of an early intervention system (EIS) for identifying problem officers?
12. What potential challenges are posed for criminal justice administrators given the spread of legal recreational-use marijuana? What will likely be the manner in which most administrators deal with the matter?

Deliberate and Decide

Liability for Failure to Protect?

On a cold winter night with a chill factor of minus 25 degrees, two municipal police officers ejected an individual (Munger) from a bar who had become extremely intoxicated. The individual was not permitted to drive home; rather, he was left by the officers to walk away from the bar clothed in only a T-shirt and jeans; he then died in an alley due to hypothermia.

Questions for Discussion

1. Were the officers *morally* responsible to see that Munger was delivered safely to his home? Explain.
2. Were the officers (and thus the agency) *legally* responsible for his death? If so, on what legal grounds? (See Notes section for the outcome of this case.[91])

Learn by Doing

1. You are enrolled in an internship with a small county sheriff's office, and after several weeks you begin to develop close friendships with some of the deputies. Eventually you learn that nearly all of the deputies are very disgruntled—and some are even irate—due to what they perceive as a lack of parity with other intracounty offices and intercounty sheriff's offices in wages and benefits, and general apathy by the county commission. They perceive a danger exists because low salaries lead to high turnover, which causes too few deputies—and too many inexperienced ones—to normally be on duty per shift. A deputy asks you if it is legally possible in your state for them to align themselves with a labor union, as well as your overall opinion concerning the pros and cons of collective bargaining and whether or not a "peaceful protest" by sheriff's personnel and their families and supporters at the county commission offices might help. What is your response?
2. Donna King has been a CO in your jail for 6 years, and one of your subordinates for 2 years. Her productivity, both in terms of quality and quantity as well as interactions with the staff and inmates, has generally been at or above standard; her performance evaluations are normally above average. In recent weeks, however, there have been rumors concerning her work; although no formal complaints have been filed, there are rumors concerning abusive treatment of inmates, not responding in a timely manner to calls by other jail staff for assistance, general lack of compliance with policies and procedures, and other matters. Today another CO contacts you to complain about her rough treatment of an inmate during booking. You decide it is time to call her into your office to discuss these matters. How will you address this situation?

Case Study

Baskerville has a population of about 100,000, with an ethnic composition of 47 percent Anglo, 38 percent African American, and 10 percent Latino. The police force, however, composed of 200 sworn officers, has only about 20 percent women and minority officers. The chief of police is receiving pressure from the mayor and the governing board to reduce crime in the central business district—where the largest percentage of minorities and lower-income residents in the city resides. The chief receives a federal grant to implement a bicycle patrol unit composed of one sergeant and five patrol officers in the central business district. The Baskerville Police Association (BPA) is the certified collective bargaining agent for all police officers and police sergeants; its agreement contains a seniority bidding clause for certain designated job assignments, but the agreement does not include a bike unit. Therefore, the city attorney has advised the chief of police that he can select the five officers and one sergeant without complying with the collective bargaining agreement. The chief, however—under pressure from the city council to ensure that women and minority officers are given preference for these new assignments—knows that if he follows the collective bargaining agreement concerning seniority, only the most senior officers and sergeants, all older white males, have a chance to win the assignments. Being stuck between the council and the BPA, the chief then posts a notice stating that all officers can apply for the new bike patrol unit, but that he will ultimately make the selection without regard to seniority. Several senior officers and sergeants then file a grievance with the BPA alleging that the chief has violated the agreement's seniority bidding provisions. Next, several female and minority officers approach the BPA president and say that the association betrayed them by not upholding their right to gain these high-profile assignments.

Questions for Discussion

1. What are the key issues in this case?
2. What steps should be taken by the police chief and union leadership in response to this crisis?
3. Who are the key stakeholders in the situation, and what are their interests?
4. What options are available to the police leadership?

Notes

1. Will Aitchison, *The Rights of Police Officers,* 3rd ed. (Portland, OR: Labor Relations Information System, 1996), p. 7.
2. Ibid.
3. Ibid.
4. Ibid.
5. Ibid., p. 8.
6. Ibid., p. 9.
7. Charles R. Swanson, Leonard Territo, and Robert W. Taylor, *Police Administration: Structures, Processes, and Behavior,* 6th ed. (Upper Saddle River, NJ: Prentice Hall, 2005), p. 517.
8. Ibid., p. 522.
9. Arnold Zack, *Understanding Fact-Finding and Arbitration in the Public Sector* (Washington, DC: U.S. Government Printing Office, 1974), p. 1.
10. Thomas P. Gilroy and Anthony V. Sinicropi, "Impasse Resolution in Public Employment," *Industrial and Labor Relations Review* 25 (July 1971–1972): 499.
11. Robert G. Howlett, "Fact Finding: Its Values and Limitations—Comment, Arbitration and the Expanded Role of Neutrals," in *Proceedings of the Twenty-Third Annual Meeting of the National Academy of Arbitrators* (Washington, DC: Bureau of National Affairs, 1970), p. 156.
12. Zack, *Understanding Fact-Finding,* p. 1.
13. Swanson, Territo, and Taylor, *Police Administration,* p. 530.
14. Ibid.
15. Ibid., p. 532.
16. Ibid., p. 534.
17. U.S. Department of Labor, Bureau of Labor Statistics, "Major Work Stoppages in 2012," January 24, 2014, http://www.bls.gov/news.release/archives/wkstp_02082013.pdf.
18. Taylor Wofford, "550 Memphis Cops Call in Sick in 'Blue Flu' Epidemic," *Newsweek*, July 18, 2014, http://www.newsweek.com/550-memphis-cops-call-sick-blue-flu-epidemic-union-pensions-healthcare-257805.
19. John H. Burpo, *The Police Labor Movement: Problems and Perspectives* (Springfield, IL: Charles C Thomas, 1971).
20. Ibid., p. xi.
21. Ibid., p. 168.
22. See Fraternal Order of Police, "About the Fraternal Order of Police," https://www.fop.net/CmsPage.aspx?id=223, and National Association of Police Organizations, "About NAPO," http://www.napo.org/.
23. Kenneth J. Peak, Larry K. Gaines, and Ronald W. Glensor, *Police Supervision and Management: In an Era of Community Policing*, 3rd ed. (Upper Saddle River, NJ: Prentice Hall, 2010), p. 282.
24. Richard P. Seiter, *Correctional Administration: Integrating Theory and Practice* (Upper Saddle River, NJ: Prentice Hall, 2002), pp. 333–334.
25. James B. Jacobs and Norma M. Crotty, *Guard Unions and the Future of Prisons* (Ithaca, NY: Institute of Public Employment, 1978), p. 41.
26. James B. Jacobs, *New Perspectives on Prisons and Imprisonment* (Ithaca, NY: Cornell University Press, 1983), p. 153.
27. Ibid., pp. 154–155.
28. U.S. Department of Justice, National Institute of Law Enforcement and Criminal Justice, *Trial Court Management Series, Personnel Management* (Washington, DC: U.S. Government Printing Office, 1979), pp. 42–47.
29. H. E. Barrineau III, *Civil Liability in Criminal Justice* (Cincinnati, OH: Pilgrimage, 1987), p. 58.
30. Ibid., p. 5.
31. Swanson et al., *Police Administration,* p. 549.
32. Ibid.
33. Zusha Elinson and Dan Frosch, "Police-Misconduct Costs Soar—Data from Big Cities Show Rising Payouts for Settlements and Court Judgments; Video Affects Cases," *Wall Street Journal* (July 16, 2015): A1.
34. Ibid.
35. Editorial, "The Laquan McDonald Case: Where Were You in April, Chicago Aldermen?," *Chicago Tribune*, December 8, 2015, http://www.chicagotribune.com/news/opinion/editorials/ct-laquan-mcdonald-chicago-aldermen-edit-1209-20151208-story.html.
36. J. David Goodman, "Eric Garner Case Is Settled by New York City for $5.9 Million," *New York Times*, July 13, 2015, http://www.nytimes.com/2015/07/14/nyregion/eric-garner-case-is-settled-by-new-york-city-for-5-9-million.html?_r=0.
37. Matt Pearce, "Growing Use of Police Body Cameras Raises Privacy Concerns," *Los Angeles Times*, September 27, 2014, http://www.latimes.com/nation/la-na-body-cameras-20140927-story.html.
38. 516 F.Supp. 1355 (W.D. Tenn., 1981).
39. *Brandon v. Holt,* 469 U.S. 464, 105 S.Ct. 873 (1985).
40. See, for example, *Black v. Stephens,* 662 F.2d 181 (1991).
41. On appeal, the Section 242 convictions were vacated, as the victim was not an inhabitant of Puerto Rico; therefore, he enjoyed no protection under the U.S. Constitution. On resentencing, in January 1991, the agents each received 50 years in prison for convictions of several other federal crimes under Title 18.
42. Andrew Conte and Brian Bowling, "Trib Investigation: Cops Often Let Off Hook for Civil Rights Complaints," *Pittsburgh Tribune-Review*, March 12, 2016, http://triblive.com/usworld/nation/9939487-74/police-rights-civil.
43. *Irwin v. Ware*, 467 N.E.2d 1292 (1984).
44. *Fudge v. City of Kansas City*, 239 Kan. 369, 720 P.2d 1093 (1986), at 373.
45. *Kendrick v. City of Lake Charles*, 500 So.2d 866 (La. App. 1 Cir. 1986).

46. *Fielder v. Jenkins*, 833 A.2d 906 (N.J. Super. A.D. 1993).
47. Isidore Silver, *Police Civil Liability* (Menands, NY: Matthew Bender, 1986), p. 4; also see *Coco v. State*, 474 N.Y.S.2d 397 (Ct.Cl. 1984); *Duvernay v. State* 433 So.2d 254 (La.App. 1983).
48. *Joseph v. State of Alaska*, 26 P.3d 459 (2001).
49. *Thomas v. Williams*, 124 S.E.2d 409 (Ga. App. 1962).
50. *Morris v. Blake*, 552 A.2d 844 (Del. Super. 1988).
51. *Davis v. City of Detroit*, 386 N.W.2d 169 (Mich. App. 1986).
52. *Monfils v. Taylor*, 165 F.3d 511 (7th Cir. 1998), cert. denied, 528 U.S. 810 (1999).
53. The U.S. Supreme Court said, in a 7–2 decision, that Gonzales could not sue the city and claim the police had violated her rights to due process. Furthermore, it held she had no constitutionally protected interest in the enforcement of the restraining order. The opinion also established that the holder of a restraining order is not entitled to any specific mandatory action by the police; rather, restraining orders only provide grounds for *arresting* the person restrained by order. See *Castle Rock v. Gonzales*, 545 U.S. 748 (2005).
54. *Seide v. State of Rhode Island*, 875 A.2d 1259 (2005).
55. Silver, *Police Civil Liability*, p. 8.
56. *Seide v. State of Rhode Island,* 875 A.2d 1259 (2005).
57. *Scott v. Harris*, 550 U.S._(2007), Docket #05-1631, at p. 13.
58. Victor E. Kappeler, *Critical Issues in Police Civil Liability*, 4th ed. (Long Grove, IL: Waveland, 2005), pp. 177–178.
59. U.S. Department of Justice, Bureau of Justice Statistics, "Jail Suicide Rates 64 Percent Lower Than in Early 1980s," October 14, 2014, http://www.bjs.gov/content/pub/press/shspljpr.cfm.
60. Ibid., p. 9.
61. Victor E. Kappeler and Rolando V. del Carmen, "Avoiding Police Liability for Negligent Failure to Prevent Suicide," *The Police Chief* (August 1991): 53–59.
62. Ibid., p. 53.
63. *Thomas v. Williams,* 124 S.E.2d 409 (Ga. App. 1962).
64. *Kanayurak v. North Slope Borough,* 677 P.2d 892 (Alaska 1984).
65. *City of Belen v. Harrell,* 603 P.2d 711 (NM: 1979).
66. *Hake v. Manchester Township,* 486 A.2d 836 (NJ: 1985).
67. *Davis v. City of Detroit,* 386 N.W.2d 169 (Mich. App. 1986).
68. *Hickey v. Zezulka,* 443 N.W.2d 180 (Mich. App. 1989).
69. *Hake v. Manchester Township,* 486 A.2d 836 (NJ: 1985).
70. Andrew Blankstein, "Nearly 20 LA Sheriff's Deputies to Be Charged in Corruption, Inmate Abuse Probe," *NBC News Investigations*, December 9, 2013, http://investigations.nbcnews.com/_news/2013/12/09/21835238-nearly-20-la-sheriffs-deputies-to-be-charged-in-corruption-inmate-abuse-probe?lite (accessed January 29, 2014).
71. V. McLaughlin and R. Bing, "Law Enforcement Personnel Selection," *Journal of Police Science and Administration* 15 (1987): 271–276.
72. Adapted from Pine Bluff, Arkansas, Police Department, *Pine Bluff Police Department Policy & Procedures Manual,* Policy No. 1100, http://www.pbpd.org/Policies/Chapter-XI/Microsoft%20Word%20-%20POL-1100%20_Standards%20of%20Conduct_.pdf.
73. Ibid.
74. *McNamara v. City of Chicago,* 700 F.Supp. 917 (ND Ill., 1988), at 919.
75. *White v. Thomas,* 660 F.2d 680 (5th Cir. 1981).
76. Robert H. Chaires and Susan A. Lentz, "Criminal Justice Employee Rights: An Overview," *American Journal of Criminal Justice* 13 (April 1995): 273–274.
77. M. Guthrie, "Using Automation to Apply Discipline Fairly," *FBI Law Enforcement Bulletin* 5 (1996): 18–21.
78. See Kappeler, *Critical Issues in Police Civil Liability*, p. 4; also see G. P. Alpert, R. G. Dunham, and M. S. Stroshine, *Policing: Continuity and Change* (Long Grove, IL: Waveland, 2006).
79. Kim M. Lersch, "Police Misconduct and Malpractice: A Critical Analysis of Citizens' Complaints," *Policing* 21 (1998): 80–96.
80. D. W. Perez, *Police Review Systems* (Washington, DC: Management Information Service, 1992).
81. Samuel Walker, Stacy O. Milligan, and Anna Berke, *Supervision and Intervention within Early Intervention Systems: A Guide for Law Enforcement Chief Executives*, Office of Community Oriented Policing Services, December 2005, http://www.policeforum.org/assets/docs/Free_Online_Documents/Early_Intervention_Systems/supervision%20and%20intervention%20within%20early%20intervention%20systems%202005.pdf; also see Samuel Walker, *Early Intervention Systems for Law Enforcement Agencies: A Planning and Management Guide,* Office of Community Oriented Policing Services, 2003, https://chicagopatf.org/wp-content/uploads/2016/02/EarlyInterventionSystemsLawEnforcement.pdf.
82. Ibid.
83. Ibid.
84. Ibid.
85. Christopher Ingraham, "Every Minute, Someone Gets Arrested for Marijuana Possession in the U.S.," *The Washington Post*, September 28, 2015, https://www.washingtonpost.com/news/wonk/wp/2015/09/28/every-minute-someone-gets-arrested-for-marijuana-possession-in-the-u-s/?utm_term=.59cb885a40cf.
86. Tim Dees, "Can Cops Smoke Marijuana in States Where It Has Been Legalized?" *Quora* (n.d.), https://www.quora.com/Can-cops-smoke-marijuana-in-states-where-it-has-been-legalized.
87. Med-Health.Net, "How Long Is THC Detectable in Urine?" December 14, 2016, http://www.med-health.net/How-Long-Is-Thc-Detectable-In-Urine.html.
88. Jonathan Kaminsky, "Seattle Police Department Loosens Rules On Marijuana Use For Recruit," February 18, 2013, http://www.huffingtonpost.com/2012/12/19/seattle-police-marijuana-rules_n_2333912.html.

89. Kevin Rector, "Davis Wants to Relax Restrictions on Past Marijuana Use for Police Recruits in Maryland," *The Baltimore Sun*, December 13, 2016, http://www.baltimoresun.com/news/maryland/crime/bs-md-ci-police-marijuana-standard-20160721-story.html.

90. Adapted from PoliceOne.com, "Police Officers Find That Dissent on Drug Laws May Come with a Price," December 3, 2011, https://www.policeone.com/drug-interdiction-narcotics/articles/4835060-Police-officers-find-that-dissent-on-drug-laws-may-come-with-a-price/.

91. In *Munger v. City of Glasgow Police Dept.* (227 F. 3d 1082, 1086-1087 (9th Cir. 2000), the court held that the officers created a danger to Munger by ejecting him and then not allowing him to return or go to his car on such a frigid night. The court also found that the officers had thus placed Munger in a position of danger. The court also determined that the police agency had a policy of taking such intoxicated individuals to their home, but that it had failed to train officers in this policy and thus was liable.

Lucadp/Shutterstock

15 Financial Administration

LEARNING OBJECTIVES

After reading this chapter, the student will be able to:

1. *delineate some basic steps in performing a workload analysis*
2. *describe some pros and cons of using civilians to stretch agency budgets and obtaining grants*
3. *define strategic planning and what role it plays in financial administration*
4. *explain how courts' budgets are unique and how judges must approach their getting funded*
5. *analyze what California's Proposition 47 did to bring about fiscal reform*
6. *define the term* budget *and how it is used*
7. *describe the meaning of a* budget cycle *and its application to budgeting*
8. *identify what is involved in formulating a budget, as well as its approval and execution*
9. *review the type of budget format used most frequently and its major advantages and component parts*

▶ Introduction

Providing criminal justice (police, courts, and corrections) services for the entire United States is an expensive undertaking: taxpayers spend about $265 billion for those services, about half of which is spent at the local (i.e., city and county) level, and about half of the total cost being spent on police protection; corrections agencies expend about 30 percent of the total, for community supervision, confinement, and rehabilitation, while courts consume about 20 percent.[1] While the general public seems to be supportive of such enormous expenditures in exchange for its safety and the adjudication and punishment of its members who transgress, it is nonetheless expected that justice administrators will be responsible stewards of those funds. Therefore, the importance of those leaders understanding all facets of financial administration cannot be overstated.

Money is the key to nearly everything criminal justice agencies do; indeed, the chief executive and staff will likely be judged on how well they compete with other governmental entities in obtaining funds necessary for meeting agency mission and goals—and how successful they were in defending their budgets against cuts. Money is the fuel that powers the organization. As Frederick Mosher observed, "Not least among the qualifications of an administrator is one's ability as a tactician and gladiator in the budget process."[2]

The **Great Recession**, a term describing the sharp decline in economic activity beginning in 2008 and lasting about 18 months, impacted justice system agencies of all levels and sizes; normally the most "safe" occupation in terms of job security found itself foundering with widespread layoffs and cutbacks. The resulting "do more with less" mentality fomented at that time has tentacles that reach out to today's agencies, creating a "new normal" for these leaders. This chapter discusses some of the recession's lingering vestiges and how to budget in these times.

Although this chapter is not intended to prepare the reader to be a fiscal analyst or an expert on the more intricate aspects of financial administration, it will provide a foundation for and insight concerning some of its basic methods and issues. Furthermore, because the police function consumes the greatest proportion of funds in the justice system and is its most visible component, we will focus on that segment of the system and include a number of policing examples herein.

To begin, we look at general areas where criminal justice administrators must develop fiscal acumen and be good stewards of their funds—to include a workload analysis and several means by which one may enhance the agency budget (e.g., grants, civilianization); we also consider the need for mobilizing stakeholders and engaging in strategic planning (to include some examples of fiscal reform). Next we focus on the heart of the chapter: budgeting, which is composed of budget definitions and uses; key elements of the budget process (formulation, approval, execution, and audit); and several budget formats. The chapter concludes with a summary, key terms and concepts, and review questions. Also included are examples, exhibits, a career profile of a budget analyst, and exercises in the Deliberate and Decide, Learn by Doing, and Case Study sections.

▶ First Things First: Enhancing Budgets and Financial Stewardship

Possessing insight into the world of fiscal affairs requires more than merely knowing how to ask for and spend monies. Therefore, next we discuss some peripheral but nevertheless important matters that bear heavily on the task of budgeting, discussed later.

Knowing What the Job Entails—and What the Competition Is Doing

workload analysis a tool to determine the time, labor, and resources required to perform an organization's operations, using historical data.

To possess financial insight and confidence, criminal justice administrators must first know what the job entails in order to provide optimal service to the community and meeting overall agency demands. Toward that end, a **workload analysis** should be completed at least every 3 years to ensure the agency has adequate staff to address the needs of the community and allow for strategic planning. A workload analysis, simply put, is a measure of an agency's staffing and deployment needs based on the demands for service that the community places on it; in policing, for example, such analysis would consider such tasks as responding to calls for service (CFS), attending training and community/departmental meetings, meal breaks, going to court, transporting prisoners, and so on. Then, with that information, staffing levels, shift schedules, beat configuration, and other related aspects of policing are better developed. (Note: In policing, many agencies strive to mimic a "recommended officers per 1,000 population" or a "national standard" for staffing; however, it is generally not useful to use such information for determining staffing needs.[3] Note, too, that for police, CFS are used instead of crime rates as workload indicators. Typically, only a small percent of a police department's CFS are crime-related in nature; much more common are CFS for order-maintenance duties. Therefore, it is far better for a police leader to divide officers' time into CFS, administrative duties, and community policing and problem-solving, and use these statistics rather than the crime rate to justify staffing requests.[4])

For the courts, a workload analysis might include some or all of the following: caseload type (e.g., criminal, civil, juvenile, industrial), assignment, amount of time spent on each case, draft opinions, the final work product must be closely reviewed by other judges within the division, participation in meetings and committee work, customer service, human resources issues, keeping current on the law, continuing legal education, public speaking/community outreach, and bar and legal association activities.[5]

In corrections, particularly prisons, staffing levels should take into account such factors as the classification system, the division of labor among types of facilities, methods of operation and service delivery, inmate programs and activities, and the status of facility physical plants.[6]

Of course, all three components should take into account the respective agency's mission and goals, organizational structure, policies and procedures, any union agreements and consent decrees (discussed in Chapter 14), contracted services, and so on. Although such an analysis can be very complicated, there are a number of resources available to assist in this endeavor.[7]

Once the staffing levels have been identified, the agency should compare its salary and benefits package to other agencies in the surrounding area. For most employees today, money alone is not a motivator; however, the absence of money can be a de-motivator. Employees soon learn how their salaries and benefits stand in comparison with other nearby agencies, and thus it is important for the agency to keep pace with the pay schedule in its labor market lest their employees leave for what they perceive as greener pastures. A simple telephone survey can be conducted of similar agencies in the area. Such surveys should include the base rate of pay, insurance, and other benefits for each community by position. Also, take into account shift configuration (e.g., eight-, ten-, or twelve-hour work schedules) and any perks such as take-home vehicles, recruitment bonuses, educational incentives, and shift differential pay.[8]

Strategies for Enhancing the Bottom Line: Growth, Grants, and Civilianization

Following are several suggestions for enhancing and stretching the budget. Although these measures will not be successful in all jurisdictions and at all times, criminal justice leaders should be sensitive to their potential as "winning strategies."

First is *population growth*, which often occurs when middle-class persons move into a city's existing area or into newly annexed areas. While middle-class residents do not typically experience high crime rates, such citizens are normally well informed, concerned about their safety and police services, and thus command greater police, courts, and corrections services. In addition, annexation (the incorporation of new territory into the domain of a city, country, or state) will sometimes bring growth to police staffing.[9]

Many criminal justice administrators have developed expertise in augmenting their operating budgets with different types of *grants*. In policing, many times expensive capital improvement budget items—upgraded communications technology including the more powerful 800 MHz radios, dispatching systems, mobile data terminals, and laptops for police vehicles—are funded by grants. Capital budgets also included expenditures for buildings, vehicles, and property. The more expensive items are typically funded by bonds and the less expensive items by grants, general funds, or asset-forfeiture funds. Police departments can access a variety of external funding sources, including state and federal grants, foundations, and business groups.[10]

Like the police, judges and prison administrators have a surprising number of funding sources available to the enterprising grant writer. Following is an overview:

- ***Justice Assistance Grants (JAG) program.*** JAG is a broad-based, competitive program with 29 funding areas; its funding is intended as "seed money" to start new programs, and funding ranges from 1 to 3 years.[11]
- ***Bureau of Justice Assistance.*** BJA has funding opportunities for treatment programs and specialty courts, drug testing and equipment, and intensive outpatient programs.[12]
- ***Office of Justice Programs.*** OJA provides a variety of types of grants geared toward implementing strategies that involve identifying the most pressing crime-related challenges and to provide information, training, and coordination for addressing these challenges.[13]
- ***The Violence Against Women Reauthorization Act of 2013.***[14] VAWA has grant programs for addressing domestic violence, dating violence, sexual assault, and stalking.[15]
- ***The Office of Juvenile Justice and Delinquency Prevention (OJJDP).*** OJJDP provides a variety of grants for research, training, and technical assistance; funding of new projects; and dissemination of information.[16]

In addition, most states have an administrative office, department of public safety, and other entities that can provide funding for a variety of purposes. There are caveats with receiving "free money" from grants, however, and criminal justice leaders should heed the adage "beware of feds bearing gifts." The major problem is simply that if local officials accept federal funding—particularly for hiring additional employees—they also promise to retain these employees and keep current staffing levels after the federal contributions expire. However, some agencies simply fail to plan adequately for the phaseout of federal assistance; then, after what is typically 3 years of grant funding, the agencies can find themselves struggling to locate the funds to do so.

A beginner's step-by-step guide for writing competitive grants is available at: http://www.policegrantshelp.com/grants101/.[17]

Finally, there has been a long-standing debate about whether or not to use, or expand, *civilianization* in criminal justice. Such debate is particularly acute in policing, as many unions, chiefs, and mayors prefer to expand the ranks of sworn personnel. Since they are not required to undergo the same comprehensive training as uniformed police, however, civilian employees can replace sworn officers in many tasks while ultimately commanding a lower salary (as well as few, if any, fringe benefits). In addition, civilianization can allow citizens to become more knowledgeable about their police and familiar with problems affecting the community.[18]

Other Causes of Budget Expansion: Sensational Incidents, Mobilized Stakeholders, Strategic Planning

The occurrence of *major crime events*—hopefully in a jurisdiction other than yours—can also bring about a loud call for more criminal justice resources. The reporting of mass killings, the murder of a police officer or judge, random shootings at schools, and so on, certainly carry an emotional element and can be a powerful rationale for making budget requests. Even when the crime rate is decreasing, violent crimes may fuel citizens' and politicians' fears.

Regarding the *mobilizing of stakeholders*, criminal justice leaders should never forget that there exists a natural constituency of neighborhood groups, civic organizations, and business groups that are concerned about crime.[19]

Finally, in addition to being a political document, as indicated above, the criminal justice agency budget is also a *planning* document. Strategic planning also became a much more integral aspect of the administrator's job since the recession. Indeed, if unlimited funds were available, planning would not be needed. The aforementioned financial crisis also had a profound effect on the ability of such agencies to plan strategically for staffing and other needs. As a result, today's agencies must view planning as more important than ever for determining staffing needs and in getting the resources to meet these needs.

Many people have difficulty understanding the concept of and need for strategic planning as it relates to finances and the future. So, take for example a high school senior who is pondering where to attend a college or university. Some preliminary questions to ponder would include: what are my aptitudes and interests? What kinds of careers fit those aptitudes and interests? How do I achieve that goal? And to achieve that goal, can I afford to go to an out-of-state school? Are scholarships available to me? Will I have to work part- or full time while in school? Can I get family help? Will I be able to afford (or even need) a car while in school? How will I pay for books, tuition, housing, and other living expenses? This is strategic planning for the short and long term.

This exercise is not unlike that of a criminal justice executive who wishes to have some better plan of taking the agency where it needs to go. Strategic planning thus means seeing both the big picture and its operational implications. Strategic thinking is, therefore, compatible with strategic planning. Both are required in any thoughtful strategy-making process and strategy formulation.[20] Strategic planning is also a leadership tool and a process; it shapes and guides what an organization is, what it does, and why it does it, with a focus on the future.[21]

Excellent examples of strategic planning abound; for example, see the strategic plan of the U.S. Department of Justice for 2014–2018 at: https://www.justice.gov/sites/default/files/jmd/legacy/2014/02/28/doj-fy-2014-2018-strategic-plan.pdf.[22]

EXHIBIT 15.1

USING PLANNING, SMART POLICING, AND FORCE MULTIPLIERS IN CAMDEN, NEW JERSEY[23]

The city of Camden, New Jersey, was struggling for survival even before the Great Recession. In addition to being the nation's poorest city (36% of residents living in poverty), its violent crime rate was more than five times that of the nation. Drug and gang crimes abounded, and 40 percent of its violent crimes were committed by youths. Many veteran as well as new officers were laid off or demoted, while others saw their salaries cut, and the agency's budget was cut by 25 percent. The police chief began seeking ways to restructure the department so as to use a smart policing strategy with remaining officers, and the first move was to eliminate or reduce specialized units and move administrative and investigative personnel to the streets. Technologies were introduced to move to a "smarter" approach that would be a force multiplier. A real-time tactical operations center was created and a gunshot location system initiated in the city's high-incident areas. Automated license-plate readers were used to detect stolen vehicles associated with criminals.

Yet, despite their best efforts, the severe budget cuts and loss of personnel resulted in rising crime rates. With fewer officers on the streets, criminals became more brazen, while citizen fear of crime, city homicides, and CFS escalated. Eventually, the city felt compelled to begin discussing a plan for consolidating its force with county agencies—a change that would save the city $14 million per year. A plan was devised whereby nearly 300 city officers would be laid off, but about half of them could be hired into the new agency through an application process. The city and county did indeed consolidate in 2013.

The key lesson to be learned from the Camden experience as other jurisdictions attempt to develop proactive responses to crime is that technology is not a substitute for police officers being deployed on the streets.

▶ Courts' Budgets, Generally

For many people, and for a long period of time, the courts have been viewed as having a "special status" as the third branch of government, possessing "the duty to protect access to justice for all … to uphold the Constitutions of our state and nation and the laws … to protect individuals' rights."[24] Indeed, courts are not opposed to suing their governing boards if believing they are not being funded sufficiently or in a sound fashion.[25]

Today, however, the recent recession has taught judges and court administrators that money trumps any special status they might hold with state or local legislators (normally a handful of whom are truly expert in budgetary matters and must be lobbied and sold on the budget request). These lawmakers are inundated with budget requests, and too often they are presented a budget request by judges in a manner perceived as an entitlement. Today, therefore, judges should invite key legislators to meet and observe courts in action, explain where the courts fit within the state's entire budget, and have plenty of data to justify their requests.[26]

▶ Thinking about Fiscal Reform: California Voters Reduce, Reinvest Prison Expenditures

Today about 2.25 million Americans are incarcerated in the United States, 1.5 million of whom are in adult correctional facilities.[27] Of the total corrections expenditures, about $80 billion per year, 80 percent is spent on maintaining these institutions.[28] Indeed, corrections spending is the third largest category of spending in most states, behind education and health care, and about one-fifth of the states spend more on corrections than on higher education.[29]

This is felt to be unsound fiscal policy: that states' financial fortunes would be stronger if they invested in education and other areas that can boost long-term economic growth, and less in maintaining high prison populations. A number of states are reconsidering their corrections policies, looking at sentencing reforms that would save money and incarcerate only those who need to be confined. California is one such state.

In November 2014, with the support of 60 percent of voters, Californians approved Proposition 47, the "Safe Neighborhoods and Schools Act," which contained a number of criminal justice reforms for reducing the state's prison population and redirecting the savings. Proposition 47:

- reclassified seven types of nonviolent drug and property offenses (included were petty theft, receiving stolen property and forging/writing bad checks when the amount involved is $950 or less) from felonies to misdemeanors for future offenders (however, current offenders in prison could petition for resentencing), shortening the maximum penalty from a prison sentence to 1 year in jail.

- mandated the state calculate the savings from the reforms each year and deposit them in a dedicated fund.
- required the savings deposited in the aforementioned fund could only be used for three purposes: 65 percent for mental health, drug treatment, and diversionary programs; 25 percent to support at-risk youth; and 10 percent for victim services.

Estimates are that the law will likely cut the state's prison population by several thousand inmates, while saving hundreds of millions of dollars annually.[30]

▶ The Budget

In this section, we focus on the more intricate parts of budgeting, to include elements, types (with several examples provided), formulation, and execution. Included is a brief explanation of the role of auditing.

A Working Definition

budget a plan, in financial terms, estimating future expenditures and indicating agency plans and policy regarding financial resources and the appropriation and expenditure of funds.

The word **budget** is derived from the old French word *bougette*, meaning a small leather bag or wallet. Initially, it referred to the leather bag in which the Chancellor of the Exchequer carried documents stating the government's needs and resources given to the English Parliament.[31] Later, it came to mean the documents themselves. More recently, *budget* has been defined as a plan stated in financial terms, an estimate of future expenditures, a policy statement, the translation of financial resources into human purposes, and a contract between those who appropriate the funds and those who spend them.[32] To some extent, all of these definitions are valid.

> In addition, the budget is a management tool, a process, and a political instrument. It is a comprehensive plan, expressed in financial terms, by which a program is operated for a given period. It includes (1) the services, activities, and projects comprising the program; (2) the resultant expenditure requirements; and (3) the resources available for their support.[33]

It is "a plan or schedule adjusting expenses during a certain period to the estimated income for that period."[34] Lester Bittel added:

> A budget is, literally, a financial standard for a particular operation, activity, program, or department. Its data are presented in numerical form, mainly in dollars—to be spent for a particular purpose—over a specified period of time. Budgets are derived from planning goals and forecasts.[35]

Although these descriptions are certainly apt, one writer warns that budgets involve an inherently irrational process: "Budgets are based on little more than the past and some guesses."[36]

As noted above, financial management of governmental agencies is clearly political. Anything the government does entails the expenditure of public funds.[37] Thus, the most important political statement that any unit of government makes in a given year is its budget. Special-interest groups, the media, politicians, and the public, with their own views and priorities, often engage in arm-twisting during the budgeting process.

▶ Key Elements: The Budget Cycle, Formulation, Approval, Execution, Audit

Administrators must think in terms of a **budget cycle**—simply put, how long a budget lasts, which is a time frame that can vary from agency to agency. In government (and, therefore, all public criminal justice agencies) the budget cycle is typically set on a fiscal-year basis. Some states have a biennial budget cycle; their legislatures, such as those in Kentucky and Nevada, budget for a 2-year period. Normally, however, the **fiscal year** is a 12-month period that may coincide with a calendar year or, more commonly, will run from July 1 through June 30 of the following year. The federal government's fiscal year is October 1 through September 30. The budget cycle is important because it drives the development of the budget and determines when new monies become available.

budget cycle a time frame that determines how long a budget lasts, which can vary from agency to agency.

fiscal year a 12-month time period that an organization uses for budgeting, forecasting and reporting.

The budget cycle consists of four sequential steps, repeated every year at about the same point in time: (1) budget formulation, (2) budget approval, (3) budget execution, and (4) budget audit.

Depending on the size and complexity of the organization and the financial condition of the jurisdiction, **budget formulation**—which involves the preparation of a budget so as to be able to allocate funds in accordance with agency priorities, plans, and programs, and to deliver necessary services—can be a relatively simple or an exceedingly difficult task; in either case, it is likely to be the most complicated stage of the budgeting process. The administrator must anticipate all types of **expenditures**—that is, payment for goods or services, to settle a financial obligation indicated by an invoice, contract, or other such document—and predict expenses related to major incidents or events that might arise. Certain assumptions based on the previous year's budget can be made, but they are not necessarily accurate. One observer noted that "every expense you budget should be fully supported with the proper and most logical assumptions you can develop. Avoid simply estimating, which is the least supportable form of budgeting."[38]

budget formulation the preparation of a budget to allocate funds in accordance with agency priorities, plans, and programs, and to deliver necessary services.

expenditure a payment for goods or services, to settle a financial obligation indicated by an invoice, contract, or other such document.

To illustrate, let us assume that a police department budget is being prepared in a city or county having a manager form of government. Long before a criminal justice agency (or any other unit of local government) begins to prepare its annual budget, the city or county manager and/or the staff have made revenue forecasts, considered how much (if any) of the current operating budget will be carried over into the next fiscal year, analyzed how the population of the jurisdiction will grow or shift (affecting demand for public services), and examined other priorities for the coming year. The manager may also appear before the governing board to obtain information about its fiscal priorities, spending levels, pay raises, new positions, programs, and so on. The manager may then send department heads a memorandum outlining the general fiscal guidelines to be followed in preparing their budgets.

On receipt of the guidelines for preparing its budget, the heads of functional areas, such as the chief of police or sheriff, have a planning and research unit (assuming a city or county is large enough to have this level of specialization) prepare an internal budget calendar and an internal fiscal policy memorandum (Table 15-1 ■ shows an internal budget calendar for a large city police department). This memo may include input from unions and lower supervisory personnel. Each bureau is then given the responsibility for preparing its individual budget request.

In small police agencies with little or no functional specialization, the chief or sheriff may prepare the budget alone or with input from other officers or the city finance officer. In some small agencies, chiefs and sheriffs may not even see their budget or assist in its preparation. Because of tradition, politics, or even laziness, the administrator may have

TABLE 15-1 Budget Preparation Calendar for a Large City Police Department

What Should Be Done	By Whom	On This Date
Issue budget instructions and applicable forms	City administrator	November 1
Prepare and issue budget message, with instructions and applicable forms, to unit commanders	Chief of police	November 15
Develop unit budgets with appropriate justification and forward recommended budgets to planning and research unit	Unit commanders	February 1
Review unit budget	Planning and research staff with unit commanders	March 1
Consolidate unit budgets for presentation to chief of police	Planning and research unit	March 15
Review consolidated recommended budget	Chief of police, planning and research staff, and unit commanders	March 30
Obtain department approval of budget	Chief of police	April 15
Forward recommended budget to city administrator	Chief of police	April 20
Review recommended budget by administration	City administrator and chief of police	April 30
Approve revised budget	City administrator	May 5
Forward budget document to city council	City administrator	May 10
Review budget	Budget officer of city council	May 20
Present to council	City administrator and chief of police	June 1
Report back to city administrator	City council	June 5
Review and resubmit to city council	City administrator and chief of police	June 10
Take final action on police budget	City council	June 20

Source: U.S. Department of Justice, National Advisory Commission on Criminal Justice Standards and Goals, *Police* (Washington, DC: U.S. Government Printing Office, 1973), p. 137.

abdicated control over the budget. This puts the agency in a precarious position indeed; it will have difficulty engaging in long-term planning and spending money productively for personnel and programs when the executive has to get prior approval from the governing body to buy items such as office supplies.

The planning and research unit then reviews the bureau's budget request for compliance with the budgeting instructions and the agency's priorities. Eventually, a consolidated budget is developed for the entire agency and submitted to the chief executive, who may meet with the planning and research unit and bureau commanders to discuss it. Personalities, politics, priorities, personal agendas, and other issues may need to be addressed; the chief or sheriff may have to mediate disagreements concerning these matters, sometimes rewarding the loyal and sometimes reducing allotments to the disloyal.[39] Requests for programs, equipment, travel expenses, personnel, or anything else in the draft budget may be deleted, reduced, or enhanced. The budget is then presented to the city or county manager. At this point, the chief executive's reputation as a budget framer becomes a factor. If the chief executive is known to pad the budget heavily, the manager is far more likely to cut the department's request than if the chief or sheriff is known to be reasonable in making budget requests, engages in innovative planning, and has a flexible approach to budget negotiations.

The city or county manager consolidates the police budget request with those from other department heads and then meets with them individually to discuss their requests further. The manager directs the city finance officer to make any necessary additions or cuts and then to prepare a budget proposal for presentation to the governing body. The general steps in budget development are shown in Exhibit 15.2.

EXHIBIT 15.2

STEPS IN BUDGET DEVELOPMENT

Following is a description of how the $1.96 billion budget for the California Highway Patrol (CHP) is typically developed. According to the budget section, "It is an all-year and year-on-year process" that begins at the level of the 8 divisions and 103 area offices/dispatch centers, where budget requests originate. The requests are dealt with one of three ways: (1) funded within the department's base budget, (2) disapproved, or (3) carried forward for review by CHP personnel.

At the division level, managers review the area requests, make needed adjustments, and submit a consolidated request to the budget section at headquarters. This section passes input from the field to individual section management staff (e.g., planning and analysis, personnel, training, and communications) for review. Budget section staff meets with individual section management staff. Within 2 or 3 months, the budget section identifies proposals for new funding that have department-wide impact and passes them on to the executive level.

The commissioner and aides review the figures along with those from other state departments and agree on a budget to submit to the governor. The governor submits this budget to the legislature, which acts on it and returns it to the governor for signature.

Source: Excerpt from "Working Out a Budget" by Hal Rubin from *Law and Order*. Copyright © 1989 by Hendon Publishing Company. Used by permission of Hendon Publishing Company.

The courts have a similar budgetary process. In a large court, the process may include five major procedures: (1) developing an internal budgetary policy, (2) reviewing budget submissions, (3) developing a financial strategy, (4) presenting the budget, and (5) monitoring the budget. Figure 15-1 ■ illustrates the relationship of the steps in the judicial budget process.

With the city or county manager's proposed budget request in hand, the governing board begins its deliberations on the budget for the entire jurisdiction. The city or county manager may appear before the board to answer questions concerning the budget; individual department heads also may be asked to appear. Suggestions for getting monies approved and appropriated include the following:

1. Have a carefully justified budget.
2. Anticipate the environment of the budget hearing by reading news reports and understanding the priorities of the council members. Know what types of questions elected officials are likely to ask.
3. Determine which "public" will be at the agency's budget hearing and prepare accordingly. Public issues change from time to time; citizens who were outraged over an issue one year may be incensed by another the next.
4. Make good use of graphics in the form of pie charts and histograms, but be selective and do not go overboard. Short case studies of successes are normal and add to the impact of graphics.
5. Rehearse and critique the presentation many times.
6. Be a political realist.[40]

After everyone scheduled has spoken, the city or county council will direct the manager to make further cuts in the budget or to reinstate funds or programs cut earlier, and so on. The budget is then approved. It is fair to say that at this stage, budgeting is largely a legislative function that requires some legal action, as a special ordinance or resolution approving the budget is passed each year by the governing board.

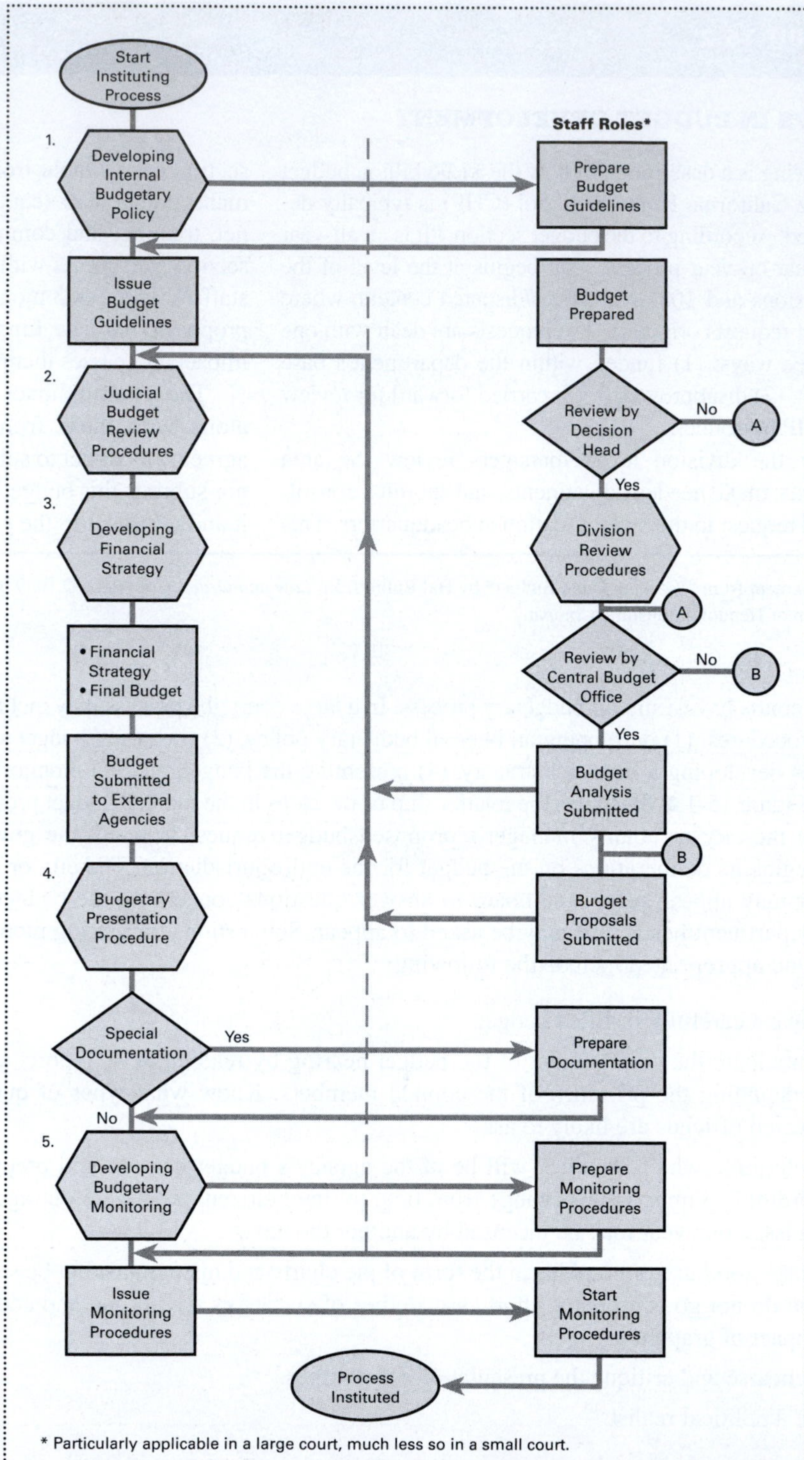
Start Instituting Process
1.
Developing Internal Budgetary Policy
Staff Roles*
Prepare Budget Guidelines
Issue Budget Guidelines
Budget Prepared
2.
Judicial Budget Review Procedures
Review by Decision Head
No
A
Yes
3.
Developing Financial Strategy
Division Review Procedures
A
• Financial Strategy
• Final Budget
Review by Central Budget Office
No
B
Yes
Budget Submitted to External Agencies
Budget Analysis Submitted
B
4.
Budgetary Presentation Procedure
Budget Proposals Submitted
Special Documentation
Yes
Prepare Documentation
No
5.
Developing Budgetary Monitoring
Prepare Monitoring Procedures
Issue Monitoring Procedures
Start Monitoring Procedures
Process Instituted
* Particularly applicable in a large court, much less so in a small court.

FIGURE 15-1 Steps in a Judicial Budgetary Process

The columns in Table 15-2 ■ indicate the budget amount requested by the chief of police, the amount recommended by the city manager, and the amount finally approved by the city council.

TABLE 15-2 Police Operating Budget ($) in a Community of 100,000 Population

Description	FY 2016–2017 Expenses	FY 2017–2018 Expenses	FY 2018–2019 Police Request	City Manager	City Council
Salaries/wages					
Regular salaries	28,315,764	28,392,639	32,221,148	32,221,148	32,221,148
Overtime	1,976,165	1,564,421	1,902,875	1,902,875	1,422,875
Severance pay	456,712	452,465	454,936	-0-	-0-
Holiday pay	790,952	1,182,158	1,396,958	1,396,958	1,396,958
Callback pay	1,205,947	1,326,534	1,476,925	1,395,241	1,395,241
Subtotals	32,745,540	32,918,217	36,916,222	36,916,222	36,436,222
Employee benefits					
Retirement	6,345,566	6,485,888	8,069,521	8,069,521	8,069,521
Group insurance	2,256,663	2,467,406	2,752,718	2,752,718	2,752,718
Life insurance	86,797	106,164	234,590	234,396	234,396
Disability insurance	1,452,885	1,588,686	2,346,909	2,346,038	2,024,398
Uniform allowance	376,079	386,827	392,750	392,750	392,750
Medicare	154,730	160,868	200,058	198,739	198,739
Long-term disability	22,583	42,974	96,517	96,517	96,517
Subtotals	10,695,303	11,238,813	14,093,063	14,090,679	13,769,039
Services and supplies					
Office supplies	124,357	98,292	102,485	102,485	102,485
Operating supplies	454,563	296,569	540,661	540,661	540,661
Repair/maintenance	496,922	390,941	466,118	466,118	466,118
Small tools	98,508	1,576	24,175	24,175	24,175
Professional services	674,263	580,359	668,765	668,765	668,765
Communications	574,757	446,200	784,906	784,906	784,906
Services and supplies					
Public utilities	222,935	232,773	242,008	242,008	242,008
Rentals	162,840	192,294	226,071	226,071	226,071
Vehicle rentals	1,668,416	2,193,926	2,363,278	2,363,278	2,169,278
Extradition	40,955	44,411	40,000	40,000	40,000
Other travel	8,649	10,123	46,500	46,500	46,500
Advertising	4,662	4,570	8,100	8,100	8,100
Insurance	656,360	1,190,257	1,884,921	1,884,921	1,884,921
Books/manuals	32,285	24,813	24,404	24,404	24,404
Employee training	94,029	60,851	-0-	-0-	-0-
Aircraft expenses	-0-	-0-	30,000	30,000	30,000
Special inventory	22,527	26,465	30,000	30,000	30,000
Other services and supplies	2,386,201	2,039,651	2,386,201	2,386,201	2,386,201
Subtotals	7,723,229	7,834,071	9,868,593	9,868,593	9,868,593
Capital outlay					
Machinery and equipment	1,144,301	204,964	-0-	-0-	-0-
Totals	52,308,373	52,196,065	60,877,878	60,875,494	60,073,854

TABLE 15-3 A Police Department's Budget Status Report ($)

Line Item	Amount Budgeted	Expenses to Date	Amount Encumbered	Balance to Date	Percentage Used
Salaries	16,221,148	8,427,062.00	-0-	7,794,086.00	52.0
Professional services	334,765	187,219.61	8,014.22	139,531.17	58.3
Office supplies	51,485	16,942.22	3,476.19	31,066.59	39.7
Repair/maintenance	49,317	20,962.53	1,111.13	27,243.34	44.8
Communications	392,906	212,099.11	1,560.03	179,246.86	54.4
Utilities	121,008	50,006.15	10,952.42	60,049.43	51.4
Vehicle rentals	1,169,278	492,616.22	103,066.19	573,595.59	51.9
Travel	23,500	6,119.22	2,044.63	15,336.15	34.7
Extraditions	20,000	12,042.19	262.22	7,695.59	61.5
Printing/binding	36,765	15,114.14	2,662.67	18,988.19	48.4
Books/manuals	12,404	5,444.11	614.11	6,345.78	48.8
Training/education	35,695	19,661.54	119.14	15,914.32	55.4
Aircraft expenses	15,000	8,112.15	579.22	6,308.63	57.9
Special investigations	15,000	6,115.75	960.50	7,922.75	47.2
Machinery	1,000	275.27	27.50	697.23	30.3
Advertising	4,100	1,119.17	142.50	2,838.33	30.8

budget execution carrying out the organization's budgeted responsibilities in a proper manner and providing an accounting of the administrator's actions with same.

The third stage of the process, **budget execution**, has several objectives: (1) to carry out the organization's budgeted objectives for the fiscal year in an orderly manner, (2) to ensure that the agency undertakes no financial obligations or commitments other than those funded by the city or county council, and (3) to provide a periodic accounting of the administrator's stewardship over the agency's funds.[41]

Supervision of the budget execution phase is an executive function that requires some type of fiscal control system, usually directed by the city or county manager. Periodic reports on accounts are an important element of budget control; they serve to reduce the likelihood of overspending by identifying areas in which deficits are likely to occur as a result of change in gasoline prices, extensive overtime, natural disasters, and unplanned emergencies (such as riots). A periodic budget status report tells the administrator what percentage of the total budget has been expended to date (Table 15-3 ■).

The prudent criminal justice administrator normally attempts to manage the budget conservatively for the first 8 or 9 months of the budget year, holding the line on spending until most fiscal crises have been averted. Because unplanned incidents and natural disasters can wreak havoc with any budget, this conservatism is normally the best course. Then the administrator can plan the most efficient way to allocate funds if emergency funds have not been spent.

audit an objective examination of the financial statements of an organization, either by its employees or an outside firm.

Finally, budgets are subject to an **audit**, which means "to verify something independently."[42] The basic rationale for an audit of a budget—which is an objective examination of the financial statements of an organization, either by its employees or by an outside firm—was described by the controller general of the United States as follows:

> Governments and agencies entrusted with public resources and the authority for applying them have a responsibility to render a full accounting of their activities. This governmental accountability should identify not only the object for which the public resources have been devoted but also the manner and effect of their application.[43]

After the close of each budget year, the year's expenditures are audited to ensure that the agency spent its funds properly. Budget audits investigate three broad areas of accountability: financial accountability (focusing on proper fiscal operations and reports of the justice agency), management accountability (determining whether funds were utilized efficiently and economically), and program accountability (determining whether the unit of government's goals and objectives were accomplished).[44]

Furthermore, financial audits determine whether funds were spent legally, the budgeted amount was exceeded, and the financial process proceeded in a legal manner. For example, auditors investigate whether funds transferred between accounts were authorized, grant funds were used properly, computations were made accurately, disbursements were documented, financial transactions followed established procedures, and established competitive bidding procedures were employed.[45] Justice administrators should welcome auditors' help to identify weaknesses and deficiencies and correct them.

▶ Budget Formats

The three types of budgets primarily in use today are the **line-item budget** (or object-of-expenditure budget), the **performance budget**, and the program (or results or outcomes) budget. Two additional types, the planning–programming–budgeting system (PPBS) and the zero-based budget (ZBB), are also discussed in the literature but are used to a lesser extent. These terms are defined and discussed later in this chapter.

line-item budget a budget format that breaks down its components into major categories, such as personnel, equipment, contractual services, commodities, and capital outlay items.

performance budget a budget that reflects the input of resources and output of services for a unit in an organization.

The Line-Item Budget

Line-item budgeting (or *item budgeting*) is the most commonly used budget format. It is the basic system on which all other systems rely because it affords control. It is so named because it breaks down the budget into the major categories commonly used in government (e.g., personnel, equipment, contractual services, commodities, and capital outlay items); every amount of money requested, recommended, appropriated, and expended is associated with a particular item or class of items.[46] In addition, large budget categories are broken down into smaller line-item budgets (in a police department, examples include patrol, investigation, communications, and jail function). The line-item format fosters budgetary control because no item escapes scrutiny.[47] Table 15-2 ■, shown earlier, demonstrates a line-item budget for police, as do Tables 15-4 ■ for a court, 15-5 for probation and parole, and 15-6 for a state prison organization. Each demonstrates the range of activities and funding needs of each agency. Note in Tables 15-2 ■, 15-5, and 15-6 how a recession affected budgets and requests from year to year in many categories, resulting in budget reductions and even some total eliminations of items previously funded. Also note some of the ways in which administrators deviated from their usual practices to save money (e.g., the police budget shows that the department found it to be less expensive to lease patrol vehicles than to buy a huge fleet).

The line-item budget has several strengths and weaknesses. Its strengths include ease of control, development, comprehension (especially by elected and other executive branch officials), and administration. Weaknesses are its neglect of long-range planning and its limited ability to evaluate performance. Furthermore, the line-item budget tends to maintain the status quo; ongoing programs are seldom challenged. Line-item budgets are based on history: This year's allocation is based on last year's. Although that allows an inexperienced manager to prepare a budget more easily, it often precludes the reform-minded chief's careful deliberation and planning for the future.

The line-item budget provides ease of control because it clearly indicates the amount budgeted for each item, the amount expended as of a specific date, and the amount still available at that date (see, e.g., Table 15-4 ■).

Virtually all criminal justice agencies are automated to some extent, whether the financial officer prepares his or her budget using a computerized spreadsheet or a clerk

TABLE 15-4 Operating Budget for a District Court in a County of 100,000 Population

Category	Amount ($)
Salaries and wages	
Regular salaries	3,180,792
Part-time temporary	19,749
Incentive/longevity	70,850
Subtotal	3,271,391
Employee benefits	
Group insurance	270,100
Worker compensation	18,470
Unemployment compensation	33,220
Retirement	612,211
Social security	15,605
Medicare	23,503
Subtotal	973,109
Services and supplies	
Computers and office equipment	62,865
Service contracts	5,000
Minor furniture/equipment	2,000
Computer supplies	15,000
Continuous forms	8,000
Office supplies	86,066
Advertising	8,550
Copy machine expenses	80,000
Dues and registration	8,000
Printing	64,000
Telephone	106,000
Training	12,000
Court reporter/transcript	535,000
Court reporter per diem	465,000
Law books/supplements	19,000
Jury trials	575,000
Medical examinations	180,000
Computerized legal research	120,000
Travel	4,500
Subtotal	2,423,981
Child support	
Attorneys and other personnel	266,480
Court-appointed attorneys	1,656,000
Grand juries	88,600
Family court services	1,762,841
Total	8,974,823

TABLE 15-5 Probation and Parole Budget ($) for a State Serving 1 Million Population

Description	FY 2016–2017 Actual	FY 2017–2018 Agency Request	FY 2018–2019 Governor's Recommendation	Legislature Approved
Personnel	26,741,104	28,290,523	26,620,991	26,540,222
Travel	824,588	824,588	824,588	802,689
Operating expenses	2,307,020	2,395,484	2,307,020	2,256,787
Equipment	20,569	8,379	8,379	8,379
Loans to parolees	8,500	8,500	8,500	8,500
Training	18,073	18,073	18,073	18,073
Extraditions	400,000	400,000	400,000	285,000
Client drug tests	224,962	224,962	224,962	224,962
Home arrest fees	224,005	224,005	224,005	228,005
Community programs	100,000	100,000	100,000	87,500
Residential confinement	896,709	1,000,709	896,709	887,663
Utilities (paid by building lessors) Totals	31,765,530	33,495,223	31,633,227	31,347,780

TABLE 15-6 Operating Budget ($) for a State Medium Security Prison with 500 Inmates

Description	FY 2016–2017 Actual	FY 2017–2018 Agency Request	FY 2018–2019 Governor's Recommendation	Legislature Approved
Personnel				
Salaries	10,051,095	10,370,979	10,186,421	10,105,533
Worker's compensation	284,362	243,462	401,198	298,016
Retirement	2,142,010	2,174,968	2,215,674	2,196,028
Recruit tests	89,447	101,528	85,692	84,972
Insurance	874,330	888,250	1,013,000	1,000,175
Retirement insurance	60,963	61,872	65,917	65,349
Unemployment compensation	12,003	12,383	12,162	12,065
Overtime	265,856	-0-	-0-	-0-
Holiday pay	250,519	258,500	254,643	251,936
Medicare	69,965	85,140	82,225	80,948
Shift differential	185,925	201,011	188,553	186,828
Standby pay	12,465	12,807	12,641	12,526
Longevity pay	28,095	28,095	28,095	28,095
Subtotals	14,327,035	14,438,995	14,546,221	14,322,471
Services and supplies				
Operating supplies	280,672	477,495	280,647	414,859
Communications/freight	8,877	10,314	10,023	10,023
Printing/copying	40,900	87,222	29,016	41,527
Equipment repair	24,385	23,542	24,817	24,817
Vehicle operation	40,405	41,601	41,016	41,016
Uniforms—custody	218,122	205,976	203,237	213,856
Inmate clothing	142,436	284,790	142,430	166,167

(continued)

TABLE 15-6 *(continued)*

Description	FY 2016–2017 Actual	FY 2017–2018 Agency Request	FY 2018–2019 Governor's Recommendation	Legislature Approved
Equipment issued	40,403	23,236	25,451	27,086
Inmate wages	66,645	102,815	65,572	82,309
Food	1,695,897	2,299,838	1,695,759	2,065,403
Postage	14,738	16,793	14,036	14,738
Telephone	44,808	43,802	42,130	44,808
Subscriptions	682	801	1,425	801
Hand tools	210	486	213	213
Subtotals	2,619,180	3,618,711	2,575,772	3,147,623
Special equipment	216,863	64,088	22,557	23,661
Grounds maintenance	250,098	409,003	238,560	285,843
Inmate law library	28,564	40,115	26,419	41,836
Special projects	103,237	16,887	16,887	16,887
Gas and power	1,054,478	1,086,604	1,005,823	1,204,335
Water	120,390	129,377	102,266	127,171
Garbage	160,035	201,240	162,436	162,436
Canine unit	23,936	4,521	8,260	4,543
Total	18,903,816	20,009,541	18,705,201	19,336,833

enters information into a database that will be uploaded to a state's mainframe computer. Some justice agencies use an automated budgeting system that can store budget figures, make all necessary calculations for generating a budget request, monitor expenditures from budgets (similar to that shown in Table 15-7 ■), and even generate some reports.

The Performance Budget

The key characteristic of a performance budget is that it relates the volume of work to be done to the amount of money spent.[48] It is input–output oriented, and it increases the responsibility and accountability of the manager for output as opposed to input.[49] This format specifies an organization's activities, using a format similar to that of the line-item budget. It normally measures activities that are easily quantified such as the number of traffic citations issued, crimes solved, property recovered, cases heard in the courtroom, and caseloads of probation officers. These activities are then compared with those of the unit that performs at the highest level. The ranking according to activity attempts to allocate funds fairly. Following is an example from a police department: The commander of the traffic accident investigation unit requests an additional three investigators, which the chief approves. Later, the chief might compare the unit's output and costs to these measures before the three investigators were added to determine how this change affected productivity.[50] An example of a police performance budget is provided in Table 15-7 ■.

The performance budget format could be used in other justice system components as well. The courts could use performance measures, such as filing cases, writing opinions, disposing of cases, and accuracy of presentence investigations.

Advantages of the performance budget include a consideration of outputs, the establishment of the costs of various justice agency efforts, improved evaluation of programs and managers, an emphasis on efficiency, increased availability of information for decision

TABLE 15-7 **Example of a Police Performance Budget**

Category		Amount
Units/activities		
Administration (chief)	Subtotal	$
Strategic planning		$
Normative planning		$
Policies and procedures formulation, etc.		$
Patrol	Subtotal	$
Calls for service		$
Citizen contacts		$
Special details, etc.		$
Criminal investigation	Subtotal	$
Suspect apprehension		$
Recovery of stolen property		$
Transportation of fugitives, etc.		$
Traffic services	Subtotal	$
Accident investigation		$
Issuance of citations		$
Public safety speeches, etc.		$
Juvenile services	Subtotal	$
Locate runaways/missing juveniles		$
Arrest of offenders		$
Referrals and liaison, etc.		$
Research and development	Subtotal	$
Perform crime analysis		$
Prepare annual budget		$
Prepare annual reports, etc.		$

making, and the enhancement of budget justification and explanation.[51] The performance budget works best for an assembly line or other organization where work is easily quantifiable, such as paving streets. Its disadvantages include its expense to develop, implement, and operate because of the extensive use of cost accounting techniques and the need for additional staff (Figure 15-2 ■ illustrates the elements used to determine the cost of providing police services); the controversy surrounding attempts to determine appropriate workload and unit cost measures (in criminal justice, although many functions are quantifiable, such reduction of duties to numbers often translates into quotas, which are anathema to many people); its emphasis on efficiency rather than effectiveness; and the failure to lend itself to long-range planning.[52]

Determining which functions in criminal justice are more important (and should receive more financial support) is difficult; therefore, in terms of criminal justice agency budgets, the selection of meaningful work units is difficult and sometimes irrational. How can a justice agency measure its successes? How can it count what does not happen?

The Program Budget

The best-known type of budget for monitoring the activities of an organization is the **program budget**, developed by the RAND Corporation for the U.S. Department of Defense. This format examines cost units as units of activity rather than as units and subunits within the organization. This budget becomes a planning tool; it demands

program budget
a budget format that examines cost units as units of activity rather than as units and subunits within the organization.

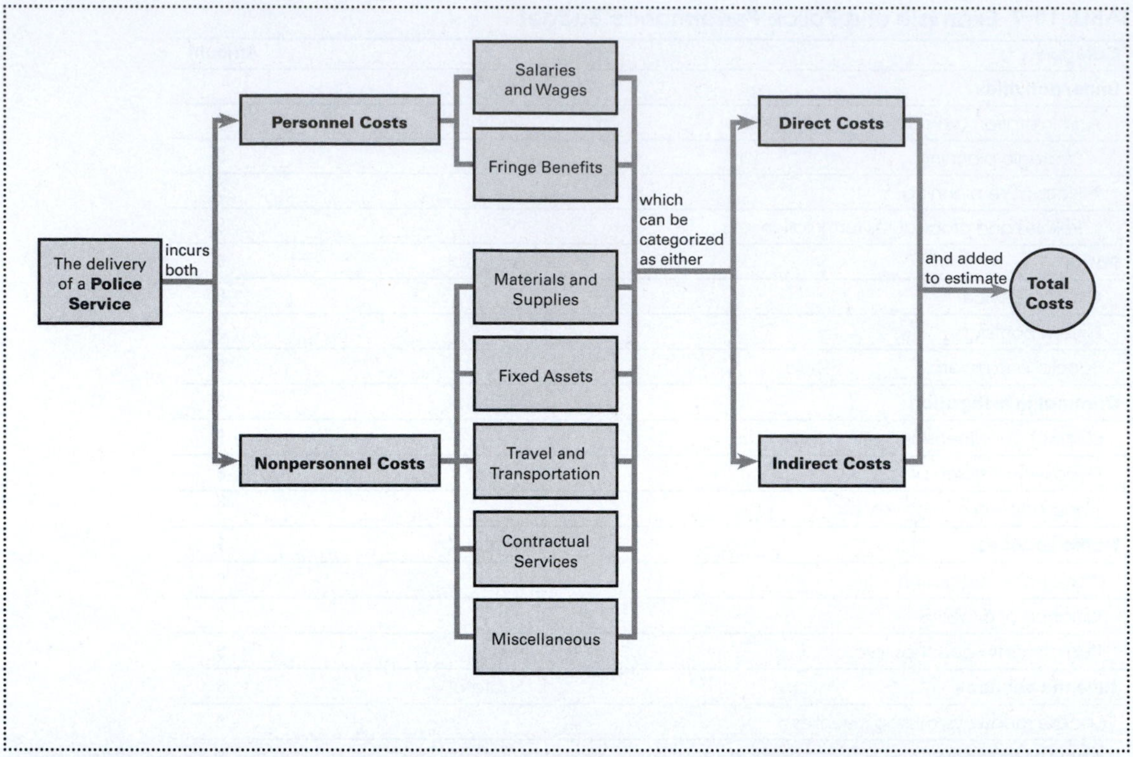

FIGURE 15-2 Elements in the Total Costs for Police Services
Source: U.S. Department of Justice, National Institute of Justice, *Measuring the Costs of Police Services* (Washington, DC: 1982), p. 20.

justification for expenditures for new programs and for deleting old ones that have not met their objectives.

Police agencies probably have greater opportunities for creating new community-based programs than do the courts or corrections agencies. Some of these include crime prevention and investigation, drug abuse education, home security, selective enforcement (e.g., drunk driving) programs, and career development for personnel. Each of these endeavors requires instructional materials or special equipment, all of which must be budgeted. For example, traffic crash investigations (TCI) may be a cost area. The program budget emphasizes output measures. Outputs for TCI include the number of accidents handled and enforcement measures taken (such as citations issued, driving under the influence of alcohol and/or drugs (DUI) and other types of arrests made, and public safety speeches given). If the budget for these programs were divided by the units of output, the administrator could determine the relative cost for each unit of output or productivity. The cost of TCI, however, entails more than just the TCI unit; patrol and other support units also engage in this program.

Thus, the program budget is an extremely difficult form to execute and administer because it requires tracking the time of all personnel by activity as well as figuring in the cost of all support services and supplies. For this reason, criminal justice agencies rarely use the program budget.[53] Some advantages of the program budget, however, include its emphasis on the social utility of programs conducted by the agency; its clear relationship between policy objectives and expenditures; its ability to provide

TABLE 15-8 Example of a Police Program Budget

Program Area		Amount
Crime prevention	Subtotal	$
Salaries and benefits		$
Operating expenses		$
Capital outlay		$
Miscellaneous		$
Traffic crash investigation	Subtotal	$
Salaries and benefits		$
Operating expenses		$
Capital outlay		$
Miscellaneous		$
Traffic crash prevention	Subtotal	$
Salaries and benefits		$
Operating expenses		$
Capital outlay		$
Miscellaneous		$
Criminal investigation	Subtotal	$
Salaries and benefits		$
Operating expenses		$
Capital outlay		$
Miscellaneous		$
Juvenile delinquency prevention	Subtotal	$
Salaries and benefits		$
Operating expenses		$
Capital outlay		$
Miscellaneous		$
Special investigations	Subtotal	$
Salaries and benefits		$
Operating expenses		$
Capital outlay		$
Miscellaneous, Etc.		$

justification for and explanation of the budget; its establishment of a high degree of accountability; and its format and the wide involvement in formulating objectives, which lead employees at all levels of the organization to understand more thoroughly the importance of their roles and actions.[54]

Examples of police and court program budgets are presented in Tables 15-8 ■ and 15-9, respectively.

PPBS and ZBB Formats

General Motors used the PPBS as early as in 1924,[55] and the RAND Corporation contributed to its development in a series of studies dating from 1949.[56] By the mid-1950s, several states were using it, and Secretary Robert McNamara introduced PPBS into the

TABLE 15-9 Example of a Court's Program Budget

Program Area		Amount
Adjudicate criminal cases	Subtotal	$
Adjudicate felony cases	Total	$
Adjudicate misdemeanor appeals	Total	$
Adjudicate civil cases	Subtotal	$
Adjudicate major civil cases	Total	$
Adjudicate minor civil cases	Total	$
Adjudicate domestic relations cases	Total	$
Adjudicate juvenile cases	Subtotal	$
Adjudicate delinquency and dependent and neglect cases	Total	$
Adjudicate crimes against juveniles	Total	$
Provide alternatives to adjudication	Subtotal	$
Divert adult offenders	Total	$
Divert juvenile offenders	Total	$
Provide security	Subtotal	$
Handle prisoner transport	Total	$
Provide courtroom security	Total	$

Source: U.S. Department of Justice, National Institute of Law Enforcement and Criminal Justice, *Financial Management* (Washington, DC: The American University, 1979), p. 41.

Defense Department in the mid-1960s.[57] By 1971, a survey revealed, however, that only 28 percent of the cities and 21 percent of the counties contacted had implemented PPBS or significant elements of it,[58] and in 1971 the federal government announced that it was discontinuing its use.

planning-programming-budgeting system (PPBS) a budgeting tool that links program to the ways and means of facilitating the program and better informing decision makers of outcomes of their actions.

PPBS is a decision-making tool that links the program under consideration to the ways and means of facilitating the program. It is thus "a long-term planning tool, better informing decision makers of the future implications of their actions, and is typically most useful in capital projects."[59] PPBS treats the three basic budget processes—planning, management, and control—as coequals. It was predicated on the primacy of planning.[60] This future orientation transformed budgeting from an annual ritual into a "formulation of future goals and policies."[61] The PPBS budget featured a program structure, **ZBB**, the use of cost-budget analysis to distinguish among alternatives, and a budgetary horizon, often 5 years.[62]

zero-based budget (ZBB) a budget format that requires managers to justify their entire budget request in detail, rather than simply using budget amounts established in previous years.

Associated with PPBS, the zero-based planning and budgeting process requires managers to justify their entire budget request in detail rather than simply to refer to budget amounts established in previous years.[63] That is, each year, all budgets begin at zero and must justify any funding. Following Peter Phyrr's use of ZBB at Texas Instruments, Governor Jimmy Carter adopted it in Georgia in the early 1970s and then as president implemented it in the federal government for fiscal year 1979. An analysis of this experience at the Department of Agriculture indicates that although its use saved $200,000 in the department's budget, it costs at least 180,000 labor hours of effort to develop.[64]

It is important to note that few organizations have budgets that are purely one format or another; therefore, it is not unusual to find that because of time, tradition, and personal preferences, a combination of several formats is used.

IN THEIR OWN WORDS

ADMINISTRATIVE ADVICE FROM THE FIELD

Name: Terri Genin

Current position/City/State: Finance Manager, Madison Police Department, Madison, Wisconsin

College attended/academic major/degree(s): University of Illinois/Nursing/B.S.N.

My primary duties and responsibilities in this position include: development, analysis, and management of the $63,500,000 annual police operating budget, oversight of payroll and purchasing functions, and management of multiple state and federal grants. Responsibilities also include serving on the department's Management Team and providing professional analytical expertise in the department's strategic planning efforts.

Personal attributes/characteristics that have proven to be most helpful to me in this position are: creativity combined with the ability to breakdown plans into small components that are more readily funded than large initiatives.

My three greatest challenges in this administrative role include:

1. Police organizations rotate command level employees on a regular basis. This rotation often results in commanders with limited financial skills that have responsibility for obtaining and managing various resources, including finances. The end result is a constant need to be training police command staff in how to be successful in managing money and obtaining support for their initiatives.
2. Elected officials often have an extremely unrealistic point of view in regards to what a police department can do to adapt to dwindling financial resources. It is very challenging to clearly explain what is realistically possible without creating barriers for future needs. In addition, the constant focus of elected officials on "boots on the street" often results in lack of resources for critical support areas, such as technology, which are necessary for officers to be effective in their work.
3. The ongoing environment of annual budget cuts has created considerable challenges in all aspects of policing. Officers and other police employees are continually being asked to provide more service with less resource options. This can often result in competition for resources and an increased level of frustration as highly motivated employees are limited in providing optimal service by a lack of funds.

Personal accomplishments during my administrative career about which I am most proud are: (1) coordinating the transition of payroll and scheduling from paper to a computerized system; (2) developing clear, concise reporting systems to effectively provide information to elected officials so that they have developed confidence in, and an understanding of, how police overtime is utilized. This has eliminated considerable acrimony and provided a framework for authorization to implement new initiatives; (3) updating grant tracking systems so that numerous federal and state grants are coordinated across several disciplines and audit reviews have resulted in positive feedback.

Advice for someone who is interested in occupying an administrative position such as mine would be: get to know rank-and-file employees, as they often have great information about potential improvements and/or new possibilities. Listen well and ask a lot of questions so that you are well prepared to explain thoroughly when others raise questions of you. Be creative. There is often more than one way to obtain resources and/or needed support for programs and initiatives, so explore a wide variety of options and timelines to obtain resources. Sometimes very simple "fixes" are more helpful to an officer than complex programs and/or purchases. Take the time and effort to educate rank-and-file officers on process and limitations as they relate to administrative functions, as this will result in greater "buy in" and reduced frustration.

Source: Used with permission from Terri Genin

Summary

This chapter has laid out the fundamentals of financial administration in criminal justice administration, to include strategies for analyzing workload, surveying other agencies in seeing what "competitors" are doing, and increasing and stretching resources. Examples were given of reducing costs and legislative enactments that are intended to reform justice system operations and budgets. This chapter's primary focus, however, was on the very important area of budgeting and included its elements, formats, and potential pitfalls. Emphases were placed on some of the lasting effects of the recent Great Recession as well as the need for administrators to develop skill in budget formulation and execution.

This chapter, in looking at the budget process and different types of budgets, noted that no single budgeting format is best; through tradition and personal preference, a hybrid format normally evolves in an organization. Nor should an administrator, under normal circumstances, surrender control of the organization's budget to another individual or body; the budget is integral to planning, organizing, and directing programs and operations.

Clearly, in these times of fiscal exigency, the justice administrator should attempt to become knowledgeable about, and recommend, sound means for reducing expenditures through changes in policy.

Key Terms and Concepts

Audit, p. 406
Budget, p. 400
Budget cycle, p. 401
Budget execution, p. 406
Budget formulation, p. 401
Civilianization, p. 396
Expenditure, p. 401
Fiscal year, p. 401
Great Recession, p. 395
Line-item budget, p. 407
Performance budget, p. 407
Planning–programming–budgeting system (PPBS), p. 414
Program budget, p. 411
Strategic planning, p. 398
Workload analysis, p. 396
Zero-based budget (ZBB), p. 414

Questions for Review

1. What are some basic purposes of, and measures in, performing a workload analysis?
2. What are some pros and cons of using civilians to stretch agency budgets? Obtaining grants?
3. What is strategic planning, and what role does it play in financial administration?
4. How are courts' budgets unique, and how must judges approach their getting funded?
5. What did California's Proposition 47 do to bring about fiscal reform?
6. What is a budget? How is it used?
7. What is a budget cycle? What is its importance in budgeting?
8. What is involved in formulating a budget? In its approval and execution?
9. Of the four budget formats used in the past, which type is used most frequently? What are its major advantages and component parts?

Deliberate and Decide

Brainstorming the Budget

Your city of 650,000 people and nearly 7,000 employees is in dire financial straits, with no end in sight unless bold actions are taken. The city or county council has held several public hearings to consider alternative courses of action to get out of the fiscal doldrums, but most such meetings result in very little agreement on how to resolve the problems.

Questions for Discussion

Look at the following options that have been proposed and debated, and *determine the pros and cons and possible ramifications of each*, as well as the numbers of citizens who would be positively or negatively affected if implemented:

1. Whether or not to lease 150 traffic speed cameras in school zones, which could generate $29 million in the first year alone.

2. Whether or not to terminate 350 city employees—about 5 percent of the total—from the city's payroll for a savings of about $25 million; or, alternatively, lay off 100 employees and offer voluntary buyouts for 300 employees for a total cost of $14 million; or simply let them leave or retire on their own terms, which would save $15 million.
3. Whether or not to restore a 4.6 percent pay cut taken from city employees 2 years ago, which would cost about $20 million.
4. Whether or not to eliminate vacant, nonpublic-safety positions ($2.6 million savings), reduce the materials and supplies budgets for all city divisions ($3.3 million savings), and reduce some health care expenses ($3.4 million).
5. Whether or not to raise property tax rates for all citizens.
6. Whether or not, as suggested by one council member, to discontinue other non-state mandated responsibilities, such as eliminating the police department and turn over those duties to the county sheriff's office.[65]

Learn by Doing

1. You are in the research and planning division of your state department of corrections. Fiscal issues are becoming a great concern as more state funding has been diverted to homeland security and court initiatives. Your director asks for some general ideas concerning what sorts of sentencing, treatment, parole, and prisoner reentry programs are being developed in similarly strapped states. What kinds of information and examples will you provide?
2. You are an assistant sheriff and thus jail administrator in a county that has only raised the tax rate in recent years to pay for jail improvements required by state and federal authorities. However, your county now finds itself in dire financial straits, primarily because the fragile "no new taxes" and a "lock 'em up" mentality have finally combined to make fiscal matters extremely tenuous. Your judges are generally sympathetic, using a Jail Alternatives Program (intensive probation, a drug court and other options) for misdemeanants to the extent possible in order to save the cost of incarcerating and transporting jail inmates. It is estimated that these programs have reduced your jail population by more than 200 people. Now, however, one of the local judges seems bent on sentencing to jail anyone who is behind on child support payments—which accounts for around 150 people in the program. It becomes clear that this policy will soon cause the jail population to explode and break the county's jail budget. You know the judge personally. What will you do to save the county's jail budget?

Case Study

The chief of police in a small (20,000 population) city has seen nearly one-third of the agency's officers leave in the last year. Budget cuts, attrition, and better salaries in other regional agencies have been the impetus for the departures. Furthermore, the city council is proposing a 15 percent cut in the police budget for the coming year. Citizens are already complaining about delays in police responses and about having to drive to the police department to make complaints or to file reports. The county sheriff has offered in the local newspaper to consolidate with the agency, or at least provide backup for the city when needed, but the chief of police believes the sheriff to be power hungry and primarily motivated by a desire to absorb the city's police force into his agency. Severe cutbacks have already been made in the Drug Abuse and Resistance Education (DARE) and gang prevention programs, and other nonessential services have been terminated. A number of concerts, political rallies, and outdoor events—all of which typically involve a number of arrests—will be held soon during the summer months and require considerable overtime. Federal grants have run out.

One of the chief's staff suggests that the chief propose to the city council a drastic reduction in the city's parks, streets, or fire department budget, those monies being transferred to the police budget. The council, in turn, already wants to explore the possibility of hiring private security services for some events. Exacerbating the situation is the fact that violent crimes are increasing in the jurisdiction.

Questions for Discussion

1. What measures could the chief implement or propose to the council to slow or eliminate the resignations of sworn personnel?
2. How might the chief obtain more revenues or, alternatively, realize some savings for the department?
3. Should the chief go public with the idea of reducing budgets in the parks or other city departments?
4. How should the chief deal with the local sheriff's offer for consolidation or assistance?

Notes

1. Bureau of Justice Statistics, *Justice Expenditure and Employment Extracts 2012*, 2012 preliminary Tables, JEEUS1201 (February 26, 2015), NCJ 248628.
2. Quoted in Charles R. Swanson, Leonard Territo, and Robert W. Taylor, *Police Administration: Structures, Processes, and Behavior,* 6th ed. (Upper Saddle River, NJ: Prentice Hall, 2005), p. 682.
3. Jeremy M. Wilson and Alexander Weiss, *A Performance-based Approach to Police Staffing and Allocation* (Washington, DC: Office of Community Oriented Policing Services, August 2012), http://a-capp.msu.edu/sites/default/files/files/041218461_Performance_Based_Approach_Police_Staffing_FINAL100112.pdf.
4. Charles K. Coe and Deborah L. Weisel, "Police Budgeting: Winning Strategies," *Public Administration Review* 61(6): 718–727.
5. As an example, see National Center for State Courts, "Colorado Court of Appeals Workload Analysis: Final Report," 2005, http://cdm16501.contentdm.oclc.org/cdm/ref/collection/ctadmin/id/1097.
6. National Institute of Corrections, *Prison Staffing Analysis: A Training Manual*, December 2008, p. 17, http://www.asca.net/system/assets/attachments/2086/staffing_analysis-1-3.pdf?1296162143.
7. For the police, see Ibid.; also see James McCabe, *An Analysis of Police Department Staffing: How Many Officers Do You Really Need?* (Washington, DC: International City/County Management Association, n.d.); for courts, see National Center for State Courts, *Workload and Resource Assessment: Resource Guide*, http://www.ncsc.org/Topics/Court-Management/Workload-and-Resource-Assessment/Resource-Guide.aspx; for corrections, particularly prisons, see National Institute of Corrections, op cit., *Prison Staffing Analysis: A Training Manual.*
8. Coe and Weisel, "Police Budgeting," p. 725.
9. Ibid., p. 723.
10. Ibid.
11. See Bureau of Justice Assistance, "The BJA Grant Writing and Management Academy," https://www.bja.gov/gwma/index.html.
12. Bureau of Justice Assistance, "Drug Court Discretionary Grant Program for United States Substance Abusers," https://www.bja.gov/Publications/2014NADCP-BJApresentation.pdf; also see http://grants.ojp.usdoj.gov:85/selector/awardDetail?awardNumber=2010-DD-BX-0537&fiscalYear=2010&applicationNumber=2010-H8086-NJ-D1&programOffice=BJA&po=BJA; Ibid., "Drug Court Discretionary Grant Program," https://www.bja.gov/ProgramDetails.aspx?Program_ID=58.
13. Office of Justice Programs, "About Us," http://www.ojp.gov/about/about.htm.
14. Pubic Law No. 113-4.
15. Office on Violence Against Women, "VAWA 2014 Summary: Changes to OVW-Administered Grant Programs," http://www.ovw.usdoj.gov/docs/vawa-2014-sum.pdf.
16. See Office of Juvenile Justice and Delinquency Prevention, "Funding," https://www.ojjdp.gov/funding/funding.html.
17. Note that while this website focuses on police agencies, most if not all of the recommendations and steps in the process will apply to courts and corrections agencies as well. See Policegrantshelp.com, "Grants 101: A Beginner's Guide to Helping Your Department Get Grants," http://www.policegrantshelp.com/grants101/.
18. "Civilianization May Improve Police Effectiveness in the Face of Budget Crisis," *Envisage Technologies*, March 29, 2016, http://www.envisagenow.com/civilianization-may-improve-police-effectiveness-in-face-of-budget-crisis/.
19. Coe and Weisel, "Police Budgeting," p. 719.
20. Ibid.
21. Internet Nonprofit Center, *What Is Strategic Planning?* (San Francisco, CA: Author, 2000), p. 1.
22. U.S. Department of Justice, *Strategic Plan, Fiscal Years 2014-2018* (n.d.), https://www.justice.gov/sites/default/files/jmd/legacy/2014/02/28/doj-fy-2014-2018-strategic-plan.pdf.
23. Police Executive Research Forum, *Policing and the Economic Downturn*, pp. 13–19, http://www.policeforum.org/assets/docs/Critical_Issues_Series/policing%20and%20the%20economic%20downturn%20-%20striving%20for%20efficiency%20is%20the%20new%20normal%202013.pdf.
24. National Center for State Courts, "State of the Judiciary Quotes Related to Budgetary Issues," http://www.ncsc.org/Information-and-Resources/Budget-Resource-Center/Budget_Funding/State-of-the-Judiciary-Quotes-Related-to-Budgetary-Issues.aspx.
25. See, for example, Bryan Lowry, "Kansas District Judge Sues State Over Court Budget Law," *The Wichita Eagle*, February 18, 2015, http://www.kansas.com/news/local/crime/article10626146.html; *City of Sparks v. Sparks Municipal Court*, 129 Nev., Advance Opinion (2013).
26. National Center for State Courts, *Funding Justice: Strategies and Messages for Restoring Court Funding* (Washington, DC: Author, 2012), pp. 10–13.
27. Bureau of Justice Statistics, *Correctional Populations in the United States, 2014*, January 21, 2016, pp. 1–2, http://www.bjs.gov/content/pub/pdf/cpus14.pdf.
28. Bureau of Justice Statistics, *Justice Expenditure and Employment Extracts 2012*, 2012 preliminary Tables, JEEUS1201 (February 26, 2015), NCJ 248628.
29. Michael Mitchell and Michael Leachman, "Changing Priorities: State Criminal Justice Reforms and Investments in Education," *Center on Budget and Policy Priorities*, October 28, 2014, http://www.cbpp.org/research/changing

-priorities-state-criminal-justice-reforms-and-investments-in-education.

30. Nancy G. Le Vigne, Samuel Bieler, Lindsey Cramer, Helen Ho, Cybele Kotonias, Debbie Mayer, Dave McClure, Laura Pacifici, Erika Parks, Bryce Peterson, and Julie Samuels, "Justice Reinvestment Initiative State Assessment Report," Urban Institute, Bureau of Justice Assistance, January 2014, http://www.urban.org/research/publication/justice-reinvestment-initiative-state-assessment-report; also see California Department of Corrections and Rehabilitation, "What You Need to Know About Proposition 47," http://www.cdcr.ca.gov/news/prop47.html.
31. James C. Snyder, "Financial Management and Planning in Local Government," *Atlanta Economic Review* (November–December 1973): 43–47.
32. Aaron Wildavsky, *The Politics of the Budgetary Process,* 2nd ed. (Boston, MA: Little, Brown, 1974), pp. 1–4.
33. Orin K. Cope, "Operation Analysis—The Basis for Performance Budgeting," in *Performance Budgeting and Unit Cost Accounting for Governmental Units* (Chicago, IL: Municipal Finance Officers Association, 1954), p. 8.
34. Lester R. Bittel, *The McGraw-Hill 36-Hour Management Course* (New York: McGraw-Hill, 1989).
35. Ibid., p. 187.
36. Robert Townsend, *Further Up the Organization: How to Stop Management from Stifling People and Strangling Productivity* (New York: Alfred A. Knopf, 1984), p. 2.
37. Roland N. McKean, *Public Spending* (New York: McGraw-Hill, 1968), p. 1.
38. Michael C. Thomsett, *The Little Black Book of Budgets and Forecasts* (New York: AMACOM, American Management Association, 1988), p. 38.
39. Swanson et al., *Police Administration,* p. 693.
40. Adapted, with some changes, from Wildavsky, *Politics of the Budgetary Process,* pp. 63–123.
41. Lennox L. Moak and Kathryn W. Killian, *A Manual of Techniques for the Preparation, Consideration, Adoption, and Administration of Operating Budgets* (Chicago, IL: Municipal Finance Officers Association, 1973), p. 5, with changes.
42. Lennis M. Knighton, "Four Keys to Audit Effectiveness," *Governmental Finance* 8 (September 1979): 3.
43. The Comptroller General of the United States, *Standards for Audit of Governmental Organizations, Programs, Activities, and Functions* (Washington, DC: General Accounting Office, 1972), p. 1.
44. Ibid.
45. Peter F. Rousmaniere (ed.), *Local Government Auditing* (New York: Council on Municipal Performance, 1979), Tables 1 and 2, pp. 10, 14.
46. Swanson et al., *Police Administration,* p. 707.
47. Allen Schick, *Budget Innovation in the States* (Washington, DC: Brookings Institution, 1971), pp. 14–15. Schick offers 10 ways in which the line-item budget fosters control.
48. Malchus L. Watlington and Susan G. Dankel, "New Approaches to Budgeting: Are They Worth the Cost?" *Popular Government* 43 (Spring 1978): 1.
49. Jesse Burkhead, *Government Budgeting* (New York: Wiley, 1956), p. 11.
50. Larry K. Gaines, John L. Worrall, Mittie D. Southerland, and John E. Angell, *Police Administration,* 2nd ed. (New York: McGraw-Hill, 2003), p. 519.
51. Swanson et al., *Police Administration,* p. 710.
52. Ibid., p. 711.
53. Gaines et al., *Police Administration,* p. 519.
54. Ibid.
55. David Novick (ed.), *Program Budgeting* (New York: Holt, Rinehart and Winston, 1969), p. xxvi.
56. Ibid., p. xxiv.
57. Council of State Governments, *State Reports on Five-Five-Five* (Chicago, IL: Author, 1968).
58. International City Management Association, *Local Government Budgeting, Program Planning and Evaluation* (Washington, DC: Author, 1972), p. 7.
59. Democracy Arsenal, "Increasing Our Security by Cutting Military Spending," http://www.democracyarsenal.org/2010/05/increasing-our-security-by-cutting-military-spending.html.
60. Allen Schick, "The Road to PPBS: The Stages of Budget Reform," *Public Administration Review* 26 (December 1966): 244.
61. Ibid.
62. Swanson et al., *Police Administration,* p. 712.
63. Peter A. Phyrr, "Zero-Base Budgeting," *Harvard Business Review* (November–December 1970): 111–121; see also E. A. Kurbis, "The Case for Zero-Base Budgeting," *CA Magazine* (April 1986): 104–105.
64. Joseph S. Wholey, *Zero-Base Budgeting and Program Evaluation* (Lexington, MA: Lexington Books, 1978), p. 8.
65. Adapted from Toby Sells, "City Council Budget Meeting: Lots of Ideas, No Easy Solutions," Scripps International Paper Group–Online, June 18, 2014, http://www.commercialappeal.com/news/2014/jun/18/city-council-budget-meeting-lots-of-ideas-no/; also see Linda Moore, "Memphis' Financial Woes Impact All of Shelby County," Scripps International Paper Group–Online, June 18, 2014, https://www.commercialappeal.com/news/2014/jun/18/memphis-financial-woes-impact-all-of-shelby/?print=1.

Oleg Zabielin/Shutterstock

16 Protecting the Homeland: Foremost Challenges for Police Chief Executives

LEARNING OBJECTIVES

After reading this chapter, the student will be able to:

1. *review the "faces" of terrorism, to include a definition, its international nature, and threats posed by homegrown extremists and lone-wolf terrorists*
2. *describe the threats posed by different types of weapons of mass destruction*
3. *relate how law enforcement has had to adapt and evolve for combating terrorism*
4. *understand the legislative measures that have been enacted in the war against terrorism*

5. *determine whether or not the use of unmanned aerial vehicles (drones) is legal and beneficial*
6. *describe the role of local police and social media in providing homeland security*

Introduction

Since September 11, 2001, there has been no cessation of attempts by would-be terrorists to attack people, significant buildings, and military objects in the United States, and bring international terrorism to our homeland. Indeed, it is no doubt a credit to those persons in our law enforcement and legislative arenas that there has not been another similar attack during these intervening years. This is the age of the determined terrorist, and the future of terrorism involves much more than planting a relatively harmless virus in a computer system or hacking into a major corporation's voicemail system.

Protecting our homeland requires specialized training and awareness for police officers of all ranks and employment of individuals with specialized, highly technological backgrounds. If the police are not prepared, these crimes could become the Achilles' heel of our society.

Even where the best-laid plans exist, we remain vulnerable—as seen in April 2013 when two **homegrown violent extremists** (defined below), al-Qaeda-influenced brothers detonated two bombs at the Boston Marathon (killing 3 people and injuring 264). Then, a December 2016 holiday party at the Inland Regional Center in San Bernardino erupted in gunfire leaving 14 dead and 22 injured; reports suggested that the planned attack was eerily similar to the bombing in Boston.[1]

What can be done (if anything) to prevent such attacks? How has law enforcement at all levels evolved to cope with such determined people bent on radicalized religious fanaticism? This chapter attempts to answer those questions.

First, we consider the international nature of terrorism and its many "faces," to include homegrown and self-radicalized lone-wolf extremists in the United States and a discussion of several types of weapons of mass destruction (nuclear, biological, chemical, conventional, and cyber). Then, we examine how law enforcement's roles and strategies have adjusted for combating terrorism, to include what federal agencies are doing, a review of legislative measures that have been enacted, and a consideration of whether the use of unmanned aerial vehicles (drones) is legal and beneficial. The role of local police is then covered, including the need for their ongoing vigilance and using social media to respond efficiently to terrorist attacks. Review questions and exercises in the Deliberate and Decide, Learn by Doing, and Case Study sections conclude the chapter.

In sum, this chapter generally sets forth the general nature of terroristic threats that law enforcement executives and other practitioners must be aware of, their new role in combatting terrorism, and the kinds of tools and practices that are available to them if they are to have even a rudimentary chance of being prepared for, and coping with what will surely be the next terrorist attack.

An International Problem

The Federal Bureau of Investigation (FBI) succinctly defines terrorism as the "unlawful use of force against persons or property to intimidate or coerce a government, the civilian population, or any segment thereof, in furtherance of political or social objectives."[2] Terrorism is defined in Title 22 of the U.S. Code, Section 2656f(d), as "premeditated, politically motivated violence perpetrated against noncombatant targets by subnational groups or clandestine agents, usually intended to influence an audience." More broadly, terrorism can be both domestic and international in nature; definitions for both are provided in the United States Code (see endnotes).[3]

According to the Global Terrorism Database, since 1970 there have been nearly 2,700 incidents involving terrorism in the United States that have involved assassination, hostage taking, armed/unarmed assault, bombing, and hijacking. This compares with nearly 15,000 such incidents occurring around the globe.[4]

At present, the most brutal terrorist organization in the world—born from an especially brutal al-Qaeda faction—is the Islamic State of Iraq and Syria (ISIS), which has become the target of a major U.S. military operation and now dominates headlines around the world.[5] Since declaring its caliphate in June 2014, the Islamic State has conducted or been involved with more than 140 terrorist attacks in 29 countries; this figure excludes such attacks in Iraq and Syria, where the carnage has taken a much deadlier toll (killing more than 2,000 people and injuring thousands more).[6] Furthermore, the year 2017 came with no perceptible letup in such attacks, including a suicide bomber in Aleppo, Syria driving into a bus convoy carrying refugees and killing at least 125 people (including 68 children);[7] indeed, the first four months of 2017 would see 387 attacks in foreign nations resulting in 2,456 fatalities.[8]

Not even the police are immune from ISIS's long reach and deadly attacks. In April 2017, a police officer died after a man with a machine gun leaped out of a car and opened fire on a police bus on Paris's most famous boulevard, the Champs-Elysees, during the French presidential election campaign. ISIS rapidly took credit for the attack, which was carried out by a French national with a long and violent criminal record (he was shot dead as he tried to make his escape).[9]

ISIS and other international terrorist (see U.S. Code definition in Note 3) groups have become more adept at recruiting "foot soldiers" through the Internet and other means—and these attacks have become increasingly focused on civilian targets, with terrorists using more traditional methods of violence such as guns and hostage taking rather than large-scale bombings.

These and other attacks also demonstrated the need for the nation's law enforcement agencies to become much more knowledgeable about terrorists' methods here and abroad, how to predict and possibly prevent future attacks, how to respond when terrorists do strike, and the importance of adopting a long-term broader view of protecting the homeland.[10]

Two Faces of U.S. Terrorism: Homegrown and Lone-Wolf Extremists

As has been demonstrated in the United States, terrorist acts can take many forms and do not always involve bombs and guns; as examples, environmental and animal activists seek to further their agendas by burning greenhouses, tree farms, logging sites, ski resorts, and mink farms. Terrorist acts are also perpetrated by hate-filled white supremacists and anti-government extremists and radical separatist groups. Such acts are often carried out by two types of terrorists that are of particular concern in the United States: the homegrown and the lone-wolf extremists, discussed next.

In December 2015, a husband and wife wearing military-style clothing and black masks entered a Christmas party for employees of the San Bernardino, California, county health department and opened fire with two assault-style weapons, killing 14 people in what was the most deadly terrorist attack in the United States since 9/11. The man and woman were parents and college graduates, solidly middle class and *sans* criminal record, and typical homegrown jihadists. And, like all other such jihadists in the United States, they were not formally affiliated with a foreign terrorist group. Such jihadists—predominantly male (93%) and averaging 29 years of age—killed 45 Americans from 2010 through 2015.[11]

Of particular concern in the United States today are such **homegrown violent extremists** (HVEs, such as the Boston bombers mentioned above), who encourage, endorse, condone, justify, or support the commission of a violent criminal act in order to achieve a political, ideological, religious, social, or economic goal. The threat posed by HVE terrorists is so daunting that in April 2017, former Department of Homeland Security secretary John Kelly admitted that he had no idea how to stop them, despite their being the "most common" threat facing the United States. (Kelly added that another threat that keeps him awake at night is the "threat against aviation," or the possibility that terrorists might shoot down an American airplane in flight.)[12] Such HVEs can include U.S.-born citizens, naturalized citizens, green card holders or other long-term residents, foreign students, or illegal immigrants wishing to commit terrorist acts inside Western countries or against Western interests abroad. Some might have been inspired by calls by the Islamic State of Iraq and the Levant (ISIL) for individual jihadists in the West to retaliate for U.S.-led airstrikes on ISIL.[13]

Homegrown violent extremists individuals who commit terrorists acts in the country they reside, but who are inspired by foreign terrorist organizations.

According to Michael Morell, twice an acting director of the Central Intelligence Agency, there is now a compelling threat from the Islamic State (ISIS) on U.S. soil: 3,500 to 5,000 "jihadist wannabes" have traveled from the United States, Western Europe, Canada, and other countries to Syria and Iraq to gain battlefield experience and have easy access to the U.S. homeland (part of at least 20,000 foreign nationals from about 90 countries who have joined ISIS). Morell states that while an attack in the United States from such fighters at the direction of ISIS has not yet occurred, "... it will." Indeed, in November 2014, an individual with sympathies for ISIS attacked two New York City police officers with a hatchet.[14]

Another type of terrorist who poses serious concern is the self-radicalized, homegrown and lone offender—individuals who appear ordinary but are driven to hateful attacks based on a particular set of beliefs without a larger group's knowledge or support.

EXHIBIT 16.1

LONE-WOLF TERRORIST ATTACK

On July 16, 2015, Muhammad Youssef Abdulazeez attacked military recruiting centers in Chattanooga, Tennessee, killing four marines. Abdulazeez first drove by the center and opened fire. He then went back to the center and opened fire and continued firing shooting 30 to 45 rounds. James Comey, then director of the FBI, stated that the shooting was motivated by terrorist propaganda. Abdulazeez ultimately was killed by responding police officers.

This incident demonstrates the randomness of lone-wolf shootings. They essentially can occur anywhere. Police departments must be able to respond at a moment's notice. Lone-wolf shootings require that police departments have response plans in place.

Source: Based on Fausset, Richard, Alan Blinder and Michael S. Schmidt, "Gunman Kills 4 Marines at Military Site in Chattanooga," New York Times, July 16, 2015.

As secretary of the Department of Homeland Security Jeh Johnson stated:

> We worry about the potential domestic-based, home-grown terrorist threat that may be lurking in our own society — the independent actor or "**lone wolf**"—those who did not train at a terrorist camp or join the ranks of a terrorist organization overseas, but who are inspired at home by a group's social media, literature or extremist ideology.[15]

lone wolf terrorist one who plans and commits violent acts alone, without any command structure and assistance from any group.

Community members are encouraged to recognize and report signs of potential self-radicalization to violence,[16] which might include individuals prominently displaying a radical Islamic jihadist (a war fought by Muslims to spread or defend their beliefs) ideology on their social media; espousing attacks on prominent symbols of the West, Christians, soldiers, and police officers; or in some other manner indicating they buy into a terrorist agenda and support radical Islamic jihad.[17]

EXHIBIT 16.2

BECOMING RADICALIZED: THE CASE OF ZACHARY CHESSER

Zachary Chesser was an average high school student in northern Virginia. He participated in his high school's Gifted and Talented program, joined his high school break-dancing team, was an avid soccer player with aspirations of getting a scholarship to play in college, and worked part time at a video rental store.

In the summer of 2008, the 18-year-old Chesser converted to Islam and quickly became radicalized, solely on the Internet. He began posting views that supported Islamist terrorist groups, watching sermons by Anwar al Awlaki, and he exchanged e-mails with the cleric about joining Al Shabab. Within weeks, he had quit his job because he "objected to working at a place that rented videos featuring naked women" and became increasingly hostile to his parents.

Soon Chesser had committed himself solely to using his computer and graphics skills to contribute to and promote violent extremist messages. He also attempted to travel to Somalia with his wife to join Al Shabab, but was unsuccessful when his mother-in-law hid his wife's passport. Next, he uploaded a video to YouTube in which he threatened the creators of the television show *South Park* after an episode depicted the Prophet Muhammad dressed in a bear costume. He then attempted to join Al Shabab once again, but was held for questioning at the airport. A few days after being questioned, Chesser was arrested for attempting to provide material support to a terrorist organization. He pled guilty to three federal felony charges—communicating threats, soliciting violent jihadists to desensitize law enforcement, and attempting to provide material support to a designated foreign terrorist organization—and was sentenced to 25 years in federal prison.[18]

The Ultimate Threat: Weapons of Mass Destruction

Weapon of mass destruction a device (explosive, chemical, biological, etc…) that can produce widespread devastation.

In terms of homeland security, the greatest threat is **weapons of mass destruction** (WMD).[19] A WMD is any explosive, incendiary, poison gas, chemical, biological, or nuclear device that can have substantial widespread devastation among human populations or structural elements.[20] WMDs can be nuclear, biological, radiological, or chemical (discussed below). WMDs have the potential capacity to cause large numbers of deaths and injuries and destruction, especially in heavily populated areas. They can cripple a city, resulting in numerous problems that could potentially last for years or decades. In fact, the primary purpose of using WMDs is not their initial death and injuries, but their residual effects that can be more destructive than the initial impact.

Nuclear Weapons

Of all the weapons of mass destruction, nuclear devices raise the most concern (as witnessed with the ongoing disquiet in the United States caused by North Korea, which has a nuclear attack against the U.S. and its territories (e.g., Guam) and defied at least four American presidents in its pursuit of nuclear and missile devices that can reach our doorstep).[21] Even a small nuclear weapon detonated in one of our large cities would result in catastrophic destruction and large numbers of casualties. Moreover, the presence of nuclear materials—radiation—would result in long-term problems for the country.

Nuclear weapons can be used in at least two ways: (1) as a so-called dirty bomb and (2) attacks on nuclear power plants. Dirty bombs use conventional explosive materials but are wrapped or contain some type of radioactive material. The conventional explosion causes the radioactive materials to be dispersed, resulting in contamination. Regarding the second form, crashing a large aircraft or using large amounts of explosives at a nuclear power plant could have the same effect as a dirty bomb except on a larger scale. Such an explosion could cause the reactor core to melt down (such as occurred at Chernobyl) or spent fuel waste to be spread across a large geographical area. The effects could be devastating, and the cleanup could take decades.

Biological Weapons

Another means of attack by terrorists involves the use of chemical/biological agents, or **bioterrorism**, which involves the release of toxic biological agents. Poisons have been used for several millennia; recent attacks using chemical/biological agents including toxins, viruses, or bacteria such as anthrax, ricin, and sarin have underscored their potential dangers and uses by terrorists today. Chemical weapons—including several types of gases—suffocate the victim immediately or cause massive burning. Biological weapons are slower acting, spreading a disease such as anthrax or smallpox through a population before the first signs are noticed. Many experts believe it is only a matter of time before chemical/biological weapons are used like explosives have been to date. All that is required is for a toxin to be cultured and put into a spray form that can be weaponized and disseminated into the population. Fortunately, such dissemination is extremely difficult for all but specially trained individuals to make in large quantities and in the correct dosage; they are also difficult to transport because live organisms are delicate.

Bioterrorism chemical/biological agents involving the release of toxic biological agents.

Chemical Weapons

Chemical weapons have different levels of toxicity and lethality. Some of the chemicals that may be used are insecticides, which have a low level of toxicity, but are readily available. On the other hand, weapons grade chemicals are potentially dangerous. Chemicals such as mustard gas, sarin, and VX are extremely lethal. As with biological weapons, the effectiveness of a chemical threat is to a large extent based on the delivery system. Large quantities of the chemical would have to be effectively released to have a significant impact.

Conventional Weapons

Radiological, biological, and chemical weapons present the greatest danger from a terrorist attack, but the terrorist attacks in the United States have been conducted using conventional weapons. Airplanes were used in the 9/11 attacks, and there have been a few incidents where knives or other bladed instruments were used. Another trend in terrorist attacks has been the use of vehicles. Firearms are the most commonly used weapon since these weapons are easily obtainable in the United States.[22] Moreover, firearms are problematic since many states allow for carrying a concealed weapon or allow people to carry firearms openly. Here, police administrators should attempt to strictly enforce all federal, state, and local gun statutes and ordinances.

Cyberterrorism—and the Asian Threat

According to INTERPOL, cybercrime is one of the fastest growing areas of crime and includes attacks against computer hardware and software, financial crimes and corruption,

cyberterrorism cybercrimes that include identity theft, attacks against computer systems, penetration of online financial systems, e-mail phishing, and so on.

and abuse, in the form of grooming or "sexploitation," especially crimes against children. Cybercrime or **cyberterrorism** includes not only highly publicized activities such as cyber hacks of elections but also such activities as identity theft, attacks against computer data and systems, the distribution of child sexual abuse images, Internet auction fraud, and the penetration of online financial services, as well as the deployment of viruses, botnets, and various e-mail scams such as phishing.[23]

Unquestionably, many people around the world are now working full time in trying to hack into online data and perpetrate related crimes; these cyberattacks are not only becoming more frequent, they are becoming more expensive to address as well; a recent study found that over a billion personal data records were breached in the United States in 2014—an increase of 78 percent over the previous year and an average of about 664,000 personal records per breach.[24]

Not withstanding the recent hacks of many states' elections by Russia, the most challenging and potentially disastrous type of cybercrime—actually, cyberespionage—now being perpetrated against the United States is by Chinese hackers, who are estimated to be responsible for the theft of 50 to 80 percent of all American intellectual property and have compromised many of the nation's most sensitive advanced weapons systems, including missile defense technology and combat aircraft. It is believed that Chinese hackers have accessed designs for more than two dozen of the U.S. military's most important and expensive weapons systems (the cost to develop plans for one aircraft alone—the F-35 Joint Strike Fighter—was $1.4 trillion). Doing so enables China to understand those systems and be able to jam or otherwise disable them. The Pentagon recently concluded that another country's computer sabotage can constitute an act of war, which could eventually lead to U.S. use of military force. China's computer hacking targets also include corporate and business secrets, and there are also concerns about threats posed to U.S. nuclear reactors, banks, subways, and pipeline companies. The specter of electricity going out for days and perhaps weeks, the gates of a major dam opening suddenly and flooding complete cities, or pipes in a chemical plant rupturing and releasing deadly gas are nightmare scenarios that keep homeland security professionals awake at night.[25]

▶ Law Enforcement Roles and Strategies

Given the above nature of terrorism in all its forms, since 9/11 law enforcement agencies have certainly been compelled to adapt so as to anticipate and address such attacks. Next we discuss how the police role has changed in these regards.

Broadly speaking, the police have four means of addressing terrorism:

1. Gathering raw intelligence on the organization's structure, its members, and its plans (or potential for the use of violence)
2. Determining what measures can be taken to counter or thwart terrorist activities
3. Assessing how the damage caused by terrorists can be minimized through rapid response and containment of the damage
4. Apprehending and convicting individual terrorists and dismantling their organizations.[26]

More specifically, current federal, state, and local strategies for addressing terrorism would include:

- The Department of Homeland Security (DHS), which has as its founding mission the protection of the United States from terrorism, which continues to work with both domestic, international, and private sector partners to protect our nation against terrorist threats while simultaneously facilitating the trade and travel that is essential to our economic security. Following are more of those related efforts:[27]

- Chemical sector
- Commercial facilities sector
- Communications sector
- Critical manufacturing sector
- Dams sector
- Defense industrial base sector
- Emergency services sector
- Energy sector
- Financial services sector
- Food and agriculture sector
- Government facilities sector
- Health care and public health sector
- Information technology sector
- Nuclear reactors, materials, and waste sector
- Transportation systems sector
- Water and wastewater systems

Figure 16-1 Types of Critical Infrastructure Assets

The National Infrastructure Protection Plan:

In 2002, the DHS published the ***National Infrastructure Protection Plan*** **(NIPP)**. This document has served as the guideline for organizing homeland security in the United States. The plan is designed to provide coordination among the numerous federal, state, and local agencies in protecting the nation's critical infrastructure and key resources. Essentially, the plan enumerates a homeland security process.[28]

National Infrastructure Protection Plan a document that serves as the guideline for organizing homeland security in the U.S.

The NIPP requires local police departments to identify the critical infrastructure assets in their jurisdiction, be they human, physical, or cyber. Figure 16-1 ■ shows the various types of critical assets as identified by the DHS. Every jurisdiction will have a number of these assets. They should be identified. Next, the level of protection each asset has in place. This can be physical security such as fences, alarms, or security personnel. Then the level of risk should be determined; what is the level of danger if the asset is compromised. Police officials should work with other government and business and corporate officials to improve security. Finally, police managers must ensure that their departments have response plans in place that coordinate with other emergency response agencies.

- National Terrorism Advisory System: In 2011, the DHS replaced the color-coded alerts of the Homeland Security Advisory System with the National Terrorism Advisory System (NTAS), designed to more effectively communicate information about terrorist threats by providing timely, detailed information to the American public. It recognizes that Americans all share responsibility for the nation's security, and should always be aware of the heightened risk of terrorist attack in the United States and what they should do.[29]
- Nationwide Suspicious Activity Reporting Initiative: This is a collaborative effort by the U.S. Department of Homeland Security, the Federal Bureau of Investigation, and state, local, tribal, and territorial law enforcement partners, to provide law enforcement with another tool to help prevent terrorism and other related criminal activity by establishing a national capacity for gathering, documenting, processing, analyzing, and sharing what is termed Suspicious Activity Reporting (SAR) information. To date, more than 229,000 frontline law enforcement personnel have received SAR training to recognize behaviors potentially related to terrorism.[30]
- The "If You See Something, Say Something" campaign, which emphasizes the importance of training frontline personnel.[31]
- Homeland Security Information Network (HSIN): HSIN is a DHS-hosted tool, which provides a secure, Internet-based network for real-time sharing of information between federal agencies and local first responders.[32]

- Grant Funding: Since fiscal year 2003, DHS has awarded more than $36 billion in preparedness grant funding based on risk to build and sustain targeted capabilities to prevent, protect against, respond to, and recover from threats or acts of terrorism.
- Screening for Airline Passengers: DHS has strengthened its in-bound targeting operations to identify high-risk travelers who are likely to be inadmissible to the United States and to recommend to commercial carriers that those individuals not be permitted to board a commercial aircraft through its Pre-Departure program.[33]
- Secure Flight: DHS implemented the TSA Secure Flight program in 2010, under which DHS conducts passenger watch list matching for 100 percent of covered U.S. aircraft operator and foreign air carrier flights flying to, from, or within the United States to identify individuals who may pose a threat to aviation or national security and designate them for enhanced screening or, as appropriate, prohibit them from boarding an aircraft. TSA now vets over 14 million passengers weekly.[34]

Joint Terrorism Task Forces multi-agency teams overseen by the FBI dedicated to address terror threats.

National Counterterrorism Center the entity which serves to integrate and analyze intelligence pertaining to terrorism (excluding domestic terrorism)

Domestic terrorism the commission of terrorist acts in one's own country, against fellow citizens.

Fusion centers entities established to analyze data and facilitate information sharing among agencies to prevent and respond to crime and terrorism

- The FBI lists terrorism as its highest priority and is the nation's lead federal law enforcement agency for investigating and preventing acts of domestic and international terrorism, and for investigating attacks involving weapons of mass destruction. The FBI is also responsible for specific terrorism-related offenses, as violence at airports, money laundering, attacks on U.S. officials, and others. The FBI also works closely with the Director of National Intelligence and other U.S. intelligence agencies to gather and analyze intelligence on terrorism and other security threats. It is the number one priority of the FBI to protect the United States and U.S. persons and interests around the world from terrorist attack.[35]
- **Joint Terrorism Task Forces (JTTF)**: Overseen by the FBI and located around the nation, JTTFs bring together more than 500 state and local agencies and 55 federal agencies (including the Department of Homeland Security, the U.S. military, Immigration and Customs Enforcement, and the Transportation Security Administration) into a single team dedicated to address terror threats of all kinds. JTTFs are essentially small cells of highly trained, locally based investigators, analysts, linguists, and SWAT experts, who chase down leads, gather evidence, make arrests, provide security for special events, conduct training, collect and share intelligence, and respond to threats and incidents at a moment's notice.[36]
- National Counterterrorism Center: Within the federal government there also exists the **National Counterterrorism Center** (NCTC), which serves to integrate and analyze all intelligence pertaining to terrorism possessed or acquired by the U.S. government (except purely **domestic terrorism**—defined as that which involves the commission of terrorist acts in one's own country, against his or her fellow citizens). It then shares its knowledge, acting as a center for joint operational planning and joint intelligence, staffed by personnel from the various agencies. NCTC is staffed by personnel from multiple departments and agencies from across the Intelligence Community. NCTC is organizationally part of the Office of the Director of National Intelligence.[37]
- Fusion Centers: State and major urban area **fusion centers** serve as focal points within the state and local environment for the receipt, analysis, gathering, and sharing of threat-related information between the federal government and state, local, tribal, and other agencies. Located in states and major urban areas throughout the country, fusion centers conduct analysis and facilitate information sharing while assisting law enforcement and homeland security partners in preventing, protecting against, and responding to crime and terrorism.[38]

Other Approaches in the Law Enforcement Toolkit

Legislative Measures

Another tool in the police toolbox for addressing terrorism involves enacting legislation to assist in the effort. Discussed next are three such legislative measures or enactments.

Immediately after the 9/11 attacks, Congress passed the Uniting and Strengthening America by Providing Appropriate Tools Required to Intercept and Obstruct Terrorism Act of 2001 (known as the **USA PATRIOT Act**), which provided a number of new investigative measures to federal law enforcement agencies. The act dramatically expanded the federal government's ability to investigate Americans without establishing probable cause for "intelligence purposes" and to conduct searches if there are "reasonable grounds to believe" there may be national security threats. Federal agencies such as the FBI and others are given access to financial, mental health, medical, library, and other records. The act was reauthorized in March 2006, providing additional tools for protecting mass transportation systems and seaports from attack: the "roving wiretap" portion and the "sneak and peek" section. The first allows the government to get a wiretap on every phone a suspect uses, while the second allows federal investigators to get access to library, business, and medical records without a court order. Then, in June 2015, Congress extended the act through 2019, but amended it to stop the National Security Agency from continuing its mass phone data collection program.[39]

USA Patriot Act a federal law which provided new investigative measures to federal law enforcement agencies to prevent and respond to terrorism.

Also aiding the fight against terrorism is the **Military Commissions Act** (MCA), which allows the president to establish military commissions to try unlawful enemy combatants; the commissions are also authorized to sentence defendants to death, and defendants are prevented from invoking the Geneva Conventions as a source of rights during commission proceedings. The law contains a provision stripping detainees of the right to file habeas corpus petitions in federal court and also allows hearsay evidence to be admitted during proceedings, so long as the presiding officer determines it to be reliable. This law also allows the Central Intelligence Agency (CIA) to continue its program for questioning key terrorist leaders and operatives—a program felt by many to be one of the most successful intelligence efforts in U.S. history.[40]

Military Commissions Act a law that allows the president to establish military commissions to try unlawful combatants.

Finally, while the **Posse Comitatus Act of 1878** prohibits using the military to execute the laws domestically, the military may be called on to provide personnel and equipment for certain special support activities, such as domestic terrorist events involving weapons of mass destruction. Furthermore, President George W. Bush directed the Department of Homeland Security secretary to develop and administer a **National Incident Management System** (NIMS). NIMS is a comprehensive document addressing response to critical incidents and providing a nationwide approach for agencies at all levels to work effectively to prepare for, prevent, respond to, and recover from domestic incidents. By adopting such a response protocol, agencies at all levels have a standard set of procedures when responding to an event. Since police departments are the first responders to an event, the procedures outlined in the NIMS should be integrated into police departments' policies. Furthermore, all federal departments and agencies must adopt and use the NIMS, and its use by state and local agencies is a condition for federal preparedness assistance.[41]

Posse Comitatus Act of 1878 a law that prohibits using the military to execute domestic laws, with some exceptions.

National Incident Management System a document outlining procedures for agency preparedness and response to domestic incidents.

Use of Unmanned Aerial Vehicles: How to Balance Security and Privacy

Another rapidly emerging issue in the fight against terrorism is the use of drones, also known as **unmanned aerial vehicles** (UAVs).

Drones are proliferating; indeed, nearly 300,000 drone owners registered their small aircraft during the initial 30 days after the Federal Aviation Administration (FAA)

Unmanned aerial vehicles also known as drones and used as a surveillance technique by law enforcement.

introduced an online registration system in December 2015, for a mere $5 fee.[42] Indeed, for the first time in U.S. history, in order for children to play with the new drone received as a Christmas or birthday gift, the "toy" must first be registered with an agency of the federal government.[43]

Drones would seem to be tailor-made for seeking out and surveilling persons who are planning or involved in terroristic activities. However, the issue concerning the use of drones came to the forefront in early 2013 during Senate confirmation hearings for President Obama's nominee to head the CIA, John Brennan. A U.S. Department of Justice (DOJ) memo came to light in which the DOJ supported Obama's legal authority to use drones as mentioned above—to target American citizens whose behavior conforms to a particular profile and are working with al-Qaeda—but with little or no oversight by Congress or the judicial system. What is evident from the hearings is that Americans are very suspicious of—and may demand that legal criteria be established for—the overflights of drones in this country as we have deployed them over Pakistan and other countries. Clearly, these are vexing security and privacy issues that our government and society must resolve, and each day the U.S. criminal justice system is closer and closer to the day when it will likewise be embroiled in those same issues.[44]

EXHIBIT 16.3

POLICE USE OF DRONES

More local law enforcement agencies are using drones and only 14 states have passed privacy legislation regulating how such agencies can use drones (requiring officers to obtain a search warrant before using drones for surveillance). Some observers describe the relative lawless time in which drone technology is emerging as a "wild west" for law enforcement.[45]

Assume you are an advisor to a presidential panel that is to make recommendations for police use of UAVs/drones, and respond to the following questions:

1. Would you support police use of drones for surveillance purposes involving serious offenses? If so, for what crime-related purposes?
2. Would you allow the police to use drones for Fourth Amendment (searches and seizures) types of operations, if legal conditions have been met?
3. Do you endorse using drones for lower-level functions, such as catching traffic speeders?
4. Would your panel be in favor of arming the drones with bullets or tear gas?
5. Do you believe drones should be used, without prior consent from any courts or other oversight body, for surveilling persons whose "profile" indicates they are a dangerous threat to security?

▶ The Role of Local Police

Need for Vigilance

In March 2015, firefighters in a Western city responded to a report of a firebomb at a fast-food restaurant. Upon arrival, they observed a broken window, a flammable material inside, and the initials "ALF" written on a drive-through sign. Recognizing the signs of possible domestic terrorism (ALF is the initials of the Animal Liberation Front, at times a very violent group in its advocacy for anything they suspect involves animal cruelty), the firefighters immediately secured the scene and contacted the Federal Bureau of Investigation.

This incident clearly demonstrates the need of all public-safety first responders—police, fire, medical, military, health, and so on—to be vigilant in identifying the signs of terrorism in today's post-9/11 society. Although the role of the federal Department of Homeland Security was discussed above, here a brief examination is provided of the role of local (municipal police and county sheriff's personnel) in protecting the homeland—a very daunting task for a nation with 3.79 million square miles, about 3,000 counties, and 2,500 cities with 10,000 or more people.[46]

Notwithstanding the many acts of terrorism committed in the United States since 9/11, most such acts are foiled, such as attempts to place bombs near public facilities or send harmful chemicals through the mail. This is not by accident; it is widely recognized that local police are key in terms of being the eyes and ears in the U.S. counterterrorism effort. Former New York City police commissioner William Bratton argues that local police also know which targets are more at risk and are best equipped to coordinate the first response to attacks. Furthermore, because they are experienced in conducting investigations, well-schooled in community policing and problem-solving, and thus possess a vast network of contacts in the community, local police are well positioned to deal with terrorist networks.[47]

Today's police agencies must not ask *whether* another terroristic attack will occur on U.S. soil, but rather *when* it will occur. They must consider the possibility of attacks by weapons of mass destruction. And, depending on their location, they must plan for the possibility that the risk of attack is high if their community has historically significant assets (e.g., Independence Hall in Philadelphia, the Alamo in San Antonio); is a center of tourism (e.g., Las Vegas); is a state capital or a major commercial, manufacturing, or financial center (e.g., Wall Street); is near a port of entry; is the site of animal research facilities; is near a large military base; or is a major site for petroleum refineries, nuclear facilities, or a transportation hub.[48]

Having Plans in Place

A primary need for local police agencies is to inculcate an organizational culture that will accept and respond to the need for terrorism preparedness so that the agency achieves a state of operational readiness. While each community stands alone in its needs and vulnerabilities (and thus it is not possible to have a "cookie-cutter" approach to terrorism readiness), being prepared minimally involves activities in three categories: processes, resources, and personnel.

1. ***Processes***—terrorism preparedness involves putting in place necessary policies and procedures that address the need for communicating, planning, and training as they involve terroristic threats;
2. ***Resources***—this entails acquiring the essential equipment, databases, and other assets for terrorism preparedness (while also avoiding unnecessary duplication of services and, often, joining with other agencies toward a regionalized approach); and
3. ***Personnel***—while it is important to emphasize that increasing personnel alone does not improve preparedness, work in fusion centers (described above) and related functions require a minimal number of staffing in an agency.[49] In addition, police executive staff should ensure that intelligence data is collected and analyzed, limit access to and parking near critical facilities, have personnel and the community be alert for suspicious packages, monitor all municipal reservoirs and wastewater treatment plants, and ensure that such related assets as command posts, public information, officer shift modification and family assistance, and equipment are in place.[50]

IN THEIR OWN WORDS

ADMINISTRATIVE ADVICE FROM THE FIELD

Name: Dora Schriro

Current position/City/State: Commissioner, Connecticut Department of Emergency Services and Public Protection[51]

College attended/academic major/degree(s): Bachelor of arts degree, Northeastern University (*cum laude*); master's of education, University of Massachusetts; doctorate of education, administration, Columbia University Teachers College; juris doctorate, St. Louis University, School of Law.

My primary duties and responsibilities in this position include: administering six agencies responsible for safety and well-being of the state's population—the Connecticut State Police, Emergency Management and Homeland Security, Scientific Services (Crime Labs), Peace Officers Standards and Training (POST), the Fire Academy, and 911 Statewide. The Department of Emergency Services and Public Protection (DESPP) employs 1,668 sworn and civilian personnel and has an annual budget of $172 million—plus grant funding of about $172 million. The commissioner establishes the department's policy and priorities, all of which are focused on protecting and improving the quality of life in Connecticut by providing a broad range of public safety and scientific services, providing training and regulatory guidance, and featuring enforcement, prevention, education, and science and technology. In my former role as Commissioner, New York City Department of Correction, I administered NYC's jail system, an agency that employs 10,440 uniform and civilian personnel and incarcerates approximately 12,000 pretrial and city sentenced inmates daily and 85,000 annually and has an annual operating budget that exceeds $1 billion. There, I established the department's policy and priorities that serve to provide constitutional and humane conditions of confinement, thereby meeting all of its statutory mandates and also to ready all of the inmates in its custody for release as civil and productive individuals.

Personal attributes/characteristics that have proven to be most helpful to me in this position are: good humor, tenacity, and a healthy dose of risk-taking.

My three greatest challenges in this administrative role include: first, integrating the work and the wisdom within and across the department's six divisions, and tapping the synergy in its six complementary agencies (an interdisciplinary approach to problem-solving is both powerful and productive); second, dedicating a public safety organization to public service with special commitments to crime victims and survivors of natural disasters as well as acts of foreign and domestic terrorism; and third, making time for myself—including tending to my garden.

Personal accomplishments during my administrative career about which I am most proud are: during my tenure as Director in Arizona, having the Department of Correction earn the only Innovations in American Government Award ever awarded for a prison-based reentry initiative; second, I successfully resolved the longest hostage-taking incident in a correctional system without any loss of life; finally, I authored the template to reform immigration detention reform, a course of action that was adopted by the U.S. Department of Homeland Security.

Advice for someone who is interested in occupying an administrative position such as mine would be: to be your best. Do your best. Be kind to everyone.

Source: Used with permission from Dora Schriro.

Finally, when an attack does occur, local police must ensure that:

- Ingress and egress from the attack site are managed, so that emergency vehicles can get to and from the scene and victims can be evacuated.
- Community policing remains in place, not only so officers can take the lead in coordinating efforts against vigilantism but also to reach out to Islamic and Arabic communities for information or help in developing informants.
- Manage and share information (not only with the public but with other assisting police, fire, military, and medical units), and give accurate instructions.[52]

Engaging the Community and Using Social Media

There are no visual or physical cues—such as dress, location, or size—which automatically identify someone as a violent **extremist** to law enforcement. For instance, someone taking a picture may be plotting an attack, or they may be a tourist. However, community members are well situated to help counter this "blend" factor by recognizing things that are out of the ordinary. By providing programs that engage the community and raise their awareness of potential indicators of radicalization to violence and of the different ways they can contact authorities to report such situations, the community can contribute to enhancing safety, and violent extremists will have a more difficult time blending in with the population. Civilians and volunteers within the department can provide law enforcement with valuable insight into ways to begin to reach out and engage the community.[53]

extremist one holding extreme or fanatical political or religious views, who might also resort to extreme action.

Community members can be made aware of the common indicators of radicalization to violence through educational campaigns and partnerships; when properly educated, parents, teachers, and peers will be in a better position to recognize early signs of radicalization to homegrown violent extremism.

Extremists also often try to recruit youth, whom they see to be the most vulnerable, for homegrown violent extremism. Thus, law enforcement's attempts to engage youth in positive relationships provide an opportunity to counter the message offered by homegrown violent extremism. Offering programs— such as police athletic leagues, youth police academies, and youth advisory councils—and sponsoring youth-specific events help law enforcement to potentially offset the allure of radicalization for some vulnerable youth.

In Boston, Massachusetts, the PortWatch program is a collaboration between public and private stakeholders to ensure public safety in and around the Port of Boston. The program was established by the chief of the Massport Police (part of the Massachusetts State Police). Partners include federal, state, and local law enforcement and regulatory agencies; private corporate security stakeholders and other private companies; and community representatives. These entities share relevant information and intelligence, which includes current trends in local, national, and international criminal or terrorist activity that may be relevant to the Port and its surrounding areas; upcoming significant events; and any operations that may impact daily routines. Law enforcement also works with private security directors to develop security awareness programs that are tailored to each company taking part in the program. In addition, PortWatch includes a training component, building on the federal "See Something, Say Something" campaign (discussed above). Employees of area hotels, restaurants, and other "soft targets" are taught how to recognize and assess suspicious behaviors, as part of enhancing the safety and security of the Port of Boston and surrounding communities.[54]

Another innovative, collaborative approach, taken by the Los Angeles Police Department (LAPD) and the Los Angeles County Sheriff's Department (LASD), provides officers and deputies with some of the most comprehensive training in what is called "countering violent extremism" (CVE). All LAPD officers and LASD deputies are trained as Terrorism Liaison Officers, attending courses on criminal networks as they pertain to terrorism and money-laundering schemes as well as extremist ideologies, in order to conduct critical analyses to help eliminate any inflammatory material and damaging instruction being taught about certain religions and individuals. The two agencies partnered with the Muslim Public Affairs Council to develop a training video for officers and deputies regarding Muslim contacts. In addition, all recruits must complete cultural competency courses that cover cultural sensitivities, common greetings in different languages, key principles and promising practices for law enforcement, and differences between religions and sects of the same religion. Furthermore, the LAPD partnered with regional representatives of the Anti-Defamation League to ensure that all of the training modules were developed with civil rights and civil liberties in mind. Site visits to places of worship are also conducted to further enhance law enforcement's understanding of the community and to build networks with attendees.

Law enforcement agencies can also engage and communicate with residents through social media. Agencies can post questions and encourage comments as a way to solicit tips and feedback and engage in dialogue with community members. Agencies can encourage residents to play an active role in addressing crime and disorder in their neighborhood by disseminating information about unsolved crimes and crime trends in the community on social media sites, effectively creating force multipliers. More information can be obtained concerning how law enforcement can use social media to engage community members by visiting the IACP Center for Social Media at www.IACPSocialMedia.org.

Summary

This chapter has described how and why, in stark terms, we are no longer safe in America. There are simply countless radical individuals, living both here and abroad, who wish at the least to do us harm and even see us dead. Their reasoning is either grounded in religion or politics: they wish to compel democratic countries such as the United States and its allies to withdraw their military forces from territories that terrorists view as their homeland. In addition, such radical militants do not like our culture, our freedom, our government, our incursions into other countries abroad to attempt to spread democracy, or anything about us, and they will use any means available to them to hurt us if they can.

The duty thus falls to law enforcement executives at all levels to develop the knowledge, means, and ability to protect us from such individuals. This chapter has set forth in brief terms how those agencies are attempting to go about that task.

Key Terms and Concepts

Bioterrorism, p. 425
Cyberterrorism, p. 426
Domestic terrorism, p. 428
Extremists, p. 433
Fusion center, p. 428
Homegrown violent extremists, p. 421
International terrorism, p. 422
Joint Terrorism Task Forces, p. 428
Legislative measures, p. 429
Lone-wolf terrorist, p. 423
Military Commissions Act, p. 429
National Counterterrorism Center, p. 428
National Incident Management System, p. 429
National Infrastructure Protection Plan, p. 427
Posse Comitatus Act of 1878, p. 429
Social media (use of), p. 434
Unmanned aerial vehicles, p. 429
USA PATRIOT Act, p. 429
Weapons of mass destruction (WMD), p. 424

Questions for Review

1. What is the definition of terrorism, per the FBI, and how is terrorism an international problem?
2. Why are homegrown and lone-wolf extremists of particular concern today?
3. How does a person become self-radicalized (using the Chesser case study)?
4. What are the kinds of activities cybercriminals engage in—and China's suspected role in cyberterrorism?
5. Why have those persons who would use bioterrorism to attack the United States thus far been largely unsuccessful?
6. What are law enforcement's four means of addressing terrorism?
7. What are some specific efforts employed by the Department of Homeland Security, FBI, and Joint Terrorism Task Forces to combat terrorism?

8. What are fusion centers?
9. What roles in combatting terrorism are played by the USA PATRIOT Act, Military Commissions Act, and Posse Comitatus Act of 1878?
10. What roles in combatting terrorism are played by each of the following?
    - Drones
    - Local police
    - Social media

Deliberate and Decide

You are a small-town police chief. Early one morning—although you don't yet know it—a man rows his small fishing boat, containing a duffel bag and two fishing rods, down the remote side of a river that runs through your city. After a slow, 30-minute ride, the fisherman approaches the dam's spillway. He then removes four interconnected backpacks from the duffel bag and lowers them into the water along the sloping spillway. A button on a control device is depressed, and a large explosion is heard for miles. The underwater explosion blows a massive hole in the earthen wall, leading to a huge avalanche of water carving a wide chasm in the dam. Within minutes, the first call of the dam break reaches you; a frantic scramble ensues as media and emergency rescue teams begin to alert everyone living downstream. Reports are also quickly coming in about people drowning near the dam. People are in a state of panic and trying frantically to escape. Several miles of roads have been wiped out.

Your task: Consider the kinds of advanced planning that could have been done to prepare for and/or prevent such a situation. Also, what would be the initial duties and responsibilities of law enforcement and other first-response personnel? The types of technologies and equipment needed? Public information responsibilities? What multiagency coordination must be accomplished?

Learn by Doing

1. Terrorists would prefer to attack critical targets—several of which exist in nearly any city or county. You, as a lieutenant in your local police agency, have been assigned to work in your countywide fusion center. The captain who oversees the unit informs you that your first task is to identify all critical targets; then, once identified, the center must consider responses for the time when a terrorist attack or other significant event occurs.
    a. What types or categories of critical infrastructure should concern you?
    b. What structures in your county do you feel should be listed as critical targets?
    c. Might local politics come into play when developing this list, especially if someone's business is (or is not) included? If so, how will you deal with it?
    d. What should your fusion center do once this list is compiled?
2. To better grasp the methods of, and problems confronted by, federal/state law enforcement agencies and local police departments, you could do no better than to seek out and interview those individuals who work in these arenas on a daily basis. Better yet, if your interests are keen in any one of these areas, you could attempt to accomplish a university-sponsored internship with one of those agencies or, perhaps, offer to volunteer your time at the agency (be forewarned, however: either of these latter objectives may not be accommodated by these agencies or, if so, would no doubt involve a thorough and lengthy background check prior to your being accepted).

Case Study

All Americans are familiar with the term and depraved acts of "9/11," especially those who are old enough to know where they were and what they were doing when first hearing about the attacks. Here are the basic facts: at about 9 A.M. on September 11, 2001, an airliner flew into the North Tower of the World Trade Center in New York City. Less than 20 minutes later another airliner tore into the South Tower. Because of the jets' speed and the amount of fuel involved, the damage caused both towers to collapse less than 90 minutes later. Then, shortly after the South Tower was struck, a third jet flew into the west side of the Pentagon, in Arlington, Virginia, and then a fourth plane went down in a field in southern Pennsylvania (its passengers, now knowing what was happening, forcing the plane down). Nearly 3,000 people died at the World Trade Center and on the four planes—surpassing the death toll at Pearl Harbor of December 11, 1941.

Questions for Discussion

1. How and why did these terrible attacks happen?
2. What contributing factors were present concerning the attackers, the military, and the intelligence agencies that allowed these unforeseen attacks to occur?

(To answer these questions, see the Executive Summary, United States Senate, 9/11 Commission, *The 9/11 Commission Report: Final Report of the National Commission on Terrorist Attacks upon the United States* (Washington, DC: U.S. Government Printing Office, July 2004), also available at: http://govinfo.library.unt.edu/911/report/911Report_Exec.pdf.)

Notes

1. Jack Dolan, Paul Pringle, and Stephen Ceasar, "San Bernardino Shooting Suspect Traveled to Saudi Arabia, Was Married, Appeared to be Living 'American Dream,' Coworkers Say," *Los Angeles Times*, December 2, 2015, http://www.latimes.com/local/lanow/la-me-ln-syed-farook-had-traveled-to-saudi-arabia-married-appeared-to-live-american-dream-co-workers-say-20151202-story.html.
2. Federal Bureau of Investigation, "What We Investigate," https://www.fbi.gov/albuquerque/about-us/what-we-investigate
3. 18 U.S.C. § 2331 states that international terrorism involves:

   > violent acts or acts dangerous to human life that violate federal or state law; that appear to be intended (i) to intimidate or coerce a civilian population; (ii) to influence the policy of a government by intimidation or coercion; or (iii) to affect the conduct of a government by mass destruction, assassination, or kidnapping; and occur primarily outside the territorial jurisdiction of the U.S., or transcend national boundaries in terms of the means by which they are accomplished, the persons they appear intended to intimidate or coerce, or the locale in which their perpetrators operate or seek asylum.

   Domestic terrorism includes activities that

   > involve acts dangerous to human life that violate federal or state law; appear intended to intimidate or coerce a civilian population; to influence the policy of a government by intimidation or coercion; or to affect the conduct of a government by mass destruction, assassination, or kidnapping; and occur primarily within the territorial jurisdiction of the U.S.
4. Global Terrorism Database, "Incidents Over Time," https://www.start.umd.edu/gtd/search/Results.aspx?start_month=0&end_month=12&start_year=2015&end_year=2015&start_day=0&end_day=31.
5. "ISIS: Trail of Terror," *ABC News*, February 15, 2015, http://abcnews.go.com/WN/fullpage/isis-trail-terror-isis-threat-us-25053190.
6. Tim Lister, Ray Sanchez, Mark Bixler, Sean O'Key, Michael Hogenmiller, and Mohammed Tawfeeq, "ISIS Goes Global: 143 Attacks in 29 Countries Have Killed 2,043," *CNN*, February 13, 2017, http://www.cnn.com/2015/12/17/world/mapping-isis-attacks-around-the-world/.
7. John Davison, "Death Toll from Aleppo Bus Convoy Bomb Attack at least 126: Observatory," *Reuters*, April 16, 2017, http://www.reuters.com/article/us-mideast-crisis-syria-idUSKB17H04Y.
8. Esri, "2017 Terrorist Attacks," April 17, 2017, https://storymaps.esri.com/stories/terrorist-attacks/?year=2017.
9. Laura Smith-Spark and Saskya Vandoorne, "Paris Shooting Casts Shadow Over Final Day of French Election Campaign," *CNN*, April 21, 2017, http://www.cnn.com/2017/04/21/europe/paris-police-shooting-champs-elysees/.
10. For a comprehensive view of terroristic activities around the world, see U.S. Senate Armed Services Committee, Worldwide Threat Assessment of the US Intelligence Community, February 26, 2015, http://www.dni.gov/files/documents/Unclassified_2015_ATA_SFR_-_SASC_FINAL.pdf.
11. Peter Bergen, "Can We Stop Homegrown Terrorists?" *The Wall Street Journal*, January 23–24, 2016, pp. C1–C2.
12. "DHS Secretary on Homegrown Terror: 'I Don't Know How to Stop That,'" *CBS News*, April 23, 2017, http://www.cbsnews.com/news/dhs-secretary-john-kelly-on-homegrown-terror-i-dont-know-how-to-stop-that/.
13. See Michael Steinbach, assistant director, Counterterrorism Division, Federal Bureau of Investigation, Statement Before the House Committee on Homeland Security Washington, DC, February 11, 2015, https://www.fbi.gov/news/testimony/the-urgent-threat-of-foreign-fighters-and-homegrown-terror; also see U.S. Department of Justice Office of Community Oriented Policing Services, Awareness Brief: Homegrown Violent Extremism (2014), http://ric-zai-inc.com/Publications/cops-w0738-pub.pdf.
14. Michael Morell, "The Gathering Threat," *Time*, May 25, 2015, pp. 20–21.
15. U.S. Department of Homeland Security, "Remarks by Secretary of Homeland Security Jeh Johnson at the Canadian American Business Council at the Canadian American Business Council," October 1, 2014, http://www.dhs.gov/news/2014/10/01/remarks-secretary-homeland-security-jeh-johnson-canadian-american-business-council.

16. U.S. Department of Homeland Security, National Terrorism Advisory System, "Bulletin," December 16, 2015, https://www.dhs.gov/ntas/advisory/ntas_15_1216_0001.
17. Matthew Clark, "There's No Such Thing as a 'Self-Radicalized' Islamic Terrorist," American Center for Law and Justice, n.d., http://aclj.org/jihad/self-radicalized-islamic-terrorist.
18. Majority and Minority Staff of the Senate Committee on Homeland Security and Governmental Affairs, Zachary Chesser: A Case Study in Online Islamist Radicalization and Its Meaning for the Threat of Homegrown Terrorism (Washington, DC: United States Senate, 2012).
19. V. Henry and D. King, "Improving Emergency Preparedness and Public–Safety Responses to Terrorism and Weapons of Mass Destruction," *Brief Treatment and Crisis Intervention* 4 (2004): 11–35.
20. Larry Gaines and Vic Kappeler, *Homeland Security* (New York: Pearson, 2012).
21. See, for example, Max Fisher, "The North Korea Paradox: Why There Are No Good Options on Nuclear Arms," *The New York Times*, April 17, 2017, https://www.nytimes.com/2017/04/17/world/asia/north-korea-nuclear-weapons-missiles-sanctions.html?_r=0.
22. M. Hamm and R. Spaaj, *Lone Wolf Terrorism in America: Using Knowledge of Radicalization Pathways to Forge Prevention Strategies* (Washington, DC: U.S. Department of Justice, 2015).
23. Interpol, "Cybercrime," http://www.interpol.int/Crime-areas/Cybercrime/Cybercrime.
24. Arjun Kharpal, "Year of the Hack? A Billion Records Compromised in 2014," *CNBC*, February 12, 2015, http://www.cnbc.com/2015/02/12/.
25. See "The World's Most Hacked," *Time,* June 8, 2015, p. 10; "Admit Nothing and Deny Everything," *The Economist*, June 8, 2013, http://www.economist.com/news/china/21579044-barack-obama-says-he-ready-talk-xi-jinping-about-chinese-cyber-attacks-makes-one (accessed June 13, 2013); Siobhan Gorman and Julian E. Barnes, "Cyber Combat: Act of War," *The Wall Street Journal*, May 30, 2011, http://online.wsj.com/article/SB10001424052702304563104576355623135782718.html (accessed June 13, 2013); Michael Riley and John Walcott, "China-Based Hacking of 760 Companies Shows Cyber Cold War," *Bloomberg Business*, December 14, 2011, http://www.bloomberg.com/news/2011-12-13/china-based-hacking-of-760-companies-reflects-undeclared-global-cyber-war.html.
26. Edward J. Tully and E. L. Willoughby, "Terrorism: The Role of Local and State Police Agencies," *National Executive Institute Associates*, May 2002, http://www.nei-associates.org/terrorism-role-local-state-pol/.
27. See U.S. Department of Homeland Security, "Preventing Terrorism Overview," July 16, 2015, http://www.dhs.gov/topic/preventing-terrorism-overview.
28. Ibid., p. 30.
29. U.S. Department of Homeland Security, "National Terrorism Advisory System," http://www.dhs.gov/national-terrorism-advisory-system.
30. Bureau of Justice Assistance, "The Nationwide SAR Initiative," https://nsi.ncirc.gov/?AspxAutoDetectCookieSupport=1.
31. U.S. Department of Homeland Security, "If You See Something, Say Something," http://www.dhs.gov/see-something-say-something.
32. U.S. Department of Homeland Security, Homeland Security Information Network (HSIN), September 23, 2015, http://www.dhs.gov/homeland-security-information-network-hsin.
33. See DHS, "Aviation Security," http://www.dhs.gov/aviation-security.
34. See Ibid.; also see a TSA video of the Secure Flight program at: https://www.tsa.gov/node/2271.
35. Federal Bureau of Investigation, "Frequently Asked Questions," https://www.fbi.gov/about-us/faqs.
36. Federal Bureau of Investigation, "Protecting America from Terrorist Attack: Our Joint Terrorism Task Forces," https://www.fbi.gov/about-us/investigate/terrorism/terrorism_jttfs
37. See National Counterterrorism Center, "Who We Are," http://www.nctc.gov/; https://www.fbi.gov/about-us/investigate/terrorism.
38. U.S. Department of Homeland Security, "State and Major Urban Area Fusion Centers," http://www.dhs.gov/state-and-major-urban-area-fusion-centers.
39. Gary Peck and Laura Mijanovich, "Give Us Security While Retaining Freedoms," *Reno Gazette Journal*, August 28, 2003, p. 9A; also see "House Approves Patriot Act Renewal," http://www.cnn.com/2006/POLITICS/03/07/patriot.act.
40. Jurist: Legal News and Research, "Bush Signs Military Commissions Act," http://jurist.law.pitt.edu/paperchase/2006/10/bush-signs-military-commissions-act.php.
41. David G. Bolgiano, "Military Support of Domestic Law Enforcement Operations: Working Within Posse Comitatus," *FBI Law Enforcement Bulletin* (December 2001), pp. 16–24.
42. James Eng, "FAA Says Nearly 300,000 Drone Owners Have Registered in First 30 Days," *NBCNews.com*, January 22, 2016, http://www.nbcnews.com/tech/tech-news/faa-says-nearly-300-000-drone-owners-have-registered-first-n502201.
43. Dronelaw.com, "The FAA's Drone Registration Requirement: A Brief Review," http://dronelaw.com/.
44. See "White House, Justice Officials Defend Drone Program After Release of Memo," *Associated Press* and *Fox News*, February 5, 2013, http://www.foxnews.com/politics/2013/02/05/senators-threaten-confrontation-with-obama-nominees-over-drone-concerns/.
45. Kaveh Waddell, "Few Privacy Limitations Exist on How Police Use Drones," *The Atlantic*, February 5, 2015, https://www.theatlantic.com/politics/archive/2015/02/few-privacy-limitations-exist-on-how-police-use-drones/458583/.
46. Michael P. Downing, "Policing Terrorism in the United States: The Los Angeles Police Department's Convergence Strategy," *The Police Chief,* February 2009,

http://www.policechiefmagazine.org/magazine/index.cfm?fuseaction=display_arch&article_id=1729&issue_id=22009.
47. Graeme R. Newman and Ronald V. Clarke, *Policing Terrorism: An Executive's Guide* (Washington, DC: U.S. Department of Justice, Office of Community Oriented Policing Services, July 2008), http://www.popcenter.org/library/reading/pdfs/policingterrorism.pdf.
48. Ibid.
49. Jeremy W. Francis, "Increasing Terrorism Preparedness of Law Enforcement Agencies," *FBI Law Enforcement Bulletin*, December 2014, https://leb.fbi.gov/2014/december/increasing-terrorism-preparedness-of-law-enforcement-agencies.
50. Ibid.
51. Although her current administrative duties revolve around homeland security and public safety, Ms. Schriro was formerly the Commissioner of the New York City Department of Correction, director of the Arizona Department of Corrections, and director of the Missouri Department of Corrections; she has taught graduate-level courses in law and criminal justice and published in the areas of corrections and immigration, innovation, and systems reform throughout her career.
52. Ibid.
53. See Jose Docobo, "Community Policing as the Primary Prevention Strategy for Homeland Security at the Local Law Enforcement Level," *Homeland Security Affairs* 1(Article 4) (June 2005), https://www.hsaj.org/articles/183.
54. See International Association of Chiefs of Police, *Using Community Policing to Counter Violent Extremism: 5 Key Principles for Law Enforcement*, 2014, pp. 17–18, http://www.theiacp.org/Portals/0/documents/pdfs/Final%20Key%20Principles%20Guide.pdf.

Maksim Kabakou/Shutterstock

17 Technologies and Tools: Toward Addressing Crime and Disorder

LEARNING OBJECTIVES

After reading this chapter, the student will be able to:

1. *describe what technologies can do for policing by examining the types of functions performed*
2. *explain the purposes and applications of crime mapping and real-time crime centers*
3. *discuss how social media and civic apps are being used to address crime and disorder*
4. *review some legal, moral, and practical considerations involving IT in policing*
5. *delineate the status of several selected technologies, including the safety of electronic control devices, facial recognition, fingerprinting, robots, and apps for crime-fighting*

▶ Introduction

Including a chapter on justice system information technologies (IT) for this (or any other) textbook is, inherently, a "risky" undertaking. Such factors as the ongoing research and rapid development of hardware and software, databases, and computers; legislative and federal court decisions (affecting their legality); the national economy; and even the social and political acceptance of technologies can radically change and render what is written today to soon be outdated. Still, with but a few exceptions—such as the fields of medicine and the defense industry—nowhere is IT developing more rapidly and posing more ethical and practical concerns than in criminal justice. Therefore, current and future criminal justice administrators must understand the nature and capabilities of today's technologies as well as their related issues, to include some of their legal, managerial, and social aspects.

Although it sounds rather cliché, because the Great Recession forced the funding spigots to contract for most criminal justice agencies, most leaders have had to work smarter and more affordably. One obvious way to do so is to use technology in more efficient ways. And while many justice system administrators might believe it difficult to afford or justify new or existing technologies in this fiscal environment, it can also be argued that it is certainly unwise to cut information technology investments and staffing. IT can serve as a "force multiplier." As a RAND report noted, it can improve the effectiveness of operations and generate cost savings.[1] Therefore, as criminal justice budgets begin to increase and return to their pre-Recession state, it would be wise to likewise increase the agency's IT capabilities to the extent possible.

Because policing is by far where the bulk of technological research and development, application, and policy implications occur, our primary focus will be on that component. This chapter begins by reviewing some means by which one can determine which IT tools to use for different police functions. (Note: Unmanned aerial vehicles, or drones, are discussed in Chapter 16 especially their use with homeland security.) Next, we consider the rationale and application of technologies for police in their problem-oriented policing efforts, and then assess the major contributions of crime mapping and real-time crime centers. We then look at how social media and civic apps are being used to address crime and disorder. Technologies that assist with various traffic-related functions are then examined, followed by a number of legal, moral, and practical considerations that accompany use of IT in policing. The status of several selected technologies (i.e., the safety of electronic control devices, facial recognition, fingerprinting, robots, and apps for crime-fighting) is then covered.

Next, we review what appears to be the major impetus in the courts: the movement toward electronic court records. Included are discussions of a model courtroom, court reporting, and case management systems. Next the field of corrections is examined, including what is being done with inmate management using video cameras and tracking devices, how inmates can benefit from mobile devices, corrections' use of social media, and the expanding field of telemedicine. Following that is a discussion of the relatively new concept, termed the Internet of Things.

A number of examples of IT applications are disseminated throughout the chapter in five exhibits. The chapter concludes with review questions and exercises in the Deliberate and Decide, Learn by Doing, and Case Study sections.

▶ Police Technologies

Much has certainly changed in policing from the day in April 1928 when a couple of young Detroit officers merged some glass tubes and copper wire in the back seat of their patrol car, creating the first car radio and thus changing police work forever. Thus was a great leap taken toward fulfilling the promise of using technology to make communities safer—while freeing officers from their red lights at intersections (which was illuminated by headquarters when they were to phone in and receive a call or information) and foot patrols—but also ending a tradition whereby beat cops knew every person in their neighborhood.[2]

In this section, we approach police use of technologies from several perspectives: knowing which IT to use in a particular type of task, IT for community policing and problem-solving, crime mapping, real-time crime centers, use of social media, and civic apps for crime-fighting. Concluding this section is a discussion of legal, moral, and practical caveats relating to police use of technologies.

Which IT Tools to Use in Policing? Consider the Type of Task Involved

One way for police leaders to view what technologies can do for policing is to categorize police activities by types of functions performed. Such a classification was developed by Hoey,[3] whose three broadly defined areas were as follows:

1. ***Support* functions**, including communication, coordination, administrative, and oversight functions, such as dispatch, personnel management, surveillance, and in-service training. Specific types of IT investments supporting these functions include:
   a. Administrative systems, including records management
   b. Communications systems, including computer-aided dispatch (a software system for call handling and dispatching, crime mapping (discussed below), data reporting and analysis, and so on), and in-car mobile data terminals
   c. Surveillance systems, including closed circuit television (CCTV) and gunshot detection systems
2. ***Reactive policing* functions**, including responding to citizens' calls for service (CFS), responding to emergencies, and conducting investigations. Specific types of related IT investments include systems intended to help law enforcement with criminal investigations, such as an Integrated Automated Fingerprint Identification System terminal; and
3. ***Proactive policing* functions,** including intelligence-driven operations, such as hotspot patrols, community-oriented engagement, and data sharing with other federal and state agencies, businesses, and partner organizations. IT investments in this area include use of intelligence systems (e.g., hotspot analysis), problem analysis, and sharing information with other state, federal, and local repositories and intel centers.

These three categories reflect key differences in strategies. They also demonstrate that before a police agency can realize any value from its IT investments, it must first understand the kinds of activities those tools are intended to assist.

This is most readily seen with proactive policing techniques: for example, while IT-based, predictive crime-pattern tools might be valuable for a department deeply involved in community policing and problem-solving, an agency that chooses to only engage in reactive answering of calls for service would find such an investment to be a waste of scarce resources. Therefore, the above classification scheme allows agencies to separate activities by the different potential effects of IT in terms of desired outcomes, and also to determine whether benefits would even be expected from particular IT investments, given departmental strategies and officer allocation decisions.[4]

IT for Problem-Oriented Policing: A Conceptual Framework

The value of employing computers for community policing and problem-solving (discussed in Chapter 4) efforts quickly became evident as soon as this philosophy began to surface. As one major city police chief put it:

> The use of high-technology equipment and applications is essential to the efficient practice of community policing. Without high technology, officers would find it difficult to provide the level and quality of services the community deserves. Computer-aided dispatching, computers in patrol cars, automated fingerprinting systems, and online offense-reporting systems are but a few examples of the pervasiveness of technology in agencies that practice community policing.[5]

To do their jobs effectively, law enforcement professionals at all levels depend on information. According to one estimate, "roughly 92% of an officer's time is spent acquiring, coalescing, or distributing information in one form or another." More modern, sophisticated policing approaches (e.g., CompStat, predictive policing, intelligence-led policing, and smart policing) are even more information-intensive and dependent. They involve not just information on crimes and perpetrators but also data on community conditions, priorities, and other factors that could shape crime prevention and responses.

In addition, problem-oriented policing requires input from (1) geographic information systems (crime data must be related to locations that result in maps and other products) and (2) problem-solving information systems (information about problem-solving efforts in order to aid officers and citizens in identifying, analyzing, and responding to substantive problems in communities).[6]

Crime Mapping

Police leaders, criminologists, sociologists, and other professionals understand that geography has a major influence on crime; indeed, crime is often highest where living conditions are at their worst. Therefore, combining geographic data with police report data and then displaying the information on a map is an effective way to analyze and predict where, how, and why crime occurs. The features and characteristics of cityscapes and rural landscapes can make it easier or more difficult for crime to occur. The placement of alleys, buildings, and open spaces, for example, affects the likelihood that a criminal will strike.

Community policing and problem-solving thus looks to simultaneously address the relationship between people and their environments—particularly those places where social ills cause real problems. Geographic analysis can help to reveal crime patterns in places, such as examining where past victims and offenders lived and where crimes occurred.[7]

GIS software used by analysts to map where crime occurs in relation to other geographic data in an effort to investigate causes of crime and develop responses.

With **geographic information systems (GIS)**, analysts map where crime occurs, combine the resulting visual display with other geographic data (such as location of schools, parks, and industrial complexes), analyze and investigate the causes of crime, and develop responses. Recent advances in statistical analysis make it possible to add more geographic and social dimensions to the analysis.[8]

Computerized crime mapping combines geographic information from global positioning satellites with crime statistics gathered by the department's computer-assisted dispatching (CAD) system and demographic data provided by private companies or the U.S. Census Bureau. The result is a picture that combines disparate sets of data for a whole new perspective on crime. Maps can thus paint a picture for crime analysts, who in turn inform officers where they need to focus their patrols.

Maps of crimes can also be overlaid with maps or layers of causative data: unemployment rates in the areas of high crime, locations of abandoned houses, population density, reports of drug activity, or geographic features (such as alleys, canals, or open fields) that might be contributing factors. Furthermore, the hardware and software are now available to nearly all police agencies for a few thousand dollars.

The National Institute of Justice's Mapping and Analysis for Public Safety (MAPS) program supports research that helps agencies use GIS to enhance public safety.[9]

Real-Time Crime Centers

Related to crime mapping and analysis is another relatively new approach, the real-time crime center (RTCC), which has the purpose of using technologies to reduce officers' reliance on paper reports and nonintegrated databases to identify crime patterns. By collecting vast amounts of crime-related data—arrest records, mug shots, and warrant information—and providing it rapidly to officers and investigators in the field, these facilities can help in investigations and protect officer safety. Soon, RTCCs may become as ubiquitous as CompStat and other such strategies.

Essentially, with RTCC police use a new information hub containing many years of voice, video, and crime data, which is translated into actionable intelligence that shows criminal activity unfolding in real time. Resembling a "mission control" center, it allows crime analysts and commanders to track the police calls as they are occurring citywide. The RTCC allows staff to notice patterns and spikes in certain activity so commanders can deploy patrol officers and detectives where they're most needed at any given time.[10]

Seattle, Washington, police chief Kathleen O'Toole called RTCC "agile policing," combining the work of police officers and crime analysts so as to adapt to the changes in the city's criminal activity.[11] The initiative can also include daily morning meetings among neighboring police agencies to share information on what anomalies or spikes they are observing. Commanders and crime analysts look at a dashboard illuminating a large screen on the wall that shows how many calls police are responding to, the priority level of each call, the nature of the calls, and where on a city map each call is coming from. The information is drawn from 911 dispatch calls, crime data, radio traffic and vehicle information data and allows the staff to visualize the call data so commanders can make operational decisions on how to deploy officers. Agencies hope this practice will allow police to halt crime sprees as they happen and stop crimes and incidents before they become more serious.[12]

Patrol officers and detectives receive information from the RTTC via radio and the computers in their patrol cars. The crime center consolidates the agency's Criminal Intelligence Section, Data Driven Policing Section, and Crime Analysis detectives into a new Intelligence and Analysts Section.[13]

Exhibit 17.1 describes how the New York and Houston police departments established and use RTCC.

EXHIBIT 17.1

NEW YORK AND HOUSTON SET UP REAL-TIME CRIME CENTER[14]

The New York Police Department's RTCC system, launched in 2005 (and recently expanded beyond homicides and firearms-related crimes to include robberies, rapes, missing persons, and other serious crimes), can comb through 120 million criminal complaints, arrests, and 911 call records dating back a decade; 5 million criminal records and parole files maintained by the state; and more than 31 million records of crime committed nationwide. RTCC also made it possible for officers to receive photographs of individuals via handheld devices, and the technology to transmit photographs to the police car laptops also became available.[15]

In Houston, for 15 years police officers lacked the ability to regularly and quickly employ databases containing huge volumes of crime and related information. Another challenge was to make the data accessible in real time. Working with a private concern, HPD developed a RTCC that makes critical information—derived from crime, jail booking, probation, and other databases—immediately available to officers responding to calls. Now, when a call comes in, integration technologies feed the incident information to the RTCC crime analysts. A report is run, pulling related historical information from the various law enforcement databases. Analysts then cross-reference that information with the details of emergency calls. Additional data on persons, vehicles, and property are pulled from internal officers' notes, as well as from external government databases. All this information can then be communicated to the responding officers while en route to the crime scene. For example, officers sent to a domestic violence incident will know if the husband is a repeat offender, has spent time in prison for similar crimes, or is permitted to carry a concealed weapon—all of which will impact the way the officer responds.[16]

Applying Social Media

Lessons from Boston's Marathon Bombing

In April 2013, two bombs exploded during Boston's annual marathon, killing three people and injuring more than 260 others. What ensued was an extraordinary manhunt and massive use of social media by law enforcement to keep the media and frightened citizens accurately informed about what was going on, via its official Twitter account. In sum, the practice was very simple and yet effective.[17]

Today, some police agencies employ full-time civilian personnel who are in charge of social media and to direct public relations through the various channels—Twitter, Facebook, YouTube—in a real-time manner. The scope of social media continues to grow, with social media also allowing police to have two-way conversations with the community, to include receiving messages from citizens about crime and disorder (including anonymous tips). It can also be used to conduct virtual "ride-alongs," with live-tweeting during an entire shift from an officer's patrol car. This gives the public a view of what police do and what is going on.[18]

Police agencies now commonly use social media for investigations, to include evidence collection (people bragging about their actions on social media sites); location of suspects (investigators "friend" suspects and track their locations); and criminal network investigations (again, gangs are prone to boast about their actions on social media sites). A good example of this use is the Albuquerque, New Mexico, Police Department, which works with private security partners to monitor tweets containing certain keywords, in order to intercept rival gangs; in one instance, police prevented the gangs from causing disruptions at a major amusement park.[19]

One concern, however, has been lodged with police use of Facebook. A Brooklyn police officer arrested a burglary gang by adding gang members as friends on Facebook. The officer tracked the gang members to their location, where they photographed the young men committing a burglary, and then arrested them.

For years, social media have been used to track criminal networks. Police methods are becoming more sophisticated, however: by combining social media, databases, and network analysis tools, police can keep track of gang activities. They not only see the status updates of youths but also view photos to determine who might be a witness in a particular case. Bystanders (potential witnesses) can also be identified from background photos that are posted, and a time-stamped photo can be relevant in an investigation. Social media also helps by identifying suspects who were friends or associates of other suspects in a crime; all of them can be brought in to be interviewed and possibly convicted of crimes.

Some teens' families complain that their kids are being unfairly labeled as criminal affiliates because of their social media connections. There have been cases where the description of a shooter was given ambiguously, for example, as "a tall light-skinned black man in a hoodie," leading to an arrest being labeled in a database as a gang member or affiliate. Also, two siblings, one who is law-abiding and the other a criminal, can be lumped together because of their computer's social connections, entered into a database of suspected criminals, and be viewed as criminals.

Civic Apps for Crime-Fighting

In 2011, the City of Chicago released to the public a large amount of city data for public consumption, including up-to-date crime incident data. This release of data into the public realm helped citizens to merge data with the police, toward bringing together the needs of safe communities with law enforcement's efforts to fight crime and improve public safety.

"Hacking" has understandably become a dirty word for most Americans and governments; however, in this context, hacking is actually a positive approach to problem-solving. Here, however, civic hacking for the public's benefit is defined as

> hands-on, citizen-driven action which produces civic innovation—it could be contributing code to an open-source civic app … or conducting a workshop with city officials to discuss how new policy could improve a neighborhood.[20]

In 2013, Chicago city officials sponsored a "safe communities" hackathon, where participants were to use new methods to query crimes, wanted lists, and mug shots, as well as graffiti problems, vacant building code violations, and even police beat boundaries. The result was a wave of apps that Chicagoans could use to track crime and improve public safety. The success of this crime hackathon spawned other such practices, some of which included contests for the best civic app. One of the winners was a mobile app that allows an injured or lost person to send out a distress notice to anyone designated as a recipient. A second companion app sends out continuous updates on the location of the individual in trouble.[21]

In Redlands, California, city officials have worked with a software firm to create an app that serves as a first step toward an eventual 311 call center for residents to report problems and complaints. In Philadelphia, the city's mobile messaging platform for public safety helps police access difficult-to-reach population groups, lets neighbors know to secure their doors if their block is getting targeted for burglaries, and reports on someone's parole. Moreover, the Virginia State Police launched a crime reporting app that is a suspicious-activity reporting tool to connect individuals, police agencies, and regional fusion centers, and collects and analyzes intelligence on criminals and terrorists. Citizens are encouraged to report suspicious photography, vehicles, or people in places that just look out of place.[22]

Some Caveats: Legal, Moral, Practical Considerations

If police leaders or students of criminal justice are looking to the courts for clear-cut guidance in the use of new technologies, particularly in the area of privacy rights, they will likely come away wanting: the law seems to be "all over the place" regarding this subject.

As examples, a U.S. district judge in Wisconsin ruled that it was reasonable for Drug Enforcement Administration agents to enter rural property without permission or a warrant to install multiple "covert digital surveillance cameras" in hopes of uncovering evidence that 30 to 40 marijuana plants were being grown in "open fields" and thus could be searched without warrants because they're not covered by the Fourth Amendment.[23] However, the United States Supreme Court held in 2012 that police attaching a global positioning system (GPS) device to a suspect's vehicle without a search warrant violates the Fourth Amendment.[24] Police use of new technologies thus possesses a wide range of unresolved issues in terms of legality. First, many IT tools are so new that the courts have not had time to rule on their constitutionality. Furthermore, in some jurisdictions different state and federal courts have handed down conflicting rulings. This means that police are often experimenting with little or no guidance from the courts about the constitutionality of their actions. In the near future, many of these constitutional questions (many of which will involve citizens' right to privacy) will be taken up by lower courts and eventually reach the U.S. Supreme Court.[25] Meanwhile, police leadership is free to test different technologies that appear to be the most useful and cost-effective.[26]

Another touchy IT issue concerns the matter of legitimacy in the eyes of the communities as they regard privacy issues. Even within a given city or county, people in different neighborhoods or regions may differ in their opinions about how to balance privacy concerns and crime-fighting.

There are a number of legislative issues that must be decided as well; oftentimes, the laws governing their use were written decades ago and do not reflect current realities. For example, most wiretap laws were written in the era of landline telephones, and many Freedom of Information laws were intended to govern the release of written documents, not video footage from police cameras.[27]

Exhibit 17.2 describes a legal conundrum that exists with regard to the use of license plate readers.

EXHIBIT 17.2

LAWSUITS ARGUING FOR/AGAINST LICENSE PLATE READERS

A license plate reader (also known as automatic license plate recognition, or ALPR, device) is a surveillance technology that can be mounted to a patrol car to capture license plate numbers during an entire patrol shift. When a suspect license plate number is read, audible and visual alarms alert the officer. To demonstrate its power, in two months' time the Denver Police Department processed 835,000 license plate images, which led to 17,000 hits for warrants, stolen vehicles, and other violations.

For obvious reasons, this technology is rapidly becoming popular as a tool. However, for many people ALPR has too little regulation against invasion of privacy. For example, the American Civil Liberties Union (ACLU) argues that ALPRs collect a lot of data that is sometimes pooled into regional sharing systems; as a result, enormous databases of innocent motorists' location information are rapidly growing. This information is often retained for years, or even indefinitely, with few or no restrictions to protect privacy rights. While not calling for a complete ban, the ACLU believes that as ALPR technology spreads, legislation and law enforcement agency policies should be adopted that will respect personal privacy and prevent the government from tracking our movements on a massive scale.[28]

Conversely, a Utah law prohibiting the use of such automated high speed cameras to photograph license plates is being challenged in a lawsuit filed in federal court by two ALPR manufacturing firms. According to the lawsuit, the Utah Automatic License Plate Reader System Act infringes on constitutionally protected speech of the First Amendment. It is also argued that license plates are public by nature and contain no sensitive or private information. Five states have already enacted legislation that is identical or similar to the Utah act.[29]

In a related litigation, in what appeared to be the first legal challenge by a private individual, in May 2015 a Virginia man sued the Fairfax County (Virginia) Police Department for collecting images of his license plate and storing them in its massive database. After learning that his license plate had been scanned by an ALPR twice in the previous year and stored in a police database, he opted to sue.[30]

According to the RAND Corporation, because the use of ALPR is legal in most states, it is unlikely that any lawsuit attacking their use would result in civil liability; however, because of their privacy implications, it is recommended that agencies establish clear policies regarding data retention and access to help address some of the privacy concerns.[31]

Selected Technologies and Policies to Watch For

Next we consider what seems to be the current state of selected IT tools for police.

Electronic Control Devices: Safe—or Not?

A 2007 study by the Wake Forest University School of Medicine—touted as "the first large, independent study to review" the overall risk and severity of injuries from electronic control devices (ECDs)—reported that 99.7 percent of nearly 1,000 cases of such uses resulted in only mild injuries, such as scrapes and bruises, or no injuries at all; only three subjects (0.3 percent) suffered injuries severe enough to need hospitalization.[32]

A more recent (2015) examination of ECDs reported different findings, however. When the Berkeley, California, city council was asked to allow its officers to carry and use ECDs, the body turned to the Stanford Law School's Criminal Justice Center for a study of the effectiveness and safety of ECDs. The resulting report questioned the ability of ECDs to minimize the use of lethal force by officers.[33]

Stanford's researchers examined more than 150 studies concerning the use of ECDs and determined that many of the claims concerning their safety and ability to reduce confrontations were not as clear-cut as has been widely accepted or portrayed. More specifically, the weapons have been found to be safe when used in the right circumstances, but they are most frequently used outside of those parameters, including when subjects are under the influence of drugs or alcohol or have mental or physical handicaps. Furthermore, they found that while ECDs do generally reduce injuries to officers, it is unclear whether the same can be said for suspects. In all, the researchers found no clear evidence that their use reduces lethal force, and that their benefits are easily overstated.

Uses of Robots

Robots are playing an increasingly important role in our lives. Consider the patrol officer's vehicle was at least partially assembled by robots, people have robot vacuum cleaners in their homes, NASA's probes are interplanetary robots, and of course the police are finding many uses of the big and small varieties.[34] Robots are now fitted with odor sensors, video capability (including night vision), a camera for photographing crime scenes, an ECD, and even the ability to engage in two-way communications.[35]

One of the most notable uses of robots was after James Eagan Holmes committed one of the worst mass shootings in American history, killing 12 people and wounding 58 at an Aurora, Colorado, movie theater in July 2012. Being informed that his apartment was booby-trapped, police officers and bomb-squad experts sent in a bomb-removal robot to disarm a tripwire guarding the apartment's front door. The robot then neutralized potential explosive devices, incendiary devices and fuel found near the door.[36]

The largest robot in the police arsenal is one used by the Los Angeles police; at 39,000 pounds, the remote-controlled vehicle can be used to lift cars and tear into buildings. With a hydraulic arm extending up to 50 feet and equipped with a claw, a forklift, or a bucket, the $1 million robot can be used for both barricade and bomb incidents. Another large robot is a vehicle that carries a shield capable of protecting 12 officers and can be used for breaching.

Submersible drones can now operate under water at depths of up to 330 feet. Equipped with a wide-angle camera, they are used by police to make fixed lawn mower-style sweeps of wide areas for body and evidence recovery.

Solving Cold Cases

South San Francisco's Police Department (SSFPD) faced a challenge. The department was asked to reopen a cold case known as the Gypsy Hill murders, which involved five homicides in multiple Bay Area locations. SSFPD was tasked with spearheading a multijurisdictional task force that included four cities as well as the FBI, and to canvass four widely dispersed neighborhoods in three separate cities.[37]

Because of the large scope of this investigation, SSFPD needed a sophisticated tool. A senior member of the force approached the city's IT department and asked them to help SSFPD develop a tool that would allow them to visualize reports from the field to expedite the collection and coordination of the investigation. A desktop app was created to track where officers in the field had visited. Key information such as time of contact, officer on site, and, most importantly, status of contact could then be entered. An interactive map was automatically updated, and once displayed on a large screen at headquarters, an entire room of officers could visually follow the investigation. Task force officers were able to record the results of the visits they made to hundreds of properties. Not only did this help command staff quickly organize the areas to visit, but it also allowed managers to assess in real time which properties should be revisited and which to target for further follow-up. This allowed same-day property revisits even by different shifts of officers. Using these and other techniques, in January 2015 Rodney Halbower was charged with two of the murders when DNA evidence linked him to the crimes.

▶ Court Technologies

For the courts, the "Holy Grail" or primary goal in terms of IT is to eventually become paperless. Helping in this and other technology-related efforts is that a number of court systems—such as those in the District of Columbia—have created what is termed a strategic management or research and development division to focus on building the court's capacity to look for innovative technologies, strategies, and evidence-based information to develop policies, enhance the administration of justice, and improve the quality of services.[38]

Next we briefly discuss this ongoing, going-paperless endeavor, a model courtroom with the latest technology, and the question of whether or not IT will replace humans in performing traditional court-reporting functions.

Why Go Paperless? Save Paper, Space, and Time

Problems of paper, space, and time have always plagued the courts, being a major source of stress, cost, and inaccuracies. A typical case file—composed of documents from litigants, attorneys, judges, court staff, the clerk's office, and other officials—makes up the "official record" that governs everything that happens. Imagine thousands of such files being generated and filed per day in a single court. In the past, only one copy of the file would be available at a given time, and it would be needed for use by many people at the same time. In addition, paper records are subject to being lost, misfiled, and even defaced or stolen.

electronic court records where incoming documents are scanned, processed (using images rather than paper), and stored in an electronic document management system.

All of the above issues have led to **electronic court records** (ECR), where incoming documents are scanned and then processed using images rather than paper; then they are stored in an electronic document management system. Since the 1990s, "electronic filing" has been a primary topic for court conferences, product information, and publications.

Exhibit 17.3 discusses benefits of electronic file sharing of court documents.

Exhibit 17.4 describes some of the kinds of technologies that are now available in U.S. courtrooms, using as a guide the newly upgraded model courtroom at the National Judicial College.

EXHIBIT 17.3

BENEFITS OF ELECTRONIC FILING OF COURT DOCUMENTS[39]

Certainly electronic court records have revolutionized the way courts conduct business, with some jurisdictions saving millions of dollars by e-filing millions of documents per year. Multiple users can simultaneously view documents from their workstations. Following are some benefits that are being realized:

- Physical space savings. No longer are hundreds if not thousands of square feet of expensive courthouse floor space consumed by the storage of paper documents.
- Speed and ease of access to the electronic court documents. Files can potentially be accessed remotely from anywhere in the world, any time of day.
- Ease of maintenance and organization of the electronic files. Court staff no longer needs to roam through file rooms with carts to gather and organize file folders.
- Secure environment for court information. Documents are no longer stolen from the public viewing area. Electronic files can be password-encrypted and advanced security measures have been developed to limit their use.
- Environmentally friendly. Electronic documents eliminate the need for literally tons of paper annually. Remote access to court documents also eliminates the need for users to physically drive to the courthouse, saving fuel and reducing carbon emissions.
- Built-in calendaring and scheduling capabilities. Case tracking is automatically provided for stored documents, making justice much better served in a timely fashion.
- Data-entry time savings. With electronic documents being read by the computer system, a great deal of data-entry time is saved. In the near future, simplified case summaries, judicial opinions, and audio recordings from all federal appellate and state supreme courts could be accessible at the touch of a button.

EXHIBIT 17.4

A PEEK INSIDE A HIGH-TECH COURTROOM: THE NATIONAL JUDICIAL COLLEGE[40]

Each year the National Judicial College, located on the campus of the University of Nevada, Reno, offers more than 50 courses on site and online for all levels and types of judges. Those judges taking courses at the campus learn firsthand how enhanced audiovisual equipment and computer software technology impacts today's courtroom. Furthermore, the NJC's Model Courtroom provides an active learning center capable of streaming instructional content to judges throughout the world.

Attorneys in the Model Courtroom can plug in their laptops to refer to notes, retrieve documents, charts, and photographs, and forward evidentiary material digitally to the presiding judge's monitor. Once the judge approves the content, the court clerk then disseminates the evidence to the LCD displays where court participants are sitting: the jury box (and the jury room), the presentation lectern, the witness stand, and the four 60″ LCDs situated in the gallery. In addition, video/audio feeds may also be relayed to the media room for reporters covering the trial, the attorney conference room (where the victim may choose to view the trial away from the defendant), and a remote-site interpreter who has been employed for non-English-speaking witnesses. During the course of a trial, attorneys and witnesses may employ the LCD's touch screen technology, which allows annotations to displayed evidence, much like a television sportscaster diagramming a football play during a broadcast.

The most visible aspect of the Model Courtroom is the proliferation of monitors, gooseneck microphones, and cameras strategically embedded throughout the room. The six cameras placed around the courtroom provide a continuous feed of images allowing the proceedings to be viewed by audiences within the court and beyond. Camera switching can be done either manually or can be triggered through voice activation. Meanwhile, all of the proceedings can be captured via digital audio and video recording for later review.

As such, the new cameras, evidence presentation tools, monitors, and computer hardware and software allow the Model Courtroom to serve as a dynamic learning center.

Will IT Ever Make Court Reporters Extinct?

Many people wonder why, in a criminal justice—and court—system that is infused with IT advances, a high-priced human being still occupies the court reporter's seat and is still a major part of court proceedings; this seems an anomaly given that court testimony could surely be taken by an electronic device.

Indeed, the court reporter has been replaced with digital recording devices in many courtrooms, but most courts have maintained the human element. However, there remain many reasons why humans are still preferred for this long-standing function.

First, there are many instances during hearings and trials when court reporters must answer before the judge, jury, attorneys, plaintiffs, and defendants. This often means reading specific portions of the official court records out loud and making notations.[41] In addition, an electronic device can hardly understand a thick foreign accent.

And while court reporters must often interrupt proceedings to get every word uttered by someone in a low tone or if more than one person is speaking at once, recording equipment cannot do that, which explains the "inaudible" entries that often punctuate court transcripts from digital recordings.[42] Cameras and tape recorders simply cannot capture every word that is uttered, but the court reporter can.

Another problem is that even if a digital recording device is used to take down the testimony, that material must still be transcribed—and no machine can do it faster than a court reporter (who often works at 220 words a minute). Also coming into play is the years-long backlog that can develop in waiting for IT-based transcriptions.[43]

Of course, using humans to transcribe court testimony leaves open the possibility of human error; occasionally, a court reporter hears one word, but writes another. In sum, however, no single system—human or machine—is perfect, but that fact might explain why IT may never fully replace the person in court (and depositions) who is responsible for taking and transcribing the testimony.[44]

Other IT Trends in Courts: Case Management Systems

Following are two additional examples of how courts are reducing time and expenditures in several court functions and streamlining their operations.

First, in Fulton County, Missouri, failure to appear (FTA) notices were a significant resource drain, with one FTA involving time to issue notices and reminders, issue warrants, arrest the defendant for FTA, investigate unresolved warrants, and even incarcerate the defendant. The county recently installed a communication system that automatically calls defendants informing them of unpaid citations, court appointments, or warrants issued. It saves the costs of physically printing and mailing notifications. Significant paper and postage costs were saved, and eventually about one-fourth of defendants responded by paying their fines online—which also has the effect of reducing foot traffic in the county courts. Most importantly, court staff found that outstanding FTA warrants were reduced by 33 percent."[45]

Furthermore, a number of courts have dedicated large amounts of time and money toward installing a unified court management system for their jurisdiction. For example, courts in Fulton County (Atlanta), Georgia, devoted 7 years' time and $15 million to create a unified case management system that combines 14 fragmented and aged systems used by the county's various criminal justice agencies. Now, all criminal justice partners can communicate and see the same information; the data flow smoothly, and a disparate, siloed environment is now a single, unified system that follows each case from arrest to disposition.[46]

▶ Corrections Technologies

Generally, technologies are being used for a wide array of purposes in institutional corrections (such as jails and prisons) and for community corrections (such as parole and probation). Advancements in video surveillance systems along with radio-frequency identification tracking devices (RFID, discussed below) combine to make institutional corrections safer and require fewer correctional personnel for surveillance. IT can safeguard the lives of both officers and inmates/clients and improve efficiency and effectiveness of correctional practices. Modern prison cameras are bullet resistant and are able to withstand both a beating by a sledgehammer and attempts by inmates to disable them during a fight or escape; portable scanners are used for detecting hidden weapons, drugs, and other contraband; monitoring inmate movements and behavior; and (in prisons and jails) alerting staff to personnel who are in trouble.

We discuss some of these and other technologies in detail, including some of their attendant concerns and problems.

Now in Limited Service

The following technologies are not yet in use routinely in correctional facilities, but they will likely become more commonplace in the near future:

- A Colorado-based company now produces a needle-free injection system for medicating and immunizing inmates. Although such devices have been on the market for years, this type was only recently approved by the U.S. Food and Drug Administration and delivers vaccine as a fine stream of fluid to puncture the skin using a single-use, sterile, disposable syringe with a reusable injector. In addition to making medical personnel and inmates safer (as well as keeping needles out of inmates' hands), it prevents needlestick injuries, which can expose health care workers to up to 20 different blood-borne pathogens.[47]
- A handheld system that is similar to a metal detector scans fully clothed people for contraband hidden under their clothing. The device uses sound waves resembling sonar to detect objects; it "listens" to the sound waves that bounce back to it, detecting hidden objects under clothing. The apparatus has successfully detected objects such as cell phones, plastic knives, guns, and credit cards.[48]
- Electronic control devices are now in use in some prisons and jails. However, because of the voluminous litigation, controversy, and even diverging research findings as to their benefits as well as harm to individuals, and which particular device is best for use in what are often small prison/jail cells and offices, it is doubtful that there will ever be a definitive answer as to their application in such settings; therefore, we will not take a side on the matter.
- Biometrics has been widely used for prison management in many parts of the world in order to track and monitor inmates. One popular, low-cost biometric approach, fingerprint recognition, is rapidly becoming a thing of the past. In its place are iris biometrics, which appears to be the technology of the future. Such a system appears to be much quicker, the most accurate, and able to be used not only to track inmates and authenticate their identities but also to verify identity prior to release and to check visitor identity prior to their having inmate contact.[49]

Lessons Learned about IT Adoption: The Woes of RFID

A technology now in use by staff in institutional corrections is called a "radio frequency identification device," or RFID. RFIDs have a tag or "chip" that can transmit data to electronic sensors. As a result, information can be provided on inmates' movements; alert staff if there is an unusual concentration of inmates in a certain area; help in investigations to determine which inmate was present in a specific part of a building at a particular time; and determine which corrections officers are closest in the event of an emergency.[50]

Although this particular device can obviously be a major asset to any correctional institution, we use it as an example of how the adoption of IT can go awry—and time and funds wasted—when users fail to understand how to properly prepare for and implement them. Such an example can provide some lessons for future criminal justice administrators and policy makers.

Recently, the National Institute of Justice (NIJ) funded an evaluation of the use of RFID in a women's prison, which was to be used for reducing sexual assaults and inmate infractions. Evaluators looked at three important aspects of its adoption:

1. users' understanding of how the technology works—the *logic* behind its use;
2. properly informing users of the product's benefits to ensure cultural buy-in and full deployment—the *fidelity* piece; and
3. having an early and ongoing assessment to identify and correct implementation problems and challenges—the *feedback loop*.[51]

Most notably, NIJ evaluators found that RFID service was inexplicably interrupted for several months, staff received minimal training in the technology's use, and bracelets to be worn by inmates were used inconsistently (at one point, 25 percent of inmates did not have bracelets); eventually, the institution restricted RFID use to perimeter control, and never actually employed the technology's most powerful feature: tailored, inmate-specific exclusionary zones (i.e., specific movements or activities that are prohibited in certain geographic areas).

Evaluators also noted that the application of RFID lacked a well-articulated logic model, and thus users failed to deploy the technology as intended. Nor was there a fidelity piece, as staff members were not informed of the nature, frequency, and context of its capabilities and operational requirements. Finally, halfway into its deployment period, the system was entirely inoperable and therefore new inmates were not even issued bracelets. Obviously, with the prison failing to monitor and document these problems routinely, the feedback loop was nonexistent as well.[52]

Together, these incidents served to represent a failure on the part of all involved parties, and serves as a good example of how IT should not be purchased if logic, fidelity, and feedback phases will not be performed.

The Continuing Problem of Cellphones in Prisons

Problems with cellphones continue to bedevil prison administrators. As examples, in 2016:

- A Georgia inmate was indicted for ordering—via cellphone—the revenge killing of a 9-month-old baby from his prison cell.
- Prisoners in Alabama rioted, taping the event with smuggled phones and posting the videos on Facebook.
- More than 50 Georgia inmates were charged with using contraband cellphones to run elaborate wire fraud and money-laundering schemes.[53]

Because the use of contraband cellphones provides inmates with unlimited access to the outside world and the ability to engage in all types of criminal activity—to intimidate witnesses, order hits on a prosecutor's family member, coordinate escapes, bribe prison officers, orchestrate gang activity, extort money from family members, defraud the elderly, and run nationwide drug rings—it is no wonder that it is illegal for inmates to possess them. However, there are many means by which they can obtain them: they bribe corrections officers, use drones to fly them in over prison walls, or smuggle them in through food delivery trucks or in underwear or legal papers. Inmates have had accomplices shoot them into prison yards using "potato guns" made out of PVC piping, toss them over prison fences, and even stuffed in the body of a dead cat.[54] Several thousand cellphones are confiscated in prisons each year in a number of states.

While prisoners are allowed to use phones, they are limited to using landline phones under the close supervision of prison officials. Furthermore, for family members on the outside, phone communication with incarcerated family members can be extremely expensive—up to $14 per minute for long-distance calls.[55]

Some responses to the problem have been developed; for example, in South Carolina, $10 million was allocated for towers to be built around the perimeters of prisons and for cameras and metal detectors to watch for contraband. California assesses a $5,000 fine for anyone supplying an inmate with a cellphone, and any inmate caught with a cellphone loses 90 days of earned "good-time credit." In Mississippi, prisons use body scanner equipment and dogs are trained to detect cellphones. Finally, several states—with the 2013 approval of the Federal Communications Commission—have begun using an "inmate call capture" system that picks up calls made from within the prison and only allows authorized calls by someone (such as a corrections officer) to go through.[56]

Use of Telemedicine

Employing **telemedicine** in correctional facilities, which is the use of telecommunications technology to remotely diagnose and treat inmates, has provided tremendous benefits. First, by providing remote inmate health consultations and treatment, the cost of transporting them to a medical facility is avoided. As state budgets contract and prisons become more crowded and older in nature, telemedicine is only expected to expand.

telemedicine the use of telecommunications technology to remotely diagnose and treat inmates.

In June 2013, the Colorado Department of Corrections teamed with a Denver medical center to launch a pilot program using videoconferencing for inmates who needed consultation. In Wyoming, where much of the state's population is remote and distant from medical facilities, telemedicine for prison inmates helps to address challenges of distance and distribution of doctors. Approximately 2,000 physician visits are conducted annually via remote connection. Similarly, the corrections department in Louisiana signed a contract to provide 17,000 annual checkups to thousands of inmates, increasing telemedicine by nearly 600 percent.[57]

Mental health services can also be provided to prisoners via mobile devices. Estimates are that a state can save $30,000 to $40,000 a month with such a system, which includes a voice platform, video software, and special videophones.

A program developed in Palm Bay, Florida, involving the police department and a trauma center, has even partnered to provide SWAT officers the ability to communicate virtually with trauma surgeons during high-risk incidents. Using a laptop or some other mobile device and a webcam, officers connect with the trauma center's secure servers. Trauma surgeons can rapidly look at the trauma injuries and give assistance to the tactical team, thus "seeing" the patient within minutes of when the injury occurred. Exhibit 17.5 discusses the benefits of telemedicine.

EXHIBIT 17.5

BENEFITS OF TELEMEDICINE

A study found that a telemedicine program led to nearly $1 billion in savings over a 10-year period while also cutting back on emergency-room and doctors' office visits by 70 percent and reducing unnecessary medical tests by 45 percent. The program also significantly cut back on prison transports, which are expensive and dangerous, while allowing staff to see patients more often, including specialists (including at remote sites all across the state of Texas). Meanwhile, costs for the program have been reduced dramatically, from $1.2 million to $600 thousand per year, while the technology has been improved. The program has been expanded to include mental health screenings, hepatitis C screenings, orthopedic and urology care, and pain management. In addition, the system is linked to an electronic medical record system, which documents the complete patient medical chart information including lab results and physician notes.[58]

Summary

"Everything we do is driven by data." This is the new mantra of many criminal justice administrators, managers, and supervisors.

This relatively new state of affairs began in policing, which was long denigrated for its resistance to alter tradition (as some used to put it, like "bending granite") but is now (and will likely continue to be) engaged in rapid, dynamic change. Since 9/11 and the subsequent emphases on homeland security, the creation of fusion centers, and the inception of CompStat (discussed in Chapter 4) in the New York Police Department in 1995—as well as the Great Recession, enhanced accountability, the expansion and affordability of technologies, and the need to "do more with less"—change is now the norm.

Therefore, intelligence-led policing, predictive policing, and "smart policing" have become the order of the day. We are also seeing these same approaches spreading and in use in courts and corrections agencies—both of which, like neighborhoods, have "hot spots" where problems are frequent and predictable.

Certainly all of the technological advances described in this chapter have made advances in problem-solving possible. And this is really a no-brainer: In order to address crime and disorder with limited resources, various uses of technological assets and analytics must be directed to the time, places, hot spots, and people where they are most sorely needed.

This is, therefore, a very exciting and challenging time to be employed in the criminal justice field; however, such entities as political governing boards, the taxpaying public, and institutions of higher education owe it to their practitioners, stakeholders, and students to keep abreast of these changing times and to have the technological capability to analyze data, perform crime analyses, understand the basics of mapping, perform trend analysis, and so on. To not do so, in the midst of this widespread sea change in crimefighting, would be to do them a great disservice.

Key Terms and Concepts

Cold cases, p. 448
Civic apps, p. 445
Crime mapping, p. 442
Electronic control devices, p. 447
Electronic court records, p. 448
Geographic information systems (GIS), p. 442
Automatic license plate recognition (ALPR), p. 446
Proactive policing functions, p. 441
Radio-frequency identification tracking (RFID), p. 451
Reactive policing functions, p. 441
Real-time crime centers, p. 443
Social media, p. 444
Support functions, p. 441
Telemedicine, p. 453

Questions for Review

1. What are some new types of databases that now exist for criminal justice agency use?
2. What are some of the good and bad applications and considerations with smartphones?
3. Regarding court technologies, what are the primary problems courts have, and what are some solutions?
4. What advances have been made in corrections regarding inmate control? Use of mobile devices?
5. What advantages are offered through the use of telemedicine?

Deliberate and Decide

A female officer comes to you alleging that her direct supervisor in the Drug Suppression Unit, who is a former lover, began sending explicit text messages to her a few weeks ago, including "I must have you" and "I am just a man. Never satisfied always wanting more."

Now, however, the sergeant is phoning her repeatedly at work to discuss personal matters and sometimes calls her offensive names. If she doesn't answer the phone, he angrily confronts her at the police station, yelling and using abusive language.

Today, she agreed to meet him in a parking lot while they were both on duty. He became angry when she refused to date him again, and he again sent her harassing text messages soon afterward. She indicates that he obviously uses GPS to track her while doing drug interdiction work, because he showed up twice yesterday where she was on a stakeout with a colleague. She claims she has brought these matters to the attention of her shift lieutenant, but so far he ignores her complaints.

Questions for Discussion

1. Is the sergeant's behavior in violation of any law? If so, specifically what?
2. What are the issues involved?
3. As her captain, what will you do about the matter?

Learn by Doing

1. As head of the research and development unit of your law enforcement agency, you are tasked to "bring the agency into the current millennium" by making recommendations concerning new technologies to be acquired. Using information provided in this chapter, select and prioritize *five* new technologies that you believe your city/county agency should obtain, including a justification for each in terms of its crime-fighting, predictive, and preventive capabilities.
2. As warden of a small minimum-custody prison facility in a remote part of the state and having an unusually high geriatric inmate population, your secretary of corrections has learned that fully one-third of your total budget is now consumed by medical and related costs (e.g., transportation to clinics and hospitals). You are ordered to come up with alternatives. What will you propose?

Case Study

You occasionally consult on justice system planning and operations, and have been contacted by a nearby county to examine its court functions. Apparently, the former court administrator (Jameson) was very popular and considered efficient because he always operated within his rather meager budget. You discover, however, that those low operating costs were due to his notion that the court did not need any "fancy gadgets," and thus the court's staff struggles to perform the court's daily functions with outmoded equipment. With Jameson now retired, the county manager (learning how antiquated the court's functions really are) supports a major upgrade, and contacts you to learn of the available court technologies that are in the marketplace.

Questions for Discussion

1. What will you report?
2. Assuming no financial restrictions, what kinds of as-yet-undeveloped technologies do you believe would be of greatest assistance to the courts?

Notes

1. Brian A. Jackson, Victoria A. Greenfield, Andrew R. Morral, and John S. Hollywood, *Police Department Investments in Information Technology Systems* (Santa Monica, CA: RAND Corporation, 2014), p. 2.
2. RAND Corporation, "How Will Technology Change Criminal Justice?," January 7, 2016, http://www.rand.org/blog/rand-review/2016/01/how-will-technology-change-criminal-justice.html.
3. Quoted in Jackson et al., *Police Department Investments in Information Technology Systems*, p. 7.
4. Ibid., p. 9.
5. Lee Brown, quote in Seaskate, Inc., "The Evolution and Development of Police Technology," http://www.police-technology.net/id59.html#.
6. Ibid.
7. Also see National Institute of Justice, "MAPS: How Mapping Helps Reduce Crime and Improve Public Safety," https://www.nij.gov/topics/technology/maps/Pages/reduce-crime.aspx.
8. Ibid.
9. In addition, a full catalog of NIJ mapping tools and databases is available at: http://www.nij.gov/topics/technology/pages/software-tools.aspx#maps; also see NIJ's "MAPS: How Mapping Helps Reduce Crime and Improve Public Safety," http://www.nij.gov/topics/technology/maps/Pages/reduce-crime.aspx.
10. Lynsi Burton, "New SPD 'Crime Center' Shows City's Activity Unfolding in Real Time," *Seattlepi.com*, October 7, 2015, http://www.seattlepi.com/local/crime/article/New-SPD-crime-center-shows-city-s-activity-6556969.php.
11. Quoted in Ibid.
12. Ibid.
13. Ibid.
14. Information Builders, "Houston Police Department Creates Real-Time Crime Center," n.d., http://www.information-builders.com/applications/houston.
15. Joseph D'Amico, "Stopping Crime in Real Time," *The Police Chief*, November 2015, http://www.policechiefmagazine.org/magazine/index.cfm?fuseaction=display&article_id=995&issue_id=92006.
16. Ibid.
17. Tod Newcombe, "Social Media: Big Lessons from the Boston Marathon Bombing," *Government Technology*, September 24, 2014; see also Edward F. Davis III, Alejandro A. Alves, and David Alan Sklansky, *Social Media and Police Leadership: Lessons from Boston* (Washington, DC: National Institute of Justice, 2014).
18. Ibid.
19. Ibid.
20. Jake Levitas, "Defining Civic Hacking," *Code for America*, June 7, 2013, http://www.codeforamerica.org/blog/2013/06/07/defining-civic-hacking/.
21. Tod Newcombe, "Civic Apps: Can They Help Fight Crime?," *Government Technology*, September 25, 2014, http://www.govtech.com/public-safety/Civic-Apps-Can-They-Help-Fight-Crime.html.
22. Ibid.
23. Declan McCullagh, "Court OKs Warrantless Use of Hidden Surveillance Cameras," *CNET*, October 30, 2012, http://www.cnet.com/news/court-oks-warrantless-use-of-hidden-surveillance-cameras/.
24. *U.S. v. Jones*, 565 U.S. ____, 132 S. Ct. 945, (2012)
25. Police Executive Research Forum, *Constitutional Policing as a Cornerstone of Community Policing* (Washington, DC: Office of Community Oriented Policing Services, 2015), p. 29, http://ric-zai-inc.com/Publications/cops-p324-pub.pdf.
26. Ibid., p. 30.
27. Ibid., p. 31.
28. American Civil Liberties Union, "Automatic License Plate Readers," 2015, https://www.aclu.org/issues/privacy-technology/location-tracking/automatic-license-plate-readers.
29. B. Shockley, "Lawsuit Challenges State of Utah Ban on License Plate Readers as Unconstitutional Censorship of Photography and Violation of 1st Amendment," *Vigilant Solutions*, February 13, 2014, http://vigilantsolutions.com/press/drn_vigilant_utah_lpr_federal_lawsuit.
30. Kim Zetter, "Virginia Man Sues Police Over License Plate Database," *Wired*, May 6, 2015, http://www.wired.com/2015/05/virginia-man-sues-police-license-plate-database/.
31. Keith Gierlack, Shara Williams, Tom LaTourrette, James M. Anderson, Lauren A. Mayer, and Johanna Zmud, *License Plate Readers for Law Enforcement: Opportunities and Obstacles* (Santa Monica, CA: RAND Corporation, 2014), p. 46, https://www.ncjrs.gov/pdffiles1/nij/grants/247283.pdf.
32. Katherine Paddock, "Study Suggests Taser Use by U.S. Police Is Safe," *Medical News Today*, October 9, 2007, http://www.medicalnewstoday.com/articles/84955.php.
33. Colleen Curry, "Tasers Might Not Reduce Lethal Force Incidents or Injuries to Suspects After All," *Vice News*, October 15, 2015, https://news.vice.com/article/tasers-might-not-reduce-lethal-force-incidents-or-injuries-to-suspects-after-all.
34. David Griffith, "Police Robots on Land and Sea," *Police*, December 28, 2015, http://www.policemag.com/channel/technology/articles/2015/12/police-robots-on-land-and-sea.aspx.
35. Brian Huber, "Wis. Police Get Robo-Cop's Help," *PoliceOne.com*, November 14, 2006, www.policeone.com/police-technology/robots/articles/1190983 (accessed March 5, 2013).
36. John Ingold, "James Holmes Faces 142 Counts, Including 24 of First-Degree Murder," *The Denver Post*, July 30, 2012, http://www.denverpost.com/breakingnews/ci_21191265/hearing-underway-man-suspected-killing-12-aurora-theater.
37. Justine Brown, "App Helps Police Manage 'Gypsy Hill' Cold Case Murder Investigation," *Government Technology*,

August 6, 2015, http://www.govtech.com/applications/App-Helps-Police-Manage-Gypsy-Hill-Cold-Case-Murder-Investigation.html.
38. See, for example, District of Columbia Courts, "Strategic Management Division," http://www.dccourts.gov/internet/system/research/main.jsf.
39. For more information about e-filing of court documents, see Thomas O-Connor, "E-Filings Making Courts More Accessible," American Bar Association, n.d., http://www.americanbar.org/content/newsletter/publications/gp_solo_magazine_home/gp_solo_magazine_index/oconnor.html; also see Missouri Courts, "Frequently Asked Questions About Electronic Filing," http://www.courts.mo.gov/page.jsp?id=46525.
40. Adapted from the National Judicial College, "The Model Courtroom," http://www.judges.org/about/the-njc-experience/model-courtroom/.
41. CourtReporterEdu.org, "In a Technological World, the Court Reporter Remains a Valuable Asset," March 5, 2015, http://www.courtreporteredu.org/2015/03/in-a-technological-world-the-court-reporter-remains-a-valuable-asset/.
42. "Man vs. Machine: Will One Become Obsolete in Law?" *Law Practice Management Advisor*, June 15, 2012, https://lawfirmsuccess.wordpress.com/2012/06/15/man-vs-machine-will-one-become-obsolete-in-law/.
43. Ibid.
44. Ibid.
45. Tyler Technologies, "Incode," http://www.tylertech.com/SuccessStories/Courts-Justice/BeltonMOIncodeClientCaseStudy.pdf.
46. See Tyler Technologies, "Fulton County Launches Odyssey Computer System," n.d., http://www.tylertech.com/SuccessStories/Courts-Justice/Fulton_County_Odyssey.pdf.
47. See Pharmajet, "Needle-Free Syringes Eliminate Needlestick Injuries, Reduce Needle Reuse and Cross-Contamination," http://pharmajet.com/needle-free-technology/.
48. Philip Bulman, "Using Technology to Make Prisons and Jails Safer," *NIJ Journal*, March 27, 2010, https://www.nij.gov/journals/262/pages/corrections-technology.aspx.
49. Iritech, Inc., "Iris Biometrics to Tighten the Prison Management," November 4, 2015, http://www.iritech.com/blog/iris-prison-management-1115/.
50. Nancy La Vigne, "Harnessing the Power of Technology in Institutional Corrections," *National Institute of Justice*, November 29, 2016, https://www.nij.gov/journals/278/Pages/harnessing-power-of-technology-in-institutional-corrections.aspx.
51. Ibid.
52. Ibid.
53. Teresa Wiltz, "States Bedeviled by Contraband Cellphones in Prisons," *Government Technology*, June 8, 2016, http://www.govtech.com/public-safety/States-Bedeviled-by-Contraband-Cellphones-in-Prisons.html.
54. Ibid.
55. David Goldman, "Government's Plan to Cut Sky-high Prison Phone Rates Is Put on Hold," *CNN*, March 9, 2016, http://money.cnn.com/2016/03/09/technology/prison-phones/.
56. Wiltz, "States Bedeviled by Contraband Cellphones in Prisons."
57. Susan Miller, "Prisons Turn to Telemedicine for Treating Inmates," *GCN*, May 21, 2014, http://gcn.com/blogs/pulse/2014/05/prisons-telemedicine-treating-inmates.aspx.
58. Gabriel Perna, "Under the Microscope: Telemedicine Care in Texas Prisons," *Healthcare Infomatics*, June 21, 2014, http://www.healthcare-informatics.com/article/under-microscope-telemedicine-care-texas-prisons.

Appendix Writings of Confucius, Machiavelli, and Lao-Tzu

The writings of certain major figures have stood the test of time. The analects of Confucius (551–479 B.C.E.) and the teachings of Machiavelli (1469–1527) are still quite popular. Many graduate and undergraduate students in a variety of academic disciplines analyze the writings of both, especially Machiavelli's *The Prince*. Both men tend to agree on many points regarding the means of governance, as the following will demonstrate. After presenting some comments from each philosopher, we will consider their application to justice administration.

Confucius often emphasized the connection between morality and leadership, saying, for example:

> He who rules by moral force is like the pole star, which remains in its place while all the lesser stars do homage to it. Govern the people by regulations, keep order among them by chastisements, and they will flee from you, and lose all self-respect. Govern them by moral force, keep order among them and they will come to you of their own accord. If the ruler is upright, all will go well even though he does not give orders. But if he himself is not upright, even though he gives orders, they will not be obeyed.[1]

Confucius also commented on the leader's treatment of subordinates: "Promote those who are worthy, train those who are incompetent; that is the best form of encouragement."[2] He also felt that leaders should learn from and emulate good administrators:

> In the presence of a good man, think all the time how you may learn to equal him. In the presence of a bad man, turn your gaze within! Even when I am walking in a party of no more than three I can always be certain of learning from those I am with. There will be good qualities that I can select for imitation and bad ones that will teach me what requires correction in myself.[3]

Unlike Confucius, Machiavelli is often maligned for being cruel; the "end justifies the means" philosophy imputed to him has cast a pall over his writings. However, although he often seems as biting as the "point of a stiletto"[4] and at times ruthless ("Men ought either to be caressed or destroyed, since they will seek revenge for minor hurts but will not be able to revenge major ones,"[5] and "If you have to make a choice, to be feared is much safer than to be loved"[6]), he, like Confucius, often spoke of the leader's need to possess character and compassion. For all of his blunt, management-oriented notions of administration, Machiavelli was prudent and pragmatic.

Like Confucius, Machiavelli felt that administrators would do well to follow examples set by other great leaders:

> Men almost always prefer to walk in paths marked out by others and pattern their actions through imitation. A prudent man should always follow the footsteps of the great and imitate those who have been supreme. A prince should read history and reflect on the actions of great men.[7]

Machiavelli's counsel also agreed with that of Confucius with regard to the need for leaders to surround themselves with persons both knowledgeable and devoted: "The first notion one gets of a prince's intelligence comes from the men around him."[8]

But, again, like Confucius, Machiavelli believed that administrators should be careful of their subordinates' ambition and greed:

> A new prince must always harm those over whom he assumes authority. You cannot stay friends with those who put you in power, because you can never satisfy them as they expected. The man who makes another powerful ruins himself. The reason is that he gets power either by shrewdness or by strength, and both qualities are suspect to the man who has been given the power.[9]

On the need for developing and maintaining good relations with subordinates, Machiavelli wrote:

> If a prince puts his trust in the people, knows how to command, is a man of courage and doesn't lose his head in adversity, and can rouse his people to action by his own example and orders, he will never find himself betrayed, and his foundations will prove to have been well laid. The best fortress of all consists in not being hated by your people. Every prince should prefer to be considered merciful rather than cruel. The prince must have people well disposed toward him; otherwise in times of adversity there's no hope.[10]

In this era of collective bargaining and a rapidly changing workforce, contemporary criminal justice administrators might do well to heed the comments of Confucius and Machiavelli.

Perhaps a leader, in the purest sense, also influences others by example. This characteristic of leadership was recognized in the sixth century B.C.E. by Lao-Tzu, who wrote:

> The superior leader gets things done
>
> With very little motion.
>
> He imparts instruction not through many words
>
> But through a few deeds.
>
> He keeps informed about everything
>
> But interferes hardly at all.
>
> He is a catalyst.
>
> And although things wouldn't get done as well
>
> If he weren't there.
>
> When they succeed he takes no credit.
>
> And because he takes no credit
>
> Credit never leaves him.[11]

Notes

1. Confucius, *The Analects of Confucius*, trans. Arthur Waley (London: George Allen and Unwin, 1938), pp. 88, 173.
2. Ibid., p. 92.
3. Ibid., pp. 105, 127.
4. Niccolo Machiavelli, *The Prince,* trans. Robert M. Adams (New York: W. W. Norton, 1992), p. xvii.
5. Ibid., p. 7.
6. Ibid., p. 46.
7. Ibid., pp. 15, 41.
8. Ibid., p. 63.
9. Ibid., pp. 5, 11.
10. Ibid., pp. 29, 60.
11. Quoted in Wayne W. Bennett and Karen M. Hess, *Management and Supervision in Law Enforcement*, 3rd ed. (Belmont, CA: Wadsworth, 2001), p. 63.

Glossary

Absolute ethics: a belief that something is good or bad, black or white, and that certain acts are inherently right or wrong in themselves, irrespective of one's culture

Accreditation: a voluntary effort by a criminal justice agency where it seeks to meet national standards in its field and thus be officially designated as accredited

Active shooter: an individual who is actively engaged in killing or attempting to kill people in a confined and populated area

Administrator: the person whose focus is on the overall organization, its mission, acquisition and use of resources, and agency relationship with external organizations and groups

Adversarial system: the legal system whereby two opposing sides present their arguments in court

Affirmative action: actions or policies that favor persons or groups who have suffered from discrimination, particularly in employment or education

Alternative dispute resolution (ADR): settling disputes outside of court, typically by negotiation, conciliation, mediation, and arbitration

Alternatives to incarceration: any form of punishment or treatment other than prison or jail time given to a convicted person

Americans with Disabilities Act: legislation making it illegal to discriminate against persons with disabilities in their recruitment, hiring, and promotion practices and then focusing on reducing forces of resistance

Appearance of impropriety: where someone creates a circumstance or situation that appears to raise questions of ethics

Arbitration: negotiation with a final and binding decision that sets the terms of the settlement and with which the parties are legally required to comply

Assessment center: a process used for promoting and hiring personnel that may include oral interviews, psychological tests, group and in-basket exercises, and writing and role-playing exercises

Audit: an objective examination of the financial statements of an organization, either by its employees or by an outside firm

Autocratic leader: leaders who are primarily authoritarian in nature and prefer to give orders rather than invite group participation

Automated records system: technologies that assist police administrators in receiving, investigating, and arriving at proper dispositions concerning employee complaints and commendations

Bioterrorism: chemical/biological agents involving the release of toxic biological agents

Bona fide occupational qualifier (BFOQ): in certain situations, a rationale for discriminating on the basis of a business necessity

***Brady* material:** evidence in the government's possession that is favorable to the accused, material to either guilt or punishment, and must therefore be disclosed to the defense; also, because of *Brady*, prosecutors must inform the defense whenever a police officer involved in their case has knowingly lied in his reports in the past

Budget: a plan, in financial terms, estimating future expenditures and indicating agency plans and policy regarding financial resources and the appropriation and expenditure of funds

Budget cycle: a time frame that determines how long a budget lasts, which can vary from agency to agency

Budget execution: carrying out the organization's budgeted responsibilities in a proper manner and providing an accounting of the administrator's actions with the same

Budget formulation: the preparation of a budget to allocate funds in accordance with agency priorities, plans, and programs, and to deliver necessary services

Bureaucracy: structuring of an organization so as to function efficiently; it includes rules, division of labor, hierarchy of authority, and expertise among its members

Case delay: an excessive amount of time passing prior to bringing a criminal case to trial

Central office: the state's central organization that oversees its prison system

Chief executive officer (CEO): the highest-ranking executive or administrator in an organization, who is in charge of its overall operation

Chief of police: the title given to the top official in the chain of command of a municipal police department

Civil liability: blame assigned to a person or organization because its employees committed negligent or other acts resulting in some type of harm

Civil Rights of Institutionalized Persons Act: a federal law protecting the rights of people in state or local correctional facilities who are mentally ill, disabled, or handicapped

Classification: the placing of inmates into the proper levels of security, housing, programming, and other aspects of their incarceration

Collective bargaining: See "negotiation"

Communication: the use of words, sounds, signs, bodily cues, or other actions to convey or exchange information, or to express ideas, to another person or group

Conflict model: holds that actors within the criminal justice system are self-serving, with pressures for success, promotion, and general accountability and resulting in fragmented efforts

Consensus model: the view of the criminal justice system in which it is assumed that all parts of the system work toward a common goal

Contingency theory: an effort to determine the fit between the organization's characteristics and its tasks and the motivations of individuals

COPPS: community-oriented policing and problem-solving, which has emerged as the dominant philosophy and strategy of policing

Correctional officer: the person responsible for the custody, safety, security, and supervision of inmates in a prison or other correctional facility

Court clerk: an officer of a court who is responsible for its clerical filings and recordkeeping, entering judgments and orders, and so on

Court of last resort: that court in a given state that has its highest and final appellate authority

Court unification: reorganizing a trial court's structure, procedures, funding, and administration to streamline operations, better deploy personnel, and improve trial and appellate processes

Courthouse violence: where individuals perpetrate violent incidents against others in courthouses, both targeted and nontargeted in nature

Courtroom civility: judges, litigants, and court actors conducting themselves appropriately so that all parties are afforded a fair opportunity to present their case

Crime control model: a philosophy that states crime must be repressed, the accused presumed guilty, legal loopholes eliminated, offenders swiftly punished, and police and prosecutors given a high degree of discretion

Criminal justice network: a view that the justice system's components cooperate and share similar goals but operate independently and compete for funding

Criminal justice nonsystem: the view that police, courts, and corrections agencies do not function harmoniously, are not a coordinated structure, and are neither efficient nor fair enough to create fear of punishment or respect for its values

Criminal justice process: the decisions and actions by an institution, offender, victim, or society that influence the offender's movement into, through, or out of the justice system

"CSI effect": the belief that a trial may be affected by television programming that creates inaccurate expectations by jurors regarding the power and use of forensic evidence

Cyberterrorism: cybercrimes that include identity theft, attacks against computer systems, penetration of online financial systems, e-mail phishing, and so on

Day reporting center: a site where offenders report to receive an array of educational or vocational, treatment, and other services, to reduce the risk factors associated with recidivism

Decor: the physical or decorative style of a setting

Decorum: correct or proper behavior indicating respect and politeness

Democratic leader: leaders who stress working within the group and strive to attain cooperation from group members by eliciting their ideas and support

Deontological ethics: a branch of ethics that focuses on the duty to act and the rightness or wrongness of actions, rather than rightness or wrongness of the consequences of those actions

Direct supervision jail: a type of design where cells are arranged in podular fashion, have an open dayroom area, and correctional officers are close to and interact with the inmates

Discipline matrix: intended to provide disciplinary actions against police officers who are consistent and fair, taking into account several variables and circumstances

Disparate treatment: treating people differently because of their age, gender, sex, or other protected status

Division of labor: a basic feature of traditional organizational theory, where specialization produces different groups of functional responsibilities

Domestic terrorism: the commission of terrorist acts in one's own country, against fellow citizens

Dress code: a set of rules, usually written as policy, specifying the required manner of dress and appearance for employees in an organization

Drug interdiction: efforts to reduce the supply and demand for drugs in prison, to include focusing on visitors, staff, mail, warehouses, gates, volunteers, and contractors

Dual court system: an organizational distinction between courts, with a federal court system and 50 individual state court systems

Due process model: the ideal that the accused should be presumed innocent and have their rights protected, while police must act only in accordance with the Constitution

Duty of care: a doctrine holding that police have a duty to protect the general public where a "special relationship" exists

Early intervention system (EIS): a means of identifying officers whose behavior is problematic, usually involving citizen complaints and improper use of force

Electronic court records: where incoming documents are scanned, processed (using images rather than paper), and stored in an electronic document management system

Ethics: moral principles governing individual and group behavior, based on ideas concerning what is morally good and bad

Exclusionary rule: the constitutional principle holding that evidence obtained illegally by law enforcement officers cannot be used against the suspect in a criminal prosecution

Expectancy theory: a theory that certain beliefs can influence effort and performance

Expenditure: a payment for goods or services, to settle a financial obligation indicated by an invoice, contract, or other such document

Fact-finding: interpretation of facts and the determination of what weight to attach to them in negotiations

Failure to protect: a form of negligence where a police officer fails to protect a person from a known and foreseeable danger

Fair Labor Standards Act (FLSA): a federal law establishing minimum wages and requiring overtime compensation in the private sector as well as state and local governmental employees

Family and Medical Leave Act (FMLA): legislation that entitles eligible employees to take unpaid, job-protected leave for specified family and medical reasons

Federal sentencing guidelines: rules for computing uniform sentencing policy; they also provide classifications of offenses and offenders, severity of crimes, and suggested punishments

Field training officer (FTO): a program designed to help new officers to transition smoothly from the recruit academy phase of their career, with a veteran officer observing and evaluating their performance in the field

First-line supervisor: the lowest yet a very important level of leadership, the supervisor directs, controls, and evaluates the work of field personnel, ensures that agency policies and procedures are followed, counsels and places employees where resources are most needed, resolves employee conflicts, and performs related duties

Force-field analysis: a process of identifying forces in support of change and those resisting change

Frivolous lawsuit: an action filed by a party or attorney who is aware it is without merit, due to a lack of legal basis or argument for the alleged claim

Fusion center: coordination of all counterterrorism elements within a jurisdiction by receiving and analyzing terrorist threat or activity information

Generation Y: sometimes termed the Millennials, persons born between 1980 and 2000

Geriatric inmates: while there is no standard definition concerning what age an inmate becomes "elderly," it is known that the aging inmate population is growing rapidly, raising medical costs and requiring special needs be met

Grant writing: preparing and submitting required documents and information for making application to funding bodies that award monies to assist eligible businesses and government agencies

Grapevine: an informal means of circulating and communicating information or gossip

Gratuities: complimentary gifts of money, services, or something of other value

Great Recession: the severe, prolonged economic downturn lasting from December 2007 to June 2009

Grievance: a real or imagined wrong or other cause for complaint by an employee concerning job-related matters

Hands-off policy: a practice by judges, in an era when they believed they had neither training nor knowledge concerning penology, allowing wardens the freedom to operate prisons as they saw fit

Hatch Acts: legislation that limits partisan political activities by governmental employees

Hawthorne effect: a theory meaning that employees' behavior may be altered if they believe they are being studied—and that management *cares*

Hierarchy of needs: Maslow's belief that people's basic and primary needs or drives are physiological (survival), safety or security, social, ego (self-esteem), and self-realization or actualization

Homegrown violent extremists: individuals who commit terrorists acts in the country they reside, but who are inspired by foreign terrorist organizations

Hostage taking: when any person—staff, visitor, or inmate—is held against his or her will by an inmate seeking to escape, gain concessions, or achieve other goals

House arrest/electronic monitoring: court-ordered punishment where a convicted or accused offender must remain in his home, usually while being remotely monitored electronically

Humanistic school: a school of psychological thought that stressed the importance of growth and self-actualization and argued that people are innately good

Inappropriate staff-inmate relationships: such correctional staff behaviors as sexual relations with inmates, providing special favors for inmates, or smuggling in contraband

Individual calendar system: a system whereby cases are assigned to a single judge who oversees all aspects of it from arraignment to pretrial motions and trial

Inferior courts: the lowest level of state courts, normally trial courts of limited jurisdiction

Inputs: an organization's committing such resources as funds, personnel/labor, and equipment toward accomplishing a goal or mission

Intelligence-led policing: a style of policing that combines crime analysis (where the "who, what, when, and where" of crime is analyzed) with intelligence analysis (which looks at the "who" of crime—the crime networks and individuals)

Intensive supervision: tight control and supervision of offenders in the community through strict enforcement of conditions and frequent reporting to a probation officer

Intermediate courts of appeals (ICAs): courts in the federal and state court systems that hear appeals, organizationally situated between the trial courts and the court of last resort

Intermediate sanctions: a range of sentencing options designed to fill the gap between probation and confinement, reduce institutional crowding, and reduce correctional costs

Internal complaints: complaints filed against employees by persons within the organization, either by one's peers or by supervisors

Job action: an activity by employees to express their dissatisfaction with a particular person, event, or condition relating to their work

Joint Terrorism Task Forces: multi-agency teams overseen by the FBI dedicated to address terror threats

Judicial (court) administration: the day-to-day and long-range activities of those persons who are responsible for the activities and functions of a court

Judicial Conference of the United States: the administrative policymaking organization of the federal judicial system

Judicial selection: the method used to nominate, select, or elect and install judges into office

Jurisdiction: the power or authority given to a court by law to hear certain kinds of cases

Jury administration: ensuring that a jury is properly composed and sustained prior to and during trials

Juvenile waiver: a provision for juvenile court judges to transfer jurisdiction over individual juvenile cases to an adult criminal court for prosecution

Laissez-faire leader: a hands-off approach to leadership, in which the organization essentially runs itself

Leadership: influencing and working with and through individuals or a group to generate activities that will accomplish organizational goals

Learning organization: an organizational culture that looks to the future to continually experiment, improve, and adapt so as to meet the challenges of a more complex role

Life without parole (LWOP): a type of sentence that can be applied to convicted adult (not juvenile) offenders, requiring that they spend the remainder of their natural life in prison

Line-item budget: a budget format that breaks down its components into major categories, such as personnel, equipment, contractual services, commodities, and capital outlay items

Lying (accepted/deviant): lying that serves legitimate purposes and lying that conceals or promotes crimes or illegitimate ends

Maintenance or hygiene factors: elements of one's career that provide one with their need to avoid pain (e.g., adequate pay, benefits, job security, decent working conditions, supervision, interpersonal relations)

Malfeasance: crimes or misconduct that officials knowingly commit in violation of state laws and/or agency rules and regulations

Manager: a person in the intermediate level of management, responsible for carrying out the policies and directives of upper-level administrators and supervising subordinate managers and employees

Master calendar system: a system whereby judges are assigned to oversee all stages of a case (preliminary hearing, arraignment, trial)

Mediation: a third party comes in to help opposing parties to settle their negotiations

Meet and confer: a comparatively weak bargaining system where employees may organize and select bargaining representatives; but if an impasse occurs, their options are limited

Mentally ill inmate: one who meets the definition and has a significant mental disorder(s), which can include schizophrenia, bipolar disorders, and major depression, among others

Merit selection/Missouri Bar Plan: a nonpartisan method of selecting judges; a nominating commission provides names of qualified persons to the governor, who chooses one person to serve

Middle manager: typically a captain or lieutenant, one who coordinates agency units' activities and sees that the administrative strategies and overall mission are carried out

Militarization: a belief held by some that local police—using military-style weapons, tactics, training, uniforms, and even heavy equipment—are becoming too militaristic in nature

Military Commissions Act: a law that allows the president to establish military commissions to try unlawful combatants

Military model: where, for example, police and many correctional officers wear uniforms, use rank designations, and have a hierarchical command structure much as the military services

Mintzberg model for CEOs: a model that delineates and defines the primary roles of a chief executive officer

Misfeasance: illegitimate acts likely committed by high-ranking officials who knowingly allow indiscretions that undermine the public interest and benefit them personally

Model Code of Judicial Conduct: (1) rules governing the conduct of judges while acting in their professional capacity; (2) standards written by the ABA to assist judges in maintaining the highest standards of judicial and personal conduct

Model of circumstantial corruptibility: a view regarding acceptance of gratuities, holding that the exchange of a gift is influenced by two elements: the roles of the giver and the receiver

Motivational factors: those psychosocial factors providing intrinsic satisfaction on the job, serving as an incentive to devote more of their time, energy, and expertise in productive behavior

National Counterterrorism Center: the entity which serves to integrate and analyze intelligence pertaining to terrorism (excluding domestic terrorism)

National Incident Management System: a nationwide system providing for levels of governments to work together to address domestic incidents

National Infrastructure Protection Plan: a document that's serves as the guideline for organizing homeland security in the U.S.

National Judicial College, The: an institute of learning in Reno, Nevada, that trains judges how to be better arbiters of justice

National Incident Management System: a document outlining procedures for agency preparedness and response to domestic incidents

Negative discipline: discipline that involves some form of punishment

Negligence: when someone's conduct creates a danger to others, often by subjecting others to a risk of harm and resulting in some form of injury

Negotiation: a dialogue between labor and management for developing a written agreement concerning such issues as working conditions, salaries, and benefits

New old penology: DiIulio's term for a shift of attention from the society of captives to the government of keepers

NIC Executive Training Program for New Wardens: training for new wardens to help grasp such areas as institutional culture, budget management, decision making, and media relations

Noble cause corruption: corruption committed in the name of good ends; when an act is committed to achieve a good end, it might still be justified

Nonfeasance: acts of omission or avoidance knowingly committed by officials who are responsible for carrying out such acts

Notorious cases: local, regional, or national civil or criminal trials either involving celebrities or particularly egregious crimes, requiring attention to jury selection and trial procedures

Organization: entities of two or more people who cooperate to achieve an objective(s)

Organizational structure: how an organization divides up its work and establishes lines of authority and communication

Organizational theory: the study of organizational designs and structures that includes the behavior of administrators and managers within organizations

Outputs: an organization's desired outcome, goods, or services

Parole: where an offender is conditionally released from prison to serve the remaining portion of a criminal sentence in the community

Peace officer: those persons having arrest authority either with a warrant or based on probable cause

Peace Officers' Bill of Rights (POBR): legislation mandating due process rights for peace officers who are the subject of internal investigations that could lead to disciplinary action

Performance budget: a budget format that is input-output oriented and relates the volume of work to be done to the amount of money spent

Personal loyalty syndrome: loyalty that can be given to unworthy peers or superiors, even when resulting in violations of constitutional provisions, legal requirements, or the public good

Planned change: rational approach to criminal justice planning that involves problem analysis, setting goals and objectives, program and policy design, developing an action plan, and monitoring and evaluation

Planning-programming-budgeting system (PPBS): a budgeting tool that links program to the ways and means of facilitating the program and better informing decision makers of outcomes of their actions

Police training officer (PTO): a relatively new program where new officers are evaluated on their application of community policing and problem-solving principles, using adult- and problem-based learning principles

Policies: written guidelines that are general in nature and serve to further the organization's philosophy and mission and help in interpreting their elements to the officers

Policymaking: (1) developing plans that are then used by an organization or government as a basis for making decisions; (2) establishing rules, principles, or guidelines to govern actions by ordinary citizens and persons in positions of authority

POSDCORB: an acronym for planning, organizing, staffing, directing, coordinating, reporting, and budgeting; this philosophy was emphasized in police management for many years

Positive discipline: a formal program that attempts to change poor employee behavior without invoking punishment

Posse Comitatus Act of 1878: a law that prohibits using the military to execute domestic laws, with some exceptions

Predictive policing: a policing strategy that integrates crime analysis, technology, intelligence-led policing, and other tactics to inform forward-thinking crime prevention strategies

Principles of good prison leadership: DiIulio's six principles for success in corrections management

Prison director: the person who sets policy for all wardens and prisons to follow in terms of management and inmate treatment

Prison industries: prison programs intended to provide productive work and skill development opportunities for offenders, to reduce recidivism and prepare offenders for reentry into society

Prison Litigation Reform Act: a law providing remedies for prison condition lawsuits and to discourage frivolous and abusive prison lawsuits

Prison Rape Elimination Act of 2003: a law mandating national data collection on the incidence and prevalence of sexual assault in correctional facilities

Prisoners' rights: the collective body of constitutional rights afforded jail and prison inmates relating to the fundamental human rights and civil liberties

Privatization: either the operation of existing prison facilities or the building and operation of new prisons by for-profit companies

Probation: where a court places an offender on supervision in the community, generally in lieu of incarceration

Problem-solving courts: special courts created to accommodate persons with specific needs and problems, such as drug, veteran, and mentally ill offenders

Procedures: specific guidelines that serve to direct employee actions, such as how to prepare investigations and conduct patrol, bookings, radio communications, and prepare reports

Program budget: a budget format that examines cost units as units of activity rather than as units and subunits within the organization

Proximate cause: due to someone's conduct, a person sustained injury or damage

Radio-frequency identification tracking (RFID): a device worn by both inmates and correctional officers for tracking purposes

Relative ethics: a belief that determining what is good or bad is relative to the individual or culture and can depend on the end or outcome of an action

Relatively identifiable boundary: an organization's goals and the public it is intended to serve

Reverse discrimination: the argument that affirmative action policies have resulted in unfair treatment for members of majority groups

Robotics: a branch of technology involving the design, construction, and function of robots

Rules and regulations: specific managerial guidelines for officers, such as not smoking in public or types of weapons to be carried on duty

SARA: for scanning, analysis, response, assessment—the logical framework for officers to respond to crime and neighborhood disorder

Scientific management: a school of management thought that is concerned primarily with the efficiency and output of an individual worker

Social entity: an organization composed of people who interact with one another and with other people

Sexual violence: any sexual act or attempted sexual act, unwanted sexual comments or advances, or acts to traffic, against a person's sexuality using coercion

Sheriff: the title given to the top official in the chain of command of a county law enforcement agency

Shock incarceration/boot camp: a short-term program where offenders experience rigorous military drill and ceremony, physical training and labor, and treatment and education to reduce recidivism and develop personal responsibility

Shock probation/parole: where a judge sends a convicted offender to prison for a short time and then suspends the remainder of the sentence, granting probation

Smart policing: a policing approach that emphasizes the use of data and analytics as well as improved crime analysis, performance measurement, and evaluation research

Social contract: a belief that people are essentially irrational and selfish, but have enough rationality to come together to form governments for self-protection

Social media: forms of electronic communication for social networking, to share information, ideas, personal messages

Span of control: the number of subordinates a chief executive, manager, or supervisor in a criminal justice organization can effectively supervise

Style theory: a theory that focuses on what leaders do and argue that leaders engage in two distinct types of behaviors: those relating to task and relationships

Succession planning: identifying and developing employees who have the potential to fill key leadership positions in the organization

Supermax prison: institutions providing the most secure levels of custody in prisons, with long-term, segregated housing for inmates who represent the highest security risks

Supervisor: typically the lowest position of leadership in an organization, one who plans, organizes, and directs staff members in their daily activities

System fragmentation: the view that members of police, courts, and corrections agencies have tremendous discretion and their own perception of the offender, resulting in goal conflict

Telemedicine: the use of telecommunications technology to remotely diagnose and treat inmates

Terrorism: the unlawful use of force against persons or property to intimidate or coerce a government or its population, so as to further political or social objectives

Theory X: the management view holding that people inherently dislike work and will avoid it, and thus negative reinforcements (punishments) and other "drivers" must be used as motivators

Theory Y: the management view holding that people inherently like to work, seek greater responsibility, and are inherently motivated rather than by punishment

Therapeutic community: drug-free residential settings relying heavily on peer influence and group processes to promote drug-free behavior

Threat assessment: a process of identifying, assessing, investigating, and managing a courthouse threat

Title 18, *U.S. Code*, **Section 242:** a law making it a criminal offense for any person acting under color of law to violate another person's civil rights

Title 42, *U.S. Code*, **Section 1983:** a law making it a civil offense for any person acting under color of law to violate another person's civil rights

Tort: the infliction of some injury on one person *by* another

Trait theory: a theory based on the notion that good leaders possess certain character traits that poor leaders do not

Trial courts: courts of original jurisdiction (or "first instance") where evidence and testimony are first introduced and findings of fact and law are made

Unit management: a corrections management approach with the larger prison population being subdivided into smaller units, felt to be more effective and to improve inmate classification

***United States Code* 21 U.S.C. §851:** a federal law allowing federal prosecutors to more heavily punish hard-core drug traffickers who have prior drug felony convictions

Unity of command: the principle holding that only one person should be in command or control of a situation or an employee

Unmanned aerial vehicles: ground-operated, powered aerial vehicles that are designed to carry nonlethal payloads for reconnaissance, command and control, and deception

USA Patriot Act: a federal law providing investigative measures to federal law enforcement agencies to prevent and respond to terrorism

Use of force: the amount of effort required by police or other criminal justice functionary to compel compliance by an unwilling subject

Use-of-force continuum: a graphic depiction of levels of force used by police to determine the type of force that is appropriate for certain types of citizen resistance

Vehicle pursuit: (1) where one or more law enforcement officers is attempting to apprehend a suspect who is evading arrest while operating a motor vehicle, usually at high speed or using other elusive means; (2) police attempts to apprehend someone in a fleeing vehicle who has indicated he or she does not intend to stop or yield

Warden: the person responsible for all activities, safety, and security of the staff and inmates within a prison

Weapon of mass destruction: a device (explosive, chemical, biological, etc…) that can produce widespread devastation

Workplace harassment: unwelcome verbal or physical conduct (whether or not of a sexual nature) that creates a hostile work environment, or a change in an employment status or benefits

Zero-based budget (ZBB): a budget format that requires managers to justify their entire budget request in detail, rather than simply using budget amounts established in previous years

Index